Minority Games

Minority Games

DAMIEN CHALLET, MATTEO MARSILI,
YI-CHENG ZHANG

This book has been printed digitally and produced in a standard specification
in order to ensure its continuing availability

OXFORD
UNIVERSITY PRESS

Great Clarendon Street, Oxford OX2 6DP

Oxford University Press is a department of the University of Oxford.
It furthers the University's objective of excellence in research, scholarship,
and education by publishing worldwide in

Oxford New York

Auckland   Cape Town Dar es Salaam   Hong Kong   Karachi
Kuala Lumpur Madrid Melbourne Mexico City   Nairobi
New Delhi Shanghai   Taipei Toronto
With offices in
Argentina Austria Brazil Chile Czech Republic France Greece
Guatemala Hungary Italy Japan South Korea Poland Portugal
Singapore Switzerland Thailand Turkey Ukraine Vietnam

Oxford is a registered trade mark of Oxford University Press
in the UK and in certain other countries

Published in the United States
by Oxford University Press Inc., New York

ISBN 978-0-19-856640-3

Printed and bound in Great Britain by CPI Antony Rowe, Chippenham and Eastbourne

Foreword

Once in a while a model problem appears that is simple to describe but offers a wealth of lessons. If the model problem is a classic—like the Ising model or the Prisoner's Dilemma—it both opens up our insight and gives us analytical pathways into an intriguing world. Challet, Marsili and Zhang's Minority Game problem is such a model. It is a classic. The game itself is easy to visualize. A number of agents wish to take some particular action, but they do not benefit if the majority of others take it too. The circumstances where this occurs may seem to be very specific, but in fact they arise *everywhere* in the economy when agents must commit in advance to something that shows diminishing returns. (Diminishing returns, that is, to the numbers committing). Financial trades must be committed to in advance, and the benefits of many strategies may be arbitraged away if others use them too. Hence the minority situation arises also in financial markets.

Damien Challet and Yi-Cheng Zhang conceived of the Minority Game in 1997. They, and their co-worker Matteo Marsili who joined them later, were intrigued not only by the problem itself, but by the possibility of applying statistical mechanics techniques to economics and game theory more generally. Over the previous two decades, physics had become adept at analyzing systems with many particles interacting heterogeneously, and markets clearly consisted of such particles—investors. But these economic "particles" reacted by attempting to forecast the outcome that would be caused by the forecasts of other particles, and to react to that in advance. They were strategic. This was a recognizable world for physicists but an intriguingly different one, and the minority game provided a pathway into it. The problem was quickly taken up by other physicists. Its formulation was simplified and progressively redefined to be closer to what physics was used to dealing with. Versions appeared, results appeared, and advances in understanding appeared. This book chronicles the progress of thought and the considerable insights gained. And it collects the papers that became the main milestones.

One distinctive feature of this work is its emphasis on phases in parameter space—different qualitative properties of the outcome that obtain under different parameter sets. Delineating phases is second nature to physicists but not to us economists, and we can learn much from this practice. In the minority game, agents align their strategies to the condition of the market: they want to choose the strategy that on average minimizes their chance of being in the majority. As a result, strategies co-organize themselves so as to minimize collective dissatisfaction. But this collective result has two phases. With few players, the recent history of the game contains some useful information that strategies can exploit. But once the number of players passes a critical value, all useful information has been used up. The properties of the outcome differ in these two regimes. Information, in fact, is central to the situation. And its role can be explicitly observed: players act as if to minimize a Hamiltonian that is itself a measure of available information. So the process by how information gets eaten up by players is made explicit, and this is another useful pathway into exploring financial markets.

Because some information is left unexploited if few players are in the market, and all information is used up as players increase past a critical number, Challet, Marsili and Zhang point out that players may enter the market until this critical number is reached. The market will therefore display self-ordered criticality. This is an important conjecture, and not just a theoretical one. It tells us that speculative investors—technical traders, at least—will seek out thin markets where possible and avoid deep ones. Markets may therefore hover on the edge of efficiency—a significant insight that can be made explicit with the techniques used here and one that is worth further investigation.

The Minority Game grew out of my El Farol bar problem, and to fill in some pre-history I should say a few words about that. Legend is indeed correct: in 1988 on Thursday nights Galway musician Gerry Carty played Irish music at El Farol, and the bar was not pleasant if crowded. Each week I mulled whether it was worth showing up, and I mulled that others also mulled. It occurred to me that situation was something like the forecasting equivalent of prisoner's dilemma. Few showing up was best; but it was in everyone's interest to be in that few. But my motivation was not to find a forecasting prisoner's dilemma. I was interested at the time in rational expectations (or forecasts) and their meaning for economics. In solving forecasting problems, economics had found it useful to imagine that everyone had the same forecasting machine and used it. You could then ask what forecasting machine would lead to agents' actions that would produce aggregate outcomes that on average would validate the machine's forecasts. This would be the rational expectations solution—the forecasting method that "rational" agents would choose. As an analytical strategy this worked, at least in the cases studied. But it bothered me. If someone were not smart enough to figure the proper forecast they would skew the outcome. Then forecasts should deviate; then I should deviate. Then others should too, and the situation would unravel. Rational expectations may have been good theory, but it was not good science. I realized that El Farol made this plain. If we postulated a "correct" bar-attendance forecasting machine that everyone coordinated on, their actions would collectively invalidate it. Therefore there could be no such correct machine. But if no deductive forecasting solution was possible, what should agents in the economy do? The problem was behaviorally ill-defined. And so were most situations involving the future in economics, I realized. This fascinated me.

In 1992 I stripped the El Farol situation to its essentials and programmed it. I wrote the problem up and presented it at the January 1994 American Economic Association meetings in a session on complexity in the economy chaired by Paul Krugman. The paper was received politely enough, but my discussant was irritated. He pointed out the problem had a solution in mixed Nash strategies: the bar-goers could toss coins to reach a satisfactory outcome. I had thought of that, but to me that missed the point. To me, El Farol was not a problem of how to arrive at a coordinated solution (although the Minority Game very much is). I saw it as a conundrum for economics: How do you proceed analytically when there is no deductive, rational solution? Defining the problem as a game lost this—all games have at least one Nash mixed-strategy equilibrium—so I resisted any game-theoretic formulation. My paper duly appeared, but economists didn't quite know what to make of it. My colleague at Santa Fe, Per Bak, did know however. He saw the manuscript and began to fax it to his physics friends. The physics community took it up, and in the hands of Challet, Marsili and Zhang, it inspired something different than I expected—the Minority Game. El Farol emphasized (for me) the difficulties of formulating economic behavior in ill-defined problems. The Minority Game emphasizes something different: the efficiency of the solution. This is as should be. The investigation reveals explicitly how strategies co-adapt and how efficiency is related to information. This opens an important door to understanding financial markets.

As I write this, there are now over 200 papers on the Minority Game, and a growing community of econophysicists who have become deeply immersed in the dynamics of markets—especially financial markets. Economists wonder at times whether all this work in physics is not just a lengthy exercise in physicists learning what economists know. It is certainly not—and indeed this book shows it is not. Modern physics can offer much to economics. Not just different tools and different methods of analysis, but different concepts such as phase transitions, critical values, and power laws. And not just the analysis of pattern at stasis, but the analysis of patterns in formation. Economics needs this. In fact economics is changing currently from an emphasis on equilibrium and homogeneity to an emphasis on the formation of pattern and heterogeneity. And so, economics in due course would be forced to use the kind of tools that are brought to bear in this book. Luckily physics is there to supply them.

The papers here and the text are an important part of a movement—looking at the economy under heterogeneity. Challet, Marsili and Zhang and the others described here have done much to power this movement, and I congratulate them for this. It is indeed a benefit to physicists and economists to have this work collected in one place.

W. Brian Arthur
Santa Fe, New Mexico.

Preface

In the twenty-first century, science seems to be taking on a more interdisciplinary approach. Walls between the disciplines are becoming porous. A natural result of this process is that many researchers with different backgrounds find themselves working on the same subject, each having his own goals and dictionary, each bringing their own methods, concepts, and notations.

Financial markets have been a subject on which the interest of many researchers from different disciplines have converged. In the past decade many economists and physicists alike have been busily studying market-related phenomena. This unprecedented surge in interest in understanding the mechanism of financial markets can be attributed not only to their ever more prominent impact on society, but also to the now much easier access to very large quantity of data.

In the meantime, physics is undergoing some profound changes as well: a significant number of physicists previously working on traditional hard science topics are shifting their attention to interdisciplinary areas bordering on biology, economics, and other social sciences. The main force behind this outflow is not so much that physicists have lost interest in physics, but the realization that there are incredibly interesting complex phenomena taking place in other disciplines which seem now within reach of the powerful theoretical tools which have been successful in physics.

There is nothing new about physicists being interested in economics or other disciplines such as biology or computer science. In economics, this is a trend which is more than a century old, many first-class economists and several Nobel laureates having a degree in physics in their earlier carrier. What is new is that nowadays physicists studying interdisciplinary subjects remain physicists and do not become economists, biologists, or computer scientists. They are interested in the wonders which such complex systems as a financial market or a protein unveil, and in understanding these systems from a different perspective.

Physicists feel uneasy about the formal mathematical approach used by theoretical economists. Their view of a financial market may be close to a black box containing frenzied people whose agitation is responsible for fluctuations of over-whelming importance. How can such a precise language as that of theorems and lemmas account for such a messy system? Fluctuations and messy (e.g. disordered) systems are very familiar to statistical physicists, who have developed powerful tools to deal with them in the last 25 years. How can such an important and interesting complex system be left in the exclusive hands of formal tools such as those of mathematical economics?

The Minority Game, which is the subject of this book, was born as an attempt to paint a physicist's picture of a financial market. It is more of a sketch, with a few raw brush-strokes trying to give the main idea. Its focus is on fluctuations, hence the agents it describes are the speculators, who are believed to be responsible for making markets so volatile.

The rules are simple: a finite number of players have to choose between two sides; whoever ends up in the minority side is a winner. By definition all players cannot be winners, and therefore they should not agree with each other as to what is the best strategy. Thus the Minority Game punishes herding and rewards diversity; the players make do with only a limited information processing capacity. Although this game is a generic model of competition between adaptive agents, it has attracted much attention as a model of financial markets, bringing appealing insights into market dynamics.

Many people from different backgrounds have contributed to the Minority Game, with more than one hundred papers published since its inception in 1997. The diversity of contributions means that even for experts it is hard to keep a comprehensive view of the whole subject, hence we believe that there is real need for this book. Instead of rewriting completely the history of the topic, which would have lead to a much more biased view, we have chosen a selection of twenty-seven papers, based not only on their importance, but also on their readability.

The Minority Game is remarkably accessible to a broad spectrum of readership. At the same time, financial market modelling touches upon many areas of social and hard sciences. We have done our best to ensure that this book will be accessible not just to physicists, but also to economists, financial market researchers and practitioners, and interested members of the general public. For this, the papers alone are not enough: for each subject area we have written introductory chapters that collectively serve to comment on and join together all the separate research papers, as well as to provide a coherent, synthetic, and hopefully pedagogical review of the subject. The content of these introductory chapters no replacement for the published papers, as the serious reader may want to go deeper into each argument by reading the original account and possibly consulting other papers referred to.

This book, after an introductory chapter, is divided into four chapters respectively describing early works, the path to the analytical solution, the relationship between the Minority Game and financial markets, and finally various extensions to the model. An appendix explains how to carry out numerical simulations and gives commented source code written in the C programming language. For reasons of space, many interesting extensions have had to be left out, but we have included an exhaustive list of publications and links to relevant websites.

Each chapter is as self-contained as possible. Each is conceived as an entry point into different areas of the vast literature, which has branched in several directions since 1997. All the chapters are intended to be accessible to a broad audience, with the possible exception of the one devoted to analytical results, in which we have sketched the different methods that can be applied to a broad range of models. So the narrative style of the first two chapters, with barely no mathematics and mostly discursive arguments, sharply contrasts with the more technical third chapter.

We would like this book to be an invitation to play with this fascinating game. At the simplest level, anyone can play the online interactive version, which is almost like a trading screen, from anywhere in the world, without a detailed knowledge of the theoretical model[1]. Human players can challenge different difficulty levels of Minority Game agents. The interactive game not only amuses players, but also provides 'experimental' data that may help us to gain some glimpses of how we humans deduct and react in a market-like setting, probing in a quantitative way some fundamental questions far beyond economics.

Then, if the reader is conversant with a minimal level of computer programming, he can start simulations, tinkering the provided code himself. More serious readers may want to explore the different ramifications of this simple mathematical model that is ready to be simulated on any computer, yet rich enough to yield the complex behavioural patterns that are characteristic of real financial markets. People confident in their mathematical prowess may discover how far one can go with analytical tools and solutions.

The standard Minority Game is well understood and a comprehensive theory of its behaviour has been developed. This allows the expert reader to play with the Minority Game, using it as a platform for all kinds of 'experiments' on market dynamics. This book shows some of the applications where ever more realistic features from the real financial markets are added on the basic game. For example, one can devise different species of players and let them interact in the same game. Will the resulting market ecology be characterized by cooperative symbiosis or competitive predator–prey interactions? The myriad applications show that the Minority Game model is a versatile tool in exploring—in a scientific way, independent of ideologies

---

[1] see http://www.unifr.ch/econophysics/minority/game

and convictions—environments populated by many agents, with bounded information capacity.

The Minority Game is an open-ended story and many new ideas and hypotheses can still be tested using this platform. If the reader takes up the challenge and starts playing with it, once some familiarity is gained, he may start asking more and more questions. Answers to some of them may be found in this book or references herein, but many may well remain open. We hope this book will help the reader, using the methods and reasoning discussed here, to find solutions.

Acknowledgements

Special thanks to W. Brian Arthur, who initiated our interest in El Farol Bar problem, and who kindly accepted to write a foreword.

Our thanks go to P. Bak, J. Berg, J.-P. Bouchaud, A. De Martino, N. F. Johnson, A. Rustichini, D. Sherrington, M. A. Virasoro, and R. Zecchina for fruitful interactions or collaborations.

We are grateful to J. Wakeling for assistance in proofreading the manuscript.

We express our gratitude to the authors and publishers of the selected papers for giving us permission to reprint their work in this book.

Contents

PART I

1. Introduction

'It's night already and I'm still sat at the trading desk, staring at the screen where the price history of the past twenty or so trading periods zigzags so teasingly. Now the trading frenzy is at its most intense, I have just scored five consecutive successful trades, a feat I never achieved previously during the whole day. I feel euphoric and invincible now, for the first time after countless hours' numb sitting I can stretch my aching neck and back, savouring the prospect of getting the upper hand of the seemingly indomitable market. In hindsight I might blame my previous bluntness on my own miscalculations: wasn't that moving average line stretching far out of the previous range, and I failed to react, for wanting to play contrarian? That double-shoulder on the trading chart was full of warning bells of imminent perils, but I stuck obstinately to my position. I saw that mini-crash coming and should have gotten out of my position way before . . . had I not been too greedy! Yet invincible I feel now, even though I'm still under for the day, having suffered huge losses during the afternoon session, and on a few times I was on the brink of being wiped out entirely of my authorized loss limit. My rival traders are invisible, for me they are just emotionless professionals ready to prey on any mistakes on my part, and on their fellow traders. But as my last straight winning track shows, I finally see through their schemes. The price history indicates that we have just come out from one of the characteristic volatility clusters—currently the slow, steady upward trend confirms my gut feeling that finally I can outsmart those cunning, bastard traders on the other side. So, invincible now, I feel the need to double my trading size, as I grow impatient at the small price increments, downside risks should be one part in a trillion, such a sure bet I shouldn't let it go. Yes, now I'm willing to bet my last shirt on this trade, as my last chance to recover my day's loss and perhaps end up with a small profit. I strike the "up" button, the price moves slightly in my direction. Even with my double leverage, the gain is insignificant, now I activate the maximum leverage, four times my normal trading size, and smash the "up" button . . . Out of the blue, the sky falls, the price inexplicably went down, way down in a previously unseen crash pattern . . . A red spot flashes, "Margin call, trade terminated". I know I just lost my last shirt.'

This could have been the recital of the daily ordeal of a tireless trader from the Foreign Currency market—some real life, legendary stories can be found in recent popular books (Krieger 1992; Niederhoffer 1998)—but it is in fact a real experience from playing an interactive version of the simple yet very rich and complex mathematical model called the *Minority Game*, which will be the main subject of this book. The above story describes the actual experience of a human player, among many computer agents, all pitted against one another. The graph on Fig. 1.1 is the 'price'

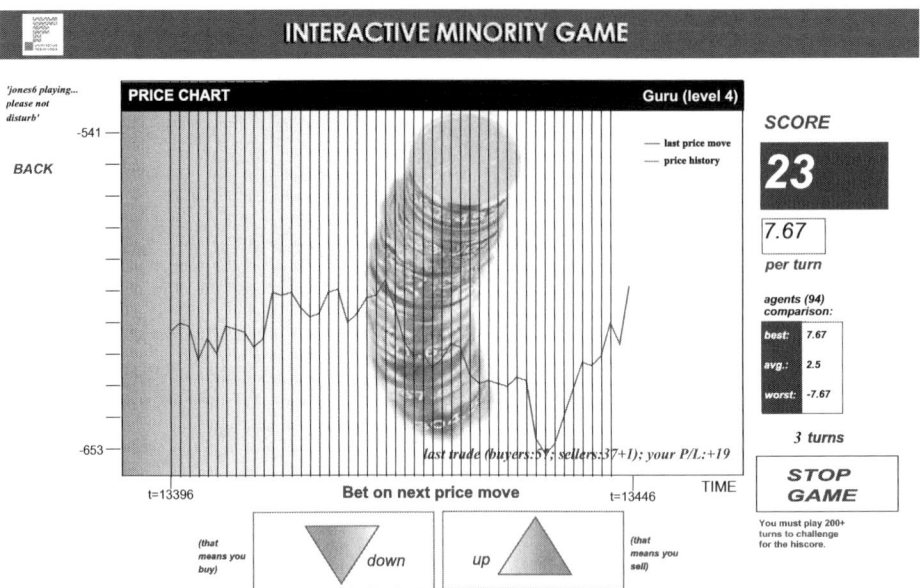

Fig. 1.1   Screenshot of the interactive minority game (www.unifr.ch/econophysics/minority/game).

history mentioned above. The Interactive Minority Game will be discussed in more detail in Chapter 5. The rules are the following: the players take bets that the price for next trading period will go up or down, and position themselves according to their convictions. The total sum of the aggregate positions of all the players determine the outcome of the next price movement, which in turn results in losses or gains depending on the respective positions taken. If most of the people buy, the price will go up, therefore it is convenient to be a seller. If the majority is on the selling side, those who buy will be on the winning side. In both cases, it pays to be in the minority, hence the name Minority Game.

There are other situations in daily life, which can be described by the Minority Game. On the other hand, financial markets are not always Minority Games. Both these issues will be discussed towards the end of this chapter. For the time being it is important to remark that Minority Game, as a model of a financial market, focuses particularly on that component of trading which is due to speculation. In order to explain the reason of this particular focus, a comment on why physicists study financial markets is in order.

1.1   Why do physicists study financial markets?

A popular tale has it that John Keynes invited Max Planck to study economic questions. After a reflection Planck declined saying the mathematics would be too difficult. At the time, it might have sounded baffling as Planck, the father of quantum mechanics, is one of the greatest physicists of the last century.

The present situation may not deserve Planck's prudence anymore. After decades of frenetic technical development of powerful mathematical tools, physics has finally evolved to a stage in which it can address questions of unprecedented complexity involving non-linear, non-equilibrium phenomena. Furthermore, massive amount of financial data has been recently made available by the advent of computers. The amount and quality of empirical information about financial market activity may even exceed that which experimental physics or biology makes available in some contexts. This has allowed empirical studies to bring to light quite remarkable regularities in the statistics of price fluctuations (Mantegna and Stanley 2000; Dacorogna et al. 2001; Bouchaud and Potters 2000). Interestingly, some of these empirical laws have features, such as power law distributions and long-range correlations, which are very similar to those of anomalous fluctuations arising in physical systems undergoing a phase transition.

It must be said that the lack in mainstream finance literature of a satisfactory model of markets' fluctuations should not be interpreted as economists having done a 'bad' job. Economics is a proud profession where, in the past three decades, more theorists have been awarded Nobel Prizes than from all the other sciences combined. To be fair, modelling economy is a much more complex subject than say, physics or even biology. 'Particles' in the economy are much harder to grasp since the modeller and the modelled are parts of the same system. The traditional method in 'hard sciences' of isolating a box, having all the external conditions specified and concentrating on the core of a few elements, is just too naïve to work. The mainstream, or neoclassical economics—which basically uses the mechanical metaphor, mimicking nineteenth century physics—is receiving ever louder criticism within the economics profession. It has been advocated a century ago by such prominent economists as Alfred Marshall (Marshall 1932) and Thorstein Veblen (Veblen 1898), and recently picked up again as a working hypothesis by the Santa Fe school, that economics should be closer in spirit to biology than to classical mechanics. Possibly it is even more complex, as economic systems evolve purposefully, changing their very interactions and rules on the run. On the other hand, statistical mechanics, a branch of theoretical physics, has in the last two decades evolved from studying crystalline materials to complex phenomena like turbulence, biological evolution, chaos, and earthquakes. It has undergone fundamental transformations both in scope and methods. Weaned long ago from the mechanical approach, it has embraced uncertainties, emergence, and catastrophes. The tools typically used would not have been recognizable only a few decades ago. For example, the methods to deal with disordered materials, that is, with heterogeneous interactions, central to the analysis of the Minority Game, were developed some 20 years ago for tackling such complex, non-linear, non-equilibrium subjects as spin-glasses. In short, mathematical tools handling a large number of degrees of freedom, connected in a random, frustrating manner, are only recently available to allow us to mount a serious attack on much harder issues like the modelling of financial markets. It would be self-serving and wrong to say that physicists can do better job at studying the economy. What seems to be true, however, is that economic study poses incredibly complex and interesting questions which are far too important to remain n the exclusive hands of mainstream economists. In addition, questions which arise in economic contexts engage the tools and the knowledge of statistical physics in yet unexplored directions. This teaches physicists something more about how fluctuations aggregate from the micro to the macroscale to produce new collective phenomena.

Physicists studying financial markets are regularly and rightly warned by economists about the rich economics literature and the risk of re-inventing the wheel. On the other hand, economists should be aware that physicists can be interested in posing quite different questions than those they would ask. And financial markets are the prototype example: They are very complicated objects. Their primary objective is to enable traders to reallocate resources efficiently: to exchange what each has or produces, including risk, with what they need. This aspect of markets, which may be the main focus for an economist, cannot by itself explain the fluctuation patterns we see. In particular, financial markets display both excess volatility and excessive trade volume, which means that only a small fraction of the fluctuations can be explained in terms of trades motivated by economic activity, the so-called fundamentals. The volume of trades in foreign exchange markets, for example, is way larger than what it should be, 90% of the daily transactions being due to speculative trading (Dacorogna et al. 2001). Any model which aims at explaining fluctuations should focus primarily on speculative trading. This is what the Minority Game is tailored for: its agents are speculators.

High volatility is a major concern for investors, because it implies risk. However, it is not strictly necessary to understand the origin of excess volatility in order to cope with it. For example, volatility clustering may not be a worry for someone interested in computing the price of an option. There is indeed a whole industry on how the Black and Scholes formula—a tool to price options in an ideal world with normal price fluctuations—can be modified in order to account for that (Bouchaud and Potters 2000). Statistical physicists instead have a special obsession for anomalous fluctuations and they cannot stand without inquiring into their origin.

1.2   Market modelling: simple yet complex

The Santa Fe institute was established with the aim of forging an unconventional place to stimulate research in diverse disciplines, with a prominent place given to economics, biology and their relationship to physics. Mitchell Waldrop's bestseller '*Complexity*' (Waldrop 1994) captures well the essential atmosphere and background, as well as the main protagonists in the founding phase. One of the main aims was to join the forces of economists and physicists to understand fundamental issues in the turbulent world economy. Led by economist Brian Arthur, the Santa Fe team came out with the 'Santa Fe Stock Market Model' (Arthur et al. 1997). This was the first *bona fide* model using heterogeneous agents to model financial markets. This challenge was later taken up by others (Caldarelli et al. 1997; Sato and Takayasu 1998; Lux and Marchesi 1999; Levy et al. 2000). These models showed that the anomalous fluctuation properties of stock markets, which have been very carefully characterized by Mantegna and Stanley (Mantegna and Stanley 2000), could be produced by the internal non-linear trading dynamics of the market. For some time, reproducing these 'stylized facts'—fat tailed distribution of returns and volatility clustering—has been very popular. The initial enthusiasm about Santa Fe stock market models and the like has faded these days because the models depend in an uncontrollable way on so many parameters that they often have unpredictable behaviour. A good thing when it gives rise to unexpected richness; a worry because, with so many parameters, one can never be sure which inputs contributed to which observed feature. More worryingly, however, there is growing unease about the general scope of the exercise: if in order to reproduce all the observed facts, we were to devise more and more refined models with an even larger set of parameters, we would likely end up with a model as complicated as the real world. Is this really what science is for? In doing so, we are still clueless as to what factors are prominent and what are the prescriptions for better regulations. In short, reproducing the real world has little to do with understanding: it is rather closer to fitting; what is needed is a dramatically simplified model, simple enough that the necessary mathematics can still be handled, yet still capturing some of the basic mechanisms of real markets. Physics has had to face similar methodological difficulties. For example, real magnetic materials are very complex to model. Take iron: each atom is already a very complex system with twenty-six electrons. A system of many iron atoms is even more complex, with emergent properties such as crystalline structure, metallic state, and magnetization. However, the Ising model (e.g. see Yeomans 1992), reducing each atom to a simple binary variable, so-called spin, and assuming a very simple spin–spin interaction, already accounts qualitatively for most of the collective behaviours. The simple Ising model served as a prototypical model to handle a very large class of phenomena successfully. What we look for is an 'Ising model' of financial markets, retaining only the key ingredients.

It has been a deep insight of Brian Arthur (Arthur 1994) that bounded rationality and heterogeneity are two essential ingredients of modelling complex systems such as speculative financial markets. Let us see why.

Speculators in financial markets are far more complex 'objects' than iron atoms because they behave purposefully, depending on their environment. In order to model purposeful behaviour, mainstream economics, in particular Game Theory, went as far as to assume that agents are fully rational. In a nutshell Game Theory (Fudenberg and Tirole 1991; Neumann and Morgenstern 1944) goes as follows: there are a few players; each tries to outsmart the others, but he must take into account what the others' reaction to his actions will be. What the player knows is of great importance, as is what they know about what other players know. It has tremendous depth and richness, but the analysis can hardly handle more than a few heterogeneous players.

To be fair, Game Theory is important in strategic decision-making, contract negotiation, etc. But modelling financial markets needs a very large number of players; for such large number Game Theory is virtually helpless to assist. Do traders make a mental model of how every other trader behaves so as to compute how he would best react to each of their actions? Can they store and process all that information to find their *best response*? Even with the best computer they could not. In the real market the amount of information is too large for anybody's capacity, be they supercomputers or finance gurus. Worse still, understanding the implications of all the pieces of information is even harder. Deductive rationality as well as full information is untenable in this context. Indeed, the Minority Game is not a game in the sense of Game Theory. Traders do not behave in such a sophisticated strategic way. Rather they make a model of the market as a whole and try to respond optimally to it. Traders play against the market not against each other. They have vastly reduced information: only the aggregate price and volume are public, information about individuals actions is denied. In addition to that, the Minority Game also assumes that the traders behave in inductively rational manner, as suggested by Arthur, rather than in a deductive way.

Dramatically simplifying the individual player's sophistication is a must, if we ever want to understand the large scale, collective behaviour. However, assuming that all the agents behave as a single 'representative agent', a traditional assumption in economics literature, is probably a non-starter. First, how can a collective behaviour qualitatively different from that of the single representative agent emerge? To make this point clear, consider an example from physics: if one studies everything possible about a few water molecules, one still does not have any clue as to when water is solid (ice), liquid, or gas (vapour). There are fundamentally new phenomena and questions that can only appear when very large numbers of the constituents aggregate. This is also true in economics: studying everything possible about a few investors gives no clues as to why there are sudden crashes in financial markets. In other words, the collective behaviour of financial markets is an *emergent* property which is the result of how fluctuations propagate through interactions from the micro to the macroscale. Emergence requires the interaction among many distinct units—the agents.

Still, just as in the case of water where molecules are identical, one may think of modelling financial markets with distinct but otherwise identical agents. After all, if there is an optimal strategy, only fools would try to deviate from it. But, as forcefully explained by Arthur with his El Farol Bar problem (Arthur 1994) there are situations where there cannot be an optimal strategy, because the chance of success of a strategy decreases with the number of agents adopting it. This forces the agents to form divergent expectations and to follow different behaviours. In these situations, the representative agent approach is doomed. Financial markets are one of these situations.

Many practitioners and scholars alike have for a long time advocated that successful trading depends more on what you do with respect to what others do, than to some hypothetical optimum benchmark. If a speculator thinks that one particular strategy is likely to lead to profits, there is no point convincing her fellow traders that she is right. The profit opportunities are fleeting: by the time the majority of the traders come to know them, they are no longer effective any more. This is why in the trading manuals it is rare that any well-documented anomaly can be substantiated upon academic, systematic checking. The same patterns would never be sustained for long; inevitably they would be transformed into other unsuspected niches.

For this reason, if we want to model speculative trading activity in financial markets it is essential to account for the full heterogeneity in the strategies of agents. This is not only because speculators may be different a priori—because they operate on different timescales (Dacorogna et al. 2001), have different beliefs, risk profiles, etc.— but because they are forced to differ.

The situation then seems hopeless: a full description of financial markets would require modelling all ingredients and will lead to uncontrollable complexity. If we want to describe heterogeneous agents, the number of parameters must grow at least as the number of agents. This is where statistical physics of disordered systems enters to rescue us: if we assume that agents are drawn at random with a particular distribution of strategies, we can still have totally heterogeneous agents with only a few parameters. Furthermore, the collective behaviour can be characterized in terms of *self-averaging* properties, which are those that do not depend on the particular realization of agents drawn. This strategy to deal with complex systems was first introduced by Paul I. Wigner for describing the statistical properties of heavy atom nuclear spectra (Wigner 1967). As Dyson puts it (Dyson 1962):

'The statistical theory will not predict the detailed [energy] level sequence of any one nucleus, but it will describe the general appearance and the degree of irregularity of the level structure that is expected to occur in any nucleus that is too complicated to be understood in detail [...] We picture a complex nucleus as a black box in which a large number of particles are interacting according to unknown laws [...] There is a strong logical expectation, though no rigorous mathematical proof, that an ensemble average will correctly describe the behaviour of one particular system which is under observation. The expectation is strong, because the system might be one of a huge variety of systems, and very few of them will deviate much from a properly chosen ensemble average'.

This approach allows the Minority Game to deal with a large number of individually distinct interacting agents, while placing draconian restrictions on the individual's capacity and behaviour. Indeed the Minority Game assumes that the complexity of the choice problem faced by the agents does not grow with the complexity of the environment they live in. Heterogeneity in agents' strategies may also introduce what physicists call *frustration*: in a nutshell, frustration means that one cannot make everyone happy, some degrees of freedom are necessarily upset and, as a result, an astronomically large number of equilibria can emerge.

It is also worth remarking that the most powerful techniques to deal with disordered systems such as spin glasses were developed with the mean-field approximation. This assumes that each spin can interact with any other, regardless of their distance. This is clearly a not-so-good approximation in physics where interactions take place only in a local neighbourhood. It is, however, very appropriate in modelling financial markets, which are the places where everyone plays with/against everyone else in a centralized fashion regardless of geographic distance.

1.3   Information efficiency and information food-chains

Information lies at the very basis of market interaction between traders in the Minority Game. For instance try to play an up-down-up-down periodic sequence in the Interactive Minority Game: you will notice that, initially, this imposes a similar oscillating behaviour in the price. However, if the machine players are sufficiently equipped, they will soon detect such regularity and trip over themselves to feast on such opportunity. This will result in the disfiguring of the initial periodic pattern, but in devouring this information the players generate secondary patterns of all sorts which provide 'food' for further speculator exploitation.

The Efficient Market Hypothesis (EMH), one of the fundamental pillars of mainstream economics, assumes that this process goes on until no detectable information is left in the signal. In other words, rational market players, if informed, would arbitrage away any profit opportunities so that no one can get extra gains from speculation. Whether or not it applies to real markets is still a hotly debated issue. The most prominent evidence in favour of EMH comes from Samuelson's notorious mathematical 'Proof that properly anticipated prices fluctuate randomly' (Samuelson 1965). While proponents are mostly mainstream theorists, most practitioners remain unconvinced.

After all, the practitioners must be up to something in their daily striving. The very fact that speculators exist, is indirect evidence of the failure of EMH in some form. From this point of view, such a sweeping mathematical proof, proves more the inadequacy of the neoclassical tool sets than gives clues to the real markets' efficiency. At any rate, the validity of the EMH remains a matter of faith without a detailed study of the ecology of a large number of heterogeneous players.

Recently, one of the authors has put up an alternative approach—the Marginally Efficient Market (MEM) theory—which takes into account the symbiotic relationship between different types of market participants (Zhang 1999). The simplest example is to divide market participants into two broad categories: producers and speculators. Producers are those players who participate largely in economic activities outside the trading market, but whose activities need market transactions; speculators focus more on the market fluctuations than producers, feeding on the information supplied by the producers' activity to make profitable trades. From an information-theoretic point of view, since producers pay less attention to the market's ups and downs, their actions effectively inject elements of predictability into the market, though inadvertently. One might say that the speculators, being more vigilant than the producers, should arbitrage the profit opportunities completely away in no time. However, the profitable opportunities have a probabilistic nature. No matter how sophisticated a speculator's strategy is, there are intrinsic risks associated with these profit opportunities. For this reason, the MEM theory asserts that because there is an information-theoretical limit, speculators can reduce the opportunity content in the market fluctuations only to a limited extent (Zhang 1999). This is tantamount to showing that the elimination of market 'inefficiencies' is impossible. On the one hand, the outside economy injects some profitable opportunities in the first place; on the other it is impossible to clean the market completely of arbitrages. Essentially, the traders form a market ecology where different types are self-arranged along an information food-chain, very much like the food-chain in the biosphere. There are interesting questions one can ask about the market ecology: how effective are the speculators? If more speculators join the market, what would be the rational reaction of producers? How long does the same pattern persist before it is arbitraged away? In the original paper (Zhang 1999) much analysis is qualitative in the sense that it is about estimates rather than precise calculations. The Minority Game provides a mathematical platform to enquire about the nature of the informational food-chain in detail.

1.4   Minority situations in economic life

This book will concentrate on modelling financial markets using Minority Game and its derivatives. But before we dive into details it is instructive to consider the broader perspective of similar situations that the Minority Game describes. Minority situations are so common that everyone can relate to them. If you drive on a crowded multilane highway, you may be tempted from time to time to switch lane, in order to economize travelling time. You figure out the lane next to you is less crowded, hence the minority choice, and decide to move over. Perhaps you will regret having made the switch, for now it turns out that the traffic flow on the lane you were in starts moving faster, and you notice several other motorists had the same otherwise clever idea as you did—thereby invalidating *a posteriori* your spotting the minority.

If you plan a holiday for a popular destination near the beach, but know that last year it was very crowded during the month of July, you might try to avoid the peak period by shifting this year's departure date forward or back a bit. That individual decisions which appears inconsequential, is actually the vital business of tourism industry: tour operators, hotels, and chartered flights all need to plan ahead. They base their estimates on the past data as well on all the trifling factors that might help them to make their guesses closer to reality. For them, the mass movement resulting from individual 'figuring out' is the most relevant factor in deciding whether or not their business is successful. They all resort to differential pricing to regulate the flow, to keep it somewhat constant.

In broader economic life, there are many other minority situations we often take for granted. The problem faced by firms considering whether to enter a market, addressed by the so-called market entry games (Bottazzi et al. 2003), are also similar to Minority Games. Also, we may notice that one profession is lacking in our town and price for that service goes up. The proverbial 'invisible hand' will see to it that the shortfall, hence minority side, will attract more potential candidates to fill the gap. Adam Smith proposed this providential mechanism as one of the cornerstones of the capitalist economy. We tend to fill in the profession that appears to be in short supply, only to find that a short time after the shortfall has turned into an oversupply, thanks to many like-minded clever people. People then become more sophisticated, considering not just the current or immediate past data but much larger parameter sets, longer historical data. However, though the simplest boom-and-bust cycles can be easily avoided, the shortfalls and oversupply almost always persist in unexpected patterns. Equilibrium, where all factors just balance each other, is to be expected only on an exceptional basis. Standard economics often concentrates on the equilibrium states, and has not sufficiently studied the fluctuation phenomena that we shall explore in this book.

We must warn readers that minority situations do not appear in all economic life, not even in the narrower sense of financial markets. In financial trading, often it is convenient to join the majority trend, not to fight against the trend. During the Internet stock follies, it was possible to reap considerable profits by going along with the explosive boom, provided one got off the trend in time. There are many other situations where success is associated with conforming with the majority.

But majority situations may actually have minority elements embedded in them. The real financial trading probably requires a mixed minority–majority strategy, in which timing is essential. The minority situations seem to prevail in the long run because speculators cannot all be winners. Indeed no boom is without end, being different from the crowd at the right time is the key to success. In a booming trend, it is the minority of those who get off first who win, the others lose.

1.5   What's next?

As we enter the more technical chapters, we shall see that the standard version of the Minority Game is more or less 'solved' and most features can be obtained analytically. The road is open to play on the Minority Game platform, to modify it in all possible ways according to need. One can change the composition of players and study all possible ecosystems of interacting market participants. For example, one can study how one species displaces another from its niche or how symbiotic relations emerge. As with any serious undertaking, to be able to exploit fully Minority Game and its ramifications there is some necessary homework to do and we hope this book will facilitate the task. The game is open ended: we hope this work will stimulate better future models of financial markets and other collective phenomena in social sciences.

It is amusing to speculate what will be the fate of the Minority Game a few years down the road. The interactive version would help it to propagate further, even away from academic circles. Just like with flight simulators, people would gauge their trading capability with the Minority Game. Eventually, some standard benchmark may be established and, similar to the IQ intelligence score, the Minority Game score may become the requisite entry ticket to Wall Street trading firms.

2. Early works

2.1 Background

The Minority Game was introduced and first studied in 1997 (Challet and Zhang 1997). Thereafter, the then tiny community of 'econophysics' caught on to it and published, in a period of merely 5 years, over one hundred papers directly concerned with it. This can be considered 'explosive' activity in economics, where typical publication times are excruciatingly slow. The reason why almost all the papers related to the Minority Game were published in interdisciplinary physics journals is that there exist multiple hurdles for outsiders like physicists publishing in the mainstream economics venues. Definitely physicists generally feel uneasy about several pillars of mainstream economic theory, such as rational expectations, the efficient market hypothesis and the notion of equilibria to name a few. This approach looks too axiomatic and formal to deal with such complex systems as, for example, financial markets. If 'econophysics' contributions have not appeared in economic journals, it is not because economists are not open-minded, but rather because econophysicists deny the very rules of the game on which mainstream academic research in economics is based. We should also note that risk-averse attitudes towards new ideas in the mainstream economics journals are particularly pronounced even towards prominent economists themselves. Think of the famous paper by Akerlof on the 'Lemons Problem' (Akerlof 1970). It had to endure more than 4 years in the refereeing process with numerous rebuttals and revisions— and 30 years later was deemed worthy of a Nobel Prize. The paper of Brian Arthur (Arthur 1990) on 'Increasing Returns' had to struggle through seven years of torture before it became the well-known benchmark paper. Physicists are maybe too spoilt to have the stamina to survive such a punishing regime. If the top-notch economists with new ideas were treated like that, what sort of welcome would be reserved for outsiders? However, it must be pointed out that in private venues, such as conferences, seminars, and workshops, the communication between economists and physicists is excellent and stimulating.

Before the Minority Game, there were quite a number of physicists already investigating various economics-related issues. The time was ripe for such investigations.

Recent years have seen a significant increase in availability of financial data, and markets became a fascination for physicists, with their seemingly chaotic dynamics—quite similar to turbulence of some sort—perhaps hiding some underlying laws. In short, in the final decade of the last century, general public awareness of economic and financial issues reached unprecedented levels and many scientists were unable to resist the temptation to try to gain a glimpse of some secret fundamental laws of nature regarding human interaction. The time was one of expansion too for the statistical physics community: with fresh successes in such 'soft-physics' disciplines as spin glasses, complexity and chaos, non-equilibrium phenomena, and self-organized criticality, they were eager to attempt new challenges outside their traditional turf.

Around this time, various groups independently proposed multiagent models for the stock market (Arthur et al. 1997; Caldarelli et al. 1997; Lux and Marchesi 1999). These were important studies which showed that interacting agent models could produce real-looking price histories, with crashes, clustered volatility, chronic bubbles, and depressions. The most serious drawback of these models was that the relevant features of the interaction were buried under so many parameters that a systematic understanding was virtually impossible. Since the market mechanisms underlying the models were intrinsically non-linear, small variations in any parameter could lead to dramatic changes and one could never be sure which aspect was responsible for which movement. Exploring a twenty-four-dimensional parameter space, which potentially hides new collective behaviour around every corner, is prohibitively difficult (and boring). In order to escape this 'dimensionality curse' and gain insight into the laws hidden behind financial fluctuations, one has to resort to a completely different strategy: start from the simplest possible model capturing the essential features of market interaction, understand it in detail and then add complications to it. This type of modelling is found frequently in physics, the prototype example being the Ising model, a miniature of real magnetic materials. It is in this spirit that we were led to the Minority Game, in the hope of having a simple yet rich platform to model various phenomena arising from real financial markets, possibly beyond. But the problem was, where to start?

2.2   Brian Arthur's El Farol Bar

Economics is not a single block! Brian Arthur is one of the original thinkers of rare courage. His work has often gone outside of the mainstream doctrine's tolerance boundaries and resulted in breakthroughs with lasting effects. He is most well known for his path-breaking work on 'increasing returns and lock-ins' (Arthur 1990). In a conversation with one of us prior to the Minority Game, he reflected on his long frustration with mainstream theory's insistence that economic agents are equipped with such rational minds as to know everything, understanding all with implicitly infinite information capacity. He wanted to return to the drawing board, to have a fresh look at agents with *bounded* rationality.

Bounded rationality was introduced by the late Herbert Simon a little over half a century ago (Simon 1981). Though its importance and relevance was widely recognized, it is difficult to model, quite simply because there are so many ways to be imperfect. We need to specify bounded rational behaviour by degree and type of imperfection. In contrast, there is only one way to be completely rational. Hence perfect, deductive rationality is straightforward to model, and has allowed mainstream economists to turn economics into a branch of applied mathematics.

Arthur came up with a model called the 'El Farol Bar' problem to illustrate the question. El Farol is an Irish bar in Santa Fe that used to have live Irish music on Thursdays. Arthur often hangs out there and it is probably there that he figured out a way of articulating his misgivings towards the 'deductive reasoning' paradigm. His paper is the first of our selection, and the story of the El Farol Bar, which is best told in his own words (Arthur 1994) (see page 115), goes roughly as follows: 'there are 100 Irish music lovers but El Farol has only 60 seats. The show is enjoyable only when fewer than 60 people show up. What should people do?'

Arthur points out that even such everyday life situations pose quite complex problems for deductive rational agents. It is quite unrealistic that people should behave as game theoretic players. This would entail each of them having to form a complete model of every other player's contingent behaviour before taking a decision.

Arthur's idea was to cook up a simple model where the agents resort to 'inductive thinking': they have a limited number of strategies—something like rules of thumb or schemata and, instead of deciding the merits of strategies prior to playing, agents would evaluate them afterwards, according to their performance, and possibly adjust their behaviour accordingly. A key aspect of Arthur's view of bounded rationality is that agents, by resorting to schemata, reduce enormously the complexity of their decision-making problem, perhaps paying for this by giving up some efficiency. 'Inductive reasoning', as a critique to the 'deductive reasoning' imposed on economic agents by mainstream economics, is the primary focus of Arthur's paper.

But the paper contains much more. A second, quite important point is that there cannot be an a priori best strategy in situations such as that occurring in the El Farol Bar. If there were, everyone would use it and find themselves unhappy, either all in the bar or all at home.[1] If agents have similar expectations about the bar attendance, and behave accordingly, these expectations are going to prove wrong. This is in marked

---

[1] This reasoning does not account for *mixed* strategies. Agents could flip a 60%–40% coin and decide accordingly whether to go or not. Maybe Arthur did not even consider real people behaving this way.

contrast with the rational expectation framework where expectations are consistent if not self-fulfilling prophecies. In a context such as that of the El Farol Bar, expectations are forced to diverge. If agents evolve at all, they are bound to become different from one another. One needs to introduce full heterogeneity across agents.

Arthur did that by assigning a distinct set of strategies to each of his agents. The strategies were rather clumsy—still to this day, we do not know exactly how large the repertoire was or whether there was any systematic characterization of the strategies. Nevertheless, the clumsy strategies serve a good purpose: his agents have very limited rationality. Their strategies have no apparent merits except being diversified. The beauty of the model is that in spite of the messy nature of the strategies and the lack of coordination among the agents, the bar attendance nevertheless evolves to the optimal value. This seems quite an achievement: agents with very limited rationality somehow collectively behave as if there is an invisible hand guiding them to the correct answer.[2]

This is quite akin to Darwin's natural selection mechanism: random mutations without apparent merits can lead the species to higher forms of life without the intervention of a 'Creator'. In this light, the mainstream deductive reasoning is the unwitting relative of the discredited creationism in biology. All the information is known a priori, the best designs are available, the fundamental value of everything is known. Arthur's El Farol Bar, from this viewpoint, is an attempt to restore the Darwinian paradigm in economics by denying such knowledge to the agents. As compensation his agents are equipped with more alternatives, akin to Darwinian over-reproduction. Selection is performed afterwards in the strategy space, according to the actual outcome of gain or loss in Arthur's model and survival of the fittest in evolution theory.[3]

Given the success of El Farol Bar model in demonstrating that inductive reasoning can indeed be quite effective, Arthur must have been satisfied with the results and felt that no further development of his model was necessary. We can deduce this from his second paper in *Science* (Arthur 1999), largely a repetition of his original paper and not reproduced here. But a statistical physicist would ask the El Farol Bar problem to explain much more, and in much more detail. This, however, requires a more precisely defined model—and this is how the Minority Game came about.

John Casti, the editor of the Santa Fe journal *Complexity* and an admirer of Arthur's work, summed up the El Farol model in an editorial thusly (Casti 1996):

So these are the components of a complex, adaptive system: a medium-sized number of intelligent, adaptive agents interacting on the basis of local information. At present, there

---

[2] Actually in Section 2.3.1 we shall see that this result is so generic that even zero-intelligence agents can achieve it.

[3] The relationship between agents learning and evolutionary models, as well as the question of whether bounded rational behaviour converges to optimal choices, has been also discussed in the economics literature (Borgers and Sarin 1997; Drew Fudenberg 1998; Rustichini 1999*a*).

appear to be no known mathematical structures within which we can comfortably ask, let alone answer, natural mathematical questions about the El Farol situation like the conjectures posed above. This situation is completely analogous to that faced by gamblers in the 17th century, who sought a rational way to divide the stakes in a game of dice when the game had to be terminated prematurely by the appearance of the police (or, perhaps, the gamblers' wives). The description and analysis of that very definite real-world problem lead Fermat and Pascal to create a mathematical formalism we now call probability theory. At present, complex systems still awaits its Pascal and Fermat.

Obviously, what was important to Fermat and Pascal was not the specific problem of dice-throwing, but rather the overall issue of how to characterise mathematically a general set of such problems. And the same is true for the El Farol situation. The problem itself is merely a cute little puzzle. But it is representative of a much broader class of problems that permeate almost every nook and cranny of the social and behavioural sciences. And it is this class of deep-reaching questions that a good formulation of the El Farol problem will help unlock. As philosopher George Gilder noted, 'The central event of the twentieth century is the overthrow of matter. In technology, economics, and the politics of nations, wealth in the form of physical resources is steadily declining in value and significance. The powers of mind are everywhere ascendant over the brute force of things'. And it is the development of a workable theory of complex systems that will be the capstone to this transition from the material to the informational. A good formulation of the El Farol problem would be a major step in this direction.

John Casti was being prophetic in 1996: he might want to check to see if, some years later, his wishes are being fulfilled.

2.3   Minority Game

With hindsight, we must say that El Farol and the Minority Game, while sharing much in spirit, serve two very different purposes. The El Farol model is about the inductive-reasoning path to equilibrium; whereas the Minority Game is mainly about fluctuations around the equilibrium. While almost any set of strategies will allow the equilibrium to be reached, fluctuations, being secondary effects, require more elaborate modelling. Secondary does not necessarily mean less important: think of financial market related phenomena where the seemingly random fluctuations hide such important information as whether markets are efficient or not, what is the nature of the interactions among agents with different aims and trading horizons, whether and why volatilities are excessive or not, and, last but not the least, whether market equilibria exist. Though very suggestive, the El Farol model is not sufficient to allow detailed study of fluctuation-related phenomena.

The steps leading from the El Farol Bar to the Minority Game might be seen as just minor modifications or detailed articulation of a fundamental insight. Yet this further detailed articulation has led to totally novel phenomena. We shall see that the advent of Minority Game, and its subsequent explosive growth of literature, has led to the exploration of a rich plethora of phenomena previously unimagined. Sometimes devil is in the details.

2.3.1   From El Farol to the Minority Game

The main obstacle to understanding in the El Farol problem lies in the definition of agents' strategies. Let us briefly recall that a strategy in the El Farol Bar problem is a rule which 'predicts' the attendance of the next week, given the information about the attendances of the past weeks. Each agent has more than one predictor, he ranks them according to their performance and follows the recommendation of the best one (attend if prediction is less than sixty remain home otherwise).

Let us take a pragmatic approach. Suppose that agents base their decisions on the last M attendance sizes. With N agents, the attendance can take $N + 1$ values each time. This makes $(N + 1)^M$ possible combinations of information about the past. If strategies are based on a prediction of the attendance given the past history, as in Arthur's paper, we have $N+1$ possible predictions for each combination of information and hence $(N + 1)^{(N+1)^M}$ possible prediction for any combination. Hence there are $(N + 1)^{(N+1)^M}$ possible predictor strategies. Searching for the best strategy in such a huge strategy space may be prohibitive. Even comparing two strategies, to find out the best one, may be a heavy task if N is large.

Before simplifying things, it is important to remark that Arthur's agents can *self-organize* close to the optimal attendance without making any effort to search or compare, as shown in Challet and Marsili (2003b). Imagine that each agent has just one predictor, taken at random from the huge set of predictors. This is equivalent to drawing at random the prediction of each agent, for each string of past outcomes. Let us generalize to a bar with a capacity of xN seats ($0 < x < 1$). For each string of past attendances, there will be approximately xN agents predicting an attendance of less than xN (because predictions are uniformly distributed in $0, \ldots, N$). Following their prediction, they will show up at the bar whereas the others will remain home. Even zero-intelligence agents, following one predictor, will make the attendance close to xN. So 'intelligence' has little to do with convergence to the optimum. Hopefully, more intelligent agents will also be able to achieve this goal, but, before giving agents more intelligence, let us observe that the variance of the attendance around the optimal one is[4] $Nx(1 - x)$. This means that typically either $\sqrt{Nx(1 - x)}$ miss an enjoyable evening, remaining home when the attendance is below xN, or a similar number go to the bar, but do not find a seat, if the attendance is above xN. The variance

---

[4] This result comes from the fact that the attendance is a binomial variable with mean xN.

of the attendance is a measure of inefficiency, so the question is, can some more intelligence help agents reduce the fluctuations?

As in the El Farol Bar, we want to give agents two or more strategies and let them decide which to use. The problem is that strategies such as those based on the forecasting rules above are too complex and their number $(N+1)^{(N+1)^M}$ is too large. What is worrying is that this number, and the complexity of strategies, increases dramatically with N. We do not expect real people to behave in a very different way in a context with $N = 100$ or $N = 105$ agents. Rather, when the number of fellow agents increases, real people tend to behave as if they were playing against the *crowd*—that is, a single mega-player—than against $N - 1$ other intelligent beings (see discussion in Rustichini (1999*b*). Furthermore, the crowd does not behave as a game-theoretic player but rather as an entity animated by an idiosyncratic will. To cut things short, if we want to model this kind of situation, we have to simplify strategies so that their complexity does not depend on N.

The first step to do this comes from observing that players in the El Farol problem are only interested in going or not going to the bar. They do not have to predict the precise attendance size, but only whether it is worthwhile to go or not. The number of strategies is then much smaller, $2^{(N+1)^M}$. This is still a very large number with still the undesirable property of depending on N. But now, why would agents consider the precise attendance size in the past in order to make a binary prediction? This seems to be vastly over-redundant information. Information encoding only the past M correct choices should be enough. Doing so reduces the number of available strategies to 2^{2^M}, which removes the undesirable dependence on N. Now the number of strategies only depends on the number of past time steps. It still increases very fast when M increases, but is constant when N increases.

This strategy simplification is the first step towards a workable version of the El Farol Bar problem. Variables and rules are systematically defined, yet they are as simple as possible so as to allow controlled study.

Second, we have seen that convergence to the bar's comfort level is not a big deal and can be achieved by simple automata. The real challenge for our agents is to reduce fluctuations. Hence, we want a model which focuses on the fluctuations of the attendance. So the second ingredient is to symmetrize the problem by assuming that the bar can contain half of the players.

We now have the minority game as it was originally defined (Challet and Zhang 1997) (see page 124). So from a narrow perspective, the Minority Game is essentially a binary symmetric version of the El Farol Bar problem. But, as an abstract model where the two choices remain unspecified, it becomes a generic model of a complex adaptive system. This makes it a platform which is easy to modify in order to focus on a particular problem by designing suitable extensions.

2.3.2   A theoretical experiment

The binary representation of the Minority Game makes everything countable and easily amenable to algebraic and geometric descriptions. The first paper is based on about a month's intense work and was hastily drafted in a week to be presented at the first econophysics conference, in Budapest. It was less than seven months after its fuzzy conception that it appeared on the library shelves. In this sense sometimes physicists are spoilt. This work was meant to be exploratory, via numerical experiments, to see if the model were rich enough to warrant further in-depth studies. The spirit of the paper is that of 'computer experiments', not that of usual 'numerical simulation' work. Indeed the model (the rules of the game, the ingredients and parameters) and the kind of phenomena to look for were all open for definition. In this new-found land the first thrust was to let our fancy roam without constraints. What opened up before our eyes was a dazzling parade of new phenomena, unheard of in our previous complexity modelling.

   Our first concern was to understand how players' information-processing capacity, here conveniently represented by the memory length M, impacted on their performance. It was also feasible to check how the size of the 'idea-bag'—that is, the number of alternative strategies each player possesses—affects performance. What we were most curious about, motivated by real markets, was to see how players of different information capacities fare when forced to cohabit. This is especially interesting since in financial markets, all sorts of different players with different abilities, different motivations and trading horizons mingle; the market is a single place for all. To understand their symbiosis is of utmost importance. Of course, much of this symbiosis could only later be systematically understood (cf. for example, Zhang 1999; Challet et al. 2000*d*). We also checked the wealth distribution within the player population, to see how and why some are statistically more successful than others.

   Without a guiding paradigm in physics or economics to address this adaptive, evolutionary system, we drew inspiration more from biology, notably Darwinian evolution theory. At the end of some period of time, the worst player was replaced by a descendant of the best one, repeatedly. He was given the same strategies, apart from occasional mutations; however, the experience of the new born baby was set to zero. In a subsequent paper, we found that the distribution of lifetimes of species reproduces the one observed in fossil records (Kauffman 1993; Challet and Zhang 1998).

   In summary, the first paper was very empirical in nature, with many more open questions than answers. The aim was to call the attention of the nascent econophysics community to a class of binary multiagent models that are more akin to models in physics than in the standard economics literature, even though the main inspiration was from Arthur's insight. Game Theory rarely provides workable models capable of handling an extremely large number of heterogeneous players at once,[5] whereas in statistical physics this extreme is the ideal limit at which to analyse and obtain solutions. It appears that financial markets are at just such an extreme where numerous anonymous players interact through a single price, everyone against everyone else. Here, we finally had a prototype model that might address challenges from real financial markets, or at least that was what we believed.

The reader can have a sample of the Minority Game dynamics by running the applets which can be found on the Internet (Challet).

2.4   Geometrical structure of the Minority Game

The physics community reacted promptly to the newly born model. Several groups raced for a better theoretical understanding of the Minority Game's rich phenomenology. Our own team at Fribourg worked initially on the geometrical approach, but later the stunning success of the algebraic approach prevailed. Two months after the publication of the Minority Game's first paper, the editors of *Europhysics News* solicited a piece for their general readership from one of us (Zhang 1999) (see page 136). With the hindsight of a few months' reflection, this occasion allowed for a better articulation of the model, as well as the first attempt to tackle the model analytically.

The key theoretical insight contained in this paper, though without a single formula, is to provide an intuitive understanding of the collective behaviour. The salient feature is to observe that, even if the strategy space is astronomically large, not all the strategies are independent. If two players use strategies which are very similar—that is, which on most occasions produce the same outcome—they tend to be in a herd. This would undermine the chance of choosing the minority side since if you have a buddy who is very like-minded, this hinders your performance. How much similarity? We needed a precise measure, which comes in conveniently as the Hamming distance between any pair of strategies. Statistical independence requires that when the Hamming distance is just halfway between the minimal and maximal values, the two strategies are said to be independent. Armed with this precise criterion, the next task is to find out, among all possible strategies, the subset of independent ones. This subset (Challet and Zhang 1998) turns out to be very small: 2^M. This gives the real effective measure of how large the strategy space is. The real relevance for the Minority Game is that, when the number of players is greater than the number of independent strategies, we are bound to have herding effects—that is, we enter a *crowded phase* as it was to be called later in statistical physics jargon. When the

---

[5] Notable exceptions are Follmer (1974) and Cohen (1998), for example.

number of players is (much) less than the number of independent strategies, the behaviour appears to be that of random players. This is because with a number of independent strategies much larger than the number of agents, the probability that two of them pick the same strategy is virtually zero. Then each player's action is completely independent of the others, hence total randomness results. For most parameter ranges, the Minority Game behaves somewhere in between, in either a crowded phase or an under-crowded phase. This suggests that the critical intrinsic parameter is the ratio of the number of agents N and the effective size 2^M of the strategy space. This analytical insight was also independently developed at about the same time by Savit et al. (1999), though from a completely different, numerical, approach. The merit of the geometric approach was not only to give an intuitive understanding of how the possibility of cooperation emerges, but also to allow Johnson's group to derive approximate expressions for the attendance fluctuations (see Section 2.5 and Johnson et al. 1999a).

2.5   Regimes and phases of the Minority Game

A few groups were also working hard to gain an understanding of the Minority Game. At about the same time as our second paper (Zhang 1998) was in preparation, we received a preprint by Savit's group from Michigan. This preprint eventually appeared in *Physical Review Letter*, albeit in a shortened version (Savit et al. 1999) (see page 140).

The highlight from their paper is a very crucial one. They introduced a key quantity in the game, the fluctuations of the attendance size, and showed that it depends only on the ratio $2^M/N$ between the number of possible histories and the number N of agents. They also introduced the notion of predictability in the Minority Game. These were major steps towards the understanding of the collective phenomena or rather in understanding what one should understand about the Minority Game.

The fluctuations are a measure of the quality of cooperation in the game. As already discussed, they measure the amount of wasted opportunities, in terms of either seats which are left empty if the attendance is low, or of agents who fail to find a seat when the attendance exceeds the comfort level.

The fluctuations show an interesting pattern which was initially classified in three regimes (see Fig. 2.1): if the number of agents is small with respect to the number of possible histories, the outcome is seemingly random, very similar to what we would expect if agents were just tossing coins to decide whether to go or not. The reason for this is that the information which agents receive about the past history is too complex for their limited processing analysis, and their behaviour 'over-fits' the fluctuations of past attendance.

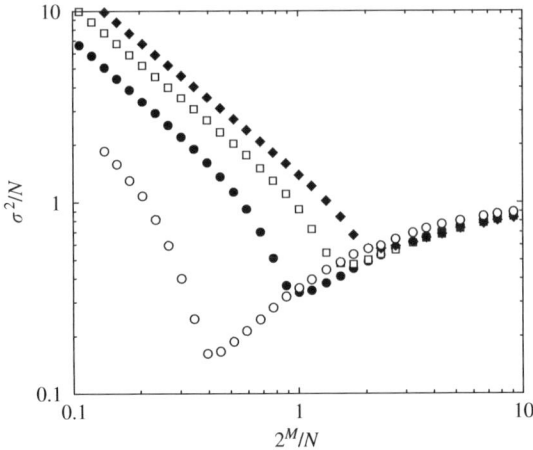

Fig. 2.1   Global efficiency σ^2/N as a function of $2^M/N$ for $S = 2, 3, 4$ from numerical simulations of the Minority Game; averages were taken after 100.2^M time steps, averaged over 100 realizations of the game ($M = 7$).

When agents are added, the fluctuations decrease and agents perform better than by choosing at random. The game enters into a regime where they manage to coordinate to reduce fluctuations. As the number of agents increases (at fixed M) the variance of fluctuations decreases further until it reaches a minimum. With only two strategies to choose between, agents manage to reduce fluctuations by a factor of more than 8. Curiously, however, their performance gets worse when they are given more strategies.

If the number of agents increases further, fluctuations rapidly increase beyond the level of random agents and the game enters into the crowded regime. The occurrence of fluctuations larger than those of random agents suggests the presence of collective fluctuations, the so-called crowd effects. The occurrence of crowd effects was beautifully demonstrated by Savit et al. who showed that, with M fixed, the variance of the attendance when agents are few is initially proportional to N, indicating that agents choose in a more or less independent way. But this behaviour crosses over to an N^2 growth when one enters the crowded regime, suggesting that choices are correlated across agents. In the crowded phase agents synchronize their actions, which is deleterious in this game.

Savit et al. (1999) also introduce the issue of predictability. Predictability measures the extent to which the knowledge of the M past outcomes of the game gives information about the next outcome. Savit shows that, when agents are few relative to the number 2^M of possible histories, the probability that the minority attends the bar, for a given past history, is spread around 50 per cent. This means that knowing the history allows for a better than random prediction of the attendance. In the crowded phase, on the contrary, the minority attends the bar in exactly 50 per cent of the cases, for any given history. Therefore no prediction is possible. The agents have eaten up all the information contained in the history of M past attendances, and the knowledge of this past is therefore useless. The history still contains some information and predictive power, but one has to look at a longer string (e.g. $M + 1$) of past attendances[6] (Challet and Zhang 1998; Hui et al. 1999; Challet et al. 2000d).

Predictability suggests that the behaviour of the Minority Game can be classified in two phases: an information rich or *asymmetric* phase, and an unpredictable or *symmetric* phase. This conclusion was put on a firmer basis in Challet and Marsili (1999) and Challet et al. (2000c), which showed that the phase transition takes place exactly where the fluctuations are minimal. It turns out that predictability plays a central role in the Minority Game. Indeed, as we will see in the following chapter, agents behave in such a way as to minimize predictability, in a mathematical form which is closely related to Shannon's information entropy.

Predictability is also the key concept which allows one to discuss market information efficiency on a quantitative basis in Minority Game models. Indeed, the insight provided by the paper of Savit might be rather familiar for traders in real financial markets. Chartists stare at price movements trying to discern any pattern they believe profitable, but exploiting profitable patterns inevitably affects their persistence and finally washes them out altogether. When the number of traders is very large, all niches are exploited, the market is unpredictable and volatility starts rising. The Minority Game makes it clear that large fluctuations are due to the absence of exploitable information, that is, to the informational efficiency of the market. This interpretation will be fully developed in Chapters 3 and 4.

2.6 Herding effects

The geometric approach of a paper by Zhang (1998) was further studied in Challet and Zhang (1998), and fully developed in e.g. (Johnson et al. 1999a; Hart et al. 2001) (see page 144) by a group from Oxford and Hong Kong, led by Neil Johnson. This approach is based on the use of the reduced strategy space defined as the subset of independent strategies discussed earlier plus the corresponding totally anticorrelated strategies. Each agent, at each time, occupies one point of this space, according to which of the 2^{M+1} reduced strategies he is using. A snapshot of the occupation of the strategy space gives us a hint about the behaviour of fluctuations in the Minority

---

[6] See Chapter 4 for a further discussion of this issue.

Game. In particular, multiple occupation at the same time of the same point in strategy space corresponds to crowd or herding effects in the Minority Game.

The fact that the average density is $N/2^{M+1}$ provides an intuitive explaination for the dependence of σ^2 in Fig. 2.1. Furthermore, the variance of the attendance is related simply to the average Hamming distance between agents in the reduced strategy space, by a linear equation (Challet and Zhang 1998; Johnson et al. 1999*a*; Challet et al. 2000*d*; Hart et al. 2001). Computing the Hamming distance is complicated in general. However, it turns out that in the reduced strategy space the Hamming distance enjoys a transitive property: if one knows the distance between strategies *a* and *b*, and between *a* and *c*, one automatically knows the distance between *b* and *c* (Challet and Zhang 1998). Hence, forcing the agents to draw their strategies from this special set, one is left with the characterization of the average strategy use. These considerations have allowed Johnson's group to derive some semi-analytic approximations to the variance of the attendance, especially in the crowded phase.

The merit of this approach is to provide intuitive tools that help one to understand the (non-) cooperative behaviour of the system. This approach has also been extended to more generic models (Gourley et al. 2003). We refer the interested reader to Hart et al. (2001) for further details.

3. Understanding the Minority Game dynamics

> even though there is apparently no science of complexity, there is much science to be learned
> from studying complex systems
>
> (Leo P. Kadanoff, (2001). [*Physics Today* **55**(8), 34, (2001)])

It is an extraordinary event in scientific research to hit by chance a model that can be solved analytically. That is even more extraordinary for a model such as the Minority Game, which was introduced and defined as a binary algorithm, without writing down a single equation. The path towards the analytic solution of the Minority Game is the subject of the present chapter. We shall see that a wide range of sophisticated tools of statistical physics—from non-equilibrium stochastic dynamics to the replica method—will be required along the way. This path is full of surprises: the non-trivial behaviour shown by early numerical simulations turns out to be only a small part of the richness of behaviours which the Minority Game has in store for us.

An operative definition of a complex system is one which, when we probe in some way, often responds in a way which defeats our intuition. These are the most interesting systems as they really teach us something new, which is not the by-product of old knowledge. The Minority Game is definitely such a complex system.

A good start to understand the Minority Game is to program it.[1] Since the computer code produces all the complexity of the Minority Game, the first step is to read the key dynamical equations from it. The second step is to simplify further the model so as to leave unaffected its generic behaviour, making an analytic treatment possible. Identifying unnecessary complications is not an easy task. For example, one a priori essential fact that a model of a financial market should capture is that traders base their strategies on processing the information about past price moves which are produced by their very actions. Very few would have guessed that such a feedback loop of information a posteriori turns out to have weak consequences on the collective behaviour (Cavagna 1999). Some other 'simplifications' actually amount

---

[1] A sample code written in C can be found in Appendix B.

in making the model apparently more complex, but remove hindrances to a mathematical approach. It is the case of the 'temperature' introduced by Cavagna et al. (1999) in order to model agents who choose in a probabilistic fashion. The Minority Game has reacted in a totally counterintuitive way to this modification, as we shall see.

These simplifications bring the Minority Game in the range of applicability of the powerful tools of statistical physics. First, by taking the average of dynamical equations, it is possible to characterize the 'average behaviour' in the stationary state. The problem can be cast into the form of the minimization of a function H with respect to the 'average behaviour' of agents.[2] Since H quantifies market predictability, in loose words we can say that agents in the Minority Game make the market as unpredictable as possible, given their strategies. This is in line with *no-arbitrage* arguments: if an agent is able to predict the market he would modify his behaviour in order to exploit this information. Therefore, in the stationary state, the agents either have no possibility to predict the market or already exploit the information they have.

The minimization of H reveals that the collective behaviour of the Minority Game features a *phase transition* as a function of the number N of agents. When there are less agents than a critical number, the price evolution seems predictable to an external agent (but not to those already playing), whereas when the number of agents is beyond the critical number, the market becomes unpredictable. This suggests that, as long as there are few participants, the market will attract more and more agents, thus approaching the critical number where the market becomes unpredictable and hence unattractive. Hence the scenario depicted by the Minority Game lends support to the conjecture that markets *self-organize at a critical point*, an issue we leave for the next chapter. Apart from predictability, the two phases have quite different properties: in the predictable phase (when there are few agents) the stationary state is unique and ergodic, that is, independent of initial conditions. When there are many agents (unpredictable phase) the stationary state is not ergodic as it remembers (i.e. depends on) the initial conditions. In particular the fluctuations in the stationary state is a decreasing function of the degree of heterogeneity of initial conditions. A further remarkable feature is that, in the unpredictable phase (many agents), adding randomness in the way agents chose, collective fluctuations decrease. This is at odd with conventional wisdom according to which collective fluctuations increase when randomness at the microscale—for example, 'temperature'—increases. Even more remarkable is the fact that in the predictable phase (few agents) collective fluctuations do not depend at all from microscopic randomness.

---

[2] That is, the frequencies with which agents play their strategies.

All these features are explained and precisely assessed in a stochastic theory of the Minority Game (Marsili and Challet 2001a). The microscopic 'temperature' affects learning rates and finally turns out to act as the inverse of a global temperature, thus explaining the unconventional dependence of fluctuations on microscopic noise. This approach, based on the neglect of time dependent volatility fluctuations, also unveils the peculiar interconnection between initial conditions and correlated fluctuations, leaving us with a complete picture of the Minority Game behaviour. Although an approximation, this theory turns out to be remarkably precise in general, except close to the phase transition in finite sytems.

We shall finally comment on a powerful alternative approach, based on the generating functional (Heimel and Coolen 2001). The extraction of quantitative results from this approach is made difficult by the mathematical complexity of the resulting equations. On the other hand, this method is rigorous and exact. Even if it does not yet provide a complete picture of how Minority Game works, the generating function is a very promising approach.

We focus on the simplest non-trivial version of the model to make the derivation as straight and simple as possible. The derivation can be extended in a straightforward manner to a number of variations on the theme, adding frills here and there on the skeleton Minority Game which we discuss. These extensions are discussed in Section 3.4. The overall picture turns out to be quite robust.

3.1   A computer code for the Minority Game dynamics

We encourage the reader to program the Minority Game on his computer.[3] A close examination of a computer code is very instructive, as it helps understand where complexity lies in the Minority Game dynamics.

If we go back to the paper by Challet and Zhang (1997) and try to translate the definition of the Minority Game [4] into a computer program, the result may look like the following:[5]

---

[3] See Appendix B for help on how to carry out numerical simulations of the Minority Game.

[4] 'Let us consider a population of N (odd) players. At each time step, everybody has to choose . . . . The player uses the strategy having the highest accumulated points for his action, he gets a real point only if the strategy used happens to win in the next play.' (Challet and Zhang, 1997: 408.)

[5] We use FORTRAN language with operators .eq. and .gt. replaced by = and > respectively for the sake of readability.

```
       . . .
C AGENTS' CHOICE
    do i=1,N
      do s=1,S
        if(points(i,s) > points(i,bestStrategy(i))) bestStrategy(i) = s
      end do
    end do
C MARKET INTERACTION
    N1=0
    do i=1,N
      N1 = N1 + side(i,bestStrategy(i), mu)
    end do
    if (N1 > N/2) then
      winSide = 0
    else
      winSide = 1
    end if
C LEARNING
    do i=1,N
      do s=1,S
        if (side(i,s,mu) = winSide) points(i,s) = points(i,s)+1
      end do
    end do
C INFORMATION UPDATE
    mu = mod(2*mu + winSide, 2**M)
       . . .
```

This code is a good starting point to analyse the dynamics: First agents choose the strategy they play—stored in the variable bestStrategy(i)—looking at the virtual points points(i,s) that each strategy s has accumulated. Agents pick the strategy with the largest number of points.[6] The side prescribed by this strategy, given the sequence mu of the last M outcomes, is stored in the table side(i,s,mu) for each agent i and each strategy s. Note that this depends on mu which encodes the history of recent games. The tables side($\cdot, \cdot, \cdot$) are drawn at random—with side(i,s,mu)=0 or 1 with equal probability—at the beginning of the game, that is, in the initialization section of the program. Once every agent has fixed his bestStrategy(i), the attendance of the two sides is computed: N1 is the number of agents who took the choice 1 and winSide is the winning side: winSide=1 if N1<N/2 and winSide=0 otherwise (we assume that N is odd). Given the outcome winSide of the game, agents update their scores points(i,s). Finally the history mu—which is an integer variable—is updated for the next time-step by the last instruction. In this way, the first M bits in the binary representation of mu are the last M values of winSide.

---

[6] In case of ties a tie-breaking rule has to be decided. The one used here is an example. Other rules can be used without affecting much the collective properties (see, for example, Appendix B).

The central quantity of interest is the difference in the attendance of the two sides:

$$A = 2 * \text{N1} - \text{N} \tag{3.1}$$

But before discussing the properties of A, let us review the key steps which have led to an analytically tractable version of the Minority Game.

3.1.1 Simplifying the Minority Game dynamics

Despite its simplicity the Minority Game as defined above, captures quite complex phenomena. The route to a thorough analytical approach has been made possible by simplifying the model still further, while preserving its rich dynamical behaviour.

1. The first step has been the observation by Cavagna (1999) (see page 156) that the fluctuations of A are left largely unaffected if the dynamics of the history

$$\text{mu} = \text{mod}(2 * \text{mu} + \text{winSide}, 2 ** \text{M}) \tag{3.2}$$

is replaced by a random draw from the integers $\{0, \ldots, 2^M - 1\}$ with uniform probability:

$$\text{mu} = \text{int}(2 ** \text{M} * \text{rand}()). \tag{3.3}$$

While μ in Eq. (3.2) encodes the *real* history, in Eq. (3.3) μ is just a random piece of information.[7]

One of the ideas behind Eq. (3.2) was to describe a closed system where agents process and react to a piece of information they themselves produce. The results of paper Cavagna (1999) suggests that this feedback is largely irrelevant. The *endogenous* information process of Eq. (3.2) may well be replaced by Eq. (3.3), which models a news arrival process of *exogenous* information 'sometimes economists express this by saying that μ is the result of a "choice of Nature" '. With exogenous information, the number of values that μ can take is not restricted to be a power of two. We call this number P henceforth, and we shall have

$$P \equiv 2^M$$

for endogenous information.

A close inspection of fig. 1 of paper by Cavagna (1999) shows that the conclusion on the irrelevance of the origin of information does not hold exactly (Challet and Marsili 2000). We shall go back to this issue in Section 3.4. At any rate, the passage

---

[7] Early works (e.g. Cavagna 1999; Challet and Zhang 1997) refer to *memory* rather than to *history*. We prefer the latter term because, strictly speaking, the memory of agents is stored in points rather than in μ.

from endogenous (Eq. 3.2) to exogenous (Eq. 3.3) information represents a great simplification of the model.

2. A further simplification of the original model is to replace the accounting of the points points(i,s) by a linear dynamics of scores $U_{i,s}(t)$. It was noticed in Johnson et al. (1998); Cavagna et al. (1999), and Challet and Marsili (1999) and later shown in Challet et al. (2000d), that this modification does not alter the qualitative behaviour of the model. In practice, this amounts to replacing the update of points points(i,s) by

$$U_{i,s}(t+1) = U_{i,s}(t) - a_{i,s}^{\mu(t)}\frac{A(t)}{N},\tag{3.4}$$

where we introduced the convenient notation

$$a_{i,s}^{\mu} = 2 * \mathtt{side(i,s,\mu)} - 1\tag{3.5}$$

for the strategy tables. Again the strategy s is rewarded [i.e. $U_{i,s}(t+1)-U_{i,s}(t) > 0$] when it predicts correctly the minority sign, that is, if $a_{i,s}^{\mu} = -\mathrm{sign}\,A(t)$, and penalized otherwise.

3. Finally it is convenient to generalize in a probabilistic fashion the way in which agents take decisions. In the original Minority Game the strategy $s_i(t)$ which agent i uses at time t is that with the highest score:

$$s_i(t) = \arg\max_s U_{i,s}(t).\tag{3.6}$$

This introduces a mathematical discontinuity with which it is hard to deal analytically. Cavagna et al. (1999) (see page 156) suggested to overcome this difficulty by resorting to a probabilistic choice model:

$$\mathrm{Prob}\{s_i(t) = s\} = \frac{e^{\Gamma U_{i,s}(t)}}{\sum_{s'} e^{\Gamma U_{i,s'}(t)}}\tag{3.7}$$

with $\Gamma > 0$. This is reminiscent of the Gibbs distribution for physicists (Yeomans 1992) and Γ appears as an 'individual inverse temperature'—whereby the name of Thermal Minority Game (Cavagna et al. 1999). Eq. 3.7 is also a very well known choice model among economists, known as the *Logit model*[8] (Luce 1959; McFadden 1981).

---

[8] The probabilistic nature of agents' choice does not necessarily imply that the agents randomize their behaviour on purpose. McFadden has indeed shown that Eq. (3.7) models individuals who maximise an 'utility' which has an implicit random idiosyncratic part $\eta_{i,s}$:

$$s_i(t) = \arg\max_s \left[\Gamma U_{i,s}(t) + \eta_{i,s}(t)\right].\tag{3.8}$$

Summarizing, the dynamics of the simplified Minority Game is described by the following equations:

$$\text{Prob}\{s_i(t) = s\} = \frac{e^{\Gamma U_{i,s}(t)}}{\sum_{s'} e^{\Gamma U_{i,s'}(t)}} \quad \text{(choices of agents)} \tag{3.9}$$

$$\text{Prob}\{\mu(t) = \nu\} = \frac{1}{P}, \quad \nu = 1, \dots, P \quad \text{(choice of Nature)} \tag{3.10}$$

$$A(t) = \sum_{i=1}^{N} a_{i,s_i(t)}^{\mu(t)} \quad \text{(market aggregation)} \tag{3.11}$$

$$U_{i,s}(t+1) = U_{i,s}(t) - a_{i,s}^{\mu(t)} \frac{A(t)}{N} \quad \text{(learning)} \tag{3.12}$$

The strategies $a_{i,s}^{\mu}$ are randomly drawn at the beginning of the game and then they are kept fixed. Hence they can be considered as fixed (quenched) disorder.

There is a further simplification which does not entail a modification of the dynamics but just a restriction. Early numerical studies have shown that varying the number S

The constant Γ is the relative weight, which agents assign to the empirical evidence accumulated in $U_{i,s}$ with respect to random idiosyncratic shocks $\eta_{i,s}$. If $\Gamma \to \infty$ agents always play their best strategy according to the scores, while if Γ decreases agents take less into account past performances. For a generic distribution $P_\eta(x) \equiv \text{Prob}\{\eta_{i,s}(t) < x\}$ we have

$$\text{Prob}\{s_i(t) = s\} = \int_{-\infty}^{\infty} dP_\eta(x) \prod_{r \neq s} P_\eta[x + \Gamma(U_{i,s} - U_{r,i})].$$

This coincides with Eq. 3.7 if $P_\eta(x) = \exp(-e^{-x})$ is the Gumbel distribution (McFadden 1981). Different distributions of $\eta_{i,s}$ lead to choice models which are different from Eq. (3.7), but the model of Eq. (3.7) is unique in that it satisfies the axiom of *independence from irrelevant alternatives*: this states that the relative odds of choices s and s' does not depend on whether another choice s'' is possible or not. In addition, there is a natural derivation of the Gumbel distribution in the case where agents want to maximize an utility function $W_i(s, \sigma_1, \dots, \sigma_n) = U_{i,s} + nV_i(\sigma_1, \dots, \sigma_n|s)$ which depends also on n variables σ_k which take g values each. The factor n in the second term implies that the weight of all variables is equivalent in decision-making. The choice behaviour with respect to the other variables, which is not of our explicit interest, is modelled in a probabilistic way. With an opportune choice of $U_{i,s}$, let us assume that $V_i(\sigma_1, \dots, \sigma_n|s)$ are i.i.d. gaussian variables with zero mean and variance v. Then, using extreme value statistics (Galambos 1987)

$$\eta_{i,s} = \max_{\{\sigma_k\}} nV_i(\sigma_1, \dots, \sigma_n|s) = V_0 + \sqrt{\frac{n}{2v \log g}} Y_{i,s},$$

where V_0 is a uninfluential constant and $Y_{i,s}$ is distributed according to the Gumbel distribution. This suggests that $\Gamma = \sqrt{(2v \log g)/n}$, that is, when there are many other choices ($n \gg 1$) σ_k which are affected by the choice of s we expect a small value of Γ and vice versa.

of strategies given to each agent, the behaviour of the Minority Game remains qualitatively the same. Actually cooperative effects manifest most strongly for $S = 2$ strategies.

Hence it is preferable to restrict attention to the case where all agents have $S = 2$ strategies (the case with $S > 2$ strategies will be discussed in Section 3.4). Challet and Marsili (1999) (see page 152) introduced a convenient notation by labelling strategy 1 as -1 and strategy 2 as $+1$ so that agent i controls the variable s_i which takes values ± 1; such a variable is called a spin in physics. The strategies of agent i can be decomposed

$$a^\mu_{i,s} = \omega^\mu_i + s_i \xi^\mu_i$$

into a constant $\omega^\mu_i = (a^\mu_{+,i} + a^\mu_{-,i})/2$ and a variable component, with $\xi^\mu_i = (a^\mu_{+,i} - a^\mu_{-,i})/2$. In binary games $|a^\mu_i| = 1$, therefore $\omega^\mu_i, \xi^\mu_i = 0, \pm 1$ but $\omega^\mu_i \xi^\mu_i = 0$. The fact that for some μ, agent i have strategies which prescribe the same action ($\xi^\mu_i = 0$ and $\omega^\mu_i \neq 0$) lies at the origin of cooperation in the game (see Section 3.4). This decomposition allows us to express $A(t)$ in a form where its dependence on the quenched disorder variables ω^μ_i, ξ^μ_i, and on the dynamical variables $s_i(t)$ is made explicit. Indeed Eq. (3.11) becomes

$$A(t) = \Omega^{\mu(t)} + \sum_{i=1}^{N} \xi^{\mu(t)}_i s_i(t), \quad \text{with } \Omega^\mu = \sum_{i=1}^{N} \omega^\mu_i. \tag{3.13}$$

A further simplification arises from the fact that only the difference between the scores of the two strategies is important in the dynamics. In other words, each agent can be described in terms of a single dynamical variable

$$Y_i(t) = \Gamma \frac{U_{+,i}(t) - U_{-,i}(t)}{2}. \tag{3.14}$$

The probability distribution of $s_i(t)$ becomes

$$\text{Prob}\{s_i(t) = \pm 1\} = \frac{1 \pm \tanh Y_i(t)}{2}. \tag{3.15}$$

Finally, the dynamics of $Y_i(t)$ is derived taking the difference of Eq. (3.12) for $s = \pm 1$:

$$Y_i(t+1) = Y_i(t) - \frac{\Gamma}{N} \xi^{\mu(t)}_i A(t). \tag{3.16}$$

The model defined in Eqs (3.10), (3.13), (3.15) and (3.16) shall be our reference model for the remaining of this chapter. Below we shall discuss its generic behaviour and the theoretical approach based on statistical physics which has allowed to understand it.

Some convenient notations

Before entering into the details, it is convenient to discuss statistical averages and to introduce the relative notations. There are two sources of randomness in the Minority Game. One is the choice of information $\mu(t)$ and the other is agents' choice of strategies $s_i(t)$. We shall be interested in the stationary state of the game.[9] Hence, for any quantity $Q(t)$, we denote by

$$\langle Q \rangle = \lim_{t_0 \to \infty} \lim_{T \to \infty} \frac{1}{T} \sum_{t=t_0+1}^{t_0+T} Q(t) \tag{3.17}$$

its average value in the stationary state. We shall also be interested in conditional averages for a particular value of the information μ. We denote it as

$$\langle Q|\mu \rangle = \lim_{t_0 \to \infty} \lim_{T \to \infty} \frac{1}{T_\mu} \sum_{t=t_0+1}^{t_0+T} Q(t)\delta_{\mu(t),\mu} \quad \text{where } T_\mu = \sum_{t=t_0+1}^{t_0+T} \delta_{\mu(t),\mu}. \tag{3.18}$$

Finally, averages over μ will be denoted by an over-line:

$$\overline{Q} = \frac{1}{P} \sum_{\mu=1}^{P} Q^\mu.$$

This notation shortens considerably some expressions. We implicitly assume that averages under the over-line are conditional on μ. So, for example

$$\overline{F(\langle Q \rangle)} = \frac{1}{P} \sum_{\mu=1}^{P} F(\langle Q|\mu \rangle).$$

Note that clearly $\langle Q \rangle = \overline{\langle Q \rangle}$ but $\langle Q \rangle^2 \neq \overline{\langle Q \rangle^2}$.

3.2 Generic behaviour of the Minority Game

Let us rephrase in mathematical terms the generic behaviour of the Minority Game sketched in the previous chapter. Early papers focused on the cooperative properties of the system in the stationary state. Symmetry arguments suggest that none of the two groups 0 or 1 will be systematically the minority one. This means that $A(t)$ will

---

[9] That a stationary state exists for the Minority Game exists can be shown observing that (i) it is a Markov process (ii) it can be approximated with a finite space Markov process (discretizing $Y_i(t)$ on a grid of Λ points) to an arbitrary precision (letting $\Lambda \to \infty$).

fluctuate around zero and $\langle A \rangle = 0$. The size of fluctuations of $A(t)$, instead, displays a remarkable non-trivial behaviour. The variance

$$\sigma^2 \equiv \langle A^2 \rangle \qquad (3.19)$$

of $A(t)$ in the stationary state is—quoting from Savit et al. (1999)—'a convenient reciprocal measure of how effective the system is at distributing resources'. The smaller σ^2 is, the larger a typical minority group is. In other words σ^2 is a reciprocal measure of the *global efficiency* of the system. This is obvious if the payoff function is linear, as in Eqs (3.12) and (3.4): in that case the total payoff given to the agents $-\sum_i a_i(t)A(t) = -A^2(t)$, hence, σ^2 measures the average total loss of the agents per time-step.

Early numerical studies (Challet and Zhang 1997, 1998; Savit et al. 1999) uncovered a remarkably rich phenomenology as a function of M and the number of agents N. Savit et al. (1999) found that the collective behaviour does not depend independently on M and N but only on the ratio

$$\alpha \equiv \frac{2^M}{N} = \frac{P}{N} \qquad (3.20)$$

between the number $P = 2^M$ of possible histories μ and the number of agents, as illustrated in Fig. 3.1. This quantity can then be called a control parameter. This means that typically $A(t) \propto \sqrt{N}$ for fixed α. When $\alpha \gg 1$ information is too complex and agents

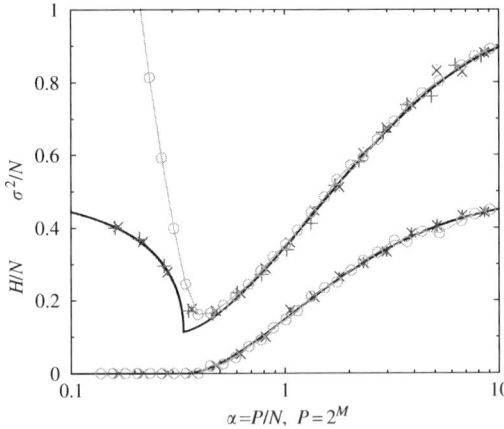

Fig. 3.1 Global efficiency σ^2/N for $P = 128$, and 256 and N ranging from $0.1P$ to $10P$. Data set with $\Gamma = 0.1$ ($+P = 128$ and $\times P = 256$) or $\Gamma = \infty$ are shown ($\circ P = 128$). Agents have two trading strategies. Each point is obtained as the average over 100 random systems in the asymptotic stationary state of the dynamics. For large N the collective properties only depend on the ratio $\alpha = P/N$. For small values of α, σ^2 is larger for fast learning ($\circ$ correspond to $\Gamma = \infty$) than for slow learning ($\times$, $+$ correspond to $\Gamma = 0.1$). The full line are the results of the theory based on the statistical mechanics approach, which is valid in the limit $P \to \infty$ and for small Γ. The predictability H/N as a function of α, for the same systems as above, is also shown at the bottom of the figure. H does not depend on Γ.

essentially behave randomly. Indeed σ^2/N converges to one—the value it would take if agents were choosing their side by coin tossing. As α decreases—which means that M decreases or the number of agents increases—σ^2/N decreases suggesting that agents manage to exploit the information in order to coordinate. But when agents become too numerous, σ^2/N starts increasing with N. Savit et al. (1999) found that, at M fixed, σ^2 increases linearly with N as long as $N \ll P$ but with a quadratic law $\sigma^2 \sim N^2$ for $N \gg P$, which implies $\sigma^2 \sim 1/\alpha$ for $\alpha \ll 1$. The behaviour for $\alpha \ll 1$ has been attributed to the occurrence of 'crowd effects', and it has been studied in some detail both numerically and by approximate methods Challet and Zhang 1998; Zhang 1998; D'Hulst and Rodgers 1999; Manuca et al. 2000; Heimel and Coolen 2001; Hart et al. 2001; Caridi and Ceva 2003.

A further interesting observation of Savit and co-workers (Savit et al. 1999) comes from their analysis of the probability

$$p^\mu = \langle \theta(A)|\mu \rangle$$

that the minority is on one given side conditional on the value of μ (here $\theta(x) = 0$ for $x < 0$ and 1 otherwise). Savit et al. observed that $p^\mu = 1/2$ for $\alpha \ll 1$: the minority was falling on either side with equal probability irrespective of μ. But when $\alpha \gg 1$ the minority happens to be more likely on one side (i.e. $p^\mu \neq 1/2$ as, for example, in Fig. 3.3), depending on the value of μ. This means that the value of $\mu(t)$ contains some information on $A(t)$ because it makes possible a better than random prediction of the minority side.

These observations were sharpened in paper (Challet and Marsili 1999) by confirming the existence of a phase transition located at the point where σ^2 attains its minimum ($\alpha_c \approx 0.34$ for $S = 2$). The transition separates a symmetric ($\alpha < \alpha_c$) from an asymmetric phase ($\alpha > \alpha_c$). The symmetry which is broken is that of the average $\langle A|\mu \rangle$ of $A(t)$ conditional on the history μ.

In the asymmetric phase, $\langle A|\mu \rangle \neq 0$ for at least one μ. Hence knowing the history $\mu(t)$ at time t, makes the sign of $A(t)$ statistically predictable. A measure of the degree of predictability is given by the function

$$H = \frac{1}{P} \sum_{\mu=1}^{P} \langle A|\mu \rangle^2 = \overline{\langle A \rangle^2}. \tag{3.21}$$

In the symmetric phase $\langle A|\mu \rangle = 0$ for all μ and hence $H = 0$.

Challet and Marsili (1999) found that, at fixed M or P, H is a decreasing function of the number N of agents[10] (see Fig. 3.1): this means that newcomers exploit

---

[10] A slightly different quantity $\theta = \frac{1}{P} \sum_{\mu=1}^{P} \langle \text{sign}(A)|\mu \rangle^2 = \overline{(2p-1)^2}$ was actually studied in Challet and Marsili (1999).

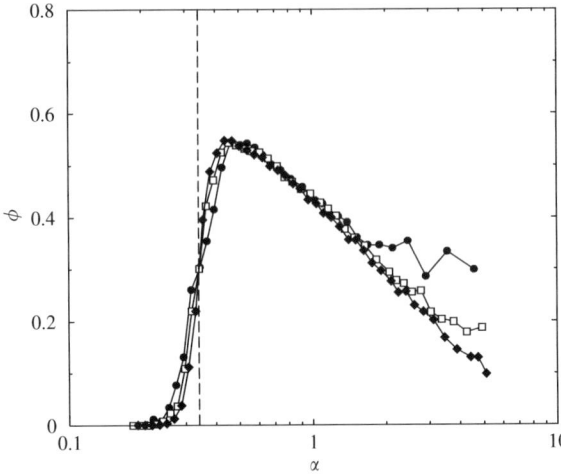

Fig. 3.2   Fraction of frozen agents versus $\alpha = P/N$ for $M = 6$ (circles), 7 (squares), and 8 (diamonds). The critical point is located at the intersection of the three curves.

the predictability of $A(t)$ and hence reduce it. The same article also introduced the concept of *frozen agents*, who always play the same strategy. The fraction ϕ of frozen agents is reported in Fig. 3.2 and it has a discontinuity which provides a very precise determination of α_c.

Finally Cavagna et al. (1999) (see page 156) observed that fluctuations σ^2 increase with Γ. That is a quite remarkable finding specially if one considers Γ as an inverse temperature as suggested by Eq. (3.9): Usually fluctuations decrease when the temperature decreases, whereas σ^2 increases when the 'temperature' $1/\Gamma$ decreases. Note that Cavagna et al. (1999) also reports a rise in σ^2 for very high 'temperatures' (i.e. for $\Gamma \ll 1$). This was later found—first in Bottazzi et al. (2003) then in Challet et al. (2000b)— to be due to lack of equilibration in numerical simulations (see also Appendix B for advice on carrying out numerical simulations).

What is also quite remarkable is that, as shown in Figs 3.1 and 3.8, σ^2 depends on Γ only for $\alpha < \alpha_c$ but not for $\alpha > \alpha_c$. Nor does H for all values of α. Furthermore, the stationary state depends on initial conditions for $\alpha < \alpha_c$ (Challet et al. 2000c; Garrahan et al. 2000; Heimel and Coolen 2001; Marsili 2001; Marsili and Challet 2001a,b): the larger the spread or the asymmetry in the initial conditions $\{Y_i(0)\}$ the smallest the value of σ^2. This dependence disappears for $\alpha > \alpha_c$ and the dynamics 'forgets' about initial conditions, as in ergodic systems (see Section 3.3.4).

These results leave us with a number of open questions that a theory of the Minority Game should address.

3.2.1   Information and predictability

The quantity H captures predictability in the Minority Game. To make this statement more precise, it is helpful to make explicit the connection with standard tools of information theory, such as the Shannon entropy. Back in Savit's paper (Savit et al. 1999), information was quantified in a 'bar graph' with the probabilities

$$p^\mu = \text{Prob}\{A(t) > 0 | \mu(t) = \mu\}$$

plotted against μ. If the bar graph is flat, with $p^\mu = 1/2$ for all μ, then the information $\mu(t)$ does not contain any information about the game's outcome. This is what happens for $\alpha \leq \alpha_c$. On the other hand for $\alpha > \alpha_c$ bars reach uneven heights $p^\mu \neq 1/2$ as in Fig. 3.3, an example that Zhang (1999) has taken from the real world. Then the market is predictable and we can quantify the information contained in μ as the difference

$$I^\mu = \log 2 - S^\mu$$

between $\log 2$, the entropy of a random bit equal to 0 or 1 with equal probability, and the entropy of the 'market bit' $b^\mu(t) = \text{sign} A(t)$ conditional on $\mu(t) = \mu$. The latter is given by

$$S^\mu = -p^\mu \log p^\mu - (1 - p^\mu) \log(1 - p^\mu).$$

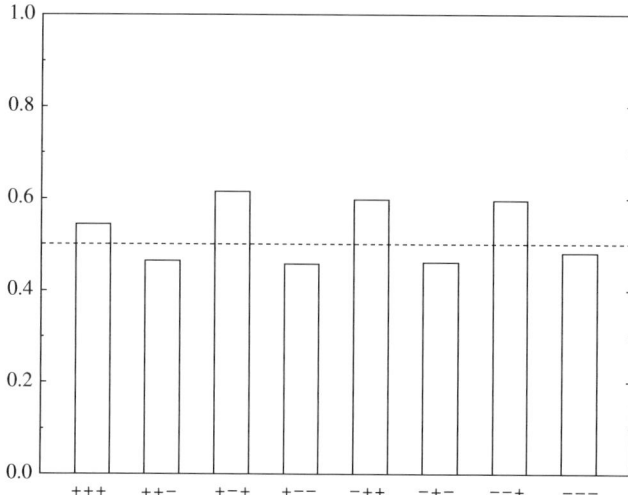

Fig. 3.3 Daily price closes of NY 400 Composite Index during 32 years. Conditional on the past observations (e.g. $+++$), this figure shows the probability p^μ to have the next day price variation to be $+$ (from Zhang 1999).

Averaging I^μ over μ we get a measure $\bar{I} = \log 2 - \bar{S}$ of the information content of the signal $\mu(t)$.

In order to establish a link between this quantity and those discussed previously, we note that, when $\mu(t) = \mu$ we have

$$A(t) = \Omega^\mu + \sum_{i=1}^{N} \xi_i^\mu s_i(t),$$

where $s_i(t)$ are chosen by agents independently from the probability distributions[11] of Eq. (3.7). Hence for $N \gg 1$, by virtue of the Central Limit Theorem (CLT), the distribution of $A(t)$ conditional on $\mu(t) = \mu$, is Gaussian with mean $\langle A|\mu \rangle$. Simple algebra shows that the variance of $A(t)$ conditional on $\mu(t) = \mu$ is well approximated, to leading order in N, by $\sigma^2 - H$. Hence we have

$$p^\mu \cong \frac{1}{2}\left[1 - \text{erf}\left(\frac{\langle A|\mu \rangle}{\sqrt{2(\sigma^2 - H)}} \right) \right].$$

This allows us to compute the information content $\bar{I}$. The average over μ can be computed by observing that $\langle A|\mu \rangle$ is also a Gaussian variable—again by the CLT—with zero average and variance H. This leads finally to a relation between information and the signal-to-noise ratio

$$\Upsilon = \frac{H}{\sigma^2 - H}$$

which reads

$$\bar{I}(\Upsilon) \cong \int_{-\infty}^{\infty} \frac{e^{-x^2/\Upsilon}}{2\sqrt{\pi \Upsilon}} \left\{ \log[1 - \text{erf}^2(x)] + \text{erf}(x) \log\left[\frac{1 + \text{erf}(x)}{1 - \text{erf}(x)} \right] \right\} \qquad (3.22)$$

$$= \frac{1}{\pi}\Upsilon - \frac{\pi - 1}{\pi^2}\Upsilon^2 + \frac{24 - 20\pi + 7\pi^2}{6\pi^3}\Upsilon^3 + O(\Upsilon^4). \qquad (3.23)$$

Figure 3.4 plots this relation and the leading behaviour for $\Upsilon \ll 1$ given by the first three terms of the power expansion (bottom). The same figure also reports the range of values of α which correspond to a certain signal-to-noise ratio Υ in the Minority Game with $S = 2$. The signal-to-noise ratio attains its maximal value $\Upsilon_{\max} \approx 1.05$ at $\alpha \approx 3.25$ and most of its variation takes place for $\alpha < 3.25$ whereas for $\alpha > 3.25$ the signal-to-noise ratio rapidly approaches a constant value $\Upsilon = 1$.

---

[11] We assume that the probability distribution of $s_i(t)$ are constant or can be considered as such. This is not true close to the phase transition which is however not the region we are interested in in this section.

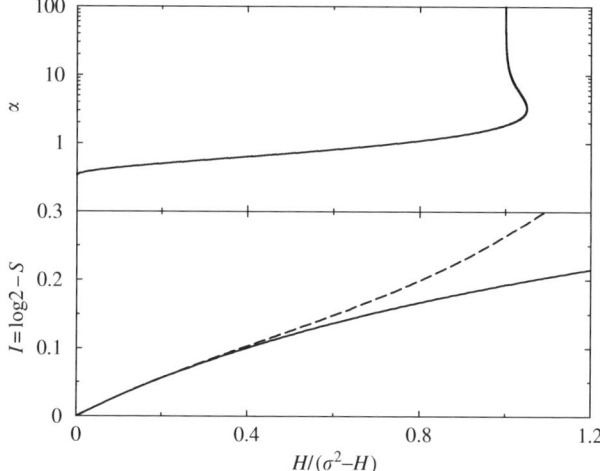

Fig. 3.4 Information content of the time series $\mu(t)$ as a function of the signal-to-noise ratio $\Upsilon = H/(\sigma^2 - H)$ (bottom). The dashed line refers to the leading power expansion up to Υ^3. Top: range of values of α where the MG with $S = 2$ attains a given signal-to-noise ratio.

3.3   Analytic approaches

The first significant attempts to understand the Minority Game dynamics have focused on the derivation of continuum time dynamical equations. This has been the subject of debate for some time. First Cavagna et al. (1999) proposed *stochastic* differential equations for time evolution of the probabilities

$$\pi_{i,s}(t) = \text{Prob}\{s_i(t) = s\},$$

which were found to be problematic in Challet et al. (2000b) (but see also Cavagna et al. 2000) and later amended in Garrahan et al. (2000) and Sherrington et al. (2002). On the other hand, Challet et al. (2000c) (see page 160) and Marsili et al. (2000) derived a *deterministic* dynamical equations by erroneously neglecting stochastic fluctuations. The asymptotic state of the dynamics was found to be related to the minima of H, which is a Lyapunov function of the deterministic dynamics. This opened the way to statistical mechanics of disordered systems because it relates the properties of the stationary state of the Minority Game to the ground state properties of a disordered spin model, which can be analysed in all details. It is remarkable that, in spite of neglecting fluctuations, this approach yields very precisely the behaviour of σ^2 and H with α, at least for $\alpha > \alpha_c$ for all values of Γ and for $\alpha < \alpha_c$ in the limit $\Gamma \to 0$. The reason for this coincidence was found in the paper (Marsili and Challet 2001a), which restores the stochastic term in the dynamics of Challet et al. (2000c) and Marsili et al. (2000) and provides a coherent picture of the Minority Game behaviour.

In addition, the generating functional approach substantiated this approach (Coolen and Heimel 2001).

It turns out that it is not necessary to derive continuum time equations in order to show that the minima of H describe several quantities in the stationary state of the Minority Game. Therefore, we shall outline the theoretical developments introducing the continuum time limit only in a second stage.

We shall keep the discussion as simple as possible and refer the reader to the relevant original papers. Many features of the rich phenomenology of the Minority Game can already be appreciated in the simple setting without information as shown in papers by Marsili (2001) and Marsili and Challet (2001b). We shall discuss this simpler case in Chapter 5 and deal with the full-fledged model here. Some of the results can also be derived with the generating functional method (Coolen and Heimel 2001; Heimel and Coolen 2001), as discussed in Section 3.3.6. Finally we shall comment on how the theory extends to several 'variations on the theme'.

3.3.1   Stationary state and minimal predictability

Taking the average of Eq. (3.16) in the stationary state one finds a dynamic equation for $\langle Y_i \rangle$. We look for solutions with $\langle Y_i \rangle \sim v_i t$. If we define

$$m_i \equiv \langle \tanh(Y_i) \rangle = \langle s_i \rangle, \tag{3.24}$$

for $t \to \infty$ we have

$$v_i = -\overline{\Omega \xi_i} - \sum_{j=1}^{N} \overline{\xi_i \xi_j} m_j. \tag{3.25}$$

Now if $v_i \neq 0$, then y_i diverges $\to \pm\infty$ and

$$m_i = \text{sign } v_i = -\text{sign} \left[\overline{\Omega \xi_i} + \sum_{j=1}^{N} \overline{\xi_i \xi_j} m_j \right] = \pm 1. \tag{3.26}$$

This means that agent i will always use the strategy $s_i(t) = m_i$ for t large enough, that is, that he or she is *frozen*. Conversely, agent i is not frozen if $\langle Y_i \rangle$ is finite, which requires $v_i = 0$, that is:

$$0 = -v_i = \overline{\Omega \xi_i} + \sum_{j=1}^{N} \overline{\xi_i \xi_j} m_j. \tag{3.27}$$

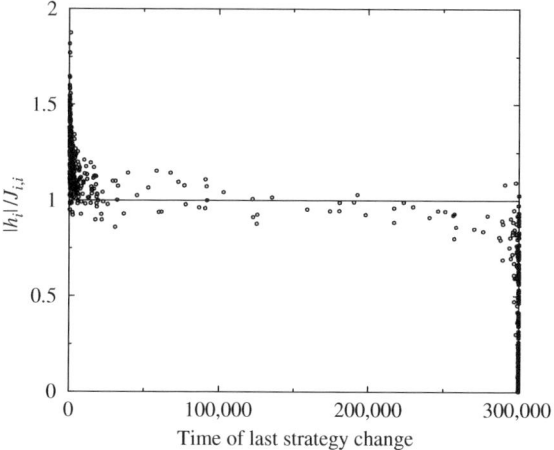

Fig. 3.5 The condition for an agent to be frozen requires that the field $h_i = \overline{\Omega \xi_i} + \sum_{j \neq i} \overline{\xi_i \xi_j} m_j$ be larger in absolute value than the self-interaction term $J_{i,i} = \overline{\xi_i^2} \simeq 1/2$. Indeed $m_i = -\text{sign}[h_i + J_{i,i} m_i]$ has only a solution when $|h_i| > J_{i,i}$. Indeed plotting the time of the last change of strategy of agents versus the ratio $|h_i|/J_{i,i}$ we see that all those agents with $|h_i| > J_{i,i}$ soon freeze onto one strategic choice. The plot refers to a simulation with $M = 8$, $N = 511$, $S = 2$, 3.10^5 iterations. Here $h_{\text{eff}} = \overline{\Omega \xi_i}$.

The presence of the self-interaction term $\overline{\xi_i^2} m_i$ in Eq. (3.27) is crucial (Challet and Marsili 1999) for the existence of non-frozen agents, as shown in Fig. 3.5. We call $\mathcal{F}$ the set of frozen agents; $\phi = |\mathcal{F}|/N$ is the fraction of frozen agents. Eqs (3.26) and (3.27) are equivalent to the solution of the constrained minimization problem

$$\min_{\{m_i\}} H, \quad m_i \in [-1, +1] \quad \forall i, \tag{3.28}$$

where

$$H = \overline{\langle A \rangle^2} = \frac{1}{P} \sum_{\mu=1}^{P} \left[\Omega^\mu + \sum_{i=1}^{N} \xi_i^\mu m_i \right]^2. \tag{3.29}$$

This is easily shown by taking the first-order derivatives of H with respect to m_i. Either $\partial H/\partial m_i = -2v_i = 0$ and then m_i takes a value in the interval $(-1, 1)$ (and agent i is not frozen) or $\partial H/\partial m_i = -2v_i \neq 0$ and then $m_i = \text{sign } v_i$.

All quantities, such as H or ϕ, which can be expressed in terms of m_i can be computed if one can solve the 'static' problem Eq. (3.28). We call m_i 'average behaviour' of agent i for short. It is represented by a so-called soft-spin in the statistical mechanics formalism.[12]

---

[12] A soft spin, as opposed to a (hard) spin $s_i = \pm 1$, is a real number $m_i \in [-1, 1]$.

The fact that the stationary state behaviour is related to the minima of the predictability H is a quite robust feature of Minority Games. This is also a natural result: Each agent is trying to predict the market outcome A with the limited capabilities—the strategies—at his disposal. The only possible stationary state is one where the outcome A is as unpredictable as possible.

The solution $\{m_i\}$ does not depend on Γ and, by Eq. (3.29), neither does H. On the contrary σ^2 cannot be expressed in terms of m_i only. Indeed

$$\sigma^2 = H + \sum_{i=1}^{N} \overline{\xi_i^2} (1 - m_i^2) + \sum_{i \neq j} \overline{\xi_i \xi_j} \langle (\tanh Y_i - m_i)(\tanh Y_j - m_j) \rangle. \quad (3.30)$$

The last term depends on fluctuation of $\tanh Y_i$ around m_i. It only involves off-diagonal correlations across different agents $i \neq j$. An analysis of fluctuations in the stationary state is necessary in order to compute this last term and hence σ^2. This requires the introduction of the continuum time limit. Let us discuss the properties of the solution to the problem (3.28). We anticipate that the effective theory which we shall develop later, and which is remarkably accurate, shows that the last term in Eq. (3.30) vanishes for $\alpha > \alpha_c$ for all values of Γ and for $\alpha \leq \alpha_c$ in the limit $\Gamma \to 0$. Accordingly, the solution of Eq. (3.28) will also allow us to compute $\sigma^2 \cong H + \sum_i \overline{\xi_i^2}(1 - m_i^2)$ in these cases.

3.3.2 The statistical mechanics analysis of stationary states and phase transition

Let us come back to the minimization problem in Eq. (3.28). The statistical properties of the solutions to this problem can be accessed using techniques of statistical mechanics. Indeed, regarding H as the Hamiltonian of a system of soft spins $\{m_i\}$, the solution to Eq. (3.28) is given by the associated ground state properties. These are studied first introducing the partition function

$$Z(\beta, \Xi) = \text{Tr}_m e^{\beta H \{m_i, \Xi\}},$$

where β is an inverse temperature, $\Xi = \{a_{i,s}^\mu\}$ denotes the quenched disorder and Tr_m stands for the integral on m_i from -1 to $+1$, for all $i = 1, \ldots, N$. This is nothing else than a generating function, from which all the statistical properties can be computed. In our case, since we are interested in the minimum of H, we shall take the limit $\beta \to \infty$ at the end of the calculus. Equation (3.28) can be rewritten as:

$$\min_{\{m_i\}} H\{m_i, \Xi\} = - \lim_{\beta \to \infty} \frac{1}{\beta} \ln Z(\beta, \Xi). \quad (3.31)$$

Rather than focusing on the solution of this problem for a particular game, that is for a given realization of the structure of interactions Ξ, we are interested in the generic properties which hold for 'typical' realizations of the game in the limit $N \to \infty$. These properties are called *self-averaging* because they hold for almost all realizations. In other words, in this limit, all the realizations of the game are characterized by the same statistical behaviour, that is, the same values for all the relevant quantities.[13] In order to study these properties, we take the average over the disorder Ξ in Eq. (3.31). This eliminates the dependence on quenched disorder but leaves us with the problem of taking the average of the logarithm of a random variable Z, which is very difficult at best. However, the replica trick (Mézard et al. 1987).

$$\langle \ln Z \rangle_\Xi = \lim_{n \to 0} \frac{1}{n} \ln \langle Z^n \rangle_\Xi \tag{3.32}$$

reduces the complexity of the calculus. In this equation, Z^n means that one replicates n times a given system, keeping the same disorder (strategies), but introducing a set of variables m_i for each replica c, denoted by $\{m_i^c\}$. One finds that (e.g. see the appendix of Challet et al. 2000d) the calculation of $\langle Z^n \rangle_\Xi$ can be reduced to an integral on a space of $n \times n$ matrices $\hat{Q}$ and $\hat{R}$, that is,

$$\langle Z^n \rangle_\Xi \propto \int d\hat{Q} d\hat{R} e^{-\beta Nnf(\hat{Q},\hat{R})} \simeq e^{-\beta Nnf(\hat{Q}^*,\hat{R}^*)}, \tag{3.33}$$

where the saddle point integration was used in the last step (note that both β and N are large). Here Q is a matrix of *order parameters* and it has elements

$$Q_{c,d} = \frac{1}{N} \sum_{i=1}^{N} m_{i,c} m_{i,d}, \tag{3.34}$$

where the indices c and d label replicas. The matrix $\hat{R}$ is introduced as a Lagrange multiplier in order to enforce Eq. (3.34).The free energy f is given by:

$$f(\hat{Q}, \hat{r}) = \frac{\alpha}{2n\beta} \text{Tr} \log \left[\hat{1} + \frac{\beta}{\alpha} \left(1 + \hat{Q} \right) \right] + \frac{\alpha\beta}{2n} \sum_{c \leq d} r_{c,d} Q_{c,d}$$

$$- \frac{1}{n\beta} \log \left[\text{Tr}_m e^{(\alpha\beta^2/2) \sum_{c \leq d} r_{c,d} m_c m_d} \right]. \tag{3.35}$$

---

[13] This also means that when the system's size increases, one has to average over less samples in numerical simulations for a given desired accuracy.

It is known that for Hamiltonian which are non-negative definite, such as $H = \overline{\langle A \rangle^2}$, the matrices $\hat{Q}^*$ and $\hat{R}^*$ which dominate the integrals in the limit $\beta N \to \infty$ have the *replica symmetric* form

$$Q^*_{a,b} = q + (Q - q)\delta_{a,b}, \qquad R^*_{a,b} = r + (R - r)\delta_{a,b}. \qquad (3.36)$$

Another consequence of the non-negativity of H is that it takes its minima on a connected set, which is either a point or a linear subspace.[14] In Chapter 5 we shall see a case where the minimized function is no more positive definite. With the *ansatz* (3.36), we can compute the free energy f and then take the limit $n \to 0$.

$$
\begin{aligned}
f^{(RS)}(Q, q, R, r) = {} & \frac{\alpha}{2\beta} \log\left[1 + \frac{\beta(Q - q)}{\alpha}\right] \\
& + \frac{\alpha}{2}\frac{1 + q}{\alpha + \beta(Q - q)} + \frac{\alpha\beta}{2}(RQ - rq) \\
& - \frac{1}{\beta}\left\langle \log \int_{-1}^{1} dm\, e^{-\beta V_z(m)} \right\rangle_z,
\end{aligned}
\qquad (3.37)
$$

where

$$V_z(m) = -\frac{\alpha\beta(R - r)}{2}m^2 - \sqrt{\alpha r}\, z\, m \qquad (3.38)$$

and the average of the last term is defined as $\langle \ldots \rangle_z = \int_{-\infty}^{\infty} dz \ldots e^{-z^2/2}/\sqrt{2\pi}$. The last term of $f^{(RS)}$ looks like the free energy of a particle in the interval $[-1, 1]$ with potential $V_z(m)$ where z plays the role of disorder. The parameters Q, q, R, and r are finally found solving the saddle point equations $\partial f^{(RS)}/\partial X = 0$ with $X = Q, q, R$, or r. The derivation of these equations is standard in disordered spin systems (Mézard et al. 1987) and are described in some more detail in Marsili et al. (2000) and Challet et al. (2000d).

The properties of the solution differ qualitatively according to whether $\alpha > \alpha_c$ or $\alpha < \alpha_c$ where

$$\alpha_c = 0.3374\ldots \quad (S = 2) \qquad (3.39)$$

is the solution of the non-linear equation $\alpha_c = \mathrm{erf}\left[\sqrt{|\log[\sqrt{\pi}(2 - \alpha_c)]|}\right]$ where $\mathrm{erf}(x)$ is the error function.

---

[14] A remarkable consequence of this will be discussed in Section 3.3.4.

3.3.3 The asymmetric phase

For $\alpha > \alpha_c$ the solution to Eq. (3.28) is unique. In parametric form, we find,

$$\lim_{N\to\infty} \frac{1}{N} \langle \min_{\{m_i\}} H\{m_i\}\rangle_\Xi = \frac{1+Q}{2(1+\chi)^2}, \qquad (3.40)$$

where the parameters Q and χ are given by

$$Q(\zeta) = 1 - \sqrt{\frac{2}{\pi}} \frac{e^{-\zeta^2/2}}{\zeta} - \left(1 - \frac{1}{\zeta^2}\right) \mathrm{erf}\left(\frac{\zeta}{\sqrt{2}}\right), \qquad (3.41)$$

$$\chi(\zeta) = \frac{\mathrm{erf}\left(\zeta/\sqrt{2}\right)}{\alpha - \mathrm{erf}\left(\zeta/\sqrt{2}\right)}, \qquad (3.42)$$

where ζ is determined by

$$\alpha = [1 + Q(\zeta)]\zeta^2, \qquad (3.43)$$

for $\alpha > \alpha_c.$[15]

The parameter $Q = \frac{1}{N}\sum_i m_i^2$ emerges in the calculation as an *order parameter*. It provides a measure of the degree of randomness of agents' behaviour: $Q = 1$ means that all agents stick to only one strategy ($m_i = \pm 1$ for all i) whereas $Q = 0$ means that they play at random ($m_i = 0$). A similar measure is given by the fraction ϕ of frozen agents, which is given, in parametric form, by

$$\phi = \lim_{N\to\infty} \frac{|\mathcal{F}|}{N} = \mathrm{erfc}(\zeta/\sqrt{2}). \qquad (3.44)$$

A more detailed information on how agents play, is given by the full probability distribution of m_i:

$$P(m) = \lim_{N\to\infty} \frac{1}{N} \sum_{i=1}^{N} \delta(m_i - m) \qquad (3.45)$$

$$= \frac{\phi}{2}\delta(m+1) + \frac{\phi}{2}\delta(m-1) + \frac{\zeta}{\sqrt{2\pi}}e^{-\zeta^2 m^2/2}.$$

---

[15] In practice, Eqs (3.41), (3.42), and (3.43) describe the $\alpha > \alpha_c$ phase in a parametric form, for $\zeta > \zeta_c$ where ζ_c is the solution of $[1 + Q(\zeta)]\zeta^2 = \mathrm{erf}(\zeta/\sqrt{2})$ (and $\zeta \to \zeta_c$ as $\alpha \to \alpha_c$).

The quantity χ emerges instead as a *response function* in the statistical mechanics approach. More precisely, it is given by

$$\chi = \lim_{\beta \to \infty} \frac{\beta(Q - q)}{\alpha} = \lim_{\beta \to \infty} \frac{\beta}{\alpha N} \sum_{i=1}^{N}(m_{i,c} - m_{i,d})^2. \qquad (3.46)$$

$Q - q$ measures the distance between two different replicas of the system, labelled by the indices c and d in the above equation. We can think of a replica as a realization of the stochastic process with given initial conditions. A finite value of χ means simply that two processes with different initial conditions converge, in the stationary state, to the same point in phase space $\{m_i\}$, that is, that $q \to Q$ as $\beta \to \infty$ in the statistical mechanics formalism. This is what we expect to occur in an ergodic Markov process. We shall see that for $\alpha < \alpha_c$ the process is not ergodic, that is, the stationary state depends on initial conditions. Indeed $\chi = \infty$ for $\alpha < \alpha_c$ as we shall see.

The behaviour of the solution as a function of α is the following: When $\alpha \gg 1$ agents behave nearly randomly $Q \approx 0$. A naive explanation is that the information encoded in μ is too complex and agents with their limited processing power are unable to detect significant patterns.

When α decreases the agents manage to exploit information in a more efficient way: Hence Q (and ϕ) increases—implying a larger specialization in the population— and H decreases. Note that a decrease in α corresponds either to a decrease in the complexity P of the information, or to an increase in the number N of agents, and thereby of their collective information-processing power. Hence at fixed P we find that as more and more agents join the game, the game's outcome becomes less and less predictable. This is a quite reasonable property for such complex adaptive systems.

Decreasing α we also find that χ increases more and more steeply. $\chi \sim (\alpha - \alpha_c)^{-1}$ diverges as $\alpha \to \alpha_c$ and correspondingly $H \sim (\alpha - \alpha_c)^2 \to 0$ (see Eq. 3.40). This singularity marks the location of a phase transition. For $\alpha > \alpha_c$ we have $H > 0$, which means that, given the information μ, the outcome $A(t)$ is probabilistically predictable, we call this an *asymmetric phase*. For $\alpha < \alpha_c$ we have $H = 0$ which means that for any μ the outcome $A(t)$ is symmetric. So we call this the *symmetric phase*.

3.3.4   The symmetric phase and dependence on initial conditions

It is worth to notice that the occurrence of a phase transition can be understood from a simple algebraic argument. Consider the set of $N(1 - \phi)$ unfrozen agents, those who have $|m_i| < 1$. In the stationary state the corresponding variables m_i must satisfy the set of linear equations:

$$\overline{\langle A \rangle \xi_i} = \overline{\Omega \xi_i} + \sum_{j=1}^{N} \overline{\xi_i \xi_j} m_j = 0.$$

There are at most P independent equations in this set because that is the rank of the matrix $\overline{\xi_i \xi_j}$. Hence as long as $N(1 - \phi) < P$ the solution is unique but when $N(1 - \phi) \geq P$ there are more variables than equations and the solution is no more unique. Notice that in this case we have $\langle A | \mu \rangle = 0$ for all μ which means $H = 0$ for $N(1 - \phi) \geq P$. We conclude that the critical threshold is given by:

$$\alpha_c = 1 - \phi(\alpha_c) \tag{3.47}$$

and that for $\alpha < \alpha_c$ the solution is no more unique, a fact at the origin of the divergence of χ in the whole $\alpha \leq \alpha_c$ phase. Note that the replica method confirms the validity of Eq. (3.47). The non-uniqueness of the stationary state implies that the properties of the Minority Game in the symmetric phase depend on the initial conditions. This was first observed in Challet et al. (2000c) then confirmed numerically in Garrahan et al. (2000). Finally Marsili and Challet (2001a) showed that it is possible to characterize this dependence in the limit $\Gamma \to 0$ where the dynamics becomes deterministic. Similar conclusions extend qualitatively to the more complex stochastic dynamics ($\Gamma > 0$), as discussed in Marsili and Challet (2001a). Before coming to that, let us mention that much insight can be gained on the dynamics in the symmetric phase by studying the limit $\alpha \to 0$ (Marsili 2001; Marsili and Challet 2001b).

In the $\alpha < \alpha_c$ phase the minimum of H is degenerate. In order to select a particular solution of $H = 0$, Marsili and Challet (2001a) add a potential $\eta \sum_i (m_i - m_i^*)^2/2$ to the Hamiltonian H. This term lifts the degeneracy and selects the equilibrium close to m_i^* in the limit $\eta \to 0$. We refer to by Marsili and Challet (2001a) for details and focus on the main results here.

Taking $m_i^* = m^* = 0$ describes symmetric initial conditions and increasing $m^* > 0$ gives asymmetric states that are reached when the initial scores are biased, that is $Y_i(0) \neq 0$. In this case, the saddle point equations of the statistical mechanics approach reduce to:

$$Q = \int_{-\infty}^{\infty} Dz m_0^2(z), \tag{3.48}$$

$$\chi = \frac{1 + \chi}{\sqrt{\alpha(1 + Q)}} \int_{-\infty}^{\infty} Dz z m_0(z), \tag{3.49}$$

where $Dz = (dz/\sqrt{2\pi})e^{-z^2/2}$ and $m_0(z) \in [-1, 1]$ is the value of m which minimizes

$$V_z(m) = \frac{1}{2}m^2 - \sqrt{\frac{1+Q}{\alpha}}zm + \frac{1}{2}\eta(1+\chi)(m-m^*)^2. \tag{3.50}$$

There are two possible solutions: one with $\chi < \infty$ finite as $\eta \to 0$ which describes the $\alpha > \alpha_c$ phase. Note that, as long as χ remains finite, the last term of Eq. (3.50) vanishes when $\eta \to 0$, hence the dependence on 'initial conditions' m^* disappears.

The second solution has $\chi \sim 1/\eta$ which diverges as $\eta \to 0$, hence the last term of Eq. (3.50) has a finite limit. This solution describes the $\alpha < \alpha_c$ phase and can be expressed in parametric form in terms of two parameters z_0 and $\epsilon_0 = cm^*/(1+c)$, where $c = \lim_{\eta \to 0} \eta\chi$. Equation (3.48) with

$$m_0(z) = \begin{cases} -1 & \text{if } z \leq -z_0 - \epsilon_0 \\ \frac{z+\epsilon_0}{z_0} & \text{if } -z_0 - \epsilon_0 < z < z_0 - \epsilon_0 \\ 1 & \text{if } z \geq z_0 - \epsilon_0 \end{cases}$$

gives $Q(z_0, \epsilon_0)$ and Eq. (3.49), which for $\chi \to \infty$ reads $\sqrt{\alpha(1+Q)} = \int Dz zm_0(z)$, then gives $\alpha(z_0, \epsilon_0)$. With $\epsilon_0 \neq 0$, that is, $m^* \neq 0$, one finds solutions with a non-zero 'magnetization' $M = \sum_i m_i/N$. This quantity is particularly meaningful, in this context, because it measures the overlap of the behaviour of agents in the stationary state with their a priori preferred strategies

$$M \equiv \int_{-\infty}^{\infty} Dz m_0(z) = \lim_{t \to \infty} \frac{1}{N} \sum_{i=1}^{N} \langle s_i(t)s_i(0) \rangle. \tag{3.51}$$

Which stationary state is reached from a particular initial condition is a quite complex issue which requires the integration of the dynamics. However, the relation between Q and M derived analytically from Eqs (3.48) and (3.51), which is a sort of 'equation of state', can easily be checked by numerical simulations of the Minority Game. Figure 3.6, from Marsili and Challet (2001a), shows that the self-overlap Q and the magnetization M computed in numerical simulations with initial conditions $y_i(0) = y_0$ for all i, perfectly match the analytic results. The inset of this figure shows how the final magnetization M and the self-overlap Q depend on the asymmetry y_0 of initial conditions.

In order to show the variability of results with initial conditions, Fig. 3.7 plots σ^2/N both for symmetric ($y_0 = 0$) and for maximally asymmetric initial conditions ($y_0 \to \infty$) in the limit $\Gamma \to 0$. The inset shows the behaviour of Q and M in the maximally asymmetric state.

Remarkably we find that σ^2/N vanishes as $\alpha \to 0$ in the maximally asymmetric state,[16] in agreement with the results of paper (Heimel and Coolen 2001).

---

[16] The relation is almost indistinguishable from a linear law $\sigma^2 = cN\alpha$ but higher order terms exist.

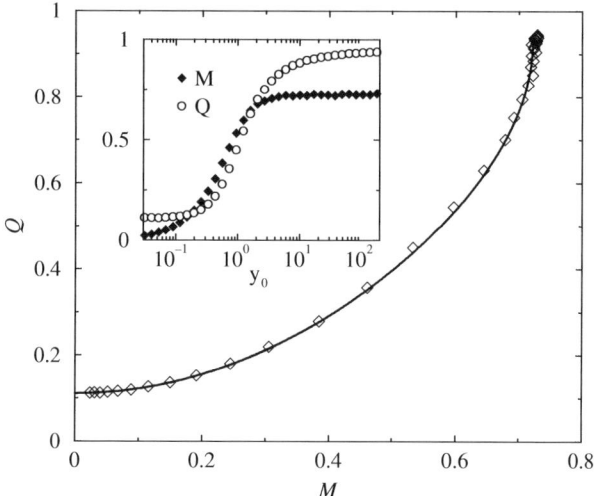

Fig. 3.6 Relation between Q and M, for $\alpha = 0.1$, derived from analytic calculation (full line) and from numerical simulations of the MG with different initial conditions y_0 ($\diamond$, $P = 32$, $N = 320$, $\Gamma = 0.1$). The inset shows the dependence of Q and M from the initial condition y_0.

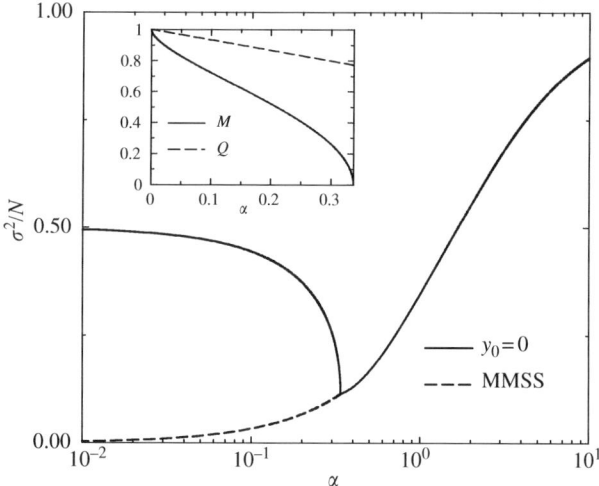

Fig. 3.7 σ^2/N for the Minority Game with initial conditions $y_0 = 0$ (full line) and $y_0 \to \infty$ (dashed line). The inset reports the behaviour of M and Q for $y_0 \to \infty$.

This means that, at fixed P, as N increases the fluctuation σ^2 remains constant. This contrast with what happens in the $y_0 = 0$ state, for $\Gamma \ll 1$, where σ^2 increases linearly with N, and with the case $\Gamma \to \infty$ where $\sigma^2 \propto N^2$ (Savit et al. 1999).

3.3.5   The continuum time limit and fluctuations in the stationary state

The study of the off-diagonal correlations $\langle s_i s_j \rangle$ requires a more refined approach. Let us go back to Eq. (3.16). The study of the dynamics of the Minority Game starts from three key observations:

(1) The scaling $\sigma^2 \sim N$, at fixed α, suggests that typically $A(t) \sim \sqrt{N}$. Hence time increments of $U_{i,s}(t)$, in Eq. (3.12) are small (i.e. of order $1/\sqrt{N}$);

(2) As shown in Challet et al. (2000b), characteristic times of the dynamics are proportional to N. Naively this is because agents need to 'test' their strategies against all $P = \alpha N$ values of μ, which requires of order P time steps.

(3) Characteristic times in the learning dynamics are also inversely proportional to Γ. The process takes a time of order $1/\Gamma$ to 'learn' a perturbation $\delta U_{i,s}$, that is, to translate it into a change in the choice probabilities Eq. (3.9) of the same order. From this perspective, Γ appears as a 'learning rate' rather than the inverse of a temperature.

The second and last observation implies that one needs to study the dynamics in the rescaled time

$$\tau = \frac{\Gamma t}{N}$$

and to introduce continuum time variables $y_i(\tau) = Y_i(t)$. The key point is that if $N \gg \Gamma$, a small time increment $d\tau \ll 1$ corresponds to a large number $\Delta t = N d\tau / \Gamma \gg 1$ of time-steps. The corresponding change $dy_i(\tau) = Y_i(t + \Delta t) - Y_i(t)$, being the sum of Δt stochastic increments, can be estimated quite precisely by the Central Limit Theorem when $\Delta t \to \infty$. Having taken the thermodynamic limit $N \to \infty$, one can take the continuum time limit $d\tau \to 0$. Note that Γ needs to be finite in this process, and the limit $\Gamma \to \infty$ can be taken at the end. In practice, numerical simulations show that the limit in which the limits $N \to \infty$ and $\Gamma \to \infty$ are taken does not matter.

We refer the interested reader to Marsili and Challet (2001a) (see page 164) for a detailed account of the derivation and jump directly to the resulting dynamical equations:

$$\frac{dy_i}{d\tau} = -\overline{\Omega \xi_i} - \sum_{j=1}^{N} \overline{\xi_i \xi_j} \tanh(y_j) + \zeta_i, \tag{3.52}$$

where $\zeta_i(\tau)$ is white noise with $\langle \zeta_i(\tau) \rangle = 0$ and

$$\langle \zeta_i(\tau)\zeta_j(\tau') \rangle = \frac{\Gamma}{N} \langle A^2 \rangle_y \overline{\xi_i \xi_j} \delta(\tau - \tau'). \tag{3.53}$$

The average $\langle \ldots \rangle_y$ in Eq. (3.53) is taken over the instantaneous probabilities $\text{Prob}\{s_i(t) = s\} = (1 + s \tanh y_i)/2$ in Eq. (3.15) of $s_i(t)$. In other words, the noise covariance depends in a non-linear and complex way on the dynamical variables $y_i(\tau)$. Hence Eqs (3.52) are complex non-linear stochastic differential equation with a time dependent noise term. They are exact in the limit $N \to \infty$ with Γ finite. This conclusion has been confirmed by the more elaborate generating functional approach of Heimel and Coolen (2001) and Coolen and Heimel (2001) (see Section 3.3.6).

A peculiar feature of these equations is that the noise strength in Eq. (3.53) is itself proportional to $\langle A^2 \rangle_y \approx \sigma^2$. This feedback effect is quite natural in hindsight: Each agent faces an uncertainty which is large when the volatility $\langle A^2 \rangle_y$ is large.

Quite remarkably, the stochastic force is proportional to Γ and that is the only place where Γ appears explicitly. Hence Γ tunes the strength of stochastic fluctuations in much the same way as temperature does for thermal fluctuations in statistical mechanics. It is significant that Γ, which is introduced as the inverse of an *individual* temperature in the definition of the model, actually turns out to play *collectively* a role quite similar to that of global temperature. This similarity will appear even more evident below.

The analysis of the stochastic dynamics is made complex by the dependence on $y_i(\tau)$, and hence on time, of Eq. (3.53). However, this time dependence comes through the volatility $\langle A^2 | \mu \rangle_y / N$, which is self-averaging unless collective fluctuations of the variables $y_i(\tau)$ arise. Challet and Marsili (2003a) expands further on this argument, showing that collective fluctuations which can sustain time dependent volatility fluctuations only arise close to the critical point and for finite size systems. Away from it, the feedback arising from time dependent volatility can be neglected assuming that

$$\overline{\langle A^2 \rangle_y \xi_i \xi_j} \approx \overline{\langle A^2 \rangle_y}\,\overline{\xi_i \xi_j} \approx \sigma^2 \overline{\xi_i \xi_j}.$$

This greatly simplifies our task by replacing Eq. (3.53) with

$$\langle \zeta_i(t)\zeta_j(t') \rangle \cong 2T\overline{\xi_i \xi_j}\delta(t - t'), \quad \text{with } T = \frac{\Gamma \sigma^2}{2N}. \tag{3.54}$$

One important point is that in going from Eq. (3.53) to (3.54) we pass from an exact to an effective theory. Note indeed that the temperature T in Eq. (3.54) depends on σ^2 which in its turn depends on the fluctuations of $y_i(\tau)$. So the theory becomes a self-consistent one. The comparison of its predictions with numerical simulations will provide a check of its validity.

Let us imagine we have solved the problem of computing m_i in the stationary state[17] and let us address the problem of computing the fluctuations of y_i. We briefly review

---

[17] We remark that for $\alpha > \alpha_c$ the solution of min H is unique and hence m_i depend only on the realization of disorder Ξ. For $\alpha < \alpha_c$ the solution is not unique, hence we also have the problem of finding which solution the dynamics selects, depending on the initial conditions.

the main steps of the analysis in Marsili and Challet (2001a) and refer the interested reader to the original paper for more details.

Using the stationary condition Eqs (3.27) and (3.54), we can write the Fokker–Planck equation for the probability distribution $P_u(y_i, i \notin \mathcal{F})$ of unfrozen agents. This satisfies a sort of fluctuation dissipation theorem: indeed both the deterministic term of Eq. (3.52) and the noise covariance Eq. (3.54) are proportional to the matrix $J_{i,j} = \overline{\xi_i \xi_j}$. This makes it possible to find a solution in the stationary state, which reads

$$P_u \propto P_{y(0)} \exp \left\{ -\frac{1}{T} \sum_{j \notin \mathcal{F}} \left[\log \cosh y_j - m_j y_j \right] \right\}, \tag{3.55}$$

where

$$P_{y(0)} \equiv \prod_{\mu=1}^{P} \int_{-\infty}^{\infty} dc^{\mu} \prod_{i=1}^{N} \delta \left[y_i - y_i(0) - \sum_{\mu=1}^{P} c^{\mu} \xi_i^{\mu} \right] \tag{3.56}$$

is a projector which imposes the constraint that the states $|y(t)\rangle = \{y_i(t)\}_{i=1}^{N}$ which are dynamically accessible must lie on the linear space spanned by the vectors $|\xi^{\mu}\rangle$ which contains the initial condition $|y(0)\rangle$. Note that Eq. (3.55) has the form of a Boltzmann distribution with temperature T, which is proportional to Γ (see Eq. 3.54).

Using the distribution Eq. (3.55), we can compute σ^2 from Eq. (3.30). In principle the third term of Eq. (3.30)

$$\Sigma(T) = \sum_{i \neq j} \overline{\xi_i \xi_j} \langle (\tanh y_i - m_i)(\tanh y_j - m_j) \rangle_T$$

(where $\langle \ldots \rangle_T$ stands for averages over P_u) depends on T which in its turn depends on σ^2 (see Eq. 3.54). Hence, the stationary state is the solution of a self-consistent problem.

For $\alpha > \alpha_c$ the number $N - |\mathcal{F}| \equiv N(1 - \phi)$ of unfrozen agents is less than P and the constraint is ineffective, that is, $P_{y(0)} \equiv 1$. Hence the dependence on initial conditions $y_i(0)$ drops out and the probability distribution of y_i factorises over i. As a consequence $\Sigma(T) \equiv 0$ vanishes identically. We conclude that, for $\alpha > \alpha_c$, $\sigma^2 = H + \sum_i \overline{\xi_i^2}(1 - m_i^2)$ only depends on m_i and is independent of Γ. This is confirmed by numerical simulations to a remarkable accuracy: Figure 3.8 shows that σ^2 changes by less than 0.3% when Γ varies over four decades.

When $\alpha < \alpha_c$, on the other hand, the constraint cannot be integrated out and the stationary distribution depends on the initial conditions. In addition $P_{y(0)}$ also introduces a correlation in the fluctuations of y_i across the agents. This leads to

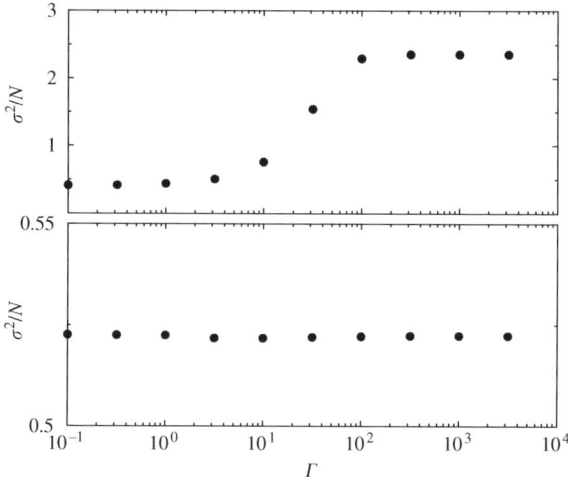

Fig. 3.8 σ^2/N as a function of Γ for a given realisation of the game with initial conditions $y(0) = 0$; $\alpha \simeq 0.1 < \alpha_c$ (upper panel, $P = 10$, $N = 101$) and $\alpha = 1.5 > \alpha_c$ (lower panel, $P = 30$, $N = 45$). Average over $10,000 P$ iterations.

a non-vanishing contribution $\Sigma(T)$ in Eq. (3.30). Hence σ^2 turns out to be the solution of the self-consistent equation:

$$\sigma^2(\Gamma) = H + \sum_{i=1}^{N} \overline{\xi_i^2}(1 - m_i^2) + \Sigma\left(\frac{\Gamma \sigma^2(\Gamma)}{2N}\right). \tag{3.57}$$

Marsili and Challet (2001a) solved these equations using Monte Carlo methods to sample the distribution P_u of Eq. (3.55). The results agree perfectly with numerical simulations of the Minority Game.

It is possible to solve Eq. (3.57) to leading order in $\Gamma \ll 1$. Marsili and Challet (2001a) show that

$$\frac{\sigma^2}{N} \cong \frac{1 - Q}{2}\left[1 + \frac{1 - Q + \alpha(1 - 3Q)}{4}\Gamma + O(\Gamma^2)\right], \tag{3.58}$$

which agrees very well with numerical simulations. Marsili and Challet (2001a) also show that a simple argument allows to understand the origin of the behaviour $\sigma^2/N \sim 1/\alpha$ for $\Gamma \gg 1$, first discussed in Savit et al. (1999). It must be observed that a correlated behaviour of agents was already hinted at by Johnson and coworkers (Johnson et al. 1999b; Hart et al. 2001), who put this effect in relation with crowd effects in financial markets.

In summary the dependence on initial conditions, cross-correlations in the behaviour of agents and dependence of aggregate fluctuations on the learning rate are intimately related in a chain of consequences. This is a remarkable and entirely novel scenario in statistical physics. These results are derived under the approximation of Eq. (3.54) but are fully confirmed by numerical simulations. This suggests that this approximation may be exact in the limit $N \to \infty$ at least far from the critical point α_c.

A quantitative study of correlated fluctuations close to the critical point has been carried out in Challet and Marsili (2003a) on the basis of a simple argument: The time dependence of the volatility becomes relevant when the deterministic part of the dynamics (see Eq. (3.52)) is small, that is, when the signal-to-noise ratio percevied by the agents falls below a given threshold. Then correlated fluctuations between y_i and y_j can be sustained by fluctuation in $\langle A^2 | \mu \rangle$. The criteria for this to occur is, in the present model (see Eq. (6) in Challet and Marsili (2003a)), $H \ll \sigma^2/\sqrt{P}$. Indeed Fig. 3.9 shows that the point where

$$\frac{H}{\sigma^2} \simeq \frac{K}{\sqrt{P}} \qquad (3.59)$$

with $K \approx 0.39$ a constant, determines quite precisely the location where numerical simulations deviate considerably from the theoretical results. Since $H \propto (\alpha - \alpha_c)^2$, we argue that the critical region where we expect anomalous fluctuations has a size which vanishes as $|\alpha - \alpha_c| \sim N^{-1/4}$ when $N, P \to \infty$. The same phenomenon also occurs in market-oriented Minority Games and is responsible for the presence of market-like large fluctuations (see Chapter 4).

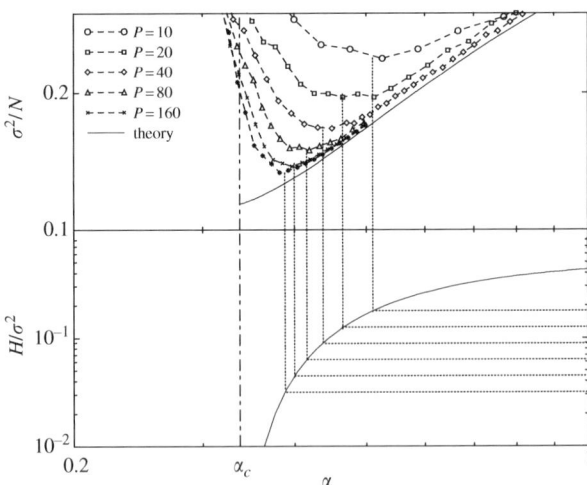

Fig. 3.9 Graphic construction to show that deviations from theoretical result occur inside the critical region defined by Eq. (3.59) ($K = 0.39$ in the figure).

We expect that Eq. (3.54) is a good approximation outside the critical region, whereas for $|\alpha - \alpha_c| \ll N^{1/4}$ one needs to take explicitly into account the time dependence of volatility.

3.3.6 The generating functional approach

A different approach, based on the generating functional has been proposed to study the Minority Game (Coolen and Heimel 2001; Heimel and Coolen 2001; (see page 176) Heimel et al. 2001). This method is dynamical in essence. Taking the average of dynamical equations over the disorder, it yields an effective dynamical theory. We include the paper by Heimel and Coolen (2001), which deals with the Minority Game with $\Gamma \to \infty$, in the list of reprints. This gives a quite detailed description of the method. We refer the interested reader first to this paper, and also to Coolen's book that goes as much into details as possible (Coolen 2004). We shall give here a brief account of the method and results.

This approach was proposed in Heimel and Coolen (2001) for a *batch* version of the Minority Game in which $\Gamma = \infty$ and the agents revise their choices $s_i(t)$ only every P time steps.[18] Later the analysis was extended to the standard—called on-line—Minority Game and later to $\Gamma < \infty$ and to a different choice rule (Coolen and Heimel 2001; Heimel et al. 2001).[19]

The idea is to write down a dynamic generating functional as a path integrals over the exact time evolution of a given configuration of scores $\{U_{i,s}\}$. After taking the average over disorder, one finds that the generating functional is dominated (in the saddle point sense) by a single 'representative' stochastic process $q(t)$—Eqs (62)–(66) of Heimel and Coolen (2001). These are quite complex self-consistent equations: Indeed the drift and diffusion term of the process $q(t)$ depend in a non-linear way on the correlation and response functions

$$C(t, t') = \langle s(t)s(t') \rangle, \qquad G(t, t') = \frac{\delta \langle s(t) \rangle}{\delta h(t')}$$

of the process $s(t)$. Here $h(t)$ is an auxiliary external field which is added to the dynamics in order to probe its response. Furthermore, the integration on the quenched disorder induces a long-term memory in the process.

A virtue of this approach has been to clarify several issues on the continuum time limit (Cavagna et al. 1999, 2000; Challet et al. 2000b,c). In particular it has shown

---

[18] Put differently agents process in a batch all information patterns μ and react to their cumulative effect.

[19] Note that as long as the average behaviour m_i is concerned, this model is identical to the online case. Indeed Eq. 3.25 are still valid. However, σ^2 differs from the online version of the game.

that characteristic times of the dynamics do indeed scale with N.[20] Furthermore, it has shown that an approach based on Fokker–Planck equation (which neglects higher order terms in the Kramers–Moyal expansion)—such as that of previous sections (Marsili and Challet 2001a)—is indeed correct. It also gives an exact derivation of the drift and diffusion terms in the continuum time description.

A drawback of the approach is that the resulting equations for $C(t, t')$ and $G(t, t')$ are too complex to be solved exactly and results are available only in limit cases or for some quantities. Assuming time translation invariance—$C(t, t + \tau) = C(\tau)$ and $G(t, t + \tau) = G(\tau)$ for $t \to \infty$—a finite integrated response

$$\lim_{t \to \infty} \int dt' G(t, t') = \chi < \infty$$

and weak long term memory (eq. (69) in Heimel and Coolen (2001), Coolen and Heimel were able to re-derive the equations of the replica approach[21] and the phase transition at $\alpha_c = 0.3374\ldots$.

It is quite interesting that the generating function approach gives a dynamical interpretation of the quantity χ as the integrated response to an infinitesimal perturbation. Then $\chi = \infty$ implies that the system 'remembers' forever a perturbation. In particular, this means that the stationary state depends on initial conditions. However, when $\chi = \infty$, for $\alpha < \alpha_c$, the self-consistent dynamic equations are much more difficult to analyse and have not yet been solved.

The generating functional approach is a quite promising tool for these systems which has also been successfully extended to more complex cases (Heimel and De Martino 2001). However, it does not yet give a clear picture of the interplay between initial conditions, correlations, and fluctuations—including the independence of σ^2 on Γ for $\alpha > \alpha_c$—such as the one given by the approach outlined in the previous sections. On the other hand, the exact representative agent process that this method allows to derive makes it possible to carry out accurate numerical simulations of the system in the thermodynamic limit (Eissfeller and Opper 1992).

3.4 Extensions

The analytic approaches discussed so far extend, in a more or less straightforward way to more complex models. Many of them lead to a quite similar generic picture characterised by a similar phase diagram. In many cases, the stationary state is related to the

---

[20] In the batch version of the game, the time is de facto rescaled by a factor P.

[21] Equations (76,77) and (78) of Heimel and Coolen (2001), with $c \equiv C(\tau \to \infty) = q = Q$ and $y = \zeta$ become equivalent to the saddle point Eqs (3.41),(3.42) and (3.43) discussed above. In addition Eq. (84) of Heimel and Coolen (2001) is exactly the expression of H in Eq. (3.40).

minimum of a functional which can be studied exactly within the replica symmetric approximation. We list here some of these extensions:

- The Minority Game with endogenous information has been studied by Challet and Marsili (2000). It turns out that for $\alpha > \alpha_c$ the behaviour of the Minority Game with endogenous information (Eq. 3.2) slightly differs from that under exogenous information (Eq. 3.3). The correction can be quantified within the analytic approach of Challet et al. (2000c) and Marsili and Challet (2001a), as shown in Challet and Marsili (2000). In brief, the dynamics of $A(t)$ induces a dynamics on $\mu(t)$ according to Eq. (3.2). $\mu(t)$ is a diffusion process on a particular graph, called after De Bruijn. The diffusion process acquires a drift for $\alpha > \alpha_c$ because $\langle A|\mu \rangle \neq 0$. This results in the fact that some value of μ arise more frequently than others, that is, the stationary state distribution ρ^μ of $\mu(t)$ is not uniform, as in the case of exogenous information ($\rho^\mu = 1/P$). These considerations can be cast into a self-consistent theory which approximately accounts for the effects of endogenous histories for $\alpha > \alpha_c$.

  For $\alpha < \alpha_c$ instead the stationary state is uniform ($\rho^\mu = 1/P$) because there is no bias ($\langle A|\mu \rangle = 0$) but correlation functions exhibit an oscillatory behaviour (fig. 2 in Challet and Marsili 1999) under endogenous information dynamics which does not arise with exogenous information. Hui et al. (1999), Challet et al. (2000d), Jefferies (2001), Metzler (2002), and Hart et al. (2002a) also discuss the issue of endogenous versus exogenous information in different variants of the Minority Game. It should be noted that there are cases where endogeneous information makes sense, for instance in models of prediction, bubbles, and crashes (Giardina and Bouchaud 2002; Lamper et al. 2002).

  Endogenous information leads to a radically different results with respect to the endogenous case when agents behave in a deterministic way (i.e. when they are all frozen). Then the induced dynamics of $\mu(t)$ is also deterministic and it locks into periodic orbits of period $\sim \sqrt{P}$ on the De Bruijn graph. The majority of the information patterns are never generated by the system. Such a situation has been discussed in Johnson et al. (1999b), Challet et al. (2000c), Marsili et al. (2000), and Challet and Marsili, 2003b (see also Chapter 5).

- This whole approach can be generalized to $S > 2$ strategies (Marsili et al. 2000). Figure 3.10 shows that σ^2/N increases with S towards the random limit $\sigma^2/N = 1$ and the phase transition $\alpha_c(S) = \alpha_c(S = 2) + S/2 - 1$ moves linearly to higher values. Giving agents more resources leads generally to a smaller efficiency, because their strategy sets are less internally correlated.

- The approach has been also generalized to include a fraction of deterministic agents—that is, agents with $S = 1$ strategy—and totally random agents. These extensions are discussed in Challet et al. (2000d) and in the next chapter.

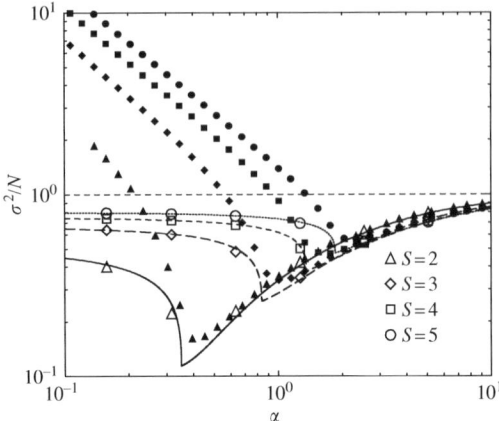

Fig. 3.10   Global efficiency σ^2/N as a function of α for $S = 2, 3, 4,$ and 5 from numerical simulations of the Minority Game with $N = 101$ agents and $\Gamma_i = \infty$ (averages were taken after $100P$ time steps), averaged over 100 realizations of $\vec{a}_i$ (small full symbols), from numerical minimization of H (large open symbols) and from the theoretical calculation (lines) with $U_{i,s}(0) = 0$.

- Cavagna et al. (1999) have proposed a generalization of the Minority Game where each agent contributes an action

$$a_i(t) = \sum_{\mu=1}^{P} a_{i,s_i}^{\mu} \eta^{\mu}(t), \tag{3.60}$$

where $\eta^{\mu}(t)$ is white noise (i.e. a Gaussian variable with zero average and unit variance, independent for each μ and t). In Cavagna et al. (1999) trading strategies a_{i,s_i}^{μ} are 'continuous', that is, they are drawn from a continuous distribution—a Gaussian—rather than from the bimodal. The idea is that the exogenous process which drives the market, or the news arrival process, is a P dimensional vector $\vec{\eta}(t)$. Agents respond to it with linear strategies, which are also P dimensional vectors $\vec{a}_{i,s}$. This model reduces to the previous one if we assume that $\vec{\eta}(t) = (\ldots, 0, 1, 0, \ldots)$ can only lay along one of the P components of the orthogonal basis and that $a_{i,s}^{\mu}$ is drawn from the bimodal distribution. In general the vector $\vec{\eta}$ probes the performance of the strategies with respect to all informations (i.e. components) μ at the same time. Challet et al. (2000b) showed that this model has the same collective behaviour (m_i) as the one discussed above. Indeed the equations which describe the stationary state of this model has the same deterministic term as Eq. (3.52).
- The agents can be allowed not to play by endowing them with a so-called $0-$strategy which prescribes not to trade, whatever μ. These models will be discussed in Chapter 4 and are characterised by a behaviour similar to that discussed here (Challet et al. 2001b; Challet and Marsili 2003a). Even if, in general, agents do not play

at all times, they all update their (virtual) payoffs simultaneously observing the market. In other words, the model is still a fully connected, mean-field model.

- The case of agents entering the market with heterogeneous weights $w_i = |a_{i,s}^\mu| \neq 1$—modelling a population where some are richer or more influential than others— has been dealt with in Challet et al. ($2000a$) and will be discussed in Chapter 4.

- Agents with a given degree of correlation between their two strategies (Challet et al. $2000d$; Sherrington et al. 2002; Sherrington and Galla 2003) also exhibit the same generic behaviour, with α_c depending on the correlation coefficient. Challet et al. ($2000d$) discuss this case within the replica approach (see also Chapter 4), while Sherrington and Galla (2003) employ generating functionals.

- Agents playing on different frequencies have been discussed in Marsili and Piai (2002). This amounts to assume that agent i plays only for a fraction f_i of information patterns μ and otherwise he does not play ($a_{i,s}^\mu = 0$). Even for broad distribution of frequencies f_i across the population of agents the phase transition persists, with α_c which depends on the distribution of f_i. Interestingly frequent players have a smaller probability of being frozen than those who play rarely.

- Information patterns with widely spread frequencies have been discussed in Challet and Marsili (2000) and Marsili and Piai (2002). Again the phase transition persists and α_c depends on the distribution of the frequencies ρ^μ with which information patterns occur. In the asymmetric phase, more frequent patterns are typically less predictable. More precisely if μ occurs with a probability $\rho^\mu = \tau^\mu / P$

$$|\langle A|\mu \rangle| \propto \frac{1}{1 + \chi \tau^\mu},$$

which also suggests that χ is the inverse of the characteristic frequency above which the market is unpredictable $\langle A|\mu \rangle \approx 0$ for $\tau^\mu \gg \chi^{-1}$).

- Minority Games with non-linear payoffs $-a_i G(A)$ have been discussed in some details in Li et al. ($2002a$) on the basis of numerical simulations and in Challet et al. ($2000d$) and Marsili and Challet, ($2001a$) analytically. Marsili and Challet, ($2001a$) show that, within a self-consistent time-independent volatility approximation, it is again possible to derive a function $\mathcal{H}$ which is minimized by agents in the stationary state. For $G(A) = -G(-A)$ and $G(A) \simeq gA + O(A^3)$ for $A \ll 1$, it is possible to argue that the location of the phase transition does not depend on $G(A)$ (Challet 2003).

- The statistical mechanics approach makes it clear that only the first two moments of the distribution of $a_{i,s}^\mu$ matter. Our results stay exactly the same for all distributions of $a_{i,s}^\mu$ with zero average and unit variance. The case of a non-zero average has been dealt with in Challet and Marsili ($2003b$).

- De Martino et al. (2003b) has shown that an additive noise in the payoff dynamics does not change the phase diagram, but it affects the fluctuations σ^2. In particular De Martino et al. (2003b) considers the case

$$U_{i,s}(t+1) = U_{i,s}(t) - a^{\mu}_{i,s} A(t) + (1 - \delta_{s,s_i(t)})\zeta_{i,s}(t), \qquad (3.61)$$

where the payoffs of strategies $s \neq s_i(t)$ which have not been played are affected by a 'measurement' noise $\zeta_{i,s}(t)$ with zero average and variance Δ. While this term does not modify the conclusion that the stationary state behaviour is related to the minimum of H, it changes the fluctuation properties. The new term $\zeta_{i,s}(t)$ removes the degeneracy of stationary states for $\alpha < \alpha_c$ thus affecting the fluctuations. Remarkably the more noisy the estimate of payoffs of agents, the less noisy the aggregate behaviour, that is, σ^2 turns out to be a *decreasing* function of Δ.

Further modifications which lead to a qualitatively different behaviour (characterized by replica symmetry breaking) or to a qualitatively different model with a similar behaviour will be discussed in the following two chapters.

4. Minority Games as market models

4.1 Introduction

In the last two chapters, we have introduced the Minority Game as a market model and shown how analytic and numerical tools reveal the richness of the standard Minority Game. But what has this model to do with financial markets? We have been speaking of market efficiency and volatility but where is the price? Where is money? What is the market mechanism?

We have presented the Minority Game as a coarse-grained model of a financial markets in which all these details are hidden, the minority rule acting as a generic agent interaction. But is the market really a Minority Game? A generic argument suggesting this conclusion, discussed in (Challet et al. 2000a), is that markets are institutions which allow agents to exchange goods. Through these exchanges, traders can reallocate their resources in order to increase their well-being, selling what they have in excess in order to buy what they prefer or need. As trading per se does not create any wealth, the market must be a zero sum game. Taking out transaction costs and other frictions (such as bid–ask spread) which are needed to reward the market maker for the service he is providing, the game becomes a Minority Game. This is particularly true of speculators, who have no special interest in the assets they trade but only on the possibility to extract profit from trading.

However, going beyond such generic arguments, making a precise connection to real markets—with prices, transactions, assets, money, and the like—is important. A comparison of real financial market with the Minority Game makes it clear that the latter cannot describe the complexity of the former in all its conditions and regimes. Hence it is important to specify clearly in which sense the Minority Game can be considered a faithful picture of a financial market. The key observation is that the Minority Game is tailored to study fluctuation phenomena and their statistical properties. Statistical physics suggests that the collective behaviour of a system of many interacting units, is qualitatively rather indifferent to microscopic details. Even a coarse grained, highly simplified description at the microscale, which however captures the relevant features of the interaction, must be able to generate collective properties similar to that of the real system. Hence our focus will not be on the precise modelling of market microstructure but rather on the qualitative nature of the interaction, with the aim of understanding in what broad circumstances a Minority Game-like interaction prevails in market activity. This is the main difference with the economics literature on market microstructure (Campbell et al. 1997) which enters into much more detail, specially when focusing on strategic issues. The validity of this approach is supported by the apparent universality of statistical regularities which are found in markets for assets, currencies, or derivatives, with quite different mechanisms, in different places of the world (Bouchaud and Potters 2000; Farmer 1999*b*; Mantegna and Stanley 2000; Dacorogna et al. 2001).

The relation between the Minority Game and different types of market mechanism will be the subject of the first section of this chapter. The bottom line is that the Minority Game describes markets only under some assumptions. However relaxing these assumptions calls for much more complex models which need to take account of the intertemporal nature of trading strategies.

Having given some motivation for regarding the Minority Game as a market model, we shall go on to explore its rich phenomenology. Modifying the parameters and/or introducing new features leads to models whose behaviours draw a cartoon of the functioning of financial markets. This picture, on which the exact results of the previous chapter give us full control, can be illustrated in terms of a market ecology.

In the end, besides a priori considerations on the appropriateness of the Minority Game, the crucial test is whether the Minority Game reproduces in a satisfactory manner the main stylized facts of financial market fluctuations a posteriori. We first give a brief account of typical properties of financial markets: the so-called stylized facts. A large part of physicists' interest in financial markets can be attributed to the striking similarity between stylized facts and fluctuation phenomena associated with phase transitions. The latter have been the subject of intense research activity in statistical physics over the past decades, as we shall recall. The Minority Game confirms the speculation, suggested by stylized facts, that real markets operate close to a phase transition. Indeed, as we shall see later in this chapter, Minority Games reproduce quite accurately the main stylized facts near a phase transition between the unpredictable (information efficient) and the predictable phases of the market. In addition, Minority Games provide a natural microscopic explanation for the volatility correlations found in real markets (Bouchaud et al. 2001). Hence the Minority Game offers a broad picture of how financial markets operate, consistent with empirical data. As expected, the above picture is quite robust with respect to modification of the model at the microscale, for example, introducing more strategies or correlations among them (Challet et al. 2000*d*), heterogeneous wealth (Challet et al. 2000*a*), frequency of trading across agents (Marsili and Piai 2002), non-linear payoffs (Marsili and Challet 2001*a*), etc.

Finally, we shall discuss some variations on the theme including a discussion on large price move forecasting, risk hedging, and option pricing in Minority Game markets, and on market models inspired by, but qualitatively different from the Minority Game. We conclude this chapter by reviewing what modifications of agent behaviour and interaction would lead to a qualitatively different scenario.

4.2   From real markets to Minority Games

In order to connect the Minority Game with financial markets, one obviously need to add a missing major ingredient: price dynamics. In the first section, we shall see that a price dynamics can be introduced in a natural way. Then we shall discuss how the Minority Game payoff emerges when speculators trade in a real market.

4.2.1   Price dynamics in market games

We focus on a market for a single asset and call $p(t)$ its price at time t. We assume that the price is driven by the difference between the number of shares being bought and sold, called the excess demand. This is the way in which the connection with price has been made in the Minority Game. Here, as well as in the following, we assume that the behaviour of the agents is restricted to the two possible actions: buy ($a_i(t) = +1$) and sell ($a_i(t) = -1$).[1] Then $A(t) = \sum_i a_i(t)$ is simply the difference between demand and supply, that is, the excess demand.

Several price formation rules, which link the excess demand $A(t)$ to price return $r(t)$, have been proposed in the literature and used in the Minority Game context. The simplest one is to suppose that the price return $r(t)$ depends linearly on $A(t)$ (Farmer 1999a)

$$r(t) \equiv \log p(t) - \log p(t-1) = \frac{A(t)}{\lambda}, \qquad (4.1)$$

where λ is sometimes called the *liquidity* and sometimes the *market depth* (Cont and Bouchaud 2000). This relationship is implicit in many early works, which refer to σ^2 as price volatility, but a plot of $\log p(t) = \sum_{t' \leq t} A(t')/\lambda$ was not shown until the paper by Johnson et al. (2000).

Let us first see how Eq. (4.1) can be justified in limit order markets. These are markets where people can submit *limit orders*, which are requests to buy or sell a given quantity of the asset at a given price. Each order can only be executed if there is an opposite matching request. It follows that while the quantity and the price of the

---

[1] This restriction is by no means necessary, but eases our discussion.

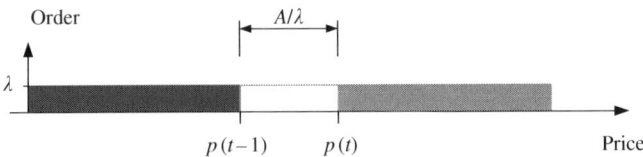

Fig. 4.1   Order density versus price as a schematic justification of Eq. (4.1). The dark grey block represents bid orders, the light grey one ask orders, and the box the executed ask orders for $A > 0$.

transaction are fixed, the time when the limit order will be executed is left undetermined (it may even be never executed). Orders waiting to be executed are stored in the *order book*; most of the time, sell orders are on the right of the last paid price $p(t - 1)$, whereas buy orders are on the left. A schematic order book is shown in Fig. 4.1.

It is also possible to submit *market orders*, which are requests to buy or sell immediately at the best price. For this kind of orders, the time and volume of transaction is fixed, but the transaction price is not known exactly in advance.

Imagine that at time $t - \epsilon$ ($0 < \epsilon \ll 1$), N market orders of size 1 arrive simultaneously on the market. Assume that $(N + A)/2$ are buy orders, and $(N - A)/2$ are sell orders. It will be possible to match $(N - |A|)/2$ buy and sell orders, and to execute them at the current price. This leaves unexecuted $|A|$ orders of one kind. If $A > 0$, they will be buy orders, else they will be sell orders. These orders will be matched with the best limit orders of the opposite type present in the order book. Now, if we assume that there is a uniform density λ of limit orders, that is, λ orders per tick,[2] the price will be displaced by a quantity A/λ, as all the orders between $p(t - 1)$ and $p(t) \equiv p(t-1) + A/\lambda$ will be executed. This is exactly what Eq. (4.1) postulates. This process can go on assuming that there are new limit orders that fill the gap between $p(t - 1)$ and $p(t)$, restoring a uniform distribution of limit orders.

The assumption of uniform order density of the order book, which is responsible for the linear relationship between A and r, is a very rough approximation, as shown in Bouchaud et al. (2002). Also the assumption on the dynamics of arrival of orders is questionable. Nonetheless, the argument above shows how excess demand drives price dynamics in a way similar to that described by Eq. (4.1).

Jefferies et al. (2001) go into some details in discussing how Eq. (4.1) needs to be modified in order to account for the presence of a market maker whose role is to absorb temporary excess demand.

Marsili (2001) (see page 260) offers a further derivation of Eq. (4.1) in a market where price is fixed by market clearing. Let us consider the market for a given asset

---

[2] Note that we are assuming that ticks are evenly spaced on a logarithmic price axis. For small price differences, this does not make a sizeable difference.

and let us assume again that traders actions, at any given time step t, are restricted to only two choices, as in the Minority Game: $a_i(t) = +1$ means that agent i invests £1 in order to buy the asset at time t, whereas $a_i(t) = -1$ means that he sells $1/p(t-1)$ units of assets, where $p(t-1)$ is the price of the last transaction. Then, the total demand is £$(N + A(t))/2$ and the total supply is $(N - A(t))/(2p(t-1))$ units of asset, where $A(t) = \sum_i a_i(t)$ as usual. Let us fix the price $p(t)$ in such a way that the demand matches the supply, that is,

$$p(t) = p(t-1)\frac{N + A(t)}{N - A(t)}. \tag{4.2}$$

If $A \ll N$, taking logarithms of both sides and keeping the leading order terms leads to an expression that is very similar to Eq. (4.1) with $\lambda = N/2$.

4.2.2 Speculative trading: payoffs and expectations

The problem of defining speculative market payoffs is a subtle one. The argument usually advocated to motivate a Minority Game like payoff $u_i^<(t) = -a_i(t)A(t)$ is that when the majority buys (sells), the price is likely to be high (low), hence it is convenient to sell (buy), that is, to be on the minority side. But high or low with respect to what? Buying some stocks of an asset at a price $p(t)$ is only profitable if one manages to sell it at a higher price $p(t')$ at a later time $t' > t$. Hence speculative market payoffs depend at least on two prices, that is, they have an inherently intertemporal nature.

Note that, if we cannot define the profit of a single transaction, we cannot define a market model as a 'single-stage game', that is one in which all the action takes place in a single time step (as in the Minority Game). In other words, if the payoffs of agents depend on two or more times, their actions also should likewise be correlated in time. Introducing an intertemporal structure in the behaviour of agents amounts to opening a Pandora box of complications in models of financial markets. Ad hoc assumptions have to be introduced anyway, at a certain level, in order to halt the resulting 'curse of complications'. This section will try to make this point clear in the simplest possible setting. This will reveal that the Minority Game results from making drastic assumptions right from the beginning, calling traders' expectations into play. This will bring us back in the realm of 'single-stage games' at the price of making a choice between Minority and Majority Games.

Let us start by considering the market payoffs within the set-up leading to Eq. (4.2). In order to do this, we need to define the *position* of each agent i introducing capital $C_i(t) = M_i(t) + p(t-1)S_i(t)$. This depends on the amount of money $M_i(t)$ and asset

$S_i(t)$ which he owns at time t, and on the current price[3] $p(t-1)$. For what we have just said, in order to define a market payoff, we need to consider a round-trip operation of two consecutive trades. The simplest ones are $a_i(t) = +1$, $a_i(t+1) = -1$ or $a_i(t) = -1$, $a_i(t+1) = +1$. The first means that agent i first buys assets for £1 at time t and then sells it back at time $t+1$ whereas the second means that he first sells $1/p(t-1)$ units of asset and then buys back for £1. Straightforward accounting and some simple algebra, shows that the position of trader i after this operations can be expressed as

$$M_i(t+2) = \begin{cases} M_i(t) - 1 + \frac{p(t+1)}{p(t)} & \text{if } a_i(t) = +1 \\ M_i(t) + \frac{p(t)}{p(t-1)} - 1 & \text{if } a_i(t) = -1, \end{cases} \tag{4.3}$$

$$S_i(t+2) = \begin{cases} S_i(t) & \text{if } a_i(t) = +1 \\ S_i(t) - \frac{1}{p(t-1)} + \frac{1}{p(t+1)} & \text{if } a_i(t) = -1, \end{cases} \tag{4.4}$$

from which we find that his capital at time $t+2$ is

$$C_i(t+2) = C_i(t) + [p(t+1) - p(t-1)]S_i(t) + \left(\frac{N - a_i(t)A(t)}{N - A(t)}\right)\left(\frac{2a_i(t)A(t+1)}{N - A(t+1)}\right)$$

$$\simeq C_i(t) + [p(t+1) - p(t-1)]S_i(t) + \frac{2}{N}a_i(t)A(t+1) + \cdots. \tag{4.5}$$

where the last line is the leading term for $A(t)$, $A(t+1) \ll N$. We recognize in the first term of Eq. (4.5) the capital gain from the transaction: this is the change in the capital due to the price change which would take place anyway, even without transactions. The last is the market payoff resulting from the pair of operations. Giardina and Bouchaud (2002) and Andersen and Sornette (2003) (see page 271) use consequently a payoff of the form

$$u_i^{\$}(t) = a_i(t)A(t+1). \tag{4.6}$$

This is why Andersen and Sornette (2003) argued that the Minority Game does not describe speculative payoffs in financial markets and called the resulting model $\$$-game. The fact that the payoff (4.6) involves two times is a natural consequence of the fact that it refers to a strategy over two periods of time. Giardina and Bouchaud (2002), Andersen and Sornette (2003) investigate what happens when the agents use Eq. (4.6), instead of the Minority Game payoff $u_i^<(t) = -a_i(t)A(t)$, to assess the validity of their strategies. The resulting model is characterized by a complex dynamics with different regimes. In some of them, the Minority Game nature of the interaction prevails,

---

[3] We use price $p(t-1)$ in the capital at time t, which is the last market price of the asset.

but more often the majority rule prevails. It is intuitive that a payoff such as (4.6) allows trends to establish and dominate the dynamics: If indeed the majority of agents plays $+1$ (or -1) for a given period of time, $A(t)$ will take a positive (negative) sign self-reinforcing the choices of agents. This is quite similar to bubble phases in real markets, where any expectation on a trend can be sustained as a self-fulfilling prophecy by the behaviour of traders. However bubbles do not last forever because traders cannot continue buying or selling forever. Sooner or later they will remain either without money or without asset. Hence Eq. (4.6) alone does not allow to define a stable market model. It is necessary to call the budget constraint explicitly into play and to model traders' behaviour when their limited amount of capital becomes a problem. This increases considerably the complexity of the model. For example, in the model of Giardina and Bouchaud (2002) 'chartist' traders revert to 'fundamentalist' strategies when the position of an agent gets close to its budget constraint. A questionable point in the $-game is that, while payoffs are defined for round-trip transactions, agents in the model do not trade that way: Eq. (4.6) is valid for agents who take $a_i(t + 1) = -a_i(t)$, but in the $-game the action $a_i(t + 1)$ is not fixed once $a_i(t)$ is chosen, but rather it is set in the same way as $a_i(t)$ on the basis of scores. We shall come back later to this point.[4]

The distinction between chartists and fundamentalists has also been discussed in Marsili (2001). This takes the viewpoint of an agent which, at time t, buys $(a_i(t) = +1)$ or sells $(a_i(t) = -1)$. Equations (4.5) and (4.6) do not allow him to estimate the validity of this action at that time, because $u_i^\$(t)$ depends on quantities which will only be known at time $t + 1$. This is indeed the heart of the game which speculators play. The way out is to invoke agents' expectations at time t about quantities at time $t + 1$. If we call $E_i[\dots|t]$ the expectation operator at time t of agent i, and apply it to Eq. (4.6), then we see that everything depends on the expectation of agent i on the future excess demand $E_i[A(t + 1)|t]$. Marsili (2001) assumes that

$$E_i[A(t + 1)|t] = -\phi_i A(t), \qquad (4.7)$$

where again the linear dependence is assumed for the sake of simplicity and can be easily generalized. Then the expected payoffs of agent i is

$$E_i[u_i^\$(t)|t] = a_i(t)E_i[A(t + 1)|t] = -\phi_i a_i(t)A(t). \qquad (4.8)$$

---

[4] A further point worth of mention is that agents in the $-game pursue exclusively capital maximization. It is not clear that the worth of a position (M_i, S_i) is given only by its capital $C_i = M_i + pS_i$. For example, if the capital is mostly in assets $M_i \ll pS_i$ the worth of the position crucially depends on the possibility to pocket the capital by selling the asset at a price close to p. This is a non-trivial issue. In general, such an unbalanced position is risky. It can be shown by straightforward algebra, that if agents account for this type of risk, for example, by maximizing $u_i(M_i, S_i) = C_i + \kappa(M_i - pS_i)^2$, the trade payoff can change sign (depending on $\kappa > 0$), that is, it may become $u_i(t) \propto -a_i(t)A(t + 1)$.

If $\phi_i > 0$ agent i expects the future movements $A(t + 1)$ to counterbalance that just occurred ($A(t)$). This is typical if he believes that price fluctuates around some equilibrium (fundamental) value p_f. A deviation out of equilibrium is likely to be followed by a restoring movement in the opposite direction. Hence Marsili (2001) calls traders with $\phi_i > 0$, fundamentalists. It is clear from Eq. (4.8) that a market of fundamentalists is a Minority Game.

On the contrary, if agent i believes that the price is following a trend, a movement $A(t)$ will likely be followed by fluctuations of the same sign, that is, $\phi_i < 0$. These agents, called 'trend followers' or 'chartists', would play a majority game, according to Eq. (4.8), when interacting.

Whatever the sign of ϕ_i is, it should be consistent with what the market actually does. If the expectation on which a trading rule is based is wrong, those using it will suffer losses, and sooner or later abandon or revise that expectation. So expectations (i.e. the variables ϕ_i) also have their own dynamics, on a timescale longer than that of trading activity.

Marsili (2001) observes that stationary states can only occur when the expectations are consistently validated by the dynamics, that is, when

$$\phi_i \simeq -\frac{\langle A(t + 1)A(t)\rangle}{\langle A^2(t)\rangle} \tag{4.9}$$

for all i. This leaves us with only the case where players are either all fundamentalist or all trend followers.[5] In a simple setting, Marsili (2001) indeed shows that both expectations $\phi_i < 0$ and $\phi_i > 0$ are self-reinforcing.

Taking Eqs (4.1) and (4.9) seriously, would suggest that markets with a positive (negative) autocorrelation of returns $\langle r(t)r(t + \tau)\rangle$ should be described by a Majority (Minority) Game on the timescale τ. If the autocorrelation changes sign with the time lag τ one would be tempted to say that markets are Majority Games on some timescales and Minority Games at other scales.[6]

Real markets are much more complex than our model and these conclusions, though suggestive, are hard to put on firm basis: In real markets the autocorrelation is very small when τ is not in the high frequency range. According to Dacorogna et al. (2001), $\langle r(t)r(t + \tau)\rangle < 0$ in foreign exchange and bond markets as long as τ is smaller than a few minutes while for larger time lags $\langle r(t)r(t + \tau)\rangle < 0$ does not exceed the noise level. Note also that $\langle r(t)\rangle \neq 0$ does not necessarily imply that the market is a Majority

---

[5] Games with a mixed population of fundamentalists and trend followers, with fixed proportions, have been studied by Marsili (2001), Martino et al. (2003a), and Challet and Galla (2003).

[6] Market microstructure studies (Campbell et al. 1997) suggest that a negative autocorrelation at high frequency is induced both by non-synchronous trading and by the presence of the bid–ask spread.

Game: Indeed speculators may effectively play a Minority Game in this case also, exploiting the fluctuations of $r(t)$ around its mean $\langle r(t) \rangle$.

Hence it is dangerous to make definite conclusions on real markets on the basis of our discussion. In the realm of theoretical market models instead, it is intuitive that agents who really enforce round trip strategies $a_i(t+1) = -a_i(t)$ such as those leading to Eq. (4.6) impose a negative autocorrelation in $A(t)$. It is quite reasonable to expect that the behaviour of a model based on Eq. (4.6), as the \$-game, will be quite similar to one where the market payoffs are given by Equation (4.8) with $\phi_i > 0$, as in the Minority Game. Marsili and Ferreira (2003) address this issue in further detail.

A model with a rich intertemporal structure, with a mixed minority–majority nature, was also introduced in Challet (2000). Slanina and Zhang (2001) (see page 276) take a different choice of market payoffs which account for the intrinsic asymmetry between asset and money. Assets carry with them the uncertainty related to price fluctuations but also yield dividends to his owner. Agents enter the market by buying a unit of asset and their payoff is positive if they manage to withdraw when the number of agents who own the asset is larger than when they entered. In addition, at each time a small fixed amount (dividend) is divided among agents who own the asset. These rules generate a complex dynamics with widely spread timescales.

Our discussion can be recast in the following conclusion: The only possibility to describe speculative markets as a single-stage game, where interaction takes place at a single point in time, is within the assumptions which led to the Minority Game. Beyond these, one needs to account explicitly for intertemporal dependencies.

4.3   Market ecology in Minority Games

In a related work (Zhang 1999), one of us argued that the financial markets have symbiotic functions for the participants. Market activities must be coupled with the outside economies so that certain players effectively inject predictive elements into the seemingly random fluctuations. These traders—the so-called producers—have a primary interest in some outside economic business and use the market for exchanging commodities. They participate in the market for their own needs in a predictable way, indifferent to small market fluctuations. On the contrary, speculators buy and sell assets without concern of their intrinsic value, solely driven by the prospects of gaining from price fluctuations. Speculators exploit the predictability introduced by producers: their trading activity 'dresses' market price fluctuations, removing predictable patterns from it. Zhang (1999) argues that in real markets, it is next to impossible to eliminate all the market inefficiencies because marginally profitable returns become meager as the market becomes unpredictable.

These two extreme types of players—producers and speculators—are very easily modelled in the Minority Game (Challet et al. 2000a,d) (see page 160, 192) producers are non-adaptive agents, they have one strategy only and play in a predictable manner. Speculators are instead adaptive, as they have more than one strategy to chose. Challet et al. (2000a,d) investigate the gain of the two types of agents as a function of their respective abundance in the market. Figure 4.2 shows the resulting picture. The first observation is that the gain of the producers is always negative, but that it increases as the number of speculators increases: hence speculators are beneficial to the producers. On the other hand the speculators obtain a positive gain (on average) provided that their number is sufficiently small and that there is enough predictability to prey on. Beyond this concentration of speculators, the average gain of speculators becomes negative even if the market remains predictable. This suggests a symbiosis: the speculators reduce the losses of the producers by providing liquidity, while the producers provide information and positive gain to the speculators. Challet et al. (2000a) investigates in detail the nature of the complex relationships among groups by analysing the effects of the introduction of a new participant of either type on the existing ones (see Fig. 4.2). We refer to that paper for a colourful picture of the resulting ecology.

One may expect the whole spectrum of agents, from producers to speculators, to be represented in a real market. Indeed even a speculator, as modelled in the basic Minority Game may inject predictability into the market. This happens when all

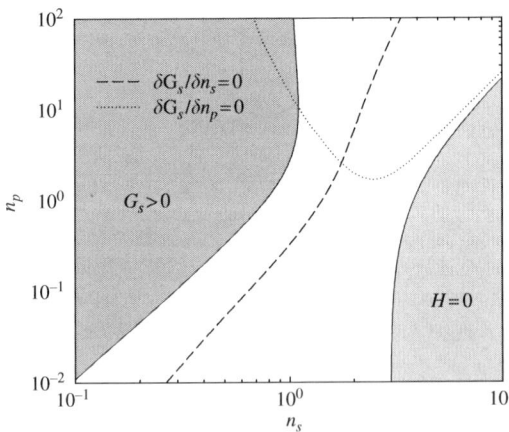

Fig. 4.2 Market ecology in the Minority Game as a function of the reduced number of speculators $n_s = N_s/P$ and producers $n_p = N_p/P$. The gain average G_p of producers is negative but it increases as n_s increases. In the symmetric phase (shaded region at bottom right) $G_p = 0$. The gain of speculators G_s is positive in the top left shaded region. Above (below) the dotted line the payoff G_s of speculators decreases (increases) with the number n_p of producers. The dashed line separates a region (left) where speculators are in competition (i.e. $G_s \searrow n_s$) from a region (right) where G_s increases with n_s.

the strategies at his disposal prescribe the same response $a_{i,1}^{\mu} = a_{i,2}^{\mu} = \ldots = a_{i,S}^{\mu}$ to a particular information pattern μ. Then his behaviour, contingent to the occurrence of that pattern, will be deterministic, hence easily predictable. The frequency with which all strategies prescribe the same action, for a particular information,[7] can be tuned by introducing a parameter as in Challet et al. (2000*d*). This allows one to model all the shades of market participants, from pure producers who act in a deterministic fashion to pure speculators with two completely opposite strategies.

When all the agents are given two opposite strategies, no pattern of predictability is injected into the game, and accordingly the asymmetric phase disappears; in addition, the price fluctuations are never smaller than those produced by agents acting randomly. Agents with opposite strategies are the most reactive as they discriminate their behaviour for all the histories μ. At the other end of spectrum, an agent with two very similar strategies behaves like an automaton; this is the least reactive kind of agents. Introducing a whole spectrum of agents with various degree of strategy correlation, defines an information food web ecology of agents which can be analyzed in detail.

The interplay between producers and speculators is also the scope of Slanina and Zhang (1999), where producers act periodically, being heterogeneous in timescales. Even though the model introduced in this paper is much more refined than that of the previous one, the same kind of symbiosis was found: namely, speculators decrease inefficiencies and price fluctuations at the advantage of producers. This paper is worth reading because it also introduces many interesting extensions that were studied later separately by many authors. The influence of noise traders, that is, traders taking a random decisions at each time step was shown to be restricted to add fluctuations (Challet et al. 2000*d*). They do not inject or remove any predictability. Speculators acting on different frequencies have been investigated in Marsili and Piai (2002). Frequent traders turn out to behave like noise traders whereas those who trade rarely take advantage of a reduced market impact (see later) and are more efficient in detecting and exploiting market asymmetries.

The nature of the relationships among market participants can also be probed by introducing one or few agents with different characteristics, such as memory $M' \neq M$ (Challet and Zhang 1997,1998; Hui et al. 1999; Challet et al. 2000*d*; Wakeling and Bak 2001), number of strategies, or asymmetric information (Challet et al. 2000*d*). Surprisingly, it turns out (Challet et al. 2000*d*) that it is worse on average to have a larger memory $M' > M$ in the predictable phase, because that provides too much information for the limited processing capabilities; the gain of an agent with $M' > M$ is positive only deep into the unpredictable phase.

---

[7] This frequency is 2^{1-S} in the Minority Game with S strategies drawn at random.

This was later explained using (anti-)persistent random walks on the graph of histories (Metzler 2002). Similarly, having more strategies, $S' > S$, than the other players is an edge for an agent in the predictable phase only if $S' \gg S$, which may be very impractical and costly.

In short, it is difficult to make money in marginally inefficient markets by only improving one's information processing abilities. However having access to information on the behaviour of others helps tremendously: knowing in advance the decision of one or more other agents, grants excess gains in a wide region of parameters. This is probably why insider trading is illegal[8] in real markets!

One unrealistic feature of the Minority Game is that it forces speculators to trade even if, with the strategies they have, they lose money. This restriction has been removed more or less independently by a number of authors (Slanina and Zhang 1999; Johnson et al. 2000; Challet et al. 2000a,d) leading to the so-called grand canonical Minority Game. This twist of the Minority Game deserves a detailed discussion which we postpone to Section 4.4.3.

All these results show the power of the Minority Game to ask simple questions and to obtain simple, or at least clear, answers. They also indicate that the Minority Game needs to be extended further in order to model real markets more closely. This is the topic of the next section.

4.4   From Minority Games to real markets

A financial market, be it for stock or foreign currency exchanges or for more complex derivatives, is characterized by a central place with many traders. Each in principle, being not aware what all his fellow traders are doing, is striving for better gains by alternating between a few actions (buy, sell, abstain, . . .). Since there is no sure optimal strategy, they need to differentiate among themselves in the strategies. Markets and Minority Games both share these essential ingredients. Beyond these few elements, however, financial markets are much more complex. Agents in particular have different time horizons, risk tolerance and expectations. They have different wealth and this evolves in time as a result of trading. Market mechanisms, rules, and operation modes also vary according to the objects being traded, geographic location, institutions, and traders needs. In spite of this, several properties of market fluctuations, the so-called stylized facts, show a remarkable indifference to these details (Dacorogna et al. 2001). Hopefully then, not all the features of realistic traders need to be included in the Minority Game in order to recover these empirical laws. It turns out that there is one key

---

[8] Insider trading occurs, for example, when brokers take advantage of the information on their clients' transactions.

variation of the basic Minority Game which makes it produce realistic fluctuation properties: allowing the agents to vary the volume of their transactions. This modification adds a new dimension to the parameter space but the phase structure of the model, characterized by a phase transition between a predictable and an unpredictable phase, remains. And it is exactly close to the phase transition that stylized facts emerge. Hence the Minority Game suggests that stylized facts are critical fluctuations of a system close to a phase transition. This interpretation deserves a brief detour on the generic nature of critical fluctuations, before entering into more details on the models.

4.4.1 Stylized facts, power laws, and phase transitions

We include the paper by Farmer (1999b) (see page 224) as it nicely sums up the main characteristic features of fluctuations in financial markets, usually called stylized facts. In short, the distribution of price returns $r(t, \Delta t) = \log p(t + \Delta t) - \log p(t)$ has fat tails which can be adequately fitted by a power law for Δt in the high frequency range (a day or less). For Δt in the range of months or years the distribution crosses over to a Gaussian. The distribution of traded volume has also a power law behaviour. With respect to time correlations, returns are uncorrelated, that is, $\langle r(t + \tau)r(t) \rangle \cong 0$ for τ larger than some minutes; hence no linear prediction is possible. The volatility instead can be predicted. Indeed days of high volatility are likely followed by days where volatility is high. More precisely, the autocorrelation of the absolute value of the returns is positive and it decays slowly with the time lag τ. This decay can be fitted with a power law with small exponents but also with other functional forms (Bouchaud, Giardina, Mézard 2001) (see also Section 4.4.3)

Power laws have a particular meaning and appeal to physicists. In the experience of statistical mechanics, the irrelevance of the collective behaviour on microscopic details becomes extreme when the system is close to a phase transition. At the phase transition point, called critical point, the system exhibit scale invariance properties in space and time which manifest in power law behaviour. Remarkably theoretical models not only reproduce the correct qualitative behaviour of real systems but also reproduce the exact values of the exponents of the power laws. These *critical* exponents relate the analytic behaviour of different quantities close to or at the phase transition. They are *universal* because their values do not depend on microscopic details but only on the qualitative nature of the interaction (which in physics is embodied in symmetries, conservation laws, and in the space dimensionality). This is remarkable because it allows us to classify the (critical) behaviour of different systems into so-called universality classes.[9]

---

[9] The simplest example of a universal behaviour is provided by limit laws in probability theory, such as the Central Limit Theorem or of its generalization to Levy laws (Mantegna and Stanley 2000). There the 'collective properties' of

Then it is sufficient to understand the behaviour of one member of a universality class to know that of all the others. Conversely, showing that a model belongs to a known universality class (e.g. by measuring its critical exponents) implies that all the known results about the latter also apply to the model. This is why physicists find power laws so exciting. The discovery of a new power law behaviour in whatever discipline relating whatever pair of quantities rings a bell in many statistical physicists minds. It is not surprising that the presence of power laws in financial markets has attracted so much attention among physicists; this is even more understandable as qualitatively and geographically different markets have similar exponents.

Hence, if the power laws observed in financial markets are the manifestation of the critical fluctuations of a system close to a phase transition, then they allow us to disclose features of the microscopic interaction and, in case, to classify market behaviour in universality classes.

This is not the only hypothesis. Indeed power laws can also arise from much more simple mechanisms, as discussed in Bouchaud (2001). In these cases, power laws, which are called generic, do not carry much information on the specific interaction mechanism. An example is Zipf's law[10] which is observed in so disparate subjects that it is really hard to think that the same mechanism is at work. Gabaix et al. (2003) offer an example of how stylized facts can be explained as generic power law behaviour.[11] There the origin of power laws is traced back, using scaling arguments, to the behaviour of big market participants (funds), who in their turn have a size whose distribution is also a power law. Without entering into a discussion of the merits of the remarkable theory of Gabaix et al., we merely remark that interaction among agents plays a marginal role in it. Everything can be explained in terms of an effective representative agent approach. There is no emergent behaviour, at the aggregate level, which is unexpected given the microscopic behaviour. By contrast, interaction plays the key role in the Minority Game and aggregate behaviour is an emergent property of a system of a priori equally sized agents.

Whether the anomalous fluctuations in financial markets have universal or only generic properties is still an open question (Bouchaud 2001). Definitely in the former case, theoretical progress requires all the sophisticated toolbox of statistical physics. This makes it a challenging endeavour which is yet in its embryonic stages at present.

---

the normalized sum of many i.i.d. random variables is independent of the details of the distribution of these variables. Only the tail behaviour of the distribution is relevant. In particular when the tail has a power law behaviour and the variance diverges, the tail exponents are 'universal'. The generalization to interacting systems is a very specialistic topic of statistical mechanics. The interested reader is referred to Huang (2001) for a more detailed account.

[10] Zipf's law is an empirical statement on the distribution of objects ranked according to some characteristic such as size. The typical statement is that size of the kth largest object is inversely proportional to k. It applies to city size, word frequency in a text, web access statistics, etc.

[11] This paper have been challenged in Farmer and Lillo (2003).

This undertaking, beyond its worth for a theory of market phenomena, sheds light on yet unexplored domains of statistical physics.

A final remark is in order. One apparent difficulty with the Minority Game picture is that outside the critical region, the Minority Game exhibits Gaussian fluctuations, at odd with what is observed in financial markets. This leaves us with the question of why markets 'self-organize' close to the phase transition. In other words, a realistic model of a financial market should be, at first sight, a Self-organized critical (SOC) model.

In order to address this issue, it is necessary to remind that in all SOC models (Jensen 1998) there are two processes with a wide separation of timescales: a slow driving process (e.g. sand deposition, grain by grain, in a sandpile) and a fast relaxation process (e.g. avalanche dynamics). The Minority Game only describes the fast process but it is not difficult to understand what the slow process is likely to be in financial markets. As long as there are few speculators in a market, this remains predictable and thus it attracts further speculators. The influx of speculators can continue until the market reaches the phase transition where it becomes unpredictable. Indeed, allowing agents not to trade if that is not favourable, as in the Grand Canonical Minority Games discussed below, one sees that the population of active traders will self-organize in a way to keep the market marginally efficient, that is, close to the phase transition.

4.4.2 Letting volume evolve I: dynamics of capitals

The volume $V(t)$ is defined as the number of shares exchanged at time t. Long range correlation of the volatility is known to be due to that of the volume (Gopikrisnan et al. 2000), which suggests that allowing the volume to evolve is a key element to reproduce realistic features in market models. The volume in the Minority Game is proportional to the number of agents in the market, weighted by the amount of capital they each invest. Therefore, there are two ways of letting the volume change in time: making the capital invested by each agent a dynamical variable and/or letting the number of active agents fluctuate.

Assigning different wealths to the agents remedies an important shortcoming of the model, as their richness and weight of the market participants in real life are definitely widely spread. More importantly, letting the wealth of agents evolve as a result of their trading activity, introduces one further 'evolutionary' element in the model: agents with 'bad' strategies will go bankrupt whereas some others will get rich. The first article to include wealth and capitals in the Minority Game is that of Slanina and Zhang (1999), followed by Farmer and Joshi (1999), Jefferies et al. (2001), Challet et al. (2000a), Giardina and Bouchaud (2002). Giardina and Bouchaud (2002) and Andersen and Sornette (2003) investigate sophisticated models and dynamic capitals are only one ingredient among many others, making it difficult to disentangle the real role of capital.

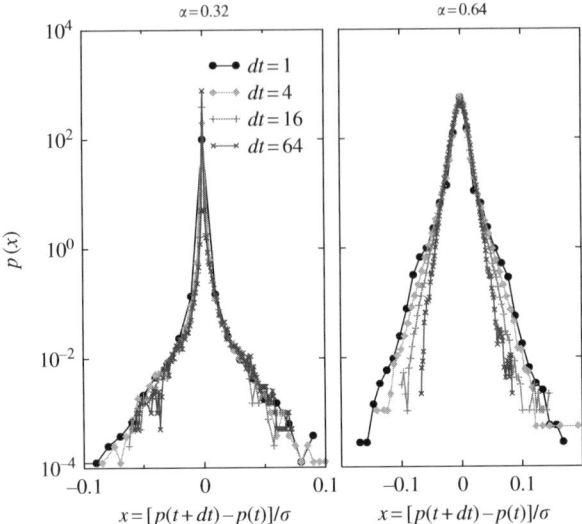

Fig. 4.3 Scaling of the probability density function $\rho_{dt}(x)$ of returns $x = [p(t + dt) - p(t)]/\sigma_{dt}$ for different time lags $dt = 1, 4, 16$, and 64 in a Minority Game market with $N_s = 100$ speculators and $N_p = 10$ producers of the model of Challet et al. (2000a). Speculators can decide not to play and those who loose all their capital are replaced by new speculators endowed with new strategies and a unit capital. The market in the left panel has $P = 32$, gives $\alpha = 0.32$, and it is close to the critical point ($\alpha_c \approx 0.3$). Indeed finite size effects are much less pronounced than for the market with $\alpha = 0.64$ (right) where the cross-over to a Gaussian behaviour is clearly visible.

Challet et al. (2000a) shows that the analytic approach can be generalized to the case where the capital (or wealth) of each agent is drawn from a given distribution and kept fixed during the whole game. However no qualitative change occurs in the collective behaviour. Then Challet et al. (2000a) moves to a model where the wealth of agents evolves depending on their success: agents invest a fixed fraction of their capital and as a result, bad performers disappear from the market, as their capital vanishes, implementing a crude kind of Darwinism. This leads to a game where successful agents cannot become too rich, because their impact increase with their wealth.[12] As a consequence, the game reaches a stationary state, which is very similar to that of a standard game: the phase transition between predictability and unpredictability still persists. But the unpredictable phase is now an absorbing phase, characterized by zero price returns $A(t) = 0$ and no market activity. Remarkably, stylized facts arise close to the critical point. The fat tails of the price return distribution have a cut-off that depends on the distance from the critical point, as clearly shown in Fig. 4.3. Interestingly, the average capital per speculator is maximal at the critical point. This suggests that

---

[12] Farmer and Joshi (1999) show that a successful agent should reduce the fraction of reinvested capital in order to reduce this effect.

at that precise point, all the information is exploited and transformed into capital. Even though analytic progress is hard with wealth dynamics, numerical simulations convincingly show that, remarkably, the overall picture of the game's behaviour is preserved.

4.4.3 Letting volume evolve II: the Grand Canonical Minority Game

The second simple extension consists in allowing the speculators to withdraw from the market if trading is not profitable. This is natural, as a speculator with a badly performing set of strategies will not get ruined using them. Rather he may continue monitoring the performance of his strategies, in case the mood of the market changes and they become profitable again. Conversely, a highly successful speculator will trade at all times. Hence, the active traders are a fraction of the total population of speculators; the rest are just watching the market waiting for the propitious time to enter.

As the number of agent is now a variable quantity, borrowing the terminology of statistical mechanics where systems with a variable number of particles are called grand canonical, such games are dubbed Grand Canonical Minority Games. The agents need to be equipped with a criterion by which they decide whether to stay in the market or to retire from it. The simplest possible rule is that agents play only if they have a strategy granting, on average, a gain larger than ϵ. Here ϵ can be seen as a benchmark, for example, an interest rate or some other return from investing elsewhere (Slanina and Zhang 1999), Johnson and co-workers independently considered $\epsilon = 0$ (Johnson et al. 2000) and then $\epsilon > 0$ (Jefferies et al. 2001). As shown in (Challet et al. 2001a), $\epsilon > 0$ is simply common sense, as agents with $\epsilon = 0$ are sure to lose some amount of money. Johnson et al. (2000) and Jefferies et al. (2001) (see page 238) were the first to show that allowing the agents not to play is enough to produce stylized facts, such as fat-tailed returns and clustered volatility. Of course, for the market to have any activity at all, the presence of producers who inject information is essential. Challet et al. (2001a) shows that the average volume of transactions indeed vanishes with the square root of the number of producers.

A more precise characterization of the phenomenology is given in Challet and Marsili (2003a) (see page 256), where the simplest Grand Canonical Minority Game is studied: all the agents have only one strategy; the only choice the speculators have is to be in or out of the market. This model can be solved analytically in the limit of infinitely many traders; the critical point turns into a line of critical points in the (α, ϵ) phase diagram which extends a point α_c, which depends on the concentration of producers, to the origin on the $\epsilon = 0$ axis. The behaviour of market as the number of speculators increases is shown in Fig. 4.4. When $\epsilon > 0$ the phase transition is

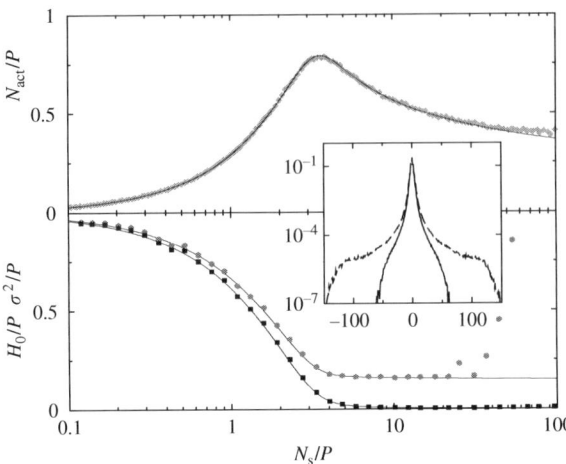

Fig. 4.4 Behaviour of the average number of active speculators (N_{act} top panel), of σ^2/P and of H/P (bottom panel) in the Grand Canonical Minority Game as a function of the relative number of speculators $n_S = N_S/P$. Speculators have only one active strategy and $\epsilon = 0.1$. They interact with $N_p = P$ producers. Full lines refer to the analytic solution whereas points are the result of numerical simulations (with $PN_S = 50{,}000$ fixed). The inset shows the histogram of $A(t)$ in two runs with $N_S/P = 20$ (full line) and $N_S/P = 50$ (solid line), and $P = 10$.

smeared and it becomes a cross-over to an almost symmetric region $H \approx 0$ for $\alpha < \alpha_c$ (i.e. for a large enough number of speculators). The exact solution for $P \to \infty$ shows that price fluctuations have a Gaussian statistics when $\epsilon > 0$: there is no traces of anomalous fluctuations similar to the stylized facts. Indeed anomalous fluctuations only occur at the phase transition, that is, for $\epsilon = 0$, in the limit $P \to \infty$. But finite systems are affected by finite size effects. This means that, for finite P, stylized facts occur in a critical region close to the phase transition, whose extend shrinks as the system's size P diverges. The inset of Fig. 4.4 moreover shows that anomalous fluctuations become stronger and stronger when the number of speculators increases. Remarkably, it is possible to determine the boundary of the critical region where large price fluctuation occur using an argument based on the signal-to-noise ratio (Challet and Marsili 2003a). In other words, one necessary condition for the emergence of large price moves is that the market's exploitable predictability falls below a given threshold.

Challet et al. (2001a) show that in densely populated markets (with $\epsilon > 0$, $\alpha < \alpha_c$) the market exhibits very wild fluctuations which in very crowded markets, such as the one of Fig. 4.5, take the form of market crashes. Grand Canonical Minority Game offer a crystalline picture of how such strong fluctuations arise. Those responsible for such large price moves are the crowd of inactive agents who just sit staring at the price.

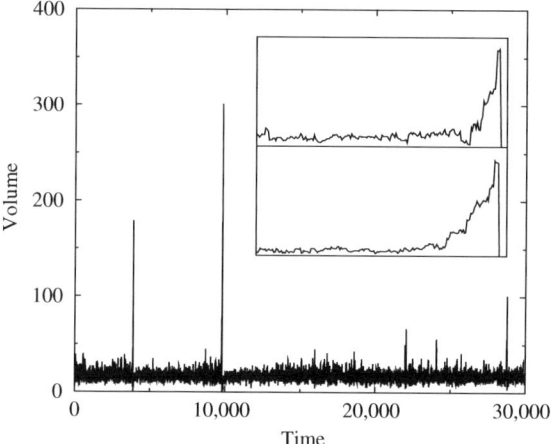

Fig. 4.5   Volume (i.e. number of active traders) in a realization of the Grand Canonical Minority Game (with $P = 32$, $N_s = 9600$ speculators with one strategy, and $\epsilon = 0.01$, and $N_p = 320$ producers). The time series in the 200 time steps before the first two crashes are shown in the inset.

The key point is that while the strategies of active traders are subject to the market's selective pressure, the strategies of those who just watch the market experience no pressure at all; in particular they 'do not feel' each other. Even worse, those with similar strategies are attracted to play in the market at the same time and they may enter the market at nearly the same time.

Of course the market is almost efficient in the long run (i.e. $H \approx 0$). However rare events where asymmetric price fluctuations persist for a certain period may occur. Such a persistent rare fluctuation will be detected by some inactive speculators staring at the market. Hence a first wave of speculators with similar strategies may enter the game at nearly the same time. The problem is that this wave can trigger a second wave of higher intensity and the latter a third, and so on. The reason is that the first wave of speculators creates a strong signal for those who sit and watch with a negatively correlated strategy in their hands. These are attracted to the market in their turn and, if the first wave of speculators endures long enough in the market before being expelled, this attraction may be strong enough to 'convince' the second wave of traders to enter the market. Actually, if it is strong enough, the second wave of traders will be even larger than the first. This second wave will, in its turn, generously inject plenty of information thus calling a third wave into the market.[13] We have a clear mechanism

---

[13] Because the strategies of the second wave is anticorrelated to those of the first, the third wave will have a large overlap with the first.

of amplification of fluctuations which can soon contaminate the majority of traders in a crazy rush in and out of the market. In order for it to be an amplifier, it only needs that the number of traders is large enough, that is, that α is small enough. Figure 4.5 shows indeed that the multiplier effect is triggered by rare fluctuations. More or less quiescent periods between crashes can last for long times.

A further manifestation of the variability of number of active agents, much milder than the onset of crashes, is volatility clustering. Bouchaud et al. (2001) (see page 251) discuss a universal mechanism for the occurrence of long time volatility correlation in the Grand Canonical Minority Game. They derive an approximation, exact for small τ, to the volume autocorrelation of the Grand Canonical Minority Game,

$$\langle V(t)V(t+\tau)\rangle \simeq \exp(-\sqrt{\tau/\tau_0}),\qquad(4.10)$$

for games with small predictability. Moreover, this functional form turns out to fit real market data to an accuracy which is at least comparable to that found elsewhere (Gopikrisnan et al. 2000) using power laws. Interestingly, this paper argues that many models that are able to reproduce clustered volatility contain a switching mechanism (for instance between types of traders; Lux and Marchesi 1999), and that this points out at a universal and realistic way of producing volatility clustering. It should be noted that this provides a microscopic explanation of volatility correlations, as opposed to traditional approaches (Gopikrisnan et al. 2000; Bacry et al. 2001).

Although much work has been done in order to get a theory of how Grand Canonical Minority Game works, a lot of work still needs to be done. Specially the critical region has thus far eluded analytic efforts.

4.5   Extensions

We end this chapter by mentioning a variety of issues on financial markets which have been addressed with models closely related to the Minority Game.

4.5.1   Information efficiency in an asset market

In efficient markets, prices 'incorporate' all information about returns from trade. But who puts the information into prices, what is the process, and when is it efficient?[14]

Berg et al. (2001) address these issues within a model of inductively rational agents trading a single asset. Agents decide whether and how many stocks to buy on the basis of some asymmetric and incomplete information they receive about the return of

[14] In the sense that there is no excess return or arbitrage opportunity.

the asset. Information efficiency in this model means that the price at which agents buy the asset becomes identical to the return they get from it. Even though the model, at first sight, is totally different from the Minority Game, it turns out to be driven by a minority-like mechanism: if the demand is too high the price is also high, hence it is not convenient to buy and conversely when few people buy, the price is low, and it is convenient to buy. Although the learning scheme is very different from that of the Minority Game, a quite similar scenario emerges: when there are few agents the market is not informationally efficient. For example, an agent who knows the private information given to others would be able to make a positive profit. As the number of agents increases, a transition takes place to an efficient market phase where prices adjust exactly to returns. All information is transferred into prices and no profit is possible anymore.

The nature of heterogeneity across agents is very different from that of the Minority Game. Rather than in trading strategies, heterogeneity enters into the information filters which agents have. In spite of this difference, the same qualitative behaviour results, suggesting that the standard Minority Game belongs to a broader class of models with similar collective properties.

4.5.2 Predicting the market and controlling risk

A particularly important question is how any *one* specific realization of the game behaves. This contrasts with the statistical physics approach which focuses on the average behaviour of many realizations. This question is obviously relevant for real-life situations, as there is for instance only one London Stock Exchange. Lamper et al. (2002) (see page 247) studied the following reverse-engineering question: given the time series of one realization of the Minority Game, is it possible to find its parameters and the strategy sets of all the agents? Surprisingly, the answer is positive for parameters. It is however only possible to gain partial and noisy knowledge about the strategy that the agents use. But Lamper et al. (2002) claims that this is enough to predict future large price changes. This suggests that the period before a crash contains forewarnings of the crash itself. In a later publication (Hart et al. 2002b), the same group found that crashes are ultimately due to a period of time where the price increases too quickly, that is, to a kind of (fast) bubble. The remedy is to weight the price downwards during this dangerous period to smoothen the crash.

Jefferies et al. (2001) (see page 238) explore further the closely related issue of how to control the risk of large changes in a system made up of many small components—a problem thus concerning a far broader range of issues than just financial markets. It is clear indeed that if some prediction, even of a statistical nature of factors which cause risk may be an important improvement. In financial markets, being able to predict the volatility of the price is already a huge improvement over considering only stationary volatility distributions. Jefferies et al. (2001) point out that this is particularly relevant in option pricing and, at least in synthetic Minority Game markets, it discusses techniques which help to reduce risks associated with emitting options.

4.5.3   Market impact

Market impact is a fundamental issue for practitioners. For traders who need to make large transactions it is of particular importance to minimize their influence on the market in order to avoid speculative attacks. Also the worth of a trading strategy is crucially affected by the market impact. To make this point clearer, let us consider the following argument. Imagine that looking at the past 10 years of history of a particular market, you come up with a strategy of daily trades which, had it been played from the beginning, with an initial capital of £1, would have delivered a cumulated gain of some thousand pounds. It is not unfrequent to find such statements in the literature (see, for example, Farmer and Lo 1999). The underlying assumption is that your dollar is so small compared to the volume of transactions that it would not have changed the price process, so you are left with the regret: 'Ah, had I only known about this strategy then!' But would things have really worked that way?

In the Minority Game we can really do the experiment: in Fig. 4.6 we let $N = 128$ agents, with $S = 2$ strategies each and $M = 6$, interact. The price is computed, as in Marsili (2001), by $p(t) = p(t-1)[N + A(t)]/[N - A(t)]$ and $p(0) = 1$. Actually the N agents are allowed to trade until they come to a stationary state and then we set our day 0 and let them play for 10 further years of 250 trading days each. Since $\alpha = 0.5$ the game is in the information rich phase: $\langle A|\mu \rangle \neq 0$ as shown by the scatter plot in the inset. The best strategy $a_{\text{best}}^{\mu} = -\text{sign}\,\langle A|\mu \rangle$ gives an expected payoff of $-\overline{a_{\text{best}} \langle A \rangle} = |\langle A \rangle| = 0.87$ per day.[15]

Now let us rewind time to day 0, inject a new agent with the strategy a_{best} and let him play. The first surprise is that now the price history is totally different. Instead of ramping up to more than 100, the price falls by a factor 20, with apparently completely different fluctuations. The second surprise is that our expected $+0.87$ gain has turned to a loss of -0.034! And finally, the introduction of this single trader washes out most of the information: $\langle A|\mu \rangle$ *after* the introduction of the new trader is a much weaker signal than it was *before* (see the inset).

---

[15] In the real market it may be reasonable to assume that the gains accumulates in a multiplicative fashion, leading to an exponential growth of the capital. In the Minority Game world discussed here we assume that capital accumulates in an additive way.

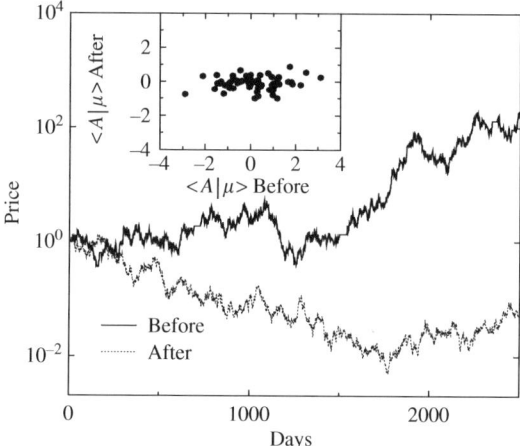

Fig. 4.6 Price history of a realization of the MG (with $N = 128$, $S = 2$, and $M = 6$) before and after the introduction of an agent with an a priori optimal strategy a_{best}^{μ}. Inset: Information content of the market before and after.

Even with the best strategy, our virtual gain turns into a loss. The reason for this debacle is that our naïve thinking neglects market impact. Market impact enters in two ways: first the new trader contributes to excess demand, that is, $A(t) \rightarrow A(t) + a_{best}^{\mu(t)}$. Second, the entry of the new trader also has an effect on the other market participants which, as a consequence, modify their behaviour (see Challet et al. 2000d for more details).

This simple example, though based on a single realization for a relatively small system, shows how the stationary state of the Minority Game is sensitive to small perturbations. In each transaction the contribution of one individual to price formation may be negligible. But over time, even a single individual can affect the price dynamics considerably. This suggests that markets self-organize to a very delicate and susceptible stationary state.

The market impact also has another subtle effect on the optimality of the trading activity of each trader. Game's optimality will be dealt with in more detail in Chapter 5. We anticipate this discussion in order to highlight the relevance of this issue for market behaviour.

Let us adopt an evolutionary metaphor in which the market is a 'primordial soup' of trading strategies fighting to occupy profitable ecological niches. Each agent has several strategies in his pool. Each time, one is used *in vivo* for trading, whereas the performance of the others is monitored *in vitro*, considering the result of virtual trades based on these strategies. Virtual here means that traders behave as *price takers*, that is, they take the market outcome $A(t)$ as given, without accounting for their contribution to it.[16] The market impact is always 'against' *in vivo* strategies, so price takers always overestimate the performance of *in vitro* strategies. So even if the strategy used *in vivo* is better than those *in vitro*, the effects of market impact can accumulate to a point where the performance of an *in vitro* strategy exceeds that of the best one. At this point, the agent will abandon the best strategy for a poorer one. Later the best strategy—monitored *in vitro*—will reveal its virtue again and the agent will switch back to it.[17]

This suboptimal behaviour may be corrected by simply awarding an extra reward to *in vivo* strategies with respect to *in vitro* ones (Challet et al. 2000c; Marsili et al. 2000; Marsili and Challet 2001b). This extra reward increases the long run payoffs of each agent individually (it is incentive compatible, as game theorists would say) and it improves global optimality in a way which is quite dramatic in efficient markets (see Fig. 5.2). This will be discussed at length in Chapter 5, where we discuss the nature of the stationary states of games depending on the degree of sophistication of agents.

For the time being, let us only anticipate that the nature of the stationary state changes radically as soon as agents depart from the naïve price-taking behaviour: the phase transition separating efficient from predictable markets disappear with the anomalous fluctuations that come with it, which we put in relation to the stylized facts. This suggests that the occurrence of fat-tails, volatility clustering, and even market crashes are due to the neglect of market impact by too many agents.

This fact seems surprising as the impact of a single agent on the aggregate seems negligible, at first sight. And indeed it is reasonable to assume that this naïve way of thinking is a likely rationale behind real traders behaving as price takers.[18] But this way of thinking is wrong because collective market behaviour may change dramatically if traders account even infinitesimally for their impact. The reason for this is that the market impact, when averaged on market fluctuations in the long run, is not negligible.

This issue will be dealt with in Chapter 5 in more detail. For the time being let us only remark that the implication for real markets is quite strong: *if* financial markets were really similar to Minority Game, as soon as traders would account for market impact, the volatility would decrease considerably. This would make traders themselves happier but also mathematical economists would rejoice because price returns would become Gaussian. Of course this would leave econophysicists disappointed, as those stylized facts which have attracted so much of their interest would disappear.

---

[16] The contribution of an agent to the market would have changed if he had followed a strategy different from that he used.

[17] For a more precise and detailed discussion we refer the interested reader to section VII of Challet et al. (2000d).

[18] Another one is probably that even if the traders are aware that they have an impact, they cannot estimate reliably.

5. Quest for better cooperation

Financial markets are the primary target for which Minority Games have been devised and studied. But at the same time, Minority Games have also been used as a tool to pose different questions.

One of these, which is to a degree contained in the original paper, is how efficiently a group of adaptive agents competing for limited resources can coordinate. The fact that agents with limited rationality and resources can perform better than by taking random decisions was regarded as a non-trivial result in early papers. This led to a 'quest for efficiency' in a series of papers aiming to find learning dynamics leading to better coordination. We include here two contributions by Hod and Nakar (2002) and Reents et al. (2001), which discuss in an elegant way simple models of agents learning and interacting through a minority mechanism. We discuss these simple models and contrast their results with those of the standard Minority Game with no information on the past history ($M = 0$ or $P = 1$).

Going somewhat further on this line of research, some authors studied how agents endowed with boolean or neural networks play the Minority Game (Kinzel et al. 2000; Paczuski et al. 2000; Wakeling and Bak 2001). These papers use the Minority Game to define frustratingly complex interaction rules among the agents and investigate how the latter cope with it, depending on their degree of rationality and sophistication.

All these works, however, do not directly pose the question of whether the agents, given their constrained capacities, play optimally or not. In game theoretic terms, playing optimally means that agents should be in a Nash equilibrium—a state where no agent can improve his payoff by adjusting his strategy if others stick to their choices. It turns out that the agents in the standard Minority Game do not converge to a Nash equilibrium because they do not play *strategically*. Putting it simply, agents behave as if they were playing against a *market* and not against $N - 1$ other agents. The key issue is that this behaviour neglects the impact that each player has on the market. A minimal requirement for a strategic behaviour is to consider the effects of one's own actions on oneself. This turns out to be enough to 'correct' the learning dynamics that then converges to a Nash equilibrium (Marsili et al. 2000; Challet et al. 2000c).

In the dynamical equations of the resulting game, the market impact plays a role similar to the cavity, self-interaction term—also called after Onsager—in spin glasses (Mézard et al. 1987). Removing this term causes replica symmetry breaking, leading to a totally novel scenario characterized by exponentially many (in N) possible equilibria. We chose the paper by Heimel and De Martino (2001) to discuss this issue on the basis of the generating functional approach. (Marsili et al. 2001) instead investigates when and how agents with a finite memory can learn to coordinate in such a complex world with so many equilibria. Spectacular effects arise when the structure of interactions is allowed to change slowly.

Although this chapter introduces a variety of extensions to the Minority Game, it does not cover all the many and ingenuous extensions that the original Minority Game has inspired. The latter are too numerous, thus making a choice inevitable. To have a better overview, the reader is advised to consult the Minority Game website (www.unifr.ch/econophysics/minority). Arbitrary as it may seem, we hope the present selection of works may serve as a useful entry into the literature growing around the Minority Game.

5.1   Cooperation in simple Minority Games

Let us go back to the very definition of the Minority Game: the choices a_i of every agent $i = 1, \ldots, N$ are aggregated into $A = \sum_{i=1}^{N} a_i$ and agents whose choice has the opposite sign of A win. Learning is missing from this definition, as it is a layer added on the top of the Minority Game itself. While the way the agents behave in the standard Minority Game was defined so as to remain close to Arthur's definition, there are many other learning schemes, some of them much simpler, some of them much more complicated.

In the standard Minority Game, the global efficiency σ^2, which also measures the total agent loss, varies but remains proportional to N. Is it the best that the agents can do? Imagine a situation where N is odd and $(N + 1)/2$ agents stick to action $a_i = +1$ whereas the rest take $a_i = -1$. This simple arrangement has $\sigma^2 = 1$ which is way better than what we found previously. Why do the agents not consider this? How can the agents coordinate to such an arrangement?[1]

It is preferable to address these simple questions in simple Minority Game models avoiding the complications of dealing with strategies, information (whether endogenous or exogenous), hence disorder. Several simple and analytically tractable models of Minority Game with $M = 0$, or $P = 1$, have been proposed (Johnson et al. 1999c;

---

[1] Note that there are very many such arrangements.

Burgos and Ceva 2000; Reents et al. 2001; Marsili and Challet 2001b), all more or less trying to find an optimal behaviour for agents.

5.1.1   Dynamics based on the last outcome

Inductive learning relies on a score, which is used to determine the probability of playing $+$ or $-$ at the next time step. Agents weigh the past outcome in their score on the same footing as all other past outcomes. Some authors considered the extreme opposite case where agents are given a piece of information and react exclusively to it in some specified way.

For instance, the piece of information that Johnson et al. (1999c) considered is simply the last winning choice: each agent plays this choice with probability p_i at next time step, and with probability $1 - p_i$ he plays the opposite. Now an agent is simply characterized by p_i. Evolution occurs when an agent j consistently underperforms: p_j is then redrawn according to some predefined rule. This is what is sometimes called the *evolutionary* Minority Game, although it is only one evolutionary scheme amongst several that have been proposed (Challet and Zhang 1997, 1998; Li et al. 2000b, c; Sysi-Aho et al. 2003). Several authors have tackled this problem analytically Lo T. S., Hui P. M., Johnson N., Theory of the evolutionary minority game, Phys. Rev. E 62, 4393 (2000). Results show that depending on the ratio R between reward and punishment, segregation (Johnson et al. 1999c) or clustering (Hod and Nakar 2002) arises in the distribution of p_i values. Both worse and better than random guessing can be obtained, depending on R (Hod and Nakar 2002) (see page 296), although the scaling of the fluctuations has not been studied yet. Quite a few papers are devoted to this variation (Johnson et al. 1999c; Burgos and Ceva 2000; Lo et al. 2000; Hod and Nakar 2002) (see the Minority Game website (Challet) for more references).

Reents et al. (2001) (see page 287) considered an even simpler dynamics: winners of the last game stick to their choice, losers individually change their minds with probability p. In other words agents react to an individual piece of information, which is whether their choice was the right one or not.[2]

This model is easy to understand: as there are $(N + |A|)/2$ losers and $|A|$ is at most of order N, the average number of changes is $p(N + |A|)/2 \sim pN$. Three regimes can be distinguished:

- $pN = x = $ constant: the number of people that change their mind does not depend on N, hence this leads to very small fluctuations $\sigma^2 \sim O(1)$

---

[2] This is in the spirit of the 'individual history' introduced in de Cara et al. (2000).

- $pN \sim O(\sqrt{N})$: the fluctuations are typically of order N, which is what happens in the original Minority Game with histories
- $p \sim O(1)$: the fluctuations are of order N^2. $A(t)$ is characterized by a double peaked distribution.

Since the model is very simple, it can be tackled analytically. We refer to Reents et al. (2001) for details.

The relationship between the number of agent switching strategy and fluctuations are generic in the Minority Game, and inductive agents with no public information ($M = 0$, or equivalently $P = 1$) are able to reproduce it as well.

5.1.2   Inductive agents with no public information

Marsili and Challet (2001b) observe that there are two separated issues in the Minority Game. One is the competitive aspect by which the agents try to exploit asymmetries in the game's outcome $A(t)$. This is the force driving to information efficiency $\langle A \rangle \approx 0$ and it has to do with predictability. The other is the coordination aspect of the game and it is related to the volatility σ^2. Loosely speaking, no agent in the Minority Game likes volatility. Furthermore, volatility increases the fluctuations in the behaviour of agents and this feeds back into the collective behaviour causing volatility build-ups.

The analysis of Marsili and Challet (2001b) was later refined in Marsili (2001). It shows that very simple models are able to explain puzzling features of the Minority Game in its full-blown complexity, such as the dependence of aggregate fluctuations (σ^2) on microscopic randomness (Γ) and on initial conditions. We give a brief outline here of the key steps, while referring the reader to a section of the paper by Marsili (2001) (Section 3) for more details. Consider a Minority Game where agents have two strategies, one to play $a_i = +1$ in response to any information, and the other to play $a_i = -1$. This can be regarded as a case where agents disregard past information (i.e. $M = 0$). The past experience of agent i is stored in the 'score' $\Delta_i(t)$: $\Delta_i(t) > 0$ means that the action $a_i = +1$ is (perceived as) more successful than $a_i = -1$ and vice versa. Accordingly agent i will play $a_i(t) = +1$ with a probability $\text{Prob}\{a_i(t) = \pm 1\} = \chi_i[\Delta_i(t)]$, which is an increasing function of Δ_i. Agents update $\Delta_i(t)$ according to

$$\Delta_i(t+1) = \Delta_i(t) - \frac{\Gamma}{N} A(t). \tag{5.1}$$

In other words: if $A(t) < 0$ agents observe that the best action was $+1$ at time t. Hence they increase Δ_i, hence the probability of playing $a_i = +1$. The role of the factor Γ/N is to modulate the strength of the response in the behaviour of agents to the stimulus $A(t)$. How does the collective behaviour depend on Γ?

Let us consider for simplicity the case where initially $\Delta_i(t = 0) = 0$ for all i and $\chi_i(x) = 1/(1 + e^{-2x})$, as in Marsili (2001). Then $\Delta_i(t)$ is independent of i for all times, and hence we may suppress the index i. For $N \gg 1$, the law of large numbers implies that $A(t)/N \simeq \tanh \Delta(t)$ so that

$$\Delta(t + 1) \simeq \Delta(t) - \Gamma \tanh \Delta(t). \tag{5.2}$$

This is a dynamical system with a fixed point $\Delta^* = 0$ which is stable only if $\Gamma < \Gamma_c = 2$. For $\Gamma > 2$ a bifurcation to orbits of period 2 occurs, that is, $\Delta(t) = (-1)^t \bar{\Delta}$ where $\bar{\Delta}(\Gamma)$ is a solution of $2x = \Gamma \tanh x$. This has dramatic effects on the collective behaviour. For $\Gamma < 2$ the system converges to a state where agents draw their actions at random, with probability $1/2$. Hence $A(t)$ has Gaussian fluctuations of magnitude $\sqrt{N}$ around zero and $\sigma^2 \simeq N$. On the contrary, for $\Gamma > 2$, the attendance oscillates between the two values $\pm N \tanh \bar{\Delta}$, which implies that $\sigma^2 \propto N^2$ is much larger than in the previous case. Note that in both cases $\langle A \rangle = 0$, but global efficiency (i.e. σ^2) is very different! Such a simple model also explains how the asymptotic state of the dynamics depends on the initial conditions. Increasing the asymmetry in initial conditions, the volatility σ^2/N decreases and Γ_c increases, thereby making the stationary state more stable (Marsili 2001).

The dependence on Γ and on initial conditions, as we saw in Chapter 3, is generic in the symmetric phase of Minority Game models (Garrahan et al. 2000; Marsili et al. 2000; Challet et al. 2000c; Heimel and Coolen 2001). It occurs as well in the efficient phase of the asset market model discussed in Berg et al. (2001).

Such a simple case contains and explains an important part of the richness of the original model, while being much simpler to solve. It clearly shows that inefficiency (high σ^2) is caused by over-reactive behaviour on the part of agents.

In the extreme case when the spread of initial conditions $\Delta_i(0)$ is very large[3] σ^2 becomes of order 1, in agreement with the numerical simulations of Garrahan et al. (2000) and Marsili and Challet (2001a) for $\alpha \to 0$. This means that agents, starting from extremely different initial conditions, finally split into two groups of equal size playing opposite actions. This outcome, however, does not come by the virtue of agents' ability to coordinate but is rather already buried in the initial conditions: roughly speaking, half of the population is convinced, right from the beginning, that $a_i = +1$ is way better than $a_i = -1$ whereas the others have opposite beliefs. Agents who learn to coordinate should form these beliefs endogenously in the course of the game. This seems to be the intuition of Arthur when he states that 'Expectations will be forced to differ' (Arthur 1994) in contexts such as the *El Farol* bar problem.

---

[3] A more precise condition is that the number of agents with initial conditions in any interval of size Γ be finite, as $N \to \infty$.

But why do the agents in the Minority Game fail to do this? The reader has to wait until Section 5.2 to learn the end of the story.

5.1.3   Minority Game and neural networks

The Minority Game provides a challenging interactive environment for adaptive agents. This has led several authors to test various known learning schemes in the Minority Game environment (Kinzel et al. 2000; Paczuski et al. 2000; Vázquez 2000; Andrecut and Ali 2001; Wakeling and Bak 2001). In particular, we shall mention adaptive random boolean networks (Paczuski et al. 2000) and neural networks (Kinzel et al. 2000; Wakeling and Bak 2001).

Random boolean networks are due to Kauffman (1993) and are basically binary strategies which are randomly interconnected. The output of the K neighbours of a given node determines its personal information and the node 'fires' or not, depending on this information. As everything is deterministic, the system locks into an orbit, whose length distribution has attracted a wide interest. Paczsuski et al. extended this model by introducing evolution. More precisely, the nodes play a minority game; regularly the worst one is redrawn at random, hence the fitness of each node is dynamically determined. At $K = 3$, the system self-organizes to a critical state with power law distributed attractor length and non-trivial intermittent behaviour. We refer to Paczuski et al. (2000) (see page 307) for further details.

The Minority Game environment has also been borrowed for interacting neural networks. Kinzel et al. (2000) (see page 311) considered perceptrons characterized by a vector of weight $\vec{w}_i$. The output of each network is a non-linear function of the scalar product $\vec{w}_i \cdot \vec{x}$ where $\vec{x}$ is the input. The non-linear function that mimicks binary lookup tables is the sign function. The perceptrons are fed with the last M minority signs and their weights are updated according to a Hebbian rule (but see also Metzler et al. 2000 for other rules). As a result Kinzel et al. find that neural networks are able to coordinate to a state with $\sigma^2 = (1 - 2/\pi)N \approx 0.363N$ in the limit of very small learning rates. We refer to Kinzel et al. (2000) and follow-ups (Metzler et al. 2000; Ein-Dor et al. 2001) for more details.

Wakeling and Bak (2001) (see page 318) borrowed the Minority Game environment to let agents endowed with *minibrains* interact. Minibrains are particular neural networks based on extremal dynamics which learn only by mistakes (Chialvo and Bak 1999; Bak and Chialvo 2001). In brief, the signal travels from input to output only through the strongest synapses, which are held responsible for the output and eventually 'punished' in case of a mismatch. As in the Minority Game, the input is the string of M past minority choices. For the simplest non-trivial network architecture, which requires an intermediary layer, Wakeling and Bak find that there is little or no advantage in having a very large memory M, when playing in a population of agents with mixed memory lengths, a result very similar to standard agents with look-up tables (Challet and Zhang 1997).

The key point which Wakeling and Bak aim at is that intelligence has to be evaluated with respect to the environment. This is exactly what the Minority Game environment was designed for, since the quality of a strategy depends entirely on those of all other agents.

5.2   Market impact and Nash equilibria

As explained above, the optimal way in which agents can play the minority game is to split into two equally sized groups taking opposite actions. If N is odd $(N + 1)/2$ agents, being in the majority, lose. But each of them cannot do better by changing side: the majority side would move with him as he switches side (unless someone else change his mind as well). No one can improve his situation by unilaterally deviating from his behaviour. This situation is exactly what game theory calls a Nash equilibrium (Fudenberg and Tirole 1991).

The Nash equilibria of the simple minority game discussed earlier, where strategies are just actions $a_i = \pm 1$, were first discussed in Marsili and Challet (2001a). Briefly, all arrangements where $N - 2k$ agents play *mixed strategies*, that is, choose $a_i = \pm 1$ at random, and the remaining $2k$ agents split into two groups of equal size taking opposite actions, are Nash equilibria. These Nash equilibria have $\sigma^2 = N - 2k$. Those k agents taking the action $a_i = +1$ can be choosen in $\binom{2k}{k}$ number of ways out of the $2k$. The number of Nash equilibria grows as 2^N; it becomes huge already for moderately large N. Those Nash equilibria with largest $k \leq N/2$ are the most efficient, with $\sigma^2 \leq 1$.

5.2.1   Learning to play Nash equilibria in simple Minority Game

Why do agents, with so many different degrees of sophistication ranging from induct-ive reasoning to neural networks, fail to reach optimal states (Nash equilibria)? The reason is that *agents in all versions of the Minority Game discussed so far do not play a game against $N - 1$ other agents. Rather, they behave as if they were playing against the process $A(t)$*. The problem becomes evident for $N = 1$: in this extreme Minority Game the agent would continue endlessly to react to himself, switching side at each round. A strategic player would do no better in terms of payoff, as he would lose whatever side he chooses. But at least he would realize that there is no way out. It may seem strange at first sight, but the fact that agents react to themselves is what hinders them from reaching an optimal Nash equilibrium even for large N. Even though for large N each agent's contribution to $A(t)$ is small, if all agents neglect it, they will fail to reach the Nash equilibrium. Marsili (2001) discusses this issue in some detail for the simple game with no information discussed earlier. It turns out that as soon as agents account, even infinitesimally, for their contribution to $A(t)$—the so-called market impact—they are able to coordinate to an optimal Nash equilibrium. More precisely, agents account for their own market impact if, instead of Eq. (5.1), they update their scores by

$$\Delta_i(t+1) = \Delta_i(t) - \frac{\Gamma}{N}[A(t) - \eta a_i(t)]. \qquad (5.3)$$

With $\eta = 1$, agents subtract their own contribution to $A(t)$. As soon as $\eta > 0$ the behaviour changes abruptly and agents learn to coordinate to a Nash equilibrium (see Marsili 2001).

A further interesting point we can learn from Eq. (5.3) is that if $\eta = 0$, $\Delta_i(t) - \Delta_i(0)$ is independent of i. Hence agents' initial heterogeneity is 'conserved' by the dynamics with $\eta = 0$. In the Δ space, the population of agents 'moves' as single block, whereas when $\eta > 0$ the population spreads widely. In simple words, Arthur's intuition (Arthur 1994) that market interaction forces heterogeneity of agents' behaviour, crucially depends on whether agents account for their market impact ($\eta > 0$) or not ($\eta = 0$).

The issue of market impact in Minority Game was first raised in Challet et al. (2000c) and Marsili et al. (2000) for the model in its full complexity. There Minority Game agents were called *naïve* as opposed to the *sophisticated* strategic players of game theory. Agents in the Minority Game naïvely neglect their market impact, assuming that it is negligible. Considering the Minority Game as a market model, they behave as *price takers*. This assumption about traders may be realistic: traders may really behave that way. But the results show that the assumption is by no means an innocent one. If all agents account for their impact the collective behaviour changes dramatically.

In particular, if agents correctly account for their market impact, they reach a Nash equilibrium.

5.2.2   Nash equilibria of the Minority Game

A Nash equilibrium is defined in terms of the strategies s_i which players can choose and in terms of the payoff matrix $u_i(s_i, s_{-i})$, where $s_{-i} = \{s_j, \ j \neq i\}$ is the usual game theoretic notation for the strategies of opponents. In the Minority Game the payoff matrix is given by

$$u_i(s_i, s_{-i}) = -\frac{1}{N} \sum_{j=1}^{N} \overline{a_{i,s_i} a_{j,s_j}} = -\frac{1}{NP} \sum_{\mu=1}^{P} \sum_{j=1}^{N} a_{i,s_i}^{\mu} a_{j,s_j}^{\mu}, \tag{5.4}$$

where $a_{i,s}^{\mu}$ are the randomly drawn look-up tables of agents.

The game theoretic interpretation of the Minority Game is discussed in Marsili et al. (2000). In brief, we imagine we deal with a single stage game with a state of the world μ which is drawn at random and Eq. (5.4) is the expected payoff.[4] Eq. (5.4) is also the expected payoff of a game where each player i is randomly matched with another one (j) to play a game with payoffs $u_i^{\mu}(s_i, s_j) = -a_{s_i,i}^{\mu} a_{s_j,j}^{\mu}$ where the state $\mu = 1, \ldots, P$ of Nature is drawn also randomly. Finally, game payoffs similar to those of Eq. (5.4) are also found in contexts where N agents compete for the exploitation of P exhaustible resources. Urban traffic, as shown in De Martino et al. (2003b), is one example.

Independently of its interpretation, the payoff matrix in Eq. 5.4 represents an interesting instance of a complex system of interacting heterogeneous agents whose rich behaviour deserves investigation in its own right. Marsili et al. (2000) found that Nash equilibria in evolutionarily stable strategies are the minima of σ^2 and each player plays pure strategies. This implies $H = \sigma^2$ (e.g. see Eq. 3.30 in Chapter 3). The study of Nash equilibria was refined in De Martino and Marsili (2001): it turns out that the characterization of the optimal Nash equilibrium, that with minimal σ^2, requires full replica symmetry breaking in the statistical mechanics approach. In simple terms, this signals the existence of a complex hierarchical organization of the Nash equilibria. De Martino and Marsili (2001) shows that the number of Nash equilibria grows exponentially with N, with a growth rate Σ which depends on α as shown in Fig. 5.1.

---

[4] In the Minority Game as well as in the El Farol bar problem, one imagines that the interaction is repeated in time, neglecting all the strategic intricacies which arise from the inter-temporal nature of repeated games (such as reputation, punishment, or signalling). It is reasonable to assume that complications of this sort play a marginal role when the number of agents is very large, as in the Minority Game. Actually El Farol bar goers consider it just too complex to undertake a strategic behaviour even in each single stage. Each of them could be better off deciding his action a_i at each stage. It is somewhat assumed that they resort to the recommendations $a_{s,i}^{\mu}$ of their look-up tables because there are implicit computational and implementation costs which make them prefer these simple, though suboptimal, rules of thumb. This is more or less the same attitude as agents in the original Minority Game. In principle, players may be forced to one of the types of behaviour prescribed by their repertoire of look-up tables by some other constraints. In this case, it is important that players do not know the value of μ before deciding which strategy to use, because otherwise they could take a decision s_i^{μ} which depends on μ.

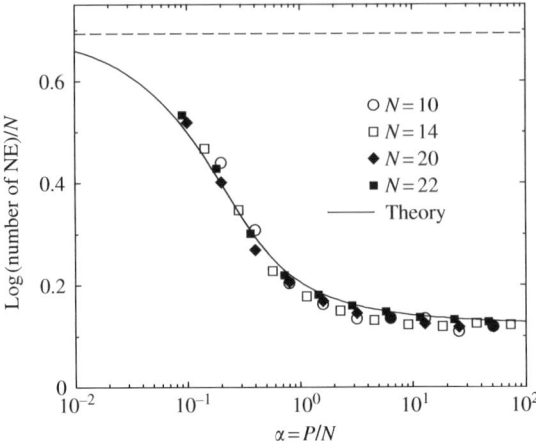

Fig. 5.1   Logarithm of the average number of Nash Equilibria divided by N as a function of α.

The properties of the Nash equilibria (NE) are quite different from those of the stationary states of the Minority Game (with naïve agents). In particular:

1. Nash equilibria are local minima of σ^2 whereas the stationary state of the Minority Game with naïve agents corresponds to minimum of H.
2. There are (exponentially) many disconnected Nash equilibria. Naïve agents reach a single stationary state, degenerate on a connected set for $\alpha < \alpha_c$.
3. Sophisticated players use pure strategies in NE whereas naïve agents alternate strategies. As a result $H = \sigma^2$ in NE whereas $H < \sigma^2$ in the original Minority Game.
4. The NE to which the learning dynamics of sophisticated agents converges is selected by the initial conditions. As the initial conditions vary the NE changes discontinuously. On the other hand, the learning dynamics of naïve agents converges to a stationary state which is unique for $\alpha > \alpha_c$ and depends *continuously* on the initial conditions for $\alpha < \alpha_c$.
5. In the stationary state of the Minority Game with naïve agents for $\alpha < \alpha_c$, a feedback of fluctuations from microscopic degrees of freedom to macroscopic quantities leads to a dependence of σ^2 on the learning rate Γ. This effect is absent for all values of α from the learning dynamics of sophisticated agents, who converge to a NE with no fluctuations.
6. The behaviour of the Minority Game with naïve agents is qualitatively the same both under endogenous and exogenous information (see Cavagna 1999) but also Challet and Marsili (2000). In contrast, the learning dynamics of sophisticated agents under endogenous information is very different from that under exogenous

information.[5] Hence the origin of information is not irrelevant when agents account for their market impact.

The fact that sophisticated agents have so many Nash equilibria at their disposal where to converge to raises interesting questions: how do agents manage to coordinate and select the same Nash equilibrium? How much time do agents need to 'learn' it? These questions are crucial in realistic cases where agents have a finite memory, that is, forget about the past. Having a finite memory may seem a further limitation but is actually a necessity to adapt optimally if the environment is changing (either because interactions change or because other agents change). A finite memory is modelled introducing a forgetting rate λ into the dynamics,

$$U_{i,s}(t+1) = \left(1 - \frac{\lambda}{N}\right) U_{i,s}(t) + \frac{\lambda}{N} u_i[s, s_{-i}(t)] \qquad (5.5)$$

by which agents learn about the payoffs $u_i[s, s_{-i}(t)]$ that they receive from strategy s. Marsili et al. (2001) have found a phase transition from a phase where agents manage to coordinate efficiently, when their memory extends sufficiently far into the past ($\lambda < 0.46\Gamma$) to a random phase where no coordination takes place. This transition, which is continuous in a stationary setting, becomes discontinuous in a 'changing world'. As Marsili et al. (2001) put it, the occurrence of a dynamical transition 'is further evidence that an analysis in terms of Nash equilibria may not be enough to predict the collective behaviour of a system. Agents may fail to coordinate [to] Nash equilibria because of purely dynamical effects.'

5.2.3 From naïve to sophisticated agents

That players should stick to just one strategy—the best one—is intuitive at first sight. Indeed the nature of the game is very similar to that of typical coordination games (Bottazzi et al. 2003). If a player has an optimal strategy, adopting this strategy is the best that he can do to reduce σ^2. This is the choice which the opponents welcome the most and that they anticipate. There is no reason why the agents should resort to mixed strategies in the Minority Game.[6] The reason why naïve agents do not stick to a single strategy in the usual Minority Game has nothing to do with game theory.

---

[5] In few words—we refer to Marsili et al. (2000) for more details—the dynamics of $\mu(t)$ become deterministic because all agents get frozen, and it locks into a periodic orbit of period $\sim\sqrt{P}$. Almost all information patterns μ', those not on the orbit, are never visited in the stationary state.

[6] The typical case where agents have strict incentives to randomize, that is, to play a mixed strategy, is the matching penny game where disclosing information about your choice makes your opponent win, whereas you lose (e.g. goal-keeper/penalty shooter interaction).

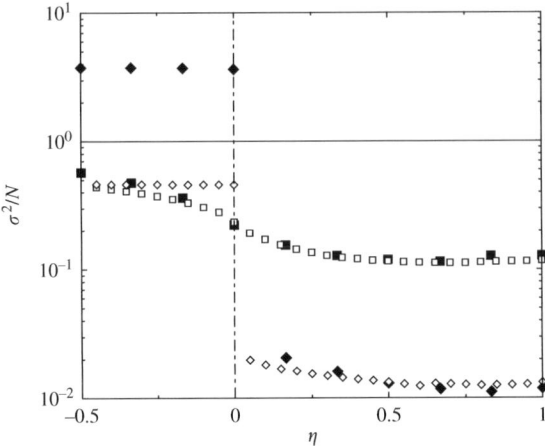

Fig. 5.2 Effect of accounting for market impact in the Minority Game with $\Gamma = \infty$ (full symbols) and $\Gamma \ll 1$ (open symbols). Squares refer to $\alpha > \alpha_c$ whereas diamonds to $\alpha < \alpha_c$.

Rather they do so because they neglect their market impact, as also explained in Section 5.2.

In order to see this, and to understand how to relate the Minority Game behaviour with that of Nash equilibria—which appears completely different—Challet et al. (2000c) suggested studying a learning dynamics

$$U_{i,s}(t+1) = U_{i,s}(t) - a_{i,s}^{\mu(t)} A(t) + \eta \delta_{s,s_i(t)} \tag{5.6}$$

with an additional term rewarding the strategy actually played by agent i. With $\eta = 0$ this clearly reproduces the behaviour of naïve agents in the Minority Game, whereas with $\eta = 1$ it reproduces the behaviour of sophisticated agents.[7] Figure 5.2 shows the dramatic influence that η has on the fluctuations in the stationary state. In the information rich phase ($\alpha > \alpha_c$) global efficiency improves smoothly with the reward η. This corresponds to crossing the full line boundary between the two phases in Fig. 5.3. But in the informational efficient phase ($\alpha < \alpha_c$), even an infinitesimal reward is able to reduce volatility by a finite amount (which amounts to crossing the dashed line in Fig. 5.3). The effect is more spectacular if agents are very reactive ($\Gamma = \infty$) than if they learn at a low rate ($\Gamma \ll 1$). What is remarkable is that the phase transition at α_c completely changes its nature for $\eta > 0$ and it disappears when agents account properly for the market impact ($\eta = 1$). This is what we alluded

---

[7] To be precise, the last term should be $+\eta a_{i,s}^{\mu(t)} a_{i,s_i(t)}^{\mu(t)}$, as observed in Mansilla (2000). However, this has the same effect as $+\eta \delta_{s,s_i(t)}$ on the long-term behaviour, because $\overline{a_{i,s} a_{i,s_i(t)}} \cong \delta_{s,s_i(t)}$.

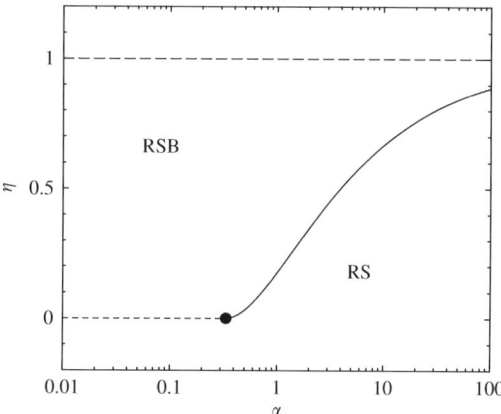

Fig. 5.3   Phase diagram of the Minority Game in the α, η plane. The phase below the line is replica symmetric and the stationary state is unique whereas above the line there are many different stationary states. The transition is continuous across the full line ($\alpha > \alpha_c$) and discontinuous across the dashed thick line ($\alpha < \alpha_c$). The stationary state has a continuous degeneracy on the line $\eta = 0$ for $0 < \alpha < \alpha_c$. The light dashed line is the locus of Nash equilibria ($\eta = 1$).

to when we stated, at the end of the previous chapter, that stylized facts disappear if agents account for their market impact.

Understanding what happens in the (α, η) space of this generalized Minority Game model requires some technicalities which we deal with in the next subsection, for the interested reader. The result is shown in Fig. 5.3 and can be summarized as follows: the properties of the Minority Game with naïve agents generalize to the whole RS region of the phase diagram. There we find a single (replica symmetric) stationary state, independent of initial conditions. Beyond the transition line in Fig. 5.3, the system has properties similar to those of Nash equilibria (replica symmetry breaking): there are many disconnected states which are selected by the choice of initial conditions. It is possible to show (Marsili et al. 2000) that σ^2 decreases and all individual payoffs increase when η increases. The transition is continuous for $\alpha > \alpha_c$, but it becomes discontinuous for $\alpha < \alpha_c$. The segment between the origin and the point (α_c, 0) is rather peculiar: the stationary state is degenerate on a continuous set and its properties change abruptly as this line is crossed. As anticipated, the interested reader can find more details in the next section.

5.2.4   The AT–MO line

The asymptotic regime of the dynamics provided by Eq. (5.6) have been related, in De Martino and Marsili (2001), to the local minima of

$$\mathcal{H}_\eta = (1 - \eta)H + \eta\sigma^2. \tag{5.7}$$

This work has shown that a phase transition separates, in the (α, η) plane, the behaviour of the Minority Game $(\eta = 0)$ from that of NE $(\eta = 1)$. At this phase transition, replica symmetry breaks down, as shown by the calculation of the stability of the replica symmetric solution.[8] The line $\eta_c(\alpha)$ above which the replica symmetric solution become unstable is shown in Fig. 5.3 and it is usually called the *AT line* after de Almeida and Thouless (1978), who first discussed it for spin glasses.

In order to understand the meaning of this result, let us focus on the Minority Game with $S = 2$ strategies per agent. In the notations of Chapter 3, the replica symmetric solution is characterized by the equality $Q = q$ of the diagonal and off-diagonal overlaps. These are defined considering two replicas of the same system corresponding to two dynamical paths starting from different initial conditions. If m_i and m_i' are the averages of the strategic choices $s_i(t)$ in the two replicas, then

$$Q - q = \frac{1}{2N} \sum_{i=1}^{N} (m_i - m_i')^2. \tag{5.8}$$

The equality $Q = q$ means that the two replicas are characterized by the same behaviour in the stationary state: $m_i = m_i'$. This indeed is what one should expect when the stationary state is unique. When the replica symmetric solution breaks down the off-diagonal overlap q takes, in principle, a whole range of values from $-Q$ to Q, signalling that beyond the line $\eta_c(\alpha)$ the minimum of $\mathcal{H}_\eta$, and hence the stationary state, are no longer unique. Different replicas, that is, dynamical realizations starting from different initial conditions, may converge to different stationary states.

The line $\eta_c(\alpha)$ can also be derived within the generating functional approach (Heimel and Coolen 2001), as shown in Heimel and De Martino (2001) (see page 300), where it is called the *memory onset* (MO) line. Indeed Heimel and De Martino show that above the MO line $\eta_c(\alpha)$ the dynamics acquire long-term memory. In loose words, for $\eta < \eta_c(\alpha)$ the dynamics always 'asymptotically forgets' perturbations in the early stages. On the contrary, for $\eta > \eta_c(\alpha)$, perturbation in the early stages of the dynamics may lead to a different stationary state: hence the system 'remembers' early perturbations. This is exactly what one should expect if at $\eta_c(\alpha)$ the uniqueness of the minimum of $\mathcal{H}_\eta$ ceases to hold.

Indeed there is a very simple derivation of the AT or MO line. At $\eta_c(\alpha)$ the unique minimum of $\mathcal{H}_\eta$ must turn into a saddle point. $\mathcal{H}_\eta$ is a quadratic function

---

[8] Actually the transition line in De Martino and Marsili (2001) is affected by a computational error, corrected in Heimel and De Martino (2001).

of the m_i,

$$\mathcal{H}_\eta = c + \sum_i g_i m_i + \sum_{i,j} m_i T_{i,j} m_j, \tag{5.9}$$

where c and g_i are constants and

$$T_{i,j} = \overline{\xi_i \xi_j}(1 - m_j^2) - \eta \overline{\xi_i^2}(1 - m_i^2)\delta_{i,j}. \tag{5.10}$$

The minimum of $\mathcal{H}_\eta$ becomes a saddle point when the smallest of the eigenvalues of $\widehat{T}$ becomes negative. Note that $\widehat{T} = \widehat{J} \cdot \widehat{D}$ where $J_{i,j} = \overline{\xi_i \xi_j} - \eta \overline{\xi_i^2}\delta_{i,j}$ and $D_{i,j} = (1 - m_i^2)\delta_{i,j}$ is diagonal. In particular, $T_{i,j} = 0$ if j is a frozen agent $(m_j = \pm 1)$, because $D_{j,j} = 0$. Hence each frozen agent corresponds to a trivial zero eigenvalue of the matrix $\widehat{T}$. The non-trivial part of the eigenvalue spectrum of T is that relative to the sector of non-frozen—or *fickle*—agents. Let $N_u = (1 - \phi)N$ be the number of fickle agents. In order to focus on the sector of fickle agents, call $\widehat{A}^{(u)}$ the $N_u \times N_u$ matrix obtained from a generic matrix $\widehat{A}$ by deleting all the $N - N_u$ rows and columns corresponding to frozen agents. The smallest eigenvalue of $\widehat{T}^{(u)}$ turns negative when the determinant of $\widehat{T}^{(u)}$ vanishes. But $\det \widehat{T}^{(u)} = \det \widehat{J}^{(u)} \det \widehat{D}^{(u)}$ and $\widehat{D}^{(u)}$ is a positive definite matrix. The minimum of H_η becomes a saddle point when the smallest eigenvalue of $\widehat{J}^{(u)}$ vanishes. The distribution of eigenvalues of matrices such as $\widehat{J}^{(u)}$, which are proportional to $\overline{\xi_i \xi_j}$, is known (e.g. see Sengupta and Mitra 1999). In particular, this allows us to compute the smallest eigenvalue of $\widehat{J}^{(u)}$, which is given by

$$\lambda_- = \frac{1}{2}\left[\left(1 - \sqrt{\frac{1-\phi}{\alpha}}\right)^2 - \eta\right]. \tag{5.11}$$

Therefore λ_- vanishes when

$$\eta_c(\alpha) = \left(1 - \sqrt{(1-\phi)/\alpha}\right)^2, \tag{5.12}$$

which is exactly the AT or MO line.[9]

This calculation can also be read as the stability analysis of stationary states for the dynamics in the continuum time limit.[10] This shows that the replica symmetric

---

[9] Heimel and De Martino (2001) report the result $1 - \phi = \alpha[1 - \eta(1 + \chi)]^2$ which coincides with Eq. (5.12). Indeed, using the saddle point equations, one finds that $\chi = 1/\sqrt{\eta} - 1$ on the line $\eta_c(\alpha)$.

[10] The dynamics in the continuum time limit reads

$$\frac{dy_i}{dt} = -\overline{\xi_i \Omega} - \sum_{j=1}^{N} \overline{\xi_i \xi_j} \tanh(y_j) + \eta \overline{\xi_i^2} \tanh y_i + \zeta_i, \tag{5.13}$$

solution becomes dynamically unstable for $\alpha < \alpha_c(\eta)$. Naively speaking, for each negative eigenvalue we have a bifurcation point of the dynamics which gives rise to the degeneracy of stationary states.

5.3   Human behaviour in the Minority Game

This book started in Chapter 1 by describing the experience of a synthetic speculator, trading his last shirt in a Minority Game market. We have described at some length how different types of agents play the Minority Game, how they compete and how they manage to coordinate. We find it appropriate to close this book, going back to real world experience, addressing the issue of how humans would play in the Minority Game.

Doing experiments with real human players is notoriously tricky in social sciences and economics (Kagel and Roth 1995). First of all human players must be coerced to play the game with the stated rules. Usually, money must be used to entice them to seriously engage themselves, or the game is imposed on students as a classroom requirement. The environment, as well as the information which players are given, must be controlled rigorously. Several research groups took on the issue of how real people play the Minority Game by gathering a small number of human players in a laboratory (Bottazzi et al. 2002; Patkowski and Ramsza 2003; Savit et al. 2003). Attempts to gather a number of human players to play simultaneously the Minority Game over a computer network were also tried. These never gained much steam as it is difficult to coordinate a not-too-small number of people to be online at the same time, let alone keep them attentive for a long time.

Laboratory experiments (Bottazzi *et al.* 2002; Patkowski and Ramsza 2003; Savit *et al.* 2003) where first aimed at measuring global quantities such as the fluctuations of the attendance, and the predictability of the outcome. All these studies agree on the human ability to coordinate. Savit et al. (2003) polled the players at the end of the rounds, asking them whether they found the experience hooking or dull; reportedly, bored players tend to take always the same action, which is beneficial for coordination.

---

where ζ_i is the stochastic force. Take the average over the ensemble of realizations $y_i(\tau)$ with the same initial conditions and define $y_i(\tau) = \operatorname{arc\,tanh} m_i + \delta y_i(\tau)$, where m_i is the solution of min $\mathcal{H}_\eta$, as in Chapter 3. Then, to linear order in δy_i, for fickle agents $|m_i| < 1$, we find

$$\frac{d\langle \delta y_i \rangle}{d\tau} = - \sum_{j \text{ fickle}} T_{i,j} \langle \delta y_j \rangle + O(\delta y^2). \tag{5.14}$$

This dynamics become unstable when $T_{i,j}$ acquires a negative eigenvalue, that is, when $\eta > \eta_c(\alpha)$.
  Note that, to this order, the dynamics is independent of Γ.

Bottazzi et al. (2002) finds that the length of the public bit-string is irrelevant to cooperation. However, feeding the players with real histories is essential (Patkowski and Ramsza 2003) as random bit-strings prohibit cooperation. Giving them no information whatsoever turns out to be an even better idea in order to achieve coordination.

The dynamics of these games in laboratory experiments is not trivial. In particular Savit et al. (2003) show that oscillations of the fluctuations occur. This seems to be due to some players changing their strategy, on longer 'evolutionary' timescales on which they explore the strategy space. These changes force other agents to change their strategy as well. This evolutionary process is not random, but rather it is biased towards simpler strategies, that is, deterministic strategies based on simpler information patterns. Indeed the simpler their strategies, the better the agents fare. The remarkable finding of Savit *et al.* is that a quite similar behaviour is found in a simple evolutionary version of the Minority Game where the worst performing agents are allowed to change their trading strategies.

Laureti et al. (2003) (see page 326) by pass the difficulties of laboratory experiments by involving only one human player at a time. He is pitted against computer-controlled players whose information capacity can be carefully dosed. Installing a web interface,[11] Laureti et al. (2003) made the Minority Game environment accessible to anyone around the globe, at any time. While players amused in trying to beat the Minority Game market, a record was kept of all the playing data, in order to gain some glimpse of players' reasoning habits from an informational point of view.

The main advantage of this setup is that experiences are easier to carry out. On the other hand, it cannot be conclusive about the ability of human beings to cooperation. Its focus is on placing the human player in a well-controlled situation in terms of game's predictability so that the ability of the human player to exploit the residual information can be measured. Human intelligence, one might say, is far superior to that of the inanimate Minority Game players. Furthermore human players are supple and intuitive. They should beat the market in a stride. But the machine players, in their defence, are strictly analytic, not blurred by the emotions that often plague human traders in real markets. What should we expect?

It should be noted that these web experiments also differ from the previous ones by the amount of available public information: The interface is designed to mimic that of a trading station. Hence the human player enjoys a view of a long price history—much more than the bit-string μ which the machine players have access to. This allows investigating not only player's efficiency in terms of payoffs, but also how much

---

[11] At www.unifr.ch/econophysics/minority/game.

information player's process, that is, how many past outcomes of the game human players regard as relevant.

The results are surprising. In brief, humans perform definitely better than computer agents deep in the symmetric phase ($\alpha < \alpha_c$) because they manage to anticipate anti-persistent behaviour of the synthetic agents. If these have trading strategies based on the past $M = 2$ or 3 outcomes, then the human trader is able to detect information over $M' = M + 1$ bit-strings and to anticipate them. This, by the way, reduces the volatility and hence it increases the gains of synthetic traders as well. When $M \geq 4$ human's ability to detect information seems to fade. Indeed human traders largely neglect the past history and resort to a highly repetitive mode of trading. $M = 3$ seems to mark the transition between these two modes of behaviour and it is remarkable that Savit et al. (2003) also find that $M = 3$ plays a crucial role. Savit and co-workers associate the special relevance of $M = 3$ with the 7 ± 2 rule, well known in psychology: this is the number of things human beings seem to be able to have in mind simultaneously. Nevertheless, when $M = 4$ and when the game is still in the symmetric phase, humans still fare better than Minority Game agents.

When the market enters into the predictable phase ($\alpha > \alpha_c$), humans are found to play in a repetitive way. This is a less efficient behaviour than that of most of the synthetic agents, but it is still better than purely random play. Though this repetitive behaviour captures some of market's predictability, it is not as efficient as that of Minority Game agents. It may be that human players revert to an oversimplified way of playing because they lack sufficient incentives for engaging more of their resources in the game. It may also be that their behaviour actually turns more sophisticated, in ways which we fail to perceive. For example, they may become responsive not only to the direction of price movements, but also to their size and maybe in an asymmetric way.

These are only hints of the many possible direction which future research on the lines of Laureti et al. (2003) can take. This opens a window on human behaviour in complex interacting environments which, with larger data sets and more refined analysis, promises quite interesting insights.

Appendix A. List of selected publications

A.1 Early works

1. Arthur, W. B. (1994). Inductive reasoning and bounded rationality: the El Farol problem. *Am. Econ. Assoc. Pap. Proc.* **84**, 406.
2. Challet, D. and Zhang, Y.-C. (1997). Emergence of cooperation and organization in an evolutionary game. *Physica A* **246**, 407.
3. Zhang, Y.-C. (1998). Evolving models of financial market. *Europhys. News* **29**, 51.
4. Savit, R., Manuca, R., and Riolo, R. (1999). Adaptive competition, market efficiency, and phase transitions. *Phys. Rev. Lett.* **82**(10), 2203.
5. Hart, M., Jefferies, P., Hui, P. M., and Johnson, N. F. (2001). Crowd–anticrowd theory of multi-agent market games. *Eur. Phys. J. B* **20**, 547.

A.2 Understanding the Minority Game dynamics

6. Cavagna, A. (1999). Irrelevance of memory in the Minority Game. *Phys. Rev. E* **59**, R3783.
7. Challet, D. and Marsili, M. (1999). Symmetry breaking and phase transition in the minority game. *Phys. Rev. E* **60**, R6271.
8. Cavagna, A., Garrahan, J. P., Giardina, I., and Sherrington, D. (1999). A thermal model for adaptive competition in a market. *Phys. Rev. Lett.* **83**, 4429.
9. Challet, D., Marsili, M., and Zecchina, R. (2000). Statistical mechanics of systems with heterogeneous agents: Minority Games. *Phys. Rev. Lett.* **84**, 1824.
10. Marsili, M. and Challet, D. (2001). Continuum time limit and stationary states of the Minority Game. *Phys. Rev. E* **64**, 056138.
11. Heimel, J. A. F. and Coolen, A. C. C. (2001). Generating functional analysis of the dynamics of the batch Minority Game with random external information. *Phys. Rev. E* **63**, 056121.

A.3   Financial markets

A.3.1   Minority Games

12. Challet, D., Marsili, M., and Zhang, Y.-C. (2000). Modeling market mechanism with Minority Game. *Physica A* **276**, 284.
13. Farmer, J. D. (1999). Physicists attempt to scale the ivory towers of finance. *Comput. Sci. Engi.*, **Nov–Dec** 26.
14. Jefferies, P., Hart, M. L., Hui, P. M., and Johnson, N. F. (2001). From market games to real-world markets. *Eur. Phys. J. B* **20**, 493.
15. Lamper, S., Howison, S., and Johnson, N. F. (2002). Predictability of large future changes in a competitive evolving population. *Phys. Rev. Lett.* **88**, 017902.
16. Bouchaud, J.-P., Giardina, I., and Mézard, M. (2001). On a universal mechanism for long-range volatility correlations. *Quant. Fin.* **1**, 212.
17. Challet, D. and Marsili, M. (2003). Criticality and market efficiency in a simple realistic model of the stock market. *Phys. Rev. E.* **68**, 036132.

A.3.2   Beyond Minority Games

18. Marsili, M. (2001). Market mechanism and expectations in minority and majority games. *Physica A* **299**, 93.
19. Andersen, J. V. and Sornette, D. (2003). The $-game. *Eur. J. Phy. B* **31**, 141.
20. Frantisek Slanina, Yi-Cheng Zhang. (2001). Dynamical spin-glass-like behavior in an evolutionary game. *Physica A* **289**, 290.

A.4   Quest for better cooperation

21. Reents, G., Metzler, R., and Kinzel, W. (2001). A stochastic strategy for the Minority Game. *Physica A* **299**, 253.
22. Hod, S. and Nakar, E. (2002). Self-segregation versus clustering in the evolutionary minority game. *Phys. Rev. Lett.* **88**, 238702.
23. Heimel, J. A. F. and De Martino, A. (2001). Broken ergodicity and memory in the Minority Game. *J. Phys. A: Math. Gen* **34**, L539–L545; 208701.
24. Paczuski, M., Bassler, K. E., and Corral, A. (2000). Self-organized networks of competing Boolean agents. *Phys. Rev. Lett.* **84**, 3185.

25. Kinzel, W., Metzler, R., and Kanter, I. (2000). Dynamics of interacting neural networks. *J. Phys. A: Math Gen.* **33**, L141.
26. Wakeling, J. and Bak, P. (2001). Intelligent systems in the context of surrounding environment. *Phys. Rev. E.* **64**: 051920.
27. P. Laureti et al. (2004). The Interactive Minority Game: a web-based investigation of human market interactions, *Physica A* **331**, 651–659.

Appendix B.   Source code

This appendix contains a sample source code for the Minority Game (MG) with linear payoff, that can be used for research. It measures σ^2/N and H/N, either for real or random histories. This source code needs the `ran2.c` routine from the Numerical Recipes (Press et al. 1993). It is very important to note that the number of iterations NIT and the equilibration time TEQ are proportional to P. It is not rare to find strange results if this prescription is not followed. From our experience, NIT $= 300P$ and TEQ $= 200P$ are reasonable choices. However if one wants to investigate finite size effects near the critical point of the standard MG, one should increases considerably TEQ, for instance TEQ $= 5000P$, because the speed of convergence to the stationary state is very slow near the critical point.

For compiling the provided code with `gcc`, type `gcc -o MG minoritygame.c` in a terminal. If this works, optimizing the executable is a good idea: type now `gcc -O3 -mcpu=i686 -o MG minoritygame.c`; change `-mcpu=i686` to `-mcpu=athlon`, `-mcpu=pentium4`, etc. depending on the type of your processor.

You can then play with the program by typing `MG` in a terminal. It indicates what argument it expects: M is the length of the history bitstring, N the number of players, S the number of strategies per agent, `NITP` the number of iteration steps in unit of P,[1] and `idum` is the seed for the random generator, and should be negative. `MG 4 101 2 500 -456345` places the system in the symmetric phase, whereas `MG 10 21 2 500 -346487238` places it in the asymmetric phase. Computing the average of σ^2/N or H/N versus α needs more work, which we leave to you.

```
#include <stdio.h>
#include <memory.h>
#include "ran2.c"

int main(int argc, char *argv[]){
  long idum,mu,nu;
  int N,S,M,P,NIT,NITP,TEQ;
  int i,j,it,winBit,A,***a,*s;
```

---

[1] The total number of iterations is `NITP*P+TEQ`

```
long **U,*avgA,*T;
double alpha,sigma2,H;

if(argc==6){
  i=1;
  M=atoi(argv[i++]);
  N=atoi(argv[i++]);
  S=atoi(argv[i++]);
  NITP=atoi(argv[i++]); /* number of iterations/P */
  idum=atoi(argv[i++]); /* random generator's seed */
}
else{
  printf("parameters:␣M␣N␣S␣NITP␣idum!!!\n\n");
  exit(-1);
}

P=1<<M; /* P=2^M */
NIT=NITP*P;
TEQ=200*P;
NIT+=TEQ;

/* memory allocation */
a=(int ***)calloc(N,sizeof(int));
s=(int *)calloc(N,sizeof(int));
U=(int **)calloc(N,sizeof(int));
avgA=(long *)calloc(P,sizeof(int));
T=(long *)calloc(P,sizeof(int));
for(i=0;i<N;i++){
  a[i]=(int **)calloc(S,sizeof(int));
  U[i]=(int *)calloc(S,sizeof(int).);
  for(j=0;j<S;j++){
    a[i][j]=(int *)calloc(P,sizeof(int));
  }
}

/* initialisation of the players */
for(i=0;i<N;i++){
  for(j=0;j<S;j++){
    for(mu=0;mu<P;mu++){
      a[i][j][mu]=2*(int)(2*ran2(&idum))-1; /* a[i][j][mu]=-1 or 1 */
    }
    U[i][j]=0; /* tabula rasa */
    s[i]=0; /* s[i] is the strategy being used by agent i */
  }
}

/* beginning of the game */
mu=(int)(ran2(&idum)*P);  /* mu(t=0) is randomly drawn */
sigma2=0;
```

```
for(it=0;it<NIT;it++){
  if(it==TEQ){                      /* resets the measured quantities */
                                    /* if the equilibration time is reached */
    sigma2=0.;
    for(nu=0;nu<P;nu++){
      avgA[nu]=0;
      T[nu]=0;
    }
  }
  A=0;                              /* A(t) */
  for(i=0;i<N;i++){
    for(j=0;j<S;j++){
      if(U[i][s[i]] == U[i][j]){
        if(ran2(&idum)<0.5){     /* breaks ties */
          s[i]=j;
        }
      }
      else{
        if(U[i][s[i]]<U[i][j]){
          s[i]=j;
        }
      }
    }
    A+=a[i][s[i]][mu];
  }
  avgA[mu]+=A;                 /* builds <A|mu> */
  T[mu]++;                     /* number of times mu appears */
  sigma2+=(double)(A*A);

  /* determination of the winning side */
  if(A>0){
    winBit=0;
  }
  else{
    winBit=1;
  }

  /* update of the strategy scores */
  for(i=0;i<N;i++){
    for(j=0;j<S;j++){
      U[i][j]+=-a[i][j][mu]*A;
    }
  }

  /* update of the history */
  mu=(2*mu)%P+winBit;   /* real histories. */
 /* mu=(int)(ran2(&idum)*P); random histories */
}
H=0.;
```

```
for (mu=0;mu<P;mu++) {
  if (T[mu]>0) {
     H+=((double)avgA[mu]*(double)avgA[mu])/(double)T[mu];
  }
}
H/=(double)((NIT-TEQ)*N);
sigma2/=(double)((NIT-TEQ)*N);

alpha=(double)P/(double)N;
printf("%e_%e_%e\n",alpha,sigma2,H);
}
```

PART II   Reprinted papers

Inductive Reasoning and Bounded Rationality

(The El Farol Problem)

W. Brian Arthur*

Santa Fe Institute, 1399 Hyde Park Road, Santa Fe, NM 87501

Given at the American Economic Association Annual Meetings, 1994
Session: Complexity in Economic Theory, chaired by Paul Krugman

The type of rationality we assume in economics—perfect, logical, deductive rationality—is extremely useful in generating solutions to theoretical problems. But it demands much of human behavior—much more in fact than it can usually deliver. If we were to imagine the vast collection of decision problems economic agents might conceivably deal with as a sea or an ocean, with the easier problems on top and more complicated ones at increasing depth, then deductive rationality would describe human behavior accurately only within a few feet of the surface. For example, the game Tic-Tac-Toe is simple, and we can readily find a perfectly rational, minimax solution to it. But we do not find rational 'solutions' at the depth of Checkers; and certainly not at the still modest depths of Chess and Go.

There are two reasons for perfect or deductive rationality to break down under complication. The obvious one is that beyond a certain complicatedness, our logical apparatus ceases to cope—our rationality is bounded. The other is that in interactive situations of complication, agents can not rely upon the other agents they are dealing with to behave under perfect rationality, and so they are forced to guess their behavior. This lands them in a world of subjective beliefs, and subjective beliefs about subjective beliefs. Objective, well-defined, shared assumptions then cease to apply. In turn,

* Santa Fe Institute, 1660 Old Pecos Trail, Santa Fe, NM 87501, and Stanford University. I thank particularly John Holland whose work inspired many of the ideas here. I also thank Kenneth Arrow, David Lane, David Rumelhart, Roger Shepard, Glen Swindle, and colleagues at Santa Fe and Stanford for discussions. A lengthier version is given in Arthur (1992). For parallel work on bounded rationality and induction, but applied to macroeconomics, see Sargent (1994).

rational, deductive reasoning—deriving a conclusion by perfect logical processes from well-defined premises—itself cannot apply. The problem becomes ill-defined.

As economists, of course, we are well aware of this. The question is not whether perfect rationality works, but rather what to put in its place. How do we model bounded rationality in economics? Many ideas have been suggested in the small but growing literature on bounded rationality; but there is not yet much convergence among them. In the behavioral sciences this is not the case. Modern psychologists are in reasonable agreement that in situations that are complicated or ill-defined, humans use characteristic and predictable methods of reasoning. These methods are not deductive, but *inductive*.

In this paper I will argue that as economists we need to pay great attention to inductive reasoning; that it makes excellent sense as an intellectual process; and that it is not hard to model. In the main part of this paper, I will present a decision problem—the 'bar problem'—in which inductive reasoning is assumed and modeled, and its implications are examined. The system that emerges under inductive reasoning will have connections both with evolution and complexity.

A.1   Thinking inductively

How *do* humans reason in situations that are complicated or ill-defined? Modern psychology tells us that as humans we are only moderately good at deductive logic, and we make only moderate use of it. But we *are* superb at seeing or recognizing or matching patterns—behaviors that confer obvious evolutionary benefits. In problems of complication then, we look for patterns; and we simplify the problem by using these to construct temporary internal models or hypotheses or *schemata* to work with.[1] We carry out localized deductions based on our current hypotheses and act on them. And, as feedback from the environment comes in, we may strengthen or weaken our beliefs in our current hypotheses, discarding some when they cease to perform, and replacing them as needed with new ones. In other words, where we cannot fully reason or lack full definition of the problem, we use simple models to fill the gaps in our understanding. Such behavior is *inductive*.

We can see inductive behavior at work in Chess playing. Players typically study the current configuration of the board, and recall their opponent's play in past games, to discern patterns (De Groot, 1965). They use these to form hypotheses or internal

---

[1] For accounts in psychological literature, see Bower and Hilgard (1981), Holland et al. (1986), Rumelhart (1980), and Schank and Abelson (1977). Not all decision problems of course work this way. Most of our mundane actions like walking or driving are subconsciously directed, and for these pattern-cognition maps directly in action. Here connectionist models work better.

models about each others' intended strategies, maybe even holding several in their minds at one time: 'He's using a Caro-Kann defense.' 'This looks a bit like the 1936 Botvinnik-Vidmar game.' 'He is trying to build up his mid-board pawn formation.' They make local deductions based on these—analyzing the possible implications of moves several moves deep. And as play unfolds they hold onto hypotheses or mental models that prove plausible, or toss them aside if not, generating new ones to put in their place. In other words, they use a sequence of pattern recognition, hypothesis formation, deduction using currently-held hypotheses, and replacement of hypotheses as needed.

This type of behavior may not be familiar in economics. But we can recognize its advantages. It enables us to deal with complication: we construct plausible, simpler models that we *can* cope with. It enables us to deal with ill-definedness: where we have insufficient definition, our working models fill the gap. It is not antithetical to 'reason,' or to science for that matter. In fact, it is the way science itself operates and progresses.

Modeling Induction

If humans indeed reason in this way, how can we model this? In a typical problem that plays out over time, we might set up a collection of agents, probably heterogeneous, and assume they can form mental models, or hypotheses, or subjective beliefs. These beliefs might come in the form of simple mathematical expressions that can be used to describe or predict some variable or action; or of complicated expectational models of the type common in economics; or of statistical hypotheses; or of condition/prediction rules ('If situation Q is observed/predict outcome or action D'). These will normally be subjective, that is, they will differ among the agents. An agent may hold one in mind at a time, or several simultaneously.

Each agent will normally keep track of the performance of a private collection of such belief-models. When it comes time to make choices, he acts upon his currently most credible (or possibly most profitable) one. The others he keeps at the back of his mind, so to speak. Alternatively, he may act upon a combination of several. (However, humans tend to hold in mind many hypotheses and act on the most plausible one (Feldman, 1962).) Once actions are taken the aggregative picture is updated, and agents update the track record of all their hypotheses.

This is a system in which learning takes place. Agents 'learn' which of their hypotheses work, and from time to time they may discard poorly performing hypotheses and generate new 'ideas' to put in their place. Agents linger with their currently most believable hypothesis or belief model, but drop it when it no longer functions well, in favor of a better one. This causes a built-in hysteresis. A belief model is clung to not because it is 'correct"—there is no way to know this—but rather because it has worked in the past, and must cumulate a record of failure before it is worth discarding. In general, there may be a constant, slow turnover of hypotheses acted upon.

We could speak of this as a system of *temporarily fulfilled expectations*—beliefs or models or hypotheses that are temporarily fulfilled (though not perfectly), that give way to different beliefs or hypotheses when they cease to be fulfilled.

If the reader finds this system unfamiliar, he or she might think of it as generalizing the standard economic learning framework which typically has agents sharing one expectational model with unknown parameters, acting upon their currently most plausible values. Here, by contrast, agents differ, and each uses several subjective models instead of a continuum of one commonly held one. This is a richer world, and we might ask whether, in a particular context, it converges to some standard equilibrium of beliefs; or whether it remains open-ended, always discovering new hypotheses, new ideas.

It is also a world that is evolutionary—or more accurately co-evolutionary. Just as species, to survive and reproduce, must prove themselves by competing and being adapted within an environment created by other species, in this world hypotheses, to be accurate and therefore acted upon, must prove themselves by competing and being adapted within an environment created by other agents' hypotheses. The set of ideas or hypotheses that are acted upon at any stage therefore coevolves.[2]

A key question remains. Where do the hypotheses or mental models come from? How are they generated? Behaviorally, this is a deep question in psychology, having to do with cognition, object representation, and pattern recognition. I will not go into it here. But there are some simple and practical options for modeling. Sometimes we might endow our agents with *focal* models—patterns or hypotheses that are obvious, simple and easily dealt with mentally. We might generate a 'bank' of these and distribute them among the agents. Other times, given a suitable model-space, we might allow the genetic algorithm or some similar intelligent search device to generate ever 'smarter' models. Whatever option is taken, it is important to be clear that the framework described above is independent of the specific hypotheses or beliefs used, just as the consumer theory framework is independent of particular products chosen among. Of course, to use the framework in a particular problem, some system of generating beliefs must be adopted.

A.2   The bar problem

Consider now a problem I will construct to illustrate inductive reasoning and how it might be modeled. N people decide independently each week whether to go to a bar that offers entertainment on a certain night. For concreteness, let us set N at 100. Space

---

[2] A similar statement holds for strategies in evolutionary game theory; but there, instead of a large number of private, subjective expectational models, a small number of strategies compete.

is limited, and the evening is enjoyable if things are not too crowded—specifically, if fewer than 60% of the possible 100 are present. There is no way to tell the numbers coming for sure in advance, therefore a person or agent: *goes*—deems it worth going— if he expects fewer than 60 to show up, or *stays home* if he expects more than 60 to go. (There is no need that utility differ much above and below 60.) Choices are unaffected by previous visits; there is no collusion or prior communication among the agents; and the only information available is the numbers who came in past weeks. (The problem was inspired by the bar El Farol in Santa Fe which offers Irish music on Thursday nights; but the reader may recognize it as applying to noontime lunch-room crowding, and to other coordination problems with limits to desired coordination.) Of interest is the dynamics of the numbers attending from week to week.

Notice two interesting features of this problem. First, if there were an obvious model that all agents could use to forecast attendance and base their decisions on, then a deductive solution would be possible. But this is not the case here. Given the numbers attending in the recent past, a large number of expectational models might be reasonable and defensible. Thus, not knowing which model other agents might choose, a reference agent cannot choose his in a well-defined way. There is no deductively rational solution—no 'correct' expectational model. From the agents' viewpoint, the problem is ill-defined and they are propelled into a world of induction. Second, and diabolically, any commonalty of expectations gets broken up: If all believe *few* will go, *all* will go. But this would invalidate that belief. Similarly, if all believe *most* will go, *nobody* will go, invalidating that belief. Expectations will be forced to differ.

At this stage, I invite the reader to pause and ponder how attendance might behave dynamically over time. Will it converge, and if so to what? Will it become chaotic? How might predictions be arrived at?

A Dynamic Model

To answer this, let us construct a model along the lines of the framework sketched above. Assume the 100 agents can individually each form several predictors or hypotheses, in the form of functions that map the past d weeks' attendance figures into next week's. For example, recent attendance might be:

>   ...   44   78   56   15   23   67   84   34   45   76   40   56   22   35

And particular hypotheses or predictors might be: *predict next week's number to be*

−the same as last week's [35]
−a mirror image around 50 of last week's [65]
−67 [67]
−a (rounded) average of the last four weeks [49]
−the trend in last 8 weeks, bounded by 0, 100 [29]

−the same as 2 weeks ago (2-period cycle detector) [22]
−the same as 5 weeks ago (5-period cycle detector) [76]
−etc. . . .

Assume each agent possesses and keeps track of a individualized set of k such focal predictors. He decides to go or stay according to the currently most accurate predictor in his set. (I will call this his *active* predictor). Once decisions are made, each agent learns the new attendance figure, and updates the accuracies of his monitored predictors.

Notice that in this bar problem, the set of hypotheses currently most credible and acted upon by the agents—the set of active hypotheses—determines the attendance. But the attendance history determines the set of active hypotheses. To use John Holland's term, we can think of these active hypotheses as forming an *ecology*. Of interest is how this ecology evolves over time.

Computer Experiments

For most sets of hypotheses, analytically this appears to be a difficult question. So in what follows I will proceed by computer experiments. In the experiments, to generate hypotheses, I first create an 'alphabet soup' of predictors, in the form of several dozen focal predictors replicated many times. I then randomly ladle out k (6 or 12 or 23, say) of these to each of 100 agents. Each agent then possesses k predictors or hypotheses or 'ideas' he can draw upon. We need not worry that useless predictors will muddy behavior. If predictors do not 'work' they will not be used; if they do work they will come to the fore. Given starting conditions and the fixed set of predictors available to each agent, the future accuracies of all predictors are predetermined. The dynamics in this case are deterministic.

The results of the experiments are interesting (Fig. 1). Where cycle-detector predictors are present, cycles are quickly "arbitraged' away so there are no persistent cycles. (If several people expect many to go because many went three weeks ago, they will stay home.) More interestingly, mean attendance converges always to 60. In fact, the predictors self-organize into an equilibrium pattern or 'ecology' in which of the active predictors, those most accurate and therefore acted upon, on average 40% are forecasting above 60, 60% below 60. This emergent ecology is almost organic in nature. For, while the population of active predictors splits into this 60/40 average ratio, it keeps changing in membership forever. This is something like a forest whose contours do not change, but whose individual trees do. These results appear throughout the experiments, robust to changes in types of predictors created and in numbers assigned.

How do the predictors self-organize so that 60 emerges as average attendance and forecasts split into a 60/40 ratio? One explanation might be that 60 is a natural 'attractor' in this bar problem; in fact if we view it as a pure game of predicting, a mixed

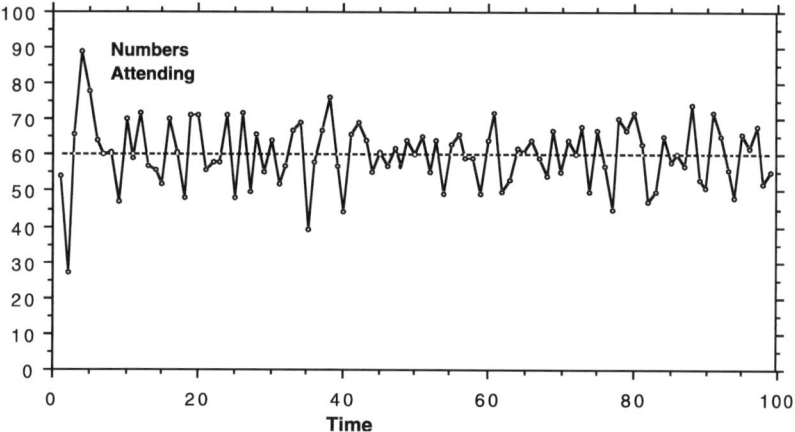

Fig. 1   Bar attendance in the first 100 weeks.

strategy of forecasting above 60 with probability 0.4 and below it with probability 0.6 is Nash. But still this does not explain how the agents approximate any such outcome, given their realistic, subjective reasoning. To get some understanding of how this happens, suppose 70% of their predictors forecasted above 60 for a longish time. Then on average only 30 people would show up. But this would validate predictors that forecasted close to 30, restoring the 'ecological' balance among predictions, so to speak. Eventually the 40%–60% combination would assert itself. (Making this argument mathematically exact appears to be non-trivial.) It is important to be clear that we do not need any 40–60 forecasting balance in the predictors that are set up. Many could have a tendency to predict high, but aggregate behavior calls the equilibrium predicting ratio to the fore. Of course, the result would fail if all predictors could only predict below 60—then all 100 agents would always show up. Predictors need to 'cover' the available prediction space to some modest degree. The reader might ponder what would happen if all agents shared the same set of predictors.

It might be objected that I lumbered the agents in these experiments with fixed sets of clunky predictive models. If they could form more open-ended, intelligent predictions, different behavior might emerge. We could certainly test this using a more sophisticated procedure, say genetic programming (Koza, 1992). This continually generates new hypotheses—new predictive expressions—that adapt 'intelligently' and often become more complicated as time progresses. But I would be surprised if this changes the above results in any qualitative way.

A.3   Conclusion

The inductive-reasoning system I have described above consists of a multitude of 'elements' in the form of belief-models or hypotheses that adapt to the aggregate environment they jointly create. Thus it qualifies as an *adaptive complex* system. After some initial learning time, the hypotheses or mental models in use are mutually co-adapted. Thus we can think of a *consistent* set of mental models as a set of hypotheses that work well with each other under some criterion—that have a high degree of mutual adaptedness. Sometimes there is a unique such set, it corresponds to a standard rational expectations equilibrium, and beliefs gravitate into it. More often there is a high, possibly very high, multiplicity of such sets. In this case we might expect inductive reasoning systems in the economy—whether in stock-market speculating, in negotiating, in poker games, in oligopoly pricing, in positioning products in the market—to cycle through or temporarily lock into psychological patterns that may be non-recurrent, path-dependent, and increasingly complicated. The possibilities are rich.

Economists have long been uneasy with the assumption of perfect, deductive rationality in decision contexts that are complicated and potentially ill-defined. The level at which humans can apply perfect rationality is surprisingly modest. Yet it has not been clear how to deal with imperfect or bounded rationality. From the reasoning given above, I believe that as humans in these contexts we use *inductive* reasoning: we induce a variety of working hypotheses, act upon the most credible, and replace hypotheses with new ones if they cease to work. Such reasoning can be modeled in a variety of ways. Usually this leads to a rich psychological world in which agents' ideas or mental models compete for survival against other agents' ideas or mental models—a world that is both evolutionary and complex.

Bibliography

Arthur, W. Brian, 'On Learning and Adaptation in the Economy,' Santa Fe Institute Paper 92-07-038, 1992.

Bower, Gordon H. and Hilgard, Ernest R., *Theories of Learning*. Englewood Cliffs: Prentice Hall, 1981.

De Groot Adriann, *Thought and Choice in Chess*, in the series *Psychological Studies*, 4. Paris: Mouton & Co., 1965.

Feldman, Julian, 'Computer Simulation of Cognitive Processes,' in Harold Borko (ed.), *Computer Applications in the Behavioral Sciences*. Englewood Cliffs: Prentice Hall, 1962.

Holland, John H., Holyoak, Keith J., Nisbett, Richard E., and Thagard, Paul R., *Induction*. Cambridge, MA: MIT Press, 1986.

Koza, John, *Genetic Programming*. Cambridge, MA: MIT Press, 1992.

Rumelhart, David, 'Schemata: the Building Blocks of Cognition,' in R. Spiro, B. Bruce, and W. Brewer (eds.), *Theoretical Issues in Reading Comprehension.* Hillsdale, NJ: Lawrence Erlbaum, 1980.

Sargent, Thomas, J., *Bounded Rationality in Macroeconomics.* Oxford University Press, 1994.

Schank, R. and Abelson, R. P., *Scripts, Plans, Goals, and Understanding: An Inquiry into Human Knowledge Structures.* Hillsdale, NJ: Lawrence Erlbaum, 1977.

ELSEVIER

Emergence of cooperation and organization in an evolutionary game

D. Challet, Y.-C. Zhang *

Institut de Physique Théorique, Pérolles, Université de Fribourg, 1700 Fribourg, Switzerland

Received 8 August 1997

Abstract

A binary game is introduced and analysed. N players have to choose one of the two sides independently and those on the minority side win. Players use a finite set of ad hoc strategies to make their decision, based on the past record. The analysing power is limited and can adapt when necessary. Interesting cooperation and competition patterns of the society seem to arise and to be responsive to the payoff function.

Keywords: Evolution; Game; Emergence of organization

Most current economics theories are deductive in origin. One assumes that each participant knows what is best for him given ·that all other participants are equally intelligent in choosing their best actions. However, it is recently realised that in the real world the actual players do not have the perfect foresight and hindsight, most often their actions are based on trial-and-error inductive thinking, rather than the deductive rationale assuming that there are underlying first principles. Whether deductive or inductive thinking is more relevant is still under debate [1].

Evolutionary games have also been studied within the standard framework of game theory [2]. However, it has been recently pointed out that the approach traditionally used in economics is not convenient to generalise to include irrationality, and an alternative Langevin-type equation is proposed [3]. As physicists, we would like to view a game with a large number of players, i.e. a statistical system, we need to explore new approaches in which the emerging collective phenomena can be better appreciated. One recent approach using bounded rationality is particularly inspiring, put forward by B. Arthur in his *El Farol* bar problem [4]. Following a similar philosophy, in this work we propose and study a simple evolutionary game.

* Corresponding author.

0378-4371/97/$17.00 Copyright © 1997 Elsevier Science B.V. All rights reserved
PII S0378-4371(97)00419-6

Table 1

Signal	Prediction
000	1
001	0
010	0
011	1
100	1
101	0
110	1
111	0

Let us consider a population of N (odd) players, each has some finite number of strategies S. At each time step, everybody has to choose to be in side A or side B. The payoff of the game is to declare that after everybody has chosen side independently, those who are in the minority side win. In the simplest version, all winners collect a point. The players make decisions based on the common knowledge of the past record. We further limit the record to contain only yes and no, e.g. side A is the winning side or not, without the actual attendance number. Thus, the system's signal can be represented by a binary sequence, meaning A is the winning side (1) or not (0).

Let us assume that our players are quite limited in their analysing power, they can only retain last M bits of the system's signal and make their next decision basing only on these M bits. Each player has a finite set of strategies. A strategy is defined to be the next action (to be in A or B) given a specific signal's M bits. An example of a strategy is illustrated in Table 1 for $M = 3$.

There are $8 (= 2^M)$ bits we can assign to the right side, each configuration corresponds to a distinct strategy, this makes the total number of strategies to be $2^{2^M} = 256$. This is indeed a fast increasing number, for $M = 2, 3, 4, 5$ it is 16, 156, 65 536, $65\,536^2$. We randomly draw S strategies for each player, and some strategies maybe by chance-shared. However, for moderately large M, the chance of repetition of a single strategy is exceedingly small. Another special case is to have all 1's (or 0's) on the RHS of the table, corresponding to the fixed strategy of stay at one side no matter what happens.

Let us analyse the structure of this minority game to see what to expect. Consider the extreme case where only one player takes a side, all the others take the other side. The lucky player gets a reward point, nothing for the others. Equally extreme example is that when $(N - 1)/2$ players at one side, $(N + 1)/2$ at the other. From the society point of view, the second situation is preferable since the whole population gets $(N - 1)/2$ points, whereas in the first example, only one point – a huge waste. Perfect coordination and timing would approach the second, disaster would be the first example. In general, we expect the population to behave between the above two extremes.

This binary game can be easily simulated for a large population of players. Initially, each player draws randomly one out of his S strategies and uses it to predict the next step; an artificial signal of M bits is also given. All the S strategies in a players's bag collect points depending if they would win or not given the M past bits, and the actual outcome of the next play. However, these points are only *virtual* points as they record the merit of a strategy as if it were used each time. The player uses the strategy having the highest accumulated points (capital) for his action; he gets a real point only if the strategy used happens to win in the next play.

In Fig. 1 we plot the actual number of attendance at side A, for a population of 1001 players, having various brain size (i.e. M bits). As one may expect, the temporal signal indeed fluctuates around the 50%. Whoever takes side A wins a point at a given time step when the signal is below 501. The precise number is not known to the players, they only know if a side is winning or not, after their bet is made. Note that large fluctuations imply large waste since still more players could have taken the winning side without harm done to the others. On the other hand, smaller fluctuations imply more efficient usage of available resources, in general this would require coordination and cooperation – which are not built-in explicitly. We see that the population having larger brains (i.e. M larger) cope with each other better: the fluctuation is indeed in decreasing order for ever increasingly "intelligent" players (i.e. $M = 6, 8, 10$). Remarkable is that each player is by definition selfish, not considerate to fellow players, yet somehow they manage to somewhat share the limited available resources.

Let us remark that the very simplest strategy by playing randomly is not included here, for generating random numbers more bits are needed. In a perfect timing, the average gain in the population would be $1/2$ per play. Waste is proportional to fluctuation's amplitude, hence the average gain is always below $1/2$ in reality. Since the game is symmetrical in A and B, one may be tempted to use the simple strategy to stay at A or B, hoping to get exactly $1/2$ gain. Let us mention if this strategy indeed rewards $1/2$ gain on average, many would imitate. Suppose that there is a group sitting at A no matter what signal is shown (this is included in the strategy space). The active players will soon recognise that they win less often choosing A than B. In fact, for them the game is no longer symmetrical and they will adopt accordingly so that the apparent advantage disappears for those sitting at one side fixed. This is similar to the arbitrage opportunities in finance: any obvious advantage will be arbitraged away – no easy "risk-free way" to make a living both for our players and those in the real world.

The advantage of the larger brain sizes over the smaller ones can be better appreciated inspecting Fig. 2 . Identical parameters ($N = 1001, S = 5$) for a mixed population having $M = 1, \ldots, 10$. We thus force unequally equiped players to play together. One may fear that the "poorly" brained players may get exploited by the more powerfully brained ones; indeed this is the case. We plot the average gain per time step after a long time. We see that within a sub-population (same M) there are better and worse performers. We have noticed that better players do not necessarily stay that way for a long time, but exceptions exist. For $M = 1$, there appears fewer points, since there are more degeneracies. As a group the more intelligent players gain more and the spread between the rich and the poor is smaller, even though the in-fighting among them is more intensified. Note that above a certain size ($M \approx 6$) the average performance

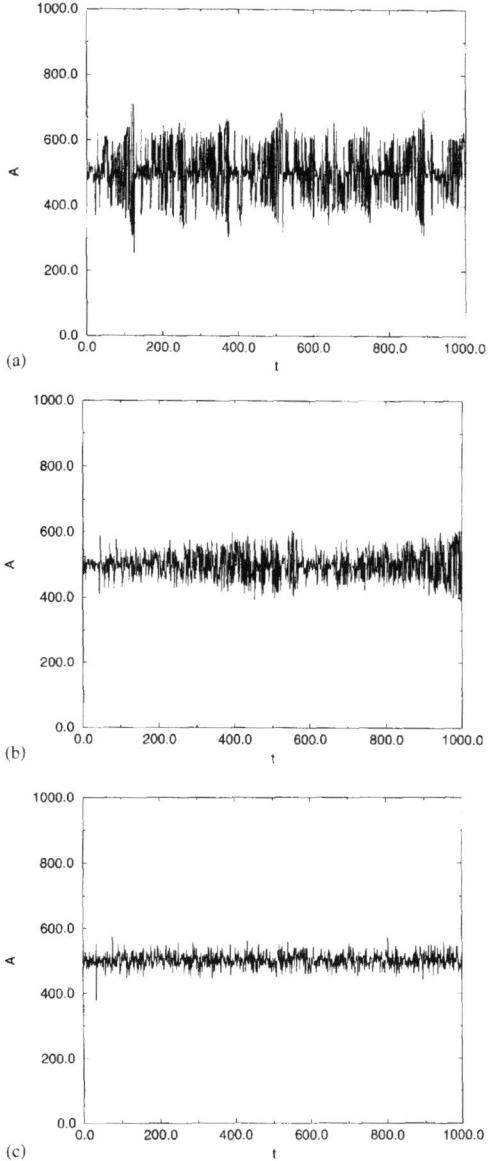

Fig. 1. Actual number of attendance at the side A against time, for a population of 1001 players, having brain size of (a) 6, (b) 8 and (c) 10 bits.

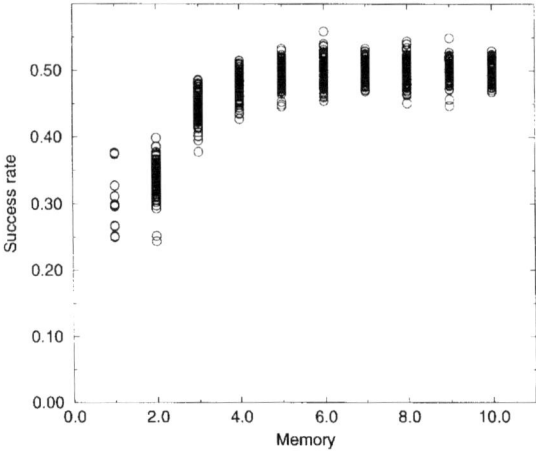

Fig. 2. Success rate of a mixed population players against their memory ($N = 1001$, $S = 5$).

of a population appears to saturate, further increasing the brain size does not seem to improve further. This is due to the simple structure of this version of the game, there is nothing more to gain. Recall that only most crude information is transmitted to the players, i.e. only yes and no, not the exact attendance number. More precise information would necessitate more analysing power, more complicated payoff functions and games also provides incentives to develop more sophisticated brains. However, in the present work, we stick to the binary functions and will report more complicated applications using neural networks elsewhere.

Of course, the game is symmetrical for A and B. This can be observed in Fig. 3 , where the histograph shows the attendance of A (hence B is the mirror image at the point $N = 501$). B. Arthur's *El Farol* problem uses 60% rule and does not give rise to new questions, and results appear to be similar.

One may argue that our payoff function is too simple, i.e. a step function without differentiating a "good" minority from a "bad" one. Let us consider the payoff function $N/x-2$, i.e. these many (nearest integer values) points awarded to every player choosing the minority side, the number of winning players being $x < N/2$. Clearly, this structure favours smaller minority. This is like in lottery you would like to be on the winning side, but even better you are alone there. The players thus face an extra type of competition, a winner would prefer less fellow winners in company. If, for instance, a player wins on a mediocre play, his winning strategies are hardly enhanced with respect to not winning at all. Globally, the population ($N = 1001$, $M = 4$) responds to having a histograph (Fig. 4) with two peaks. Although the jackpot (winning alone) is very appealing, this is very unlikely to happen since the fellow players are just as intelligent. The players need a sizeable gain to get motivation to win. There appears to

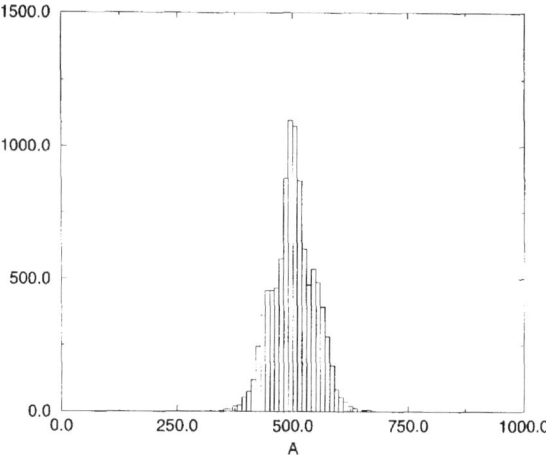

Fig. 3. Histograph of the attendance of A ($N = 1001$, $M = 8$, $S = 5$).

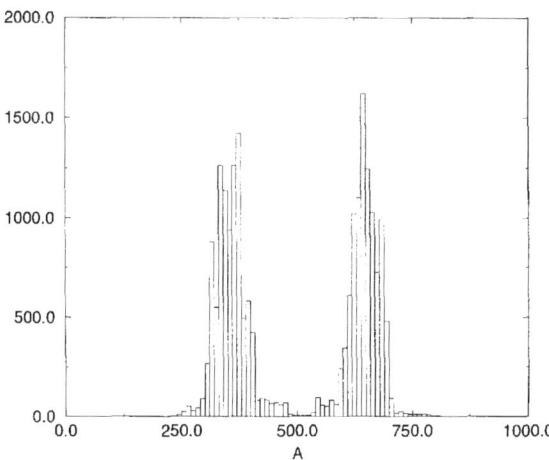

Fig. 4. Histograph of the attendance of A for a $N/x - 2$ payoff ($N = 1001$, $M = 4$, $S = 5$).

be a compromise that they effectively (not through any enforceable agreement) agree to show up on the minority side a smaller number of players. What is remarkable here is that entropy, i.e. the most likely configuration, does not favour the distribution in Fig. 4. The players manage to defy entropy; in other words, to get themselves organised to occupy less unlikely configurations.

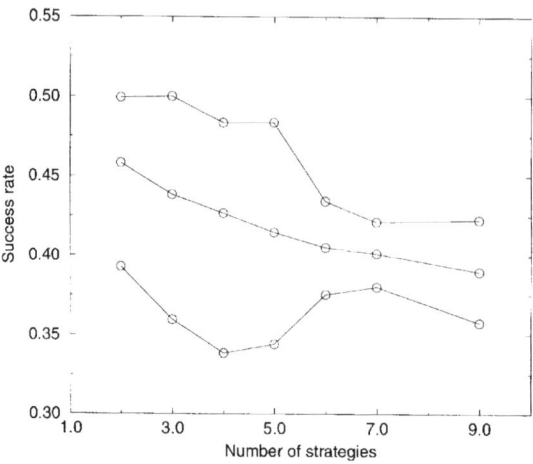

Fig. 5. Success rate against the number of strategies ($N = 1001$, $M = 5$).

One may enquire what happens if the players are provided with a bigger "idea bag" with more alternative strategies. In Fig. 5 we show the results for various populations ($N = 1001$, $M = 5$) with $S = 2, 3, \ldots, 9$. We see that, in general, with increasing number of alternatives the players tend to perform worse. What happens is that the players tend to switch strategies often and are more likely to get "confused", i.e. some outperforming strategy may distract the player's attention, after being chosen turns out to be underperforming. We recognise this has also to do with the observation time, currently a player switches immediately if another strategy has one virtual point more than that in use. If a higher threshold is set, then the hinderance by increasing the number of alternatives can be in part avoided. In the neural network version of our game, just one network (with adjustable weights) is given to a player. Let us recall that in a recent study, Borkar et al. [5] have proven that in an evolutionary game players tend to specialise in a single strategy, even though alternatives exist.

In Fig. 6 we plot the switching rate against the success rate for various populations. The general tendency that the oftener one switches, less successfull one would end up. The phase space seems to be highly fragmented and many substructures appear, this having to do with the binary nature of our game.

It is also instructive to follow the performance record. In Fig. 7, we select 3 top players, 3 bottom players and 3 randomly chosen players. They are chosen at the last time step and we trace back their past record. Their capital gains are scaled such that the average gain (over the population) appears in an almost horizontal line. We see that the general tendency for best and worst players are rather consistent even though setbacks for the best and bursts for the worst do occur. Notice that the gap between the

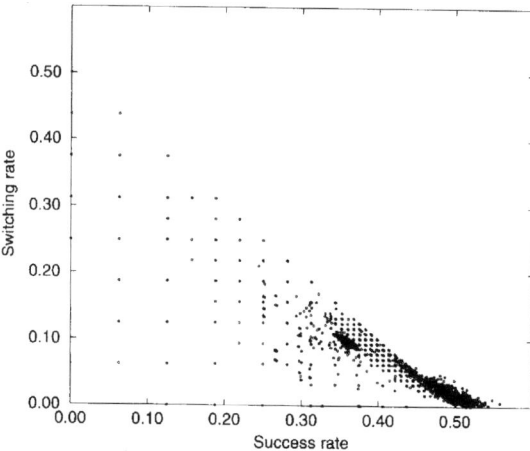

Fig. 6. Switching rate against the success rate for various populations.

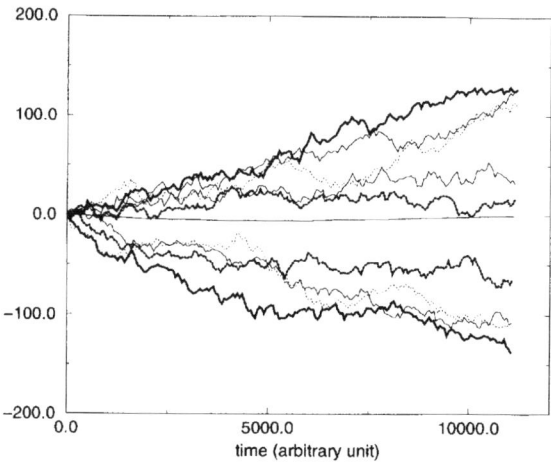

Fig. 7. Performance record of the 3 best, the 3 worst and 3 randomly chosen players ($N = 1001$, $M = 10$, $S = 5$).

rich and the poor appears to increase linearly with time, though reversion is possible but the poor players in general are doomed to stay poor.

Another result enhances this conclusion: one may blame bad players for their bad strategies. In order to check whether there are really good and bad strategies, we plot the virtual gains of all the strategies in the population. In Fig. 8 we see three different

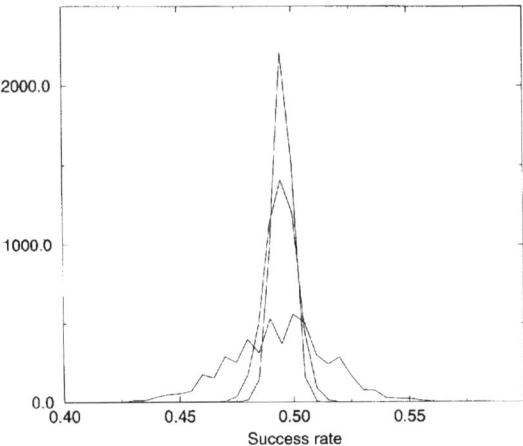

Fig. 8. Different distributions of the average value of all the strategies with increasing iterations numbers (1000, 5000 and 10000), showing that all strategies are equivalent in the $t \to \infty$ limit.

distributions of the average (time) gains. The longer the time the more concentrate is the distribution, indicating that the relative values of the strategies are about the same. Indeed, it can be analytically shown that all the strategies are equivalent to each other, since our game is symmetrical in A and B. So the bad players are bad because they have used the strategies inopportunely and are unlucky, also their specific composition is to blame. Note that a player is only distinguished from others by this composition, if two players have the same composition, they are clone sisters. In that case, initial conditions can still set them apart and they may know different fortunes only in the beginning.

The above discussion calls for a genetic approach in which the poor players are regulary weeded out from the game and new players are introduced to replace the eliminated ones. Let us consider our minority game generalised to include the Darwinist selection: the worst player is replaced by a new one after a finite time steps, the new player is a clone of the best player, i.e. it inherits all the strategies but with corresponding virtual capitals reset to zero. This is analogous to a new born baby, though having all the predispositions from the parents, it does not inherit their knowledge.

To keep a certain diversity, we introduce mutation possibility in cloning. We allow one of the strategies of the best player to be replaced by a new one. Since strategies are not just recycled among the players any more, the whole strategy phase space is available for selection. We expect this population is capable of "learning" since self-destructive, obviously bad players are weeded out with time, fighting is among so-to-speak the best players. Indeed, in Fig. 9 we observe that the learning has emerged in time. Fluctuations are reduced and saturated, this implies the average gain for everybody is improved but never reaches the ideal limit. What would happen if no mutation

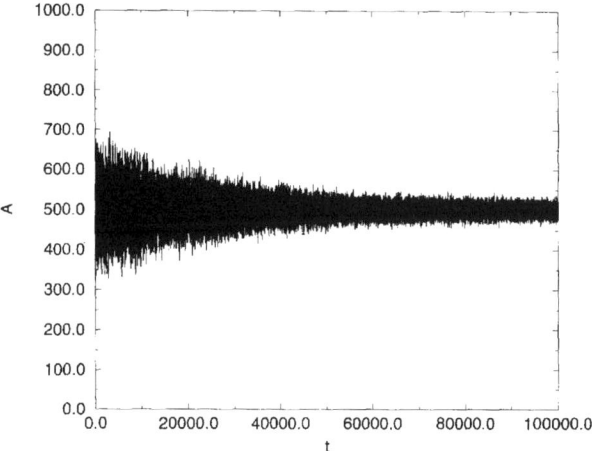

Fig. 9. Temporal attendance of A for the genetic approach showing a learning process.

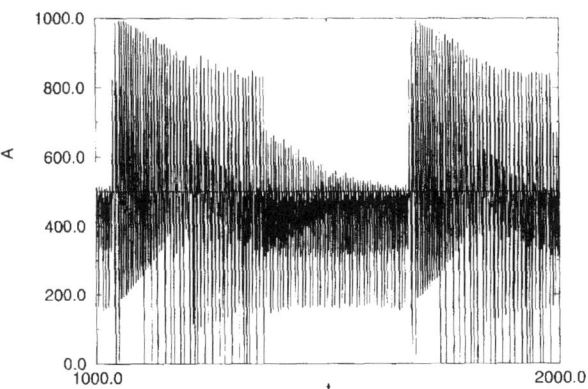

Fig. 10. Temporal attendance of A of an "pure" population.

is allowed and cloning is perfect? Eventually, population is full of the clone copies of the best player, each may still differ in their decision since the virtual capitals in their idea-bag can be different. In Fig. 10 we plot the performance of such a "pure" population; there appears tremendous waste and all strange things go loose. Indeed, the results from inbreeding look rather incestous.

As a last experiment we start the population very "simple-minded", say $M = 2$. We allow in the cloning process mentioned above an additional feature that a bit of memory can be added or subtracted for the cloned new player, with a small probability. We

416

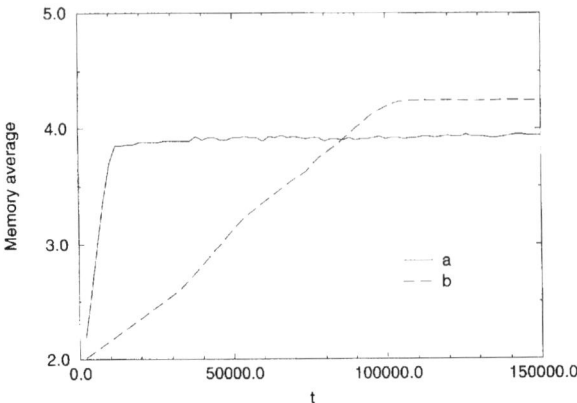

Fig. 11. Temporal record of the memory average starting from $M = 2$ population for $N - 101$ (a) and $N = 1001$ (b) $(S = 5)$.

want to be sure that the rules are such that this structural mutation is strictly neutral, i.e. does not favour bigger brains over the smaller ones; we leave this to the invisible hand of evolution to decide. Indeed, something remarkable takes place: in Fig. 11 we plot the average brain size in the population started with $M = 2$, for population of $N = 101$ and $N = 1001$. The temporal record shows that there is an "arm race" among the players. We know by now that the more brain power leads to advantage, so in the evolution of survival-of-the-fittest the players develop bigger brains to cope with ever-aggressive fellow players. However, such an evolution appears to saturate and the "arm race" to settle at a given level. The saturation values are not universal, having to do with the time intervals of reproduction. In general, the larger brains need longer time to learn. Larger population ($N = 1001$) needs more powerful brains to sustain the apparent equilibrium than the smaller population ($N = 1001$), also the learning rate (the slope in Fig. 11) is smaller. We mention *en passant* that population's brain sizes do not concentrate on one value, only the average value is plotted. Some players manage to make do quite happily with a relatively small brain.

To conclude, what can we learn from these simple numerical experiments? First of all, the economical behaviour in the real-world seems to call for a general approach to systematically study the evolutionary nature of games. There are few most relevant questions to address: (1) Given each agent's selfishness what is his cooperative and cognitive skills in the course of competition? (2) What is the emerging collective behaviour that is the society's performance without an enforceable authority? (3) How can our *visible* hand modify the rules of the game (payoff functions) such that the global response may appear more cooperative? (4) How does evolution puts its *invisible* hand to work? Clearly, our study is far from answering all these. What we have presented in this work is not just an oversimplied model, but a general approach to ask the right questions. This approach, as the reader can readily convince himself, is very open to all sorts of variations. It is easy to include other situation-motivated payoff functions and game structures, there are qualitatively new questions to be asked when more realistic games are studied. It is a theoretical physicist's dream to have an Ising-type model, though oversimplified, and yet to capture some essential points of the real world. Our minority game may be indeed the simplest of the kind.

Our model is by design without fundamentals and insider information. Players are forced to fight each other. With the Darwinism included, everyone has to keep improving in order to survive – the *red-queen* effect. Unlike some examples in standard game theory, there is no commonly accepted optimal strategy (analogous to physical systems without obvious ground states). A rational approach is helpless here. Yet the emerging society appears to have a certain organisation. Even though the players care only their own gain, cooperation and timing does seem to spontaneously arise. Note that our learning mechanism is different from the traditional neural network studies, where a *pre-assigned* task like a pattern is given and performance is measured on how precisely the original is restored. Here the task is self-appointed and no ending is defined.

We may even speak of the emergence of intelligence. If the analysing power of the players can adapt to the increasingly challenging task (survival amongst ever-aggressive fellow players and larger number of players), the population seems to evolve to more equipped, larger brains appear to dominate and available resources are better explored, i.e. less fluctuation and waste in the attendance number. This is not unsimilar to the study of the prebiotic evolution: in the promodial soup only very simple organisms exist. Evolution allows these organisms to add one new feature (and reduce an existing one) from time to time. More complex organisms cope with the survival task better, on average, and more and more refined organisms spontaneously appear out of the monotonous soup [6].

We thank Matteo Marsili for helpful conversations. This work has been supported in part by the Swiss National Foundation through the Grant No. 20-46918.96.

References

[1] K. Arrow, D. Pines, P.W. Anderson (Eds.), The Economy as an Evolving Complex System, Addison-Wesley, Redwood City, 1988.
[2] J.W. Weibull, Evolutionary Game Theory, MIT Press, Cambridge, 1995.
[3] M. Marsili, Y.-C. Zhang, Fluctuations around Nash equilibria in game theory, Physica A 245 (1997) 181.
[4] W.B. Arthur, Inductive reasoning and bounded rationality, Am. Econ. Assoc. Papers and Proc. 84, 1994, pp. 406–411.
[5] V.S. Borkar, S. Jain, G. Rangarajan, Dynamics of individual specialization and global diversification in communities, preprint, Bangalore, IISc-CTS-3/97, 1997.
[6] Y.-C. Zhang, Quasispecies evolution of finite population, Phys. Rev. E 55 (1997) R3815.

Evolving Models of Financial Markets

The physics of financial markets is an emerging science. In the second part of a guide to this new field, one of its exponents, **Yi-Cheng Zhang** of Fribourg University, outlines the theory behind some of his own models of the market-place

A new trend has arisen recently: more and more physicists have been attracted to economy-related problems. Evidence of this is the growth in the numbers of papers in physics journals devoted to theoretical and applied issues in economics and finance. In addition, fresh PhDs and seasoned researchers alike are finding careers in finance, new journals are being launched and conferences organized.

Trespassing on the domain of others is a notorious activity of physicists: their insatiable curiosity steadily pushes them into their near and far neighbours' territories such as biology, economics and other natural and social disciplines.

The current predilection seems to be for economics, especially finance. One can probably recognise two reasons for the interest. Firstly, physicists' tools are much in demand and so-called 'technical analysis' has become more and more complex so that an experienced physicist can offer skills that traditionally-trained economists lack. Secondly, such research topics present fundamental, intellectual challenges where the aim is to understand the basic mechanism. In this essay we shall concentrate on this second aspect. Moreover, we shall limit ourselves to modelling mechanisms of financial markets.

What Makes it Interesting

To appreciate why economics is interesting for physicists and what challenges there are, one has to know about the currently accepted theory in the economics field. I will not pretend to summarize the state-of-the-art here; a critical appraisal can be found in the Santa Fe proceedings (The Economy as an Evolving Complex System, ed. P.W. Anderson, K. Arrow and D. Pines, Redwood City, Addison-Wesley 1988). If one looks into the economics literature as a physicist, one may get the strange feeling that the theory is detached

from the experiment. On the one hand, the theory is extremely refined and self-consistent with little effort made to compare it with empirical evidence; on the other hand, the experiments (ie market traders at work) are extensively performed with little reference to the theory. It is revealing to see how George Soros, one of the top players in global finance, considers the theory. His very success is an embarrassment to the orthodox theory; he considers it to be hardly relevant (see Alchemy of Finance, J. Wiley & Sons, New York 1994).

In short, current prevailing theory assumes equilibrium and its descriptions are mostly static. Little is said of how equilibrium can be attained, if it is attainable at all. Such descriptions look like 'mean field' theory of physics. The dynamics of markets can be found nowhere. However, insight gained in statistical mechanics, especially in non-equilibrium processes, may inspire a physicist to have a try in formulating a sort of dynamic theory for some economic processes.

There is no shortage of data. But data of crashes, for example, defy explanation. One is tempted to compare the current state of affairs to thermodynamics before Boltzmann or even Carnot – the framework has not yet been established. One does not know how to put the pieces of empirical law together to form a coherent picture. But let us not carry this comparison too far, since economics provides less precise data, and the fundamental elements are *thinking agents* as compared to the obedient particles in thermodynamics. One can never hope to get a future economic theory as quantitative and predictive as those of physical laws (Traders would die of joy if they could foretell prices as well as we can predict the weather). However, this should not deter us from

searching for a framework to understand some basic phenomena qualitatively.

While hoping not to offend our colleagues, we might say that current research in statistical mechanics is somewhat stagnant, in contrast to the exciting times of the 70s and 80s. The 'soft' science of economics presents new challenges, new problems and new ways of thinking; it can teach us some new secrets of how Nature works.

How to build a model

Lacking a general framework one has to search for models in the dark. Before we present our own choice, let us recall that our aim has to be very modest; the best one can have is a sort of paradigm. One also has to keep the model as simple as possible, in order to say something general. One has in mind here the Ising Model which, despite its oversimplification, still offers insight into real magnetism; or the BTW Self-Organized Criticality Model (see P. Bak, C. Tang, and K. Wiesenfeld; Self-Organized Criticality *Phys. Rev. Lett.* 60 (1988) 2347), which apparently applies only to ideal sand piles but turns out to offer insight into many natural phenomena.

Let us list a minimal set of ingredients that are indispensable for modelling markets:

- A large number of independent agents participating in a market.
- Each agent has some choice available when making a decision.
- The aggregate activity results in a market price, which is known to all agents.
- Agents use this public price history to make their decisions.

We omit from the ingredients two important factors. One, no fundamental news (ie economic news from the outside world) reaches the market traders besides news of their own trading activity; and two, agents do not believe in any theory (ie traders do not derive their predictions from an established theory, but use some *ad hoc* personal rules; they learn from their own experience, and believe that the price history contains information). In this way we can begin to study the inherent dynamics of a market, in the absence of external influences, even though real economies have both internal and external components.

W. B. Arthur has advocated the so-called 'inductive thinking' approach (see Inductive Reasoning and Bounded

We thank the author and The European Physical Society for granting us permission for reprinting this paper.

Rationality, *Am. Econ. Assoc. Papers and Proc.* 84 (1994) p 406–411) which corresponds to the opinion of a minority in economics. His idea is that since an agent cannot use theory to make a decision, his (or her) only choice is to learn from his own experience, as many a trader would attest to. Our own model is inspired from Arthur's El Farol problem, described in the above paper. We shall illustrate our ideas using two models. The first (the minority model) is intended to reveal the rich intrinsic market dynamics and general issues; the second (the trading model) is an attempt to apply the basic ideas to an artificial market.

The Minority Model

The simplest model we can think of is defined in the form of an evolutionary game. Let us consider a population of N (odd number) players. The game evolves discretely in time steps. At each time step, everybody has to choose to be on either side A or B. The payoff of the game is that, after everyone has chosen sides independently, those who are on the side of the minority win. In the simplest version all winners receive one point. Players make decisions based on the past record, which is common knowledge. But the past record only records which side was the winning side, without the actual attendance number.

The time series (the sides chosen or won) can be represented by a binary sequence, 1 or 0 meaning A or B is the chosen or winning side. Let us assume that our players are quite limited in their analysing power; they can only remember the last M bits of the system's results and can only make their next decision based on these M bits. Each player has a finite set of available strategies, S. A strategy is defined as the next action (to choose either A, B; or rather 1, 0) given a specific past record (of M bits). An example of one strategy is illustrated in *table* 1 for $M = 3$.

There are 8 (= 2^M) bits we can assign to the decision. Each configuration of 8 bits corresponds to a distinct strategy, this makes the total number of strategies $2^{2^M} = 256$. This is indeed a fastly increasing number, for $M = 2, 3, 4, 5$ it is 16, 256, 65536, 655362.

We randomly draw S strategies for each player from this pool. All S strategies in a player's bag can collect points depending on whether they would win or not given the past M bits and the actual outcome of the next play. However, these are only *virtual* points as they record the merit of a

strategy as if it were used. The player actually puts into play the strategy which has accumulated the most virtual points, and gets a real point only if this strategy used happens to win in the next play. The method of using alternative strategies makes the players adaptive to the market. A player thus tends to maximize his capital (accumulated points) and his performance is judged only on his time averaged capital gain.

Several remarks are in order. By the very definition of minority, agents are not encouraged to form commonly-agreed views on the market. This is like real market trading: bears and bulls live together. In real trading it is often observed that a minority of traders first get into a trend (buying or selling), then the majority get dragged in. When the minority anticipates correctly and gets out of the trend in time, it pockets the profit at the expense of the majority. There are limited resources available for competition. If the players manage to coordinate well, per play they can expect $(N - 1)/2$ points, the maximum gain possible. Since our players are selfish, no explicit coordination is imposed and their fate is left to the market. The important question is whether they can somehow learn to spontaneously cooperate. $S = 1$ simplifies further the model so that, instead of the players, the strategies compete directly. The outcome is a trivial deterministic set of results. The extra layer of complexity at the player's level ensures adaptability.

This binary model is very suitable for numerical experiments. Damien Challet, a graduate student at Fribourg, implemented the game on a computer. (The preliminary results are reported in D. Challet and Y.-C. Zhang, Emergence of Cooperation in an Evolutionary Game, *Physica A* 246

record	decision
000	1
001	0
010	0
011	1
100	1
101	0
110	1
111	0

Table 1 An example strategy. The decision on which side to choose next is based on the last three winning sides (the record). If the last three wins were 001, then the decision would be 0. The eight decisions together make up the strategy

(1997) 407). Note the word 'experiment' instead of 'simulation' is used at the beginning of this paragraph. This is to emphasize that we did not have precise goals at the start – as in an exploratory experiment the players are let loose to play and we observe. But we were rather amazed by the complex, rich consequences of the model.

There are just three parameters in the model: N, M and S. However, there are hidden parameters, which is illustrated by looking at the total number of strategies. At first glance this number seems so huge that even for realistic parameter values, say $M = 10$, this number would be regarded as infinite ($2^{2^M} > 10^{300}$) for all practical purposes. And the number is so large that you would not expect changing it to have any effect on the model. But numerical experiments show that this is not the case. Depending on N the market has distinct behaviour, $M = 10$ can, in fact, be too large or too small for achieving coordination.

How can such a large number (10^{300}) still be relevant in this model? This apparently large number *is* irrelevant in the model; a much smaller (but hidden) parameter is actually responsible for the dynamics. A more refined analysis of the strategy space shows this.

Boolean 'Genetic' Space

It is instructive to represent the strategy space on a 2^M-dimensional Boolean hypercube. The $N_{tot} = 2^{2^M}$ distinct strategies are on the points (corners) of the hypercube. (This has a striking similarity with the construction of S. Kauffman's Boolean NK network, *see* The Origins of Order, Oxford University Press, New York 1993). Consider two neighbouring strategies which differ only in one bit (*ie* differ in one decision).

We say that the Hamming distance between the two strategies is one. The two strategies almost always predict the same outcome when acting on the past record: out of 2^M possibilities there is only one exception. Therefore, distinct strategies can be highly correlated. And players using correlated strategies tend to obtain the same decision, thus hindering their chance of finding the minority side. Among the N_{tot} strategies there is a huge redundancy. If two strategies are uncorrelated, their decision outcomes should match with 1/2 probability. This is possible if their Hamming distance is 1/2 of the maximal value (2^M). We are thus led to count mutually uncorrelated strategies. This count will provide a crucial measure of diversity (or independence) of the N_{tot} strategies.

We recall now some useful basic properties of a hypercube. There is a subset of 2^M pairs of points (out of N_{tot}) in which, for each pair, the Hamming distance is maximum (2^M). They are anti-correlation pairs in the sense that the two strategies of a pair always predict opposite actions. All other Hamming distances among these $N_o = 2^{M+1}$ points are 2^{M-1}, ie mutually independent. In other words, these N_o points are composed of two groups of 2^M points each. Within the group the strategies are completely independent. Some of the cross-group links can be anti-correlated.

It is this reduced number N_o which plays an important role in the model. If the number of strategies in the population (NS) is larger than N_o then the players have to use strategies which are positively correlated. The herd effect (of most agents doing the same thing) is unavoidable despite the adaptability of the players, and will result in fluctuations larger than random chance would warrant, which leads to a waste of the limited resources. On the other hand, if $NS << N_o$ then the 'independent' subset of strategies indeed appears to be independent. NS cannot sample enough of the N_o strategies, the anti-correlation Hamming distances are hardly represented (they appear with probability proportional to NS/N_o). The players in this case will appear as if they were using random strategies, independent from each other. Most interesting is the critical case when $NS \sim N_o$, ie when the reduced set is more or less covered by the population. The majority of their mutual Hamming distances implies independence, but a small part (about the square-root of the total) implies anti-correlation. This means that the players behave almost independently, the small number of anti-correlation Hamming distances help them to obtain opposite decisions. This is beneficial for everybody since coordinated avoidance makes the players more evenly distributed on the two sides, and the limited resources are better exploited. There are, therefore, three distinct phases:

1. The overcrowded phase, $NS > N_o$, where positive correlation is inevitable. The herd effect makes it worse for everybody.

2. A cooperative or critical region, $NS \sim N_o$ where the strategies used by N players are mostly independent (plus some anti-correlation links which achieve mutual

avoidance). The resource is better shared.

3. A random region $NS << N_o$ where anti-correlation is hardly present, and strategies appear to be independent.

A recent numerical study is in qualitative agreement with the above analytical result (*see* R. Savit, R. Manuca and R. Riolo, Adaptive Competition, Market Efficiency, Phase Transitions and Spin-Glasses *Michigan Univ. Pre-print*, December 1997).

Darwinism and Evolution

Between the over-competitive and random phases lies the critical region, $NS \sim N_o$, where cooperation emerges. This reminds us of Kauffman's often quoted motto "adaptation toward the edge of chaos". The competing population has different phases of collective behaviour, depending on the choice of N, M and S. We see from the above discussion that adaptation gives an evolutionary pressure

━━━━━━━━━━━━━━

Many an investor figures out his chances by simulation, and is then attracted to markets if he believes he has an edge. But often the subsequent participation can be disappointing

━━━━━━━━━━━━━━

to players' strategies, and they tend to be as diversified as possible. In the $NS > N_o$ region this pressure, or tendency, is frustrated since the strategy space (the hypercube) is too crowded. To relieve this pressure, one may want to change S or M for fixed N. Changing S is not very efficient. Increasing M is highly effective because of the exponential dependence.

However, we would like to let the population evolve to this cooperative region without fine tuning the parameters. To this end we introduce another level of adaptation by adding Darwinism to this game of competition. The worst player is periodically eliminated from the game; the best player is allowed to produce an offspring. The new born player is a clone copy of his parent, but with his virtual capital reset to zero. And a small mutation rate is assumed to ensure genetic diversity – one of his inherited strategies is replaced. The total population is kept constant without loss of generality. The newly drawn strategy can have its M changed by one unit. This permits the players to find the best suitable M. The population can

nevertheless reach a stationary state, clearly with inhomogeneous M. In short, the population is able to evolve without outside intervention and self-organize itself to find the critical region $NS \sim N_o$ which is beneficial for everybody.

Another interesting variant is to let the strategies fight directly without the players as intermediaries ($S = 1$). In order to have non-trivial dynamics going on, we allow a large number (N_t) of randomly drawn strategies to participate in the game passively, only a small number of strategies of the total ($N_a << N_t$) actively play. The passive strategies observe the system's posting board and count their virtual gain (as if they had taken part in the game). If one strategy's simulated gain is above a certain threshold, say a benchmark average of the actual game, it is bullish enough to come to the fore by becoming an active strategy. The worst strategies recede to the status of passive observers. Each strategy has two balance sheets, one for the accumulated real gain during its active playing periods; another for simulated gain counted from the last time it was relegated to the observer pool. In this variant the Darwinistic evolutionary pressure is also operative. Positively correlated strategies may do well as observers, but do poorly in actual play. Therefore, their active appearance is bound to be brief. Most interesting is to let the number of active strategies N_a free, everyone is allowed to actively play, and the market should decide how many actually do. Clearly, inhomogeneous M is better and mutation should also be operative in order to keep an adequate diversity. The system is like a grand-canonical ensemble. A large pool of observers is also a realistic feature of markets. Many an investor figures out his chances by simulation, and is then attracted to markets if he believes that he has an edge. But often the subsequent participation can be disappointing.

A Prototype Trading Model

The minority model, though very rich, still lacks some of the most basic features of a real market; the price, for example, which is determined by the aggregate supply and demand. We want to keep the above general ingredients to build a more specific trading model. In a trading model players have to decide when to buy and sell, just like taking sides A or B in the minority model. However, the payoff is not a fixed rule, it depends on the price movement which is in turn determined by the players' trading. In the modern market of stocks, currencies, and commodities, trading patterns are becoming more and more global. Market-moving information is available to everybody. However, not all the participants interpret the information in the same way and react at the same time delay. In fact, every participant has a certain fixed framework for facing external events. And it is well known that the global market is far from being at equilibrium, the collective behaviour of the market can occasionally have violent bursts.

Let us define our model more precisely. Each player is initially given the same amount of capital in two forms: cash and stock. There is only one stock in this model. All trading consists of switching back and forth between cash and this stock. Each player has a strategy that makes recommendations for buying or selling a certain amount of stock at the next time step. This depends solely on the price history. Player i's strategy is an arbitrary non-linear function, $F_i(p_t, p_{t-1}, \ldots)$, positive (or negative) values suggest the amount of buying (or selling). The aggregate trading decides the price at the next time tick, p_{t+1}, using the law of supply and demand. Darwinism is also implemented here.

The results of this model are quite encouraging (see G. Caldarelli, M. Marsili and Y.-C. Zhang, A Prototype Model of

Stock Exchange, *Europhys. Lett.* 40 (1997) 479). Despite the simplicity and the arbitrariness of the strategies, an extremely rich price history is created. A sample of P_t is shown in *figure* 1, which shows fluctuations of all sizes. During long runs, depending on the parameters, crashes occasionally occur with no warning. New features appear here with respect to the minority model. Even though the same self-organized structure is used here, the system does not appear to reach equilibrium, there is hardly any limit to the range of the price fluctuations. This is due partly to the continuous strategy space, as well as the law of supply and demand.

We have discussed two models of self-organized systems, in which players compete in a common market-place using the results produced by their own activities. We argue that this general scenario should also be present in real markets.

Open Questions and Perspectives

As one would expect from the early stages of any emergent scientific discipline – it has been baptised 'econophysics' – many different models have been proposed. We feel the current need is to learn how to ask the right questions about economic processes. By asking the right questions and by trying to answer them, we have to explore many seemingly isolated models and empirical laws to be able to set up a

workable framework. Already, at the level of the simplest minority model, we see that many interdisciplinary subjects have without intention been touched upon, including self-organized criticality, population and Darwinism, ecology, information science, glasses and spin-glasses (*see* A Random Walk in Search of the Glass Transition in this issue), Kauffman's NK model and auto-catalysis, game theory (Prisoner's dilemma pits two players against each other, the minority game is a natural generalisation). Many of these relations deserve further study. Besides some relevance to economics, continuing this exercise of model building and playing is certainly rewarding.

The author would like to thank G. Caldarelli, D. Challet and M. Marsili for a fruitful collaboration

Thoughts on what econophysicists should be doing, written by Marcel Ausloos, appear on page 70, and are followed by a reply from Yi-Cheng Zhang

Past issue
See the last issue of
Europhysics News (29 1)
which carried an article
on the Caldarelli-Marsili-
Zhang model

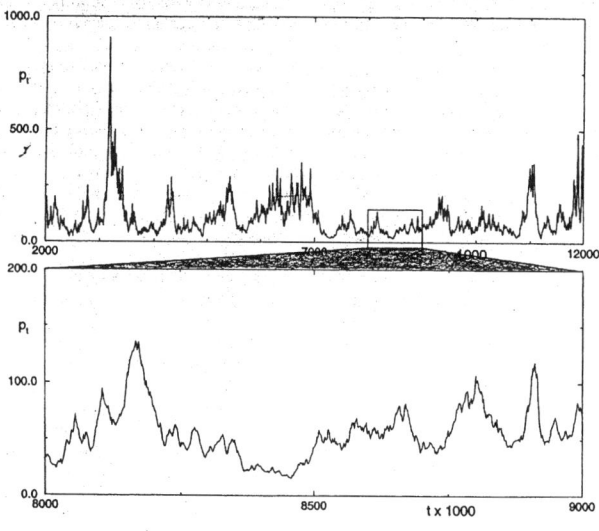

Fig 1 Price history of an artificial trading model. Fluctuations in the price look the same no matter what timescale is used, which is also true of real market data. In fact, the statistical properties of this artificial price index are in reasonable agreement with real data (*see* Mantegna and Stanley, *Nature* 379 (1995) 46)

Adaptive Competition, Market Efficiency, and Phase Transitions

Robert Savit, Radu Manuca, and Rick Riolo

Program for the Study of Complex Systems and Physics Department, University of Michigan, Ann Arbor, Michigan 48109

(Received 3 August 1998)

In many social and biological systems agents simultaneously and adaptively compete for limited resources, thereby altering their environment. We analyze a simple model that incorporates fundamental features of such systems. If the space of strategies available to the agents is small, the system is in a phase in which all information available to the agents' strategies is traded away, and agents' choices are maladaptive, resulting in a poor collective utilization of resources. For larger strategy spaces, the system is in a phase in which the agents are able to coordinate their actions to achieve a better utilization of resources. The best utilization of resources occurs at a critical point, when the dimension of the strategy space is on the order of the number of agents. [S0031-9007(99)08619-6]

PACS numbers: 02.50.Le, 05.65.+b, 05.70.Fh, 87.23.Ge

Most systems in the biological and social sciences involve interacting agents, each making behavioral choices in the context of an environment that is formed, in large part, by the collective action of the agents themselves, and with no centralized controller acting to coordinate agent behavior. In the most interesting cases, the agents have heterogeneous strategies, expectations, and beliefs [1]. In some cases, the agents' strategies may be self-validating, at least for a limited time. For example, in the financial markets a widespread belief that a commodity will rise in price may perforce result in a price rise for that commodity. But unless there are fundamental reasons for the price rise, such bubbles eventually burst, so that widely shared strategies are often self-defeating in the long run. Thus, in many systems successful agents will employ strategies that differentiate them from their competitors. Furthermore, from the point of view of overall system performance, the best strategy sets are those that result in coordinated resource utilization so that average agent experience is relatively good, and resources are consumed near their limiting rates. Examples of systems in which agents seek to differentiate themselves from their competitors, and in which coordinated allocation of resources is critical, include firms searching for profitable technological innovations, ecological communities [2], routers sending packets over the internet [3], and humans deciding on which night to go to a popular bar [1].

Although these systems are enormously complicated, there are fundamental properties which are shared by all of them. To understand such systems, we must first understand the dynamics imposed by their most basic common properties.

The simple model of competition we discuss here [4] consists of N agents playing a game as follows: At each time step of the game, each of the N agents joins one of two groups, labeled 0 or 1. Each agent that is in the minority group at that time step is awarded a point, while each agent belonging to the majority group gets nothing. An agent chooses which group to join at a given time step based on the prediction of a strategy. The strategy uses information from the historical record of which group was the minority group as a function of time. A strategy of memory m is a table of two columns and 2^m rows. The left column contains all of the 2^m possible combination of m 0's and 1's, while each entry in the right column is a 0 or a 1. To use this strategy, an agent observes which groups were the minority groups during the immediately preceding m time steps, and finds that string of 0's and 1's in the left column of the table. The corresponding entry in the right column contains that strategy's determination of which group (0 or 1) the agent should join during the current time step.

In each of the games discussed here, all strategies used by all of the agents have the same value of m. At the beginning of the game each agent is randomly assigned s (>1) of the 2^{2^m} possible strategies, chosen with replacement [5]. For its current play the agent chooses its strategy that would have had the best performance over the history of the game until that time. Ties between strategies are decided by a coin toss. Because the agents each have more than one strategy, the game is adaptive in that agents can choose to play different strategies at different moments of the game in response to changes in their environment. Because the environment (i.e., the time series of minority groups) is created by the collective action of the agents themselves, and because the relative rankings of the agents' strategies depend on their previous successes, this system has strong collective feedback.

This system may be though of as a very simple model for a number of different situations in the social and biological sciences. In particular, this system can be interpreted as a kind of very simple "protomarket," driven by a simple supply-demand dynamic [6].

We report here the results of this game for a range of values of N (odd), m, and $s = 2$. The qualitative results also hold for other values of s that are not extremely large [7]. We must also create a short (of order m) random history of 0's and 1's, so that the strategies can be initially evaluated. The asymptotic statistical results of any run do not materially depend on what this random string is.

0031-9007/99/82(10)/2203(4)$15.00

To understand the behavior of this system, consider the time series of the number of agents belonging to group 1, which we will call L_1. (This information is not available to the agents but it is available to the researchers.) The mean of this series is generally close to $N/2$ for all values of N, m, and s, so the standard deviation σ of this time series is a convenient reciprocal measure of how effective the system is at distributing resources, on average, since the smaller σ is, the larger a typical minority group is.

The behavior of σ is quite remarkable. In Fig. 1, we plot σ for these time series as a function of m for $N = 101$ and $s = 2$. For each value of m, 32 independent runs were performed. The horizontal dashed line in this graph is at the value of σ for the random choice game (RCG), i.e., for the game in which each agent randomly chooses 0 or 1, independently and with equal probability at each time step. Note the following features: (1) For small m, the average value of σ is very large (much larger than in the RCG). In addition, for $m < 6$ there is a large spread in the σ's for different runs with different (random) initial distributions of strategies to the agents, but with the same m. (2) There is a minimum in σ at $m = 6$ at which σ is less than the standard deviation of the RCG. We shall refer to the value of m at which the σ vs m curve (for fixed N) has its minimum as m_c. Also, for $m \geq m_c$, the spread in the σ's appears to be small relative to the spread for $m < m_c$. (3) As m increases beyond 6, σ slowly increases, and for large m approaches the value for the RCG.

The system clearly behaves in a qualitatively different way for small and large m. To understand the dynamics in these two regions, consider the (binary) time series of minority groups G, the data publicly available to the agents. To study the information content of G, consider $P(1 \mid u_k)$, the conditional probability to have a 1 immediately following some specific string, u, of k elements. Recall that in a game played with memory m, the strategies use only the information encoded in strings of length m to make their

choices. In Fig. 2, we plot $P(1 \mid u_k)$ for G generated by a game with $m = 4$, $N = 101$, and $s = 2$. Figure 2(a) shows the histogram for $k = m = 4$ and Fig. 2(b) shows the histogram for $k = 5$. Note that the histogram is quite flat at 0.5 in Fig. 2(a), but is not flat in Fig. 2(b). Thus, for any strategy with memory (less than or equal to 4, the history of minority groups contains no predictive information about which will be the minority group at the next time step. But recall that this time series itself was generated by players playing strategies with $m = 4$. Therefore, in this sense, the market is efficient [8] and no strategy using memory (less than or equal to 4 can, over the long run, have a success rate better than 50%. But G is not a random (IID) sequence. There is information in G, as indicated by the fact that the histogram in Fig. 2(b) is not flat. However, that information is not available to the strategies of the agents playing the $m = 4$ game who collectively generated G in the first place. We shall refer to this property as "strategy efficient" to distinguish it from other kinds of market efficiency [8].

We can repeat this analysis for $m \geq 6$ ($N = 101$, $s = 2$). For this range of m, the corresponding histogram for $k = m$ is not flat, as we see in Fig. 3 for the $m = 6$ game. In this case, there is significant information available to the strategies of the agents playing the game with memory m and the market is not efficient in this sense.

How does the system behavior depend on N? One finds, plotting σ vs m for each fixed N, that in all cases one obtains a graph with a shape similar to that of Fig. 1, but

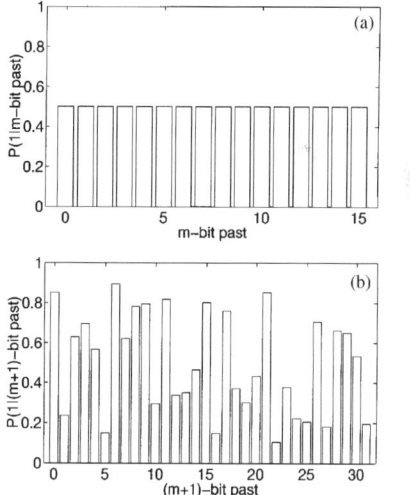

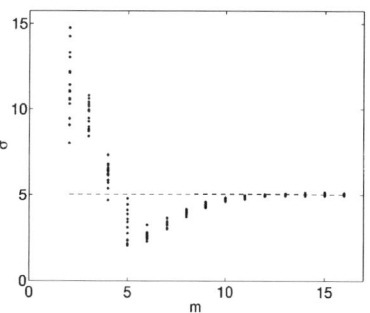

FIG. 1. σ as a function of m for $N = 101$ and $s = 2$, showing 32 independent runs of 10 000 time steps for each value of m. The value of σ for each run is indicated by a dot. The horizontal dashed line is at the value of σ for the random game described in the text.

FIG. 2. (a) A histogram of the conditional probability $P(1 \mid u_k)$ with $k = 4$ for the game played with $m = 4$. The bin numbers, when written in binary form, yield the strings u. (b) A histogram of the conditional probability $P(1 \mid u_k)$ with $k = 5$ for the game played with $m = 4$.

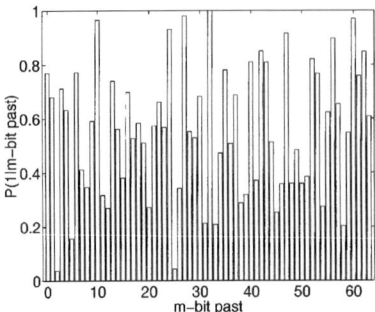

FIG. 3.   A histogram of the conditional probability $P(1\,|\,u_k)$ with $k = 6$ for the game played with $m = 6$. The bin numbers, when written in binary form, yield the strings u.

in which the position of the minimum, m_c, is proportional to $\ln N$. In addition, σ and the spread in σ behave in very simple ways as a function of N. Generally, for fixed $m < m_c$, both σ and the standard deviation of the σ's (defined as $\Delta\sigma$) are proportional to N, whereas for fixed $m \geq m_c$ both σ and $\Delta\sigma$ are proportional to $N^{1/2}$.

The transition between these very different behaviors is at $m_c \sim \ln N$. We have found [6], using mean-field-like arguments, that to a first approximation σ^2/N is a function only of $2^m/N \equiv z$. To see this explicitly, we plot in Fig. 4 σ^2/N as a function of z on a log-log scale for various N and m (with $s = 2$). Note that all of the data fall on a nearly universal curve. The minimum of this curve is near $2^{m_c}/N \equiv z_c \approx 0.5$, and separates the two different phases. The slope for $z < z_c$ approaches -1 for small z, while the slope for $z > z_c$ approaches zero for large z, consistent with the results of Fig. 4 [9]. Because σ^2/N depends only on z, it is clear that, for any fixed z, σ is proportional to $N^{1/2}$, both above and below z_c. In addition, it can be shown that, for fixed z, $\Delta\sigma$ is approximately independent

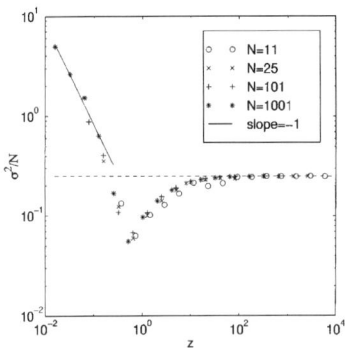

FIG. 4. σ^2/N as a function of $z \equiv 2^m/N$ for various values of N, on a log-log scale.

of N, approaching a z-dependent constant as $N \to \infty$. In the $N \to \infty$ limit, $\Delta\sigma$ is large for small values of z and decreases monotonically with increasing z. It is unclear whether or not $\Delta\sigma$ is nonanalytic at z_c.

The two phase structure we have observed is due to competition between two different effects. First, there is an embedded periodic dynamics which results in strong positive correlations in the responses of the agents to subsequent occurrences of a given string of length m in G. For small m, it can be shown [6] that the system's response to any given m history in G is largely independent of its response to other m strings. In this phase, odd occurrences of a given m string in G result in a subsequent minority group whose size is close to $N/2$, while even occurrences result in very small minority groups. Moreover, the minority group that follows an even occurrence of a given m string in G is opposite that of the preceding odd occurrence of that same string. This gives rise to a "bursty" structure in L_1 with larger, order N excursions from the mean separated by smaller excursions of order $N^{1/2}$.

It is the response of the system to the even occurrence of strings that gives rise to the large deviations from the mean in L_1, and are responsible for the fact that, in the strategy-efficient, small m phase, σ (as well as $\Delta\sigma$) is proportional to N for fixed m. This dynamic also explains the flat conditional probability distributions such as those shown in Fig. 2(a). Consecutive (odd-even) occurrences of a given string produce opposite responses in the sequence of minority groups. Consequently, the conditional probabilities will be very close to 0.5 for all m strings, for a game with small enough m. Using a simple random walk argument [6], one can show that for values of $m \geq m_c$ this period-two dynamics ceases to dominate.

The second effect, and possibly the most remarkable feature of this system, is the emergent coordination among the agents' responses to different strings of length m which works, for large enough m, to reduce σ below the value it would have in a RCG. For m near m_c, the contribution of the periodic dynamics diminishes, and we uncover this remarkable emergent property which gives rise to an improvement in overall utilization of the resource. The region of greatest effective coordination (smallest σ) is when $z = 2^m/N$ is of order one. Coordination diminishes and σ approaches the RCG result as m increases beyond m_c. This can be qualitatively understood by recalling that each chosen strategy carries with it fixed responses to 2^m different strings of length m. Thus, the ranking of strategies by each agent must coordinate the agents' responses to 2^m different strings. As m increases, for fixed N, it becomes increasingly difficult for the agents to coordinate all of their responses (systemwide there are only N choices that can be made to try to satisfy 2^m conditions), and the system's behavior will look increasingly random as m increases for fixed N.

Despite this apparent random behavior for large m, the system is not in a Nash equilibrium for large m, nor generally for any other value of m. That σ is consistent with RCG at large m is not due to a Nash equilibrium mixed strategy that one would have in the RCG. In fact, there is increasing information in G as m increases [6]. There are many Nash equilibria in a minority game, but they are not achieved by the dynamics of this system.

It is also quite remarkable that σ^2/N lies on a universal curve as a function of the scaling variable $z = 2^m/N$ (Fig. 4). Since m_c is proportional to ln N, we are led to the intriguing idea that for maximum coordination N should be roughly the same size as the *dimension* of the strategy space.

It is clear that the behavior of the system is qualitatively different for m above and below m_c. However, it is unclear whether that difference is the result of a singularity (and, thus, a bona fide phase transition at m_c) or a crossover effect, even in the limit $N \rightarrow \infty$ with z fixed. In Ref. [6] we show that information theoretic measures, including the entropy, appear to be nonanalytic at m_c (at least for large s), suggesting that a phase transition does exist, at least in the large s limit. It may also be that the phase change is accompanied by a change from a period to a nonperiodic (possibly chaotic) state [6,10].

In an effort to begin to understand the universality of our results, we have studied some models which are variations of the one described here, differing, for example, in the length of the history over which the strategies are evaluated, the nature of the publicly available information, or in some of the details of the way in which the agents choose among their strategies. While some details of the results change [6,11], the general structure remains the same. In particular, Fig. 4 is largely unchanged.

The model's general two-phase structure, with maximum utilization of resources at the phase transition (when the dimension of the strategy space is of the order of the number of agents playing the game), may well be a characteristic that transcends the class of simple models we have studies. Thus, the size of the available strategy space may be of practical significance for the structure of many systems such as financial markets and ecological systems.

Although the behavior we have elucidated is very intriguing, one must remember that there are many effects that may play a major role in specific systems and which could alter the emergent structure, fundamentally. For example, while this model is adaptive, it is not evolutionary. There is no discovery of new strategies by the agents, no mutation, no recombination, and no sex. Strong evolutionary dynamics may drastically alter the phase structure of the system. Nevertheless, any analysis of more complicated specific systems, which share the general competitive dynamics we have discussed here, must take account of the type of structure we have described.

Finally, and perhaps most importantly, our work raises the question: What really are the fundamental terms in which we ought to think about N-agent adaptive systems? For example, the fact that, for $m < m_c$, σ is so strongly dependent on the initial distribution of strategies suggests that a meaningful specification of σ must include a speci-

fication of the spread in the variance. This suggests the need for care in interpreting data from adaptive systems, or from their simulations. For the *cognescenti*, this suggests an intriguing analogy with spin glasses [12] in which the agents' random, but fixed, strategies are analogous to the frozen-in impurities found in a spin glass. In any case, it is certainly true that the phenomenon of frustration, which is at the core of glassy behavior, plays a significant role in competitive games of the sort described here.

The fact is that there is no well-developed epistemology for complex adaptive systems, and we are still quite unsure of what the important issues are or the most robust ways of characterizing the dynamics of such systems. But the study of simple statistical models, and the elucidation of the variety of behaviors which they manifest, can lead us toward a deeper understanding of how to properly frame the questions that we can sensibly ask, and sensibly answer, for complex systems.

[1] W. Brian Arthur, Am. Econ. Assoc. Papers Proc. **84**, 406–411 (1994).

[2] *Ecology and Evolution of Communities,* edited by M. L. Cody and J. M. Diamond (Harvard University, Cambridge, MA, 1975).

[3] *Coordination of the Internet,* edited by B. Kahin and J. Keller (MIT, Cambridge, MA, 1997).

[4] D. Challet and Y.-C. Zhang, Physica (Amsterdam) **246A**, 407 (1997).

[5] The dynamics of adaptivity are crucial to our results. It is thus essential that $s > 1$ so that the agents have more than one strategy with which to play. For $s = 1$, the game devolves into a game with a trivial periodic structure.

[6] R. Manuca, Y. Li, R. Riolo, and R. Savit, University of Michigan Program for the Study of Complex Systems Report No. PSCS-98-11-001 (to be published), available at http://www.pscs.umich.edu/RESEARCH/pscs-tr.html..

[7] The dependence of the results of the game on s are interesting and are discussed in Ref. [6]. However, the qualitative picture we present here obtains for $s \ll 2^{2^m}$.

[8] Classic references on market efficiency are written by E. F. Fama [J. Finance **25**, 383 (1970); **46**, 1575 (1991).] The sense in which the market is efficient here is subtle. The flat probability distribution means that the market is informationally efficient with respect to the strategies. But the market is not necessarily efficient with respect to the agents. Since the agents can switch their strategies, they could, in principle, use different strategies at different times and have a better than random success rate. In fact, in this phase the opposite happens and the agents' choices are maladaptive. See also Ref. [6].

[9] For different values of s there are systematic changes in the shape of this scaling curve, although the qualitative structure is similar. These are discussed further in Ref. [6].

[10] This may fall in the class of voting games discussed in D. Meyer and T. Brown, Phys. Rev. Lett. **81**, 1718 (1998).

[11] Y. Li, R. Riolo, and R. Savit (to be published).

[12] See, for example, *Spin Glasses,* edited by K. Fischer and J. Hertz (Cambridge University, Cambridge, England, 1991). See also Ref. [6].

THE EUROPEAN
PHYSICAL JOURNAL B

EDP Sciences
© Società Italiana di Fisica
Springer-Verlag 2001

Crowd-anticrowd theory of multi-agent market games

M. Hart[1,a], P. Jefferies[1], P.M. Hui[2], and N.F. Johnson[1]

[1] Physics Department, Oxford University, Oxford, OX1 3PU, UK
[2] Physics Department, Chinese University of Hong Kong, Shatin, Hong Kong, PR China

Received 28 August 2000 and Received in final form 23 September 2000

Abstract. We present a dynamical theory of a multi-agent market game, the so-called Minority Game (MG), based on crowds and anticrowds. The time-averaged version of the dynamical equations provides a quantitatively accurate, yet intuitively simple, explanation for the variation of the standard deviation ('volatility') in MG-like games. We demonstrate this for the basic MG, and the MG with stochastic strategies. The time-dependent equations themselves reproduce the essential dynamics of the MG.

PACS. 87.23.Ge Dynamics of social systems – 01.75.+m Science and societ – 02.50.Le Decision theory and game theory – 05.40.-a Fluctuation phenomena, random processes, noise, and Brownian motion

Agent-based games have great potential application in the study of fluctuations in financial markets. These fluctuations exhibit fascinating statistical properties [1]. Any realistic agent-based market models will necessarily be complex because of the need to incorporate real-world market factors. In reference [2] we present a discussion of such market games. In this paper we concern ourselves with the simple, yet non-trivial, Minority Game (MG) of Challet and Zhang [3,4] which is the fundamental building block for our more realistic market games [2]. The MG comprises an odd number of agents N choosing repeatedly between option 0 (*e.g.* buy) and option 1 (*e.g.* sell). The winners are those in the minority group, *e.g.* sellers win if there is an excess of buyers. The outcome at each timestep represents the winning decision, 0 or 1. A common bit-string of the m most recent outcomes is made available to the agents at each time-step [5]. The agents randomly pick s strategies at the beginning of the game, with repetitions allowed - each strategy is a bit-string of length 2^m which predicts the next outcome for each of the 2^m possible histories. Agents reward successful strategies with a (virtual) point. At each turn of the basic MG, the agent uses her most successful strategy, *i.e.* the one with the most virtual points. Here we develop a dynamical theory for MG-like games based on the formation of crowds and anticrowds.

The number of agents holding a particular combination of strategies can be written as a $D \times D \times \ldots$ (s terms) dimensional matrix Ω, where D is the total number of available strategies. For $s = 2$, this is simply a $D \times D$ matrix where the entry (i, j) represents the number of agents who picked strategy i and then j. The strategy labels are given by the decimal representation of the strategy plus unity, for example the strategy 0101 for $m = 2$ has strategy label

5+1=6. Ω is fixed at the beginning of the game ('quenched disorder') and can represent either the full strategy space or the reduced strategy space [3], depending on the choice of D. Σ is another time-independent matrix, containing all the strategies in the required space in their binary form: $\Sigma_{r,h+1}$ describes the prediction of strategy r given the history h (where h is the decimal corresponding to the m-bit binary history string).

We introduce a vector $\mathbf{n}(t)$: this contains the number of agents using each strategy at time t, in order of increasing strategy label. The vector $\mathbf{S}(t)$ contains the virtual score for each strategy at time t in order of increasing strategy label. The vector $\mathbf{R}(t)$ lists the strategy label in order of best-to-worst virtual points score at time t; if any strategies are tied in points then the strategy with the lower-value label is listed first. The vector $\boldsymbol{\rho}(t)$ shows the rank of the strategy listed in order of increasing strategy label at time t. Hence $\mathbf{R}(t)$ and $\boldsymbol{\rho}(t)$ can be found from $\mathbf{S}(t)$ using simple sort operations. The vector $\mathbf{n}(t)$ is the sum of two terms

$$\mathbf{n}(t) = \mathbf{n}^0(t) + \mathbf{n}^d(t). \tag{1}$$

Here $\mathbf{n}^0(t)$ gives the number of agents using each strategy; however where any strategies are tied in virtual score, $\mathbf{n}^0(t)$ assumes that the agent will use the strategy with the lower-value label by virtue of the definition of $\mathbf{R}(t)$. The term $\mathbf{n}^d(t)$ accounts for tied strategies, and hence provides a correction to $\mathbf{n}^0(t)$. $\mathbf{n}^0(t)$ is given by

$$\mathbf{n}^0(t)_r = \sum_{i=\rho(t)_r}^{2^{m+1}} [\widehat{F}(\Omega)]_{r,R(t)_i} \tag{2}$$

a e-mail: michael.hart@physics.ox.ac.uk

where $[\widehat{F}(\Omega)]_{\alpha,\beta} = \Omega_{\alpha,\beta} + \Omega_{\beta,\alpha} - \delta_{\alpha,\beta}\Omega_{\alpha,\beta}$. The vector $\mathbf{n}^d(t)$ is given by

$$\mathbf{n}^d(t)_r = \sum_{r' \neq r} \delta_{s(t)_{r'},s(t)_r} \mathrm{Sgn}(r - r')\mathrm{Bin}_{r',r} \quad (3)$$

where: $\mathrm{Bin}_{r',r} \sim B[(\widehat{F}(\Omega))_{r',r}, \frac{1}{2}]$ and $\mathrm{Bin}_{r',r} = \mathrm{Bin}_{r,r'}$. The standard notation Bin represents the binary distribution. Note the condition $\mathrm{Bin}_{r',r} = \mathrm{Bin}_{r,r'}$ which guarantees conservation of agents, as in the basic MG. The outcome parameter $\Upsilon(t)$ denotes which choice, 0 or 1, is the minority (and hence winning) decision at time t:

$$\Upsilon(t) = \mathcal{H}[-[\mathbf{n}(t)^T \Sigma']_{h(t)+1}] \quad (4)$$

where $\Sigma' = 2\Sigma - 1$. The history, i.e. bit-string of the m most recent outcomes, and the virtual scores of the strategies are updated as follows:

$$h(t+1) = 2[h(t) - 2^{m-1}\mathcal{H}[h(t) - 2^{m-1}]] + \Upsilon(t) \quad (5)$$

where $\mathcal{H}$ is the Heaviside function, and

$$\mathbf{S}(t+1) = \mathbf{S}(t) + \Sigma'_{h(t)+1}[2\Upsilon(t) - 1]. \quad (6)$$

Equations (1-6) are a set of time-dependent equations which reproduce the essential dynamics of the basic MG, and can be easily extended to describe MG generalizations. Iterating these equations is equivalent to running a numerical simulation, but is far easier and can even be done analytically. A slight difference may arise as a result of the method chosen for tie-breaking between strategies with equal virtual points: a numerical program will typically break this tie using a separate coin-toss for each agent, whereas the dynamical equations group together those agents using the same pair of strategies and then assign a proportion of that group to a particular strategy using a coin-toss. This difference is typically unimportant.

As an example of the implementation of these equations, consider a time t_e during the following game: $m = 2$, $s = 2$ and $N = 101$ in the reduced strategy space, with a strategy configuration Ω and strategy score given as follows:

$$\Omega = \begin{pmatrix} 2 & 3 & 2 & 3 & 5 & 3 & 1 & 1 \\ 1 & 3 & 2 & 2 & 2 & 1 & 2 & 1 \\ 1 & 0 & 2 & 0 & 1 & 3 & 1 & 3 \\ 1 & 1 & 0 & 1 & 1 & 0 & 1 & 3 \\ 4 & 5 & 1 & 1 & 2 & 0 & 0 & 0 \\ 2 & 1 & 2 & 1 & 0 & 2 & 0 & 4 \\ 1 & 2 & 1 & 2 & 0 & 0 & 2 & 4 \\ 1 & 2 & 2 & 1 & 1 & 1 & 1 & 2 \end{pmatrix}$$

$$\mathbf{S}(t_e) = \begin{pmatrix} 3 \\ -1 \\ -3 \\ 1 \\ -1 \\ 3 \\ 1 \\ -3 \end{pmatrix}, \text{ with } \Sigma = \begin{pmatrix} 0 & 0 & 0 & 0 \\ 0 & 0 & 1 & 1 \\ 0 & 1 & 0 & 1 \\ 0 & 1 & 1 & 0 \\ 1 & 0 & 0 & 1 \\ 1 & 0 & 1 & 0 \\ 1 & 1 & 0 & 0 \\ 1 & 1 & 1 & 1 \end{pmatrix}.$$

Using these values for Ω and $\mathbf{S}(t_e)$ we can obtain values for $\mathbf{n}(t)$ and ultimately $\mathbf{S}(t_e + 1)$. Ω and $\mathbf{S}(t_e)$ imply that

$$\mathbf{n}^0(t_e) = \begin{pmatrix} 31 \\ 15 \\ 7 \\ 13 \\ 5 \\ 15 \\ 13 \\ 2 \end{pmatrix}, \text{ while } \mathbf{n}^d(t_e) = \begin{pmatrix} -3 \\ -2 \\ -5 \\ 0 \\ 2 \\ 3 \\ 0 \\ 5 \end{pmatrix} \text{ with}$$

probability $p = \frac{105}{524288}$, hence yielding $\mathbf{n}(t_e)$ when summed. (When two strategies are tied, agents holding these strategies each flip a coin to decide which strategy to use. The separate probabilities obtained for the allocation of agents between all tied strategies, when multiplied together, yield the probability p of this $\mathbf{n}^d(t)$ being chosen.)

Suppose $h(t_e) = 2$, i.e. the last two minority groups were '1' then '0'. Hence $\Upsilon(t_e) = 0$, $h(t_e + 1) = 0$ and consequently

$$\mathbf{S}(t_e + 1) = \begin{pmatrix} 4 \\ -2 \\ -2 \\ 0 \\ 0 \\ 2 \\ 2 \\ -4 \end{pmatrix}.$$

An expression for the time-averaged quantity called the 'volatility' (standard deviation of the number of agents choosing one particular group) can be easily found using the above formalism:

$$\sigma_{\mathrm{MG}} = \frac{\left[\sum_{t=t_1}^{t_2}\left[\varepsilon(t) - \bar{\varepsilon}\right]^2\right]^{\frac{1}{2}}}{t_2 - t_1} \quad (7)$$

where $\varepsilon(t) = [\mathbf{n}(t)^T \Sigma]_{h(t)+1}$ and $\bar{\varepsilon}$ is the time-average of $\varepsilon(t)$ from time t_1 to t_2. Here t_1 and t_2 denote the time window over which the volatility is calculated. In the reduced

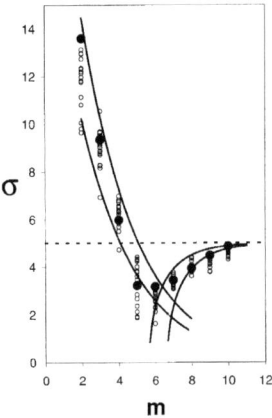

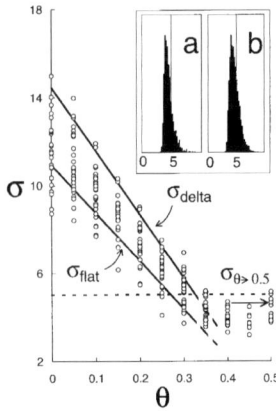

Fig. 1. Theoretical crowd-anticrowd calculation (solid circles) and numerical simulations (open circles) for the standard deviation σ in basic MG with $s = 2$ and $N = 101$. 16 numerical runs are shown for each m. Solid lines correspond to analytic expressions representing special cases within the time-averaged crowd-anticrowd theory of reference [6].

Fig. 2. Theoretical crowd-anticrowd calculation and numerical simulations (circles) for σ vs. the probability parameter θ in the stochastic MG. Here $N = 101$, $m = 2$ and $s = 2$. Monotonically decreasing solid lines correspond to analytic expressions σ_{delta} and σ_{flat} (see text). Dashed line shows random coin-toss value. Solid arrow indicates theoretical value $\sigma_{\theta \to 0.5} = 4.7$ for $\theta \to 0.5$. Inset shows distribution of σ values at $\theta = 0.5$ for several thousand randomly-chosen initial strategy configurations: (a) numerical simulation, (b) semi-analytic theory of reference [8].

strategy space [3] a similar quantity to this standard deviation can also be written down using our previously introduced (time-averaged) crowd-anticrowd framework [6]:

$$\sigma_{\text{CA}} = \frac{\sum_{t=t_1}^{t_2} \left[\frac{1}{4} \sum_{r=1}^{2^m} [\mathbf{n}(t)_r - \mathbf{n}(t)_{2^{m+1}+1-r}]^2 \right]^{\frac{1}{2}}}{t_2 - t_1}. \qquad (8)$$

For a given run of the game $\sigma_{\text{MG}} \neq \sigma_{\text{CA}}$, however these quantities become quantitatively the same (within the limits of sample size) when averaged over initial configurations of strategies [6]. σ_{CA} mirrors the semi-analytic approach introduced to motivate the time-independent crowd-anticrowd theory of reference [6] (see Fig. 1 of Ref. [6]). Indeed, the dynamical equations can be linked more formally with our previous time-averaged approach [6]. Consider a simple example where no two strategies are tied in virtual points and there are an equal number of agents having each possible pairing of strategies (low m limit and reduced strategy space), i.e. all elements in Ω are equal and non-zero. It is then easy to show that $\mathbf{n}^0(t)_r$ reduces to $\mathbf{n}^0{}_r = \frac{N}{(2^{m+1})^2}[1 + 2(2^{m+1} - \rho(t)_r)]$; this is precisely the vector of the quantity n_r introduced in reference [6] now written in order of increasing strategy label. If we allow for tied strategies, $\mathbf{n}^d(t)$ will be non-zero thus reducing the size of large crowds and increasing the size of the smaller crowds (and hence anticrowds), thereby leading to a smaller standard deviation than if the effect of $\mathbf{n}^d(t)$ had been neglected.

We now turn to a comparison between the standard deviation or 'volatility' σ obtained from numerical sim-

ulations and our (time-averaged) crowd-anticrowd theory. We start with the basic MG. Figure 1 shows the spread of numerical values for different numerical runs (open circles), the full crowd-anticrowd theoretical calculation (large solid circles) and various limiting analytic curves (solid lines) for which closed-form expressions were given reference [6]. Fuller details are provided in reference [6]. The time-averaged dynamics can be described using a quantity $P(r' = \bar{r})$ which represents the probability that any strategy r' is the anti-correlated partner of strategy r [6]. To produce the limiting analytic curves in Figure 1, $P(r' = \bar{r})$ is taken to be either a delta-function or a flat distribution. The full theory takes the relevant form of $P(r' = \bar{r})$ from the game. The agreement is very good, confirming that our theory captures the essential economics.

In a variant of the basic MG, agents pick which strategy to use stochastically at each timestep. Focusing on $s = 2$, numerical simulations [7] found that the larger-than-random σ in the 'crowded' regime (i.e. small m) becomes smaller-than-random when the strategy-picking rule is made increasingly stochastic. Our crowd-anticrowd theory provides a quantitative explanation of this effect. Let θ be the probability that the agent uses the worst of her $s = 2$ strategies. Figure 2 shows a comparison between numerical simulation (open circles) and analytic expressions (monotonically-decreasing solid lines) obtained using our crowd-anticrowd theory (full details are given in Ref. [8]). These analytic expressions vary in their choice of $P(r' = \bar{r})$: the upper line σ_{delta} in Figure 2 assumes a delta function while the lower line σ_{flat} assumes a flat distribution. The theory agrees well in the range $\theta = 0 \rightarrow 0.35$ and provides a quantitative, yet physically intuitive, explanation for the previously unexplained transition in σ from larger-than-random to smaller-than-random as θ increases.

Above $\theta = 0.35$, the numerical data tend to flatten off while the analytic expressions predict a decrease in σ as $\theta \rightarrow 0.5$. This is because the analytic theory averages out the fluctuations in strategy-use at each time-step. In reference [8] we showed how to correct this shortcoming of the analytic theory. Consider $\theta = 0.5$; Figure 2 inset (a) shows the measured numerical distribution in σ for $\theta = 0.5$, while inset (b) shows the result from the semi-analytic procedure introduced in reference [8]. The two distributions are in good agreement. Note that the non-zero average (4.7 for $N = 101, m = 2$ and $s = 2$) for each distribution lies *below* the random coin-toss limit $\sqrt{N}/2$. It is also possible to perform a fully analytic calculation of the average σ_θ in the $\theta \rightarrow 0.5$ limit [8]; this value (which is also 4.7 for $N = 101, m = 2$ and $s = 2$) is shown in Figure 2.

In summary, we have demonstrated that the crowd-anticrowd approach can be applied to explain many aspects of MG games, yielding both time-averaged and time-dependent theories (see also Ref. [9]).

We thank A. Short for useful discussions.

References

1. J.-P. Bouchaud, M. Potters, *Théorie des Risques Financières* (Alea-Saclay, Eyrolles, 1998); R.N. Mantegna, H.E. Stanley, *An Introduction to Econophysics: Correlations and Complexity in Finance*; Y. Liu, P. Gopikrishnan, P. Cizeau, M. Meyer, C-K, Peng, H.E. Stanley, Phys. Rev. E **60**, 1390 (1999).

2. P. Jefferies, M. Hart, N.F. Johnson, Eur. Phys. J. B, this issue.

3. D. Challet, Y.C. Zhang, Physica A **246**, 407 (1997); *ibid.* **256**, 514 (1998); *ibid.* **269**, 30 (1999); D. Challet, M. Marsili, Phys. Rev. E **60**, R6271 (1999); D. Challet, M. Marsili, R. Zecchina, Phys. Rev. Lett. **84**, 1824 (2000).

4. See http://www.unifr.ch/econophysics for a detailed account of previous work on agent-based games such as the Minority Game.

5. See D. Challet, M. Marsili, cond-mat/0004196 for demonstrations confirming the relevance of the actual memory, in contrast to the claim of A. Cavagna, Phys. Rev. E **59**, R3783 (1999).

6. M. Hart, P. Jefferies, N.F. Johnson, P.M. Hui, cond-mat/0005152.

7. A. Cavagna, J.P. Garrahan, I. Giardina, D. Sherrington, Phys. Rev. Lett. **83**, 4429 (1999); J.P. Garrahan, E. Moro, D. Sherrington, cond-mat/0004277.

8. M. Hart, P. Jefferies, N.F. Johnson, P.M. Hui, Phys. Rev. E **63**, 017102 (2001).

9. N.F. Johnson, P.M. Hui, D. Zheng, M. Hart, J. Phys. A **32**, L427 (1999); N.F. Johnson, M. Hart, P.M. Hui, Physica A **269**, 1 (1999).

PHYSICAL REVIEW E

STATISTICAL PHYSICS, PLASMAS, FLUIDS, AND RELATED INTERDISCIPLINARY TOPICS

RAPID COMMUNICATIONS

The Rapid Communications section is intended for the accelerated publication of important new results. Since manuscripts submitted to this section are given priority treatment both in the editorial office and in production, authors should explain in their submittal letter why the work justifies this special handling. A Rapid Communication should be no longer than 4 printed pages and must be accompanied by an abstract. Page proofs are sent to authors.

Irrelevance of memory in the minority game

Andrea Cavagna*

Theoretical Physics, University of Oxford, 1 Keble Road, Oxford OX1 3NP, United Kingdom

(Received 15 December 1998)

By means of extensive numerical simulations, we show that all the distinctive features of the minority game introduced by Challet and Zhang [Physica A **256**, 514 (1998)] are completely independent of the memory of the agents. The only crucial requirement is that all the individuals must possess the same information, irrespective of whether this information is true or false. [S1063-651X(99)50204-3]

PACS number(s): 05.90.+m, 87.10.+e

Originally inspired by the "El Farol" problem stated by Arthur in [1], a model system has been introduced in [2] for the adaptive evolution of a population of interacting agents, the so-called minority game. This is a toy model where inductive, rather than deductive, thinking, in a population of bounded rationality, gives rise to cooperative phenomena.

The setup of the minority game is the following: N agents have to choose at each time step whether to go in room 0 or 1. Those agents who have chosen the less crowded room (minority room) win, the others lose, so that the system is intrinsically frustrated.

A crucial feature of the model is the way by which agents choose. In order to decide in what room to go, agents use strategies. A strategy is a choosing device; that is, an object that processes the outcomes of the winning room in the last m time steps (each outcome being 0 or 1) and accordingly to this information prescribes in what room to go in the next step. The so-called memory m defines 2^m potential past histories (for instance, with $m=2$ there are four possible pasts, 11, 10, 01, and 00). A strategy is thus formally a vector R_μ, with $\mu = 1, \ldots, 2^m$, whose elements can be 0 or 1. The space Γ of the strategies is a hypercube of dimension $D = 2^m$ and the total number of strategies is 2^D.

At the beginning of the game each agent draws randomly a number s of strategies from the space Γ and keeps them

forever, as a genetic heritage. The problem is now to fix which one, among these s strategies, the agent is going to use. (We will consider only the nontrivial case $s>1$.) The rule is the following. During the game the agent gives points to *all* his/her strategies according to their potential success: at each time step a strategy gets a point only if it has forecast the correct winning room, regardless of whether or not it has actually been used. At a given time the agent chooses among his/her s strategies the most successful one up to that moment (i.e., the one with the highest number of points) and uses it in order to choose the room. The adaptive nature of the game relies on the time evolution of the best strategy of each single agent. In this way the game has a well-defined deterministic time evolution, which only depends on the initial distribution of strategies and on the random initial string of m bits necessary to start the game.

Among all the possible observables, a special role is played by the variance σ of the attendance A in a given room [2]. We can consider, for instance, room 0 and define $A(t)$ as the number of agents in this room at time t. We have

$$\sigma^2 = \lim_{t \to \infty} \frac{1}{t} \int_{t_0}^{t} dt' \left(A(t') - \frac{N}{2} \right)^2, \quad (1)$$

where $N/2$ is the average attendance in the room and t_0 is a transient time after which the process is stationary [2,3]. In all the simulations presented in this Rapid Communication

---

*Electronic address: a.cavagna1@physics.ox.ac.uk

1063-651X/99/59(4)/3783(4)/$15.00
PRE <u>59</u>   R3783

$t=t_0=10\,000$ has been taken for a maximum value of $N=101$ and it has been verified that the averages were saturated over these times.

The importance of σ (called *volatility* in a financial context) is simple to understand: the larger σ is, the larger the global waste of resources by the community of agents. Indeed, only with an attendance A as near as possible to its average value is there the maximum distribution of points to the whole population. Moreover, from a financial point of view, it is clear that a low volatility σ is of great importance in order to minimize the risk.

If all the agents were choosing randomly, the variance would simply be $\sigma_r^2=N/4$. An important issue is therefore: under what conditions is the variance σ *smaller* than σ_r? In other words, is it possible for a population of selfish individuals to collectively behave in a better-than-random way? What has been found first in [3] is that the volatility σ as a function of m has a remarkable behavior, since actually *there is a regime where σ is smaller than the random value σ_r*. In this phase the collective behavior is such that less resources are globally wasted by the population of agents. A deep understanding of this feature is therefore important.

From the very definition of the model and from the behavior of $\sigma(m)$ described above, it seems clear that the memory m is a crucial quantity for the two following reasons. First, from a geometrical point of view, m defines the dimension of the space of strategies Γ and therefore it is related to the probability that strategies drawn randomly by different agents could give similar predictions: the larger m is, the bigger Γ is and the lower the probability is that different players have some strategies in common. Since the nonrandom nature of the game relies on the presence of correlated choices, that is, exactly on the possibility that different agents use the same strategies, it follows that for very large m the game proceeds in a random way [3–6]. (This argument works at a fixed number of agents N. Otherwise, the relevant variable will be $2^m/N$. We discuss this point later.)

Second, m is supposed to be a real memory. Actually, the whole game is constructed around the role of m as a memory: at time t agents use strategies which process the last m events in the past. As a consequence of this, a new minority room will come out and at time $t+1$ there will be a new m-bits past which will differ from the old one for the outcome at time t. Thus, agents, or better, strategies, choose by remembering the last m steps of time history, so that m is a natural time scale of the system. Due to this, an explanation of the behavior of $\sigma(m)$ has been proposed in [3], where the decay rate of the time correlations in the system is compared and related to m, thus supporting the key interpretation of m as a real memory. This memory role of m complicates greatly the nature of the problem, since it induces an explicits dynamical feedback in the evolution of the system, such that the process is not local in time.

The purpose of this Rapid Communication is to show that the memory of the agents is irrelevant. We shall prove that there is no need for an explicit time feedback in order to obtain all the distinctive features of the model. In order to prove this statement we consider the same model introduced in [2] and described above, but with the following important difference: at each time step, the past history is just *invented*;

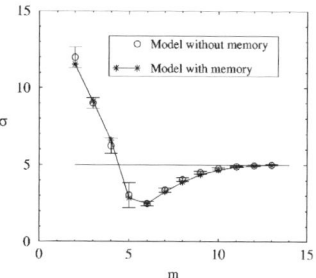

FIG. 1. Model without memory vs model with memory. The variance σ as a function of m for $s=2$. The horizontal line is the variance σ_r of the random case. The number of agents is $N=101$. Average is over 100 samples. Errors bars are shown only for the model without memory, while the line just connects the points of the memory model.

that is, a random sequence of m bits is drawn, to play the role of a fake time history. This is the information that all the agents process with their best strategies to choose the room. As we are going to show, this oblivious version of the model gives exactly the same results as the original one, thus proving that the role of m is purely geometrical.

In Fig. 1, the variance σ as a function of m is plotted for both the case with and the case without memory. The two models give the same results, not only qualitatively, but also quantitatively (see also the data of [3–6]). In particular, the minimum of σ as a function of m is found even without memory and cannot therefore be related to it.

The dependence of the whole function $\sigma(m)$ on the individual number of strategies s is another important point. It has been shown for the first time in [4] the larger the value of s is, the shallower the minimum of this curve is. In Fig. 2 we show that this same phenomenon occurs for the model without memory.

From a technical point of view, note that once the role of m as a memory is eliminated, the only quantity involved in the actual implementation of the model is D, the dimension of the space of strategies Γ. Therefore, instead of drawing a

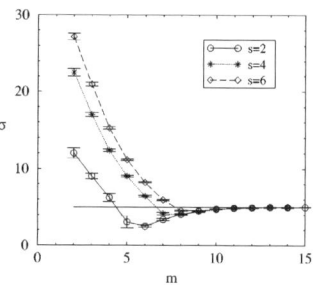

FIG. 2. Model without memory. Variance σ as a function of m, at different values of s, $N=101$. Average is over 100 samples. Lines are just a guide for the eye.

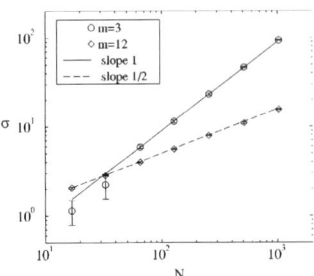

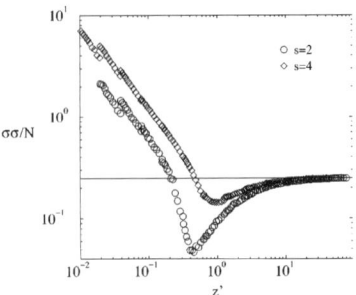

FIG. 3. Model without memory. Variance σ as a function of the number of agents N, for different values of m, at fixed $s=2$. Average is over ten samples. The full line is $\sigma \sim N$, while the dashed line is $\sigma \sim N^{1/2}$.

FIG. 4. Model without memory. Plot of σ^2/N as a function of the scaling parameter $z'=2D/sN$. The number of agents N varies from $N=51$ to $N=101$, while D varies from $D=2$ to $D=4096$. The individual number of strategies s ranges over two values $s=2$ and $s=4$. Average is over 50 samples.

random sequence of m bits, it is much easier to draw a random component $\mu \in [1,D]$ to mimic the past history: each agent uses component μ of his/her best strategy to choose the room. The main consequence of this is that there is no need for being $D=2^m$, since we can choose any integer value of D. In [5] a method has been introduced by which it is possible to consider noninteger values of m in the model with memory. This is useful, since it permits one to study the shape of $\sigma(m)$ around its minimum, with a better resolution in m. In the present context, it is trivial to consider noninteger values of m, since we simply have $m=\log_2 D$. In this way results identical to [5] are obtained.

Once s is fixed, let m_c be the value of m where the minimum of $\sigma(m)$ occurs. In [3] it has been pointed out that for $m<m_c$ the variance σ grows as N, where N is the number of agents, while for $m>m_c$ it grows as $N^{1/2}$. In Fig. 3, σ as a function of N is plotted for the model without memory. The same behavior as in the model with memory is found.

An interesting question is whether σ is a function of a single scaling variable z constructed with m, N, and s. It has been shown in [3] that by considering as a scaling variable $z=2^m/N=D/N$ all the data for σ at various m and N collapse on the same curve. In this case the relevant parameter is thus the dimension D of Γ, over the number N of playing strategies. On the other hand, a different scaling variable has been proposed in [4]; that is, $z'=2\times 2^m/sN=2D/sN$. In this way, the relevant parameter would be the density on Γ of the *total* number of strategies sN. In Fig. 4 we plot σ^2/N as a function of z', at different values of D, N, and s, for the model without memory. We see that the correct scaling parameter is z and not z', since the data with different values of s collapse on different curves. The same result is obtained if we perform the simulation with the memory (see [5]). The two models give once again the same results. Note from Fig. 4 that the scaling is not perfect at very low values of z'; that is, for very small D. This is just a trace of the integer nature of the model.

From what is shown above it is reasonable to conclude that in order to obtain all the crucial features of the minority game, the presence of an individual memory of the agents is irrelevant. The parameter m still plays a major role, but only for being related to the dimension $D=2^m$ of the strategies space Γ. A consequence of this fact is that any attempt to

explain the properties of this model, relying on the role of m as a memory, can hardly be correct. On the other hand, as already said, the geometrical role of m remains. Indeed, some recent attempts to give an analytic description of the model (see [4,6,9]) are only grounded in geometrical considerations about the distribution of strategies in the space Γ and go, therefore, in our opinion, in the correct direction.

The most important result of the present Rapid Communication is the existence of a regime where the whole population of agents still behaves in a better-than-random way, even if the information they process is completely random, that is wrong if compared to the real time history. *The crucial thing is that everyone must possess the same information.* Indeed, if we invent a different past history for each different agent, no coordination emerges at all and the results are the same as if the agents were behaving randomly (this can be easily verified numerically). In other words, if each individual is processing different information, the features of the system are completely identical to the random case, irrespective of the values of m and s.

The conclusion is the following: the crucial property is not at all the agents' memory of the real time history, but rather the fact that they all share the same information, however false or true this is. As a consequence, there is no room in this model for any kind of forecasting of the future based on the "understanding" of the past.

We hope this result will be useful for a future deeper understanding of this kind of adaptive system. Indeed, before trying to explain the rich structure of a quite complicated model, it is important in our opinion to clear up what the truly necessary ingredients of such a model are and what, on the contrary, is just an irrelevant complication that can be dropped. In the case of the so-called memory (or brain size, or intelligence), m, there also has been a problem of terminology: given the original formulation of the model, it seemed that the very nature of a variable encoding the *memory* or the *intelligence* of the agents, could warrant by itself a relevance to it [2–8], relevance which, as we have seen, was not deserved. Notwithstanding this, we still consider the present model to be very interesting and far from trivial.

Finally, let us note that the passage from a model with memory to a model without memory is equivalent to replacing a deterministic but very complicated system with a stochastic but much simpler one which, nevertheless, gives the same results as the original case and which is therefore indistinguishable from it for all practical purposes. The use of a stochastic/disordered model to mimic a deterministic/ordered one, is similar in spirit to what happens in the context of glassy systems, where some disordered models of spin glasses are often used in order to have a better understanding of structural glasses, which contain in principle no quenched disorder [10].

The author wishes to thank Erik Aurell, Francesco Bucci, Juan P. Garrahan, John Hertz, and David Sherrington for useful discussions and, in particular, Irene Giardina for many suggestions and for reading the manuscript. He also wishes to thank NORDITA (Copenhagen), where part of this work was done, for their kind hospitality. This work was supported by EPSRC Grant No. GR/K97783.

[1] W. B. Arthur, Amer. Econ. Assoc. Papers and Proc. **84**, 406 (1994).

[2] D. Challet and Y.-C. Zhang, Physica A **246**, 407 (1997).

[3] R. Savit, R. Manuca, and R. Riolo, e-print adap-org/9712006.

[4] D. Challet and Y.-C. Zhang, Physica A **256**, 514 (1998).

[5] R. Manuca, Y. Li, R. Riolo and R. Savit; e-print adap-org/9811005.

[6] N. F. Johnson and M. Hart, e-print cond-mat/9811227.

[7] N. F. Johnson, S. Jarvis, R. Jonson, P. Cheung, Y. R. Kwong, and P. M. Hui, Physica A **256**, 230 (1998).

[8] N. F. Johnson, P. M. Hui, R. Jonson, and T. S. Lo, e-print cond-mat/9810142.

[9] Y.-C. Zhang, Europhys. News **29**, 51 (1998).

[10] See, for a recent account on this topic, M. Mézard and G. Parisi, e-print cond-mat/9812180, and references therein.

Phase transition and symmetry breaking in the minority game

Damien Challet[1] and Matteo Marsili[2]

[1]Institut de Physique Théorique, Université de Fribourg, CH-1700 Fribourg, Switzerland
[2]Istituto Nazionale per la Fisica della Materia, Unitá di Trieste SISSA, V. Beirut 2-4, Trieste I-34014, Italy

(Received 30 June 1999)

We show that the minority game, a model of interacting heterogeneous agents, can be described as a spin system and displays a phase transition between a symmetric phase and a symmetry broken phase where the game's outcome is predictable. As a result a "spontaneous magnetization" arises in the spin formalism.
[S1063-651X(99)50912-4]

PACS number(s): 02.50.Le, 05.40.−a, 64.60.Ak, 89.90.+n

Market interactions among economic agents give rise to fluctuation phenomena, which are raising much interest in statistical physics [1,2]. The search for a toy system to study agents with marketlike interactions has led to the definition of the minority game (MG) [2,3], a model inspired by Arthur's "El Farol" problem [4], which embodies some basic market mechanisms [2] while keeping the mathematical complexity to a minimum.

In short, the MG is a repeated game where N agents have to decide which of two actions (such as buy or sell) to make. With N odd, this procedure identifies a *minority action* as that chosen by the minority. Agents who took the minority action are rewarded by one payoff unit, whereas the majority of agents looses one unit. Agents do not communicate one with the other and they have access to a "public information," related to past game outcomes, represented by one of P possible patterns.

The strategic point of view of game theory may require, in a case like this, a prohibitive computational task for each of the agents [5]. That is specially true if N and P are very large and agents have no complete information on the detailed mechanism that determines their payoffs, the identity of their opponents, or even their number N. In such complex strategic situations, which are similar to those that agents face in stock markets [2,6], agents may prefer to simplify their decision task by looking for simple behavioral rules that prescribe an action for each of the P possible patterns. This may be particularly advantageous if computational costs exist.

This behavior, called *inductive reasoning* in Ref. [4], is the basis of the MG [2,3]: each agent has a pool of S rules which prescribe an action for each of the P patterns. At each time, she follows her best rule (see below for a more precise definition). These rules, called strategies below, are initially drawn at random among all possible rules, independently for each agent in order to model agents' heterogeneity of beliefs and behaviors.

Numerical simulations [3,7,8] have shown that this system displays a *cooperative* phase for large values of the ratio $\alpha = P/N$: With respect to the simple "random agent" state, where each agent just tosses a coin to choose her action, agents are better off because they get to enstablish a sort of coordination. For small values of α agents receive, on average, poorer payoffs than in the random agent state, a behavior that has been related to crowd effects in markets [2,7,8].

A qualitative understanding of this behavior has been given in terms of geometric considerations [2,9].

In this Rapid Communication we show that the model can be described as a spin system and, as $\alpha = P/N$ varies, it undergoes a dynamical phase transition with symmetry breaking. The symmetry that gets broken is the equivalence between the two actions: in the symmetric phase ($\alpha < \alpha_c$) both actions are taken by the minority with the same frequency (e.g., there are, on average, as many buyers as sellers). For $\alpha > \alpha_c$, in each of the P possible states, the minority does more frequently an action than the other one, i.e., the game's outcome is asymmetric. An asymmetry in the game's outcome is an opportunity that an agent could in principle exploit to gain. This is called an *arbitrage* in economics and it bears a particularly relevant meaning (see discussions in [2,7]). The asymmetry for $\alpha > \alpha_c$ naturally suggests an order parameter and is related to a "phase separation" in the population of agents: while for $\alpha < \alpha_c$ all agents use all of their strategies, for $\alpha > \alpha_c$ a finite fraction ϕ of the agents ends up using only one strategy which, in the spin formalism, is the analog of spontaneous magnetization. The point α_c also marks the transition from persistence (for $\alpha > \alpha_c$) to antipersistence ($\alpha < \alpha_c$) of the game's time series.

Let us start from a sharp definition of the model: We use $+$ and $-$ to denote the two possible actions, so that a generic action is a sign. At each time t, the information available to each agent is the string $\mu_t = (\chi_{t-1}, \ldots, \chi_{t-M})$ of the last M actions taken by the minority. This, in our notation, is a string of M minority signs $\chi_{t-k} \in \{\pm 1\}$. There are $P = 2^M$ possible such strings, which we shall label by an index $\mu = 1, \ldots, P$ [10]. The index μ_t corresponding to $(\chi_{t-1}, \ldots, \chi_{t-M})$ shall be called the present *history*, for short. For each history μ, a strategy a specifies a fixed action a^μ. Each agent $i = 1, \ldots, N$ has $S = 2$ strategies, denoted by $a_{\pm,i}$, which are randomly drawn from the set of all 2^P possible strategies (the generalization to $S>2$ strategies will be discussed below). We define

$$\omega_i^\mu = \frac{a_{+,i}^\mu + a_{-,i}^\mu}{2}, \quad \xi_i^\mu = \frac{a_{+,i}^\mu - a_{-,i}^\mu}{2}$$

so that the strategies of agent i can be written as $a_{s_i,i}^\mu = \omega_i^\mu + s_i \xi_i^\mu$ with $s_i = \pm 1$. If $\omega_i^\mu \neq 0$, then $\xi_i^\mu = 0$ (and vice versa) and the player always takes the decision ω_i^μ whenever the

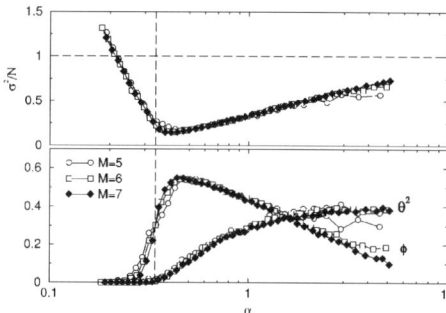

FIG. 1. Top: σ^2/N vs $\alpha = P/N$ for $P = 2^M$ with $M = 5$, 6, and 7. Bottom: θ^2 and ϕ versus α for the same system sizes P. The vertical dashed line is at $\alpha = 0.34 \approx \alpha_c$.

history is μ. The current best strategy of agent i, which she shall adopt at time t, is that which has the highest cumulated payoff. Let us define $\Delta_{i,t} \equiv U_{i,t}^{(+)} - U_{i,t}^{(-)}$ as the difference between the cumulated payoffs $U_{i,t}^{(\pm)}$ of strategies $+$ and $-$ for agent i at time t. Therefore, her choice is given by

$$s_i = \mathrm{sgn}\,\Delta_{i,t}, \qquad (1)$$

where ties ($\Delta_{i,t} = 0$) are broken by coin tossing. The difference in the population of agents choosing the $+$ and the $-$ sign, at time t, is then

$$A_t = \sum_{i=1}^{N} a_{s_i,i}^{\mu_t} = \Omega^{\mu_t} + \sum_{i=1}^{N} \xi_i^{\mu_t} s_i, \qquad (2)$$

where $\Omega^{\mu} = \Sigma_i \omega_i^{\mu}$. The sign chosen by the minority gives the *minority sign* at time t

$$\chi_t = -\mathrm{sgn}\,A_t \qquad (3)$$

and this determines the new history μ_{t+1}, which corresponds to the string $(\chi_t, \ldots, \chi_{t-M+1})$ [10]. Finally, each agent i rewards those of her strategies which have predicted the right sign $(a_{s,i}^{\mu_t} = \chi_t)$ updating the cumulated payoffs $U_{i,t+1}^{(\pm)} = U_{i,t}^{(\pm)} + a_{\pm,i}^{\mu_t} \chi_t$. This implies that the cumulated payoff difference $\Delta_{i,t}$ is updated according to

$$\Delta_{i,t+1} = \Delta_{i,t} + 2\chi_t \xi_i^{\mu_t}. \qquad (4)$$

Equations (1)–(4) update the state $\{\mu_t, \Delta_{i,t}\}$ of the system from t to $t+1$. With an initial condition (e.g., $\mu_0 = 1$, $\Delta_{i,0} = 0$, $\forall i$) the dynamics of the MG is completely specified. The "quenched" variables $\{\Omega^{\mu}, \xi_i^{\mu}\}$ play here the same role as disorder in statistical mechanics [11].

An important quantity in the MG is the variance $\sigma^2 = \langle A^2 \rangle$ of the difference A in the sizes of the two populations, where $\langle \cdot \rangle$ is a time average in the stationary state of the process specified by Eqs. (1)–(4). The number of winners, at each time step, is $(N - |A|)/2 \approx (N - \sigma)/2$ so that smaller fluctuations σ^2 correspond to larger global gain. A population of random agents would yield $\sigma^2 = N$. Numerical simulations [3,7,8] (see Fig. 1) show that, for $\alpha = P/N$ large

enough, agents with inductive reasoning manage to behave globally better (i.e., $\sigma^2 < N$) than random agents, whereas $\sigma^2 > N$ for small α (see Fig. 1). However, no singularity (and no order parameter) has been yet identified in order to locate a phase transition.

As shown in Ref. [12], to a good approximation one can neglect the coupling of the dynamics of $\Delta_{i,t}$ and μ_t and replace the dynamics of the latter by random sampling of the history space, i.e., $\mathrm{Prob}(\mu_t = \mu) = 1/P$, $\forall \mu$. This simplifies considerably our discussion since then

$$\sigma^2 \simeq \frac{1}{P} \sum_{\mu=1}^{P} (\Omega^{\mu})^2 + 2\sum_{i=1}^{N} h_i \langle s_i \rangle + \sum_{i,j=1}^{N} J_{i,j} \langle s_i s_j \rangle, \quad (5)$$

where $\langle \cdot \rangle$ stands for a time average and

$$h_i = \frac{1}{P} \sum_{\mu=1}^{P} \Omega^{\mu} \xi_i^{\mu}, \quad J_{i,j} = \frac{1}{P} \sum_{\mu=1}^{P} \xi_i^{\mu} \xi_j^{\mu}. \qquad (6)$$

The field h_i measures the difference of correlation of the two strategies with Ω^{μ}, whereas the coupling $J_{i,j}$ accounts for the interaction between agents as well as for agents self-interaction ($J_{i,i}$). The structure of the couplings (6) is reminiscent of neural networks models [11], where ξ_i^{μ} play the role of memory patterns. This similarity confirms the conclusion of Refs. [2,7,9] that the relevant parameter is the ratio $\alpha = P/N$ between the number of patterns and the number of spins.

The key element that is at the origin of the behavior of the model is the fact that for each history μ, there are agents which always take the same decision. This gives rise to the time independent contribution Ω^{μ} in A, which produces a bias in the value of χ_t whenever $\mu_t = \mu$. A measure of this bias, is given by the parameter

$$\theta = \sqrt{\frac{1}{P} \sum_{\mu=1}^{P} \langle \chi | \mu \rangle^2}, \qquad (7)$$

where $\langle \chi | \mu \rangle$ is the conditional average of χ_t given that $\mu_t = \mu$. Loosely speaking, θ measures the presence of information or arbitrages in the signal χ_t. If $\theta > 0$ an agent with strategies of "length" $M = \log_2 P$ can detect and exploit this information if one of her strategies is more correlated with $\langle \chi | \mu \rangle$ than the other. More precisely, we observe that if $v_i \equiv \langle \Delta_{i,t+1} - \Delta_{i,t} \rangle \neq 0$, then $\Delta_{i,t} \approx v_i t$ grows linearly with time, and the agent's spin will always take the value $s_i = \mathrm{sgn}\,v_i$. We shall call this a *frozen* agent, since her spin variable is frozen. We find

$$v_i = \langle \chi_t \xi_i^{\mu_t} \rangle \simeq \frac{1}{P} \sum_{\mu=1}^{P} \langle \chi | \mu \rangle \xi_i^{\mu} \propto -h_i - \sum_{j=1}^{N} J_{i,j} \langle s_j \rangle, \quad (8)$$

where the last equation relies on an expansion of $\langle \chi | \mu \rangle$ to linear order in A [13].

It is instructive to consider first the case where other agents choose by coin tossing (i.e., $\langle s_j \rangle = 0$ for $j \neq i$) so that $v_i \propto -h_i - J_{i,i} \langle s_i \rangle$. If $v_i \neq 0$, then $s_i = \mathrm{sgn}\,v_i = -\mathrm{sgn}(h_i + J_{i,i} \langle s_i \rangle)$. But this last equation has a solution only if $|h_i| > J_{i,i}$, whereas otherwise $|\langle s_i \rangle| < 1$ and $v_i = 0$. Note that $J_{i,i} \approx 1/2$ and that h_i can be approximated by a Gaussian variable with zero average and variance $(4\alpha)^{-1}$. This means that $|h_i| \ll J_{i,i}$ for $\alpha \gg 1$, which implies that most agents have $\langle s_i \rangle \approx 0$ in this limit and we can indeed neglect agent-agent interaction. This allows one to compute the probability for an agent to be frozen,

$$\phi = P\{|h_i| > J_{i,i}\} \propto e^{-\alpha/2}, \tag{9}$$

for $\alpha \gg 1$. Numerical simulations show that ϕ $\propto e^{-(0.37 \pm 0.02)\alpha}$ indeed decays exponentially. As $\alpha \to \infty$, the random agents limit is attained because $\langle s_i \rangle \to 0$ for all i and $\langle s_i s_j \rangle = \langle s_i \rangle \langle s_j \rangle$ for $i \neq j$. By Eq. (5) we find $\sigma^2 = \sum_\mu (\Omega^\mu)^2 / P + \sum_i J_{i,i} \approx N$.

The same argument applies in general, with the difference that the "bare" field h_i must be replaced by the "effective" field $\bar{h}_i = h_i + \sum_{j \neq i} J_{i,j} \langle s_j \rangle$. In order for agent i to get frozen, her effective field $\bar{h}_i$ must overcome the self-interaction $J_{i,i}$, i.e., $|\bar{h}_i| > J_{i,i} \approx 1/2$. If this condition is met, $s_i = -\operatorname{sgn} \bar{h}_i$. It can also be shown that a frozen agent will, on average, receive a larger payoff than an unfrozen agent [14]. Loosely speaking, one can say that a frozen agent has a *good* and a *bad* strategy and the good one remains better than the bad one even when she actually uses it. On the contrary, unfrozen agents have two strategies, each of which seems better than the other when it is not adopted. In this sense, symmetry breaking in $\langle \chi | \mu \rangle$ induced a sort of breakdown in the *a priori* equivalence of agents' strategies.

A quantitative analysis of the fully interacting system shall be presented elsewhere [14]. For the time being we shall discuss the behavior of the system on the basis of extensive numerical simulations. Figure 1 reports the behavior of θ, ϕ and σ^2 as functions of α for several values of P. As α decreases, i.e., as more and more agents join the game, the arbitrages opportunities, as measured by θ decrease. In loose words, agents' exploitation of the signal Ω^μ weakens its strength by screening it with their adaptive behavior. If the number N of agents is small compared to the signal "complexity" $P = 2^M$, agents exploit only partially the signal Ω^μ, whereas if $N \gg P$ then Ω^μ is completely screened by agents' behavior and $\theta = 0$. As Figure 1 shows the parameter θ displays the characteristic behavior of an order parameter with a singularity at $\alpha_c \approx 0.34$. Accordingly, also the fraction ϕ of frozen agents drops to zero as $\alpha \to \alpha_c^+$. The comparison between different system sizes in Fig. 1 strongly suggests that ϕ drops discontinuously to zero at α_c (and it also gives the value of α_c). The vanishing of ϕ is clearly a consequence of the fact that θ also vanishes at α_c. Indeed if $\langle \chi | \mu \rangle = 0$ for all μ, by Eq. (8), also $v_i = 0$ for all i, so that $\Delta_{i,t}$ remains bounded and $|\langle s_i \rangle| < 1$.

The transition can also be understood in terms of the variables $\Delta_{i,t}$ as an "unbinding" transition as $\alpha \to \alpha_c^-$: For $\alpha < \alpha_c$ a "bound state" exists with finite $\Delta_{i,t}$, which corresponds to the fact that the equations $v_i = 0$, $i = 1, \ldots, N$ admit a solution with $|\langle s_i \rangle| < 1$, $\forall i$ [14] (only P of the equations $v_i = 0$ are linearly independent). For $\alpha > \alpha_c$ this is no longer true and the population separates: a fraction ϕ of variables $\Delta_{i,t}$ acquire a constant "velocity" $v_i \neq 0$ (with $|\langle s_i \rangle| = 1$), whereas for the remaining agents $v_i = 0$, $\Delta_{i,t}$ remains bounded and $|\langle s_i \rangle| < 1$.

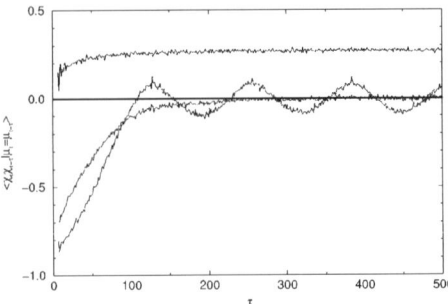

FIG. 2. Temporal correlation of χ_t on the same history, $\langle \chi_t \chi_{t+\tau} | \mu_t = \mu_{t+\tau} \rangle$, averaged over all histories vs τ (10^6 iterations, $M = 6$, $\alpha = 0.5$, 0.22, and 0.1)

It is suggestive to observe that $v_i \propto -(\partial \sigma^2 / \partial s_i)$ so that the dynamics of the minority game is actually similar to a spin dynamics with Hamiltonian σ^2. Indeed either the spin is frozen in the direction that minimizes $-s_i v_i(s_i)$, or its average $\langle s_i \rangle$ is such that $v_i = 0$. This then explains why cooperation occurs in the MG. A closer analysis, to be reported elsewhere [14], reveals that indeed the stationary state of the MG is described by the ground state properties of an Hamiltonian very similar to σ^2. Finite size scaling suggests that σ^2 has a minimum at α_c with a discontinuity in its derivative (see Fig. 1). These conclusions are indeed confirmed by exact results [14]. It is worth stressing, however, that the qualitative aspects of the transition are already captured at the simple level of approximation of Eq. (8).

Let us go back to Fig. 1. Above α_c agents do not fully exploit the information Ω^μ and, as a result, $\langle \chi | \mu \rangle \neq 0$. Figure 2 shows that χ_t shows persistence in time, in the sense that when $\mu_t = \mu_{t+\tau}$ the minority signs χ_t and $\chi_{t+\tau}$ tend to be the same. This persistence disappears, $\langle \chi_t \chi_{t+\tau} | \mu_t = \mu_{t+\tau} \rangle \to 0$ as α decreases and it turns into anti-persistence for smaller α. The oscillatory behavior in Fig. 2 has indeed period $2P$, which means that typically when the population comes again on the same history μ it tends to do the opposite of what it did the time before. Even if finite size effects do not allow a definite conclusion, it is quite likely that this change in time correlations also occurs at α_c [14]. Time correlations, even though of opposite nature, are present both above and below α_c. These are like arbitrages in a market which could be exploited by agents. In this sense the market is *efficient*, i.e., arbitrage free, only for $\alpha = \alpha_c$.

The same qualitative behavior is expected when agents have $S > 2$ strategies. Again for a given history μ it may happen that all the S agent's i strategies prescribe the same action: agent i will do that action no matter what strategy she has chosen. As S increases, this will occur for a smaller and smaller number of histories (more precisely with a probability 2^{1-S}). This shall correspond to a weaker signal Ω^μ, which is in complete agreement with the observation [7,9] of shallower features for larger S. Note that for each agent it would be rewarding to increase the number of strategies because they would have more chances to outguess χ_t. At the same time, if all agents increase S the game becomes less rewarding for all of them, at least for $\alpha > \alpha_c$. This situation is typical of games, such as the *tragedy of commons*, where many agents interact through a global resource [15].

The condition $v_i = 0$ for the bound state in the symmetric phase involves P equations with $(S-1)N$ variables. This suggests that in general the scaling parameter is $\alpha = P/[(S-1)N]$. The curve σ^2/N as a function of $\alpha = P/[(S-1)N]$ collapse remarkably well one on the other for $\alpha \lesssim \alpha_c$ (especially for $S>2$) but not for $\alpha > \alpha_c$ [e.g., in the large α behavior $\phi \propto e^{-C(S)\alpha}$ we found $C(2) \approx 0.37$, $C(3) \approx 1.50$ and $C(4) \approx 2.90$].

Our approach also implies that no coordination is possible if agents have $S=2$ opposite strategies ($a_{+,i}^\mu = -a_{-,i}^\mu$) because then $\Omega^\mu = 0$. Numerical simulations show that indeed $\sigma^2 \gtrsim N$ for all $\alpha > 0$ in this case.

The same qualitative behavior also occurs in a wide range of related models. First, total freezing occurs in majority models. Note indeed that changing the sign of Eq. (3) would also change the sign in Eq. (8). In particular the self-interaction $J_{i,i}$ changes sign so that it becomes favorable for each agent to stick to only one strategy anyway. The model is therefore trivial. More interesting models are obtained keeping the "frustration" effects of the MG but changing the definition of payoffs in Eq. (4). It can be shown [14] that the phase transition and the large α behavior are quite robust features of minority games (see, e.g., [13]).

In summary, we find that a phase transition occurs in the minority game. The cooperative phase ($\alpha > \alpha_c$) is characterized by the presence of a fraction ϕ of frozen agents (who use only one strategy), unexploited arbitrages ($\langle \chi | \mu \rangle \neq 0$), and persistence in the global signal χ_t. In the symmetric phase ($\alpha < \alpha_c$) inductive dynamics is inefficient: agents adopt strategies when they are no longer good. There is no arbitrage (for strategies of length M) to exploit and the signal shows anti-persistence.

We acknowledge Y.-C. Zhang for enlightening discussions, useful suggestions, and for introducing us to the minority game. This work was partially supported by Swiss National Science Foundation Grant No. 20-46918.98.

---

[1] P. W. Anderson, K. Arrow, and D. Pines, *The Economy as an Evolving Complex System* (Addison-Wesley, New York, 1988); *Econophysics: an Emerging Science*, edited by J. Kertesz and I. Kondor (Kluwer, Dordrecht, 1998).

[2] Y.-C. Zhang, Europhys. News **29**, 51 (1998).

[3] D. Challet and Y.-C. Zhang, Physica A **246**, 407 (1997).

[4] W. B. Arthur, Am. Econ. Assoc. Papers Proc. **84**, 406 (1994).

[5] A strategic player has to consider, for any given strategy she can actually play, how each of her opponents would react knowing that she is playing that strategy, and how that affects her payoff. On this basis, which assumes that also her opponents behave the same, she has to find out what the best strategy is. See, e.g., D. Fudenberg and J. Tirole, *Game Theory* (MIT Press, Cambridge, MA, 1991).

[6] Y.-C. Zhang, e-print cond-mat/9901243.

[7] R. Savit, R. Manuca, and R. Riolo, Phys. Rev. Lett. **82**, 2203 (1999); e-print adap-org/9811005.

[8] N. F. Johnson *et al.*, Physica A **256**, 230 (1998).

[9] D. Challet and Y.-C. Zhang, Physica A **256**, 514 (1998); N. F. Johnson *et al.*, e-print cond-mat/9811227.

[10] An example of labeling is binary coding. μ_{t+1} is then given by: $\mu_{t+1} = [2\mu_t + 1 + \chi_t/2] \mathrm{mod}\, P$.

[11] M. Mezard, G. Parisi, and M. A. Virasoro, *Spin Glass Theory and Beyond* (World Scientific, Singapore, 1987).

[12] A. Cavagna, Phys. Rev. E **59**, R3787 (1999) has shown that replacing the dynamics of μ_t by random sampling does not change, to a very good approximation, the behavior of the model. The assumption that each history μ is sampled with the same frequency is strictly true only in the symmetric phase $\alpha < \alpha_c$ but it holds qualitatively also for $\alpha > \alpha_c$.

[13] This approximation is justified by the fact that the "linear" minority model obtained replacing Eq. (4) by $\Delta_{i,t+1} = \Delta_{i,t} - A_t \xi_i^{\mu_t}$ gives results very similar to those presented here. An analytic derivation is also possible from the identity $\langle \chi | \mu \rangle = 2\,\mathrm{Prob}(A^\mu < 0 | \mu) - 1$ [14].

[14] D. Challet, M. Marsili, and R. Zecchina (unpublished).

[15] G. Hardin, Science **162**, 1243 (1968).

Thermal Model for Adaptive Competition in a Market

Andrea Cavagna,* Juan P. Garrahan,† Irene Giardina,‡ and David Sherrington§

Theoretical Physics, University of Oxford, 1 Keble Road, Oxford OX1 3NP, United Kingdom
(Received 29 March 1999; revised manuscript received 13 July 1999)

New continuous and stochastic extensions of the minority game, devised as a fundamental model for a market of competitive agents, are introduced and studied in the context of statistical physics. The new formulation reproduces the key features of the original model, without the need for some of its special assumptions and, most importantly, it demonstrates the crucial role of stochastic decision making. Furthermore, this formulation provides the exact but novel nonlinear equations for the dynamics of the system.

PACS numbers: 02.50.Le, 05.65.+b, 05.70.Fh, 87.23.Ge

There is currently much interest in the statistical physics of nonequilibrium frustrated and disordered many-body systems [1]. Even relatively simple microscopic dynamical equations have been shown to lead to complex cooperative behavior. Although several of the interesting examples are in areas traditionally viewed as physics, it is growingly apparent that many further challenges for statistical physics have their origins in other fields such as biology [2] and economics [3]. In this Letter we discuss a simple model whose origin lies in a market scenario and show that not only does it exhibit interesting behavior in its own right, but also it yields an intriguingly unusual type of stochastic microdynamics of potentially more general interest.

The model we will introduce is based on the minority game (MG) [4], which is a simple and intuitive model for the behavior of a group of agents subject to the economic law of supply and demand, which ensures that in a market the profitable group of buyers or sellers of a commodity is the minority one [5]. From the perspective of statistical physics, these problems are novel examples of frustrated and disordered many-body systems. Agents do not interact directly but with their collective action determine a "price" which in turn affects their future behavior. Quenched disorder enters in that agents have randomly chosen but fixed strategies determining their individual responses to the same stimuli. Frustration enters in that, due to the global minority constraint, not all the individual inclinations can be satisfied simultaneously. The consequent cooperative behavior is reminiscent of that of spin glasses [6] and of the random equipartitioning problem [7], but there are important conceptual and technical differences.

The setup of the MG in the original formulation of [4] is the following: N agents choose at each time step whether to "buy" (0) or "sell" (1). Those agents who have made the minority choice win; the others lose. In order to decide what to do, agents use strategies which prescribe an action given the set of winning outcomes in the last m time steps. At the beginning of the game, each agent draws s strategies randomly and keeps them forever. As they play, the agents give points to all their strategies according to their potential success in the past, and at each time step they employ their currently most successful one (i.e., the one with the highest number of points).

The most interesting macroscopic observable in the MG is the fluctuation σ of the excess of buyers to sellers. This quantity is equivalent to the price volatility in a financial context and it is a measure of the global waste of resources by the community of the agents. We therefore want σ to be as low as possible. An important feature of the MG, observed in simulations [8], is that there is a regime of the parameters where σ is *smaller* than the value σ_r which corresponds to the case where each agent is buying or selling randomly. Previous studies have considered this feature from a geometrical and phenomenological point of view [9]. Our aim, however, is to enable a full analytic solution.

One of the major obstacles to an analytic study of the MG in its original formulation is the presence of an explicit time feedback via the memory m. Indeed, when the information processed at each time step by the agents is the *true* history, that is the result of the choices of the agents in the m previous steps, the dynamical evolution of the system is non-Markovian and an analytic approach to the problem is very difficult.

A step forward in the simplification of the model has been made in [10], where it has been shown that the explicit memory of the agents is actually irrelevant for the global behavior of the system: when the information processed by the agents at each time step is just *invented* randomly, having nothing to do with the true time series, the relevant macroscopic observables do not change. The significance of this result is the following: the global information on which the individual agents act provides a mechanism for them to interact effectively with one another; the crucial ingredient for the volatility to be reduced below the random value [11] appears to be that the agents must all react to the *same* piece of information, irrespective of whether this information is true or false [12]. This result has an important technical consequence, since the explicit time feedback introduced by the memory disappears: the agents respond now to an instantaneous random piece of information, i.e., a noise, so that the process has become stochastic and Markovian.

0031-9007/99/83(21)/4429(4)$15.00   © 1999 The American Physical Society   4429

The model can be usefully simplified even further and at the same time generalized and made more realistic. Let us first consider the binary nature of the original MG. It is clear that from a simulational point of view a binary setup offers advantages of computational efficiency, but unfortunately it is less ideally suited for an analytic approach [13]. More specifically, if we are interested in the analysis of time evolution, integer variables are usually harder to handle. Moreover, the geometrical considerations that have been made on a hypercube of strategies of dimension 2^m for the binary setup [9] become more natural and general if the strategy space is continuous. Finally, in the original binary formulation of the MG there is no possibility for the agents to fine tune their bids: each agent can choose to buy or sell, but they cannot choose by *how much*. As a consequence, also the win or loss of the agents is not related to the consistency of their bids. This is another unrealistic feature of the model, which can be improved. For all these reasons, we shall now introduce a continuous formulation of the MG.

Let us define a strategy $\vec{R}$ as a vector in the real space $\mathbb{R}^D$, subject to the constraint, $\|\vec{R}\| = \sqrt{D}$. In this way, the space of strategies Γ is just a sphere and strategies can be thought of as points on it. The next ingredient we need is the information processed by strategies. To this aim, we introduce a random noise $\vec{\eta}(t)$, defined as a unit-length vector in $\mathbb{R}^D$, which is δ correlated in time and uniformly distributed on the unit sphere. Finally, we define the response $b(\vec{R})$ of a strategy $\vec{R}$ to the information $\vec{\eta}(t)$, as the projection of the strategy on the information itself,

$$b(\vec{R}) \equiv \vec{R} \cdot \vec{\eta}(t). \tag{1}$$

This response is nothing else than the *bid* prescribed by the particular strategy $\vec{R}$. The bid is now a continuous quantity, which can be positive (buy) or negative (sell).

At the beginning of the game, each agent draws s strategies randomly from Γ, with a flat distribution. All the strategies initially have zero points and in operation the points are updated in a manner discussed below. At time step t, each agent i uses his/her strategy with the highest number of points $\vec{R}_i^\star(t)$. The *total bid* is then

$$A(t) \equiv \sum_{i=1}^{N} b_i(t) = \sum_{i=1}^{N} \vec{R}_i^\star(t) \cdot \vec{\eta}(t), \tag{2}$$

We have now to update the points. This is particularly simple in the present continuous formulation. Let us introduce a time dependent function $P(\vec{R}, t)$ defined on Γ, which represents the points P of strategy $\vec{R}$ at time t. We can write a very simple and intuitive time evolution equation for P,

$$P(\vec{R}, t + 1) = P(\vec{R}, t) - A(t) b(\vec{R})/N, \tag{3}$$

where $A(t)$ is given by Eq. (2). A strategy $\vec{R}$ is thus rewarded (penalized) if its bid has an opposite (equal) sign

to the total bid, as the supply-demand dynamics requires. Now the win or the loss is proportional to the bid.

It is important to check whether the results obtained with this continuous formulation of the MG are the same as in the original binary model. The main observable of interest is the variance (or volatility) σ in the fluctuation of A, $\sigma^2 = \lim_{t \to \infty} \frac{1}{t} \int_{t_0}^{t_0+t} dt' A(t')^2$. Indeed, we shall not consider any quantity related to individual agents. We prefer to concentrate on the global behavior of the system, taking more the role of the market regulator than that of a trading agent. The main features of the MG are reproduced: first, we have checked that the relevant scaling parameter is the reduced dimension of the strategy space $d = D/N$; second, there is a regime of d where the variance σ is smaller than the random value σ_r, showing a minimum at $d = d_c(s)$, and, moreover, the minimum of $\sigma(d)$ is shallower the higher is s [9] (see Fig. 1). It can be shown that *all* the other standard features of the binary model are reproduced in the continuous formulation.

An interesting observation is that there is no need for $\vec{\eta}(t)$ to be random at all. Indeed, the only requirement is that it must be *ergodic*, spanning the whole space Γ, even in a deterministic way. Moreover, if $\vec{\eta}(t)$ visits just a subspace of Γ of dimension $D' < D$, everything in the system proceeds as if the actual dimension was D': the *effective* dimension of the strategy space is fixed by the dimension of the space spanned by the information.

Relations (2) and (3) constitute a closed set of equations for the dynamical evolution of $P(\vec{R}, t)$, whose solution, once averaged over $\vec{\eta}$ and over the initial distribution of the strategies, gives in principle an exact determination of the behavior of the system. In practice, the presence of the "best-strategy" rule, i.e., the fact that each agent uses

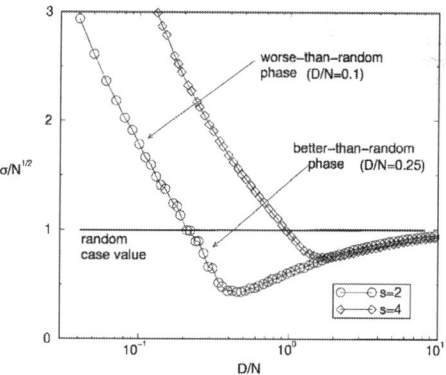

FIG. 1. Continuous formulation: The scaled variance $\sigma/\sqrt{N}$ as a function of the reduced dimension D/N, at $s = 2$ and $s = 4$. The horizontal line is the variance in the random case. The total time t and the initial time t_0 are 10 000 steps. Average over 100 samples, $N = 100$.

the strategy with the highest points, makes the handling of these equations still difficult. From the perspective of statistical physics it is natural to modify the deterministic nature of the above procedure by introducing a thermal description which progressively allows stochastic deviations from the best-strategy rule, as a temperature is raised. We shall see that this generalization is also advantageous, both for the performance of the system in certain regimes and for the development of convenient analytical equations for the dynamics. In this context the best-strategy original formulation of the MG can be viewed as a zero temperature limit of a more general model.

Hence, we introduce the thermal minority game (TMG), defined in the following way. We allow each agent a certain degree of stochasticity in the choice of the strategy to use at any time step. For each agent i the probabilities of employing his/her strategy $a = 1, \ldots, s$ is given by

$$\pi_i^a(t) \equiv \frac{e^{\beta P(\vec{R}_i^a, t)}}{Z_i}, \qquad Z_i \equiv \sum_{b=1}^{s} e^{\beta P(\vec{R}_i^b, t)}, \qquad (4)$$

where P are the points, evolving with Eq. (3). The inverse temperature $\beta = 1/T$ is a measure of the power of *resolution* of the agents: when $\beta \to \infty$ they are perfectly able to distinguish which are their best strategies, while for decreasing β they are more and more confused, until for $\beta = 0$ they choose their strategy completely at random. What we have defined is therefore a model which interpolates between the original best-strategy MG ($T = 0$, $\beta = \infty$) and the random case ($T = \infty$, $\beta = 0$). In the language of game theory, when $T = 0$ agents play "pure" strategies, while at $T > 0$ they play "mixed" ones [14].

We now consider the consequences of having introduced the temperature. First, let us fix a value of d belonging to the worse-than-random phase of the MG (see Fig. 1) and see what happens to the variance σ when we switch on the temperature. We know that for $T = 0$ we must recover the same value as in the ordinary MG, while for $T \to \infty$ we must obtain the value σ_r of random choice. But in between a very interesting thing occurs: $\sigma(T)$ is not a monotonically decreasing function of T, but there is a large intermediate temperature regime where σ is *smaller* than the random value σ_r (see Fig. 2). The meaning of this result is the following: even if the system is in a MG phase which is worse than random, there is a way to significantly decrease the volatility σ below the random value σ_r by *not* always using the best strategy, but rather allowing a certain degree of individual error.

The temperature range where the variance is smaller than the random one is more than 2 orders of magnitude large, meaning that almost every kind of individual stochasticity of the agents improves the global behavior of the system. Furthermore, if we fix d at a value belonging to the better-than-random phase, but with $d < d_c$, a similar range of temperature still improves the behavior of the system, decreasing the volatility even below the MG value (inset of Fig. 2).

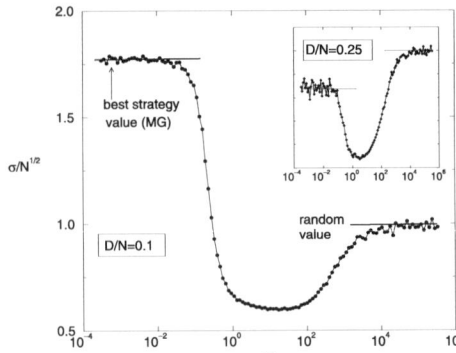

FIG. 2. TMG: The scaled variance $\sigma/\sqrt{N}$ as a function of the temperature T, at $D/N = 0.1$, for $s = 2$. In the inset we show $\sigma(T)/\sqrt{N}$ for $D/N = 0.25$.

These features can be seen also in Fig. 3, where we plot σ as a function of d at various values of the temperature. In addition, this figure shows further effects: (i) the improvement due to thermal noise occurs only for $d < d_c$; (ii) there is a crossover temperature $T_1 \sim 1$, below which temperature has very little effect for $d > d_c$; (iii) above T_1 the optimal $d_c(T)$ moves continuously towards zero and $\sigma(d_c)$ increases; (iv) there is a higher critical temperature $T_2 \sim 10^2$ at which d_c vanishes, and for $T > T_2$ the volatility becomes monotonically increasing with d.

We turn now to a more formal description of the TMG. Once we have introduced the probabilities π_i^a in Eq. (4) we can write a dynamical equation for them. Indeed, from

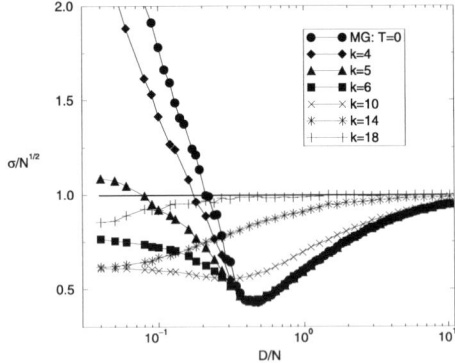

FIG. 3. TMG: The scaled variance $\sigma/\sqrt{N}$ as a function of the reduced dimension D/N, at different values of the temperature $T = 2^k \times 10^{-2}$, for $s = 2$.

Eq. (3), after taking the continuous-time limit, we have

$$\dot{\pi}_i^a(t) = -\beta \pi_i^a(t) a(t) \left(\vec{R}_i^a - \sum_{b=1}^{s} \pi_i^b(t) \vec{R}_i^b \right) \cdot \vec{\eta}(t),$$
(5)

where the normalized total bid $a(t)$ is given by

$$a(t) = N^{-1} \sum_{i=1}^{N} \vec{r}_i(t) \cdot \vec{\eta}(t).$$
(6)

Now $\vec{r}_i(t)$ is a stochastic variable, drawn at each time t with the time dependent probabilities set $[\pi_i^1, \ldots, \pi_i^s]$. Note the different notation: $\vec{R}_i^a$ are the *quenched* strategies, while $\vec{r}_i(t)$ is the particular strategy drawn at time t by agent i from the set $[\vec{R}_i^1, \ldots, \vec{R}_i^s]$ with instantaneous probabilities $[\pi_i^1(t), \ldots, \pi_i^s(t)]$. In order to better understand Eq. (5), we recall that $b_i^a(t) = \vec{R}_i^a \cdot \vec{\eta}(t)$ is the bid of strategy $\vec{R}_i^a$ at time t [Eq. (1)] and therefore the quantity $w_i^a(t) \equiv -a(t) b_i^a(t)$ can be considered as the *win* of this strategy [cf. Eq. (3)]. Hence, we can rewrite Eq. (5) in the following more intuitive form:

$$\dot{\pi}_i^a(t) = \beta \pi_i^a(t)[w_i^a(t) - \langle w \rangle_i],$$
(7)

where $\langle w \rangle_i \equiv \sum_{b=1}^{s} \pi_i^b(t) w_i^b(t)$. The meaning of Eq. (7) is clear: the probability π_i^a of a particular strategy $\vec{R}_i^a$ increases only if the performance of that strategy is better than the instantaneous *average* performance of all the strategies belonging to the same agent i with the same actual total bid.

Relations (5) and (6) are the exact dynamical equations for the TMG. They do not involve points nor memory, but just stochastic noise and quenched disorder, and they are local in time. From the perspective of statistical mechanics, this is satisfying and encouraging. However, these equations differ fundamentally from conventional replicator and Langevin dynamics. First, although our equations look like replicator equations, they are not deterministic [15] and the Markov-propagating variables are themselves probabilities. Second, there are two sorts of stochastic noises, as well as quenched randomness. Third, and more importantly, the stochastic noises enter nonlinearly, one independently for each agent via probabilistic dependence on the π themselves, the other globally and quadratically. They thus provide interesting challenges for fundamental transfer from microscopic to macroscopic dynamics, including an identification of the complete set of relevant macroobservables [16] (as well as the volatility). We shall address the problem of finding a solution of the TMG equations in a future work.

Finally, let us note that the TMG is not only suitable for the description of market dynamics: any natural system where a population of individuals organizes itself to optimize the utilization of some resources can be described by such a model. We hope that our model will give more insight into this kind of natural phenomena.

We thank L. Billi, P. Gillin, N. F. Johnson, I. Kogan, and P. Love for useful discussions. This work was supported by EPSRC Grant No. GR/M04426 and EC Grant No. ARG/B7-3011/94/27.

*Email address: a.cavagnal@physics.ox.ac.uk
†Email address: j.garrahan1@physics.ox.ac.uk
‡Email address: i.giardina1@physics.ox.ac.uk
§Email address: d.sherrington1@physics.ox.ac.uk

[1] See, e.g., J.-P. Bouchaud, L. F. Cugliandolo, J. Kurchan, and M. Mézard, in *Spin Glasses and Random Fields,* edited by A. P. Young (World Scientific, Singapore, 1998); *Nonequilibrium Statistical Mechanics in One Dimension,* edited by V. Privman (Cambridge University, Cambridge, England, 1997).

[2] See, e.g., *Physics of Biomaterials,* edited by T. Riste and D. Sherrington (Kluwer Academic Press, Dordrecht, 1996); *Landscape Paradigms in Physics and Biology,* edited by H. Frauenfelder *et al.* (North-Holland, Amsterdam, 1997).

[3] *The Economy as an Evolving Complex System,* edited by P. W. Anderson, K. Arrow, and D. Pines (Addison-Wesley, Redwood City, CA, 1988).

[4] D. Challet and Y.-C. Zhang, Physica (Amsterdam) **246A,** 407 (1997).

[5] See, e.g., W. B. Arthur, Am. Econ. Assoc. Papers Proc. **84,** 406 (1994); Science, **284,** 107 (1999).

[6] M. Mézard, G. Parisi, and M. A. Virasoro, *Spin Glass Theory And Beyond* (World Scientific, Singapore, 1986).

[7] See, for example, J. R. Banavar, D. Sherrington, and N. Sourlas, J. Phys. A **20,** L1 (1987), and references therein.

[8] R. Savit, R. Manuca, and R. Riolo, Phys. Rev. Lett. **82,** 2203 (1999).

[9] D. Challet and Y.-C. Zhang, Physica (Amsterdam) **256A,** 514 (1998); Y.-C. Zhang, Europhys. News **29,** 51 (1998); N. F. Johnson, M. Hart, and P. M. Hui, Physica (Amsterdam) **269A,** 1 (1999); R. D'hulst and G. J. Rodgers, Physica (Amsterdam) **270A,** 222 (1999).

[10] A. Cavagna, Phys. Rev. E **59,** R3783 (1999).

[11] The effective interactions among agents produce the best compromise in a manner reminiscent of a spin glass: the volatility can become less than random just as the energy of a spin glass is less than that of a paramagnet.

[12] In economics, such a situation is described as *sun-spot* equilibrium. See, e.g., M. Woodford, Econometrica **58,** 277 (1990). (We thank M. Marsili for drawing our attention to sun spots.)

[13] See, however, D. Challet and M. Marsili, cond-mat/9904071.

[14] J. Hofbauer and K. Sigmund, *Evolutionary Games and Population Dynamics* (Cambridge University, Cambridge, England, 1998).

[15] Stochastic learning processes are described by replicator equations only if the continuous-time limit is taken in a particular way. See T. Börgers and R. Sarin, J. Econ. Theory **77,** 1 (1997).

[16] A. C. C. Coolen, S. N. Laughton, and D. Sherrington, Phys. Rev. B **53,** 8184 (1996).

Statistical Mechanics of Systems with Heterogeneous Agents: Minority Games

Damien Challet,[1] Matteo Marsili,[2] and Riccardo Zecchina[3]

[1] *Institut de Physique Théorique, Université de Fribourg, CH-1700 Fribourg, Switzerland*
[2] *Istituto Nazionale per la Fisica della Materia (INFM), Trieste-SISSA Unit, Via Beirut 2-4, I-34014 Trieste, Italy*
[3] *The Abdus Salam International Centre for Theoretical Physics, Strada Costiera 11, P.O. Box 586, I-34100 Trieste, Italy*

(Received 27 April 1999; revised manuscript received 30 June 1999)

We study analytically a simple game theoretical model of heterogeneous interacting agents. We show that the stationary state of the system is described by the ground state of a disordered spin model which is exactly solvable within the simple replica symmetric ansatz. Such a stationary state differs from the Nash equilibrium where each agent maximizes her own utility. The latter turns out to be characterized by a replica symmetry broken structure. Numerical results fully agree with our analytical findings.

PACS numbers: 02.50.Le, 05.20.Dd, 64.60.Ak, 87.23.Ge

Statistical mechanics of disordered systems provides analytical and numerical tools for the description of complex systems, which have found applications in many interdisciplinary areas [1]. When the precise realization of the interactions in a heterogeneous system is expected not to be crucial for the overall macroscopic behavior, then the system itself can be modeled as having random interactions drawn from an appropriate distribution. Such an approach appears to be very promising also for the study of systems with many heterogeneous agents, such as markets, which have recently attracted much interest in the statistical physics community [2,3]. Indeed it provides a workable alternative to the so-called *representative agent* approach of microeconomic theory, where, assuming that agents are identical, one is lead to a theory with one single (representative) agent [4].

In this Letter, we present analytical results for a simple model of heterogeneous interacting agents, the so-called minority game (MG) [3,5], which is a toy model of N agents interacting through a global quantity representing a market mechanism. Agents aim at anticipating market movements by following a simple adaptive dynamics inspired at Arthur's *inductive reasoning* [6]. This is based on simple *speculative* strategies that take advantage of the available public information concerning the recent market history, which can take the form of one of P patterns. Numerical studies [3,7–9] have shown that the model displays a remarkably rich behavior. The relevant control parameter [3,7] turns out to be the ratio $\alpha = P/N$ between the "complexity" of information P and the number N of agents, and the model undergoes a phase transition with symmetry breaking [8] independently of the origin of information [9].

We shall limit the discussion on the interpretation of the model—which is discussed at some length in Refs. [3,7]—to a minimum and rather focus on its mathematical structure and to the analysis of its statistical properties for $N \gg 1$. Our main aim is indeed to show that the model can be analyzed within the framework of statistical mechanics of a disordered system [1].

We find that dynamical steady states can be mapped onto the ground state properties of a model very similar to that proposed in Ref. [10] in the context of optimal dynamics for attractor neural networks. There [10] one shows that the minimization of the interference noise is equivalent to maximizing the dynamical stability of each device composing the system. Conversely, we show that the individual utility maximization in interacting agent systems is equivalent to the minimization of a global function. We also find that different learning models lead to different patterns of replica symmetry breaking.

The model is defined as follows [8]: Agents live in a world which can be in one of P states. These are labeled by an integer $\mu = 1, \ldots, P$ which encodes all the information available to agents. For the moment being, we follow Ref. [9] and assume that this information concerns some external system so that μ is drawn from a uniform distribution $\varrho^\mu = 1/P$ in $\{1, \ldots, P\}$. Each agent $i = 1, \ldots, N$ can choose between one of two *strategies*, labeled by a spin variable $s_i \in \{\pm 1\}$, which prescribes an *action* $a_{s_i,i}^\mu$ for each state μ. Strategies may be "look up tables," behavioral rules [3,6], or information processing devices. The actions $a_{s,i}^\mu$ are drawn from a bimodal distribution $P(a_{s,i}^\mu = \pm 1) = 1/2$ for all i, s, and μ, and they will play the role of quenched disorder [1]. Hence, there are only two possible actions, such as "do something" ($a_{s,i}^\mu = 1$) or "do the opposite" ($a_{s,i}^\mu = -1$). It is convenient [8] to make the dependence on s explicit in $a_{s,i}^\mu$, introducing ω_i^μ and ξ_i^μ so that $a_{s,i}^\mu = \omega_i^\mu + s\xi_i^\mu$ [11]. If agent i chooses strategy s_i and her opponents choose strategies $s_{-i} \equiv \{s_j, j \neq i\}$, in state μ, she receives a payoff,

$$u_i^\mu(s_i, s_{-i}) = -a_{s_i,i}^\mu G(A^\mu), \qquad (1)$$

where, defining $\Omega^\mu = \sum_j \omega_j^\mu$,

$$A^\mu = \sum_j a_{s_j,j}^\mu = \Omega^\mu + \sum_j \xi_j^\mu s_j. \qquad (2)$$

The function $G(x)$, which describes the market mechanism, is such that $xG(x) > 0$ for all x so that the total payoff to agents is always negative: the majority of agents

0031-9007/00/84(8)/1824(4)$15.00
© 2000 The American Physical Society

receives a negative payoff whereas only the minority of them gain. Note that the agent-agent interaction, which comes from the aggregate quantity $G(A^\mu)$, is of mean-field character.

The game defined by the payoffs in Eq. (1) can be analyzed along the lines of game theory [12] by looking for its Nash equilibria in the strategies space $\{s_j, j = 1, \ldots, N\}$. Before doing this, we prefer to discuss the dynamics of *inductive agents* following Refs. [3,7,8]: There, the game is repeated many times and agents try to estimate empirically which of the two strategies they have is the best one, using past observations. More precisely, each agent i assigns a *score* $U_{s,i}(t)$ to her sth strategy at time t, and we assume, as in Ref. [13], that she chooses that strategy with probability [14]

$$\pi_{s,i}(t) \equiv \mathrm{Prob}\{s_i(t) = s\} = Ce^{\Gamma U_{s,i}(t)}, \qquad (3)$$

with $C^{-1} = \sum_{s'} e^{\Gamma U_{s',i}(t)}$ and $\Gamma > 0$. The scores are initially set to $U_{s,i}(0) = 0$, and they are updated as

$$U_{s,i}(t + 1) = U_{s,i}(t) - a_{s,i}^{\mu(t)} G(A^{\mu(t)})/P. \qquad (4)$$

The idea is that if a strategy s has predicted the right sign, i.e., if $a_{s,i}^\mu = -\mathrm{sgn}G(A^\mu)$, its score, and, hence, its probability of being used, increases. Note that $a_{s,i}^\mu G(A^\mu)$ in Eq. (4) is *not* the payoff $u_i^\mu(s, s_{-i})$ which agent i would have received if she had actually played strategy $s \neq s_i(t)$. Indeed $G(A^\mu)$ depends on the strategy $s_i(t)$ that agent i has actually played through A^μ. Agents in the MG neglect this effect and behave as if they were facing an external process $G(A^\mu)$ rather than playing against other $N - 1$ agents. This may seem reasonable for $N \gg 1$ since the relative dependence of aggregate quantities on each agent's choice is expected to be small. We shall see below [see Eq. (11)] that this is not true: If agents consider the impact of their actions on A^μ, the collective behavior changes considerably.

We focus on the linear case $G(x) = x$, which allows for a simple treatment. Other choices, such as the original one, $G(x) = \mathrm{sgn}x$, lead to similar conclusions, as will be discussed elsewhere [15]. With this choice, the total losses of agents is $-\sum_i u_i^\mu = (A^\mu)^2$. The time average σ^2 of $(A^\mu)^2$ is shown in Fig. 1, as a function of $\alpha \equiv P/N$. The system shows a complex behavior characterized, among other things, by a phase transition at $\alpha_c \simeq 0.34$ [8], where σ^2 shows a cusp and a small α phase where σ^2 increases with Γ [13].

In order to uncover this behavior, let us focus on the long time behavior of the dynamics. The key observation is that, in the long run, the score of a strategy depends on its performance in all P states. Hence, the behavior of agents will change systematically only on time scales of order P. This suggests introduction of the rescaled time $\tau = t/P$. As $P \to \infty$, any finite interval $d\tau = \Delta t/P$ is made of infinitely many time steps, and we can use the law of large numbers to approximate time averages with statistical averages over the variables $\mu(t)$ and $s_i(t)$ from their respective distributions ϱ^μ and $\pi_{s,i}$. We henceforth

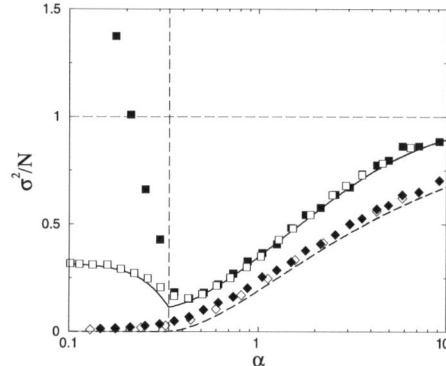

FIG. 1. σ^2/N versus $\alpha = P/N$ for $P = 2^6$ for inductive dynamics (full squares), for the numerical minimization of Eq. (7) (open squares), corrected inductive dynamics (full diamonds), and the ground state of σ^2 (open diamonds). The full and the dashed lines are the corresponding analytic results. Averages are taken over 200 realizations.

use the notation $\bar{o} = \sum_\mu \varrho^\mu o^\mu$ for averages over μ and $\langle \cdot \rangle$ for averages on $s_i(t)$, and we define $m_i(\tau) \equiv \langle s_i(t) \rangle$. With this notation, σ^2 reads

$$\sigma^2 = \overline{\langle A^2 \rangle} = \overline{\Omega}^2 + \sum_i [\overline{\xi_i^2} + 2\overline{\Omega \xi_i} m_i]$$
$$+ \sum_{i \neq j} \overline{\xi_i \xi_j} m_i m_j, \qquad (5)$$

where we have used statistical independence of s_i, i.e., $\langle s_i s_j \rangle = m_i m_j + (1 - m_i^2)\delta_{i,j}$. The evolution of scores $U_{s,i}$ in continuum time τ is obtained iterating Eq. (4) for $\Delta t = Pd\tau$ time steps. Using Eq. (3) in the form $m_i = \tanh[\Gamma(U_{+1,i} - U_{-1,i})]$, we find

$$\frac{dm_i}{d\tau} = -2\Gamma(1 - m_i^2)\left[\overline{\Omega \xi_i} + \sum_j \overline{\xi_i \xi_j} m_j\right]. \qquad (6)$$

This can be easily written as a gradient descent dynamics $dm_i/d\tau = -\Gamma(1 - m_i^2)(\partial H/\partial m_i)$ which minimizes the Hamiltonian

$$H = \overline{\langle A \rangle^2} = \sigma^2 - \sum_i \overline{\xi_i^2}(1 - m_i^2). \qquad (7)$$

As a function of m_i, H is a positive definite quadratic form, which has a unique minimum. This implies that *the stationary state of the MG is described by the ground state properties of H*. It is easy to see [15] that H is closely related to the order parameter $\theta = \sqrt{\overline{\langle \mathrm{sgn}A \rangle^2}}$ introduced in [8], which is a measure of the system predictability [8]. Indeed $H \propto \theta^2$ when θ is small, suggested that inductive agents actually minimize predictability rather than their collective losses σ^2.

It is possible to study the ground state properties of H in Eq. (7) using the replica method [1]. First, we introduce an inverse temperature β [16] and compute the average over the disorder variables $\Xi = \{a_{s,i}^\mu\}$ of the partition function of n replicas of the system, $\langle Z^n \rangle_\Xi$. Next, we perform an analytic continuation for noninteger values of n, thus obtaining $\langle \ln Z \rangle_\Xi = \lim_{n \to 0} \frac{\langle Z^n \rangle_\Xi - 1}{n}$. The "free energy" $F_{ID} = -\langle \ln Z \rangle_\Xi / \beta$ depends on the overlap matrix $Q_{a,b} = \langle m_i^a m_i^b \rangle$ $(a, b = 1, \ldots, n, a \neq b)$ and on the order parameter $Q_a = (1/N)\sum_i (m_i^a)^2$, together with their Lagrange multipliers $r_{a,b}$ and R_a, respectively. F_{ID} can be calculated using a saddle point method that, within the replica symmetric (RS) ansatz $Q_{a,b} = q$, $r_{a,b} = r$ (for all $a < b$), and $Q_a = Q$, $R_a = R$ (for all a), leads to

$$F_{ID} = \frac{\alpha}{2}\,\frac{1 + q}{\alpha + \beta(Q - q)} + \frac{\alpha}{2\beta}\log\left[1 + \frac{\beta(Q - q)}{\alpha}\right]$$
$$+ \frac{\beta}{2}(RQ - rq)$$
$$- \frac{1}{\beta}\int d\Phi(\zeta)\log\int_{-1}^{1} ds\, e^{-\beta V(s|\zeta)},$$

where $V(x\,|\,\zeta) = \beta(r - R)(x^2/2) - \sqrt{r}\,\zeta x$, and Φ is the normal distribution. The ground state properties of H are obtained solving the saddle point equations [1] in the limit $\beta \to \infty$. Figure 1 compares the analytic and numerical findings for σ^2. For $\alpha > \alpha_c = 0.337\,40\ldots$, the solution leads to $Q = q < 1$ and a ground state energy $H_0 > 0$. $H_0 \to 0$ as $\alpha \to \alpha_c^+$ and $H_0 = 0$ for $\alpha \leq \alpha_c$.

This confirms the conclusion $\langle A^\mu \rangle = 0 \; \forall \mu$ [8] (or $\theta = 0$) for $\alpha \leq \alpha_c$ and it implies the relation

$$\sigma^2 = \sum_i \overline{\xi_i^2}(1 - m_i^2) \cong \frac{N}{2}(1 - Q), \qquad \alpha \leq \alpha_c. \tag{8}$$

The RS solution is stable against replica symmetry breaking (RSB) for any α, as expected from positive definiteness of H. Following Ref. [10], we compute the probability distribution of the strategies, which for $\alpha > \alpha_c$ is bimodal and it assumes the particularly simple form

$$\mathcal{P}(m) = \phi(z)[\delta(m - 1) + \delta(m + 1)]$$
$$+ \frac{z}{\sqrt{2\pi}}e^{-(zm)^2/2}, \tag{9}$$

with $z = \sqrt{\alpha/(1 + Q)}$ (Q taking its saddle point value) and where $\phi(z) = [1 - \mathrm{erf}(z/\sqrt{2})]/2$ is the fraction of frozen agents (those who always play one and the same strategy). Below α_c, $\mathcal{P}(m)$ is continuous, i.e., $\phi = 0$ in agreement with numerical findings [8].

At the transition the spin susceptibility $\chi = \lim_{\beta \to \infty}\beta(Q - q)$ diverges as $\alpha \to \alpha_c^+$, and it remains infinite for all $\alpha \leq \alpha_c$. This is because the ground state is degenerate in many directions (zero modes) and an infinitesimal perturbation can cause a finite shift in the equilibrium values of m_i. This implies that in the long run the dynamics (6) leads to an equilibrium state which depends on the initial conditions $U_{s,i}(t = 0)$. The underconstrained nature of the system is also responsible

for the occurrence of antipersistent effects for $\alpha < \alpha_c$ [8]. The periodic motion in the subspace $H = 0$ is probably induced by inertial terms $d^2 U_{s,i}/d\tau^2$ which we have neglected, and which require a more careful study of dynamical solutions of Eqs. (3) and (4). It is, however, clear that the amplitude of the excursion of $U_{+1,i}(t) - U_{-1,i}(t)$ decreases with Γ, by the smoothing effect of Eq. (3). When this amplitude becomes of the same order of $1/\Gamma$ antipersistence is destroyed, which explains the sudden drop of σ^2 with Γ found in Ref. [13].

A natural question arises: Is this state individually optimal, i.e., it is a Nash equilibrium of the game where agents maximize the expected utility $\bar{u}_i = -\overline{a_{s,i}A}$? One way to find the Nash equilibria is to consider stationary solutions of the multipopulation replicator dynamics [17]. This takes the form of an equation for the so-called *mixed* strategies, i.e., for the probabilities $\pi_{s,i}$ with which agent i plays strategy s. In terms of $m_i = \pi_{+,i} - \pi_{-,i}$, with a little algebra, these equations [17] read

$$\frac{dm_i}{d\tau} = (1 - m_i^2)\frac{\partial \bar{u}_i}{\partial m_i}. \tag{10}$$

Observing that $\partial \bar{u}_i/\partial m_i = -\partial\sigma^2/\partial m_i$, we can rewrite Eq. (10) as a gradient descent dynamics which minimizes a global function which is *exactly* the total loss σ^2 of agents. Nash equilibria then correspond to the local minima of σ^2 in the domain $[-1, 1]^N$. The quadratic form σ^2 is not positive definite, which means that there shall be many local minima and the Nash equilibrium is not unique. It is easy to see [15] that Nash equilibria are in *pure* strategies, i.e., $m_i^2 = 1 \; \forall i$, which implies $\sigma^2 = H$, by Eq. (7). A detailed characterization of the Nash equilibria shall be given elsewhere [15]. The best Nash equilibrium can be studied applying the replica method to σ^2 for $\beta \to \infty$. The multiplicity of Nash equilibria (metastable states) manifests itself in the occurrence of replica symmetry breaking for any $\alpha > 0$ with a nonvanishing σ^2/N [15]. The simple RS solution, though incorrect, provides a close lower bound $F_{NE}^{(RS)} = F_{ID} + \frac{1}{2}(1 - Q)$ to σ^2/N for $\beta \to \infty$ (see Fig. 1). For $\alpha > 1/\pi$, we have $Q = q = 1$ and $F_{NE}^{(RS)}$ $(\beta = \infty) = [1 - 1/\sqrt{\pi\alpha}]^2$ positive, whereas $1 = Q < q$ and $F_{NE}^{(RS)} = 0$ for $\alpha < 1/\pi$.

Figure 1 shows that in a Nash equilibrium agents perform much better than in the MG. This is the consequence of the fact that agents do not take into account their impact on the market (i.e., on A^μ) when they update the scores of their strategies by Eq. (4). It is indeed known [18] that reinforcement-learning dynamics based on Eq. (3) is closely related to the replicator dynamics and, hence, it converges to rational expectation outcomes, i.e., to Nash equilibria. More precisely, Ref. [18] suggests that this occurs if Eq. (4) is replaced with

$$U_{i,s}(t + 1) = U_{i,s}(t) + u_i^{\mu(t)}[s, s_{-i}(t)]/P. \tag{11}$$

Now $U_{s,i}(t)$ is proportional to the cumulated payoff that agent i would have received had she always played strategy s (with other agents playing what they actually played) until time t. As Fig. 1 again shows, this leads to results which coincide with those of the Nash equilibrium. It is remarkable that the (relative) difference between Eqs. (4) and (11) is small, i.e., of order $1/A^\mu \sim 1/\sqrt{N}$. Yet, it is *not negligible* because, when averaged over all states μ, it produces a finite effect, especially for $\alpha < \alpha_c$, and it effects considerably the nature of the stationary state. This term has the same origin of the cavity reaction term in spin glasses [1]. In order to follow Eq. (11), agents need to know the payoff they would have received for any strategy s they could have played. That may not be realistic in complex situations where agents know only the payoffs they receive and are unable to disentangle their contribution from $G(A^\mu)$. However, agents can account approximately for their impact on the market by adding a cavity term $+\eta \delta_{s,s_i(t)}$ to Eq. (4) which "rewards" the strategy $s_i(t)$ used with respect to those $s \neq s_i(t)$ not used. The most striking effect of this new term, as discussed elsewhere [15] in detail, is that for $\alpha < \alpha_c$ an *infinitesimal* $\eta > 0$ is sufficient to cause RSB and to reduce σ^2/N by a *finite* amount.

Thus far, the information $\mu(t)$ was randomly and independently drawn at each time t from the distribution $\varrho^\mu = 1/P$. In the original version of the MG [3], μ is instead endogenously determined by the collective dynamics of agents: $\mu(t)$ indeed labels the sequence of the last $M = \log_2 P$ "minority" signs, i.e., $\mu(t + 1) = [2\mu(t) + 1]_{\text{mod}P}$ if $A^{\mu(t)} > 0$, and $\mu(t + 1) = [2\mu(t)]_{\text{mod}P}$ otherwise. The idea [3] is that the information refers to the recent past history of the market, and agents try to guess trends and patterns in the time evolution of the process $G(A^{\mu(t)})$. We may say that $\mu(t)$ is *endogenous* information, since it refers to the market itself, as opposed to the *exogenous* information case discussed above.

Numerical simulations [9] show that the collective behavior of the MG, based on Eq. (4), under endogenous information is the same as that under exogenous information. Within our approach, the relevant feature of the dynamics of $\mu(t)$ is its stationary state distribution ϱ^μ. The key point is that a finite fraction $1 - \phi$ of agents behave stochastically ($m_i^2 < 1$) because $Q < 1$. As a consequence, A^μ has stochastic fluctuations of order $\sqrt{N(1 - Q)}$ which are of the same order of its average $\langle A^\mu \rangle \sim \sqrt{H}$. With endogenous information, these fluctuations of A^μ induce a dynamics of $\mu(t)$ which is ergodic in the sense that typically each μ is visited with a frequency $\varrho^\mu \simeq 1/P$ in the stationary state [15]. The situation changes completely when agents follow Eq. (11). Indeed the system converges to a Nash equilibrium where agents play in a deterministic way, i.e., $m_i^2 = 1$ (or $Q = \phi = 1$). The noise due to the stochastic choice of s_i by Eq. (3) is totally suppressed. The system becomes deterministic and the dynamics of $\mu(t)$ locks into some periodic orbit. The ergodicity assumption then breaks down: Only a small number $\bar{P} \ll P$ of patterns μ are visited in the stationary state of the system, whereas the others never occur ($\varrho^\mu = 0$). This leads to an effective reduction of the

parameter $\alpha \to \tilde{\alpha} = \bar{P}/N$, which further diminishes σ^2. Numerical simulations show that $\bar{P} \propto \sqrt{P}$ which imply that $\tilde{\alpha} \to 0$ in the limit $P = \alpha N \to \infty$, i.e., $\sigma^2/N \to 0$.

In summary, we have shown how methods of statistical physics of disordered systems can successfully be applied to study models of interacting heterogeneous agents. Our results extend easily to more general models [15] and, more importantly, the key ideas can be applied to more realistic models of financial markets, where heterogeneities arise, e.g., from asymmetric information.

We acknowledge J. Berg, A. De Martino, S. Franz, F. Ricci-Tersenghi, S. Solla, M. Virasoro, and Y.-C. Zhang for discussions and useful suggestions. This work was partially supported by Swiss National Science Foundation Grant No. 20-46918.98.

---

[1] M. Mezard, G. Parisi, and M. A. Virasoro, *Spin Glass Theory and Beyond* (World Scientific, Singapore, 1987).

[2] P. W. Anderson, K. Arrow, and D. Pines, *The Economy as an Evolving Complex System* (Addison-Wesley, Reading, MA, 1988); *Econophysics: An Emerging Science,* edited by J. Kertesz and I. Kondor (Kluwer, Dordrecht, 1998).

[3] D. Challet and Y.-C. Zhang, Physica (Amsterdam) **246A**, 407 (1997); Y.-C. Zhang, Europhys. News **29**, 51 (1998).

[4] A. Mas-Colell, M. D. Whinston, and J. R. Green, *Microeconomic Theory* (Oxford University, New York, 1995).

[5] See www.unifr.ch/econophysics for a complete collection of references on the minority game.

[6] W. B. Arthur, Am. Econ. Assoc. Papers Proc. **84**, 406 (1994).

[7] R. Savit, R. Manuca, and R. Riolo, Phys. Rev. Lett. **82**, 2203 (1999).

[8] D. Challet and M. Marsili, Phys. Rev. E **60**, R6271 (1999).

[9] A. Cavagna, Phys. Rev. E **59**, R3783 (1999).

[10] N. Brunel and R. Zecchina, Phys. Rev. E **49**, R1823 (1994).

[11] Both ω_i^μ and ξ_i^μ take values in $\{0, \pm 1\}$ but they are not independent: $\omega_i^\mu \xi_i^\mu = 0$ and $\omega_i^\mu + \xi_i^\mu \neq 0$ for all i, μ.

[12] D. M. Kreps, *Game Theory and Economic Modelling* (Oxford University, New York, 1990).

[13] A. Cavagna, J. P. Garrahan, I. Giardina, and D. Sherrington, Phys. Rev. Lett. **83**, 4429 (1999).

[14] See, e.g., M. Marsili, Physica (Amsterdam) **269A**, 9 (1999).

[15] M. Marsili, D. Challet, and R. Zecchina, cond-mat/9908480; D. Challet, M. Marsili, and Y.-C. Zhang (to be published).

[16] β is introduced as a device to study the minima of H and it should not be confused with Γ. Equation (6) suggests that Γ is not an inverse temperature, in this context, but rather the learning rate. However, a system with a finite memory—i.e., replacing Eq. (4) by $U_{s,i}(t + 1) = (1 - \epsilon)U_{s,i}(t) - a_{s,i}^{\mu(t)}G(A^{\mu(t)})$—is described by the properties of H at a finite temperature $\beta = \Gamma/\epsilon$.

[17] J. W. Weibull, *Evolutionary Game Theory* (MIT, Cambridge, MA, 1995).

[18] A. Rustichini (to be published); D. Fudenberg and D. K. Levine, *The Theory of Learning in Games* (MIT, Cambridge, MA, 1998).

1827

Continuum time limit and stationary states of the minority game

Matteo Marsili

Istituto Nazionale per la Fisica della Materia (INFM), Trieste-SISSA Unit, Via Beirut 2-4, Trieste 34014, Italy

Damien Challet

Theoretical Physics, Oxford University, 1 Keble Road, Oxford OX1 3NP, United Kingdom

(Received 17 February 2001; revised manuscript received 29 June 2001; published 30 October 2001)

We discuss in detail the derivation of stochastic differential equations for the continuum time limit of the minority game. We show that all properties of the minority game can be understood by a careful theoretical analysis of such equations. In particular, (i) we confirm that the stationary state properties are given by the ground state configurations of a disordered (soft) spin system, (ii) we derive the full stationary state distribution, (iii) we characterize the dependence on initial conditions in the symmetric phase, and (iv) we clarify the behavior of the system as a function of the learning rate. This leaves us with a complete and coherent picture of the collective behavior of the minority game. Strikingly we find that the temperaturelike parameter, which is introduced in the choice behavior of *individual* agents turns out to play the role, at the *collective* level, of the inverse of a thermodynamic temperature.

DOI: 10.1103/PhysRevE.64.056138   PACS number(s): 02.50.Le, 05.40.−a, 64.60.Ak, 89.90.+n

I. INTRODUCTION

Even under the most demanding definition, the minority game (MG) [1,2] definitely qualifies as a complex system. The MG can be regarded as an Ising model for systems of heterogeneous adaptive agents, which interact via a global mechanism that entails competition for limited resource, as found, for instance, in biology and financial markets. In spite of more than three years of intense research, its rich dynamical behavior is still the subject of investigations; many variations of the basic MG are being proposed, each uncovering new surprising regions of phase space.

Most importantly, Refs. [3–7] have shown that much theoretical insight can be gained on the behavior of this class of models, using nonequilibrium statistical physics and statistical mechanics of disordered systems. The approach of Refs. [3–6] rests on the assumption that, in a continuum time limit (CTL), the dynamics of the MG can be described by a set of *deterministic* equations. From these, one derives a function H that is minimized along all trajectories; hence, the stationary state of the system corresponds to the ground state of H, which can be computed exactly by statistical mechanics techniques. This approach has been challenged in Refs. [8,9], which have proposed a *stochastic* dynamics for the MG, thus leading to some debate in the literature [10,11].

In this paper, our aim is to analyze in detail the derivation of the CTL in order to clarify this issue. We show that a proper derivation of the CTL indeed reconciles the two approaches: the resulting dynamical equations—Eqs. (15)–(17) below, which are our central result—are indeed *stochastic*, as suggested in Refs. [8,9], but still the stationary state of the dynamics is described by the minima of the function H, as suggested in Refs. [3,4]. We then confirm the analytic results derived previously. In few words, our analysis follows two main steps: first, we characterize the average behavior of agents by computing the frequency with which they play their strategies. This step can be translated in the study of the ground state properties of a soft spin disordered Hamiltonian.

Second, we characterize the fluctuations around the average behavior. To do this, we explicitly solve the Fokker-Planck equation associated with the stochastic dynamics.

The results we derive are the following.

(1) We derive the full probability distribution in the stationary state. Remarkably we find that the parameter that is introduced as a temperature in the individual choice model turns out to play the role of the inverse of a global temperature.

(2) For $\alpha > \alpha_c$ the distribution factorizes over the agents whereas in the symmetric phase ($\alpha < \alpha_c$) agents play in a correlated way. In the latter case, the correlations contribute to the stochastic force acting on agents. We show how the dependence of global efficiency on individual temperature found in Ref. [8] arises as a consequence of these correlations.

(3) We extend the analytic approach of Refs. [3,4] to the $\alpha < \alpha_c$ phase and asymmetric initial conditions. The dependence on the initial conditions in this phase, first noticed and discussed in Refs. [3,4], has been more recently studied quantitatively in Refs. [9,7]. We clarify the origin of this behavior and derive analytic solutions in the limit $\Gamma \to 0$.

(4) We show that the stronger the initial asymmetry in agents' evaluation of their strategies, the larger is the efficiency and the more stable is the system against crowd effects [12].

(5) We derive the Hamiltonian of MGs with nonlinear payoffs.

This leaves us with a coherent picture of the collective behavior of the minority game, which is an important reference framework for the study of complex systems of heterogeneous adaptive agents.

II. THE MODEL

The dynamics of the MG is defined in terms of dynamical variables $U_{s,i}(t)$ in discrete time $t=0,1,\ldots$. These are scores, propensities or "attractions" [14], which each agent

$i = 1, \ldots, N$ attaches to each of his possible choices $s = 1, \ldots, S$. Each agent takes a decision $s_i(t)$ with

$$\text{Prob}\{s_i(t) = s\} = \frac{e^{\Gamma_i U_{s,i}(t)}}{\sum_{s'} e^{\Gamma_i U_{s',i}(t)}}, \qquad (1)$$

where $\Gamma_i > 0$ appears as an "individual inverse temperature." The original MG corresponds to $\Gamma_i = \infty$ [1] and was generalized later to $\Gamma_i \equiv \Gamma < \infty$ [8].

The public information variable $\mu(t)$ is given to all agents; it belongs to the set of integers $(1, \ldots, P)$ and can either be the binary encoding of the last M winning choices [1], or drawn at random from a uniform distribution [15]; we stick to the latter case for sake of simplicity.[1] The action $a_{s_i(t),i}^{\mu(t)}$ of each agent depends on its choice $s_i(t)$ and on $\mu(t)$. The coefficients $a_{s,i}^{\mu}$, called strategies, play the role of quenched disorder: they are randomly drawn signs $(\text{Prob}\{a_{s,i}^{\mu} = \pm 1\} = 1/2)$, independently for each i, s, and μ. On the basis of the outcome

$$A(t) = \sum_{i=1}^{N} a_{s_i(t),i}^{\mu(t)}, \qquad (2)$$

each agent updates his scores according to

$$U_{s,i}(t+1) = U_{s,i}(t) - a_{s,i}^{\mu(t)} \frac{A(t)}{P}. \qquad (3)$$

The idea of this equation is that agents reward [$U_{s,i}(t+1) > U_{s,i}(t)$] those strategies that would have predicted the *minority sign*—$A(t)/|A(t)|$. The MG was initially proposed with a nonlinear dependence on $A(t)$, i.e., with a dynamics $U_{s,i}(t+1) = U_{s,i}(t) - a_{s,i}^{\mu(t)} \text{sgn}[A(t)]$. This leads to qualitatively similar results. The extension of our theory to nonlinear cases is dealt with in Appendix A. We shall not discuss any longer the interpretation of the model, which is discussed at length elsewhere [4,17–19].

The sources of randomness are in the choices of $\mu(t)$ by nature and of $s_i(t)$ by agents. These are fast fluctuating degrees of freedom. As a consequence also, $U_{s,i}(t)$ and hence the probability with which agents chose $s_i(t)$ are subject to stochastic fluctuations. Our analysis will indeed focus on the characterization of the low-frequency fluctuations of $U_{s,i}$ by integrating out the high-frequency fluctuations of $\mu(t)$ and $s_i(t)$. This will become clearer in the next section. For the time being let it suffice to say that there are two levels of fluctuations, that of "fast" variables $\mu(t)$ and $s_i(t)$ and that of "slow" degrees of freedom $U_{s,i}(t)$.

The key parameter is the ratio $\alpha = P/N$ [18] and the two relevant quantities are

$$\sigma^2 = \langle A^2 \rangle, \qquad H = \frac{1}{P} \sum_{\mu=1}^{P} \langle A|\mu \rangle^2, \qquad (4)$$

which measure, respectively, global efficiency and predictability.[2]

Generalizations of the model, where agents account for their market impact [3,4], where deterministic agents—so-called producers—are present [5], or where agents are allowed not to play [20–24], have been proposed. Rather than dealing with the most generic model, which would depend on too many parameters, we shall limit our discussion to the plain MG. Furthermore, we shall specialize, in the second part of the paper, to the case $S = 2$, which lends itself to a simpler analytic treatment. The analysis carries through in obvious ways to the more general cases discussed in Refs. [4,5,3,24].

III. THE CONTINUUM TIME LIMIT

Our approach, which follows that of Refs. [3,4], is based on two key observations.

(1) The scaling $\sigma^2 \sim N$, at fixed α, suggests that typically $A(t) \sim \sqrt{N}$. Hence time increments of $U_{s,i}(t)$ in Eq. (3) are small (i.e., of order $\sqrt{N}/P \sim 1/\sqrt{N}$).

(2) Characteristic times of the dynamics are proportional to P. Naively this is because agents need to "test" their strategies against all P values of μ, which requires of the order of P time steps. More precisely, one can reach this conclusion by measuring relaxation or correlation times and verifying that they indeed grow linearly with P (see Ref. [10]).

The second observation implies that one needs to study the dynamics in the rescaled time $\tau = t/P$. This makes our approach differ from that of Refs. [8,9], where the time is not rescaled.

In order to study the dynamics for $P, N \gg 1$ at fixed α, we shall focus on a fixed small increment $d\tau$ such that $P d\tau = \alpha N d\tau \gg 1$. This means that we take the continuum time limit $d\tau \to 0$ *only after* the thermodynamic limit $N \to \infty$. We focus only on the leading order in N. Furthermore, we shall also consider Γ_i finite and

$$\Gamma_i d\tau \ll 1, \qquad (5)$$

which means that the limit $\Gamma_i \to \infty$ should be taken after the limit $d\tau \to 0$. The orders in which these limits are taken, given the agreement with numerical simulation results, does not really matter: as we shall see differences only enter in the finite size corrections. We shall come back later to these issues.

Iteration of the dynamics for $P d\tau$ time steps, from $t = P\tau$ to $t = P(\tau + d\tau)$ gives

$$u_{s,i}(\tau + d\tau) - u_{s,i}(\tau) = -\frac{1}{P} \sum_{t=P\tau}^{P(\tau + d\tau) - 1} a_{s,i}^{\mu(t)} A(t), \qquad (6)$$

where we have introduced the functions $u_{s,i}(\tau) = U_{s,i}(P\tau)$.

---

[1] Both prescriptions lead to qualitatively similar results for the quantities we study here. See [16] for more details.

[2] Averages $\langle \cdots \rangle$ stand for time averages in the stationary state of the process. Then $\langle \cdots | \mu \rangle$ stands for time averages conditional on $\mu(t) = \mu$.

Let us separate a deterministic $(du_{s,i})$ from a stochastic $(dW_{s,i})$ term in this equation by replacing

$$a_{s,i}^{\mu(t)} A(t) = \overline{a_{s,i} \langle A \rangle_\pi} + X_{s,i}(t). \tag{7}$$

Here and henceforth, we denote averages over μ by an overline

$$\overline{R} = \frac{1}{P} \sum_{\mu=1}^{P} R^\mu,$$

while $\langle \cdots \rangle_\pi$ stands for an average over the distributions

$$\pi_{s,i}(\tau) = \frac{1}{Pd\tau} \sum_{t=P\tau}^{P(\tau+d\tau)-1} \frac{e^{\Gamma_i U_{s,i}(t)}}{\sum_r e^{\Gamma_i U_{r,i}(t)}}, \tag{8}$$

which is the frequency with which agent i plays strategy s in the time interval $P\tau \leq t < P(\tau+d\tau)$.

Notice that $\pi_{s,i}(\tau)$ will themselves be stochastic variables, hence we also define the average on the stationary state as

$$\langle \cdots \rangle = \lim_{\tau_0, T \to \infty} \frac{1}{T} \int_{\tau_0}^{\tau_0+T} d\tau \langle \cdots \rangle_{\pi(\tau)}, \tag{9}$$

where the average inside the integral is performed with the probabilities $\pi_{s,i}(\tau)$.

Hence

$$u_{s,i}(\tau+d\tau) - u_{s,i}(\tau) = du_{s,i}(\tau) + dW_{s,i}(\tau)$$
$$= -\overline{a_{s,i} \langle A \rangle_\pi} d\tau$$
$$+ \frac{1}{P} \sum_{t=P\tau}^{P(\tau+d\tau)-1} X_{s,i}(t). \tag{10}$$

Now the first term is of order $d\tau$ as required for a deterministic term. In addition it remains finite as $N \to \infty$ [25].

The second term is a sum of $Pd\tau$ random variables $X_{s,i}(t)$ with zero average. We take $d\tau$ fixed and N very large, so that $Pd\tau \gg 1$ and we can use limit theorems. The variables $X_{s,i}(t)$ are independent from time to time, because both $\mu(t)$ and $s_j(t)$ are drawn independently at each time. Hence $X_{s,i}(t)$ for $P\tau \leq t < P(\tau+d\tau)$ are independent and identically[3] distributed. For $Pd\tau \gg 1$ we may approximate the second term $dW_{s,i}$ of Eq. (10) by a Gaussian variable with zero average and variance,

$$\langle dW_{s,i}(\tau) dW_{r,j}(\tau') \rangle = \frac{\delta(\tau-\tau')}{P^2} \sum_{t=P\tau}^{P(\tau+d\tau)} \langle X_{s,i}(t) X_{r,j}(t) \rangle_\pi$$
$$= \delta(\tau-\tau') d\tau \frac{\langle X_{s,i}(t) X_{r,j}(t) \rangle_\pi}{P},$$

---
[3]Strictly speaking, $s_i(t)$ is drawn from the distribution in Eq. (1) and not from $\pi_{s,i}$ of Eq. (8). However, these two distributions differ by a negligible amount as long as the condition (5) holds (see later).

where the $\delta(\tau-\tau')$ comes from independence of $X_{s,i}(t)$ and $X_{r,j}(t')$ for $t \neq t'$ and the fact that $X_{s,i}(t)$ are identically distributed in time leads to the expression in the second line. Now

$$\frac{\langle X_{s,i}(t) X_{r,j}(t) \rangle_\pi}{P} = \overline{\frac{a_{s,i} a_{r,j} \langle A^2 \rangle_\pi}{P}} - \overline{\frac{a_{s,i} \langle A \rangle_\pi a_{r,j} \langle A \rangle_\pi}{P}}. \tag{11}$$

The second term always vanishes for $N \to \infty$ because $a_{s,i} \langle A \rangle_\pi$ is of order N^0 [25]. In the first term, instead,

$$\langle A^2 | \mu \rangle_\pi = N + \sum_{k \neq l=1}^{N} \sum_{s',r'} a_{s',k}^\mu a_{r',l}^\mu \pi_{s',k} \pi_{r',l} \tag{12}$$

is of order N, which then gives a positive contribution in Eq. (11) for $N \to \infty$.

Equation (12) leads to a stochastic dynamics where the noise covariance depends on the stochastic variables $u_{s,i}(\tau)$ themselves. The complications that result from this fact can be avoided if one takes the approximation

$$\langle A^2 | \mu \rangle_\pi \approx \overline{\langle A^2 \rangle} \equiv \sigma^2. \tag{13}$$

This approximation can be justified naively by observing that the dependence on $\pi_{s,i}$ of the correlations only involves the global quantity $\langle A^2 | \mu \rangle_\pi / P$ for which one expects some sort of self-averaging properties. Numerical results suggest that terms that are ignored by Eq. (13) are negligible for $N \gg 1$, but we were unable to prove this in general [26].

Within this approximation the correlation, for $N \gg 1$ becomes

$$\langle dW_{s,i}(\tau) dW_{r,j}(\tau') \rangle \cong \frac{\sigma^2}{\alpha N} \overline{a_{s,i} a_{r,j}} \delta(\tau-\tau') d\tau. \tag{14}$$

Note that, for $r \neq s$ or $j \neq i$, correlations $\langle dW_{s,i}(\tau) dW_{r,j}(\tau') \rangle \propto \overline{a_{s,i} a_{r,j}} \sim 1/\sqrt{N}$ vanish as $N \to \infty$. However, it is important to keep the off-diagonal terms because they keep the dynamics of the phase space point $|U(t)\rangle = \{U_{s,i}(t)\}_{s=1,\ldots,S,\ i=1,\ldots,N}$ constrained to the linear space spanned by the vectors $|a^\mu\rangle = \{a_{s,i}^\mu\}_{s=1,\ldots,S,\ i=1,\ldots,N}$, which contains the initial condition $|U(0)\rangle$. The original dynamics of $U_{s,i}(t)$ indeed posses this property.

It is important to remark that the approximation (13) makes our approach a self-consistent theory for σ^2. We introduce σ^2 as a constant in Eq. (13), which then has to be computed self-consistently from the dynamic equations.

Summarizing, the dynamics of $u_{s,i}$ is described by a continuum time Langevin equation,

$$\frac{du_{s,i}(\tau)}{d\tau} = -\overline{a_{s,i} \langle A \rangle} + \eta_{s,i}(\tau), \tag{15}$$

$$\langle \eta_{s,i}(\tau) \rangle = 0, \tag{16}$$

056138-3

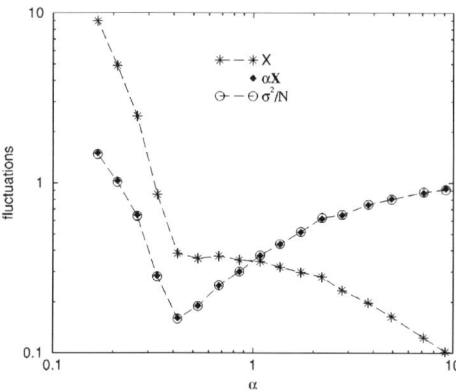

FIG. 1. Noise strength averaged over all agents (stars); when it is multiplied by α (diamonds), one recovers σ^2/N (circles) ($P = 32$, $S = 2$, $300P$ iterations, $\Gamma = \infty$, average over 50 samples). Dashed lines are for eye guidance only.

$$\langle \eta_{s,i}(\tau) \eta_{r,j}(\tau') \rangle \cong \frac{\sigma^2}{\alpha N} \overline{a_{s,i} a_{r,j}} \delta(\tau - \tau'). \tag{17}$$

Equation (15), given its derivation, has to be interpreted in the Ito sense. The expression for the noise strength confirmed by Fig. 1, where the measure of $X = \Sigma_{i,s} \langle (X_{i,s}^2) \rangle/(PNS)$ in a MG is reported; note that these numerical simulations were done for $\Gamma = \infty$ and confirm Eq. (17) is valid even for $\alpha < \alpha_c$. Figure 2 compares the results of numerical simulations of the MG, as a function of Γ, with those of a semianalytic solution of Eqs. (15)–(17), to be discussed later. The agreement of the two approaches shows that Eqs. (15)–(17) are valid even in the symmetric phase ($\alpha \lesssim \alpha_c$) for all values of Γ.

The instantaneous probability distribution of s, in the continuum time limit, reads

$$\pi_{s,i}(\tau) = \frac{e^{\Gamma_i u_{s,i}(\tau)}}{\sum_r e^{\Gamma_i u_{r,i}(\tau)}}. \tag{18}$$

This and Ito calculus then lead to a dynamic equation for $\pi_{s,i}(\tau)$. We prefer to exhibit this for $\Gamma_i = \Gamma$ and using the rescaled time $t = \Gamma \tau$,

$$\frac{d\pi_{s,i}}{dt} = -\pi_{s,i}[\overline{a_{s,i}\langle A \rangle} - \vec{\pi}_i \cdot \overline{\vec{a}_i\langle A \rangle}] + \frac{\sigma^2 \Gamma}{\alpha N} \pi_{s,i}(\pi_{s,i} - \vec{\pi}_i^2)$$

$$+ \sqrt{\Gamma} \pi_{s,i}(\eta_{s,i} - \vec{\pi}_i \vec{\eta}_i). \tag{19}$$

The first term in the right-hand side comes from the deterministic part of Eq. (15), the second from the Ito term (where we neglected terms proportional to $\overline{a_{i,s} a_{i,s'}} \sim 1/\sqrt{N}$ for $s \neq s'$), and the third from the stochastic part. It is clear that, in the limit $\Gamma \to 0$ the last two terms vanish and the dynamics becomes deterministic.

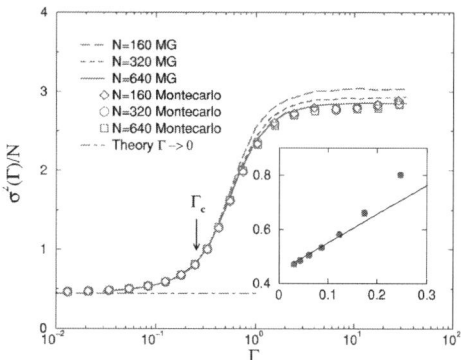

FIG. 2. Global efficiency σ^2/N versus Γ for $\alpha = 0.1 < \alpha_c$ and different system sizes. Lines refer to direct simulations of the MG with $N = 160$, 320, and 640. Finite size effect for $\Gamma \gg 1$ are evident. Symbols refer instead to the solution of the self-consistent equation (36) for the same system sizes. For both methods and all values of N, σ^2 is averaged over 100 realizations of the disorder. The arrow marks the location of Γ_c predicted by Eq. (34). In the inset, the theoretical prediction, Eq. (37), on the leading behavior of σ^2/N for $\Gamma \ll 1$ (solid line) is tested against numerical simulations of the MG (points) for the same values of N.

We see then that Γ tunes the strength of stochastic fluctuations in much the same way as temperature does for thermal fluctuations in statistical mechanics. The "individual inverse temperature" Γ should indeed more correctly be interpreted as a learning rate.[4] Furthermore, it plays the role of a "global temperature." We shall pursue this discussion in detail below for the case $S = 2$.

At this point, let us comment on the limit $\Gamma \to \infty$, which is of particular importance since it corresponds to the original MG. It is clear that in the limit $\Gamma \to \infty$ the dynamical Eqs. (19) become problematic. The origin of the problem lies in the order in which the limits $N \to \infty$ and $\Gamma \to \infty$ is performed. Indeed in Eq. (8) $U_{s,i}(t) \approx u_{s,i}(\tau) + O(d\tau)$ for $P\tau \leq t < P(\tau + d\tau)$. Therefore, as long as $\Gamma d\tau \ll 1$ the difference between Eq. (8) and $\pi_{s,i}$ in Eq. (18) is negligible. In practice, in order to satisfy both $\Gamma d\tau \ll 1$ and $P d\tau \gg 1$, one needs $\Gamma \ll P$. When this condition is not satisfied the instantaneous probability (1) fluctuates very rapidly at each time step. Equation (8) averages out these high-frequency fluctuations so that, even for $\Gamma = \infty$, the distribution $\pi_{s,i}(\tau)$ of Eq. (8) is not a discontinuous step function of $u_{s,i}(\tau)$, as suggested by Eq. (18). High-frequency fluctuations contribute to the functional form of $\pi_{s,i}$ on $u_{s,i}$, which will differ from Eq. (18).

Summarizing, when we let $\Gamma \to \infty$ only after the limit $N \to \infty$ has been taken, no problem arises. There is no reason to

---

[4]This is an *a posteriori* learning rate. Indeed $1/\Gamma$ is the time the dynamics of the scores needs in order to learn a payoff difference. From a different viewpoint, Γ tunes the randomness of the response of agents. The larger the randomness, the longer it takes to average fluctuations out.

believe that results change if the order of the limits is interchanged. This expectation, as we shall see, is confirmed by numerical simulations (see Fig. 2): direct numerical simulations of the MG deviate from the prediction of Eqs. (15)–(17) only for finite size effects that vanish as $N \to \infty$.

Equations (15)–(17) are our central result. We shall devote the rest of the paper to discuss their content and to show that all of the observed behavior of the MG can be derived from these equations.

IV. STATIONARY STATE

Let us take the average, denoted by $\langle \cdots \rangle$, of Eq. (15) on the stationary state (SS). Let

$$f_{s,i} = \langle \pi_{s,i} \rangle$$

be the frequency with which agent i plays strategy s in the SS. Then we have

$$v_{s,i} \equiv \left\langle \frac{du_{s,i}}{d\tau} \right\rangle = -\overline{a_{s,i}\langle A \rangle}, \quad \langle A | \mu \rangle = \sum_{j,s'} f_{s',j} a_{s',j}^{\mu}.$$

Given the relation between $\pi_{s,i}$ and $u_{s,i}$ and considering that the long-time dynamics of $u_{s,i}$ in the SS is $u_{s,i}(\tau) = \text{const} + v_{s,i}\tau$, we have that (i) each strategy that is played in the SS by agent i must have the same "velocity" $v_{s,i} = v_i^*$ and (ii) strategies that are not played (i.e., with $f_{s,i}=0$) must have $v_{s,i} < v_i^*$. In other words

$$-\overline{a_{s,i}\langle A \rangle} = v_i^* \quad \forall\ i,s \quad \text{such that} \quad f_{s,i}>0, \quad (20)$$

$$-\overline{a_{s,i}\langle A \rangle} \leq v_i^* \quad \forall\ i,s \quad \text{such that} \quad f_{s,i}=0. \quad (21)$$

Consider now the problem of constrained minimization of H in Eq. (4), subject to $f_{s,i} \geq 0$ for all s,i and the normalization conditions. Introducing Lagrange multipliers λ_i to enforce $\Sigma_s f_{s,i}=1$ for all i, this problem reads

$$\min_{\{f_{s,i} \geq 0\}} \left\{ \langle A \rangle^2 - \sum_{i=1}^{N} \lambda_i \left(1 - \sum_{s=1}^{S} f_{s,i} \right) \right\}. \quad (22)$$

Taking derivatives, we find that if $f_{s,i}>0$ then $\overline{a_{s,i}\langle A \rangle} + \lambda_i = 0$ whereas if $f_{s,i}=0$ then $\overline{a_{s,i}\langle A \rangle} + \lambda_i \geq 0$. These are exactly Eqs. (20) and (21) where $v_i^* = \lambda_i$. We then conclude that the two problems, Eqs. (20) and (21) and Eq. (22) are one and the same problem.[5] In other words $f_{s,i}$ can be computed from the constrained minimization of H as proposed in Refs. [3,4].

---

[5]Indeed both problems can be put in the form of a linear complementarity problem [27],

$$f_{s,i} \geq 0,$$

$$\sum_{j,s'} \overline{a_{s,i}a_{s',j}} f_{s',j} + v_i^* \geq 0,$$

$$f_{s,i} \left[\sum_{j,s'} \overline{a_{s,i}a_{s',j}} f_{s',j} + v_i^* \right] = 0.$$

This problem has a solution for all values of v_i^* because of non-negativity of the matrix $\overline{a_{s,i}a_{s',j}}$, see Ref. [27].

Hence the statistical mechanics approach based on the study of the ground state of H is correct. This approach gives the frequency $f_{s,i}$ with which agents play their strategies.

We remark once more that H is a function of the stationary state probabilities $f_{s,i}$. Also note that

$$\tilde{H}\{\pi_{s,i}\} = \sum_{i,j=1}^{N} \sum_{s,s'=1}^{S} \overline{a_{s,i}a_{s',j}} \pi_{s,i}\pi_{s',j}$$

as a function of the instantaneous probabilities $\pi_{s,i}$ is *not* a Lyapunov function of the dynamics. The dynamical variables $\pi_{s,i}(t)$ are subject to stochastic fluctuations of the order of $\sqrt{\Gamma_i}$ around their average values $f_{s,i}$. Only in the limit $\Gamma_i \to 0$, when the dynamics becomes deterministic and $\pi_{s,i} \to f_{s,i}$, the quantity $\tilde{H}\{\pi_{s,i}\}$ becomes a Lyapunov function.

The solution to the minimization of H reveals two qualitatively distinct phases [3,4] that are separated by a phase transition occurring as $\alpha \to \alpha_c$. We discuss qualitatively the behavior of the solution for a generic S and leave for the next section a more detailed discussion in the simpler case $S=2$.

A. Independence on Γ for $\alpha > \alpha_c$

When $\alpha > \alpha_c$ the solution to Eq. (22) is unique and $H > 0$. Hence $f_{s,i}$ does not depend on Γ, neither does H. In addition we shall see that

$$\langle \pi_{s,i}\pi_{s',j} \rangle = \langle \pi_{s,i} \rangle \langle \pi_{s',j} \rangle = f_{s,i}f_{s',j} \quad \text{for } i \neq j, \quad (23)$$

implying that

$$\sigma^2 \equiv N + \sum_{i \neq j} \sum_{s,r} \overline{a_{s,i}a_{r,j}} \langle \pi_{s,i}\pi_{r,j} \rangle$$

does not depend on Γ either. Hence the solution $\{f_{s,i}\}$ uniquely determines all quantities in the SS, as well as the parameters that enter into the dynamics [notice the dependence on σ^2 in Eq. (17)]. In particular, σ^2 does not depend on Γ.

B. Dependence on Γ and on initial conditions for $\alpha < \alpha_c$

For $\alpha < \alpha_c$ the solution to the minimization problem is not unique: there is a connected set of points $\{f_{s,i}\}$ such that $H = 0$. Let us first discuss the behavior of the system in the limit $\Gamma \to 0$, where the dynamics becomes deterministic. The dynamics reaches a stationary state $\{f_{s,i}\}$ that depends on the initial conditions.

In order to see this, let us introduce the vector notation $|v\rangle = \{v_{s,i}, s=1, \ldots, S, i=1, \ldots, N\}$. Then for all times $|u(\tau)\rangle$ is of the form

$$|u(\tau)\rangle = |u(0)\rangle + \sum_{\mu=1}^{P} |a^{\mu}\rangle C^{\mu}(\tau),$$

where $C^{\mu}(\tau)$ are P functions of time.

If there are vectors $\langle v |$ such that $\langle v | a^{\mu} \rangle = 0$ for all μ, then $\langle v | u(\tau) \rangle = \langle v | u(0) \rangle$, i.e., the components of the scores will not change at all along these vectors. As a result the SS will depend on initial conditions $|u(0)\rangle$. These vectors $\langle v|$ exist exactly for $\alpha<\alpha_c$ [4], because the "dimensionality" of the vectors $|u(\tau)\rangle$ is larger than P.[6]

The picture is made even more complex by the fact that for $\alpha<\alpha_c$, when Γ is finite, Eq. (23) does not hold. Hence σ^2 has a contribution, which depends on the stochastic fluctuations around $f_{s,i}$. The strength of these fluctuations, given by Eqs. (17) and (19), depends on Γ and σ^2 itself. We face, in this case, a self-consistent problem: σ^2 enters as a parameter of the dynamics but should be computed in the stationary state of the dynamics itself. Therefore, the solution to this problem and hence σ^2 depends on Γ. The solution $\{f_{s,i}\}$ to the minimization of H should also be computed self-consistently. As a result, the SS properties acquire a dependence on Γ.

The condition (23), which is similar to the *clustering* property in spin glasses [28], plays then a crucial role. We show below how the condition (23), the dependence on initial conditions, and on Γ enter into the detailed solution for $S=2$. By similar arguments our conclusion can be generalized to all $S>2$.

V. THE CASE $S=2$

We work in this section with the simpler case of $S=2$ strategies, labeled by $s=\pm$. We also set $\Gamma_i=\Gamma$ for all i. Following Refs. [3,13] we introduce the variables

$$\xi_i^\mu=\frac{a_{+,i}^\mu-a_{-,i}^\mu}{2},\quad \Omega^\mu=\sum_{i=1}^N\frac{a_{+,i}^\mu+a_{-,i}^\mu}{2}.$$

Let us rescale time $t=\Gamma\tau$ and introduce the variables

$$y_i(t)=\Gamma\frac{u_{+,i}(\tau)-u_{-,i}(\tau)}{2}.$$

Then, using Eq. (8), the dynamical equations (15)–(17) become

$$\frac{dy_i}{dt}=-\overline{\xi_i\Omega}-\sum_{j=1}^N\overline{\xi_i\xi_j}\tanh(y_j)+\zeta_i,\qquad(24)$$

$$\langle\zeta_i(t)\zeta_j(t')\rangle=\frac{\Gamma\sigma^2}{\alpha N}\overline{\xi_i\xi_j}\delta(t-t').\qquad(25)$$

The Fokker-Planck (FP) equation for the probability distribution $P(\{y_i\},t)$ under this dynamics reads

---

[6]In order to compute the dimensionality of the vectors $|u\rangle$ we have to take into account the N normalization conditions and the fact that strategies that are not played ($f_{s,i}=0$) should not be counted. So if there are $N_>$ variables $f_{s,i}>0$, the relevant dimension of the space of $|u\rangle$ is $N_>-N$. Hence vectors $\langle v|$ orthogonal to all $|a^\mu\rangle$ exist for $N_>-N>P$, i.e., for $\alpha<\alpha_c=N_>(\alpha_c)/N-1$.

$$\frac{\partial P(\{y_i\},t)}{\partial t}=\sum_{i=1}^N\frac{\partial}{\partial y_i}\left\{\overline{\xi_i\Omega}+\sum_{j=1}^N\overline{\xi_i\xi_j}\tanh(y_j)\right.$$

$$\left.+\frac{1}{\beta}\sum_{j=1}^N\overline{\xi_i\xi_j}\frac{\partial}{\partial y_j}\right\}P(\{y_i\},t),\qquad(26)$$

where we have introduced the parameter

$$\beta=\frac{2\alpha N}{\Gamma\sigma^2}.\qquad(27)$$

Multiply Eq. (26) by y_i and integrate over all variables. Using integration by parts, assuming that $P\to0$ fast as $y_j\to\infty$, one gets

$$\frac{\partial}{\partial t}\langle y_i\rangle=-\overline{\xi_i\Omega}-\sum_{j=1}^N\overline{\xi_i\xi_j}\langle\tanh(y_j)\rangle.$$

Let us look for solutions with $\langle y_i\rangle\sim v_it$ and define $m_i=\langle\tanh(y_i)\rangle$. Hence for $t\to\infty$ we have

$$v_i=-\overline{\xi_i\Omega}-\sum_{j=1}^N\overline{\xi_i\xi_j}m_j.\qquad(28)$$

Now, either $v_i=0$ and $\langle y_i\rangle$ is finite or $v_i\neq0$, which means that $y_i\to\pm\infty$ and $m_i=\mathrm{sgn}\,v_i$. In the latter case ($v_i\neq0$) we say that agent i is *frozen* [13], we call $\mathcal{F}$ the set of frozen agents and $\phi=|\mathcal{F}|/N$ the fraction of frozen agents.

As in the general case, the parameters v_i for $i\in\mathcal{F}$ and $m_i\equiv\langle\tanh(y_i)\rangle$ for $i\notin\mathcal{F}$ are obtained by solving the constrained minimization of

$$H=\frac{1}{P}\sum_{\mu=1}^P\left[\Omega^\mu+\sum_{i=1}^N\xi_i^\mu m_i\right]^2.$$

When the solution of $\min H$ is unique, i.e., for $\alpha>\alpha_c$, the parameters m_i depend only on the realization of disorder $\{\xi_i^\mu,\Omega^\mu\}$, and their distribution can be computed as in Ref. [3]. When the solution is not unique, i.e., for $\alpha<\alpha_c$, we are left with the problem of finding which solution the dynamics selects. Let us suppose that we have solved this problem (we shall come back later to this issue) so that all m_i are known.

Using the stationary condition Eq. (28), we can write the FP equation for the probability distribution $P_u(y_i,i\in\mathcal{F})$ of unfrozen agents. For times so large that all agents in $\mathcal{F}$ are indeed frozen [i.e., $s_i(t)=\mathrm{sgn}\,v_i$] this reads

$$\frac{\partial P_u}{\partial t}=\sum_{i\notin\mathcal{F}}\frac{\partial}{\partial y_i}\sum_{j\notin\mathcal{F}}\overline{\xi_i\xi_j}\left\{\tanh(y_j)-m_j+\frac{1}{\beta}\frac{\partial}{\partial y_j}\right\}P_u.$$

This has a solution

$$P_u\propto\exp\left\{-\beta\sum_{j\notin\mathcal{F}}[\ln\cosh y_j-m_jy_j]\right\}.\qquad(29)$$

Finally we have to impose the constraint that $|y(t)\rangle = \{y_i(t)\}_{i=1}^{N}$ must lie on the linear space spanned by the vectors $|\xi^\mu\rangle$, which contains the initial condition $|y(0)\rangle$. This means that

$$P_u \propto \mathcal{P}_{y(0)} \exp\left\{ -\beta \sum_{j \notin \mathcal{F}} [\ln \cosh y_j - m_j y_j] \right\}, \quad (30)$$

where the projector $\mathcal{P}_{y(0)}$ is given by

$$\mathcal{P}_{y(0)} \equiv \prod_{\mu=1}^{P} \int_{-\infty}^{\infty} dc^\mu \prod_{i=1}^{N} \delta\left[y_i - y_i(0) - \sum_{\mu=1}^{P} c^\mu \xi_i^\mu \right]. \quad (31)$$

We find it remarkable that Γ, which is introduced as the inverse of an *individual* "temperature" in the definition of the model, actually turns out to be proportional to β^{-1} [see Eq. (27)], which plays *collectively* a role quite similar to that of temperature.

Using the distribution Eq. (30), we can compute

$$\sigma^2 = H + \sum_{i=1}^{N} \overline{\xi_i^2}(1 - m_i^2) + \sum_{i \neq j} \overline{\xi_i \xi_j} \langle (\tanh y_i - m_i) \times (\tanh y_j - m_j) \rangle. \quad (32)$$

This depends on β, i.e., on σ^2 itself by virtue of Eq. (27). The stationary state is then the solution of a self-consistent problem. Let us analyze in detail the solution of this self-consistent problem.

A. $\alpha > \alpha_c$

For $\alpha > \alpha_c$ the solution of $\min H$ is unique, and hence m_i depends only on the realization of the disorder. In addition, the number $N - |\mathcal{F}| \equiv N(1 - \phi)$ of unfrozen agents is less than P and the constraint is ineffective, i.e., $\mathcal{P}_{y(0)} \equiv 1$. The scores $|y\rangle$ of unfrozen agents span a linear space, which is embedded in the one spanned by the vectors $|\xi^\mu\rangle$. Hence the dependence on initial conditions $y_i(0)$ drops out. Therefore, the probability distribution of y_i factorizes as in Eq. (29). Then the third term of Eq. (32), which is the only one that depends on β, vanishes identically. We conclude that, for $\alpha > \alpha_c$, σ^2 only depends on m_i and is hence independent of Γ as confirmed by numerical simulations.

Summarizing, for $\alpha > \alpha_c$ one derives a complete solution of the MG by finding first the minimum $\{m_i\}$ of H and then by computing σ^2, β, and the full distribution of y_i from Eq. (29).

B. $\alpha \leq \alpha_c$: Dependence on Γ and crowd effects

When $\alpha < 1 - \phi$, on the other hand, the solution of $\min H$ is not unique. Furthermore, the constraint cannot be integrated out and the stationary distribution depends on the initial conditions.

Numerical simulations [8] show that σ^2 increases with Γ for $\alpha < \alpha_c$ (see Fig. 2). This effect has been related to crowd effects in financial markets [12]. References [6] has shown that crowd effects can be fully understood in the limit α

$\rightarrow 0$: as Γ exceeds a critical learning rate Γ_c, the time-independent SS becomes unstable and a *bifurcation* to a period-2 orbit occurs. Neglecting the stochastic term ζ_i, Ref. [6] shows that this picture can be extended to $\alpha > 0$ [7] This approach suggests a crossover to a "turbulent" dynamics for $\Gamma > \Gamma_c$, where

$$\Gamma_c(\alpha) = \frac{4}{(1 + \sqrt{\alpha})^2(1 - Q)} \quad (34)$$

and

$$Q = \frac{1}{N} \sum_{i=1}^{N} m_i^2.$$

Both Q and Γ_c can be computed exactly in the limit $N \rightarrow \infty$ within the statistical mechanics approach [3,6].

This approach however (i) does not properly takes into account the stochastic term, (ii) does not explain what happens for $\Gamma > \Gamma_c$, and (iii) does not explain why such effects occur only for $\alpha < \alpha_c$.

The stochastic dynamics derived previously gives detailed answers to all these issues. We first restrict attention to symmetric initial conditions $y_i(0) = 0$ and then discuss the dependence on initial conditions. The choice of $y_i(0) = 0 \forall i$ is convenient because it allows one to use this same symmetry to identify the solution $\{m_i\}$ to the minimization of H, independently of Γ. To be more precise, one can introduce a "magnetization"

$$M \equiv \lim_{t \to \infty} \frac{1}{N} \sum_{i=1}^{N} \langle s_i(t) s_i(0) \rangle = \frac{1}{N} \sum_{i=1}^{N} m_i, \quad (35)$$

which measures the overlap of the SS configuration with the initial condition. Symmetric initial conditions are related to $M = 0$ SS. These are the states we focus on. The solution is derived in two steps: (1) find the minimum $\{m_i\}$ of H with $M = 0$, (2) compute self-consistently σ^2. The numerical pro-

---

[7] The idea of Ref. [6] is the following: imagine that our system is close to a SS point y_i^* at time $t = t_k$, when $\mu(t) = 1$. Will the system be close to y_i^* when the pattern $\mu = 1$ occurs again the next time $t' = t_{k+1}$? To see this, let us integrate Eq. (24) from $t = t_k$ to t_{k+1}. In doing this we (i) neglect the noise term (i.e., $\zeta_i = 0$) and (ii) assume that $\tanh y_i(t) \approx \tanh y_i(t_k)$ stays constant in the integration time interval. This latter assumption is similar to the recently introduced [7] batch version of the MG, where agents update their strategies every P time steps. This leads to the study of a discrete time dynamical system

$$y_i(t_{k+1}) = y_i(t_k) - \Gamma\left\{ \Omega \overline{\xi_i} + \sum_{j=1}^{N} \overline{\xi_i \xi_j} \tanh[y_j(t_k)] \right\}, \quad (33)$$

where the factor Γ comes because $t_{k+1} - t_k$ is on average equal to Γ. The linear stability of fixed point solutions is analyzed setting $y_i(t_k) = y_i^* + \delta y_i(k)$ and computing the eigenvalues of the linearized map $\delta y_i(k+1) \approx \sum_j T_{i,j} \delta y_j(k)$. There is a critical value of Γ above which the solution y_i^* become unstable, which is given by Eq. (34).

cedure for solving the problem is the following: given the realization of disorder $\{\xi_i^\mu, \Omega^\mu\}$, step (1)—finding the minimum $\{m_i\}$ of H—is straightforward. For step (2) we sample the distribution (30) with the Monte Carlo method[8] at inverse temperature β and measure the β-dependent contribution of σ^2 in Eq. (32),

$$\Sigma(\beta) = \sum_{i \neq j} \overline{\xi_i \xi_j} \langle (\tanh y_i - m_i)(\tanh y_j - m_j) \rangle_\beta .$$

Here $\langle \cdots \rangle_\beta$ stands for an average over the distribution (30) with parameter β. Finally we solve the equation

$$\sigma^2(\Gamma) = \sigma^2(0) + \Sigma\left[\frac{2\alpha N}{\Gamma \sigma^2(\Gamma)}\right]. \tag{36}$$

This procedure was carried out for different system sizes and several values of Γ. The results, shown in Fig. 2, agree perfectly well with direct numerical simulations of the MG. Actually Fig. 2 shows that, for $\Gamma \gg 1$, the solution of the self-consistent equation (36) suffers much lesser finite size effects than the direct numerical simulations of the MG. Figure 2 also shows that, even if only approximate, Eq. (34) provides an useful estimate of the point where the crossover occurs.

It is possible to compute $\sigma^2(\Gamma)$ to leading order in $\Gamma \ll 1$. The calculation is carried out in Appendix B in detail. The result is

$$\frac{\sigma^2}{N} \cong \frac{1-Q}{2}\left[1 + \frac{1-Q+\alpha(1-3Q)}{4\alpha}\Gamma + O(\Gamma^2)\right]. \tag{37}$$

The inset of Fig. 2 shows that this expression indeed reproduces quite accurately the small Γ behavior of σ^2. Note finally that Eq. (36) has a finite solution $\sigma^2(\infty) = \sigma^2(0) + \Sigma(0)$ in the limit $\Gamma \to \infty$. Furthermore, it is easy to understand the origin of the behavior $\sigma^2/N \sim 1/\alpha$ for Eq. (36). Because of the constraint, when $\overline{\xi_i \xi_j}$ is positive (negative) the fluctuations of $\tanh(y_i) - m_i$ are positively (negatively) correlated with $\tanh(y_j) - m_j$. If we assume that $\langle[\tanh(y_i) - m_i][\tanh(y_j) - m_j]\rangle \approx c\overline{\xi_i \xi_j}$ for some constant c, we find $\Sigma \approx c\sum_{i \neq j} \overline{\xi_i \xi_j}^2$. This leads easily to $\Sigma/N \approx c/(4\alpha)$, which explains the divergence of σ^2/N as $\alpha \to 0$ for $\Gamma \gg 1$.

---

[8]The Monte Carlo procedure follows the usual basic steps: (i) A move $y_i \to y_i + \epsilon \xi_i^\mu$ is proposed with μ and ϵ drawn at random, (ii) the "energy"

$$E\{y_i\} = \sum_{i=1}^{N} [\ln \cosh y_i - m_i y_i]$$

of the new configuration is computed, and (iii) the move is accepted with a probability equal to $\min(1, e^{-\beta \Delta E})$, where ΔE is the "energy" difference.

C. Selection of different initial conditions in the replica calculation

As discussed above, the stationary state properties of the MG in the symmetric phase depend on the initial conditions. Can the statistical mechanics approach to the MG [3,4] be extended to characterize this dependence for $\Gamma \ll 1$? If this is possible, how do we expect the resulting picture to change when Γ increases? We shall first focus on the first question (i.e., $\Gamma \ll 1$) and then discuss the second.

Of course one can introduce the constraint on the distribution of y_i in the replica approach in a straightforward manner. This leads, however, to tedious calculations. We prefer to follow a different approach. In the $\alpha < \alpha_c$ phase the minimum of H is degenerate, i.e., $H = 0$ occurs on a connected set of points. Each of these points corresponds to a different set of initial conditions, as discussed above. In order to select a particular point with $H = 0$ we can add a potential $\eta \Sigma_i (s_i - s_i^*)^2/2$ to the Hamiltonian H, which will favor the solutions closer to s_i^*, and then let the strength η of the potential go to zero. This procedure lifts the degeneracy and gives us the statistical features of the equilibrium close to s_i^*.

The nature of the stationary state changes as the asymmetry in the initial conditions changes. If we take $s_i^* = s^*$, the state at $s^* = 0$ describes symmetric initial conditions and increasing $s^* > 0$ gives asymmetric states.

The saddle point equations of the statistical mechanics approach of Ref. [3] can be reduced to two equations,

$$Q = \int_{-\infty}^{\infty} Dz \, s_0^2(z), \tag{38}$$

$$\chi = \frac{1+\chi}{\sqrt{\alpha(1+Q)}} \int_{-\infty}^{\infty} Dz \, z s_0(z), \tag{39}$$

where $Dz = (dz/\sqrt{2\pi})e^{-z^2/2}$, $s_0(z) \in [-1,1]$ is the value of s that minimizes

$$V_z(s) = \frac{1}{2}s^2 - \sqrt{\frac{1+Q}{\alpha}}zs + \frac{1}{2}\eta(1+\chi)(s-s^*)^2, \tag{40}$$

and $\chi = \beta(Q-q)/\alpha$ is a "spin susceptibility." There are two possible solutions. One with $\chi < \infty$ finite as $\eta \to 0$, which describes the $\alpha > \alpha_c$ phase. The other has $\chi \sim 1/\eta$, which diverges as $\eta \to 0$. This solution describes the $\alpha < \alpha_c$ phase. We focus on this second solution, which can be conveniently parametrized by two parameters z_0 and ϵ_0. We find

$$s_0(z) = \begin{cases} -1 & \text{if } z \leq -z_0 - \epsilon_0 \\ \dfrac{z + \epsilon_0}{z_0} & \text{if } -z_0 - \epsilon_0 < z < z_0 - \epsilon_0 \\ 1 & \text{if } z \geq z_0 - \epsilon_0 \end{cases}$$

Indeed Eq. (38) gives $Q(z_0, \epsilon_0)$ and Eq. (39), which for $\chi \to \infty$ reads $\sqrt{\alpha(1+Q)} = \int Dz z s_0(z)$, then gives $\alpha(z_0, \epsilon_0)$.

With $\epsilon_0 \neq 0$ one finds solutions with a nonzero "magnetization" $M = \langle s_i \rangle$. This quantity is particularly meaningful,

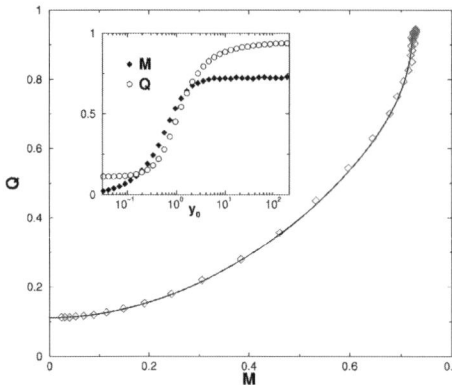

FIG. 3. Relation between Q and M, for $\alpha=0.1$, derived from analytic calculation (full line) and from numerical simulations of the MG with different initial conditions y_0 ($\Diamond$: $P=32, N=320, \Gamma =0.1$). The inset shows the dependence of Q and M on the initial condition y_0.

in this context, because it measures the overlap of the behavior of agents in the SS with their *a priori* preferred strategies,

$$M \equiv \int_{-\infty}^{\infty} Dz\, s_0(z) = \lim_{t\to\infty} \frac{1}{N} \sum_{i=1}^{N} \langle s_i(t) s_i(0) \rangle. \quad (41)$$

Note indeed that one can always perform a "gauge" transformation in order to redefine $s=+1$ as the initially preferred strategy. This amounts to taking $y_i(0) \geq 0$ for all i.

Which SS is reached from a particular initial condition is, of course, a quite complex issue that requires the integration of the dynamics. However, the relation between Q and M derived analytically from Eqs. (38) and (41) can easily be checked by numerical simulations of the MG. Figure 3 shows that the self-overlap Q and the magnetization M computed in numerical simulations with initial conditions $y_i(0) = y_0$ for all i, perfectly match the analytic results. The inset of this figure shows how the final magnetization M and the self-overlap Q in the SS depend on the asymmetry y_0 of initial conditions.

Let us finally discuss the dependence on Γ for asymmetric initial conditions. Equation (34) provides a characteristic value of Γ as a function of α and Q. This theoretical prediction is tested against numerical simulations of the MG in Fig. 4: when plotted against Γ/Γ_c, the curves of σ^2/N obtained from numerical simulations approximately collapse one onto the other in the large Γ region. Figure 4 suggests that Γ_c in Eq. (34) provides a close lower bound for the onset of saturation to a constant σ^2 for large Γ. We find it remarkable that a formula such as Eq. (34), which is computed in the limit $\Gamma \to 0$, is able to predict the large Γ behavior.

With respect to the dependence on initial conditions, we observe that Γ_c is an increasing function of Q and hence it increases with the asymmetry y_0 of initial conditions. Hence, for a fixed Γ, the fluctuation-dependent part Σ of σ^2 de-

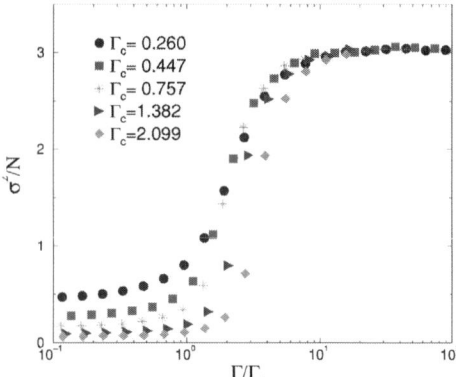

FIG. 4. Global efficiency σ^2/N versus Γ/Γ_c for $\alpha=0.1 < \alpha_c$, $N=160$ agents, and different initial conditions y_0. The value Γ_c is computed from Eq. (34) and is shown in the legend.

creases with y_0 because it is an increasing function of Γ/Γ_c. This effect adds up to the decrease of the Γ-independent part of σ^2 discussed previously.

Figure 4 also shows that the $\Gamma \gg \Gamma_c$ state is independent of initial conditions y_0. This can naively be understood observing that stochastic fluctuations induce fluctuations δy_i that increase with Γ. For $\Gamma \gg 1$ the asymmetry y_0 of initial conditions is small compared to stochastic fluctuations δy_i and hence the system behaves as if $y_0 \approx 0$.

D. The maximally magnetized stationary state

The maximally magnetized SS (MMSS), obtained in the limit $y_0 \to \infty$, is also the one with the largest value of Q, and hence with the smallest value of $\sigma^2 = N(1-Q)/2$. σ^2/N is plotted against α both for symmetric $y_0=0$ initial conditions and for maximally asymmetric ones $y_0 \to \infty$ in Fig. 5. The inset shows the behavior of Q and M in the MMSS.

Remarkably we find that σ^2/N vanishes linearly with α in the MMSS.[9] This means that, at fixed P, as N increases the fluctuation σ^2 remains constant. This is in contrast with what happens in the $y_0=0$ state for $\Gamma \ll \Gamma_c$, where σ^2 increases linearly with N, and with the case $\Gamma \gg \Gamma_c$, where $\sigma^2 \propto N^2$ [18,6]. Note also that the lowest curve of Fig. 5 also gives an upper bound to the σ^2 of Nash equilibria (see Refs. [3,4,29]).

The MMSS is also the most stable state against crowd effects: if we put $Q(\alpha, y_0=\infty) \cong 1 - c\alpha$, as appropriate for the MMSS, we find that $\Gamma_c \sim 1/\alpha$ diverges with α.

VI. CONCLUSIONS

We have clarified the correct derivation of continuous time dynamics for the MG. This on the one hand reconciles the two current approaches [3,9]. On the other it leads to a

---

[9]This result was also found analytically in [7]

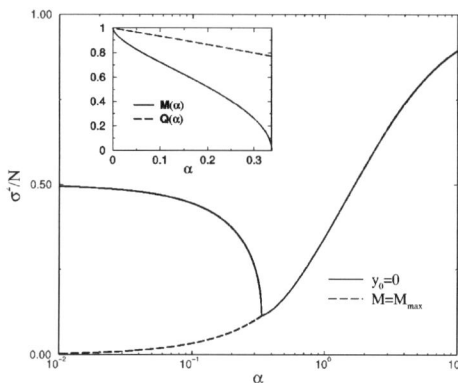

FIG. 5. σ^2/N for the MG with initial conditions $y_0 = 0$ (full line) and $y_0 \to \infty$ (dashed line). The inset reports the behavior of M and Q in the $y_0 \to \infty$ SS. Note that Q is linear in α.

complete understanding of the collective behavior of the MG. We confirm that stationary states are characterized by the minimum of a Hamiltonian, which measures the predictability of the game. For $\alpha > \alpha_c$ we find a complete analytic solution, whereas for $\alpha < \alpha_c$ the statistical mechanics approach of Ref. [3] is valid for $\Gamma \to 0$. It is, in principle, possible to introduce the new elements discussed here in the approach of Ref. [3] and to derive a full analytic solution. We have indeed derived the first term of the series expansion for $\Gamma \ll 1$, which agrees perfectly with numerical data. The extension of the approach of Ref. [3] involves lengthy calculations and it shall be pursued elsewhere.

Finally we note that the results derived in this paper generalize to more complex models. It is worth remarking that the solution to the FP equation is no more factorizable, in general, when agents account for their market impact as in Refs. [3,6,4]. Hence, as long as there are unfrozen agents, we expect that the stationary state depends on Γ. However, when the agents take fully into account their market impact, all of them are frozen and the conclusion that agents converge to Nash equilibria remains valid.

ACKNOWLEDGMENTS

We acknowledge constructive discussions with A.C.C. Coolen, A. Engel, J.P. Garrahan, J.A.F. Heimel, and D. Sherrington.

APPENDIX A: NONLINEAR MINORITY GAMES

Take a generic dynamics

$$U_{s,i}(t+1) = U_{s,i}(t) - a_{s,i}^{\mu(t)} g[A(t)],$$

where $g(x)$ is some function. When we carry out the limit to continuous time we find a deterministic term, which is proportional to $-\overline{a_{s,i}\langle g(A)\rangle}$. The stationary state conditions then read

$$v_i = -\overline{a_{s,i}\langle g(A)\rangle} \quad \text{if} \quad f_{s,i} > 0$$

and

$$v_i > -\overline{a_{s,i}\langle g(A)\rangle} \quad \text{if} \quad f_{s,i} = 0.$$

For any fixed μ, $A(t)$ is well approximated by a Gaussian variable with mean

$$\langle A|\mu\rangle = \sum_{i,s} f_{s,i} a_{s,i}^\mu$$

and variance $D = \sigma^2 - H$. Here we neglect dependences on μ. Also we treat D as a parameter and neglect its dependence on the stationary state probabilities $f_{s,i}$. Hence we can write

$$\langle g(A)|\mu\rangle = \int_{-\infty}^{\infty} \frac{dx}{\sqrt{2\pi}} e^{-x^2/2} g(\langle A|\mu\rangle + \sqrt{D}x).$$

The stationary state conditions of the dynamics above can again be written as a minimization problem of the functional

$$H_g = \frac{1}{P} \sum_{\mu=1}^{P} \int_{-\infty}^{\infty} \frac{dx}{\sqrt{2\pi}} e^{-x^2/2} G\left(\sum_{i,s} f_{s,i} a_{s,i}^\mu + \sqrt{D}x\right)$$

with

$$g(x) = \frac{dG(x)}{dx}$$

and $D = \sigma^2 - H$, which must be determined self-consistently.

Indeed taking the derivative of H_g with respect to $f_{s,i}$ and imposing the constraint $f_{s,i} \geq 0$ and normalization, we arrive at exactly the same equations that describe the stationary state of the process.

The Hamiltonian for the original MG is derived setting $g(x) = \text{sgn}\, x$, which leads to

$$H_{\text{sign}} = \frac{1}{P} \sum_{\mu=1}^{P} \left[\frac{1}{\sqrt{\pi}} e^{-\langle A|\mu\rangle^2/D} + \frac{\langle A|\mu\rangle}{\sqrt{D}} \text{erf}\left(\frac{\langle A|\mu\rangle}{\sqrt{D}}\right) \right].$$

The analysis of stochastic fluctuations can be extended to nonlinear cases in a straightforward manner. Again the key point is that the dynamics is constrained to the linear space spanned by the vectors $|a^\mu\rangle$. For $\alpha > \alpha_c$ we have no dependence on initial conditions. However, it is not easy to show, in general, that the distribution of scores factorizes across agents. This means that there may be a contribution of fluctuations to σ^2—i.e., $\Sigma > 0$—so we cannot rule out a dependence of σ^2 on Γ. Numerical simulations for $g(x) = \text{sgn}\, x$ show that such a dependence, if it exists, is very weak. Anyway even though σ^2 only depends on $f_{s,i}$, the minimization problem depends on $D = \sigma^2 - H$, which must then be determined self-consistently.

For $\alpha < \alpha_c$ the dependence on initial conditions induces a correlation of scores across agents. As a result σ^2 depends on Γ just as in the linear case discussed above.

APPENDIX B: SMALL Γ EXPANSION

For $\Gamma \ll 1$ it is appropriate to consider $\beta \gg 1$ and to take

$$y_i = \text{arc tanh } m_i + \frac{z_i}{\sqrt{\beta}}$$

so that $\beta[\ln \cosh y_i - m_i y_i] \simeq \frac{1}{2}(1 - m_i^2)z_i^2 + O(\beta^{-1/2})$. Hence we have to sample a distribution

$$P\{z_i\} \propto \exp\left[-\frac{1}{2}\sum_i (1 - m_i^2)z_i^2 \right],$$

where z_i has the form

$$z_i = \sum_{\mu=1}^{P} c^\mu \xi_i^\mu .$$

It is convenient to express everything in terms of the coefficients c^μ. Their pair distribution function (PDF) is derived from that of z_i and it reads

$$P\{c^\mu\} \propto \exp\left[-\frac{1}{2}\sum_{\mu, \nu} c^\mu T^{\mu, \nu} c^\nu \right],$$

$$T^{\mu, \nu} = \sum_{i=1}^{N} (1 - m_i^2)\xi_i^\mu \xi_i^\nu .$$

From this we find $\langle c^\mu c^\nu \rangle = [T^{-1}]^{\mu, \nu}$.

Now we split the term $\Sigma(\beta)$ into two contributions,

$$\Sigma(\beta) = \overline{\left\langle \left[\sum_{i=1}^{N} \xi_i(\tanh y_i - m_i) \right]^2 \right\rangle} + \sum_{i=1}^{N} \overline{\xi_i^2[m_i^2 - (\tanh y_i)^2]},$$

and work them out separately. For the first we use

$$\sum_{i=1}^{N} \xi_i^\mu(\tanh y_i - m_i) = \frac{1}{\sqrt{\beta}}\sum_\nu T^{\mu, \nu} c^\nu$$

so that

$$\overline{\left\langle \left[\sum_{i=1}^{N} \xi_i(\tanh y_i - m_i) \right]^2 \right\rangle} = \frac{1}{\beta P}\sum_{\mu, \nu, \gamma} T^{\mu, \nu} T^{\mu, \gamma}\langle c^\nu c^\gamma \rangle$$

$$= \frac{\text{Tr } T}{\beta P} \cong \frac{1-Q}{2\beta}N.$$

Within the approximation $(1 - 3m_i^2) \approx (1 - 3Q)$ we are able to derive a closed expression also for the second term,

$$\sum_{i=1}^{N} \overline{\xi_i^2[m_i^2 - (\tanh y_i)^2]} = \frac{1}{\beta}\sum_{i=1}^{N} \overline{\xi_i^2(1 - m_i^2)(1 - 3m_i^2)\langle z_i^2 \rangle}$$

$$\approx \frac{\alpha}{\beta}\frac{1 - 3Q}{2}N.$$

Hence we find

$$\Sigma(\beta) \cong \left[\frac{1-Q}{2} + \frac{1-3Q}{2}\alpha\right]\frac{1}{\beta} + O(\beta^{-2}).$$

This equation and Eq. (27) lead to Eq. (37).

[1] D. Challet and Y.-C. Zhang, Physica A **246**, 407 (1997); e-print adap-org/9708006.

[2] See the web page on minority games http://www.unifr.ch/econophysics

[3] D. Challet, M. Marsili, and R. Zecchina, Phys. Rev. Lett. **84**, 1824 (2000); e-print cond-mat/9904392.

[4] M. Marsili, D. Challet, and R. Zecchina, Physica A **280**, 522 (2000); e-print cond-mat/9908480.

[5] D. Challet, M. Marsili, and Y.-C. Zhang, Physica A **276**, 284 (2000); e-print cond-mat/9909265.

[6] M. Marsili and D. Challet, Adv. Compl. Sys. **4**, 3 (2001); e-print cond-mat/0004376; e-print cond-mat/0004196.

[7] J.A.F. Heimel and A.C.C. Coolen, Phys. Rev. E **63**, 056121 (2001); e-print cond-mat/0012045.

[8] A. Cavagna, J.P. Garrahan, I. Giardina, and D. Sherrington, Phys. Rev. Lett. **83**, 4429 (1999); e-print cond-mat/9903415.

[9] J.P. Garrahan, E. Moro, and D. Sherrington, Phys. Rev. E **62**, R9 (2000).

[10] D. Challet, M. Marsili, and R. Zecchina, Phys. Rev. Lett. **85**, 5008 (2000); e-print cond-mat/0004308.

[11] A. Cavagna, J.P. Garrahan, I. Giardina, and D. Sherrington, Phys. Rev. Lett. **85**, 5009 (2000); e-print cond-mat/0005134.

[12] M. Hart, P. Jefferies, P. Hui, and N.F. Johnson, e-print cond-mat/0008385.

[13] D. Challet and M. Marsili, Phys. Rev. E **60**, 6271 (1999); e-print cond-mat/9904071.

[14] The learning process belongs to the class of models described in C. Camerer and T.-H. Ho, Econometrica **67**, 827 (1999) with $\phi = \kappa = \delta = 1$.

[15] A. Cavagna, Phys. Rev. E **59**, R3783 (1999).

[16] D. Challet and M. Marsili, Phys. Rev. E **62**, 1862 (2000).

[17] Y.-C. Zhang, Europhys. News **29**, 51 (1998).

[18] R. Savit, R. Manuca, and R. Riolo, Phys. Rev. Lett. **82**, 2203 (1999); e-print adap-org/9712006.

[19] D. Challet, A. Chessa, M. Marsili, and Y.-C. Zhang, Quant. Fin. **212**, 1 (2001); e-print cond-mat/0011042.

[20] F. Slanina and Y.-C. Zhang, Physica A **272**, 257 (1999); e-print cond-mat/9906249.

[21] P. Jefferies, M.L. Hart, P.M. Hui, and N.F. Johnson, Int. J. Theor. Phys. **3**, 3 (2000); e-print cond-mat/9910072.

[22] T.S. Lo, P.M. Hui, and N.F. Johnson, e-print cond-mat/0008387.

[23] J.-P. Bouchaud, I. Giardina, and M. Mezard, e-print cond-mat/0012156.

[24] D. Challet, M. Marsili, and Y.-C. Zhang, Physica A **294**, 514 (2001); e-print cond-mat/0101326.

[25] Indeed $a_{s,i}^{\mu}\langle A|\mu\rangle_{\pi}$ is of order $\sqrt{N}$ but its sign fluctuates. When we average over $P \sim N$ different μ, we get a quantity of order N^0. We are implicitly assuming that $\overline{\langle A\rangle}\simeq0$, which definitely holds for large times.

[26] We thank J. A. F. Heimel for pointing out this issue.

[27] Katta G. Murty, *Linear Complementarity, Linear and Nonlinear Programming* (Heldermann-Verlag, Berlin, 1988).

[28] M. Mezard, G. Parisi, and M. A. Virasoro, *Spin Glass Theory and Beyond* (World Scientific, Singapore, 1987).

[29] A. De Martino and M. Marsili, e-print cond-mat/0007397 (2000).

Generating functional analysis of the dynamics of the batch minority game with random external information

J. A. F. Heimel and A. C. C. Coolen

Department of Mathematics, King's College London, The Strand, London WC2R 2LS, United Kingdom
(Received 4 December 2000; published 24 April 2001)

We study the dynamics of the batch minority game, with random external information, using generating functional techniques introduced by De Dominicis. The relevant control parameter in this model is the ratio $\alpha = p/N$ of the number p of possible values for the external information over the number N of trading agents. In the limit $N \to \infty$ we calculate the location α_c of the phase transition (signaling the onset of anomalous response), and solve the statics for $\alpha > \alpha_c$ exactly. The temporal correlations in global market fluctuations turn out not to decay to zero for infinitely widely separated times. For $\alpha < \alpha_c$ the stationary state is shown to be nonunique. For $\alpha \to 0$ we analyze our equations in leading order in α, and find asymptotic solutions with diverging volatility $\sigma = O(\alpha^{-1/2})$ (as regularly observed in simulations), but also asymptotic solutions with vanishing volatility $\sigma = O(\alpha^{1/2})$. The former, however, are shown to emerge only if the agents' initial strategy valuations are below a specific critical value.

DOI: 10.1103/PhysRevE.63.056121   PACS number(s): 02.50.Le, 87.23.Ge, 05.70.Ln, 64.60.Ht

I. INTRODUCTION

The minority game has been the subject of much (and at times heated) debate in the physics literature recently. It was originally introduced in [1], as a variation of the El Farol-Bar problem [2], to serve as a simple model for a situation where adaptive agents are competing for limited resources. It has since attracted much attention, especially as a model for financial markets (see, e.g., [3]). The players in the minority game are trading agents who, at every stage of the game, have to make a decision whether to buy or to sell, on the basis of both publicly available information (i.e., past market dynamics, weather forecasts, political developments, or stock prices) and their personal strategies. Those agents who find themselves having made the minority decision make a profit, while those agents who opted for the majority choice lose money. After each round all agents revalue their strategies. There are many variations on the precise implementation of this game, yet most share the same main features of the emerging market fluctuations. The important control parameter in the model is the ratio $\alpha = p/N$ of the number p of possible values for the external information over the number N of trading agents. If this ratio α is very large, the agents exhibit essentially random behavior. This is reflected in the fluctuations of the total bid, which is the sum of all buyers minus the sum of all sellers. If less external information is available (or used) to base decisions upon, i.e., for reduced α, the mismatch between buyers and sellers is found to decrease, and the market behaves more efficiently. This behavior is now understood quite well on the basis of the replica calculations in [4–6] and the crowd-anticrowd theory of [7]. The situation is much less clear, however, when α becomes very small. One possibility is that the market becomes extremely efficient, and the number of buyers almost equals the number of sellers. Another possibility is that the mismatch between buyers and sellers diverges if the amount of shared (i.e., external) information becomes small, and the market becomes extremely inefficient (see, e.g., [8,9]).

In this paper we solve the dynamics for the original many-agent model, using the exact generating functional (or path integral) techniques introduced in [10]. After defining the rules of the game we derive in the limit $N \to \infty$ an equivalent description in terms of an effective stochastic non-Markovian single-agent process, for which we calculate the first time steps. For sufficiently large values of α, we can solve the statics exactly under the assumption of absence of anomalous response. We calculate the point α_c where this assumption breaks down, resulting in a phase transition; our value for α_c is identical to that found in [4]. The present dynamical approach allows us to study the behavior of the market below α_c. In this region there exist persistent non-static solutions that cannot be studied by the methods of [4]. Below α_c the market is nonergodic and the initial conditions of the agents determine the final stationary state of the market [4,5,13]. For $\alpha \to 0$ we calculate the market volatility to leading order in α for the case where the agents are initialized with only weak strategy preferences, leading to a diverging volatility with exactly the scaling exponent $\sigma = O(\alpha^{-1/2})$ predicted in [9] on the basis of heuristic arguments. We find a critical value for the initial strategy valuations above which this solution no longer exists and is replaced by an alternative solution with a vanishing volatility of the form $\sigma = O(\alpha^{1/2})$. Our dynamical approach allows in addition for the calculation of the two-time correlations in the global market fluctuations, by definition inaccessible with equilibrium methods (replica or otherwise), which are found to have a persistent component. Numerical simulations confirm our theoretical results convincingly.

II. MODEL DEFINITIONS

There are N agents playing the game. We will only consider the case where N is very large, and ultimately take the limit $N \to \infty$. The agents are labeled with roman indices i, j, k, etc. At iteration round l all agents are given the same (as yet unspecified) piece of external information $I_{\mu(l)}$, chosen randomly from a total number $p = \alpha N$ of possible values, i.e., $\mu(l) \in \{1, \ldots, \alpha N\}$. In the original model [1] the history of the actual market is used as the information given to the agents; however, in [11] it was shown that random

1063-651X/2001/63(5)/056121(16)/$20.00   **63** 056121-1   ©2001 The American Physical Society information gives (almost) the same volatility. Each agent i has S strategies $\mathbf{R}_{ia} = (R_{ia}^1, \ldots, R_{ia}^{\alpha N}) \in \{-1,1\}^{\alpha N}$ at her disposal with which to determine how to convert the external information into a trading decision, with $a \in \{1, \ldots, S\}$. Each component R_{ia}^μ is selected randomly and independently from $\{-1,1\}$ before the start of the game, with uniform probabilities, and remains fixed throughout the game. The strategies thus introduce quenched disorder into the model. Each strategy of every agent is given an initial valuation or payoff $p_{ia}(0)$. The choice made for these initial values will turn out to be crucial for the emerging behavior of the market. Given a choice $\mu(l)$ made for the external information presented at the start of round l, every agent i selects the strategy labeled by $\bar{a}_i(l)$ that for trader i has the highest payoff value at that point in time, i.e., $\bar{a}_i(l) = \arg\max p_{ia}(l)$, and subsequently makes a binary bid $b_i(l) = R_{i\bar{a}_i(l)}^{\mu(l)}$. The (rescaled) total bid at stage l is defined as $A(l) = N^{-1/2}\Sigma_i b_i(l)$. Next all agents update the payoff values of each strategy a on the basis of what would have happened if they had played that particular strategy:

$$p_{ia}(l+1) = p_{ia}(l) - R_{ia}^{\mu(l)} A(l).$$

The minus sign in this expression has the effect that strategies that would have produced a minority decision are rewarded.

This setup so far allows for an arbitrary number of strategies S. The qualitative behavior of the market fluctuations, however, is found to be very much the same for all nonextensive numbers of strategies larger than 1 [12,9]. We therefore present results here only for the $S=2$ model, where the equations can be simplified considerably upon introducing for each agent the instantaneous difference between the two strategy valuations $q_i(l) = [p_{i1}(l) - p_{i2}(l)]/2$ as well as their common part $\boldsymbol{\omega}_i = (\mathbf{R}_{i1} + \mathbf{R}_{i2})/2$ and the difference between the strategies $\boldsymbol{\xi}_i = (\mathbf{R}_{i1} - \mathbf{R}_{i2})/2$. The strategy actually selected in round l can now be written explicitly as a function of $s_i(l) = \mathrm{sgn}[q_i(l)]$, viz., $\mathbf{R}_{i\bar{a}_i(l)} = \boldsymbol{\omega}_i + s_i(l)\boldsymbol{\xi}_i$, and the evolution of the difference will now be given by

$$q_i(l+1) = q_i(l) - \xi_i^{\mu(l)}\left[\Omega^{\mu(l)} + N^{-1/2}\sum_j \xi_j^{\mu(l)} s_j(l)\right], \quad (1)$$

with $\Omega = N^{-1/2}\Sigma_j \boldsymbol{\omega}_j \in \mathfrak{R}^{\alpha N}$. It has been observed in numerical simulations (see, e.g., [13]) that the magnitude of the market fluctuations remains almost unchanged if a large number of bids are performed before a reevaluation of the strategies is carried out. This is the motivation for us to study a modified (and simpler) version of the dynamics of the game, where, rather than allowing the strategy payoff valuations to be changed at each round, only the accumulated effect of a large number of market decisions is used to change an agent's strategy payoff valuations. This amounts to performing an average in the above dynamic equations over the choices to be made for the external information. If we also change the time unit accordingly from l (which

measured individual rounds of the game) to a new unit t which is proportional to the number of payoff validation updates, we arrive at

$$q_i(t+1) = q_i(t) - h_i - \sum_j J_{ij}s_j(t), \quad (2)$$

where $J_{ij} = \boldsymbol{\xi}_i \cdot \boldsymbol{\xi}_j / N\tau^2$ and $h_i = \boldsymbol{\xi}_i \cdot \boldsymbol{\Omega} / \sqrt{N}\tau^2$, and with $\tau^2 = \langle(\Omega^\mu)^2\rangle = \langle(\xi_i^\mu)^2\rangle = \langle(\omega_i^\mu)^2\rangle$; here $\tau^2 = \frac{1}{2}$. The above particular choice of time scaling has been made only because it gives the simplest equations later. To make a connection with the original game, one must interpret the evolution of the $q_i(t)$ as described by Eq. (2) as the accumulated effect of order N iterations in the original model. Equation (2) defines the version of the minority game analyzed in this paper. Note that Eq. (2) cannot be converted into a continuous time equation, upon replacing $[q_i(t+1) - q_i(t)]/\sqrt{N}$ by dq_i/dt. A number of agents change their preferred strategy at every iteration of Eq. (2). The size of their q's will be of the order of (half) the step size. In the continuous time limit, in contrast, this step size is lost; yet any discretization used to integrate the continuous time differential equation obtained will effectively reintroduce an (arbitrary) scale for the q's. We regard Eq. (2) as the equivalent of what in the neural network literature would be called the "batch" version of the conventional "on-line" minority game. For a more detailed discussion concerning the validity of a continuous time differential equation for the thermal minority game we refer to [14,4,15]. Finally, the magnitude of the market fluctuations, or *volatility*, is given by $\sigma^2 = \langle A^2\rangle - \langle A\rangle^2$. From the starting point $A(l) = N^{-1/2}\Sigma_i[\omega_i^{\mu(l)} + s_i(l)\xi_i^{\mu(l)}]$ and on the time scales of the process (2), one easily derives

$$\langle A\rangle = \frac{1}{\alpha N\sqrt{N}}\sum_i s_i \sum_\mu \xi_i^\mu + O\left(\frac{1}{\sqrt{N}}\right), \quad (3)$$

$$\langle A^2\rangle = \frac{1}{2} + \frac{1}{\alpha N}\left[\sum_i h_i s_i + \frac{1}{2}\sum_{ij} s_i J_{ij} s_j\right] + O\left(\frac{1}{\sqrt{N}}\right). \quad (4)$$

Purely random trading corresponds to $\langle A\rangle = 0$ and $\sigma^2 = 1$. We will also define a more general object, the volatility matrix $\Xi_{tt'}$,

$$\Xi_{tt'} = \langle[A_t - \langle A_t\rangle][A_{t'} - \langle A_{t'}\rangle]\rangle, \quad (5)$$

which measures the temporal correlations of the market fluctuations. Note that $\sigma_t^2 = \Xi_{tt}$. In the case where the average bid $\langle A\rangle$ is zero (which will turn out to happen in the present model), the volatility measures the efficiency of the market. Zero volatility implies that supply and demand are always at the same level, and that the market is extremely efficient. A large volatility implies large mismatches between supply and demand, and is the signature of an inefficient market.

III. THE GENERATING FUNCTIONAL

There are two compelling reasons for studying the dynamics of the minority game (MG). First, dynamical techniques do not rely on the presence of a Lyapunov function, so that the MG can be studied for small α. Secondly, it is clear from simulations [13] (see also the figures below) that, at least on the relevant time scales, the stationary state of the minority game can depend quite strongly on the initial conditions. One canonical tool to deal with the dynamics of the present problem is generating functional analysis as introduced by De Dominicis [10], originally developed in the disordered systems community (to study spin glasses, in particular). This formalism allows one to carry out the disorder average (which here is an average over all strategies) and take the $N \to \infty$ limit exactly. The final result of the analysis is a set of closed equations, which can be interpreted as describing the dynamics of an effective "single agent" [10,16]. Due to the disorder in the process, this single agent will acquire an effective "memory," i.e., she will evolve according to a nontrivial non-Markovian stochastic process.

First we rewrite Eq. (2) as a Chapman-Kolmogorov equation describing the temporal evolution of an ensemble of markets:

$$p_{t+1}(\mathbf{q}) = \int d\mathbf{q}' \, W(\mathbf{q}|\mathbf{q}') p_t(\mathbf{q}'),$$

where, in the absence of noise, the transition probability density is simply

$$W(\mathbf{q}|\mathbf{q}') = \prod_i \delta\left(q_i - q_i' + h_i + \sum_j J_{ij} s_j' \right)$$

$$= \int \frac{d\hat{\mathbf{q}}}{(2\pi)^N} \exp\left[\sum_i i\hat{q}_i\left(q_i - q_i' + h_i + \sum_j J_{ij} s_j' \right) \right]$$

with the shorthand $s_j' = \text{sgn}[q_j']$. The moment generating functional for a stochastic process of the present type is defined as

$$Z[\boldsymbol{\psi}] = \left\langle \exp\left[i \sum_t \sum_i \psi_i(t) q_i(t) \right] \right\rangle$$

$$= \int \prod_t \left[d\mathbf{q}(t) W(\mathbf{q}(t+1)|\mathbf{q}(t)) \right] p_0(\mathbf{q}(0))$$

$$\times \exp\left[i \sum_t \sum_i \psi_i(t) q_i(t) \right].$$

By taking suitable derivatives of the generating functional with respect to the conjugate variables $\boldsymbol{\psi}$, one can generate all moments of $\mathbf{q}$ at arbitrary times. Upon introducing the two short hand notations

$$w_t^\mu = \frac{1}{\tau\sqrt{N}} \sum_i \hat{q}_i(t)\xi_i^\mu, \quad x_t^\mu = \frac{1}{\tau\sqrt{N}} \sum_i s_i(t)\xi_i^\mu,$$

as well as $D\mathbf{q} = \prod_{it}[dq_i(t)/\sqrt{2\pi}]$, $D\mathbf{w} = \prod_{\mu t}[dw_t^\mu/\sqrt{2\pi}]$, and $D\mathbf{x} = \prod_{\mu t}[dx_t^\mu/\sqrt{2\pi}]$ (with similar definitions for $D\hat{\mathbf{q}}$, $D\hat{\mathbf{w}}$, and $D\hat{\mathbf{x}}$, respectively), the generating functional takes the following form:

$$Z[\boldsymbol{\psi}] = \int D\mathbf{w}\,D\hat{\mathbf{w}}\,D\mathbf{x}\,D\hat{\mathbf{x}} \exp\left\{ i \sum_{t\mu} [\hat{w}_t^\mu w_t^\mu + \hat{x}_t^\mu x_t^\mu \right.$$

$$\left. + w_t^\mu(\Omega^\mu/\tau + x_t^\mu)] \right\} \int D\mathbf{q}\,D\hat{\mathbf{q}}\, p_0(\mathbf{q}(0))$$

$$\times \exp\left\{ \frac{-i}{\tau\sqrt{N}} \sum_{\mu i} \xi_i^\mu \sum_t [\hat{w}_t^\mu \hat{q}_i(t) + \hat{x}_t^\mu s_i(t)] \right\}$$

$$\times \exp\left(i \sum_{ti} \{\hat{q}_i(t)[q_i(t+1) - q_i(t) - \theta_i(t)] \right.$$

$$\left. + \psi_i(t) q_i(t)\} \right), \tag{6}$$

where we have introduced auxiliary driving forces $\theta_i(t)$ to generate averages involving $\hat{q}_i(t)$ (these can be removed later).

IV. DISORDER AVERAGING

At this stage we can carry out the disorder averages, to be denoted as $\overline{\cdots}$, which involve the variables $\xi_i^\mu = \tau^2(R_{i1}^\mu - R_{i2}^\mu)$ and $\Omega^\mu = N^{-1/2}\tau^2\Sigma_j(R_{j1}^\mu + R_{j2}^\mu)$ only. For times that do not scale with N one obtains

$$\overline{\exp\left(\frac{i}{\tau}\sum_{t\mu} w_t^\mu \Omega^\mu - \frac{i}{\tau\sqrt{N}}\sum_{\mu i} \xi_i^\mu \sum_t [\hat{w}_t^\mu \hat{q}_i(t) + \hat{x}_t^\mu s_i(t)] \right)}$$

$$= \prod_{i\mu} \overline{\exp\left(\frac{i\tau}{\sqrt{N}} \sum_t \{w_t^\mu(R_1+R_2) - (R_1-R_2)[\hat{w}_t^\mu \hat{q}_i(t) + \hat{x}_t^\mu s_i(t)]\} \right)}$$

$$= \exp\left(-\frac{1}{2}\sum_{\mu tt'} [w_t^\mu w_{t'}^\mu + \hat{w}_t^\mu L_{tt'} \hat{w}_{t'}^\mu + 2\hat{x}_t^\mu K_{tt'} \hat{w}_{t'}^\mu + \hat{x}_t^\mu C_{t,t'} \hat{x}_{t'}^\mu] + O(N^0) \right),$$

where we have introduced $C_{tt'}=N^{-1}\sum_i s_i(t)s_i(t')$, $K_{tt'}=N^{-1}\sum_i s_i(t)\hat{q}_i(t')$, and $L_{tt'}=N^{-1}\sum_i \hat{q}_i(t)\hat{q}_i(t')$. We isolate these functions via the insertion of appropriate δ functions (in integral representation), and define the corresponding shorthand notation $DC=\Pi_{tt'}[dC_{tt'}/\sqrt{2\pi}]$, $DK=\Pi_{tt'}[dK_{tt'}/\sqrt{2\pi}]$, and $DL=\Pi_{tt'}[dL_{tt'}/\sqrt{2\pi}]$ (with similar definitions for $D\hat{C}$, $D\hat{K}$, and $D\hat{L}$, respectively). Upon assuming simple initial conditions of the form $p_0(\mathbf{q})=\Pi_i p_0(q_i)$, the i-dependent terms in the disorder-averaged generating functional (6) are now found to factorize fully over the N traders, and we arrive at an expression of the following form:

$$\overline{Z[\boldsymbol{\psi}]}=\int [DC\,D\hat{C}][DK\,D\hat{K}][DL\,D\hat{L}]e^{N[\Psi+\Phi+\Omega]+O(N^0)}.\tag{7}$$

The subdominant $O(N^0)$ term in the exponent is independent of the generating fields $\{\psi_i(t)\}$ and $\{\theta_i(t)\}$. There are three distinct leading contributions to the exponent in Eq. (7). The first is a "bookkeeping" term, linking the two-time order parameters to their conjugates:

$$\Psi=i\sum_{tt'}[\hat{C}_{tt'}C_{tt'}+\hat{K}_{tt'}K_{tt'}+\hat{L}_{tt'}L_{tt'}].$$

The second reflects the statistical properties of the players' arsenal of strategies:

$$\Phi=\alpha\ln\left[\int Dw\,D\hat{w}\,Dx\,D\hat{x}\exp\left(i\sum_t[\hat{w}_t w_t+\hat{x}_t x_t+w_t x_t]\right)\right.$$

$$\times\exp\left(-\frac{1}{2}\sum_{tt'}[w_t w_{t'}+\hat{w}_t L_{tt'}\hat{w}_{t'}+2\hat{x}_t K_{tt'}\hat{w}_{t'}\right.$$

$$\left.\left.+\hat{x}_t C_{tt'}\hat{x}_{t'}]\right)\right].\tag{8}$$

The third term, which contains the generating fields, will describe the (now stochastic) evolution of the strategy valuations $q(t)$ of a single effective agent:

$$\Omega=\frac{1}{N}\sum_i\ln\left[\int Dq\,D\hat{q}\,p_0(q(0))\right.$$

$$\times\exp\left(i\sum_t \hat{q}(t)[q(t+1)-q(t)-\theta_i(t)]\right)$$

$$\times\exp\left(i\sum_t \psi_i(t)q(t)-i\sum_{tt'}[s(t)\hat{C}_{tt'}s(t')\right.$$

$$\left.\left.+s(t)\hat{K}_{tt'}\hat{q}(t')+\hat{q}(t)\hat{L}_{tt'}\hat{q}(t')]\right)\right]$$

with $s(t)=\mathrm{sgn}[q(t)]$, $Dq=\Pi_t[dq(t)/\sqrt{2\pi}]$, $Dw=\Pi_t[dw_t/\sqrt{2\pi}]$, and $Dx=\Pi_t[dx_t/\sqrt{2\pi}]$ (and similar definitions for $D\hat{q}$, $D\hat{w}$, and $D\hat{x}$). The form of Eq. (7) is suitable for a saddle-point integration in the thermodynamic limit $N\to\infty$. With a modest amount of foresight we define $G_{tt'}=-iK_{tt'}$. Upon taking derivatives with respect to the generat-

ing fields $\{\theta_i(t),\psi_i(t)\}$, and using the built-in normalization $\overline{Z[\mathbf{0}]}=1$, we find that at the relevant saddle point

$$C_{tt'}=\lim_{N\to\infty}\frac{1}{N}\sum_i\overline{\langle s_i(t)s_i(t')\rangle},\tag{9}$$

$$G_{tt'}=\lim_{N\to\infty}\frac{1}{N}\sum_i\frac{\partial}{\partial\theta_i(t')}\overline{\langle s_i(t)\rangle},\tag{10}$$

$$L_{tt'}=\lim_{N\to\infty}\frac{1}{N}\sum_i\frac{\partial^2}{\partial\theta_i(t)\partial\theta_i(t')}\overline{Z[\mathbf{0}]}=0.\tag{11}$$

The first two are recognized as representing disorder-averaged and site-averaged correlation and response functions. At this stage the generating fields are in principle no longer needed. We will put $\psi_i(t)=0$ and $\theta_i(t)=\theta(t)$, and find our expression for Ω simplifying to

$$\Omega=\ln\left[\int Dq\,D\hat{q}\,p_0(q(0))\right.$$

$$\times\exp\left(i\sum_t \hat{q}(t)[q(t+1)-q(t)-\theta(t)]\right)$$

$$\times\exp\left(-i\sum_{tt'}[s(t)\hat{C}_{tt'}s(t')+s(t)\hat{K}_{tt'}\hat{q}(t')\right.$$

$$\left.\left.+\hat{q}(t)\hat{L}_{tt'}\hat{q}(t')]\right)\right].\tag{12}$$

Extremization of the extensive exponent $\Psi+\Phi+\Omega$ of Eq. (7) with respect to $\{C,\hat{C},K,\hat{K},L,\hat{L}\}$ gives the saddle-point equations

$$C_{tt'}=\langle s(t)s(t')\rangle_\star,\qquad G_{tt'}=\frac{\partial\langle s(t)\rangle_\star}{\partial\theta(t')},\tag{13}$$

$$\hat{C}_{tt'}=\frac{i\partial\Phi}{\partial C_{tt'}},\quad \hat{K}_{tt'}=\frac{i\partial\Phi}{\partial K_{tt'}},\quad \hat{L}_{tt'}=\frac{i\partial\Phi}{\partial L_{tt'}},\tag{14}$$

whereas $L_{tt'}=0$. The effective single-trader averages $\langle\cdots\rangle_\star$, generated by taking derivatives of Eq. (12), are defined as follows (note that $s(t)=\mathrm{sgn}[q(t)]$):

$$\langle f[\{q\}]\rangle_\star=\frac{\int Dq\,M[\{q\}]f[\{q\}]}{\int Dq\,M[\{q\}]},$$

$$M[\{q\}]=p_0(q(0))\exp\left(-i\sum_{tt'}s(t)\hat{C}_{tt'}s(t')\right)$$

$$\times\int D\hat{q}\exp\left(-i\sum_{tt'}\hat{q}(t)\hat{L}_{tt'}\hat{q}(t')\right)$$

$$\times\exp\left(i\sum_t \hat{q}(t)\left[q(t+1)-q(t)-\theta(t)\right.\right.$$

$$\left.\left.-\sum_{t'}\hat{K}^T_{tt'}s(t')\right]\right).\tag{15}$$

Upon elimination of $\{\hat{C},\hat{K},\hat{L}\}$ via Eq. (14), we have now obtained exact closed equations for the disorder-averaged correlation and response functions in the $N \to \infty$ limit: namely, Eq. (13), with the effective single-trader measure (15).

V. SIMPLIFICATION OF THE SADDLE-POINT EQUATIONS

The above procedure is quite insensitive to changing model details; alternative choices made for the statistics of traders' strategies would simply lead to a different form for the function Φ (8), whereas changing the update rules for the strategy valuations of the traders (e.g., by making these non-deterministic, as in [14,4]) would affect only the details of the term Ω (12). We now work out our equations for the present choice of model. Focusing first on Φ, we perform the x_t integrals, yielding $\Pi_t \delta[\hat{x}_t + w_t]$, and after performing the remaining $\hat{x}$ integrations we get

$$\Phi = \alpha \ln \int Dw \, D\hat{w} \exp\left(i \sum_t \hat{w}_t w_t\right)$$

$$\times \exp\left(-\frac{1}{2} \sum_{tt'} [w_t w_{t'} + \hat{w}_t L_{tt'} \hat{w}_{t'} - 2 w_t K_{tt'} \hat{w}_{t'}]\right.$$

$$\left. + w_t C_{tt'} w_{t'}]\right).$$

The Gaussian integration over $\{w_t\}$ gives

$$\Phi = -\frac{1}{2} \alpha \ln \det D + \alpha \ln \int \prod_t \left[\frac{d\hat{w}_t}{\sqrt{2\pi}}\right]$$

$$\times \exp\left(-\frac{1}{2} \sum_{tt'} \hat{w}_t L_{tt'} \hat{w}_{t'}\right)$$

$$\times \exp\left(-\frac{1}{2} \sum_{tt'} \hat{w}_t [(1-iK)^T D^{-1} (1-iK)]_{tt'} \hat{w}_{t'}\right),$$

where the entries of the matrix D are given by $D_{tt'} = 1 + C_{tt'}$. We now take the derivative of Φ with respect to $L_{tt'}$, as dictated by Eq. (14), and subsequently put all $L_{tt'} \to 0$. This gives

$$\hat{L} = -\frac{1}{2} i \alpha (1-iK)^{-1} D (1-iK^T)^{-1},$$

and $\lim_{L \to 0} \Phi = -\alpha \operatorname{Tr} \ln(1-iK)$, so that

$$\hat{K}^T = -\alpha(1-iK)^{-1}, \quad \hat{C} = 0.$$

We now write our final result in terms of the response function (10), via the identity $K = iG$, and find our effective single-trader measure $M[\{q\}]$ of Eq. (15) reducing to

$$p_0(q(0)) \int D\hat{q}$$

$$\times \exp\left(-\frac{1}{2} \alpha \sum_{tt'} \hat{q}(t)[(1+G)^{-1} D(1+G^T)^{-1}]_{tt'} \hat{q}(t')\right)$$

$$\times \exp\left(i \sum_t \hat{q}(t)\left[q(t+1) - q(t) - \theta(t)\right.\right.$$

$$\left.\left. + \alpha \sum_{t'} (1+G)^{-1}_{tt'} s(t')\right]\right). \tag{16}$$

This describes a stochastic single-agent process of the form

$$q(t+1) = q(t) + \theta(t) - \alpha \sum_{t' \leq t} (1+G)^{-1}_{tt'} \operatorname{sgn}[q(t')]$$

$$+ \sqrt{\alpha} \, \eta(t). \tag{17}$$

Causality ensures that $G_{tt'} = 0$ for all $t' \geq t$ [so that $(1 + G)^{-1}_{tt'} = 0$ for $t' > t$], and $\eta(t)$ is a Gaussian noise with zero mean and with temporal correlations given by $\langle \eta(t) \eta(t') \rangle = \Sigma_{tt'}$:

$$\Sigma = (1+G)^{-1} D (1+G^T)^{-1}. \tag{18}$$

The correlation and response functions defined by Eqs. (9) and (10) are the dynamic order parameters of the problem, and must be solved self-consistently from the closed equations

$$C_{tt'} = \langle \operatorname{sgn}[q(t)q(t')] \rangle_\star, \quad G_{tt'} = \frac{\partial \langle \operatorname{sgn}[q(t)] \rangle_\star}{\partial \theta(t')}. \tag{19}$$

Note that $M[\{q\}]$ as given by Eq. (16) is normalized, i.e., $\int Dq \, M[\{q\}] = 1$, so the associated averages reduce to $\langle f[\{q\}]_\star \rangle = \int Dq \, M[\{q\}] f[\{q\}]$. The solution of Eq. (19) can be calculated numerically with arbitrary precision, without finite size effects, using a technique described in [17].

Finally, in Appendix A we calculate the disorder-averaged rescaled average bid $\langle A_t \rangle$ and volatility matrix $\Xi_{tt'} = \langle A_t A_{t'} \rangle - \langle A_t \rangle \langle A_{t'} \rangle$, for $N \to \infty$, as defined previously in Eqs. (3) and (5). Note that objects such as $\langle A_t \rangle$ must asymptotically become self-averaging, i.e., independent of the microscopic realization of the disorder; hence $\langle A_t \rangle \langle A_{t'} \rangle \to \langle A_t \rangle \langle A_{t'} \rangle$ for $N \to \infty$. We find the satisfactory result that the average bid is zero, and that the volatility matrix (and thus also the ordinary single-time volatility $\sigma_t^2 = \Xi_{tt}$) is proportional to the covariance matrix (18) of the noise in the dynamics (17) of the effective single agent:

$$\lim_{N \to \infty} \langle A \rangle_t = 0, \quad \lim_{N \to \infty} \Xi_{tt'} = \frac{1}{2} \Sigma_{tt'}. \tag{20}$$

Thus the noise term $\eta(t)$ in the single-agent process (17) represents the overall market fluctuations, and the covariance matrix (18) informs us of both single-time volatility and the temporal correlations of the market fluctuations.

VI. THE FIRST TIME STEPS

For the first few time steps it is possible to calculate the order parameters (correlation and response functions) and the volatility explicitly, starting from the effective single-trader measure (16). Note that $D_{tt'} = 1 + C_{tt'}$ and that $C_{tt} = 1$ for any t. Significant simplifications can be made by using causality. For instance, we always have $(1+G)^{-1} = \sum_{n \geq 0} (-1)^n G^n$, with causality enforcing

$$[G^n]_{tt'} = 0 \quad \text{for } t' > t - n. \tag{21}$$

At $t = 0$ this immediately allows us to conclude that $\Sigma_{00} = D_{00} = 2$. We now obtain from Eq. (16) the joint statistics at time $t = 1$:

$p(q(1)|q(0))$

$$= \frac{\exp(-\{q(1) - q(0) - \theta(0) + \alpha \, \text{sgn}[q(0)]\}/4\alpha)}{2\sqrt{\alpha\pi}}. \tag{22}$$

Equation (22), in turn, allows us to calculate $C_{10} = \langle \text{sgn}[q(0)q(1)] \rangle_\star$ and $G_{10} = \partial\langle \text{sgn}[q(1)] \rangle_\star / \partial\theta(0)$:

$$C_{10} = -\int dq(0) p(q(0))$$
$$\times \text{erf}\left[\frac{\sqrt{\alpha}}{2} - \frac{|q(0)| + \theta(0)\text{sgn}[q(0)]}{2\sqrt{\alpha}}\right],$$

$$G_{10} = -\frac{1}{\sqrt{\alpha\pi}}\int dq(0) p(q(0))$$
$$\times \exp\{-[\alpha \, \text{sgn}[q(0)] - q(0) - \theta(0)]^2/4\alpha\}.$$

We can now move to the next time step, again using Eq. (21), where we need the noise covariances Σ_{11} and Σ_{10}:

$$\Sigma_{10} = \sum_{tt'} [1 - G + O(G^2)]_{1t} D_{tt'}[1 - G^T + O(G^T)^2]_{t'0}$$
$$= 1 + C_{10} - 2G_{10},$$

$$\Sigma_{11} = \sum_{tt'} [1 - G + O(G^2)]_{1t} D_{tt'}[1 - G^T + O(G^T)^2]_{t'1}$$
$$= 2 - 2G_{10}[1 + C_{01}] + 2[G_{10}]^2.$$

Although this procedure can in principle be repeated for an arbitrary number of time steps, generating exact expressions for the various order parameters iteratively, the results become increasingly complicated when larger times are involved.

It is interesting, however, to inspect further some special limits. We first turn to the (trivial) case where α is very small, $p(q(0)) = \delta[q(0) - q_0]$, and q_0 is finite. Provided $|q_0| \gg \sqrt{\alpha}$ as $\alpha \to 0$, we immediately deduce from the above results that $\lim_{\alpha \to 0} C_{10} = 1$, $\lim_{\alpha \to 0} G_{10} = 0$, and $\lim_{\alpha \to 0} \Sigma_{10} = \lim_{\alpha \to 0} \Sigma_{11} = 2$. Hence we find in leading order in α that $q(1) = q(0)$ and $\eta(1) = \eta(0)$. One easily repeats the argument

for larger times, and finds that, without perturbations, both the system variables $q(t)$ and the noise variables $\eta(t)$ will remain frozen for times $t \ll 1/\sqrt{\alpha}$, the only remaining uncertainty in the noise being the realization of $\eta(0)$:

$$q(t) = q_0 + t\sqrt{\alpha}\,\eta(0) + O(\alpha t) \quad (\alpha \to 0).$$

If $\text{sgn}[q_0] \neq \text{sgn}[\eta(0)]$, the system will "defreeze" at the first instance where $t > |q_0/\eta(0)\sqrt{\alpha}|$. Since $\eta(0)$ is a zero average Gaussian variable, one should therefore for small α expect half of the population of traders (those with nonprofitable initial random strategy choices) to commence strategy chances at time scales $t = O(\alpha^{-1/2})$, whereas the other half will continue playing the game with their (for now profitable) initial strategy choices at least up to $t = O(\alpha^{-1})$.

It is also interesting to analyze the case where the game is initialized in a *tabula rasa* manner (which appears to have been common practice in the literature), i.e., $p(q(0)) = \delta[q - q_0]$ with $q_0 = 0^+$, and where we have no perturbation fields, i.e., $\theta(t) = 0$. Now the above results reduce to

$$C_{10} = -\text{erf}[\tfrac{1}{2}\sqrt{\alpha}], \quad G_{10} = (\alpha\pi)^{-1/2}e^{-\alpha/4},$$

$$\Sigma_{10} = 1 - \text{erf}[\tfrac{1}{2}\sqrt{\alpha}] - \frac{2}{\sqrt{\alpha\pi}}e^{-\alpha/4},$$

$$\Sigma_{11} = 2 - \frac{2}{\sqrt{\alpha\pi}}e^{-\alpha/4}(1 - \text{erf}[\tfrac{1}{2}\sqrt{\alpha}]) + \frac{2}{\alpha\pi}e^{-\alpha/2}.$$

The negative value of the correlation function C_{10} implies that for short times the traders will exhibit a tendency to alternate their (two) strategies. Let us now inspect the limiting behavior of the above expressions for large and small values of α. For large α one obtains

$$\lim_{\alpha \to \infty} C_{10} = -1, \quad \lim_{\alpha \to \infty} G_{10} = \lim_{\alpha \to \infty} \Sigma_{10} = 0.$$

For small α, on the other hand, we find

$$C_{10} = -\frac{\sqrt{\alpha}}{\sqrt{\pi}} + O(\alpha^{3/2}), \quad G_{10} = \frac{1}{\sqrt{\alpha\pi}} + O(\sqrt{\alpha}),$$

$$\Sigma_{10} = 1 - \frac{2}{\sqrt{\alpha\pi}} + O(\sqrt{\alpha}), \quad \Sigma_{11} = \frac{2}{\alpha\pi} - \frac{2}{\sqrt{\alpha\pi}} + O(\alpha^0).$$

So $\eta(1) = O(\alpha^{-1/2})$, whereas $\eta(0) = O(\alpha^0)$. We also find

$$\left\langle \left[\eta(1) + \frac{\eta(0)}{\sqrt{\alpha\pi}}\right]^2 \right\rangle = \Sigma_{11} + \frac{2}{\sqrt{\alpha\pi}}\Sigma_{10} + \frac{1}{\alpha\pi}\Sigma_{00} = O(\alpha^0),$$

from which it follows that $\eta(1) = -\eta(0)/\sqrt{\alpha\pi} + O(\alpha^0)$, and hence we can write the first steps of the effective single-agent equation (17) as

$$q(1) = q(0) - \alpha \, \mathrm{sgn}[q(0)] + \sqrt{\alpha} \, \eta(0)$$

$$= \sqrt{\alpha} \, \eta(0) + O(\alpha),$$

$$q(2) = q(1) - \alpha \, \mathrm{sgn}[q(1)] + \alpha G_{10} \, \mathrm{sgn}[q(0)] + \sqrt{\alpha} \, \eta(1)$$

$$= - \eta(0)/\sqrt{\pi} + O(\sqrt{\alpha}).$$

Thus also $C_{20} = \langle \mathrm{sgn}[q(0)q(2)] \rangle_\star = O(\sqrt{\alpha})$ and $C_{21} = \langle \mathrm{sgn}[q(1)q(2)] \rangle_\star = -1 + O(\sqrt{\alpha})$. We observe that for small α the first two time steps are driven predominantly by the noise component in Eq. (17). This noise component increases in strength and starts oscillating in sign, resulting in an effective agent that is increasingly likely to alternate its strategies. Equivalently, this implies that in the initial N-agent system an increasing *fraction* of the population of agents will start alternating their strategies.

Let us finally inspect the initial behavior of Eq. (17) for the intermediate regime where $p(q(0)) = \delta[q - q_0]$ with $q_0 = O(\sqrt{\alpha})$, to which (as we have seen) also for $q_0 = O(\alpha^0)$ about half of the traders will automatically be driven in due course. We now put $q_0 = \sqrt{\alpha} \bar{q}_0$ and find in leading order

$$C_{10} = \mathrm{erf}[\tfrac{1}{2} |\bar{q}_0|] + \cdots, \quad G_{10} = \frac{1}{\sqrt{\alpha \pi}} e^{-\bar{q}_0^2/4} + \cdots,$$

$$\Sigma_{10} = -\frac{2}{\sqrt{\alpha \pi}} e^{-\bar{q}_0^2/4} + \cdots, \quad \Sigma_{11} = \frac{2}{\alpha \pi} e^{-\bar{q}_0^2/2} + \cdots.$$

Thus we have $\langle [\, \eta(1) + (\alpha \pi)^{-1/2} e^{-\bar{q}_0^2/4} \eta(0)]^2 \rangle = 0$, so also $\eta(1) = -(\alpha \pi)^{-1/2} e^{-\bar{q}_0^2/4} \eta(0)$, in leading order for $\alpha \to 0$. This then, together with $q(1) = O(\sqrt{\alpha})$ [which immediately follows from Eq. (22)], leads us to

$$q(2) = - \pi^{-1/2} e^{-\bar{q}_0^2/4} \eta(0) + O(\sqrt{\alpha}).$$

We thus find that for $q_0 = O(\sqrt{\alpha})$ also the initial conditions are more or less washed out by the internal noise generated by the process, within just two iteration steps.

VII. THE STATIONARY STATE FOR $\alpha > \alpha_c$

For general α, not necessarily small, the arguments used in the second part of the previous section do not hold. In a stationary state, along with agents that will change strategy (almost) every cycle, there will generally also be agents finding themselves consistently in the minority group, which will consequently play the same strategy over and over again. For the latter "frozen" group (a term introduced in [18]), the differences between the valuations of the two available strategies (i.e., the values of q_i) will grow more or less linearly in time, whereas the "fickle" agents will have values for q_i very close to zero. In order to separate the two groups efficiently we introduce the rescaled values $\bar{q}_i(t) = q_i(t)/t$. Frozen agents will be those for which $\lim_{t \to \infty} \bar{q}_i(t) \neq 0$. Similarly, the effective single-agent process (17) is transformed via $\bar{q}(t) = q(t)/t$, where now the quantity

$\phi = \lim_{\epsilon \to 0} \lim_{t \to \infty} \langle \theta[|\bar{q}(t)| - \epsilon] \rangle_\star$ will give the asymptotic fraction of frozen agents in the original N-agent system, for $N \to \infty$. The dynamical equation of the rescaled effective agent can be written as

$$\bar{q}(t) = \frac{1}{t} \bar{q}(1) + \frac{\sqrt{\alpha}}{t} \sum_{t' < t} \eta(t')$$

$$- \frac{\alpha}{t} \sum_{t' < t} \sum_{t''} (1 + G)^{-1}_{t' t''} \, \mathrm{sgn}[\bar{q}(t'')]. \qquad (23)$$

If the game has reached a stationary state, then $G_{tt'} = G(t - t')$, $C_{tt'} = C(t - t')$, and $\Sigma_{tt'} = \Sigma(t - t')$, by definition. We will assume in this section that the stationary state is one without anomalous response, i.e., temporary perturbations will not influence the stationary state and decay sufficiently fast, such that $\lim_{t \to \infty} \Sigma_{t \leqslant \tau} G(t) = k$ exists. This condition will be met if there is just one ergodic component; it is the dynamical equivalent of replica symmetry being stable (see, e.g., [19]) in a detailed balance model. We now define $\bar{q} = \lim_{t \to \infty} \bar{q}(t)$ (assuming this limit exists) and take the limit $t \to \infty$ in Eq. (23). Under the assumption of absent anomalous response, we can use the two lemmas in Appendix B to simplify the result to

$$\bar{q} = - \frac{\alpha}{1 + k} s + \sqrt{\alpha} \, \eta \qquad (24)$$

with the averages $s = \lim_{\tau \to \infty} \tau^{-1} \Sigma_{t \leqslant \tau} \, \mathrm{sgn}[\bar{q}_t]$ and $\eta = \lim_{\tau \to \infty} \tau^{-1} \Sigma_{t \leqslant \tau} \eta(t)$. The variance of the zero-average Gaussian random variable η follows from Eq. (18):

$$\langle \eta^2 \rangle = \lim_{\tau, \tau' \to \infty} \frac{1}{\tau \tau'} \sum_{t \leqslant \tau} \sum_{t' \leqslant \tau'} [(1 + G)^{-1} D (1 + G^T)^{-1}]_{tt'}$$

$$= (1 + k)^{-2} \left[1 + \lim_{\tau, \tau' \to \infty} \frac{1}{\tau \tau'} \sum_{t \leqslant \tau} \sum_{t' \leqslant \tau'} C_{tt'} \right]$$

$$= (1 + k)^{-2} [1 + \langle s^2 \rangle]. \qquad (25)$$

Note that $\langle s^2 \rangle = \lim_{\tau \to \infty} \tau^{-1} \Sigma_{t \leqslant \tau} C(t) = c$.

The effective agent is frozen if $\bar{q} \neq 0$, in which case $s = \mathrm{sgn}[\bar{q}]$. This solves Eq. (24) if and only if $|\eta| > \sqrt{\alpha}/(1 + k)$. If $|\eta| < \sqrt{\alpha}/(1 + k)$, on the other hand, the agent is not frozen; now $\bar{q} = 0$ and $s = (1 + k) \eta/\sqrt{\alpha}$. We can now calculate $c = \langle s^2 \rangle$ self-consistently, upon distinguishing between the two possibilities:

$$c = \left\langle \theta \left[|\eta| - \frac{\sqrt{\alpha}}{1 + k} \right] \right\rangle + \left\langle \theta \left[\frac{\sqrt{\alpha}}{1 + k} - |\eta| \right] \frac{(1 + k)^2 \eta^2}{\alpha} \right\rangle.$$

Working out the Gaussian integrals describing the statics of η with variance (25) then gives

$$c = 1 - \left(1 - \frac{1 + c}{\alpha} \right) \mathrm{erf} \left[\sqrt{\frac{\alpha}{2(1 + c)}} \right] - 2 \sqrt{\frac{1 + c}{2 \pi \alpha}} e^{-\alpha/2(1 + c)}. \qquad (26)$$

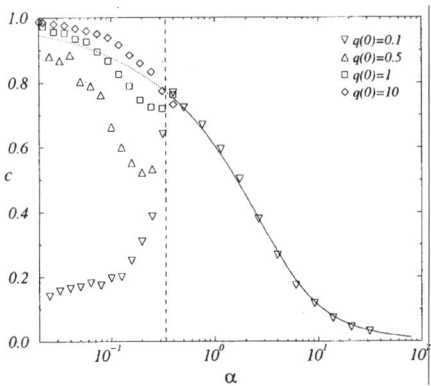

FIG. 1. Asymptotic average $c = \lim_{\tau \to \infty} \tau^{-1} \Sigma_{t \leqslant \tau} C(\tau)$ of the stationary covariance. The markers are obtained from individual simulation runs performed with a system of $N = 4000$ agents and various homogeneous initial valuations [where $q_i(0) = q(0)$], and in excess of 1000 iteration steps. The solid curve to the right of the critical point is the theoretical prediction, given by the solution of Eq. (26). The dotted curve to the left is its continuation into the $\alpha < \alpha_c$ regime (where it should no longer be correct).

From this equation the value of c can be obtained numerically. For large α the solution behaves as $c \sim \alpha^{-1}$. In Figs. 1 and 2 we show the solution of Eq. (26) and the fraction ϕ of frozen agents, given according to the theory by $\phi = \langle \theta[|\eta| - \sqrt{\alpha}/(1+k)] \rangle = 1 - \mathrm{erf}[\sqrt{\alpha/2(1+c)}]$, as functions of α, together with the values for c and ϕ as obtained by carrying out numerical simulations of the minority game. One observes excellent agreement between theory and experiment above a critical value α_c, which we will calculate below.

From the time-averaged asymptotic correlation c we next move on to calculate the integrated response $k = \lim_{\tau \to \infty} \Sigma_{t \leqslant \tau} G(t)$. Since the occurrence of the Gaussian noise term $\eta(t)$ in Eq. (17) is (apart from a factor α) similar to that of an external field, we can write the response function as $G_{tt'} = \alpha^{-1/2} \langle \partial \, \mathrm{sgn}[q(t)]/\partial \eta(t') \rangle_\star$. Integration by parts in this expression generates

$$\langle \partial \, \mathrm{sgn}[q(t)]/\partial \eta(t') \rangle_\star = \sum_{t''} \Sigma_{t' t''}^{-1} \langle \mathrm{sgn}[q(t)] \eta(t'') \rangle_\star$$

and hence,

$$\sqrt{\alpha} \sum_{t''} \langle \eta(t) \eta(t'') \rangle G_{t't'}^T = \langle \mathrm{sgn}[q(t)] \eta(t') \rangle_\star. \quad (27)$$

Averaging over the two times t and t' now gives, in a stationary state, upon using again the assumption of absent anomalous response and the familiar notational conventions $s = \lim_{\tau \to \infty} \tau^{-1} \Sigma_{t \leqslant \tau} \mathrm{sgn}[q(t)]$ and $\eta = \lim_{\tau \to \infty} \tau^{-1} \Sigma_{t \leqslant \tau} \eta(t)$

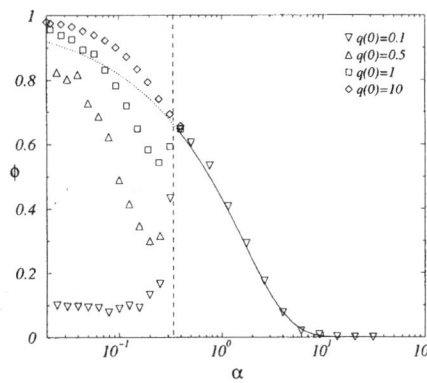

FIG. 2. Fraction $\phi = 1 - \mathrm{erf}[\sqrt{\alpha/2(1+c)}]$ of frozen agents in the stationary state. The markers are obtained from individual simulation runs performed with a system of $N = 4000$ agents and various homogeneous initial conditions, where $q_i(0) = q(0)$, and in excess of 1000 iteration steps. The solid line to the right of the critical point is the theoretical prediction, obtained from the solution of Eq. (26). The dotted curve to the left is its continuation into the $\alpha < \alpha_c$ regime (where it should no longer be correct).

$$\langle s \, \eta \rangle = \sqrt{\alpha} \lim_{\tau \to \infty} \frac{1}{\tau} \sum_{t' \leqslant \tau} \sum_{t''} \langle \eta \eta(t'') \rangle G_{t''t'}^T$$

$$= k \sqrt{\alpha} \langle \eta^2 \rangle. \quad (28)$$

The variance $\langle \eta^2 \rangle$ is given in Eq. (25). We calculate the remaining object $\langle s \, \eta \rangle$ similarly to our calculation of c, by distinguishing between frozen and nonfrozen agents and by using the two identities $s = \mathrm{sgn}[\eta]$ (for frozen agents) and $s = \eta(1+k)/\sqrt{\alpha}$ (for the nonfrozen ones), both of which follow immediately from Eq. (24). This results in

$$\langle s \, \eta \rangle = \left\langle \theta \left[|\eta| - \frac{\sqrt{\alpha}}{1+k} \right] |\eta| \right\rangle + \left\langle \theta \left[\frac{\sqrt{\alpha}}{1+k} - |\eta| \right] \frac{\eta^2(1+k)}{\sqrt{\alpha}} \right\rangle$$

$$= \frac{1+c}{(1+k)\sqrt{\alpha}} \, \mathrm{erf} \left[\sqrt{\frac{\alpha}{2(1+c)}} \right].$$

Insertion into Eq. (28), together with Eq. (25), then gives the desired expression for the integrated response:

$$\frac{1}{k} = \frac{\alpha}{\mathrm{erf}[\sqrt{\alpha/2(1+c)}]} - 1 \quad (29)$$

with the value of c to be determined by solving Eq. (26). Equivalently, using $\phi = 1 - \mathrm{erf}[\sqrt{\alpha/2(1+c)}]$, we get

$$k = \frac{1-\phi}{\alpha - 1 + \phi}. \quad (30)$$

The integrated response k is positive and finite, and hence our solution (based on this property) is exact, for $\alpha > \alpha_c$.

Here α_c is the point at which k diverges, which is found to happen when the fraction of fickle agents equals α. According to Eqs. (26) and (29), we can write α_c as $\alpha_c = \mathrm{erf}[x]$, where x is the solution of the transcendental equation

$$\mathrm{erf}[x] = 2 - \frac{1}{x\sqrt{\pi}} e^{-x^2}. \tag{31}$$

This equation is identical to that derived in [4] (for a stochastic version of the game) using replica calculations. The resulting value is $\alpha_c \approx 0.337\,40$. Below α_c there might well be multiple ergodic components, i.e., more than one stationary solution of our fundamental order parameter equations (19).

VIII. STATIONARY VOLATILITY FOR $\alpha > \alpha_c$

In contrast to the persistent order parameter c and its relative k, the volatility matrix (5), to be calculated within our theory from expressions (18) and (20) and in a stationary state of the Toeplitz form $\Xi_{tt'} = \Xi(t-t')$, generally involves both long-term and short-term fluctuations. This becomes apparent when we work out $\Xi(t)$ using Eq. (18) and the results of Appendix B. We separate in the functions C and G the persistent from the nonpersistent terms, i.e., $C(t) = c + \tilde{C}(t)$ and $G(t) = \tilde{G}(t)$ (there is no persistent response for $\alpha > \alpha_c$), and find

$$2\Xi(t) = \frac{1+c}{(1+k)^2} + \lim_{\tau \to \infty} \frac{1}{\tau} \sum_{u \leqslant \tau} \sum_{t't''} (1+\tilde{G})^{-1}_{u+t\,t'} \tilde{C}_{t't''}$$
$$\times (1+\tilde{G}^T)^{-1}_{t''u}. \tag{32}$$

Clearly, the asymptotic (stationary) value of the volatility $\sigma^2 = \Xi(0)$ cannot be expressed in terms of persistent order parameters only. It requires solving our coupled saddle-point equations (19) for $C_{tt'}$ and $G_{tt'}$ for large times but finite temporal separations $t-t'$. The persistent market correlations, however, are found to be expressible in terms of persistent order parameters:

$$\Xi(\infty) = \frac{1+c}{2(1+k)^2}. \tag{33}$$

Above α_c, this quantity can be recognized as the "energy" per agent H/N used in the replica calculations [4]. In order to find the volatility we separate the correlations at stationarity into a frozen and a fickle contribution:

$$C(t-t') = \phi \langle \mathrm{sgn}[\tilde{q}(t)\tilde{q}q(t')\rangle_{\mathrm{fr}} + (1-\phi)\langle \mathrm{sgn}[\tilde{q}(t)\tilde{q}(t')]\rangle_{\mathrm{fi}}$$
$$= \phi + (1-\phi)\langle \mathrm{sgn}[\tilde{q}(t)]\mathrm{sgn}[\tilde{q}(t')]\rangle_{\mathrm{fi}}$$

and hence

$$\tilde{C}(t-t') = \phi - c + (1-\phi)\langle \mathrm{sgn}[\tilde{q}(t)]\mathrm{sgn}[\tilde{q}(t')]\rangle_{\mathrm{fi}}.$$

Insertion into Eq. (32) and putting $t=0$ then gives

$$2\sigma^2 = \frac{1+\phi}{(1+k)^2} + (1-\phi)\lim_{\tau \to \infty} \frac{1}{\tau} \sum_{t \leqslant \tau} \sum_{t't''} (1+\tilde{G})^{-1}_{tt'}$$

$$\times \langle \mathrm{sgn}[\tilde{q}(t')]\mathrm{sgn}[\tilde{q}(t'')]\rangle_{\mathrm{fi}}(1+\tilde{G}^T)^{-1}_{t''t}$$

$$= \frac{1+\phi}{(1+k)^2} + (1-\phi)\lim_{\tau \to \infty} \frac{1}{\tau}$$

$$\times \sum_{t \leqslant \tau} \left\langle \left\{ \sum_{t' \leqslant t} (1+\tilde{G})^{-1}_{tt'} \mathrm{sgn}[\tilde{q}(t')] \right\}^2 \right\rangle_{\mathrm{fi}}. \tag{34}$$

We note that the sum $\sum_{t' < t}(1+\tilde{G})^{-1}_{tt'} \mathrm{sgn}[\tilde{q}(t')]$ is the retarded self-interaction term in Eq. (17). Such a term is a familiar ingredient of disordered systems with "glassy" dynamics (see, e.g., [20]), and generally acts as the mechanism that drives the system to a frozen state. Hence, self-consistency of the distinction between frozen and fickle traders dictates that the retarded self-interaction term can be large for frozen traders, but must be small (if not absent) for fickle ones. Our approximation now consists in consequently disregarding the retarded self-interaction for the fickle traders:

$$\sum_{t' < t} (1+\tilde{G})^{-1}_{tt'} \mathrm{sgn}[\tilde{q}(t')] \approx 0 \quad \text{for } |\eta| < \frac{\sqrt{\alpha}}{1+k}.$$

Thus we retain for fickle traders only the instantaneous $t' = t$ term in $\sum_{t' \leqslant t}(1+\tilde{G})^{-1}_{tt'} \mathrm{sgn}[\tilde{q}(t')]$, and find the (exact) expression (34) being replaced by the approximation

$$\sigma^2 = \frac{1+\phi}{2(1+k)^2} + \frac{1}{2}(1-\phi). \tag{35}$$

This turns out to be a surprisingly accurate approximation of the volatility for $\alpha > \alpha_c$, as can be observed in Fig. 3.

Only in the limit $\alpha \to \infty$ can we expect to be able to go beyond Eqs. (33) and (35), and work out expressions (32) and (34) exactly. This requires calculating the response function $\tilde{G}(\tau)$ for small τ, which we will set out to do next. Since we assume absent anomalous response we may choose trivial initial conditions. We also choose the perturbation fields $\theta(t)$ to be nonzero only for a given time $t-\tau$, where $\tau > 0$. From Eq. (17) we now derive

$$\mathrm{sgn}[q(t)] = \mathrm{sgn}\left[\frac{\theta(t-\tau)}{t\sqrt{\alpha}} + \frac{1}{t}\sum_{t' \leqslant t} \eta(t') \right.$$
$$\left. - \frac{\sqrt{\alpha}}{t} \sum_{t''t'' \leqslant t} (1+G)^{-1}_{t't''} \mathrm{sgn}[q(t'')] \right]. \tag{36}$$

Hence, for vanishingly small perturbations $\theta(t-\tau)$, and upon taking the $t \to \infty$ limit,

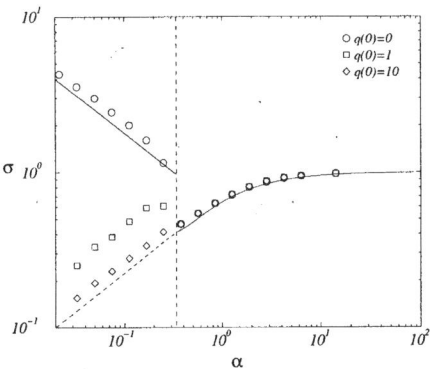

FIG. 3. The volatility σ as a function of the relative number α $=p/N$ of possible values for the external information. The markers are obtained from individual simulation runs performed with a system of $N=4000$ agents and various homogeneous initial conditions, where $q_i(0)=q(0)$, and in excess of 1000 iteration steps. The solid curve for $\alpha>\alpha_c$ is the approximate expression (35). Below α_c the approximate asymptotic solutions of Eqs. (61) (solid) and (62) (dashed) are drawn.

$$\tilde{G}(\tau)=-\frac{2\sqrt{\alpha}}{1+k}\lim_{t\to\infty}\frac{1}{t}\sum_{t'\leqslant t}\left\langle\delta\left[\eta-\frac{s\sqrt{\alpha}}{1+k}\right]\left[\frac{\partial\,\mathrm{sgn}[q(t')]}{\partial\theta(t'-\tau)}\right]\right\rangle$$

$$+2\left\langle\delta\left[\eta-\frac{s\sqrt{\alpha}}{1+k}\right]\left[\lim_{t\to\infty}\frac{1}{t}\sum_{t'\leqslant t}\frac{\partial\eta(t')}{\partial\theta(t-\tau)}\right]\right\rangle.$$

We observe that $\eta=s\sqrt{\alpha}/(1+k)$ is precisely the condition for a trader to be fickle, in the language of the effective single agent. Secondly, from causality it follows that $\lim_{t\to\infty}t^{-1}\sum_{t'\leqslant t}\partial\eta(t')/\partial\theta(t-\tau)=\lim_{t\to\infty}t^{-1}\sum_{t'=t-\tau+1}^{t}$ $\times\partial\eta(t')/\partial\theta(t-\tau)=0$. Hence our result can in a stationary state be written as

$$\tilde{G}(\tau)=-\frac{2\sqrt{\alpha}(1-\phi)}{1+k}\lim_{t\to\infty}\left\langle\frac{\partial\,\mathrm{sgn}[q(t)]}{\partial\theta(t-\tau)}\right\rangle_{\mathrm{fi}}.\qquad(37)$$

For $\alpha\to\infty$ our stationary order parameter equations give $(1-\phi)/(1+k)\to1$. Furthermore, for $\alpha\to\infty$ all traders will become fickle, so $\langle\partial\,\mathrm{sgn}[q(t)]/\partial\theta(t-\tau)\rangle_{\mathrm{fi}}\to\tilde{G}(\tau)$. This leaves for $\alpha\to\infty$ only the trivial solution for Eq. (37): $\lim_{\alpha\to\infty}\tilde{G}(\tau)=0$ for all τ. Insertion into our exact expression (32) for the stationary volatility matrix gives

$$\lim_{\alpha\to\infty}\Xi(t)=\frac{1}{2}+\frac{1}{2}\lim_{\alpha\to\infty}\tilde{C}(t)$$

and hence

$$\lim_{\alpha\to\infty}\lim_{t\to\infty}\sigma=1.\qquad(38)$$

This is the random trading limit.

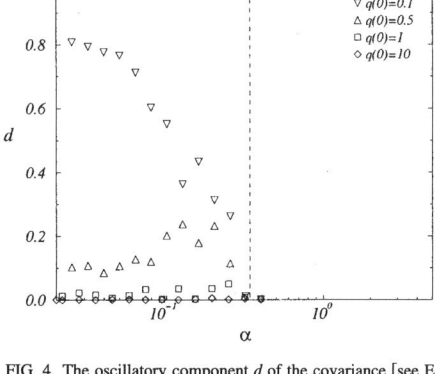

FIG. 4. The oscillatory component d of the covariance [see Eq. (40)]. The markers represent the results of individual simulations, performed with $N=4000$ agents and various homogeneous initial conditions, where $q_i(0)=q(0)$, and after in excess of 1000 iteration steps.

IX. THE STATIONARY STATE FOR $\alpha<\alpha_c$

When the amount of external information available for agents to base their actions upon (i.e., the value of α) becomes small, the behavior of the market is found to become strongly dependent on initial conditions. Numerical simulations show that below α_c the sequence $\Sigma_{t'}G_{tt'}$ is unbounded, and that within the limits of experimental accuracy:

$$\lim_{t\to\infty}\sum_{t'}(1+G)_{tt'}^{-1}=0,\qquad(39)$$

$$C_{t+\tau,t}=c+d(-1)^{\tau}\quad\text{for }\tau\neq0\qquad(40)$$

(with $C_{tt}=1$, by definition). Figure 4 shows the asymptotic values of d as measured during numerical simulations, for different values of α and $q(0)$. One clearly observes the dependence on initial conditions, as already seen in e.g., simulations of Ref. [13].

We will now use Eqs. (39) and (40) as *ansätze*, i.e., we will construct special self-consistent stationary state solutions of the fundamental order parameter equations (19) which obey Eqs. (39) and (40), as well as the stationary conditions $C_{tt'}=C(t-t')$ and $G_{tt'}=G(t-t')$. First we analyze the statistical properties of the Gaussian noise $\eta(t)$ in the single-agent equation (17). From Eqs. (39) and (40) it follows that the noise covariance matrix (18) obeys

$$\lim_{t\to\infty}\langle\eta(t+\tau)\eta(t)\rangle=(-1)^{\tau}d\gamma^2+(1-c-d)$$

$$\times\sum_t(1+G)^{-1}(t+\tau)(1+G)^{-1}(t),$$

$$(41)$$

in which

$$\gamma=\sum_t(1+G)^{-1}(t)(-1)^t.\qquad(42)$$

From Eq. (41) one can derive, in turn, that the noise variables must asymptotically take the form

$$\eta(t)=(-1)^t \gamma z \sqrt{d}+\xi(t)\sqrt{1-c-d}, \quad t\to\infty, \quad (43)$$

where z and $\{\xi(t)\}$ are zero-average Gaussian variables, with $\langle z^2\rangle=1$, $\langle z\xi(t)\rangle=0$, and

$$\lim_{t\to\infty}\langle\xi(t+\tau)\xi(t)\rangle=\sum_t (1+G)^{-1}(t+\tau)(1+G)^{-1}(t).$$

From Eq. (39) we know that $\lim_{\tau\to\infty}\lim_{t\to\infty}\langle\xi(t+\tau)\xi(t)\rangle=0$, i.e., in the stationary state the $\xi(t)$ decorrelate for large temporal separations. For sufficiently large t, and without external perturbations, Eq. (17) now acquires the form

$$q(t+1)=q(t)+\gamma z\sqrt{\alpha d}(-1)^t+\xi(t)\sqrt{\alpha(1-c-d)}$$

$$-\alpha\sum_{t'\leqslant t}(1+G)^{-1}_{tt'}\,\mathrm{sgn}[q(t')]. \quad (44)$$

Frozen agents are those for which $\mathrm{sgn}[q(t)]$ is independent of time; due to Eq. (39) these will not experience the last term in Eq. (44). However, due to the properties of the noise in the $\alpha<\alpha_c$ regime (and in contrast to the situation with $\alpha>\alpha_c$), even frozen agents will now have $\lim_{t\to\infty}q(t)/t=0$. Insertion into Eq. (44) shows that frozen solutions of the following form exist:

$$q(t)=q-\tfrac{1}{2}\,\gamma z\sqrt{\alpha d}(-1)^t \quad (45)$$

provided $\mathrm{sgn}[q(t)]=\mathrm{sgn}[q]$ for all t, so q and d must obey

$$d=1-c, \quad |q|>|\tfrac{1}{2}\,\gamma z\sqrt{\alpha d}|. \quad (46)$$

Oscillating agents, on the other hand, are those for which $\mathrm{sgn}[q(t)]=\hat{\sigma}(-1)^t$, with $\hat{\sigma}=\pm1$. Insertion into Eq. (44) shows that oscillating solutions of the following form exist:

$$q(t)=q+\tfrac{1}{2}\,\gamma\hat{\sigma}[\alpha-z\hat{\sigma}\sqrt{\alpha d}](-1)^t \quad (47)$$

provided $\mathrm{sgn}[q(t+1)]=-\mathrm{sgn}[q(t)]$ for all t, so q and d must obey

$$d=1-c, \quad \gamma[\alpha-z\hat{\sigma}\sqrt{\alpha d}]>0, \quad |q|<\tfrac{1}{2}\,\gamma[\alpha-z\hat{\sigma}\sqrt{\alpha d}]. \quad (48)$$

Note that, if rigorously frozen and/or rigorously oscillating agents were asymptotic solutions of Eq. (44), then the correlations would come out as $C(\tau)=\phi+(1-\phi)(-1)^\tau$ (with ϕ, as before, denoting the fraction of frozen agents), and we would find $c+d=1$. Figures 1 and 4, however, show that this simple relation holds only near $\alpha=0$. Away from $\alpha=0$ there will therefore be solutions describing fickle agents that change strategy at intervals intermediate between 1 (oscillating) and infinity (frozen). This can be understood on the basis of Eq. (44), where due to the noise term $\xi(t)$ (with a finite temporal correlation length) there will for $c+d<1$ always be a nonzero probability of nearly frozen agents changing strategy occasionally, and of nearly oscillating agents not changing strategy occasionally.

X. THE LIMIT $\alpha\to0$

Let us finally investigate the situation near $\alpha=0$ more closely, where we may use the experimental observation that $c+d\approx1$, which implies that all agents will be either frozen or oscillating. We put $c=\phi$ (the fraction of frozen agents) and $d=1-\phi$, and choose homogeneous initial conditions with $q(0)>0$. We now find $\eta(t)=(-1)^t \gamma z\sqrt{(1-\phi)}$ and our two solution types are given by

$$q(t)=\begin{cases} q-\tfrac{1}{2}\,\gamma z\sqrt{\alpha(1-\phi)}(-1)^t, & \text{frozen,}\\ |q|<\tfrac{1}{2}\,\gamma[\alpha-z\hat{\sigma}\sqrt{\alpha(1-\phi)}], & \text{oscillating,}\end{cases}$$

provided the following conditions for existence are met:

$$|q|>|\tfrac{1}{2}\,\gamma z\sqrt{\alpha(1-\phi)}|, \quad \text{frozen,}$$

$$|q|<\tfrac{1}{2}\,\gamma[\alpha-z\hat{\sigma}\sqrt{\alpha(1-\phi)}], \quad \text{oscillating,} \quad (49)$$

$$\gamma\sqrt{\alpha}>\gamma z\hat{\sigma}\sqrt{1-\phi}. \quad (50)$$

Near $\alpha=0$ we also know, due to $c+d=1$, that

$$\langle\eta(t+\tau)\eta(t)\rangle=(-1)^\tau(1-\phi)\gamma^2, \quad t\to\infty, \quad (51)$$

$$\eta(t)=(-1)^t \gamma z\sqrt{1-\phi}, \quad t\to\infty, \quad (52)$$

and that $\lim_{t\to\infty}\sigma^2=\tfrac{1}{2}(1-\phi)\gamma^2$. In order to eliminate the remaining parameters γ and ϕ we note that time translation invariance guarantees the validity of the relation $\Sigma_t(G^n)(t)(-1)^t=[\Sigma_t G(t)(-1)^t]^n$, and hence

$$\gamma=(1+\Gamma)^{-1}, \quad \Gamma=\sum_t G(t)(-1)^t. \quad (53)$$

The quantity Γ can, in turn, be expressed in terms of γ upon inserting Eqs. (51) and (52) into Eq. (27). We obtain

$$\sqrt{\alpha}(1-\phi)\gamma(1-\gamma)(-1)^\tau=\lim_{t\to\infty}\langle\mathrm{sgn}[q(t+\tau)]\eta(t)\rangle_\star.$$

Working out the average on the right-hand side, by separating frozen from fickle solutions, gives for large t

$$\langle\mathrm{sgn}[q(t+\tau)]\eta(t)\rangle_\star=\phi\langle\mathrm{sgn}[q(t+\tau)]\eta(t)\rangle_{\mathrm{fr}}+(1-\phi)$$

$$\times\langle\mathrm{sgn}[q(t+\tau)]\eta(t)\rangle_{\mathrm{fi}}$$

$$=\gamma\sqrt{(1-\phi)}(-1)^\tau\{\phi(-1)^t$$

$$\times\langle\mathrm{sgn}[q]z\rangle_{\mathrm{fr}}+(1-\phi)\langle\hat{\sigma}z\rangle_{\mathrm{fi}}\}.$$

Since in a stationary state the correlation function $\langle\mathrm{sgn}[q(t)]\eta(t')\rangle_\star$ can only depend on $t-t'$, we must conclude that $\langle\mathrm{sgn}[q]z\rangle_{\mathrm{fr}}=0$ and that either

$$\lim_{\alpha\to0}\gamma(1-\phi)=0 \quad \text{or} \quad \gamma=1-\sqrt{(1-\phi)/\alpha}\langle\hat{\sigma}z\rangle_{\mathrm{fi}} \quad (54)$$

(in leading order for $\alpha\to0$). Multiplication of both sides of the second equation in (54) by $\gamma\sqrt{\alpha}$ shows that it automatically ensures the validity of the second condition of Eq. (50). The first equation of (54) will satisfy the second condition of Eq. (50) as long as $\gamma > 0$.

In order to proceed we need to calculate the persistent term q in the proposed solutions, which can be seen as representing their effective initial conditions. It incorporates both the true initial conditions and the effects of the transients of the dynamics, which initially will not be of the simple form (44). Exact evaluation would require solving our order parameter equations for arbitrary times, which is not feasible. However, one can proceed for now on the basis of the postulate that the properties of the long-term attractors (viz., the Gaussian variable z) are uncorrelated with the value of q. The conditions (49) and (50) then simply state whether a value of q, generated independently of z according to some distribution $P(q)$, is compatible with a given attractor. Although we will not be able to generate all possible stationary solutions of the process (17), we will show how two qualitatively different solutions, one with a diverging volatility for $\alpha \to 0$ and one with a vanishing volatility for $\alpha \to 0$, can both be extracted from our equations.

The first type of solution is obtained for $\lim_{\alpha \to 0} \phi = \phi_0 < 1$. Now one finds, in leading order in α, that $\hat{\sigma} = -\text{sgn}[\gamma z]$ and that $\gamma = \langle |z| \rangle_{\text{fi}} \sqrt{(1-\phi_0)}/\alpha$. The conditions (49) and (50) reduce in leading order to the complementary pair

$$|q| > \tfrac{1}{2} \gamma |z| \sqrt{\alpha(1-\phi_0)}, \quad \text{frozen}, \tag{55}$$

$$|q| < \tfrac{1}{2} \gamma |z| \sqrt{\alpha(1-\phi_0)}, \quad \text{oscillating}. \tag{56}$$

This, in turn, allows us to calculate ϕ_0 and $\langle |z| \rangle_{\text{fi}}$:

$$\phi_0 = \int dq\, P(q) \int \frac{dz}{\sqrt{2\pi}} e^{-z^2/2} \theta[|q| - \tfrac{1}{2}\gamma|z|\sqrt{\alpha(1-\phi)}]$$

$$= \int dq\, P(q)\, \text{erf}\left[\frac{\sqrt{2}|q|}{\gamma\sqrt{\alpha(1-\phi)}} \right],$$

$$\langle |z| \rangle_{\text{fi}} = \int \frac{dq\, P(q)}{1-\phi_0} \int \frac{dz|z|}{\sqrt{2\pi}} e^{-z^2/2}$$

$$\times \theta[\tfrac{1}{2}\gamma|z|\sqrt{\alpha(1-\phi_0)} - |q|]$$

$$= \frac{\sqrt{2}}{(1-\phi_0)\sqrt{\pi}} \int dq\, P(q) e^{-2q^2/\gamma^2\alpha(1-\phi_0)}.$$

We eliminate γ in favor of $\sigma = \tfrac{1}{2}\sqrt{2}\gamma\sqrt{1-\phi_0}$ and end up with the following simple closed equation for σ:

$$\sigma = \int dq\, P(q) \frac{e^{-q^2/\sigma^2\alpha}}{\sqrt{\alpha\pi}}. \tag{57}$$

The associated value for ϕ_0 then follows from

$$\phi_0 = \int dq\, P(q)\, \text{erf}\left[\frac{|q|}{\sigma\sqrt{\alpha}} \right]. \tag{58}$$

Finally, we can use our observations regarding the first few time steps (Sec. VI) of the process in order to obtain an estimate for $P(q)$. These showed for small α that initially (i) for small $|q(0)| = O(\sqrt{\alpha})$ the system is driven toward the oscillating state, (ii) for large $|q(0)| = O(\alpha^0)$ the system tends to freeze, (iii) the transient processes are dominated by the (Gaussian) noise term in Eq. (17), and (iv) the noise term is automatically being "amplified" (either via a diverging response function, or via accumulation over time) to an effective $O(\alpha^0)$ contribution. Note that (i) and (ii) confirm that q can indeed be seen as the sum of $q(0)$ and the net effect of the transient processes, and that (iii) and (iv) subsequently suggest representing the transient processes by adding a single effective Gaussian variable. Hence for small α it would appear sensible to write $P(q) = (\Lambda\sqrt{2\pi})^{-1}e^{-[q-q(0)]^2/2\Lambda^2}$, which converts Eqs. (57) and (58) into

$$\sigma^2\alpha + 2\Lambda^2 = \frac{1}{\pi} e^{-2q^2(0)/(\sigma^2\alpha + 2\Lambda^2)}.$$

We conclude that σ can be written in terms of the solution y of a transcendental equation

$$\sigma = \frac{1}{\sqrt{\alpha}} \left[\frac{2q^2(0)}{y} - 2\Lambda^2 \right]^{1/2}, \quad 2q^2(0) = \frac{y}{\pi} e^{-y}. \tag{59}$$

For $|q(0)| \to 0$ we find that $\sigma = (\alpha\pi)^{-1/2}\sqrt{1 - 2\pi\Lambda^2}$; hence we must obviously require $\Lambda^2 < 1/2\pi$. The associated value for ϕ_0 then follows from

$$\phi_0 = \int Dx\, \text{erf}\left[\frac{|q(0) + \Lambda x|}{\sigma\sqrt{\alpha}} \right]. \tag{60}$$

Since we cannot calculate or estimate the width Λ of the effective Gaussian noise term without solving our order parameter equations for short times [Λ could even depend on $q(0)$], it is quite satisfactory that several interesting properties of the solution are found to be independent of Λ. For instance, one always finds a diverging volatility of the form $\sigma = O(\alpha^{-1/2})$, and there is a critical value $q_c = (2\pi e)^{-1/2} \approx 0.242$ such that for $|q(0)| > q_c$ the solution no longer exists. This solution is clearly the type of volatile state that has been reported regularly (see, e.g., [8,9]) upon observing numerical simulations. We have now found, however, that whether or not it will appear depends critically on the choice made for the initial conditions. Numerical simulations indeed appear to support the existence and predicted magnitude of a critical value $q_c \approx 0.242$ (see Fig. 5); fully conclusive experiments, however (with even smaller values of α), would require impractical amounts of CPU time and/or memory in order to meet the requirements $p \to \infty$ and $N \to \infty$ for increasingly small values of α, and are presently ruled out. In the limit $q(0) \to 0$ one can easily carry out the integrals in Eq. (60), giving $\Lambda = (2\pi)^{-1/2}\sin[\tfrac{1}{2}\pi\phi_0]$. Elimination of Λ via insertion into $\sigma = (\alpha\pi)^{-1/2}\sqrt{1 - 2\pi\Lambda^2}$ then leads to the simple relation

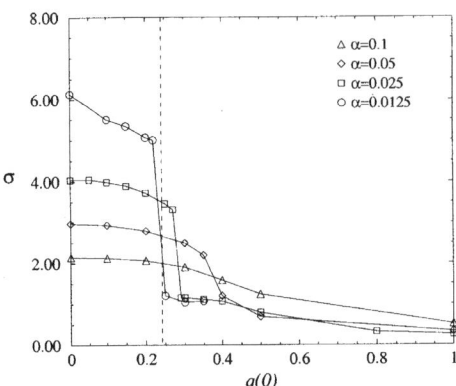

FIG. 5. Experimental evidence in support of the existence of a critical value for the initial strategy valuation $q(0)$ below which a high-volatility solution exists. The connected markers represent the results of measuring the volatility in individual simulations, performed with $N=4000$ agents and initial conditions where $q_i(0) = q(0)$, and after in excess of 1000 iteration steps. CPU time and memory limitations prevent us from doing reliable and conclusive experiments for $\alpha < 0.0125$; the available data, however, are clearly not in conflict with our theoretical prediction $q_c \approx 0.242$ (vertical dashed line), which follows from Eq. (59).

$$\sigma = \frac{\cos[\frac{1}{2}\pi\phi_0]}{\sqrt{\alpha\pi}} + O(\alpha^0), \quad \alpha, q(0) \to 0. \quad (61)$$

This is the high-volatility solution shown in the $\alpha < \alpha_c$ regime of Fig. 3, with ϕ_0 as measured in simulations (see, e.g., Fig. 2). The power of α in Eq. (61) is observed to be correct. The observed difference between theory and experiment with regard to the prefactor can be understood as a reflection of our approximation $c + d \approx 1$; this amounts to disregarding deviations from the idealized purely frozen or purely oscillating behavior, which can indeed be expected to give an approximate theory that (even for small α) slightly underestimates the volatility.

We note that the condition $\lim_{\alpha \to 0} \phi < 1$ for the above reasoning to apply can in fact be weakened to $\lim_{\alpha \to 0} \alpha/(1 - \phi) = 0$. The above solution ceases to hold, however, at the point where the fraction ϕ of frozen agents scales as $\phi = 1 - \kappa\alpha + O(\alpha^2)$, in which case we have to turn to the first option in Eq. (54), rather than the second. This is consistent with our previous observation that small values of $|q(0)|$ lead to a relatively small fraction of frozen agents (and a large volatility), whereas for large $|q(0)|$ such a solution will break down in favor of states with a larger fraction of frozen agents. Since we can now no longer use the second equation in (54) to determine γ and hence find the volatility $\sigma = \frac{1}{2}\sqrt{2}\gamma\sqrt{1-\phi}$, we have to return to Eq. (53). A fully frozen state, for which for $\alpha \to 0$ will indeed be described by this second type of solution (since $\lim_{\alpha \to 0} \phi = 1$), must necessarily have $G(t>0) = g$. This is consistent with our *ansätze*, since it gives

$$(1+G)^{-1}(t) = -g(1-g)^{t-1}, \quad t > 0,$$

which implies $\Sigma_{t \geqslant 0}(1+G)^{-1}(t) = 0$, provided $0 < g < 2$. We can now calculate γ from Eq. (53) and find $\lim_{\alpha \to 0} \gamma = 2/(2-g)$. Thus we obtain, provided $2 - g = O(\alpha^0)$,

$$\sigma = \frac{\sqrt{2\kappa}}{2-g}\sqrt{\alpha} + O(\alpha), \quad \kappa = \lim_{\alpha \to 0}\frac{1-\phi}{\alpha}.$$

We also note that the scaling property $\phi = 1 - O(\alpha)$ implies that $P(0) = \lim_{q \to 0} P(q) = O(\sqrt{\alpha})$, since all q values of order $q = O(\sqrt{\alpha})$ will contribute to the fraction $1 - \phi$ of fickle agents, giving $1 - \phi = O(P(0)\sqrt{\alpha})$. We can now calculate $\lim_{\alpha \to 0} g$ upon explicitly inspecting the effect of a perturbation of a frozen state. Since $G(t>0) = g$ we may restrict ourselves to considering the effect on $\text{sgn}[q(t+1)]$ of a perturbation at time t, giving in leading order for $\alpha \to 0$

$$\lim_{\alpha \to 0} g = \lim_{\alpha \to 0} \lim_{\theta \to 0} \left\langle \frac{\partial}{\partial\theta} \text{sgn}[q + \tfrac{1}{2}\alpha\gamma z\sqrt{\kappa}(-1)^t + \theta] \right\rangle$$

$$= 2 \lim_{\alpha \to 0} \langle \delta[q + \tfrac{1}{2}\alpha\gamma z\sqrt{\kappa}(-1)^t] \rangle$$

$$= 2 \lim_{\alpha \to 0} P(0) = 0.$$

Hence, since the frozen state has $q = O(\alpha^0)$, we find $\lim_{\alpha \to 0} \gamma = 1$ and

$$\sigma = \tfrac{1}{2}\sqrt{2\kappa\alpha} + O(\alpha), \quad \alpha \to 0. \quad (62)$$

Explicit calculation of the prefactor in Eq. (62) would require taking our calculations beyond the leading order in α, in order to find κ. Equation (62) is the low-volatility solution shown in the $\alpha < \alpha_c$ regime of Fig. 3, with κ as measured in simulations (see, e.g., Fig. 6). Again the power of α in Eq. (62) is observed to be correct. The remaining difference between theory and experiment with regard to the prefactor can again be understood as a reflection of our approximation $c + d \approx 1$, which induces a structural underestimation of the volatility.

XI. DISCUSSION

In this paper we have solved a "batch" version of the minority game with random external information, using generating functional analysis (or dynamic mean field theory) as introduced by De Dominicis, which allows one to carry out the disorder averages in a dynamical context. Since the dynamics of the game is not described by a detailed balance type of stochastic process, equilibrium statistical mechanical tools cannot be applied directly. Phase transitions (if present) must be of a dynamical nature. The disorder in the minority game consists of the microscopic realization of the repertoire of randomly drawn trading strategies of the N agents. Upon taking the limit $N \to \infty$ one ends up with an exact non-Markovian stochastic equation describing the dynamics of an effective single agent (17), whose statistical properties are identical to those of the original system (averaged over all realizations of the disorder). The key control parameter in

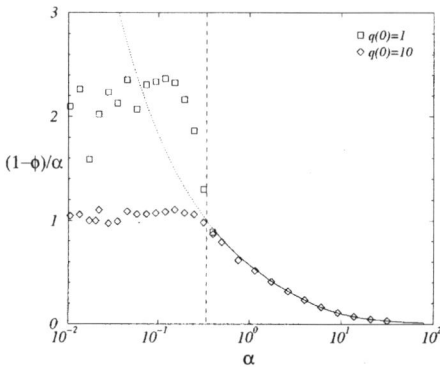

FIG. 6. Experimental evidence for the existence of the limit $\kappa = \lim_{\alpha \to 0}(1 - \phi)/\alpha$ for the low-volatility solution. The markers are obtained from individual simulation runs performed with a system of $N = 4000$ agents and initial valuations of the form $q_i(0) = q(0) > q_c$ (to evoke the low-volatility state), and in excess of 1000 iteration steps. The solid curve to the right of the critical point is the theoretical prediction, obtained from the exact equations (26) and $\phi = 1 - \mathrm{erf}[\sqrt{\alpha/2(1+c)}]$ describing the $\alpha > \alpha_c$ regime (the dotted curve to the left is its continuation into the $\alpha < \alpha_c$ regime (where it should indeed no longer be correct).

this problem is the ratio $\alpha = p/N$ of the number of possible values of the external information over the number of agents.

We find a phase transition at $\alpha_c \approx 0.337\,40$, signaled by the onset of anomalous response, in agreement with the value reported recently in [4]. The method used in [4] depends on the fact that for their stochastic version of the minority game a Lyapunov function exists. Our approach does not have this constraint and can be easily applied to those variations of the game where a Lyapunov function is not available, thus opening up a wider range of models for analysis (see, e.g., [3]). Above α_c (where anomalous response is absent) we can solve the stationary state of the system exactly, giving exact expressions for quantities such as the fraction of frozen agents (which is zero for $\alpha \to \infty$ but increases with decreasing α), the persistent two-time correlations, and the persistent correlations in the total bid. The volatility (which is itself not an order parameter of the system) can be calculated to a very good approximation. Above α_c, our method and that of [6,4] are likely to describe the same behavior [21]. Below α_c, i.e., in the region of complex dynamics (inaccessible by the replica approach [15]), our present method still applies. In this region we demonstrate the existence of multiple stationary states, and derive expressions for the relevant observables in leading order in α as $\alpha \to 0$. We show, more specifically, that the occurrence and practical observability of a diverging volatility for $\alpha \to 0$ (as reported in, e.g., [8,9]) is crucially dependent on the overall degree of a priori preference for specific strategies exhibited by the agents at $t = 0$, which may explain the different observations regarding the $\alpha \to 0$ behavior that have been reported in the literature [13]. More specifically, our theory points at the

existence of a critical value for the initial strategy valuations, above which the system will revert to a state with vanishing volatility. Our theoretical predictions find quite satisfactory confirmation in numerical simulations.

The fact that we can analyze the stationary state of Eq. (17), in spite of it describing a non-Markovian stochastic process, suggests that the present method should also be suitable to deal with models where the external information depends on time, or on the previous behavior of the agents, as in the original model [1,22].

ACKNOWLEDGMENTS

We would like to thank Andrea Cavagna and David Sherrington for introducing us to the minority games and Matteo Marsili for a discussion of previous work done. J.A.F.H. wishes to thank King's College London Association for financial support.

APPENDIX A: EXPRESSIONS FOR AVERAGE BID AND VOLATILITY

First we calculate $\lim_{N \to \infty} \overline{\langle A_t \rangle}$ using expression (3). We note that we obtain $\langle A_t \rangle$ simply by making the replacement $\exp[i \sum_{ti} \psi_i(t) q_i(t)] \to (\tau \alpha N) \sum_\mu x_t^\mu$ in the right-hand side of Eq. (6). The disorder average is carried out as before, but instead of Eq. (7) we now obtain

$$\overline{\langle A_t \rangle} = \tau \int [DC\,D\hat{C}][DK\,D\hat{K}][DL\,D\hat{L}]$$

$$\times e^{N[\Psi+\Phi+\Omega]+O(N^0)} e^{-\Phi/\alpha} \int Dw\,D\hat{w}\,Dx\,D\hat{x}\, x_t$$

$$\times \exp\left(i \sum_s [\hat{w}_s w_s + \hat{x}_s x_s + w_s x_s] \right)$$

$$\times \exp\left(-\frac{1}{2} \sum_{ss'} [w_s w_{s'} + \hat{w}_s L_{ss'} \hat{w}_{s'} \right.$$

$$\left. + 2\hat{x}_s K_{ss'} \hat{w}_{s'} + \hat{x}_s C_{ss'} \hat{x}_{s'}] \right),$$

where we have used permutation invariance with respect to μ (after the disorder average). The integral is dominated by the familiar saddle point. Since the $O(N^0)$ term in the exponent is identical to that in Eq. (7), we can now simply use the identity $\overline{Z[\mathbf{0}]} = 1$ to show that

$$\lim_{N \to \infty} \overline{\langle A_t \rangle} = \tau e^{-\Phi/\alpha} \int Dw\,D\hat{w}\,Dx\,D\hat{x}\, x_t$$

$$\times \exp\left(i \sum_s [\hat{w}_s w_s + \hat{x}_s x_s + w_s x_s] \right)$$

$$\times \exp\left(-\frac{1}{2} \sum_{ss'} [w_s w_{s'} + 2i\hat{x}_s G_{ss'} \hat{w}_{s'} \right.$$

$$\left. + \hat{x}_s C_{ss'} \hat{x}_{s'}] \right) = 0. \tag{A1}$$

The last step follows immediately from the antisymmetry of the integrand under overall reflection.

To determine the disorder-averaged volatility matrix, which for $N \to \infty$ becomes identical to $\overline{\langle A_t A_{t'} \rangle}$ due to Eq. (A1) and the self-averaging property, we first work out the dominant terms in Eq. (5). Using $\lim_{N \to \infty} (\alpha N)^{-1} \Sigma_\mu \Omega_\mu^2 = \frac{1}{2}$, we obtain the relatively simple expression

$$\lim_{N \to \infty} \langle A_t A_{t'} \rangle = \lim_{N \to \infty} \frac{1}{2\alpha N} \sum_\mu \langle [x_t^\mu + \Omega^\mu / \tau][x_{t'}^\mu + \Omega^\mu / \tau] \rangle.$$

We calculate this average by making the replacement $\exp[i\Sigma_{ti} \psi_i(t) q_i(t)] \to (2\alpha N)^{-1} \Sigma_\mu \langle [x_t^\mu + \Omega^\mu / \tau][x_{t'}^\mu + \Omega^\mu / \tau] \rangle$ on the right-hand side of Eq. (6). Repeated integration by parts over the w_t^μ shows that we may equivalently put $\exp[i\Sigma_{ti} \psi_i(t) q_i(t)]$ $\to (2\alpha N)^{-1} \Sigma_\mu \hat{w}_t^\mu \hat{w}_{t'}^\mu$. Following the steps we also took in calculating $\langle A \rangle$ now gives

$$\lim_{N \to \infty} \overline{\langle A_t A_{t'} \rangle} = \frac{1}{2} e^{-\Phi/\alpha} \int Dw\, D\hat{w}\, Dx\, D\hat{x}\, \hat{w}_t \hat{w}_{t'} \exp\left(i \sum_s [\hat{w}_s w_s + \hat{x}_s x_s + w_s x_s] \right)$$

$$\times \exp\left(-\frac{1}{2} \sum_{ss'} [w_s w_{s'} + 2i\hat{x}_s G_{ss'} \hat{w}_{s'} + \hat{x}_s C_{ss'} \hat{x}_{s'}] \right)$$

$$= \frac{1}{2} \frac{\int D\hat{w}\, \hat{w}_t \hat{w}_{t'} \exp\left(-\frac{1}{2} \Sigma_{ss'} \hat{w}_s [(1+G)^T D^{-1}(1+G)]_{ss'} \hat{w}_{s'} \right)}{\int D\hat{w} \exp\left(-\frac{1}{2} \Sigma_{ss'} [(1+G)^T D^{-1}(1+G)]_{ss'} \hat{w}_{s'} \right)}$$

$$= \frac{1}{2} [(1+G)^{-1} D(1+G^T)^{-1}]_{tt'}. \tag{A2}$$

APPENDIX B: CONSEQUENCES OF ABSENCE OF ANOMALOUS RESPONSE

Lemma 1. Consider two bounded sequences of real numbers A_t and b_t. Because b_t is bounded, there exists a number b such that $\lim_{\tau \to \infty} (1/\tau) \Sigma_{t \leq \tau} b_t = b$. Define $a_\tau = \Sigma_{t \leq \tau} A_t$, and assume that $\lim_{\tau \to \infty} a_\tau = a$. Then

$$\lim_{\tau \to \infty} \frac{1}{\tau} \sum_{t \leq \tau} \sum_{t' \leq t} A_{t-t'} b_{tt'} = ab.$$

Proof. Upon substituting $t \to t + t'$ we find

$$\frac{1}{\tau} \sum_{t \leq \tau} \sum_{t' \leq t} A_{t-t'} b_{t'} = \frac{1}{\tau} \sum_{t' \leq \tau} b_{t'} \sum_{t \leq \tau - t'} A_t = \frac{1}{\tau} \sum_{t \leq \tau} a_{\tau-t} b_t.$$

The sequences $\{a\}$ and $\{b\}$ are bounded, so there exist numbers C_a and C_b such that $|a_t| < C_a$ and $|b_t| < C_b$ for all $t \geq 0$. The sequence $\{a\}$ converges to a, so for any $\epsilon > 0$ there exists a K such that for all $t > K$ $|a_t - a| < \epsilon/3 C_b$. We now choose M such that for all $\tau > M$ $|(1/\tau) \Sigma_{t \leq \tau} b_t - b| < \epsilon/3 |a|$ and $KC_a C_b / \tau < \epsilon/3$. Then we find for all $\tau > M$

$$\left| \frac{1}{\tau} \sum_{t \leq \tau} a_{\tau-t} b_t - ab \right|$$

$$= \left| \frac{1}{\tau} \sum_{t=\tau-K}^{\tau} a_{\tau-t} b_t + \sum_{t < \tau - K} a_{\tau-t} b_t - ab \right|$$

$$\leq \left| \frac{1}{\tau} \sum_{t=\tau-K}^{\tau} a_{\tau-t} b_t \right| + \left| \frac{1}{\tau} \sum_{t < \tau - K} (a_{\tau-t} - a) b_t \right.$$

$$\left. - a\left(b - \frac{1}{\tau} \sum_{t < \tau - K} b_t \right) \right|$$

$$\leq \frac{KC_a C_b}{\tau} + \left| \frac{1}{\tau} \sum_{t < \tau - N} (a_{\tau-t} - a) b_t \right|$$

$$+ |a| \left| b - \frac{1}{\tau} \sum_{t < \tau - K} b_t \right| \leq \epsilon.$$

Hence the limit is as claimed. ■

Lemma 2. Suppose $G_{st} = G(s-t) \in \mathfrak{R}$, where $G(t) = 0$ for all $t < 0$ and with $\lim_{\tau \to \infty} \Sigma_{t \leq \tau} G(t) = k$, and suppose $\lim_{\tau \to \infty} \tau^{-1} \Sigma_{t \leq \tau} s(t) = s$. Then for all $n \in \mathbb{N}$

$$\lim_{\tau \to \infty} \frac{1}{\tau} \sum_{t=1}^{\tau} \sum_{t'} (G^n)_{tt'} s(t') = k^n s.$$

Proof. The proof proceeds by induction. For $n=0$, the statement is trivially true. Suppose now that it is true for all $n \leq m$. Then

$$\lim_{\tau \to \infty} \frac{1}{\tau} \sum_{t=1}^{\tau} \sum_{t'} (G^{m+1})_{tt'} s(t')$$

$$= \lim_{\tau \to \infty} \frac{1}{\tau} \sum_{t=1}^{\tau} \sum_{t'' \leq t} G(t-t'') \sum_{t' \leq t''} (G^m)_{t''t'} s(t').$$

The sequence $b_t = \sum_{t' \leq t} (G^m)_{tt'} s(t')$ satisfies the conditions of Lemma 1, application of which gives

$$\lim_{\tau \to \infty} \frac{1}{\tau} \sum_{t=1}^{\tau} \sum_{t'} (G^{m+1})_{tt'} s(t') = k k^m s = k^{m+1} s.$$

Hence the claim holds for $m+1$, and by induction it is now proved for all n. ∎

[1] D. Challet and Y.-C. Zhang, Physica A **246**, 407 (1997).

[2] W. Arthur, Am. Econ. Assoc. Papers Proc. **84**, 406 (1994).

[3] D. Challet, http://www.unifr.ch/econophysics/minority (an extensive annotated collection of work on the minority game).

[4] D. Challet, M. Marsili, and R. Zecchina, Phys. Rev. Lett. **84**, 1824 (2000).

[5] M. Marsili, D. Challet, and R. Zecchina, Physica A **280**, 522 (2000).

[6] A. De Martino and M. Marsili, J. Phys. A **34**, 2525 (2001).

[7] N. F. Johnson, M. Hart, and P. Hui, e-print cond-mat/9811227; M. Hart, P. Jefferies, P. Hui, and N. F. Johnson, Eur. Phys. J. B (to be published); M. Hart, P. Jefferies, and N. F. Johnson, J. Phys. A (to be published).

[8] R. Savit, R. Manuca, and R. Riolo, Phys. Rev. Lett. **82**, 2203 (1999).

[9] R. Manuca, Y. Li, R. Riolo, and R. Savit, University of Michigan Technical Report No. pscs-98-11-001 (unpublished); R. Manuca, Y. Li, R. Riolo, R. Savit, e-print adap-org/9811005.

[10] C. De Dominicis, Phys. Rev. B **18**, 4913 (1978).

[11] A. Cavagna, Phys. Rev. E **59**, R3783 (1999).

[12] D. Challet and Y.-C. Zhang, Physica A **256**, 514 (1998).

[13] J. P. Garrahan, E. Moro, and D. Sherrington, Phys. Rev. E **62**, R9 (2000).

[14] A. Cavagna, J. P. Garrahan, I. Giardina, and D. Sherrington, Phys. Rev. Lett. **83**, 4429 (1999); see also the comments by Challet *et al.*, e-print cond-mat/0004308, and the reply by Cavagna *et al.*, e-print cond-mat/0005134.

[15] M. Marsili and D. Challet, Adv. Complex Syst. 3-I (2001).

[16] H. Sompolinsky and A. Zippelius, Phys. Rev. B **25**, 6860 (1982).

[17] H. Eissfeller and M. Opper, Phys. Rev. Lett. **68**, 2094 (1992).

[18] D. Challet and M. Marsili, Phys. Rev. E **60**, R6271 (1999).

[19] M. Mézard, G. Parisi, and M. Virasoro, *Spin Glass Theory and Beyond* (World Scientific, Singapore, 1987).

[20] K. H. Fischer and J. A. Hertz, *Spin Glasses* (Cambridge University Press, Cambridge, 1991).

[21] M. Marsili (private communication).

[22] D. Challet and M. Marsili, Phys. Rev. E **62**, 1862 (2000).

www.elsevier.com/locate/physa

Modeling market mechanism with minority game

Damien Challet[a],[*], Matteo Marsili[b], Yi-Cheng Zhang[a]

[a]*Institut de Physique Théorique, Université de Fribourg, 1700 Fribourg, Switzerland*
[b]*Istituto Nazionale per la Fisica della Materia (INFM), Trieste-SISSA Unit, V. Beirut 2-4,*
Trieste I-34014, Italy

Received 17 September 1999

Abstract

Using the minority game model we study a broad spectrum of problems of market mechanism. We study the role of different types of agents: producers, speculators as well as noise traders. The central issue here is the information flow: producers feed in the information whereas speculators make it away. How well each agent fares in the common game depends on the market conditions, as well as their sophistication. Sometimes there is much to gain with little effort, sometimes great effort virtually brings no more incremental gain. Market impact is also shown to play an important role, a strategy should be judged when it is actually used in play for its quality. Though the minority game is an extremely simplified market model, it allows to ask, analyze and answer many questions which arise in real markets. © 2000 Elsevier Science B.V. All rights reserved.

1. Introduction

Recently, it became possible to study markets of heterogenous agents, in particular in the form of the so-called minority games (MG) [1,2]. Since long-time practitioners of the market, as well as some economists have criticized the main-stream economics where a so-called representative agent plays the central role. Many prominent economists like Herbert Simon [3], Richard Day and Brian Arthur [4] have been forceful proponents of the "bounded rationality" and "inductive thinking". However, though many people join in unison in their criticism of the main stream, their alternative approaches and models do not command consensus yet.

The MG is inspired by Arthur's "*El Farol*" model [4], which shows for the first time how the equilibrium can be reached using inductive thinking. Whereas *El Farol* model is about the equilibrium, our MG model is about fluctuations. In a sense MG

* Corresponding author. Fax: +41-26-300-9758.
E-mail address: damien.challet@unifr.ch (D. Challet)

gives us a powerful tool to study detailed pattern of fluctuations, the equilibrium point is trivial by design. It is the fluctuations that play the dominant role in economic activities, like the market mechanism. MG allows us to study in a precise manner the approach to equilibrium, how the agents try to outsmart each other, for their selfish gain, compete for the available marginal information (any deviation from the mid-point represents exploitable advantage). It is for this residual margin that all the agents fight for, resembling the real markets. The importance to market mechanism is primordial, as any practitioner can attest. Neo-classical economics would tell us that the MG, as in a competitive market, does not offer consistent gain, based on the efficient market hypothesis (EMH). However, if some agents stop playing (i.e. choosing dynamically among the two sides), they will give away information that the other more diligent dynamic agents make use of. This means that equilibrium can be only dynamically maintained, any relaxing would imply a relative disadvantage. It is not that the same thing occurs in real markets?

Studying a model of market mechanism opens up many detailed questions, which practitioners have to face constantly but the main-stream economists do not have any clue to answer them. For instance, in a model like MG agents interact with each other through a common market, what information each agent brings in? What gain each agent takes out? How sophisticated should an agent be? What is realizable gain objective? What is the role of noise traders? How about insider trading (an agent processing privileged information about fellow agents)? What is the market impact of an otherwise clever strategy? The list is obviously endless. The point we want to make here is that with so little to start with, and with so many questions relevant to real markets one can hope for a qualitative answer.

After two years since the MG's birth, during which much work has revealed its extremely rich structure [5], an analytical approach leading to its exact solution has been found [6,7]. Unfortunately, the main progress is still confined in the physics community. We hope that, with this paper, this will change: The aim is to convince people, including economists hopefully, that many concrete questions about market mechanisms can be asked and answered, in precise and analytical way, using the approach of Refs. [6,7]. In fact the MG can be used as a flexible platform and different handles can be added and manipulated almost at will. To achieve our goal, the analytic approach shall be supplemented by numerical simulations to confirm its validity. More technical parts and heavy calculations shall be dealt with in the appendices.

2. Main results

Here below we give a list of salient points of our paper:

(1) *Diversification of ideas.* If an agent has different alternative strategies, it is better to have them diversified, i.e., not too much correlated. We show the effects of diversification.

285

(2) *Markets have two types of agents: producers and speculators.* The former do not have alternative strategies; the latter are represented by the normal agents of the standard MG. Producers provide information into the market, upon which speculators feed. For the first time it is possible to demonstrate that producers and speculators need each other, they live in a symbiosis. However, benefits to each group are not equal, depending on the parameters.

(3) *Agents are not obliged to play, if they do not see a possible gain.* We generalize MG to let agents have the option of not playing. In the presence of producers, markets appear to be attractive and more speculators are drawn into the fore.

(4) *Noise traders.* One may wonder if some traders decide to be pure noise traders, i.e., they use completely random strategy, what is the "harm" done to other market participants (producers and speculators), as well as to themselves. In the information rich phase, they appear to increase volatility and in the herding-effect phase, they actually make the market perform better.

(5) Despite the fact that agents start equally equipped, there are better and worse agents and the rank of the agents has an interesting non-Gaussian "bar-code" structure.

(6) Sometimes it pays to increase the capacity of an agent's brain, say add one more unit in M. This will give enormous advantage to the better-equipped agent in the crowded phase (or symmetric phase), where information on the range M is exhausted, whereas such a feature becomes a disadvantage in the information-rich phase.

(7) *Does it pay to have more strategies as alternatives? In general yes.* Here we calculate the relative advantage by having more alternatives. We also show that, due to self-market impact, the imagined gain differs from the real gain, a fact known too well to market practitioners. Even each agent has many alternatives, they actually use only a small number of them.

(8) *Some agents may get illegal information about others.* It is just like a stock broker who knows his clients' orders before execution. Hence, he has privileged information and should be barred from trading. An agent who spies on fellow agents enjoys trading advantages. We measure how much is this effect, as the number of fellow agents whom you spy increases, how much would be your gain.

3. Formalism and review

Our model of market consists of N agents which, for simplicity, can take only one of two actions, such as "buy" and "sell" at each time step t. We represent this assuming that each agent $i=1,\ldots,N$, at time t, can either do the action $a_i(t)=+1$ or the opposite action $a_i(t)=-1$. Given the actions of all agents, the gain of agent i is given by

$$g_i(t) = -a_i(t)A(t) \quad \text{where } A(t) = \sum_{j=1}^{N} a_j(t). \tag{1}$$

This equation models the basic structure of market interaction where each agent's payoffs are determined by the action taken and by a global quantity $A(t)$, which is usually a price and it is determined by all of them. For simplicity, we assume here a linear dependence of $g_i(t)$ on $A(t)$. Other choices, such as $g_i(t) = -a_i(t)\operatorname{sign} A(t)$ in Refs. [1,8,9], can be taken without affecting qualitatively the results we shall discuss below. This interaction clearly rewards the minority of agents (those who took the action $a_i(t) = -\operatorname{sign} A(t)$) who gain an amount $|A(t)|$ and punishes the majority by a loss $-|A(t)|$, hence the name minority game [1]. There are always more losers than winners and agents have no way of knowing what the majority will do before taking their actions.

All agents have access to public information which is represented by an integer variable μ taking one of P values. At time t information "takes the value" $\mu(t)$. We shall also call $\mu(t)$ history since originally this information has been introduced as encoding the record of the past $M = \log_2 P$ signs of $A(t)$ with M bits. It has however been shown [10] that if $\mu(t)$ is randomly drawn in $\{1,\dots,P\}$ one recovers the same results (see also the discussion in Refs. [6,7]). We shall henceforth consider this second, simpler case. When having access to some information, agents can behave differently for different values of $\mu(t)$, eventually because of their personal beliefs on the impact that information $\mu(t)$ shall have on the outcome of the market, $A(t)$. Strictly speaking $A(t)$ only depends on what agents do, so $\mu(t)$ has no direct impact on the market. However, if agents behavior depends on $\mu(t)$ also $A(t)$ shall depend on it, and we denote it by $A^{\mu(t)}(t)$.

How do agents choose actions under information $\mu(t)$? If agents expect that $\mu(t)$ contains some information on the market, they will consider *forecasting strategies* which for each value of μ suggest which action a^μ shall be done. There are 2^P such strategies, and we assume, for the time being, that each agent just picks S such rules randomly (with replacement) from the set of all 2^P strategies. The action of agent i if she follows her sth strategy and the information is μ is denoted by $a^\mu_{s,i}$. Therefore, if $s_i(t)$ is the choice made (in a way we shall specify below) by agent i at time t, her action becomes $a_i(t) \to a^{\mu(t)}_{s_i(t),i}$ and correspondingly, her gain [Eq. (1)] becomes

$$g_i(t) = -a^{\mu(t)}_{s_i(t),i} A^{\mu(t)}(t) \quad \text{where } A^{\mu(t)}(t) = \sum_{j=1}^{N} a^{\mu(t)}_{s_j(t),j} \,. \tag{2}$$

In this paper, we mainly focus on $S = 2$. This case contains all the richness of the model and allows a more transparent presentation. All the results discussed below can be extended to $S > 2$ along the lines of Ref. [7]. For $S = 2$ we can adopt a notation where each agent controls a variable $s_i \in \{\downarrow,\uparrow\}$, with the identification $\uparrow = +1$ and $\downarrow = -1$. This is useful to distinguish strategies s_i from actions a_i. It is convenient to introduce the variables

$$\omega_i^\mu = \frac{a^\mu_{\uparrow,i} + a^\mu_{\downarrow,i}}{2}, \qquad \xi_i^\mu = \frac{a^\mu_{\uparrow,i} - a^\mu_{\downarrow,i}}{2} \,. \tag{3}$$

With these notations, the action taken by this agent in reaction to the history μ is

$$a^\mu_{i,s_i} = \omega_i^\mu + \xi_i^\mu s_i \,, \tag{4}$$

so ω_i^μ represents the part of i's strategies which is fixed, whereas ξ_i^μ is the variable part. We also define $\Omega^\mu = \sum_i \omega_i^\mu$ so that

$$A^\mu(t) = \sum_{i=1}^N a_{i,s_i(t)}^\mu = \Omega^\mu + \sum_{i=1}^N \xi_i^\mu s_i(t) \,. \tag{5}$$

Each agent updates the cumulated virtual payoffs of all her strategies according to

$$U_{s,i}(t+1) = U_{s,i}(t) - A^{\mu(t)}(t) a_{i,s}^{\mu(t)} \tag{6}$$

The quantity $U_{i,s}$ is a "reliability index" which quantifies the agent i's perception of the success of her sth strategy. $U_{i,s}(t)$ is the *virtual* cumulated payoff that agent i would have received up to time t if she had always played strategy s (with others playing the strategies $s_j(t')$ which they actually played at times $t' < t$). *Virtual* here means that this is not the real cumulated payoff but rather that *perceived* by agent i. These differ, as explained below and in Ref. [7], because agents neglect their impact on the market (i.e., the fact that if they had indeed always played s the aggregate quantity $A(t)$ would have been different).

Inductive dynamics [4,1] consists in assuming that agents trust and use their most reliable strategy, which are those with the largest virtual score:

$$s_i(t) = \arg \max_{s \in \{\uparrow,\downarrow\}} U_{i,s}(t) \,. \tag{7}$$

More generally, one can consider a probabilistic choice rule – the so called *Logit* model [11] – such that $P(s_i(t) = s) \propto \exp[\Gamma U_{s,i}(t)]$, (see [12,6,7]). Then Eq. (7) is recovered in the limit $\Gamma \to \infty$. As in Ref. [13], we find it useful to introduce the variables $\Delta_i(t) = U_{i,\uparrow} - U_{i,\downarrow}$. Their dynamics reads

$$\Delta_i(t+1) = \Delta_i(t) - A^{\mu_t}(t) \xi_i^{\mu_t} \tag{8}$$

and Eq. (7) becomes

$$s_i(t) = \operatorname{sign} \Delta_i(t) \,. \tag{9}$$

3.1. Notations on averages

We define the temporal average of a given time-dependent quantity $R(t)$ as

$$\langle R \rangle = \lim_{T \to \infty} \frac{1}{T} \sum_{t=1}^T R(t) \,. \tag{10}$$

This quantity can be decomposed into conditional averages on histories, that is

$$\langle R^\mu \rangle = \lim_{T \to \infty} \frac{P}{T} \sum_{t=1}^T R(t) \delta_{\mu(t),\mu} \,. \tag{11}$$

Note that the factor P and the relation $\langle \delta_{\mu(t),\mu} \rangle = 1/P$ imply that $\langle R^\mu \rangle$ is a conditional average. More precisely, it is the temporal average of the quantity $R(t)$ subject to the condition that the actual history $\mu(t)$ was [1] μ. Finally, averages over the histories μ of a quantity R^μ are defined as

$$\bar{R} \equiv \frac{1}{P} \sum_{\mu=1}^{P} R^\mu .$$ (12)

3.2. Quantities of interest

With these notations, let us now discuss the main quantities which characterize the stationary state of the system. The main free parameter, as first observed in Ref. [8], is

$$\alpha = \frac{P}{N}$$ (13)

and we shall eventually consider the thermodynamic limit where $N, P \to \infty$ with α fixed. The first quantity of interest is

$$\sigma^2 \equiv \overline{\langle A \rangle^2} = \bar{\Omega}^2 + 2 \sum_{i=1}^{N} \overline{\Omega \xi_i} \langle s_i \rangle \langle s_i \rangle + \sum_{i,j} \overline{\xi_i \xi_j} \langle s_i s_j \rangle .$$ (14)

This equals the total loss of agents

$$-\sum_i \langle g_i \rangle = \sigma^2 ,$$ (15)

so it is a measure of global waste. It also quantifies the volatility of the market, i.e., the fluctuations of the quantity $A(t)$, and is related to the average "distance" between agents (see Appendix A). Even though $\langle A \rangle = 0$, by symmetry, it may happen that for a particular μ, the aggregate quantity $A(t)$ is nonzero on average, i.e., that $\langle A^\mu \rangle \neq 0$. In order to quantify this asymmetry, we introduce the quantity

$$H \equiv \overline{\langle A \rangle^2} = \bar{\Omega}^2 + 2 \sum_{i=1}^{N} \overline{\Omega \xi_i} \langle s_i \rangle \langle s_i \rangle + \sum_{i,j} \overline{\xi_i \xi_j} \langle s_i \rangle \langle s_j \rangle .$$ (16)

Note that the only difference with σ^2 lies in the diagonal terms $(i = j)$ of the last sum. Indeed, we assume that $\langle s_i s_j \rangle = \langle s_i \rangle \langle s_j \rangle$ for $i \neq j$, whereas [2] $\langle s_i^2 \rangle \equiv 1 \neq \langle s_i \rangle^2$. Indeed, we can write

$$\sigma^2 = H + \sum_{i=1}^{N} \overline{\xi_i^2}(1 - \langle s_i \rangle^2) .$$ (17)

If $H > 0$, the game is asymmetric: At least for some μ one has that $\langle A^\mu \rangle \neq 0$. This implies that there is a *best* strategy $a_{\text{best}}^\mu = -\text{sign}\langle A^\mu \rangle$ which in principle could give a

---

[1] This implies that the number of iterations must be proportional to P in any numerical simulation.
[2] This amounts to say that the fluctuations in time of s_i around its average $\langle s_i \rangle$ are uncorrelated with $s_j - \langle s_j \rangle$. This assumption fails when crowd effects occur, i.e., in the symmetric phase, and our theory will accordingly fail to describe these effects.

positive gain $|\langle A \rangle| - 1$.[3] In economic terms we may say that the system is not *arbitrage free*, and that H is a measure of the perceived arbitrage opportunities present in the market. As a function of $\alpha - P/N$ the system displays a *phase transition* with symmetry breaking [13]: For $\alpha > \alpha_c$ the symmetry between the two signs of $A(t)$ is broken.

H plays a particular important role because in Refs. [6,7] it has been shown that the inductive dynamics is equivalent to a dynamics which minimizes H in the dynamical variables $m_i = \langle s_i \rangle$. Therefore, the ground-state properties of the Hamiltonian H yields the stationary state of the system. H is a spin-glass Hamiltonian where $\overline{\Omega \xi_i}$ are the local magnetic fields and $\overline{\xi_i \xi_j}$ the coupling between two agents. These play the same role as *quenched* disorder in spin glasses. This system is of *mean field* type since interactions $\overline{\xi_i \xi_j}$ are infinite ranged. For this reason, the statistical mechanics approach to disordered systems [14,15] via the replica method yields exact results for these models (see Appendix C).

The behavior of each agent is completely determined by the difference of her cumulated payoffs Δ_i. For long times, $\Delta_i \simeq v_i t$, where

$$v_i = \langle \Delta(t+1) - \Delta_i(t) \rangle = -2\langle A \rangle \overline{\xi_i} \, . \tag{18}$$

If $v_i \neq 0$, agent i shall stick to only one strategy $s_i = \text{sign } v_i$, whereas if $v_i = 0$, she will sometimes use her $\uparrow$ strategy and sometimes her $\downarrow$ one. This is quantified by m_i, and a global measure of the fluctuations in the strategic choices of agents is given by

$$Q = \frac{1}{N} \sum_{i=1}^{N} m_i^2 \, . \tag{19}$$

This quantity also emerges naturally from the replica approach where it plays a key role.

4. Speculators with diversified strategies

In the standard MG, it is assumed that the agents draw all their strategies randomly, and independently. One can argue that the agents can be less simple-minded so that they first draw a strategy, and then following their needs or what seems the best for them, draw the others strategies. For instance, if $S = 2$, an agent can believe that one strategy is enough and sticks to it (or takes two same strategies). On the contrary, an agent might believe that it is better to have one strategy and another one which is quite opposite. More generally, we suppose that all the agents[4] draw their second strategy according to

$$P(a_\uparrow^\mu = a_\downarrow^\mu) = c \quad \forall \mu \, . \tag{20}$$

---

[3] Here the -1 comes from the fact that if the strategy is actually played $A^\mu \to A^\mu + a_{\text{best}}^\mu$ and "in principle" means that A^μ would also change as a result of the fact that other agents would also react to the best strategy agent.

[4] This can be generalized to a c for each agent; exact results also arise from the replica calculus.

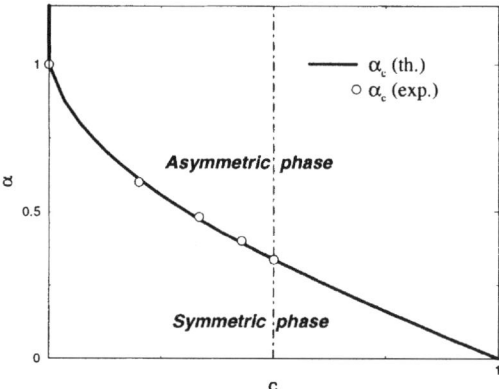

Fig. 1. Phase diagram of the minority game with diversified strategies. The phase transition in the standard MG corresponds to the dash-dotted vertical line $c = \frac{1}{2}$. The circle are numerical data.

The parameter c counts the average fraction of histories for which the agents' choices are biased, that is, the average correlation between their two strategies. The standard MG corresponds to the independent case $c = \frac{1}{2}$, while having only one strategy is obtained with $c = 1$. The other very special case is $c = 0$: all agents have two opposite strategies, thus there is no asymmetry in the outcome. As a result, the game is always in the symmetric phase: as α is varied, no phase transition occurs. Increasing c has two effects: on the one hand, it increases the bias of the outcome $\Omega^\mu \sim \sqrt{cN}$, on the other, it reduces the ability of the agents of being adaptative, since they learn something about the game only when $\xi_i^\mu \neq 0$ (see Eq. (8)), which happens in average for $(1 - c)P$ histories. The fact that the biases depend on c too implies that the second-order phase transition also occurs when this parameter is varied. With the replica formalism (see Appendix C), one gets the phase diagram of the MG with parameter c (see Fig. 1). In the standard MG, one varies α (dot-dashed vertical line). If one fixes α and changes c, the symmetry is also broken (any horizontal line). Note that if $c = 0$ and $\alpha > 1$, an infinitesimal c breaks the symmetry of the game.

5. Speculators and producers

Real markets are not *zero sum* games [16]. The fact that most participants are interested in playing is beyond doubt. In real markets the participants can be grossly divided into two groups: speculators and producers [16]. Producers can be characterized by those using the market for purposes other than speculation. They need market for hedging, financing, or any ordinary business. They thus pay less or no attention to "timing the market". Speculators, on the other hand, join the market with the aim of exploiting the marginal profit pockets. The two groups were shown to live in symbiosis [16]: the former inject information into the market prices, and the latter make a living

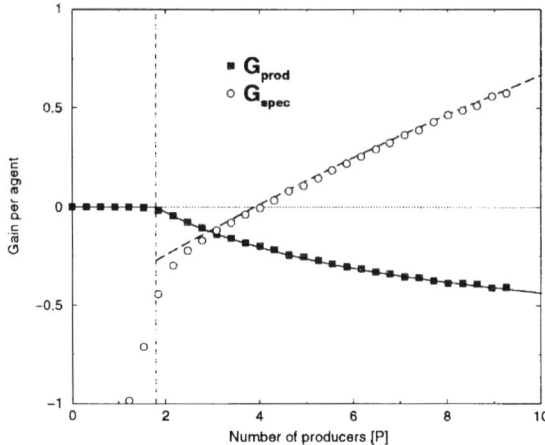

Fig. 2. Gain of producers and speculators versus the number of producers (in P unit); the number of speculators is fixed at $N = 641$ ($c = 0$, $M = 8$, $S = 2$, $\alpha = 0.4$, average over 200 realizations). The lines are theoretical predictions.

carefully exploiting this information. One may wonder why do producers let themselves be taken advantage of. Our answer is that they have other, probably more profitable business in mind. To conduct their business, they need the market, and their expertises and talents in other areas give them still better games to play. Speculators, being less capable in other areas, or by choice, make do exploiting the "meager margin" left in the competitive market.

In our MG, these general questions can be studied in detail. Producers will be limited in choice, their activities outside the game are not represented. We define a *speculator* as an normal agent, and a *producer* as an agent limited to one strategy. Thus, the latter have a fixed pattern in their market behavior and put a measurable amount of information into the market, which is exploited by the speculators. We take a population of N speculators and always define $\alpha = P/N$. We add ρN heterogeneous producers, so that ρ is the fraction of producers per speculator. The outcome is then

$$A^\mu = A^\mu_{\text{spec}} + A^\mu_{\text{prod}} .$$ (21)

The bias induced by the producers adds to the one caused by the speculators, so that the total bias is of order $\sqrt{(c + \rho)N}$. Therefore, the phase transition can be obtained at fixed P by varying either N, c, or the number of producers. Let us begin with the last possibility. We fix $c = 0$, $P = 2^8$, $N = 641$ and plot the gains of the speculators and producers as a function of the number of producers (see Fig. 2). In the symmetric phase, the speculators wash out all the available information, thus, by symmetry, the gain of the producers (squares) is zero. As the number of producers increases, the gain of the speculators (circles) stays negative but grows monotonically, while the gain of the producers remains zero as long as the symmetry of the outcome is not broken. When the number of producers reaches a critical value, the speculators are

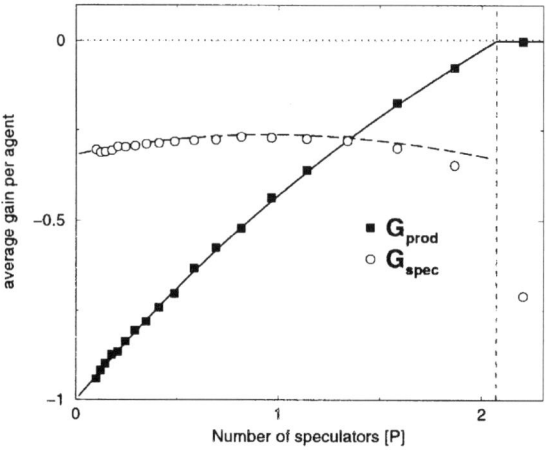

Fig. 3. Gain of producers and speculators versus the number of speculators (in P unit); the number of producers is fixed at 64 ($c = 0$, $M = 8$, $S = 2$, average over 200 realizations). The lines are theoretical predictions.

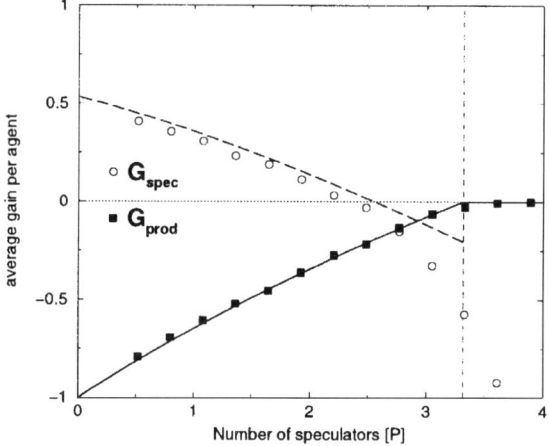

Fig. 4. Gain of producers and speculators versus the number of speculators (in P unit); the number of producers is fixed at 256 ($c = 0$, $M = 6$, $S = 2$, average over 200 realizations). The lines are theoretical predictions.

no more able to remove all the available information, therefore the (second-order) phase transition occurs (dashed line). Beyond this point, the producers lose more and more, while some (frozen) speculators gain more than zero in average (see Section 8). At one point, the gains of speculators and producers are the same. Finally, there are enough producers to make the gain of the speculators positive on average.

As illustrated by Figs. 3 and 4, if the number of speculators changes and that of producers is fixed the behavior is qualitatively the inverse of that of Fig. 2: The gain of producers increases as the number of producers grows; similarly, the gain of the speculators decreases when N increases for sufficiently large N. If there are not enough producers, the game is always negative sum for the speculators, and their gain has a maximum (see Fig. 3).

We now expose exact analytical results concerning the gain of the two types of agents. They rely on the generalization of the approach of Refs. [6,7]: the calculus is carried out in detail in Appendix C. Let us introduce G_{spec}, the total gain of the speculators and G_{prod}, the one of the producers. From Eq. (15)

$$G_{spec} + G_{prod} = -\sigma^2 . \tag{22}$$

The results depend on the ratio ρ between the number of producers, on the number of speculators and on c, the parameter introduced in the previous section. We obtain

$$\frac{\sigma^2}{N} = \frac{c + \rho + (1 - c)Q}{(1 + \chi)^2} + (1 - c)(1 - Q) , \tag{23}$$

where χ is the magnetic susceptibility of the system, and Q is defined in Section 3.2. These two quantities depend on α and on $(1 + \rho)/(1 - c)$ (see Appendix C). The average gain per producer is

$$\frac{G_{prod}}{\rho N} = -\frac{1}{1 + \chi} \tag{24}$$

and the average gain per speculator is

$$\frac{G_{spec}}{N} = -\frac{c + \rho + (1 - c)Q}{(1 + \chi)^2} - (1 - c)(1 - Q) + \frac{\rho}{1 + \chi} . \tag{25}$$

Figs. 2–4 completely agree with analytical results; note that the small deviations are finite size effects. The fact that the gains of producers and speculators only depend on the ratio ρ and not on how many producers and speculators there are in the game explains why Figs. 3 and 4 look very much like the inverse of Fig. 2.

As it emerges for the replica calculus, the critical point α_c only depends[5] on $(1 + \rho)/(1 - c)$ (see Fig. 5), that is, on the distribution of the quenched disorder. Numerical data (circles) completely agree with our results. The vertical line corresponds to the standard MG ($\rho = 0$ and $c = \frac{1}{2}$). A more intuitive version of this phase diagram is shown in Fig. 6 for $c = 0$.

The game becomes favorable, on average, for the speculators when their average gain is greater than zero. Using Eq. (25), one can plot the curve of zero sum gain for the speculators (see Fig. 6). One can see that the number of producers must be greater than $1.868\ldots P$ (this value depends on c) in order to make the game positive sum for the speculators; this is consistent with numerical simulations (Figs. 3 and 4).

The main message of these results is that producers always benefit from the presence of speculators, and reversely: both types of agents live in symbiosis. Indeed, the

---

[5] This explains why evolutionary schemes that preserve the distribution of the quenched disorder have the same α_c [17], while others that involve Darwinism, shift α_c [1,9].

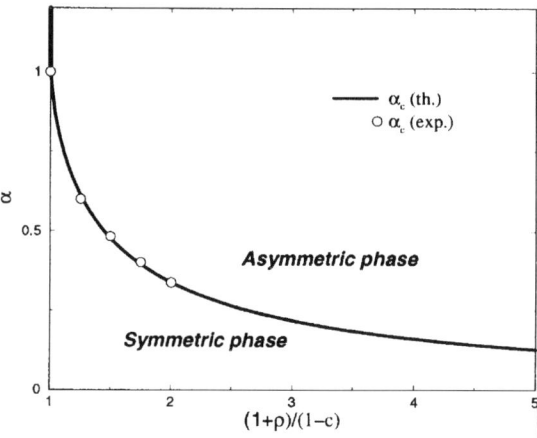

Fig. 5. Phase diagram $\alpha_c[(1 + \rho)/(1 - c)]$.

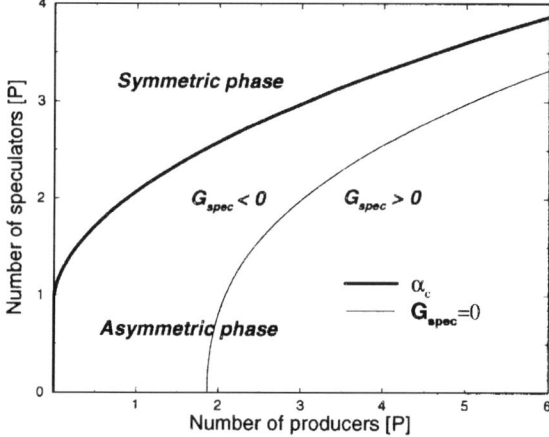

Fig. 6. Phase diagram, and zero sum game for speculators with $c = 0$ at a fixed P.

producers introduce systematic biases into the market, and without speculators, their losses would be proportional to these biases. The speculators precisely try to remove this kind of bias, reducing also systematic fluctuations in the market, thus reducing the losses of the producers and their own losses. Moreover, the efforts of speculators yield a positive gain only if the number of producers is sufficiently large. In this respect the symmetric phase, where producers do not lose and speculators lose a lot, is unrealistic: real speculators would rather withdraw from a market which is in this phase, thus increasing α, and recovering the asymmetric phase. This suggests that a grand-canonical MG is much more realistic.[6] Here we briefly present an over-simplified

---

[6] See also [18,19].

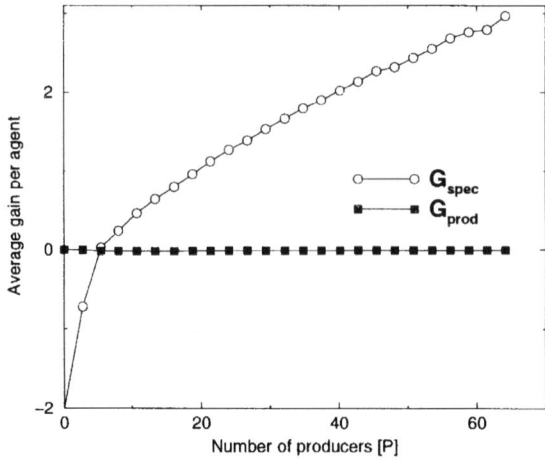

Fig. 7. Average gain per agent versus the number of producers (in P units) in the grand canonical MG ($N = 107$, $M = 5$, $\alpha = 0.3$, $S = 2$, $c = \frac{1}{2}$, average over 500 realizations).

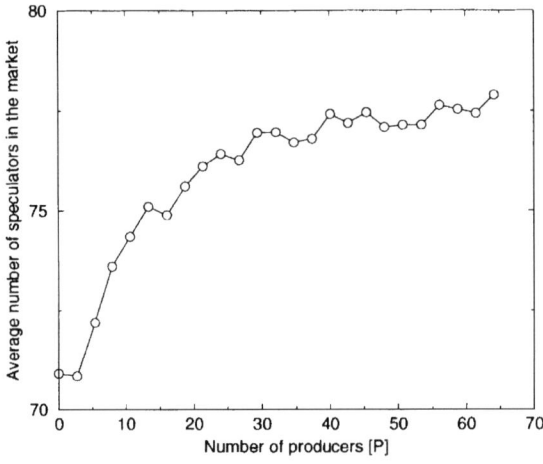

Fig. 8. Average number of speculators versus the number of producers (in P units) in the grand canonical MG ($N = 107$, $M = 5$, $\alpha = 0.3$, $S = 2$, $c = \frac{1}{2}$, average over 500 realizations).

"grand-canonical" MG. An agent enters into the market only when she has a strategy with virtual points greater than zero. As a result, the game is always in the asymmetric phase, but almost at the transition point: the average losses of the producers are always extremely small (see Fig. 7). When the number of producers increases, the a priori asymmetry of the outcome increases, and more and more agents actually play the game (see Fig. 8), thus in this situation, the producers give incentives to play to the speculators. Accordingly, the average gain of the speculators, is much higher in this grand-canonical MG than in the corresponding canonical MG.

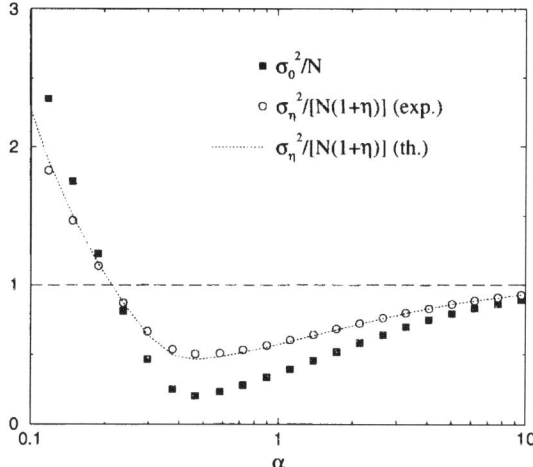

Fig. 9. Normalized variance of the outcome with (opaque circles and without (black squares) noise traders; the dotted line is the naive theoretical prediction. Inset: difference of variances with and without noise traders ($N = 101$ speculators, 50 noise traders, average over 1000 realizations).

6. Speculators, producers and noise traders

The debate about what the noise traders do to a competitive market is not closed [20]. In the economics literature a noise trader is not very precisely defined. Sometimes they are synonym with speculators. We define noise traders in the following way: they choose their actions without any basis. Compared with speculators, who analyze carefully the market information, noise traders take action in a purely random way (see Appendix C). Noise traders may be speculators who base their action on astrology, on "fengshui", or on some "random number generators". Our present model allows us to evaluate the influence of noise traders on the market. They increase the market volatility σ^2, as shown in Fig. 9 and in Appendix C. Therefore, in principle, they do harm to themselves as well as to other participants. Actually, in the linear-payoff version that we consider, the average gain of speculators and producers is not much affected by noise traders, since $\langle A_{\mathrm{noise}} \rangle = 0$. However, it is easy to see that in the original version, where $g_i(t) = -a_i(t) \operatorname{sign} A(t)$, payoffs are reduced by the presence of noise traders (see Appendix D).

Our numerical results of Fig. 9 also shows that deep in the symmetric phase, noise traders reduces the volatility per agent $\sigma^2/(N + N_{\mathrm{noise}})$, when this becomes bigger than one. This is easy to understand assuming that the only effect of noise traders is to increase σ^2 by a constant equal to $N_{\mathrm{noise}} \equiv \eta N$. Let σ_0^2/N be the volatility per agent, without noise traders ($\eta = 0$) and σ_η^2 that with noise traders. The variation in the volatility per agent in the presence of noise traders is

$$\frac{\sigma_\eta^2}{N(1+\eta)} - \frac{\sigma_0^2}{N} \simeq \frac{\sigma_0^2 + \eta N}{N(1+\eta)} - \frac{\sigma_0^2}{N} = \frac{1 - \sigma_0^2/N}{1 + 1/\eta} \ . \tag{26}$$

As illustrated by Fig. 9, numerical simulations globally confirm these conclusions, but also show that the effects of the noise traders are more pronounced than those predicted by theory.

7. Market impact

In order to quantify the impact of an agent on the market let us first consider the case of an *external* agent with S strategies: This agent does not take part in the game but just observes it from the outside. From this position, each of her strategies gives an average [7] *virtual* gain

$$u_s = -\overline{a_s \langle A \rangle}, \quad s = 1, \dots, S. \tag{27}$$

Given that the strategies a_s^μ are drawn randomly, u_s are independent random variables. Since u_s is the sum of $P \gg 1$ independent variables $a_s^\mu \langle A^\mu \rangle / P$, their distribution is Gaussian with zero mean and variance

$$\text{Var}(u_s) = \frac{1}{P^2} \sum_{\mu=1}^{P} \text{Var}(a_s^\mu) \langle A^\mu \rangle^2 = \frac{H}{P}.$$

Clearly, one of these strategies, that with $u_{s^*} = \max_s u_s$, is superior to all others. [8] It would be most reasonable for this agent to just stick to this strategy.

However, the same agent *inside* the game will typically use not only strategy s^*. This is because every strategy, when used, delivers a *real* gain which is reduced with respect to the virtual one by the "market impact". Imagine the "experiment" of injecting the new agent in a MG. Then $\langle A^\mu \rangle \to \langle A^\mu \rangle + a_s^\mu$, where, in a first approximation, we neglect the reaction of other agents to the new-comer. Then the real gain of the new-comer is

$$g_s \cong -\overline{a_s \langle A \rangle} - \langle a_s a_s \rangle = u_s - 1. \tag{28}$$

The agent will then update the scores $U_s(t)$ with the real gain g_s for the strategy she uses and with the virtual one $u_{s'} = g_{s'} + 1 - \overline{a_s a_{s'}}$, for the strategies she does not use (in the following, we neglect the term $\overline{a_s a_{s'}}$). Therefore, inductive agents over-estimate the performance of the strategies they do not play. Then if strategy s is played with a frequency p_s, the virtual score increases *on average* by

$$\delta U_s = U_s(t+1) - U_s(t) = p_s g_s + (1 - p_s)(g_s + 1)$$
$$= g_s - p_s + 1 \tag{29}$$

at each time step (on average). If the agent ends up playing only n out of her S strategies with some frequency $p_s > 0$, it must be that the virtual score increases δU_s are all equal for these strategies and the virtual scores of strategies not played are lower.

---

[7] The average is meant over a long time here.

[8] The distribution of u_{s^*} can be easily computed using extreme statistics. For $S \gg 1$ typically $u_{s^*} \simeq \sqrt{2H \log(S)/P}$.

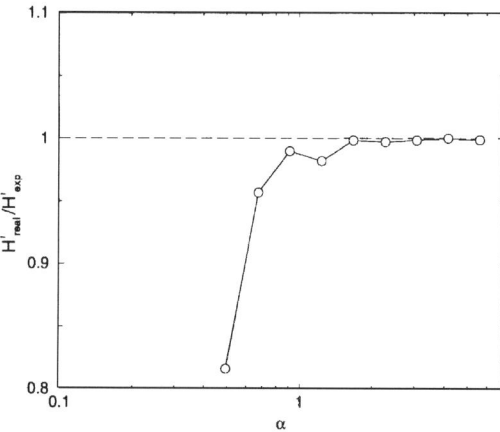

Fig. 10. Ratio of real H' over approximated $H' \simeq H - 2\overline{|\langle A \rangle|} + 1$ versus α ($N = 101$, average over 100 realizations).

More precisely, let $s = 1, \ldots, n$ label the strategies which are played and $r = n + 1, \ldots, S$ those which are not played. It must be that

$$\delta U_s = g_s - p_s + 1 = v, \quad s = 1, \ldots, n, \tag{30}$$

$$\delta U_r = g_r + 1 < v, \quad r = n + 1, \ldots, S. \tag{31}$$

These equations yield the number n of strategy that this agent will use. Normalization of p_s in the first equation gives the average virtual gain v of the agent, which is

$$v = \frac{1}{n} \sum_{s=1}^{n} g_s - \frac{1}{n} + 1. \tag{32}$$

Using $p_s = g_s + 1 - v$, we can compute the real gain of the inductive agent $g = \sum_{s=1}^{n} p_s g_s$.

Summarizing, we find that inductive agents mix their best strategy with less-performing ones. This is a consequence of the fact that they neglect their impact on the market.

So far, we did not take into account the reaction of other agents to the new-comer. In order to quantify this effect, let us consider a MG in the asymmetric phase, and let us add a new agent with the *best* strategy $a^\mu = -\text{sign} \langle A^\mu \rangle$. This gives us an idea of this effect in the extreme case and we expect that for a randomly drawn strategy the effect will be smaller. Neglecting the reaction of other agents, we find that the available information with the new-comer should be $H' \simeq H - 2\overline{|\langle A \rangle|} + 1$. Fig. 10 shows that the reaction of all agents is indeed negligible, except near the critical point, where H is of the order of 1.

8. Gain

In this section we show how the behavior and the gain of each agent (speculator as well as producer) depends on her microscopic constitution and on the asymmetry of the outcome $A(t)$ in the asymmetric phase. Let us denote the gain of agent i by g_i; by definition,

$$g_i = -\overline{\langle Aa_i \rangle} \,. \tag{33}$$

In the asymmetric phase, since the stationary state is mean field, $\langle s_i s_j \rangle = m_i m_j$. Consequently, by expanding Eq. (33) one obtains

$$
\begin{aligned}
g_i &= -\overline{\langle A \rangle \omega_i} - \overline{\langle A s_i \rangle \xi_i} \\
&= -\overline{\langle A \rangle \omega_i} - \overline{\langle A \rangle \xi_i m_i} - \overline{\xi_i^2 (1 - m_i^2)} \,.
\end{aligned}
\tag{34}
$$

Remember that the stationary behavior of agent i is described by $v_i = -2\overline{\langle A \rangle \xi_i}$ (see Section 3). If an agent is non-frozen, $v_i = 0$, while $m_i = -\text{sign}\, v_i$ otherwise, hence the gain of a generic agent i is

$$g_i = -\overline{\langle A \rangle \omega_i} + |\overline{\langle A \rangle \xi_i}| - \overline{\xi_i^2 (1 - m_i^2)} \,. \tag{35}$$

Note that the second term of the above equation vanishes for a non-frozen agent j and therefore

$$g_j = -\overline{\langle A \rangle \omega_j} - \overline{\xi_j^2 (1 - m_j^2)} \quad \text{non-frozen} \,. \tag{36}$$

On the other hand, the third term of Eq. (35) vanishes if agent k is frozen:

$$g_k = -\overline{\langle A \rangle \omega_k} + |\overline{\langle A \rangle \xi_k}| \quad \text{frozen} \,. \tag{37}$$

In Eqs. (36) and (37), the gain of each agent is expressed as her internal constitution, allowing us to interpret what does the gain of a general agent depends on. In both equations, the first term $-\overline{\langle A \rangle \omega_i}$, which represent how much the agents lose due to their bias, is on average negative, due to the impact this bias has on the market. The second term in Eq. (36) is always negative, and represents the losses due to the switching between strategies, which, as shown above, arises from the neglect of market impact. Since the probability distribution function of m_i is not Gaussian [6], this term gives rise to an non-Gaussian distribution of g_j for non-frozen agents. The average gain of the rth best agent is represented in Fig. 11.

By contrast, the term $\overline{\xi_k^2 (1 - m_k^2)}$ disappears for a frozen agent because $m_k^2 = 1$. It is replaced by $|\overline{\langle A \rangle \xi_k}|$ which is always positive and which measures how well agent k exploits the available information. Therefore, in average, the frozen agents gain more than the non-frozen ones. This is clearly illustrated in Fig. 12 which also shows that Eqs. (36) and (37) are exact. Finally, a producer is of course frozen, and her gain is always lower than zero in this phase, since she has $|\overline{\langle A \rangle \xi_k}| = 0$.

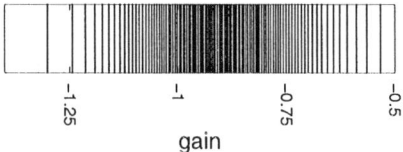

Fig. 11. Bar-code structure of the rth best agent's gain ($\alpha=10$, $M=10$, $S=2$, average over 300 realizations).

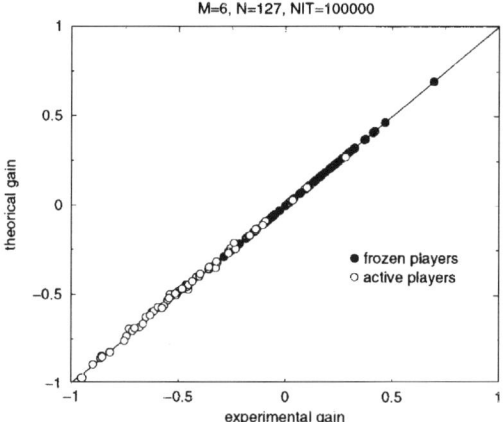

Fig. 12. Theoretical gain versus experimental gain showing that the frozen agents gain more than the active ones ($\alpha=0.5$, $M=6$).

9. Privileged agent or insider-trading

In this section we consider a MG where a particular agent has different characteristics. In particular, we address the question of what additional resources would be advantageous for this agent and in which circumstances. In the first subsection, we consider an agent with S' strategies (with $S' > S$, where S is the number of strategies assigned to other agents). The last two subsections are devoted to the study of effects of asymmetric information, in which an agent has access to privileged information which the other cannot access. This can be achieved in several ways. First, we consider the case of a pure population with memory M and one agent with a longer memory M'. Then we consider the case of an agent who knows, in advance, how a subset of agents plays.

9.1. An agent with S' strategies

In the symmetric phase, no matter how many strategies an agent has, there is no possibility of gaining. Therefore we focus in this section on the asymmetric phase.

As shown in Section 7, inductive agents over-estimate the performance of the strategies they do not play.

Let us consider now the case where an agent with S' strategies enters into a MG. As shown in Section 7, to a good approximation, the value of H/P is the only relevant information we need to retain of the stationary state of the MG without the special agent. This quantity encodes all other informations such as the number of producers, the number of strategies played by the agents in the MG and the value of α.

We carried out numerical simulations, and compared it to the analytical results derived in Section 7. These are shown in Fig. 13, for $H/P = 0.5$, and 14, for $H/P = 1$. The virtual gain v is always larger than the actual gain g. Even though g is less than the gain agents would get playing only their best strategy $E[g_{s^*}]$ (maximal gain), it is not much smaller and has the same leading behavior $g \propto \sqrt{\ln S}$.

Numerical simulations agree well with analytical results, apart from finite size effects which become more pronounced if H/P is small.[9]

Figs. 13 and 14 refer to values of H/P which are realistic of MG with producers. A moderately large S' suffices to obtain a positive gain $g > 0$. With $S = 2$ and without producers $H/P \sim 0.1$ at most. For these values the analytic approach suggests that, even playing only her best strategy an agent would need $S' > 750$ strategies to have a positive gain, whereas inductive agents would need more than $S' \simeq 2400$ strategies to obtain a positive gain. The same agent would find that her virtual gain becomes positive with only $S' > 8$ strategies. These results for $H/P = 0.1$ suffer from strong finite size effects (which indeed are of the order of P/H). One would need system sizes N which are well beyond what our computational resources allow to confirm these conclusions.

It is also interesting to observe that the number of strategies actually used by the inductive agent increases with S (sub-linearly) and it decreases as H/P increases (see Figs. 13 and 14). That means that if there is more exploitable information in the system, agent's behavior becomes more peaked on the best strategy.

9.2. $M' > M$

Let us consider the case of a pure population with memory M and one agent with a longer memory [10] M'. Fig. 15 plots the gain of such an agent with $M' = M + 1$ as a function of α. The average gain of all agents is also shown for comparison. In the asymmetric phase the special agent receives a lower payoff, which can be understood by observing that she has a number of histories $P' = 2^{M'} = 2P$ bigger than that of the pure population. Thus her effective $\alpha' = 2\alpha$ is larger, which is detrimental in the asymmetric phase.

The gain of the special agent is the same as that of normal agents at the point where there is neither persistence, nor anti-persistence ($\alpha \simeq 0.25$ for $M = 3$, and α_c in the thermodynamic limit).

---

[9] This is mostly due to the term which we have neglected in Section 7: it is typically of the order of P/H.
[10] In this kind of numerical simulations, one has to keep the dynamics of histories.

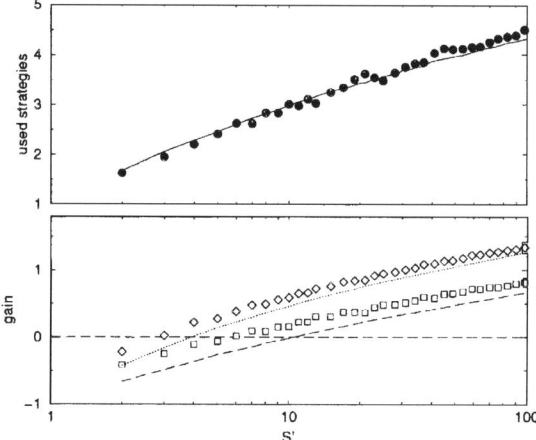

Fig. 13. Upper graph: average number of played strategies (circles) versus S'. Below: average virtual (diamonds) and actual (squares) gains versus S' for $H/P=0.5$, from top to below (averages over 500 realizations). The lines are theoretical predictions.

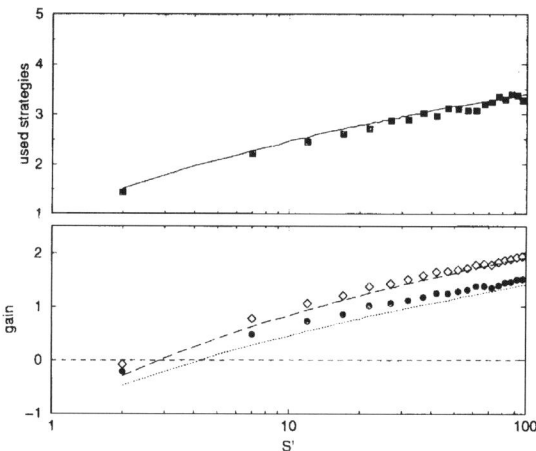

Fig. 14. Upper graph: average number of played strategies (squares) versus S'. Below: average virtual (diamonds) and actual (circles) gains versus S' for $H/P=1$, from top to below (averages over 500 realizations). The lines are theoretical predictions.

In contrast, in the symmetric phase, the game is symmetric for normal agents but their anti-persistent behavior produces arbitrages who can be exploited by agents having a bigger memory. Indeed, as α decreases, the available information $H_{M'}$ for the privileged agent grows.[11] As a result the gain of the privileged agent becomes larger than that of other agents and as α becomes small enough, it becomes positive.

---

[11] $H_{M'}$ is defined as $H = \overline{\langle A \rangle^2}$, but with an average over $\mu' = 1,\ldots,2P$.

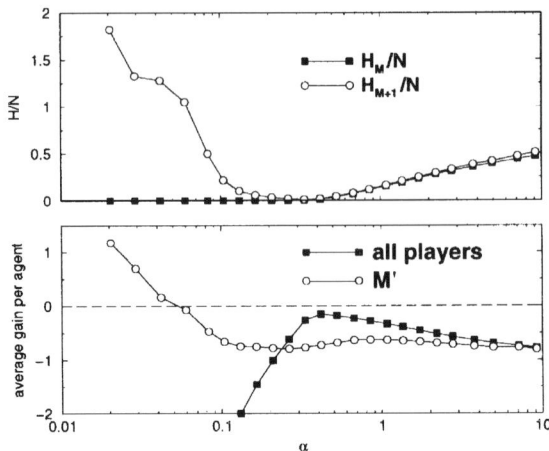

Fig. 15. Upper graph: normalized available information for M and $M + 1$. Lower graph: Gain of an agent with $M + 1$ within a pure population with $M = 3$ ($S = 2$, average over 3000 realizations).

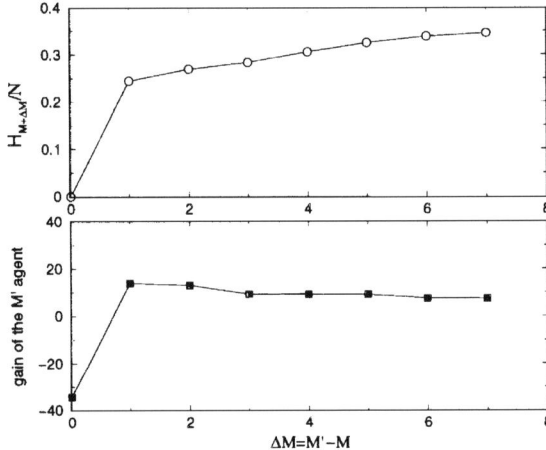

Fig. 16. Gain of an agent with $M' = M + \Delta M$ within a pure population with $M = 3$ ($\alpha = 0.1$, average over 1000 realizations).

Can the anti-persistence be exploited even more if one increases M'? Fig. 16 answers clearly no. This is not surprising since again the effective α is bigger and bigger as M' is increased. At the same time, the available information increases, but too slowly.

9.3. Espionage

Some agents may have access to some information about other agents. This is the case of a stock broker who knows his clients' orders before execution, hence he has privileged information and should be barred from trading. When there is no available

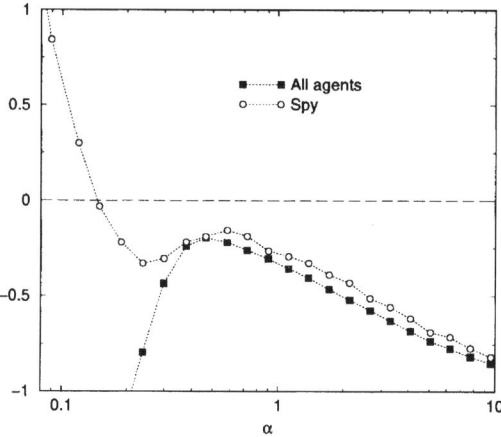

Fig. 17. Gain of a spy and average gain of all agents versus α ($N = 101$, $N_B = 3$, $100P$ iterations, average over 100 realizations).

information, as in the symmetric phase, an agent who has access to asymmetric information can expect at least to lose much less than the other agents, or even have a positive gain. Also, since having access to a little information is greatly preferable to no information at all, only a very limited amount of information is needed to get a considerable advantage. Suppose that agent b knows the sign $s_{\mathscr{B}}$ of the aggregate actions of a subset $\mathscr{B}$ of other agents. Let $B = |\mathscr{B}|$ be the number of agents in $\mathscr{B}$. Then $s_{\mathscr{B}}(t) = \operatorname{sign} \sum_{i \in \mathscr{B}} a_i(t)$. She can exploit this supplementary information by having two virtual values $U_{b,s}^{+}(t)$ and $U_{b,s}^{-}(t)$ for each of her strategies. In other words, if agent b knows that $s_{\mathscr{B}}(t) = +1$ before having to choose, she takes her decision according to the scores $U_{b,s}^{+}(t)$, that is,

$$s_b(t) = \arg \max_{s=1,\ldots,S} U_{b,s}^{+}(t), \tag{38}$$

she updates the scores of her strategies according to

$$U_{b,s}^{+}(t+1) = U_{b,s}^{+}(t) - a_{b,s}^{\mu(t)} A^{\mu(t)} \tag{39}$$

and analogously if $s_{\mathscr{B}}(t) = -1$.

What is the kind of the supplementary information this agent has access to?

Since the outcome is anti-persistent in the symmetric phase and persistent in the asymmetric phase, only at the critical point there is no long-term correlation in the outcome [13]. Accordingly, the spy always gains more than the average, except at the critical point where she gains the same (see Fig. 17). With this setting, the agent has access in particular to the anti-persistence of the symmetric phase, explaining why even if only one agent is spied, the gain of the broker is much bigger (Fig. 18).

Finally, the comparison between the two types of asymmetric information we have considered shows that it is much more interesting to spy than to have a larger memory:

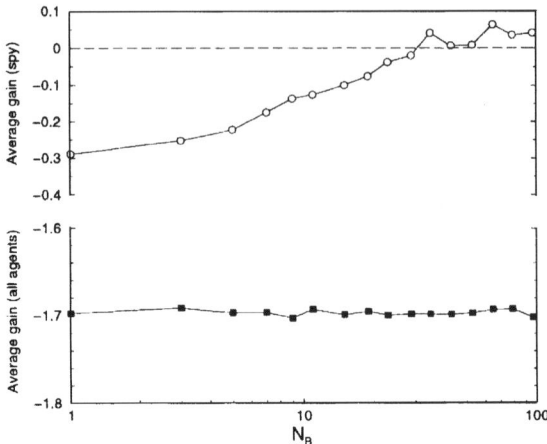

Fig. 18. Gain of a spy versus the number of spied agents ($N=1001$, $\alpha=0.15$, average over 1000 realizations).

in the former case, one is sure to win more than the normal agents, except at the critical point.

10. Conclusions

In this work we have shown how to ask questions about real market mechanisms in a toy model. In spite of the severe simplification of the MG, with little modification one is able to study a broad spectrum of problems which could be dreamed of previously. The central result is to show that agents with limited rationality (or limited information processing power) can only make a market marginally efficient. To the first approximation one can say that these inductive players can maintain an approximate equilibrium, which is the central result of the El-Farol model. But studying carefully the fluctuations one finds that the fact that the market is more or less efficient does not imply that one can stop playing and sit at a randomly chosen site. Doing so would make the model less efficient. It is around this residual (marginal) inefficiency that the players are busy about.

With the introduction of producers the game can be of positive sum. We have shown how producers and speculators live in a symbiosis: producers are passive players who do not try to switch strategies. The reason is that they voluntarily give up the speculation opportunities because they have outside business in mind. Thus, producers inject information that the eager speculators are just happy to feed on. The speculators, while making away profits, perform a social function by providing liquidity thus reducing producers' market impact. We believe this is also true in real markets. Numerous other results show that it is now possible to systematically study markets with heterogeneous agents, with real questions in mind.

Appendix A. Geometric and algebraic approaches to the MG

This appendix is devoted to giving intuitive but rigorous views of what happens in the MG.

A.1. Geometric approach to the MG

The global behavior of the MG, measured by σ^2, can be quite well understood with a geometrical approach. Indeed, it is directly related to a much more intuitive geometrical concept: the Hamming distance between agents [9], which is defined as follows for agents i and j:

$$\overline{d_{i,j}} = \overline{\frac{(a_i - a_j)^2}{4}} = \frac{1}{2} - \frac{1}{2}\overline{a_i a_j} . \tag{A.1}$$

It is worthwhile to note that $1 - \overline{d_{i,j}}$ equals the probability that both agents take the same action for a randomly drawn history, so for an agent, maximizing her distance with respect to all other agents is equivalent to maximizing her gain. Since the game is dynamical, one has to consider the time average of the actual Hamming distance between those two agents

$$\overline{\langle d_{i,j}\rangle} = \tfrac{1}{2} - \tfrac{1}{2}\overline{\langle a_i a_j\rangle} . \tag{A.2}$$

The average Hamming distance per agent is then

$$\overline{\langle d\rangle} = \frac{1}{N(N-1)}\sum_{i,j}\overline{\langle d_{i,j}\rangle} = \frac{1}{2} - \frac{1}{2N(N-1)}\sum_{i,j}\overline{\langle a_i a_j\rangle} . \tag{A.3}$$

The relationship between the distance and the fluctuations arises naturally by rewriting the latter as

$$\sigma^2 = N + \sum_{i\neq j}\overline{\langle a_i a_j\rangle} , \tag{A.4}$$

that is, as a sum over random fluctuations and correlations. Putting Eqs. (A.3) and (A.4) together, one finds

$$\frac{\sigma^2}{N} = 1 - 2(N-1)\left(\frac{1}{2} - \overline{\langle d\rangle}\right) . \tag{A.5}$$

This equation [12] links the geometrical [9,12] and the analytical approaches [6,13]. It states that finding the average Hamming distance between the agents is equivalent to determining σ^2 by the analytical tools used in [6,7,13]. In general, it is impossible to find the average distance with a geometrical approach due to the fact that the Hamming distance is not transitive. [13] However, in the so-called reduced space of strategies (RSS) [9], the distance is transitive, consequently Johnson et al. could find an approximate

---

[12] It is exact for any S; even more, it remains exact if agents do not have the same number of strategies.
[13] The knowledge of $d_{i,j}$ and $d_{i,k}$ does not allow that of $d_{j,k}$.

analytical expression of $\overline{\langle d \rangle}$, and, by implicitly using Eq. (A.5) (which is straightforward in the RSS), they also gave an approximative expression of σ^2 [21]. An equation quite similar to Eq. (A.5) also appears in [22], where it is shown that perceptrons playing the MG can cooperate.

A.2. Algebraic approach to the phase transition

We expose the algebraic origin of the phase transition. As it has been recalled, the agents actually try to minimize the available information H [6,7], and can actually cancel it when $\alpha < \alpha_c$. Let us see why. Since H is a sum of P non negative averages $\overline{\langle A \rangle}^2$, $H = 0$ only if all averages are zero, namely $\overline{\langle A \rangle} = 0 \ \forall \mu$, or equivalently

$$\sum_{i=1}^{N} \xi_i^{\mu} \langle s_i \rangle = -\Omega^{\mu} \quad \forall \mu . \tag{A.6}$$

These are P linear equations in N variables. However, the N variables $m_i = \langle s_i \rangle$ are restricted to the $[-1, 1]$ interval. Above α_c there are $N\phi$ variables which are frozen at the boundary of this interval ($m_i = \pm 1$). Therefore there are $(1 - \phi)N$ free variables only. As shown in Refs. [6,7], the point α_c marks the transition below which the system of equations (A.6) becomes degenerate, i.e., when there are more variables than equations. Exactly at α_c the number of free variables $(1 - \phi)N$ exactly matches the number of equations P. Dividing this equation by N gives an equation for α_c,

$$\alpha_c = 1 - \phi \tag{A.7}$$

which is indeed confirmed numerically to a high accuracy.

When $\alpha < \alpha_c$, there are more free variables (N indeed) than equations: the solutions of Eq. (A.6) then belong to a subspace of dimension $N - P$. This allows the anti-persistent behavior to take place, because the system is free to move on this subspace. In the special case $c = 0$, since there is no bias $\Omega^{\mu} = 0$. The linear system of equation is then homogeneous and the solution $\langle s_i \rangle = 0$ for all i always exists. In particular, if $\alpha > 1$, this solution is unique, hence $\sigma^2/N = 1$. When $\alpha < 1$, a subspace of solutions of dimension $N - P$ arises, and the anti-persistent behavior also takes place. Note that in this case, the system is always in the symmetric phase, therefore there is no phase transition.

This argument easily generalizes to $S > 2$ strategies [7]. If agents use, on average, $n(S)$ strategies (and $S - n(S)$ are never used) the number of free variables is $Nn(S)$. There are P plus N equations which these have to satisfy, where the latter N comes from the normalization condition on the frequency with which each strategy is used. At the critical point, these two numbers are equal, and we find

$$n_c(S) = \alpha_c(S) + 1 . \tag{A.8}$$

At the critical point nearly one half of the strategies yield positive virtual gain and are used, whereas the others are not used [7]. From this we find

$$\alpha_c(S) \cong \alpha_c(2) + \frac{S}{2} - 1 . \tag{A.9}$$

This shows that actually α_c grows linearly with S, but in a slightly less-simple way than that previously believed [2,9,13,21].

Let us now show how the behavior of the agents is related to persistence/anti-persistence. We define W as the average over the agents of v_i^2:

$$W = \frac{1}{N} \sum_{i=1}^{N} (v_i)^2 \tag{A.10}$$

$$= \lim_{T \to \infty} \frac{1}{T^2} \sum_{t,t'=1}^{T} \sum_{i=1}^{N} \frac{1}{N} \xi_i^{\mu(t)} \xi_i^{\mu(t')} A(t)A(t') , \tag{A.11}$$

since the ξ_i^μ are independently drawn,

$$\frac{1}{N} \sum_{i=1}^{N} \xi_i^{\mu(t)} \xi_i^{\mu(t')} = (1 - c)\delta_{\mu(t),\mu(t')} + O(1/\sqrt{N}) . \tag{A.12}$$

Thus for large N

$$W \simeq \lim_{T \to \infty} \frac{1}{T} \sum_{t=1}^{T} \overline{\langle A(t)A(t - \tau)|\mu(t) = \mu(t - \tau) \rangle} , \tag{A.13}$$

where $\overline{\langle A(t)A(t - \tau)|\mu(t) = \mu(t - \tau)\rangle}$ means that the average is taken over time $\tau = 0,\ldots,t - 1$ for all t and τ such that $\mu_t = \mu_{t-\tau}$, and summed over all histories. A closely related quantity was first studied in Ref. [13] where it was shown to quantify anti-persistence in the symmetric phase.

Note that this equation implies that there can be no frozen agents unless the outcome exhibits persistence (i.e., $\overline{\langle A(t)A(t - \tau)|\mu(t) = \mu(t - \tau)\rangle} \neq 0$), which agrees with the analysis of [13]. In this case we find

$$W \simeq \frac{H}{N} . \tag{A.14}$$

Furthermore, the condition of freezing $v_i \neq 0$ is equivalent to [13]

$$\overline{\xi_i \xi_i} < |\tilde{h}_i| , \tag{A.15}$$

where $\tilde{h}_i = \overline{\Omega \xi_i} + \sum_{j \neq i} \overline{\xi_i \xi_j} \langle s_j \rangle$. It is worthwhile to see that $\overline{\xi_i \xi_i}$ is the internal hamming distance. Eqs. (A.13) and (A.14) give global conditions whether there can be frozen players or not, while Eq. (A.15) give conditions on individual freezing.

Appendix B. The MG in biology

The MG model has another important application in biology: the sex ratio of 50 : 50. In the widely read book of Richard Dawkins "Selfish Gene" [23], the Fischer theory was brilliantly explained: if in the offspring pool either males or females were in minority, reproductive strategies for giving birth to a member in that minority would enjoy a genetic advantage linearly proportional to the deviation from the 50 : 50 ratio.

The stable ratio is thus dynamically maintained. Brian Arthur's "El Farol" model, is also of the same genre, to show that using alternative strategies can lead to equilibrium. MG goes one step further: while the equilibrium point is previously solved in different contexts by Fisher, Arthur et al., we concentrate on more refined questions.

Appendix C. Replica method for the MG

For the sake of generality, we consider three different population of agents:

(1) The first population is composed of N *speculators*. These are adaptive agents and they have each two *speculative* strategies $a_{\uparrow,i}^{\mu}$, $a_{\downarrow,i}^{\mu}$ for $i=1,\ldots,N$ and $\mu=1,\ldots,P$. These are drawn at random from the pool of all strategies, independently for each agent. We allow a correlation among the two strategies of the same agent:

$$P(a_{\uparrow},a_{\downarrow}) = \frac{c}{2}[\delta_{a_{\uparrow},+1}\delta_{a_{\downarrow},+1} + \delta_{a_{\uparrow},-1}\delta_{a_{\downarrow},-1}] + \frac{1-c}{2}[\delta_{a_{\uparrow},-1}\delta_{a_{\downarrow},+1} + \delta_{a_{\uparrow},-1}\delta_{a_{\downarrow},+1}].$$

(C.1)

Note that, for $c=0$ agents choose just one strategy $a_{\uparrow}$ and fix $a_{\downarrow}=-a_{\uparrow}$ as its opposite, whereas for $c=1$ they have one and the same strategy $a_{\uparrow}=a_{\downarrow}$. The original random case [1,8] corresponds to $c=\frac{1}{2}$. These agents assign scores $U_{s,i}(t)$ to each of their strategies and play the strategy $s_i(t)$ with the highest score, as discussed in the text. Therefore for speculators

$$a_{\text{spec}}(t) = a_{s_i(t),i}^{\mu(t)}.$$

(C.2)

(2) Then we consider $N_{\text{prod}}^{\text{indep}} = \rho N$ *producers*: They have only one randomly and independently drawn strategy b_i^{μ} so

$$a_{\text{prod}}(t) = b_i^{\mu(t)}.$$

(C.3)

Producers have a predictable behavior in the market and they are not adaptive. Instead of ρN *independent* producers one can also consider $N_{\text{prod}}^{\text{dep}}$ correlated producers who all have the same predictable behavior b_{prod}^{μ}.

(3) Finally, we consider ηN *noise traders*. These are defined as agents whose actions are given by

$$a_{\text{noise}}(t) = \text{random sign}.$$

(C.4)

Each noise trader as a random number generator which is independent of those other agents.

It has been shown [6,7] that the stationary state properties of the MG are described by the ground state of H. Note that this approach fails however to reproduce the anti-persistent behavior which is at the origin of crowd effects in the symmetric phase. In our case

$$A(t) = A_{\text{spec}}(t) + A_{\text{prod}}(t) + A_{\text{noise}}(t),$$

(C.5)

where

$$A_{\text{spec}}(t) = \sum_{j=1}^{N} a_{s_j(t),j}^{\mu(t)} \tag{C.6}$$

and

$$A_{\text{prod}}(t) = \sum_{j=1}^{\rho N} b_j^{\mu(t)} \equiv A_{\text{prod}}^{\mu(t)} \tag{C.7}$$

and $A_{\text{noise}}(t) = 2k(t) - \eta N$, where $k(t)$ is a binomial random variable with $P(k) = \binom{\eta N}{k} 2^{-\eta N}$. Since $H = \overline{\langle A \rangle^2}$ and the contribution of noise traders to $\langle A^\mu \rangle$ vanishes $\langle A_{\text{noise}} \rangle = 0$, the collective behavior of the system is independent of η. Noise traders shall contribute a constant ηN to σ^2 and will not affect other agents. This only holds in the asymmetric phase (see text). We can then reduce to the study of speculators and producers only.

Let us define, for convenience, $A^\mu = A_{\text{spec}}^\mu + \lambda A_{\text{prod}}^\mu$, where

$$A_{\text{spec}}^\mu = \sum_{i=1}^{N} \left[a_{\uparrow,i}^\mu \frac{1+s_i}{2} + a_{\downarrow,i}^\mu \frac{1-s_i}{2} \right] \tag{C.8}$$

and A_{prod}^μ is given in Eq. (C.7). Here s_i is the dynamical variable controlled by speculator i. We shall implicitly consider directly time-averaged quantities, so s_i is a real variable in $[-1,1]$ rather than a discrete one. The parameter λ is inserted so that, once we have computed the energy $H = \overline{(A_{\text{spec}} + \lambda A_{\text{prod}})^2}$ we can compute the total gain G_{prod} of producers by

$$G_{\text{prod}} \equiv -\overline{A A_{\text{prod}}} = -\frac{1}{2} \frac{\partial H}{\partial \lambda}\bigg|_{\lambda=1} .$$

The gain of speculators is obtained subtracting this contribution and that of noise traders from the total gain $-\sigma^2$

$$G_{\text{spec}} = -\sigma^2 + \eta N - G_{\text{prod}} . \tag{C.9}$$

C.1. Replica calculation

The zero temperature behavior of the Hamiltonian H can be studied with spin-glass techniques [15,14]. We introduce n replicas of the system, each with dynamical variables $s_{i,c}$, labeled by replica indices $c, d = 1, \ldots, n$. Then we write replicated partition function

$$\langle Z^n(\beta) \rangle = \text{Tr}_s \prod_{\mu,c} \langle e^{-\beta/P(A_c^\mu)^2} \rangle_{a,b} , \tag{C.10}$$

where the average is over the disorder variables $a_{s,i}^\mu$, b_i^μ and Tr_s is the trace on the variables $s_{i,c}$ for all i and c. Following standard procedures [15,14], we introduce a Gaussian variable z_c^μ so that we can linearize the exponent in Eq. (C.10). This allows us to carry out the averages over a's and b's explicitly. Then we introduce new variables $Q_{c,d}$ and $r_{c,d}$ with the identity

$$1 = \int dQ_{c,d}\,\delta\left(Q_{c,d} - \frac{1}{N}\sum_i s_{i,c}s_{i,d}\right)$$

$$\propto \int dr_{c,d}\,dQ_{c,d}\,e^{-\alpha\beta^2/2r_{c,d}(NQ_{c,d}-\sum_i s_{i,c}s_{i,d})}$$

for all $c \geqslant d$, which allow us to write the partition function (to leading order in N) as

$$\langle Z^n(\beta)\rangle = \int d\hat{Q}\,d\hat{r}\,e^{-Nn\beta F(\hat{Q},\hat{r})}$$

with

$$F(\hat{Q},\hat{r}) = \frac{\alpha}{2n\beta}\,\mathrm{Tr}\log\hat{T} + \frac{\alpha\beta}{2n}\sum_{c\leqslant d} r_{c,d}Q_{c,d} - \frac{1}{n\beta}\log[\mathrm{Tr}_s\,e^{\alpha\beta^2/2\sum_{c\leqslant d}r_{c,d}s_c s_d}].$$

$$(C.11)$$

The matrix $\hat{T}$ is given by

$$T_{a,b} = \delta_{a,b} + \frac{2\beta}{\alpha}[c + \rho + (1 - c)Q_{a,b}].$$

For *correlated* producers we would have obtained the same result but with $\rho \to \rho + \rho^2 N\varepsilon^2$, where ε measures the bias of producers towards a particular action for a given μ, or equivalently the correlation between the actions of two distinct producers. More precisely, ε^2 is the average of $b_i^\mu b_j^\mu$ for $i \neq j$ and for all μ. Therefore, the limit $\rho \to \infty$ also corresponds to a small share of producers $\rho \ll 1$ with a small bias $\varepsilon \neq 0$. Note that a bias $\varepsilon \sim \sqrt{N}$ corresponds indeed to $\sim N$ independent producers. Equivalently $\sim \sqrt{N}$ correlated producers, with ε finite are equivalent to $\sim N$ independent producers.

With the replica symmetric ansatz

$$Q_{c,d} = q + (Q - q)\delta_{c,d}, \qquad r_{c,d} = 2r + (R - 2r)\delta_{c,d}$$

the matrix $\hat{T}$ has $n - 1$ degenerated eigenvalues $\lambda_0 = 1 + 2(1 - c)\beta(1 - q)/\alpha$ and one eigenvalue equal to $\lambda_1 = 2\beta[c + \rho + (1 - c)q]/\alpha n + 1 + 2(1 - c)\beta(1 - q)/\alpha$ therefore, after standard algebra,

$$F^{(\mathrm{RS})}(q,r) = \frac{\alpha}{2\beta}\log\left[1 + \frac{2(1 - c)\beta(Q - q)}{\alpha}\right] + \frac{\alpha[c + \rho + (1 - c)q]}{\alpha + 2(1 - c)\beta(Q - q)}$$

$$+ \frac{\alpha\beta}{2}(RQ - rq) - \frac{1}{\beta}\left\langle\log\int_{-1}^{1}ds\,e^{-\beta V_z(s)}\right\rangle,$$

$$(C.12)$$

where we found it convenient to define the "potential"

$$V_z(s) = -\frac{\alpha\beta(R - r)}{2}s^2 - \sqrt{\alpha r}\,zs$$

$$(C.13)$$

so that the last term of $F^{(\mathrm{RS})}$ looks like the free energy of a particle in the interval $[-1,1]$ with potential $V_z(s)$ where z plays the role of disorder.

The saddle point equations are given by

$$\frac{\partial F^{(\mathrm{RS})}}{\partial q} = 0 \Rightarrow r = \frac{4(1-c)[c+\rho+(1-c)q]}{[\alpha+2(1-c)\beta(Q-q)]^2} , \tag{C.14}$$

$$\frac{\partial F^{(\mathrm{RS})}}{\partial Q} = 0 \Rightarrow \beta(R-r) = -\frac{2(1-c)}{\alpha+2(1-c)\beta(Q-q)} , \tag{C.15}$$

$$\frac{\partial F^{(\mathrm{RS})}}{\partial R} = 0 \Rightarrow Q = \langle\!\langle s^2 \rangle\!\rangle , \tag{C.16}$$

$$\frac{\partial F^{(\mathrm{RS})}}{\partial r} = 0 \Rightarrow \beta(Q-q) = \frac{\langle\!\langle sz \rangle\!\rangle}{\sqrt{\alpha r}} , \tag{C.17}$$

where $\langle\!\langle \cdot \rangle\!\rangle$ stands for a thermal average over the above-mentioned one-particle system.

In the limit $\beta \to \infty$ we can look for a solution with $q \to Q$ and $r \to R$. It is convenient to define

$$\chi = \frac{2(1-c)\beta(Q-q)}{\alpha} \quad \text{and} \quad \zeta = -\sqrt{\frac{\alpha}{r}}\beta(R-r) \tag{C.18}$$

and to require that they stay finite in the limit $\beta \to \infty$. The averages are easily evaluated since, in this case, they are dominated by the minimum of the potential $V_z(s) = \sqrt{\alpha r}(\zeta s^2/2 - zs)$ for $s \in [-1,1]$. The minimum is at $s = -1$ for $z \leqslant -\zeta$ and at $s = +1$ for $z \geqslant \zeta$. For $-\zeta < z < \zeta$ the minimum is at $s = z/\zeta$. With this we find

$$\langle\!\langle sz \rangle\!\rangle = \frac{1}{\zeta}\,\mathrm{erf}\!\left(\frac{\zeta}{\sqrt{2}}\right) \tag{C.19}$$

and

$$\langle\!\langle s^2 \rangle\!\rangle = Q = 1 - \sqrt{\frac{2}{\pi}}\frac{e^{-\zeta^2/2}}{\zeta} - \left(1 - \frac{1}{\zeta^2}\right)\mathrm{erf}\!\left(\frac{\zeta}{\sqrt{2}}\right) . \tag{C.20}$$

With some more algebra, one easily finds

$$\chi = \left[\alpha/\mathrm{erf}\!\left(\frac{\zeta}{\sqrt{2}}\right) - 1\right]^{-1} . \tag{C.21}$$

Finally, ζ is fixed as a function of α by the equation

$$\sqrt{\frac{2}{\pi}}\frac{e^{-\zeta^2/2}}{\zeta} + \left(1 - \frac{1}{\zeta^2}\right)\mathrm{erf}\!\left(\frac{\zeta}{\sqrt{2}}\right) + \frac{\alpha}{\zeta^2} = \frac{1+\rho}{1-c} . \tag{C.22}$$

Note that ζ only depends on the combination $(1+\rho)/(1-c)$ which runs from $1 -$ for $\rho = c = 0$, i.e., no producers and "perfect" speculators – to ∞. The latter limit occurs either if $c \to 1$, i.e., when speculators become producers, or if $\rho \to \infty$ (many producers).

Eq. (C.21) means that χ diverges when $\alpha \to \alpha_c(\rho,c)^+$, which then implies that at the critical point

$$\mathrm{erf}\!\left(\frac{\zeta}{\sqrt{2}}\right) = \alpha = \alpha_c . \tag{C.23}$$

313

Substituting this in the other saddle point equations, yields the following equation for $\zeta = \zeta_c$:

$$\sqrt{\frac{2}{\pi}}\frac{e^{-\zeta_c^2/2}}{\zeta_c} + \operatorname{erf}\left(\frac{\zeta_c}{\sqrt{2}}\right) = \frac{1+\rho}{1-c} \,. \tag{C.24}$$

The free energy, at the saddle point, for $\beta \to \infty$, is

$$F^{\text{(RS)}} = \frac{c + (1-c)Q + \rho}{(1+\chi)^2} \,, \tag{C.25}$$

where Q and χ take their saddle point values, Eqs. (C.20) and (C.21).

The gain of producers, from Eq. (C.12), is

$$\frac{G_{\text{prod}}}{N} = -\frac{\rho}{1+\chi} \tag{C.26}$$

and that of speculators is obtained from Eq. (C.9).

At α_c $\chi \to \infty$ so that $F^{\text{(RS)}} \to 0$. Note that the loss of producers vanishes $L_{\text{prod}} \to 0$ as $\alpha \to \alpha_c$, whereas the loss of speculators $L_{\text{spec}} = (1-Q)/2$ is always positive below α_c.

The phase diagram is shown in Fig. 5. here we discuss some limits.

Appendix D. The sign MG

The original MG [1] is defined with payoffs

$$g_i = -a_i(t)\operatorname{sign} A(t) \tag{D.1}$$

Over a long period of time T, the change in $\Delta_i(t)$ is given by

$$\frac{\Delta_i(t+T) - \Delta_i(t)}{T} = \frac{-2}{T}\sum_{\tau=t}^{T-1} \xi_i^{\mu(\tau)}\operatorname{sign} A(\tau)$$

$$\simeq \frac{-2}{P}\sum_{\mu=1}^{P} [2\operatorname{Prob}\{A(\tau) > 0 | \mu(\tau) = \mu\} - 1]\xi_i^\mu \,. \tag{D.2}$$

Then, for any fixed μ, the relevant quantity is the probability that $A(t) > 0$, when $\mu(t) = \mu$. This can be computed within our mean-field approximation: Indeed if $\langle s_i \rangle = m_i$ we can regard s_i as a random variable with distribution

$$P(s_i = \pm 1) = \frac{1 \pm m_i}{2} \,.$$

Then, the relation $A^{\mu(t)}(t) = \Omega^\mu + \sum_{i=1}^{N} \xi_i^\mu s_i$ implies that we can consider A^μ as a Gaussian variable with variance

$$\operatorname{Var}(A^\mu) = \sum_{i=1}^{N} \xi_i^{\mu 2}(1 - m_i^2) + \eta N \,.$$

314

This allows us to compute

$$\text{Prob}\{A(\tau) > 0 | \mu(\tau) = \mu\} = \frac{1}{2}\text{erfc}\left(\frac{\langle A^\mu \rangle}{\sqrt{2\text{Var}(A^\mu)}}\right) .$$

Note that close to the critical point α_c, $\langle A^\mu \rangle$ is very small compared to $\text{Var}(A^\mu)$, which means that it is legitimate to expand the erfc function to a linear order. This gives us back a linear minority game, but with

$$g_i = -\frac{a_i(t)A(t)}{\sqrt{2\text{Var}(A^\mu)}}. \tag{D.3}$$

Note, then that when η increases the gains for each speculator decreases. This is actually true even away from α_c. It is indeed easy to check that $\langle \text{sign}\, A(t) \rangle$ decreases as η increases.

References

[1] D. Challet, Y.-C. Zhang, Physica A 246 (1997) 407 (adap-org/9708006).
[2] Y.-C. Zhang, Europhys. News 29 (1998) 51 (cond-mat/9803308).
[3] H. Simon, Models of Bounded Rationality, MIT Press, Cambridge, 1997.
[4] W.B. Arthur, Amer. Econ. Assoc. Papers Proc. 84 (1994) 406 (http://www.santafe.edu/arthur/Papers/El_Farol.html).
[5] See the Minority Game's web page on http://www.unifr.ch/econophysics.
[6] D. Challet, M. Marsili, R. Zecchina, preprint, cond-mat/9904392.
[7] M. Marsili, D. Challet, R. Zecchina, preprint, cond-mat/9908480.
[8] R. Savit, R. Manuca, R. Riolo, Phys. Rep. Lett. 82(10) (1999) 2203 (adap-org/9712006).
[9] D. Challet, Y.-C. Zhang, Physica A 256 (1998) 514 (cond-mat/9805084).
[10] A. Cavagna, preprint, cond-mat/9812215, 1998.
[11] R.D. Luce, Individual Choice Behavior: A Theoretical Analysis, New York, Wiley, 1959.
[12] A. Cavagna, J.P. Garrahan, I. Giardina, D. Sherrington, preprint, cond-mat/9903415, 1999.
[13] D. Challet, M. Marsili, preprint, cond-mat/9904071.
[14] M. Mezard, G. Parisi, M.A. Virasoro, Spin Glass Theory and Beyond, World Scientific, Singapore, 1987.
[15] V. Dotsenko, An Introduction to the Theory of Spin Glasses and Neural Networks; World Scientific Publishing, Singapore, 1995.
[16] Y.-C. Zhang, Physica A 269 (1999) 30 (cond-mat/9901243).
[17] Y. Li et al., preprints, cond-mat/9903415 and cond-mat/9906001.
[18] M. Marsili, R. Zecchina, forthcoming.
[19] N.F. Johnson et al., forthcoming.
[20] J.B. Delong, A. Schleifer, L.H. Summers, R.J. Waldmann, Noise trader risk in financial markets, J. Political Econ. 98 (1990) 703.
[21] N.F. Johnson et al., preprint, cond-mat/9811227.
[22] W. Kinzel, R. Metzler, I. Kanter, preprint, cond-mat/9906058.
[23] R. Dawkins, The Selfish Gene, Oxford Univ. Press, New York, 1976.

PHYSICISTS ATTEMPT TO SCALE THE IVORY TOWERS OF FINANCE

Physicists have recently begun doing research in finance, and even though this movement is less than five years old, interesting and useful contributions have already emerged. This article reviews these developments in four areas, including empirical statistical properties of prices, random-process models for price dynamics, agent-based modeling, and practical applications.

During the past decade or so, many physicists have gone to Wall Street to work in finance. While the commonly heard statement that "Wall Street is the biggest single recruiter of physics PhDs" appears to be an urban legend, physicists working as *quants*—quantitative analysts—are now unquestionably common in large investment banks and other financial businesses.

More recently, a countermovement has emerged as physicists have begun writing research papers on finance and economics. While this work has yet to have a major impact on mainstream economics research, papers on finance are appearing with some frequency in physics journals, with a few publications in major science journals such as *Nature*, and occasionally even in economics journals. A new movement sometimes called *econophysics* has been established. Recently, about 200 people participated in the Third Annual Applications of Physics in Financial Analysis Conference (http://www.nbi. dk/APCA), held at Dublin's Trinity College in July 1999, where speakers included both practitioners and academics.

In the last five years, roughly 30 recent physics PhDs have addressed finance topics with their doctoral research. To paraphrase Jean-Phillipe Bouchaud, a pioneer in this area and the advisor of several such students: "Somebody has to train all the physics graduates going into banking and finance, and we want it to be us, not people from other disciplines. To do this we need to establish a scientific presence in the field." There is a widespread feeling among members of this movement that finance offers fertile terrain for physicists. It might be possible, for instance, to describe the aggregate behavior of financial agents using the tools of statistical physics. Combined with a fresh point of view, this might lead to some good science.

Not surprisingly, the few economists who have paid any heed at all view the entry of physicists into economics with considerable skepticism. Economics and finance, like physics, depend on a depth of domain-specific knowledge that takes years to master. Many physicists working in this area are poorly versed in the finance and economics literature. The point of view and problem-solving approach are quite different. The problems presented in modeling the physical and social worlds are not the same, and it is not obvious that methods that work well in physics will also work well in economics. With some justification, many economists think that the entry of physicists into their world reflects merely audac-

1521-9615/99/$10.00 © 1999 IEEE

J. DOYNE FARMER
Santa Fe Institute

26

We thank the author and the Institute of Electrical and Electronics Engineers, Inc. for granting us permission to reprint this paper.

ity, hubris, and arrogance. Physicists are not known for their humility, and some physicists have presented their work in a manner that plays into this stereotype. The cultural barrier between the two groups will be difficult to overcome.

This schism was already evident at a conference held at the Santa Fe Institute in 1988 titled "The Economy as an Evolving Complex System."[1] Roughly half the participants were economists and the other half physicists. Although many of the physicists were largely ignorant of economics, that did not prevent them from openly criticizing the economists. At one point, Nobel laureate Phil Anderson said, "You guys really believe that?" At another point, Larry Summers (now Secretary of the Treasury) accused physicists of having a "Tarzan complex." This was not just a turf war. Whether due to nature or nurture, this conference clearly showed that there is a deep epistemological divide between physicists and economists that is difficult to cross.

In this article, I am going to attempt a brief critical review of some of the work done in the past four or five years by physicists working on problems in finance. I will not discuss work that might be more broadly called economics, because I am too ignorant to do so. In the spirit of full disclosure, I should make my biases clear at the outset: My interest in finance stems from trading financial instruments at Prediction Company, where I was one of the founders, using directional forecasting models based on time-series analysis of historical data. According to many mainstream economists, the highly statistically significant profits we made should have been impossible. My view of finance relies at least as much on conversations with traders as with academics. More importantly, my formative religious training was in physics. I am thus a highly biased reviewer. My only claim to impartiality is a wide exposure to fields outside of physics and a lack of involvement in the early stages of the econophysics movement; as a new entrant with many ideas of my own, my hope at the outset was that none of the juicy problems had been solved yet.

The topics presented at the Dublin econophysics conference included a variety of subjects, ranging from metaphorical models to empirically driven practical applications. I will single out a few highlights, dividing the presentations into four categories: empirical statistical regularities in prices, random-process models, agent-based models for price formation and market evolution, and practical applications, such as option pricing, risk control, and portfolio formation.

This article was explicitly commissioned to review work by physicists—a theme defined by cultural history and kinship relations rather than by the subject of scientific investigation. I write this review with some reluctance. I believe that disciplinary boundaries are dangerous and disciplines should be broken down or wholly eliminated. At the risk of spoiling the dramatic thread of this story, my conclusion in reviewing this work is that it indeed has value. That does not mean that I wish to argue that economists should move over and let physicists rule. Rather, I think that physicists have something to contribute, and I hope to encourage physicists and economists to work together.

Empirical statistical regularities in prices

The distribution of price fluctuations is one of the most basic properties of markets. For some markets the historical data spans a century at a daily timescale, and for at least the last decade every transaction is recorded. Nonetheless, the price distribution's functional form is still a topic of active debate. Naively, central-limit theorem arguments suggest a Gaussian (normal) distribution. If $p(t)$ is the price at time t, the *log-return* $r_\tau(t)$ is defined as $r_\tau(t) = \log p(t + \tau) - \log p(t)$. Dividing τ into N subintervals, the total log-return $r_\tau(t)$ is by definition the sum of the log-returns in each subinterval. If the price changes in each subinterval are independent and identically distributed (IID) with a well-defined second moment, under the central limit theorem the cumulative distribution function $f(r_\tau)$ should converge to a normal distribution for large τ.

For real financial data, however, convergence is very slow. While the normal distribution provides a good approximation for the center of the distribution for large τ, for smaller values of τ— less than about a month—there are strong deviations from normality. This is surprising, given that the autocorrelation of log-returns is typically very close to zero for times longer than about 15 to 30 minutes.[2,3] What is the nature of these deviations from normality and what is their cause?

The actual distribution of log-returns has *fat tails*. That is, there is a higher probability for extreme values than for a normal distribution. As one symptom of this, the fourth moment is larger than expected for a Gaussian. We can measure this deviation in a scale-independent manner by using the *kurtosis* $k = \langle (r - \langle r \rangle)^4 \rangle / \langle (r - \langle r \rangle)^2 \rangle^2$ ($\langle \ \rangle$ in-

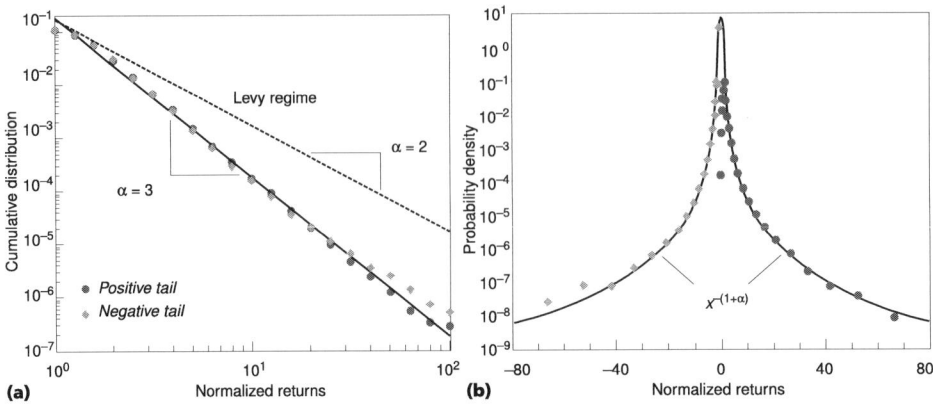

Figure 1. Fat tails in price fluctuations: (a) Cumulative distribution of the positive and negative tails for normalized log-returns r_τ of 1,000 of the largest US companies for 1994–1995, with $\tau = 5$ minutes.[12] The returns are normalized by dividing by the standard deviation for each company during this period. The solid line is a regression fit in the region $2 < r <$ 80. (b) The probability density function of the normalized returns. The values in the center of the distribution arise from the discreteness in stock prices, which are important for small price movements.

dicates a time average). In the early 1960s, Benoit Mandelbrot[4] (now famous as the grandfather of fractals) and Eugene Fama[5] (now famous as the high priest of efficient market theory) presented empirical evidence that f was a *stable Levy distribution*. The stable Levy distributions are a natural choice because they emerge from a generalization of the central limit theorem. For random variables that are so fat-tailed that their second moment doesn't exist, the normal central limit theorem no longer applies. Under certain conditions, however, the sum of N such variables converges to a Levy distribution.[3] The Levy distributions are characterized by a parameter $1 \leq \mu \leq 2$, where $\mu = 2$ corresponds to the special case of a normal distribution. For $\mu < 2$, however, the stable Levy distributions are so fat-tailed that their standard deviation and all higher moments are infinite—that is, $\langle r^q \rangle = \infty$ for $q \geq 2$. In practice, this means that numerical estimates of any moment $q = 2$ or higher will not converge. Based on daily prices in different markets, Mandelbrot and Fama measured $\mu \approx 1.7$, a result that suggested that short-term price changes were indeed ill-behaved: if the variance doesn't exist, most statistical properties are ill-defined.

Subsequent studies demonstrated, however, that the behavior is more complicated than this.[6–12] First, for larger values of τ, the distribution becomes progressively closer to normal. Second,

investigations of larger data sets (including work by economists in the late '80s and early '90s[6–8]) make it clear that large returns asymptotically follow a power law $f(r) \sim |r|^{-\alpha}$, with $\alpha > 2$. This finding is incompatible with the Levy distribution. The difference in the value of α is very important: with $\alpha > 2$, the second moment (the variance) is well defined. A value $2 < \alpha < \infty$ is incompatible with the stable Levy distribution and indicates that simply generalizing the central limit theorem with long tails is not the correct explanation.

Physicists have contributed to this problem by studying really large data sets and looking at the scalings in close detail. A group at Olsen and Associates, led by Michel Dacorogna, studied intraday price movements in foreign exchange markets.[9] Another group at Boston University, led by Rosario Mantegna and Eugene Stanley, has studied the intraday movements of the S&P index.[10,11] More recently, they studied the five-minute returns of 1,000 individual stocks traded on the AMEX, NASDAQ, and NYSE exchanges, over a two-year period involving roughly 40 million records.[12] In this case, they observed the power-law scaling over about 90 standard deviations (see Figure 1). For larger values of $|r|$, these results dramatically illustrate that $f(r)$ is approximately a power law with $\alpha \approx 3$. Thus, the mean and variance are well-defined, the kurtosis clearly diverges, and the behavior of the skewness is not so clear.

Power-law scaling is not new to economics. The power-law distribution of wealth discovered by Vilfredo Pareto (1848–1923) in the 19th century predates any power laws in physics.[13] And indeed, since Pareto, the existence of power laws has been controversial. One underlying reason is that power-law probability distributions are necessarily approximations. An inverse power-law cumulative distribution $f(r) \sim |r|^{-\alpha}$ with an exponent $\alpha > 0$ is not integrable at zero, and similarly, with an exponent $\alpha \leq 0$, it is not integrable at infinity. Thus, a power-law probability distribution cannot be exactly true for a variable with an unbounded range. When they apply at all, power-law distributions are necessarily only part of a more complete description, valid within certain limits. (See the "Power law distribution of wealth" sidebar for more on this topic.[14])

Another reason for skepticism about power laws in economics is that sloppy statistical analysis has led to mistakes in the past. In the 1980s, there was considerable interest in the possibility that price changes might be described by a low-dimensional chaotic attractor. Physics and biology have many examples where the existence of low-dimensional chaos is unambiguous. Why not economics? Based on a numerical computation of fractal dimension, several researchers claimed to observe low-dimensional chaos in price series. Such computations are done by measuring the coarse-grained size of a set, in this case a possible attractor of returns in a state space whose variables are lagged returns, as a function of the scale of the coarse-graining. If this behaves as a power law in the limit where the scale is small, it implies low-dimensional chaos. But it is very easy to be fooled when performing such calculations. It is critical to test against a carefully formulated null hypothesis.[15] More careful statistical analysis by José Scheinkman and Blake LeBaron showed that the claims of low-dimensional chaos in price series were not well-justified.[16] While nonlinearity is clearly present, there is no convincing evidence of low-dimensionality. The power-law scaling that people thought they saw was apparently just an artifact of the finite size of their data sets.

The power law for large price moves is a very different story. To detect a chaotic attractor based on its fractal dimension in state space requires a test of the distribution's fine-grained, microscopic properties. Low-dimensional chaos is a very strong hypothesis, because it would im-

ply deep structure and short-term predictability in prices. A power law in the tails of the returns, in contrast, is just a statement about the frequency of large events and is a much weaker hypothesis. This becomes clear in the context of extreme value theory. For simplicity, consider the positive tail $r \to \infty$. Under very general conditions, there are only three possible limiting behaviors, which we can classify based on the tail index α:

1. There is a maximum value for the variable. The distribution vanishes for values greater than this maximum, and $\alpha < 0$.
2. The tails decay exponentially and $1/\alpha = 0$ (an example is a normal distribution).
3. There are fat tails that decay as a power law with $\alpha > 0$.

Price returns must be in one of these three categories, and the data clearly points to choice 3 with $\alpha > 2$.[2,6-12] Surprisingly, this implies that the price-formation process cannot be fully understood in terms of central limit theorem arguments, even in a generalized form. Power-law tails do obey a sort of partial central limit theorem: For a random variable with tail exponent α, the sum of N variables will also have the same tail exponent α.[17] This does not mean that the full distribution is stable, however, because the distribution's central part, as well as the power law's cutoff, will generally vary. The fact that the

Power-law distribution of wealth

Sorin Solomon and various collaborators have proposed an interesting idea for understanding the power-law distribution of wealth. An old approach to such an understanding entails modeling an agent's wealth at any given time as a multiplicative random process. By taking logarithms, it is clear that in the absence of any constraints such a process will tend toward log-normal distribution. When the mean is small compared to the standard deviation, an approximate power-law distribution for large wealth arises. The problem is that the tail exponent $\alpha = 1$, whereas the observed exponent varies, but can be above 2 or even 3. Solomon and his colleagues suggest that we can fix this problem by renormalizing for drifts in total wealth and imposing a constraint that there is a minimum relative wealth below which no one is allowed to drop. The exponent of the power law is then $\alpha = 1/(1 - c)$, where c is the minimum wealth expressed as a fraction of the mean wealth. The Pareto exponent should thus be higher for countries that have a higher floor of minimum income, meaning a stronger welfare system.

distribution's shape changes with τ makes it clear that the random process underlying prices must have nontrivial temporal structure, as I'll discuss next. This complicates statistical analysis of prices, both for theoretical and practical purposes, and gives an important clue about the behavior of economic agents and the price-formation process. But unlike low-dimensional chaos, it does not imply that the direction of price movements is predictable. (Also see the "Power-law scaling" sidebar.[18])

The search for a random process model of prices

Price fluctuations are not identically distributed. Properties of the distribution, such as the variance, change in time. This is called *clustered volatility*. While the autocorrelation of log-returns, $\rho(\tau) \sim \langle r_\tau(t + \tau)r_\tau(t)\rangle$, is generally very small on timescales longer than a day, this is not true for the volatility (which can be defined, for example, as r^2 or $|r|$). The volatility on successive days is positively correlated, and these correlations remain positive for weeks or months. Clustered volatility can cause fat tails in $f(r)$. For example, the sum of normally distributed variables with different variances has a high kurtosis (although it does not have power-law tails).[3] To understand the statistical properties of price changes, we need a more sophisticated model that accounts for the probability distribution's temporal variation.

Clustered volatility is traditionally described by simple ad hoc time-series models with names that include the letters ARCH (for AutoRegressive Conditional Heteroscedasticity).[19,20] Such models involve linear relationships between the square or absolute value of current and past log-

returns. Volatility at one time influences volatility at subsequent times. ARCH-type models can be effective for forecasting volatility, and there is a large body of work devoted to problems of parameter estimation, variations on the basic model, and so forth. ARCH models are not compatible with all of the empirical properties of price fluctuations, however.

A good price-fluctuations model should connect the behavior on multiple timescales. A natural test is the behavior of moments, in this case $\langle |r_\tau|^q \rangle$ as a function of q and τ. Several groups report approximate power-law scaling with τ, with different slopes for each value of q, as Figure 2 shows.[21,22] In the jargon of dynamical systems theory, this suggests a fractal random process. A slope that is a linear function of q implies a simple fractal process, and a slope that is a nonlinear function of q implies a *multifractal* or *multiscaling* process. Indeed, several different calculations seem to show that the slope varies nonlinearly with q, suggesting that the price process is multifractal.

These results have suggested a possible analogy to turbulence.[21] Under this analogy, velocity plays the role of the logarithm of price and length plays the role of time. The hypothesis is that there is an analogy between the Kolmogorov energy cascade, through which large vortices break up into smaller vortices, and an *information cascade*, in which financial agents with more money or longer-term strategies influence financial agents betting smaller sums over shorter spans of time, inducing a cascade of volatility. This view is reinforced by Alain Arneodo, Jean-Francois Muzy, and Didier Sornette, who use a wavelet decomposition of volatility and an analysis in terms of mutual information to argue that there is indeed a cascade of volatility from large to small scales.[23]

While this is an exciting and interesting idea, caution is in order. As Mantegna and Stanley discussed, turbulence and price fluctuations differ in many important ways.[2] There is a possible alternative explanation for the complicated scaling behavior of price fluctuations.[24,3] Numerous studies show clearly that the autocorrelation function for volatility decays as a power law, $g(\tau) \sim \tau^{-\nu}$, with ν somewhere in the range $0.1 < \nu < 0.3$.[2,3,21–28] In this case, Jean-Phillipe Bouchaud, Marc Potters, and Martin Meyer show that the higher moments automatically scale as sums of power laws with different slopes. Asymptotically, the dominant power law has an exponent proportional to q, but for smaller values of τ, another power law whose exponent is a nonlinear function of q might dominate. Thus, there is apparent multifractal behav-

---

Power-law scaling

Stanley's group at Boston University has discovered a new power-law scaling that economists apparently had not previously observed. They show that the fluctuations in the growth rates of companies of size S follow a power law $S^{-\beta}$, with $\beta \approx 0.2$ The growth-rate fluctuation is measured by the standard deviation of the distribution of a variety of different quantities, including sales, number of employees, assets, and several other measures. Furthermore, they observe a similar power law with approximately the same exponent for the GNPs of countries. This result is particularly interesting because it is not explained by standard theories (and they have proposed a new theory).

ior, even though asymptotically the process is just a simple fractal, with all the moments determined by the scaling of a single moment. For a short data set, a simple fractal process might look like a multifractal process due to slow convergence.

At this point, we can't say which of these two explanations is correct. Unlike fluid turbulence, where multifractal scaling is supported by strong theoretical evidence and by analysis of very large data sets, the situation in finance is still not clear. Resolution of this problem will await analysis of longer data sets and development of better theoretical models.

One thing that does seem clear is that conventional ARCH-type models are incompatible with the scaling properties of price fluctuations.[2,3] While ARCH-type models can indeed give rise to fat-tailed probability distributions with $\alpha > 2$, they cannot explain other properties of the price fluctuations.[28] ARCH-type models fit at a given timescale τ do not appear to do a good job of explaining the volatility at a different timescale τ. Furthermore, conventional ARCH models do not have asymptotic power-law decay in the volatility autocorrelation function. The most likely explanation is that ARCH models are misspecified—their simple linear structure is not general enough to fully capture the real temporal structure of volatility. Given that they are completely ad hoc models, this is not surprising.

There are still missing pieces and several open questions to be answered before we will have a good random-process model linking the behavior of prices across a range of different time scales. Physicists have contributed to the theory and data analysis leading to the current understanding. They have also contributed an interesting new hypothesis; even if the analogy to turbulence turns out to be wrong, it has already stimulated interesting alternatives. But to have a good theory of how prices behave, we will need to explain the behavior of the agents on whom they depend. See the "Agent-based models" sidebar for a discussion of these models.

Practical applications

Let's now look at some of the practical applications that have come out of the physics community. Physicists have taken the fat tails of the price distribution seriously and explored their implications in several areas, such as risk control, portfolio formation, and option pricing. In addition, they have made use of results on random matrices to provide some insight into the prob-

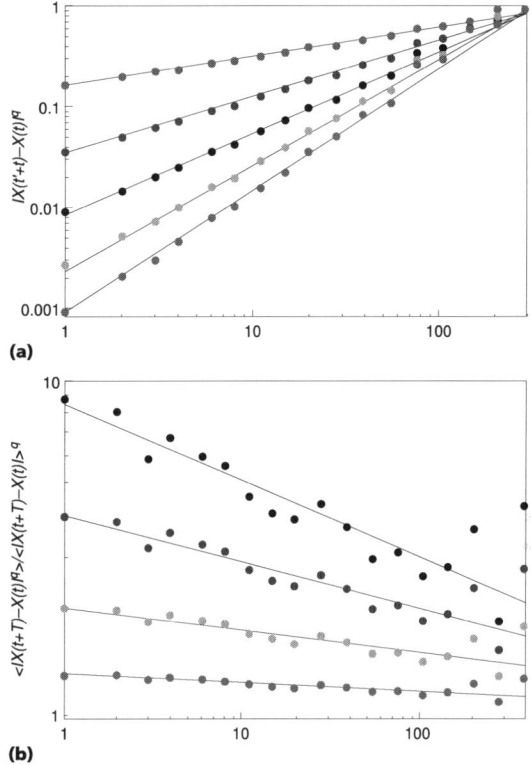

(a)

(b)

Figure 2. Power-law scalings: (a) The mean moment of the absolute daily returns $\langle |r_\tau|^q \rangle$ plotted as a function of τ for several different values of q ranging from 0.5 (top) to 2.5 (bottom).[22] In a log-log representation these appear to be approximately straight lines, suggesting power-law behavior. Furthermore, the variation of this line's slope with q looks nonlinear, suggesting multifractal behavior. (b) As a test of this, the ratio $\langle |r|^q \rangle / \langle |r| \rangle^q$, which is constant for a simple fractal, but not for a multifractal for q = 1.5–3 (bottom to top).

lem of estimating correlation matrices between different assets.

Perhaps the most direct consequence of fat tails is their impact on risk control. With fat tails, the probability of extreme events can be orders of magnitude larger than it is with a normal distribution. For a fat-tailed distribution, the variance is an inadequate and potentially misleading indicator of risk. Failure to take this into account can be disastrous. This was dramatically illustrated in October 1998 by the near failure of Long Term Capital Management, which was apparently at least in part due to a lack of respect for fat tails.

Agent-based models

The elementary building blocks of financial markets are human agents, each buying and selling based on his or her own point of view. To have a full and fundamental description of markets requires models that take intelligence, learning, and complex decision making into account, not to mention emotion, irrationality, and intuition.

The traditional view in economics is that financial agents are completely rational with perfect foresight. Markets are always in equilibrium, which in economics means that trading always occurs at a price that conforms to everyone's expectations of the future. Markets are efficient, which means that there are no patterns in prices that can be forecast based on a given information set. The only possible changes in price are random, driven by unforecastable external information. Profits occur only by chance.

In recent years this view is eroding.[1] Modern economic theory assumes bounded rationality.[2] Equilibria are dynamic, driven by agents' changing perceptions of each others' actions. Allowance is made for the possibility of reasonable excess profits for agents who perform services, such as reducing risk or processing information. The *behavioral economists* have presented evidence of irrational behavior and market anomalies that historically would have allowed excess profits.[3] Anecdotal evidence suggests that some individuals might indeed make statistically significant excess profits.

It is fair to say that the physicists studying these problems tend toward the more radical end of the spectrum. While bounded rationality is a nice idea, it is only part of the story. People are not identical finite-capacity calculating machines differing only in their utility functions. Equally important is the diversity of viewpoints induced by nature and nurture. Formulating successful predictive models is extremely difficult and requires both hard work and intelligence. To make a good model, it is necessary to specialize, which stimulates diversification of financial strategies. As a result, financial agents are very heterogeneous. Some agents are more skilled than others, and the excess profits of such agents are not necessarily reasonable. The behavioral economists are clearly right that people are not fully rational and that this can play an important role in setting prices.[3,4] But where do we go from there? Despite the idiosyncrasies of human psychology, is there a *statistical mechanics* that can explain some of the statistical properties of the market, and perhaps take such idiocyncracies into account?

Agent-based modeling offers one approach to addressing these problems.[5] Efforts in this direction range from simple, metaphorical models, such as those of evolutionary game theory,[6] to complicated simulations, such as the Santa Fe Institute stock market model.[7,8] The SFI model, which was a collaboration between two economists, a physicist, and a computer scientist, was a significant accomplishment. It demonstrated that many of the dynamical properties of real markets, such as clustered volatility and fat tails, emerge automatically when a market simulation allows the views of the participants to be dynamic. It was a good start, but in part because of the complexity of the numerical simulations, it left many unanswered questions.

The minority game

The minority game represents the opposite end of the spectrum. Despite its simplicity, it displays some rich behavior. While the connection to markets is only metaphorical, its behavior hints at the problems with the traditional views of efficiency and equilibrium. The minority game was originally motivated by Brian Arthur's El Farol problem.[9,10] El Farol is a bar in Santa Fe, near the original site of the Santa Fe Institute, which in the old days was a popular hangout for SFI denizens. In the El Farol problem, a fixed number of agents face the question of whether or not to attend the bar. If the bar is not crowded, as measured by a threshold on the total number of agents, an agent wins if he or she decides to attend. If the bar is too crowded, the agent wins by staying home. Agents make decisions based on the recent record of total attendance at the bar. This problem is like a market in that each agent tries to forecast the behavior of the aggregate and that no outcome makes everyone happy.

The minority game introduced by Damien Challet and Yi-Cheng Zhang is a more specific formulation of the El Farol problem.[11-15] At each timestep, N agents choose between two possibilities (for example, A and B). A historical record is kept of the number of agents choosing A; because N is fixed, this automatically determines the number who chose B. The only information made public is the most popular choice. A given time step is labeled "0" if choice A is more popular and "1" if choice B is more popular. The agents' strategies are lookup tables whose inputs are based on the binary historical record for the previous m timesteps. Strategies can be constructed at random by simply assigning random outputs to each input (see Table A).

Each agent has s possible strategies, and at any given time plays the strategy that has been most successful up until that point in time. The ability to test multiple strategies and use the best strategy provides a simple learning mechanism. This learning is somewhat effective—for example, asymptotically A is chosen 50% of the time. But because there is no choice that

Table A. Example of a strategy for the minority game. The input is based on the attendance record for the m previous timesteps, 0 or 1, corresponding to which choice was most popular. In this case $m = 2$. The output of the strategy is its choice (0 or 1). Outputs are assigned at random.

Input	Output
0 0	1
0 1	0
1 0	0
1 1	1

satisfies everyone—indeed, no choice that satisfies the majority of the participants—there is a limit to what learning can achieve for the group as a whole.

When $s > 1$, the sequence of 0s and 1s corresponding to the attendance record is aperiodic. This is driven by switching between strategies. The set of active strategies continues to change even though the total pool of strategies is fixed. For a given number of agents, for small m the game is efficient, in that prediction is impossible, but when m is large, this is no longer the case. In the limit $N \to \infty$, as m increases there is a sharp transition between the efficient and the inefficient regime.

The standard deviation of the historical attendance record, σ, provides an interesting measure of the average utility. Assume that each agent satisfies his or her utility function by making the minority choice. The average utility is highest when the two choices are almost equally popular. For example, with 101 agents the maximum utility is achieved if 50 agents make one choice and 51 the other. However, it is impossible to achieve this state consistently. There are fluctuations around the optimal attendance level, lowering the average utility. As m increases, σ exhibits interesting behavior, starting out at a maximum, decreasing to a minimum, and then rising to obtain an asymptotic value in the limit as $m \to \infty$ (see Figure A). The minimum occurs at the transition between the efficient and inefficient regimes.

The distinction between the efficient and inefficient regimes arises from the change in the size of the pool of strategies present in the population, relative to the total number of possible strategies. The size of the pool of strategies is sN. The number of possible strategies is 2^{2^m}, which grows extremely rapidly with m. For example, for $m = 2$ there are 16 possible strategies, for $m = 5$ there are roughly 4 billion, and for $m = 10$ there are more than 10^{300}—far exceeding the number of elementary particles in the universe. In contrast, with $s = 2$ and $N = 100$, there are only 200 strategies actually present in the pool. For low m, when the space of strategies is well-covered, the conditional probability for a given transition is the same for all histories—there are no patterns of length m. But when m is larger, so that the strategies are only sparsely filling the space of possibilities, patterns remain. We can interpret this as meaning that the market is efficient for small m and inefficient for large m.

The El Farol problem and minority game is a simple game with no solution that can satisfy everyone. This is analogous to a market where not everyone profits on any given trade. Studies of the minority game suggest that the long-term behavior is aperiodic: the aggregate behavior continues to fluctuate. In

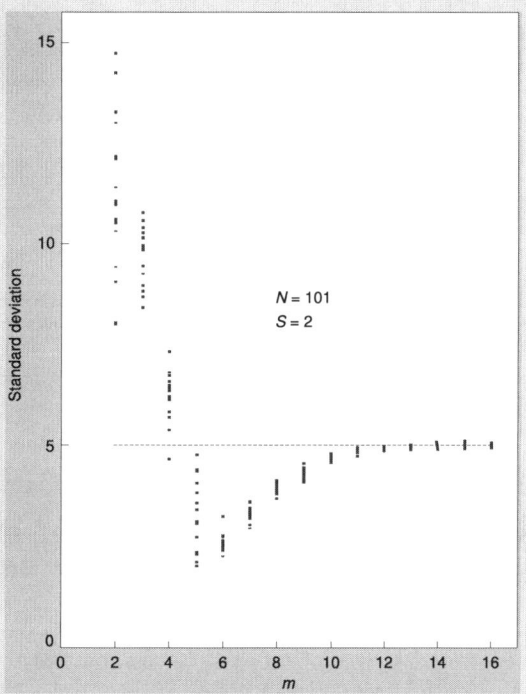

Figure A. For the minority game, the standard deviation of the attendance σ is plotted as a function of the memory length of the strategies.[12] σ is not zero, reflecting the fact that there are irregular oscillations in the attendance, with corresponding variations in the mean utility of the players of the game.

contrast to the standard view in economics, such fluctuations occur even in the absence of any new external information.

Connections to financial markets

While the results for the minority game are elegant and interesting in their own right, the connection to financial markets is only metaphorical. There are no prices and no trading in the minority game, and by definition a market is a place where prices are adjusted as trading takes place. Profits in markets are not made by being in the minority, but rather by anticipating the majority. To go past the metaphorical level, we must study models of markets that involve buying and selling assets and must be able to incrementally modify such models by adding successively more realism. There have been several steps in this direction.[16–26] These models involve a definition of agents, who make trading decisions, and a price-formation rule that determines how the price changes in response to these decisions. There is a feedback between these two processes: decisions affect prices, which affect decisions, and so forth. As a result, the prices and agents can display interesting dynamics.

Many dynamic trading models attempt to use strategies patterned after strategies actually used in real markets (as opposed to arbitrary, abstract strategies that have often been used in other game-theoretic models). The decisions are based on information internal to the market, such as prices and their history, and possibly information external to the market, and can be public (such as prices) or private (such as conversations between traders).

Despite the wide variation in financial-trading strategies, we can classify many of them into broad groups. Strategies that depend only on the price history are called *technical trading* or *chartist* strategies. The minority game strategies are technical-trading strategies (although not of a type that is widely used). *Trend-following strategies* are a commonly used special case of technical strategies in which the holdings of the asset positively correlate with past price movements. *Value* or *fundamental* strategies are strategies based on perceived value—that is, a model for what something ought to be worth, as opposed to its current price. The perceived value is inherently subjective, and from the point of view of the models discussed here is considered external information. Value strategies tend to buy when an asset is undervalued and sell when it is overvalued.

Many authors have studied trend and value strategies, with a variety of differences in the details of the implementations. Certain conclusions seem to emerge that are independent of the details. For example, trend strategies tend to induce trends and therefore positive autocorrelations in the price,[23] which was also evident in earlier work by economists.[27] Several new features, however, are apparent with a simple price formation rule that were not recognized in earlier studies by economists because of the more cumbersome framework they used to formulate the problem. For example, trend-following strategies also induce oscillations because, to keep risk bounded, strategies are formulated in terms of positions (holdings), whereas changes in price are caused by orders, which are changes in positions. Thus, the price dynamics have second-order, oscillatory terms.[23] Earlier studies also showed that trends are self-reinforcing—that trend strategies tend to induce trends in the market.[27] Some have mistaken this to mean "the more the merrier"—that the profits of trend strategies are enhanced by other identical trend strategies. A more careful analysis disproves this. While trend strategies indeed create profit opportunities, these opportunities are for *other* trend strategies, not for the *same* trend strategy.

A study of value-investing strategies also shows some interesting results.[23] Not surprisingly, most sensible value strategies induce negative autocorrelations in the price. Some

value strategies cause prices and perceived values to track each other. But surprisingly, many sensible value strategies do not have this property. Another interesting set of questions concerns the case where the perceived values are heterogeneous (that is, people have different opinions about what something is worth). If all the strategies are linear, the market behaves just as though there were a single agent whose perceived value is the mean of the all the diverse values. If the strategies are nonlinear, however, the diversity of views results in *excess volatility*.[28]

All of the models I've discussed show certain generic phenomena, such as fat tails and clustered volatility, and preliminary results suggest that it might be possible to provide a quantitative explanation for some of the statistical properties of prices. For example, simulations by Thomas Lux and Michele Marchesi[21] (an economist and a physicist) use trend-following and value-investing strategies. They let agents switch from one group to the other. They observe power-law scaling in the tails of the log-returns, with a tail exponent $\alpha \approx$ 3, similar to that observed in real data. Other simulations also find power-law scaling in the tails in models that allow diffusion of private information.[26] For all of the models discussed in this sidebar, which allow dynamic interactions between prices and decisions, the problem is not, "How do we get realistic deviations from normality and IID behavior?" but rather, "How do we determine the necessary and sufficient conditions, and how do we identify which factors actually drive such effects in real markets?"

All of these models show variations in the price, reminiscent of boom-bust cycles. One source of these irregular cycles is the interaction between trend and value strategies. We can describe one such scenario roughly as follows: Suppose the market is strongly undervalued. The value investors buy, thereby raising the price. As the price rises, it creates a trend, causing trend followers to buy, raising the price even further. As the price becomes overvalued, the value investors sell, the trend is damped, and the trend followers eventually sell, and so on. In practice, there are many other effects and the resulting oscillations are highly irregular. See Figure B for an example illustrating the qualitative similarity of the resulting oscillations to those seen in real data. This example suggests that it would be interesting to try to develop more quantitative models of this type to see whether they are useful for prediction.

An economist would criticize the results in the studies I've cited for several reasons. A minor point concerns questions of whether the price-formation process some of these models use is sufficiently realistic. Use of an entirely ad hoc price-formation rule might cause inefficiencies or spurious dynamical effects. My results elsewhere have answered this criticism in part.[23] Perhaps more persuasively, all of these dynamic trading models have qualitative features such as clustered volatility and fat tails in common, even though the strategies and in some cases the price formation rules are quite different. So far, no careful

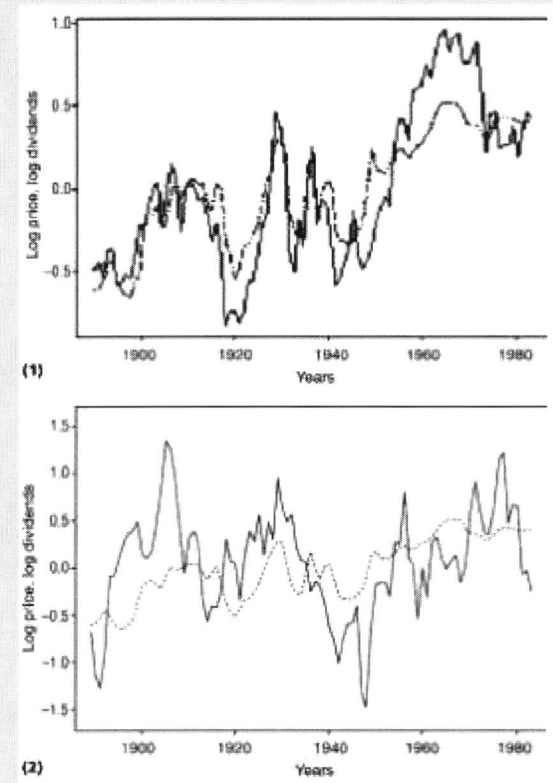

(1)

(2)

Figure B. A comparison of the fluctuations in price and value of US stocks to an agent-based simulation:[23] (a) the logarithm of the S&P index (solid), adjusted for inflation, compared to the logarithm of the mean dividend (dashed), which can be used as a crude measure of perceived value; (b) an agent-based simulation, using the same perceived value. The agents include a mixture of value and trend strategies. The relative population of the two groups is adjusted so that the net autocorrelation of the returns is zero, and the total population is adjusted to roughly match volatility. Otherwise there has been no attempt to adjust parameters or match initial states. The point is purely qualitative: For both the real data and the simulation, the price and the perceived value undergo large oscillations around each other, as the market becomes alternately underpriced and overpriced.

studies have compared different methods of price formation or determined which market properties depend on the method of price formation. Perhaps the main contribution of physicists here has been the use of really simple methods for price formation, within which the dynamics are obvious and simple examples are easily solved analytically.

As a stronger criticism, many of these models contain only limited mechanisms for individual agents to learn, or perhaps more important, selection mechanisms that allow the agent population as a whole to learn. With appropriate selection mechanisms under standard dogma, the market should become efficient and the price should be random (or at least random enough that it is impossible for any agent to make profits).

Shareen Joshi and I have partially addressed this criticism.[24] We use a simple price-formation rule and employ the same representation of strategies discussed earlier for the minority game. For $s > 1$, the sequence of prices is aperiodic. We also add the ability for agents to reinvest their profits and accumu-

late capital, which provides a mechanism driving the market toward efficiency. Starting from an arbitrary initial state, the agents with profitable strategies accumulate capital. As this happens, their market impact increases, driving their profits down. The system approaches an attractor that in some respects resembles a classic economic equilibrium. Prices fluctuate irregularly.

Although asymptotically the capital of each agent ceases to increase, fluctuating around a mean value, before this state is reached agents with superior strategies accumulate capital. Unlike a classic equilibrium, the fluctuations are not driven by external information—the fluctuations are generated completely internally. Furthermore, the efficiency is only partial: for a reasonably large value of the memory, the entropy of the prices never approaches its maximum value. There are always patterns remaining in prices, representing profit-making opportunities for new strategies.

This study of dynamic agent-based trading models is still in its infancy, and many interesting problems remain to be addressed. To make these models more convincing. more work is needed to make them more realistic and better grounded in economic theory.

References

1. J.D. Farmer and A.W. Lo, "Frontiers of Finance: Evolution and Efficient Markets," *Proc. Nat'l Academy of Science,* Vol. 96, NAS, Washington, D.C., 1999, pp. 9991–9992.

The growing awareness of fat tails is changing the way people characterize risk. Ten years ago, sophisticated quantitative trading firms characterized risk in terms of standard deviations. Increasingly, this is changing to Value at Risk (VaR), the size of the loss that would be experienced with an unfavorable move of a given probability.[3] The probability level chosen is generally rather small— for example, 1%, where the normal begins to be a poor approximation. With a good estimate of the probability distribution of the returns on all the assets, we can use Monte Carlo methods to make a VaR estimate. This can be time-consuming, however. Jean-Phillipe Bouchaud and Marc Potters have recently offered an alternative.[29]

This method uses the optimal fluctuation method from physics to simplify VaR calculations by taking advantage of the fat tails. They expand the VaR in a Taylor series in terms of the derivatives of the value of a portfolio with respect to factors (such as principal values) and show that when the tails decay as a power law, higher derivatives can be neglected and a few factors usually dominate. This simplifies the VaR calculation, but more importantly, gives a better understanding of what risks depend on and how different risk factors interact.

Dealing with fat tails properly can also be important for constructing portfolios. The classic Markowitz approach is to maximize returns subject to a constraint on the variance of the portfolio. Although portfolio theory is often cited as one of the great achievements of modern finance theory, mean-variance portfolios tend to perform poorly in practice. Even if we assume that the underlying assets have a normal distribution, the portfolio weights and portfolio performance are so sensitive to estimation errors that the amount of data required to get good estimates can be prohibitive. This problem is much worse in the presence of fat tails.

Didier Sornette, Propsero Simonetti, and Jorgen Anderson recently introduced a new approach to portfolio formation that explicitly takes fat tails into account.[30] They make a change of variables into normally distributed coordinates using a simple numerical procedure and use the correlation matrix in these coordinates to form the portfolio. The resulting procedure is stabler and better conditioned than the usual mean-variance approach. They show that minimizing variance often increases large risks, as measured for example by VaR. With fat tails, an adequate prediction of the risks relies much more on a correct description of the tail structure than on the correlations between the assets.

The implications of fat tails are important for option pricing. An option is a financial instrument that gives the holder the option to buy or sell at a given price (the *strike price*) at a later time (the *expiration date*). The value of an option depends on the strike price and expiration date, as well as on the underlying asset's statistical properties. The standard method of pricing options using the Black-Scholes formula assumes that the log-returns of the underlying asset are normally distributed. Under the Black-Scholes formula, we can compute the price of the option for a given volatility, or alternatively, the formula can be inverted to compute the implied volatility based on the option price.

According to the Black-Scholes formula, the

2. T.J. Sargent, *Bounded Rationality in Economics*, Clarendon Press, Oxford, UK, 1993.

3. W.F.M. deBondt and R.H. Thaler, "Financial Decision Making in Markers and Firms: A Behavioral Perspective," *Handbooks in Operations Research and Management Science*, Vol. 9, Elsevier Science, New York, 1995.

4. R. Shiller, "Human Behavior and the Efficiency of the Financial System," *Handbooks in Macroeconomics, Vol. 2*, Elsevier Science, New York, 1999.

5. B. LeBaron, "Agent-Based Computational Finance: Suggested Readings and Early Research," to appear in *J. Economic Dynamics and Control*, 1999.

6. J.W. Weibull, *Evolutionary Game Theory*, MIT Press, Cambridge, Mass., 1996.

7. W.B. Arthur et al., "Asset Pricing under Endogenous Expectations in an Artificial Stock Market," *The Economy as an Evolving, Complex System II*, Addison-Wesley, Reading, Mass., 1997.

8. B. LeBaron, W.B. Arthur, and R. Palmer, "Time Series Properties of an Artificial Stock Market," *J. Economic Dynamics and Control*, Vol. 23, 1999, pp. 1487–1516.

9. W.B. Arthur, "Inductive Reasoning and Bounded Rationality," *Am. Economic Assoc. Papers and Proc.*, Vol. 84, 1994, 406–411.

10. W.B. Arthur, "Complexity and the Economy," *Science*, Vol. 238, 1999, pp. 107–109.

11. D. Challet and Y.-C. Zhang, "Emergence of Cooperation and Organization in an Evolutionary Game," *Physica A*, Vol. 246, 1997, p. 407.

12. R. Savit, R. Manuca, and R. Riolo, "Adaptive Competition, Market Efficiency, Phase Transitions, and Spin-Glasses," *Physical Review Letters*, Vol. 82, 1999, p. 2203.

13. N.F. Johnson, M. Hart, and P.M. Hui, "Crowd Effects and Volatility in a Competitive Market," 1998; http://xxx.lanl.gov/cond-mat/ 9811227.

14. D. Challet , M. Marsili, and R. Zecchina, "Theory of Minority Games," 1999; preprint http://xxx.lanl.gov/cond-mat/99014392.

15. A. Cavagna et al., "A Thermal Model for Adaptive Competition in a Market," 1999;

implied volatility should be independent of the strike price. In practice, however, the implied volatility depends strongly on the strike price. For many assets, such as stocks, options with strike prices that are in the money (near the current price) have lower implied volatilities than those with strike prices that are out of the money. The implied volatility plotted against the strike price looks like a noisy parabola called the *smile*. The smile makes it clear that real option prices deviate from the Black-Scholes formula.

The Black-Scholes pricing theory has two remarkable features:

- the hedging strategies eliminate risk entirely, and
- the option price does not depend on the average return of the underlying asset.

There are very special properties that are only true under the assumption of normality. With a more realistic distribution for the underlying returns, risk in option trading cannot be eliminated and the correct option price depends on the full distribution of the underlying asset, including its mean. Physicists have played a leading role in developing practical and simple risk-return methods for pricing options in a more general context that takes into account deviations from normality, as well as transaction costs.[31,32] These are based on the principle that the proper option price minimizes (but does not eliminate) risk. In fact, in practice the residual risk is rather large, certainly much larger than the zero risk predicted by the Black-Scholes procedure. This results in good predictions of the

smile. The "implied kurtosis" from such procedures also agrees reasonably well with the historical kurtosis. Furthermore, this procedure does a good job of predicting the dependence of the option price on the mean return, which is important to many practitioners, who might have views about the mean return. Science and Finance, a company consisting largely of physicists, has developed software employing these principles, which a major bank known for their expertise in pricing options is using.

Another interesting application in a somewhat different direction concerns the computation of correlation matrices. Correlation matrices are important for many reasons. Correlations are generally very important for hedging risks, for example, to optimize a portfolio using the conventional Markowitz approach. The correlation matrix for N assets has $(N(N-1))/2$ independent values. Thus the computation of a correlation matrix is poorly determined for any large value of N unless the effective length T of the data sets is enormous. For example, to estimate the daily correlations of the stocks in the S&P index, just to have the number of data points equal the number of free parameters would require about 500 years of stationary data. The S&P index has not existed that long, the composition of companies is constantly changing, and the nature of companies changes, so that the relevance of price history in the distant past is questionable. Five to 10 years is typically the largest sensible value of T for most practical applications. Estimation errors are a big problem.

To understand the structure of correlation matrices in such a highly random setting, physicists have recently applied the theory of random ma-

http://xxx.lanl.gov/cond-mat/9903415.

16. A. Rieck, "Evolutionary Simulation of Asset Trading Strategies," *Many-Agent Simulation and Artificial Life*, E. Hillebrand and J. Stender, eds., IOS Press, Amsterdam, 1994, pp. 112–136,

17. M. Levy, N. Persky, and S. Solomon, "The Complex Dynamics of a Simple Stock Market Model," *Int'l J. High Speed Computing*, Vol. 8, 1996, p. 93.

18. G. Caldarelli, M. Marsili, and Y.C. Zhang, "A Prototype Model of Stock Exchange," *Europhysics Letters*, Vol. 40, 1997, p. 479.

19. M. Youssefmir, B.A. Huberman, and T. Hogg, "Bubbles and Market Crashes," *Computational Economics*, Vol. 12, 1998, pp. 97–114.

20. P. Bak, M. Paczuski, and M. Shubik, "Price

Variations in a Stock Market with Many Agents," *Physica A*, Vol. 246, 1997, pp. 430–453.

21. T. Lux and M. Marchesi, "Scaling and Criticality in a Stochastic Multiagent Model of Financial Market," *Nature*, Vol. 397, 1999, pp. 498–500.

22. J.-P. Bouchaud and R. Cont, "A Langevin Approach to Stock Market Fluctuations and Crashes," *European Physics J. B*, Vol. 6, 1998, pp. 543–550.

23. J.D. Farmer, *Market Force, Ecology, and Evolution*, Santa Fe Inst. Working Paper 98-12-117, SFI, Santa Fe, N.M., 1998; http://xxx.lanl.gov/adapt-org 9812005.

24. J.D. Farmer and S. Joshi, *Evolution and*

Efficiency in a Simple Technical Trading Model, SFI Working Paper 99-10-071, Santa Fe Inst., Santa Fe, NM, 1999.

25. D. Stauffer and D. Sornette, "Self-Organized Percolation Model for Stock Market Fluctuations," 1999; http://xxx.lanl.gov/cond-mat/9906434.

26. G. Iori, "A Microsimulation of Traders Activity in the Stock Market: The Role of Heterogeneity, Agents' Interactions, and Trade Frictions," 1999; http://xxx.lanl.gov/adp-org/0005005.

27. J.B. Delong et al., "Positive Feedback and Destabilizing Rational Speculation," *J. Finance*, Vol. 45, 1990, pp. 379–395.

28. R. Shiller, *Market Volatility*, MIT Press, Cambridge, Mass., 1989.

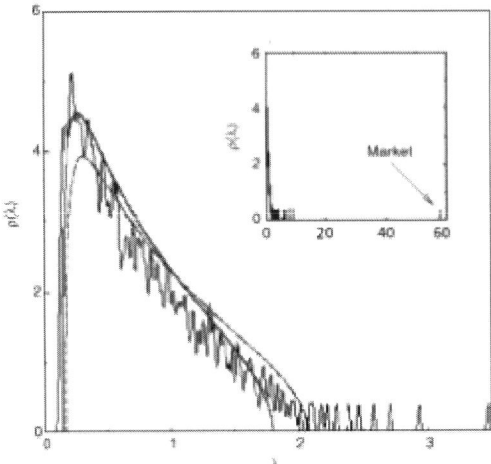

Figure 3. Smoothed density of the eigenvalues λ of an empirical correlation matrix for the returns of 406 companies in the S&P index, for the period 1991–1996.[33] For comparison, this is plotted against the theoretical density of eigenvalues if the matrix is completely random except for its largest eigenvalue (dotted line). A better fit is obtained by fitting parameters, as shown in the solid line. The inset shows the same thing when the largest eigenvalue, which corresponds to the overall market movement, is included.

trices, extensively developed in nuclear physics and elsewhere.[33,34] The eigenvalues and eigenvectors of random matrices approach a well-defined functional form in the limit $N \to \infty$. It is then possible to compare the distribution of empirically determined eigenvalues to the distribution that would be expected if the data were completely random, as shown in Figure 3. For the correlation matrix of 406 companies in the S&P index, in a computation based on daily data from 1991 to 1996, only seven out of 406 eigenvalues are clearly significant with respect to a random null hypothesis. This suggests that we can improve estimates by setting the insignificant eigenvalues to zero, mimicking a common noise-reduction method used in signal processing.

I have omitted quite a lot from this short review. Some of this is good work that is either out of the few main themes developed here or that is too complicated to explain with a small amount of space. Some is work that is either of poor quality or simply crazy, as is typical of new fields. It also reflects a difference between the intellectual cultures of physics and economics. Physics tends to be less restrictive about publication. In physics, publications appear more rapidly and peer review is typically not as strict. There is more emphasis on creativity and less on rigor. This is perhaps one of the luxuries of natural science, where theory is easily tested against data. Since their inception, it seems that mystics, cabalists, and alchemists have been attracted to the financial markets, and there

are many such people who, knowing some mathematics, will always hover around any group that will pay them the courtesy of listening. In any case, a field should be judged by its best work, rather than its worst work.

At the Dublin conference, I was initially disturbed that almost all the speakers were physicists. This was apparently intentional. The conference's organizers felt that during the formative stages it is important not be too critical. Let new ideas grow and see where they lead; thinning can take place later. In the early stages, too much harsh criticism from economists might be counterproductive. Given the conservatism of many economists, there is some good sense to this. But the time is rapidly approaching when physicists who want to do serious work in finance need to interact more closely with economists. There were many bright people in Dublin and many good ideas. There was also sometimes a lack of grounding. Many of the physicists knew very few empirical facts about markets and were largely ignorant of the literature in economics and finance. Some of the work there focused on problems that might be fun from a mathematical point of view, but are not very relevant to understanding financial markets.

There are many fresh ideas in the work of physicists that have been missing or underrepresented in economics. These will lead to new and interesting work, and I expect rapid progress in the next few years. This will come as physicists do the hard work to master the domain knowledge. Physicists like me need to fully understand what has already been done by economists and stop reinventing the wheel. There have already been several good collaborations between physicists and economists, and hopefully there will be many more. While there is a hard core of conservative economists who will never accept these new ideas, they will eventually die. The beauty of the scientific method is that ultimately it is always possible for new ideas to gain acceptance if they are right. Prediction of empirical data based on elegant, concise scientific theories will ultimately triumph over dogma and myopia. There is no shortage of empirical data to test theories in finance and economics. The challenge for physicists is to understand the real problems, and produce theories that fit the data. A good start has been made, but the real challenges and adventures lie ahead. ⬛

Acknowledgement

I would like to thank Erik Aurell, Jean-Philippe Bouchaud, Michel Dacorogna, Blake LeBaron, David Sherrington, Didier Sornette, Francois Schmitt, and Eugene Stanley for valuable comments, and Andrew Lo for commissioning this article.

References

1. P.W. Anderson, J.K. Arrow, and D. Pines, eds., *The Economy as an Evolving Complex System*, Addison-Wesley, Redwood City, Calif., 1988.

2. R.N. Mantegna and H.E. Stanley, *Introduction to Econophysics: Correlations and Complexity in Finance*, Cambridge Univ. Press, Cambridge, UK, 1999.

3. J.-P. Bouchaud and M. Potters, *Theory of Financial Risk: From Statistical Physics to Risk Management*, Cambridge Univ. Press, Cambridge, UK, http://www.science-finance.fr.

4. B.B. Mandelbrot, "The Variation of Certain Speculative Prices," *J. Business*, Vol. 36, 1963, pp. 394–419.

5. E.F. Fama, "The Behavior of Stock Market Prices," *J. Business*, Vol. 38, 1965, pp. 34–105.

6. V. Akgiray, G.G. Booth, and O. Loistl, "Stable Laws Are Inappropriate for Describing German Stock Returns," *Allegemeines Statistisches Archiv.*, Vol. 73, 1989, pp. 115–121.

7. K.G. Koedijk, M.M.A. Schafgans, and C.G. De Vries, "The Tail Index of Exchange Rate Returns," *J. Int'l Economics*, Vol. 29, 1990, pp. 93–108.

8. T. Lux, "The Stable Paretian Hypothesis and the Frequency of Large Returns: An Examination of Major German Stocks," *Applied Financial Economics*, Vol. 6, 1996, pp. 463–475.

9. U.A. Müller, M.M. Dacorogna, and O.V. Pictet, "Heavy Tails in High-Frequency Financial Data," *A Practical Guide to Heavy Tails*, R.J. Adler, R.E. Feldman, and M.S. Taqqu, eds., Birkhäuser, Boston, 1998, pp. 382–311.

10. R.N. Mantegna and H.E. Stanley, "Scaling Behavior in the Dynamics of an Economic Index," *Nature*, Vol. 376, 1995, pp. 46–49.

11. P. Gopikrishnan et al., "Scaling of the Distribution of Fluctuations of Financial Market Indices," 1999; http://xxx.lanl.gov/cond-mat/ 9905305.

12. V. Plerou et al., "Scaling of the Distribution of Price Fluctuations of Individual Companies," 1999; http://xxx.lanl.gov/cond-mat/ 9907161.

13. J. Eatwell, M. Milgate, and P. Newman, *The New Palgrave: A Dictionary of Economics 3*, MacMillan Press, London, 1991.

14. O. Malcai, O. Biham, and S. Solomon, "Power-Law Distributions and Levy-Stable Intermittent Fluctuations in Stochastic Systems of Many Autocatalytic Elements," *Physical Rev. E*, Vol. 60, No. 2, 1998, pp. 1299–1303.

15. J. Theiler et al., "Testing for Nonlinearity in Time Series: The Method of Surrogate Data," *Physica D*, Vol. 58, 1992, pp. 77–94.

16. J. Scheinkman and B. LeBaron, "Nonlinear Dynamics and Stock Returns," *J. Business*, Vol. 62, 1989, pp. 311–338.

17. W. Feller, *An Introduction to Probability Theory and Its Applications*, Vol. 2, Wiley & Sons, New York, 1971.

18. Y. Lee et al., "Universal Features in the Growing Dynamics of Complex Organizations," *Physical Rev. Letters*, Vol. 81, No. 15, 1998, pp. 3275–3278.

19. R.F. Engle, "Autoregressive Conditional Heteroskedasticity with Estimations of the Variance of UK Inflation," *Econometrica*, Vol. 50, 1982, pp. 987–1002.

20. J.Y. Campbell, A.W. Lo, and A.C. MacKinlay, *The Econometrics of Financial Markets*, Princeton Univ. Press, Princeton, N.J., 1997.

21. S. Ghashghaie et al., "Turbulent Cascades in Foreign Exchange Markets," *Nature*, Vol. 381 1996, pp. 767–770.

22. F. Schmitt, D. Schertzer, and S. Lovejoy, "Multifractal Analysis of Foreign Exchange Data," *Applied Stochastic Models and Data Analysis*, Vol. 15, 1999, pp. 29–53.

23. A. Arneodo, J.-F. Muzy, and D. Sornette, "'Direct' Causal Cascade in the Stock Market," *European Physical J. B*, Vol. 2, 1998, pp. 277–282.

24. J.-P. Bouchaud, M. Potters, and M. Meyer, "Apparent Multifractality in Financial Time Series," 1999; http://xxx.lanl.gov/ cond-mat/ 9906347.

25. U.A. Müller et al., "Statistical Study of Foreign Exchange Rates, Empirical Evidence of a Price Scaling Law, and Intraday Analysis," *J. Banking and Finance*, Vol. 14, 1990, pp. 1189–1208

26. M.M. Dacaragona et al., "A Geographical Model for the Daily and Weekly Seasonal Volatility in the Foreign Exchange Market," *J. Int'l Money and Finance*, Vol. 12, 1993, pp. 413–428.

27. Z. Ding, C.W.J. Granger, and R.F. Engle, "A Long Memory Property of Stock Returns and a New Model," *J. Empirical Finance*, Vol. 1, 1993, p. 83.

28. P. Embrechts, C. Kluppelberg, and T. Mikosch, *Modelling Extremal Events*, Springer-Verlag, Berlin, 1997.

29. J.-P. Bouchaud and M. Potters, "Worst Fluctuation Method for Fat Value-at-Risk Estimates," 1999; http://xxx.lanl.gov/ cond-mat/ 9909245.

30. D. Sornette, P. Simonetti, and J.V. Andersen, "Field Theory for Portfolio Optimization: "Fat Tails" and Nonlinear Correlations," 1999; http://xxx.lanl.gov/cond-mat/9903203.

31. J.-P. Bouchaud and D. Sornette, "The Black-Scholes Option Pricing Problem in Mathematical Finance: Generalization and Extensions for a Large Class of Stochastic Processes," *J. Physics*, Vol. 4, 1994, pp. 863–881.

32. J.-P. Bouchaud, G. Iori, and D. Sornette, "Real-World Options: Smile and Residual Risk," *Risk 9*, Mar. 1996, pp. 61–65.

33. L. Laloux et al., "Noise Dressing of Financial Correlation Matrices," 1998; http://xxx.lanl.gov/cond-mat/9810255.

34. V. Plerou et al., "Universal and Nonuniversal Properties of Cross-Correlations in Financial Time Series," 1999: http://xxx. lanl.gov/cond-mat/9902283.

J. Doyne Farmer is the McKinsey Professor at the Santa Fe Institute. In 1991, together with Norman Packard, he founded Prediction Company, a firm whose business is automatic trading of financial instruments using time series-based directional forecasting methods. He worked in the Theoretical Division and at the Center for Nonlinear Studies at Los Alamos National Laboratories, where he was Oppenheimer Fellow and founder of the Complex Systems Group. He received a BS from Stanford University and a PhD from the University of California at Santa Cruz, both in physics. Contact him at the Santa Fe Inst., 1399 Hyde Park Rd., Santa Fe, NM 87501.

THE EUROPEAN
PHYSICAL JOURNAL B
EDP Sciences
© Società Italiana di Fisica
Springer-Verlag 2001

From market games to real-world markets

P. Jefferies[1,a], M.L. Hart[1], P.M. Hui[2], and N.F. Johnson[1]

[1] Department of Physics, Oxford University, Parks Rd, Oxford, OX13PU, UK
[2] Physics Department, Chinese University of Hong Kong, Shatin, Hong Kong, PR China

Received 30 August 2000

Abstract. This paper uses the development of multi-agent market models to present a unified approach to the joint questions of how financial market movements may be simulated, predicted, and hedged against. We first present the results of agent-based market simulations in which traders equipped with simple buy/sell strategies and limited information compete in speculatory trading. We examine the effect of different market clearing mechanisms and show that implementation of a simple Walrasian auction leads to unstable market dynamics. We then show that a more realistic out-of-equilibrium clearing process leads to dynamics that closely resemble real financial movements, with fat-tailed price increments, clustered volatility and high volume autocorrelation. We then show that replacing the 'synthetic' price history used by these simulations with data taken from real financial time-series leads to the remarkable result that the agents can collectively learn to identify moments in the market where profit is attainable. Hence on real financial data, the system as a whole can perform better than random. We then employ the formalism of Bouchaud in conjunction with agent based models to show that in general risk cannot be eliminated from trading with these models. We also show that, in the presence of transaction costs, the risk of option writing is greatly increased. This risk, and the costs, can however be reduced through the use of a delta-hedging strategy with modified, time-dependent volatility structure.

PACS. 01.30.Cc Conference proceedings – 05.45.Tp Time series analysis – 05.65.+b Self-organized systems

1 Introduction

Agent-based models of complex adaptive systems are attracting significant interest across a broad range of disciplines [1]. An important application receiving much attention within the physics community, is the study of fluctuations in financial time-series [2]. Currently many different agent-based models exist in the 'econophysics' literature, each with its own set of implicit assumptions and interesting properties [3–6]. In general these models exhibit some of the statistical properties that are reminiscent of those observed in real-world financial markets: fat tailed distributions of returns, clustered volatility and so on. These models, despite their differences draw on several of the same key ideas; feedback, frustration, adaptability and evolution.

The Minority Game (MG) introduced by Challet and Zhang [7] offers possibly the simplest paradigm for a system containing these key features. Unlike the sophisticated model of Lux [3] there is no external noise process simulating information arrival. Nor is there any element of agents sharing local information as in the model of Cont and Bouchaud [4]. The MG simply comprises of an odd number of agents N choosing repeatedly between the options of buying (1) and selling (0) a quantity of a risky

asset. The resource level of this asset is finite and therefore the agents will compete to buy low and sell high. This gives the game its 'minority' nature; an excess of buyers will force the price of the asset up, consequently the minority of agents who have placed sell orders receive a good price at the penalty of the majority who end up buying at an over-inflated price. The MG agents act with inductive reasoning, using strategies that map the series of recent (binary) asset price fluctuations to an investment decision for the next time-step. In an attempt to learn from their past mistakes the agents constantly update the 'score' of their strategies and use only the most successful one to make their prediction.

The basic assumptions of this system are minimal but the resultant dynamics show a richness and diversity that has been the focus of much recent study . However, the MG as a realistic market model has many shortcomings:

- All agents trade at each time-step
- All agents trade equal quantities
- The system resource level is fixed
- Agent diversity is typically limited.

Many of these as well as other interesting extensions (such as agents having the ability to learn of their own market impact [5]) have been studied separately and are discussed in [2]. This paper aims to jointly develop many of these

[a] e-mail: p.jefferies@physics.ox.ac.uk

extensions to the basic MG in an attempt to build a minimal and yet realistic market model.

The development and study of market models from a physicist's standpoint is motivated by the desire to learn what key interactions are responsible for phenomena observed in the real-world system, the financial marketplace. However, the scope for using such market models is not simply limited to qualitative phenomenological studies. The models may be extended or manipulated to explore quantitatively the emergence of empirical scaling laws. Alternatively, the approach to 'critical' self-organized, or stable states may be examined [13]. These are just a few of the uses which could be categorized as 'theoretical' study. What then can these models be used for on a more 'practical' or perhaps commercial level?

Recently we have been working on the possibility of using these market models in a similar way to the way in which a meteorologist may use a model of atmospheric dynamics; *i.e.* condition the models with observed data and let them run into the future to extract probabilistic forecasts. These forecasts may then be used for not only speculative gain but also for more insightful risk management and portfolio optimization. Section 2 of this text will expand on the idea of using the MG as a market model, detailing the extensions needed, Section 3 will then explore two different market-making mechanisms, assessing the resultant dynamics, Section 4 will detail how these models may be used for predictive purposes and Section 5 will focus on risk and portfolio optimization.

2 The MG as a market model

2.1 The basic MG

As mentioned in the previous section, the MG formulation captures some of the behavioral phenomena that are thought to be of importance in financial markets; those of competition, frustration, adaptability and evolution. It is also a 'minimal' system of only few parameters:

N = Number of agents

m_i = 'Memory' of agent i

s_i = Number of strategies held by agent i.

The *memory* of an agent is the number of bits of the most recent past global history that are used by a strategy in order to form a prediction. The agents are assigned their s_i strategies at the start of the game and are not allowed to replace them at any point. Each agent uses the historically most successful of her strategies to form a prediction, the predictions of all agents are then pooled and the global history is updated with the prediction of the minority group.

A single *strategy* maps each of the 2^m possible 'histories' to a prediction. Thus there are 2^{2^m} different possible binary strategies. However, many of the strategies in this space are largely similar to one another (*i.e.* are separated by a small Hamming distance). It has been

shown [14] that the principle features of the MG are reproduced in a smaller *Reduced Strategy Space* of 2^{m+1} strategies wherein any two strategies are separated by a Hamming distance of either 2^m or 2^{m-1} (*i.e.* are *anti-correlated* or *un-correlated*). If the number of strategies in play *i.e.* Ns is greater than 2^{m+1} then the game is said to be in the *crowded'* phase, in contrast $Ns \ll 2^{m+1}$ represents the *dilute* phase.

The properties of the crowded and dilute phases of the game are quite different and could be thought of as representing different regimes of a market. In the crowded phase there will at any one time be a large number of agents who are using the same (best) strategy and so will flood into the market as large groups, producing large swings in supply and demand and a consequently high volatility. If the memory of the agents is larger such as to render $Ns \sim 2^{m+1}$ then the groups of agents using the same (best) strategy (*crowds*) will be smaller. There will also be groups of agents who are forced to use the anti-correlated (worst) strategy, these can be thought of as *anti-crowds* as they cancel the market action of the *crowds*. This cancellation effect causes a reduction in the market volatility. In the dilute phase it is very unlikely that any agents will hold the same strategies and so the market behaves more randomly and can be modelled well as a group of independent coin-tossers. A theory based on these crowding effects reproduces quantitative results for the market volatility in the basic and so called 'thermal' MG across the full range of parameters N, m, s. For more details of this the reader is referred to [12,15]. This 'Crowd, Anticrowd Theory' may also be put to use in the formulation of an entirely analytical set of dynamical mapping equations that reproduce the MG [16]. These equations can be analyzed in several interesting limiting cases to unveil the dynamics underlying microscopic behavior in different regimes of the game. They may also be used in the analysis of approaches to unstable behavior in these types of games (and possibly the real market itself). Our preliminary studies have identified that there can be at least two different 'types' of build up to a large movement (or 'crash'). Further work is currently underway to investigate the various 'types' of crash that can occur

2.2 The grand-canonical MG

In the basic MG agents must either buy or sell at every time-step. In a real market however, traders are likely to wait on the sidelines until they are reasonably confident that they are able to make a profit with their next trade. They will observe the market passively, mentally updating their various strategies, until their confidence overcomes some threshold value – then they will jump in and make a trade. We now demonstrate an extension to the basic MG which attempts to incorporate this general behavioral pattern.

The primitive binary agents of the basic MG keep a tally of the *virtual* score $r_{S,i}$ of each of their s_i strategies, +1 for a correct prediction and −1 for an incorrect prediction and *virtual* in the sense that the strategy is scored

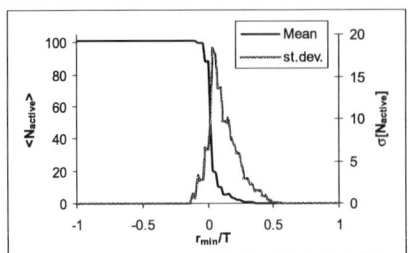

Fig. 1. Mean and standard deviation in the number of active agents N_{active} (game parameters $N = 101$, $m = 2$, $s = 2$, $T = 50$).

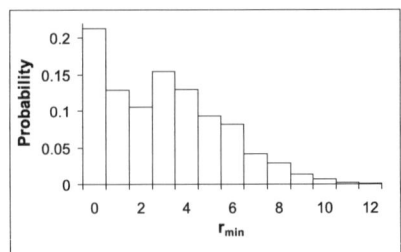

Fig. 2. Distribution of threshold values r_{min} after 6000 time-steps (game parameters $N = 151$, $m = 3$, $s = 2$, $T = 50$, $\lambda = 0.07$).

whether it is played or not. They may also keep a tally of their own personal prediction success score r_i. It is reasonable that each agent i has a finite time horizon T_i over which these success scores are monitored; this is equivalent to a 'sunken losses' approach. We now make the simplest possible generalization which is to introduce a threshold value r_{min} in either r or r_S below which an agent would choose to not trade. In this case, the agent continues to update her strategy scores r_S but now adds a 0 to her personal score tally r. With this extension, the number of agents actively trading at each time-step N_{active} will vary throughout the game. This feature is reminiscent of the Grand-Canonical-Ensemble in statistical mechanics.

If an agent's threshold to play lies at the lower end of the range $-T \leq r_{min} \leq T$ then we would expect the agent to play a large proportion of the time as her best strategy will have invariably scored higher than this threshold. Conversely, for high r_{min}, the agent will scarcely play at all. We would thus expect to see a transition occur between these two regimes at intermediate values of the threshold. Figure 1 shows the time-averaged number of active agents $\langle N_{active} \rangle$ and the standard deviation of this quantity as a function of r_{min} for a uniform population of $N = 101$ $m = 2$, $s = 2$ agents who record scores over $T = 50$ time-steps. Here r_{min}, the threshold to play, is based on the agent's strategy score $r_{S,i}$ such that an agent only plays if $\max{[\{r_{S,i}\}]} > r_{min}$. A similar transition effect is also seen if the threshold is based on prediction success score r_i.

The behavior of $\langle N_{active} \rangle$ can be reproduced to a coarse approximation by assuming that the strategy scores $r_{S,i}$ undergo independent binomial random walks:

$$r_S \sim 2\mathrm{Bin}\left[T, \frac{1}{2}\right] - T.$$

This gives:

$$\langle N_{active} \rangle \approx N\left(1 - P\left[r_S < r_{min}\right]^s\right)$$
$$\sigma^2\left[N_{active}\right] \approx N\left(1 - P\left[r_S < r_{min}\right]^s\right)P\left[r_S < r_{min}\right]^s.$$

This approximation captures the essence of the transition mentioned in the paragraph above. However, the behavior

of r_S is in reality far from that of a random walk. In the crowded regime r_S is strongly mean-reverting and in the dilute regime of the game it has a strong drift component, also the increments in individual strategy scores can be highly correlated. The approximation becomes better for $T \gg 2^m$, where many of these effects become averaged out.

With intermediate values for r_{min} this modified MG produces very interesting dynamics [17], for instance there can be moments of extreme illiquidity followed by a rush to the market causing huge swings in supply and demand. There are also noticeable 'ranging' and 'break-out' periods and other patterns familiar to market traders [18].

We now extend this model to allow r_{min} to be dynamic. Here each agent decides on her own threshold in a manner dependent on her current internal state variables. This allows an enhanced element of evolution within the model and more closely resembles behavioral models of markets wherein levels of confidence are time-dependent. We choose to make r_{min} a function of the agent's personal success rate r_i. Asserting that agents are rational and risk-averse implies that $r_{min} > 0$ and that $\frac{dr_{min,i}}{dr_i} \leq 0$ *i.e.* never play a strategy that has lost more times than won and take fewer risks if losing. Following basic utility theory we therefore arrive at: $r_{min,i} = \max\left[0, -\left(r_i - \lambda.\sigma\left[r_i\right]\right)\right]$ (where $\sigma\left[r_i\right]$ is the player's standard deviation of success and λ is their coefficient of risk-aversion). As agents' success rates vary in time, then so will their threshold values and we see an overall evolution towards a diverse population as shown in Figure 2.

This version of the 'Grand-Canonical' MG forms the basic framework for our development of a market model. The following subsection will outline the further necessary extensions to the model that, when combined, form our 'realistic' market model.

2.3 Agent diversity and wealth

It is a simple extension of the model developed in the text above to include agent heterogeneity in terms of wealth, investment size and investment strategy. As it stands, each trade made by an agent is the exchange of one quanta of a riskless asset for one quanta of a risky one, irrespective of the agent's wealth or the price of the asset. Also, agents always trade as 'value' investors, seeking to buy low and sell high at each time-step. We now generalize this framework to introduce a more realistic heterogeneity between investors.

We first allot each agent i a quantity of each asset, riskless $B_i[0]$ and risky $S_i[0]$. When a trade is made, it is made at the market price of $p[t] \pm \delta[t]$ where $\delta[t]$ corresponds to a spread raised by the marketmaker (the market-making mechanism is the subject of the next section). We now re-assert the assumption that investors are risk-averse and will therefore trade amounts proportional to their absolute wealth. We also assume that the amount they trade will be in proportion to their confidence in the strategy they intend to use. It is helpful at this stage to define a measure of this confidence c_i

$$c_i[t] = \frac{\max[r_{S,i}[t]] - r_{\min}[t]}{T_i}$$

thus $-2 < c_i < 1$ but the agent only plays if $c_i > 0$. Buy operations are then represented by:

$$B_i[t+1] = B_i[t]\left(1 - c_i[t]\frac{p[t+1] + \delta[t+1]}{p[t] + \delta[t]}\right)$$

$$S_i[t+1] = S_i[t] + \frac{c_i[t]\,B_i[t]}{p[t] + \delta[t]}$$

and sell operations by:

$$B_i[t+1] = B_i[t] + c_i[t]\,S_i[t]\,(p[t+1] - \delta[t+1])$$
$$S_i[t+1] = S_i[t](1 - c_i[t]).$$

Wealthy agents make large transactions and thus will have a high market impact (in a system where price movement size is an increasing function of order size *c.f.* Eq. (1)) whereas poor agents effectively form a background 'noise' of small trades. Of course poor agents may grow rich or vice-versa. When agents have lost all their assets, they can no longer trade, this represents the bankruptcy of that agent. This situation happens extremely rarely in these models and so we have not sought to implement a system for the re-generation of new agents. Figure 3 shows the average distribution of agents' wealth as measured by $B[t] + S[t].p[t]$ (*i.e.* the probabilities are averaged over time).

As well as the diversity in agents' trade size, there can also be a diversity in investment strategy. Within the framework presented here, investment strategies can fall into the two broad classes; *value* and *trend*. A *value* investor aims at each time-step to make a profit from buying low and selling high, a *trend* investor on the other hand aims to buy an upward moving asset and sell a downward mover. A population purely of value investors will have a minority-game character, a population of trend investors will create a majority-game of self-fulfilling prophecies. In general, the population of traders will be a combination of these types and thus the character of the market (minority or majority) is unclear. We are currently testing

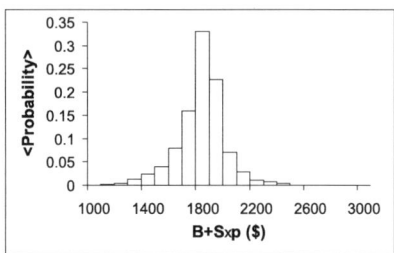

Fig. 3. Time averaged PDF of agent's wealth as measured by $B[t] + S[t]\,p[t]$ (Game parameters $N = 151$, $m = 3$, $s = 2$, $T = 50$, $\lambda = 0.07$). Original allocation of wealth; $B[0] = 1000$ \$, $S[0] = 100$, $p[0] = 10$ \$.

how the proportion of each investor type alters the global dynamics and stability of the market.

3 The market-making mechanism

3.1 Walrasian auction

The simplest type of market-making process is that of a Walrasian auction. This is a popular model in the economics community (and actually the system used in the London Metals Exchange). In a Walrasian auction investors take part in a price setting process by submitting orders to buy or sell the risky asset based on a theoretical price. The level of this theoretical price is changed until the supply and demand for the asset exactly match and the market can be cleared, then the process repeats.

We can use our market model to simulate a simplified version of this process in the following way. First of all we assume that the supply and demand are in equilibrium at each time-step. The resulting equilibrium price for the risky asset then must be equal to the current demand-value of stocks sought divided by the number of risky assets offered. This gives:

$$p[t+1] = \frac{\sum\limits_{i,\text{Buyers}} c_i[t]\,B_i[t]}{\sum\limits_{i,\text{Sellers}} c_i[t]\,S_i[t]}.$$

It is clear then that this process is unstable: if there are no buyers the price falls to zero and if there are no sellers it will rise to infinity! Even though these situations happen rarely in a run of the market model, the resulting dynamics still show an inherent instability and the fluctuations are excessive as well as exhibiting a strong anti-persistence. This situation arises because we are asserting that the buy and sell pressures are in equilibrium at each time-step. Of course this is far from the reality and we must extend the market-making mechanism to accommodate the real out-of-equilibrium process.

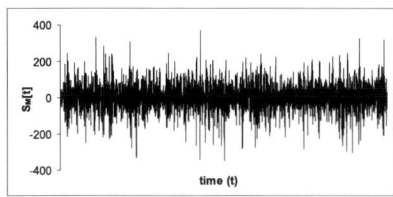

Fig. 4. Market-maker's stock $S_M[t]$ over 6000 turns (total stock in market 15100).

3.2 Non-equilibrium market

If the supply of risky assets does **not** exactly match the demand at each time-step then the market will either not clear, or the market-maker will take a position in the asset himself in order to fill the orders. In reality it is most likely that a combination of these scenarios occurs, the market maker will want to fill as many orders as possible and take the spread but he will not allow himself to incur a large position. There are many ways in which this type of behavior could be modelled, we limit ourselves here to looking at one particular system.

Let us start by implementing the price setting rule of Bouchaud-Cont-Farmer [4,6]:

$$p[t+1] = p[t]\, e^{\frac{\text{Buys}[t] - \text{Sells}[t]}{\text{Liquidity}}} \qquad (1)$$

where: $\begin{matrix}\text{Buys}\\\text{Sells}\end{matrix}[t] = \sum_{i \begin{subarray}{l}\text{Buyers}\\\text{Sellers}\end{subarray}} S_i[t+1] - S_i[t]$, and liquidity

is a constant set by the market-maker. This rule prevents the market-maker being arbitraged but leaves his inventory ($B_M[t]$ and $S_M[t]$) as unbounded. Over many runs of such a market simulation we would expect the market-maker's mean inventory to be zero. What we really require on the other hand is that his mean inventory in a particular run be zero. We therefore propose the following extension to equation (1):

$$p[t+1] = p[t]\, e^{\frac{\text{Buys}[t] - \text{Sells}[t] - S_M[t]}{\text{Liquidity}}}. \qquad (2)$$

This implies that if the market-maker is accruing a net long position in the risky asset, he'll start lowering the price in order to attract buyers into the market and *vice versa*. This mechanism works remarkably well and we find that $S_M[t]$ under this new rule is strongly mean-reverting as shown in Figure 4.

With equation (2) however the market maker can be arbitraged by the agents; the strategy buy, wait, sell or vice-versa will make money as long as enough agents do it at the same time. The agents in these systems learn to exploit this very quickly (an interesting result in itself) and the result is a negative drift to the market-maker's money $B_M[t]$. There are several mechanisms that the market-maker may exploit to overcome this; he can raise a spread or he can reduce the liquidity. We employ the first of

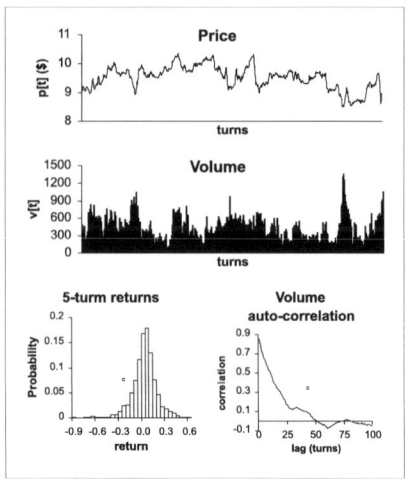

Fig. 5. Price and volume statistics for a single run of the market simulation (parameters $N_{\text{value}} = 101$, $N_{\text{trend}} = 50$, $m = 3$, $s = 2$, $T = 20$, $\lambda = 0.07$).

these mechanisms, updating the spread proportionally to $-\frac{\langle B_M[t]\rangle}{\langle v[t]\rangle}$ where $v[t]$ is the volume of transactions defined as $v[t] = \sum_{i=1}^{N} S_i[t+1] - S_i[t]$. The means $\langle B_M[t]\rangle$ and $\langle v[t]\rangle$ are taken over a time-length T_M which is kept large compared with $\{T_i\}$ such as to average over local extreme behavior such as momentary illiquidity. This mechanism for raising a spread may not be highly efficient but it does maintain the market-maker's mean wealth close to the desired zero point by raising the spread if he starts losing money. The $1/v[t]$ dependence stabilizes this process somewhat by sharing the job of paying for the market-maker's deficit over the current number of market participants.

We now have a complete and arguably 'realistic' model and may begin to investigate its properties. We are at present looking at how different statistical properties of the model-market are dependent on its parameters. We seem to find however that some statistical features are in general present over very large parameter ranges. These are the types of feature that are associated with 'real' markets: High excess kurtosis of returns with weak decay over time, volatility clustering, high volume autocorrelation etc. as shown in Figure 5.

4 Prediction from market-models

The market-models introduced in Section 2 consist of a population of adaptive agents who attempt to predict the future movement of an asset price. Recently, we have been

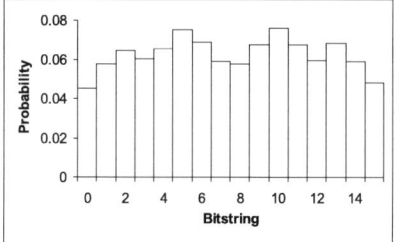

Fig. 6. Occurence probability of 4-bit strings in the price-sign history $h[t]$ generated from 10 years of hourly \$/Yen FX-rate data.

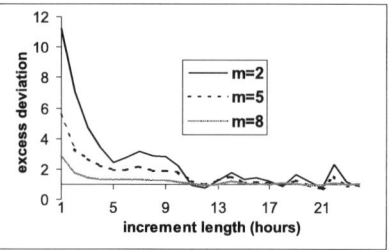

Fig. 7. $\sigma^{\text{real}}_{\text{Bitstring}}/\sigma^{\text{random}}_{\text{Bitstring}}$ as a function of price increment length for $m = 2, 5, 8$ (dataset \$/Yen FX-rate between 1990–99).

investigating the accuracy of these predictions when the synthetic self-generated global history of asset movements is replaced with a real financial time series.

The first step in this process is to generate binary information from the given financial time-series. This can be done in many ways in order to investigate the predictability of different aspects of the movement. We choose here to examine the sign of movements and hence our information history $h[t]$ becomes:

$$h[t] = H[p_{\text{real}}[t] - p_{\text{real}}[t-1]]$$

where $H[x]$ is the Heaviside function. If $p_{\text{real}}[t] = p_{\text{real}}[t-1]$ then we assign $h[t]$ a 0 or 1 randomly. Before we begin to look at how the agent-models perform with this new information set, let us first examine some of its properties. The agents examine chunks of the information set h of length m bits in order to make a prediction. If we look at the occurrence rate of $m+1$ length bit-strings we can therefore infer the success rate of strategies. For example Figure 6 shows the occurrence probability of 4-bit strings; *i.e.* 3 memory bits ($m = 3$) and one prediction bit. The bit-strings are enumerated by their decimal value *e.g.* 0011 → 3. We can infer that the strategy {10101010} (which is the $m = 1$, {10} *i.e.* anti-persistent strategy) will have the highest success rate as 000 is more often followed by a 1, 001 by a 0 etc.

As we decrease the sampling rate on our data-set so as to look at the signs of price increments over longer periods, we find that the most successful strategy becomes less well defined and tends to swap regularly. It is no longer the case that a simple anti-persistent strategy is the best. Also as we increase the memory m and look at longer bit-strings, we find that the 'information content' of the bit-string occurrence histograms gets 'washed away' in the mixing of low m probabilities. This implies that the most dominant physical process is a low m process. Figure 7 shows these two effects by examining the excess standard deviation of the bit-string distributions *i.e.* $\sigma^{\text{real}}_{\text{Bitstring}}/\sigma^{\text{random}}_{\text{Bitstring}}$ where

$$\sigma^{\text{random}}_{\text{Bitstring}} = \frac{\sqrt{L(2^{m+1}-1)}}{2^{m+1}},$$ where L is the length of the data-set.

In the agent simulations, $h[t]$ plays the same role as before, with strategies and agents being scored for predic-

tion success in the same fashion as detailed in Section 2. Of course now the feedback has been removed from the model, it bears more resemblance to a system of genetic algorithms. The key important difference though is the fact that this system of independent agents has a large built in frustration: the agents aren't allowed to replace poorly performing strategies. Although this at first appears to be a handicap, it can in fact be a strength. In systems where there is not necessarily a 'correct' strategy to employ, there is an advantage in having many currently non-optimal strategies in play as this gives greater adaptability. We have compared the prediction success of these types of model with those employing simple Bayesian update of the probability of a given outcome for a given history and found the former to be much more powerful. Figure 8 shows the time-series of the \$/Yen FX-rate between 1990-99, below this is a plot of the cumulative noncompounded profit attained from using the agent model's predictions to trade hourly. The trading strategy employed is simply to put the original investment amount on either the \$ or the Yen side of the market and take it off again at the end of the hour, banking the profit in a zero interest account. This is clearly an unrealistic strategy as transaction costs would be penalizing, however it is used in order to demonstrate simply that the agent-model performs better than random (around 54% prediction success rate)[1]. The two profit lines on Figure 8 represent two different uses of the independent predictions of the agents. The lower line corresponds to the case where the investment is split equally between all agents, the upper line is for the case where the agents' predictions are pooled together with a non-linear function. This demonstrates that the population as a compound entity can perform much better than the sum of its individual parts. This kind of phenomena has been termed 'collective intelligence' in the past.

Arguably the most interesting phenomena of models such as the MG arise from the strong feedback mechanism. In replacing the self-generated $h[t]$ with an external

---

[1] We have run these models with randomly generated information histories $h[t]$ and were able to reject the null hypothesis that the mean prediction success rate with real data was random.

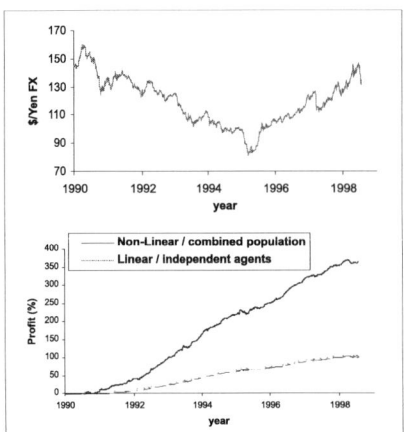

Fig. 8. $/Yen FX-rate 1990–99 (top) and cumulative non-compounded profit from using agent predictions both independently and collectively (bottom).

process we disable that feedback. The system is still however able to function as a weak predictor. It appears that the prediction success rate can be raised by invoking again a feedback within the system. It is probable that this feedback forces a more efficient learning process to take place. These effects are the subject of our current studies.

We have hence demonstrated the success of the agent-based models in direct prediction of the sign of the next price increment. However, we can also implement the models in a different way by 'training' them on historical data of a particular asset movement and then using the artificial market-making process to run the models forward into the future. If this is done with an ensemble of such models, each having a different initial allocation of strategies, we can form a distribution of likely future asset price levels. Typically the resulting distributions are fat tailed and can have considerable skewness quite in contrary to more standard economic models. This information can not only be of use in speculation but also in risk control and portfolio management.

5 Risk management

5.1 Implied future risk from agent-models

The control of risk in financial investment should be of equal importance to the realization of profit. Most current theories of risk control rely on the implicit assumption that future behavior of the market will be like its past behavior. This assumption is continually being brought into question when banks and investors seem to be 'caught out' by events that past distributions seemed to imply

were impossible. There thus may be room here for risk-control models that rely more on possible emergent future behavior than on historic data.

Using agent-based models in the way mentioned at the close of Section 4 gives us distributions for likely future price levels based on what microscopically might happen. This may be just the type of forward-casting model that could be of use here. We must first however develop a framework within which we can use the type of information that these models give us. Much of risk-control concerns itself with the use of derivative instruments, we therefore follow this direction but take pause to note that a similar methodology can be used for analyzing any portfolio of assets.

Several years ago Bouchaud and Sornette developed a framework for examining and controlling the risk inherent in writing derivative contracts [19]. This formalism explicitly deals with future asset movements in a probabilistic, path-dependent fashion *i.e.* does not rely on any random-walk model etc. This makes the formalism ideal for combining with the forward-casting agent-models.

The formalism examines the variation in future wealth ΔW_T from holding a certain portfolio, for example short one euro-call contract of price C_0 maturity T and strike X and long $\phi_t [S_t]$ hedging assets in the underlying which is at price S_t at time t:

$$\Delta W_T = C_0 - \max [S_T - X, 0] + \sum_{t=0}^{T} \phi_t [S_t] (S_{t+1} - S_t). \tag{3}$$

The variance of this wealth process (which is used as a measure of risk) is then found analytically for a general underlying movement. For our models, this can be done in a Monte-Carlo fashion using each member of the model ensemble to generate a ΔW_T. Doing this we could also look at other measures of risk such as VAR etc. This process generates a more insightful measure of risk based on likely future microscopic behavior.

The control of this risk is the next issue. Bouchaud and Sornette's variance of the wealth process can be minimized with respect to the hedging strategy $\phi_t [S_t]$. The full details are given in [20]; the result is a risk-minimizing 'optimal strategy' given by:

$$\phi_t [S_t] = \int_X^{\infty} \frac{(S_T - S_t) \langle \delta S_{S_t, t \to S_T, T} \rangle}{\langle \delta S_t^2 \rangle} P [S_T | S_t] \, dS_T. \tag{4}$$

Using the forward-casting agent-models we obtain $P [S_T | S_t]$ (the probability of the underlying moving from value S_t to S_T) by counting the number of members of the (large) model ensemble that cast paths passing near both these two values (price space S is discretized for this purpose). Similarly $\langle \delta S_{S_t, t \to S_T, T} \rangle$ is found as the mean increment at time t of paths passing near S_t and S_T, $\langle \delta S_t^2 \rangle$ is simply the mean squared increment at time t of all paths. The resulting reduction in risk when using this 'optimal strategy' with historical distributions is well documented [20]; the effects are similar with the agent-models future-cast distributions. The important difference to note is that the risk being minimized is the microscopically derived future risk rather than a measure assuming the continuity of past behavior.

5.2 Transaction costs

We now digress slightly and examine the effect of transaction costs on the risk control process discussed in the previous paragraphs. Bouchaud and Sornette's formalism is easily couched in discrete time, accounting for the fact that continuous trading is un-physical due to transaction cost and brokerage inefficiencies. However, transaction costs themselves have not explicitly been accounted for in the wealth process, therefore their effect on risk-control cannot be gauged. We address this point here by adding a term to equation (3) in order to include a general transaction cost structure.

$$\Delta W_T \rightarrow \Delta W_T + \sum_{t=0}^{T} k_1$$
$$+ (k_2 + k_3 S_t) \left| \phi_t [S_t] - \phi_{t-1} [S_{t-1}] \right|.$$

We now again proceed to find the variance of this wealth process as a gauge of risk. We find that the approximation of $|\phi_t [S_t] - \phi_{t-1} [S_{t-1}]| \approx \frac{\partial \phi_t}{\partial S_t} |\delta S_t|$ holds reasonably well as the time dependence of $\phi_t [S_t]$ is weak. This allows us to formulate an analytical correction term to Bouchaud and Sornette's expression for risk (full details will be presented elsewhere).

$$R \rightarrow R + \sum_{t=1}^{T} \left(\begin{array}{c} \int_{-\infty}^{\infty} \langle \delta S_t^2 \rangle (k_2 + k_3 S_t)^2 \\ \times \left(\frac{\partial \phi_t}{\partial S_t} \right)^2 P[S_t|S_0] \, dS_t \\ - \left(\int_{-\infty}^{\infty} \langle |\delta S_t| \rangle (k_2 + k_3 S_t) \right. \\ \left. \times \frac{\partial \phi_t}{\partial S_t} P[S_t|S_0] \, dS_t \right)^2 \end{array} \right) \quad (5)$$
$$+ \sum_{ti \neq tj} \iint_{-\infty}^{\infty} \left(\begin{array}{c} \langle |\delta S_{ti}| \rangle \langle |\delta S_{tj}| \rangle \\ \times (k_2 + k_3 S_{ti}) (k_2 + k_3 S_{tj}) \\ \times \frac{\partial \phi_{ti}}{\partial S_{ti}} \frac{\partial \phi_{tj}}{\partial S_{tj}} P[S_{ti}|S_0] \\ \times (P[S_{tj}|S_{ti}] - P[S_{tj}|S_0]) \end{array} \right) \, dS_{ti} dS_{tj}.$$

The first line of equation (5) represents the sum of independent transaction costs variances whereas the second line represents the covariance between transaction costs. The covariance terms become very large as we execute more transactions. This non-local behavior leads to a divergence of the risk as we go toward continuous time as shown in Figure 9. Clearly if we are to minimize risk now the answer is not to simply re-hedge more often.

The minimization of risk with respect to a choice of hedging strategy $\phi_t [S_t]$ is now highly complex and in general path-dependent as might be expected from equation (5). However, we may use perturbation theory to obtain approximate solutions. We find that the risk and

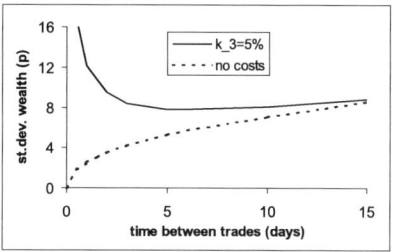

Fig. 9. Standard deviation of the wealth process (risk) as a function of trading time (length of time between trades). 30-day at-the-money European option $vol = 7.37$ p/day.

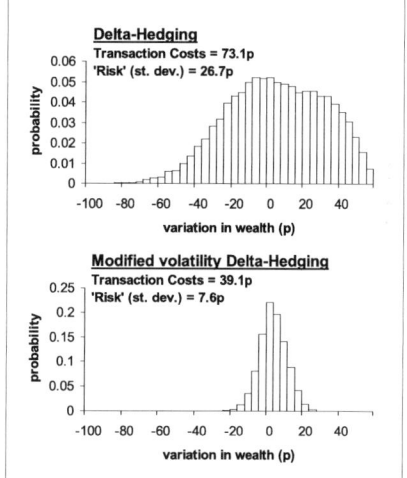

Fig. 10. Simulated distribution of wealth for portfolio short one 30-day euro-call, at the money, $vol = 7.37$ p/day and long $\phi_t [S_t]$ of the underlying with transaction costs at $k_3 = 5\%$. $\phi_t [S_t]$ according to Black-Scholes Delta (top) and with modified volatility as described in the text (bottom).

transaction costs are reduced greatly using a volatility correction to equation (4) of the form:

$$\langle \delta S_t^2 \rangle \rightarrow \gamma [t] \langle \delta S_t^2 \rangle.$$

The form of $\gamma [t]$ as a function of time is amusingly that of a smile, much like the volatility correction in strike price to the Black-Scholes delta that is implied by equation (4) itself. The origins of these two 'volatility smiles' are of course very different. Using this correction, for portfolios where transaction costs are likely to be high, we see a dramatic reduction in the risk and also in the absolute transaction costs. Figure 10 demonstrates this for a particular option.

6 Conclusion

We have presented here a development from the basic minority game, to a full market model. We have attempted to capture the behavioral aspects of market-making and agent-participation in a thorough and yet simplistic fashion. From this model we have then shown behavior reminiscent of 'real' financial asset movements with fat-tailed distributions of returns, clustered volatility and high volume autocorrelation.

We then moved on to show how these types of agent-based models perform in a predictive capacity when we replace the self-generated synthetic asset-price history with a real financial asset movement. We showed that as independent entities, the agents were able to function in a manner similar to an inefficient genetic algorithm and thus exploit the residual information present in the asset movement's sign. We then went on to show that when combined as a population, the agents were able to perform as a much stronger predictor, suggesting an element of collective-intelligence. We then outlined another manner in which ensembles of these models can be used to forecast future asset-price levels in a probabilistic manner.

Lastly, we showed how output from the agent-models could be used in a portfolio management setting in order to measure and control risk. We went on to demonstrate that the addition of transaction costs to Bouchaud and Sornette's formalism for risk management led to a greatly increased risk for high-frequency trading. We then presented a volatility correction to the 'optimal strategy' that could be used to reduce this excess risk and also reduce transaction costs.

Our aim is to develop a general understanding and framework for investigating and exploiting financial markets based on microscopic models of agent interactions. It is hoped that the work presented here represents positive and significant steps toward this goal.

We thank Mr A. Short for many useful discussions

References

1. W.B. Arthur, Science **284**, 107 (1999).
2. http://Www.Unifr.Ch/Econophysics. Econophysics website.
3. T. Lux, Nature **397**, 498 (1999).
4. R. Cont, J.P. Bouchaud, *Herd behavior and aggregate fluctuations in financial markets*, cond-mat/9712318v2.
5. M. Marsili, D. Challet, *Trading behavior and excess volatility in toy markets*, cond-mat/0004376.
6. J.D. Farmer, *Market force, ecology, and evolution*, Santa Fe Inst. Working Paper 98-12-117.
7. D. Challet, Y.C. Zhang, Physica A **246**, 407 (1997).
8. R. Savit, R. Manuca, R. Riolo, Phys. Rev. Lett. **82**, 2203 (1999).
9. A. Cavagna, J.P. Garrahan, I. Giardina, D. Sherrington, Phys. Rev. Lett. **83**, 4429 (1999).
10. R. D'hulst, G.J. Rodgers, Physica A **270**, 514 (1999).
11. D. Challet, M. Marsili, *Relevance of memory in minority games*, cond-mat/0004196.
12. M. Hart, P. Jefferies, N.F. Johnson, *Crowd-anticrowd theory of the minority game*, cond-mat/0005152.
13. R. D'Hulst, G.J. Rodgers, Physica A **280**, 554 (2000).
14. D. Challet, Y.C. Zhang, Physica A **256**, 514 (1998).
15. M. Hart, P. Jefferies, N.F. Johnson, *Stochastic strategies in the minority game*, cond-mat/0006141.
16. M. Hart, P. Jefferies, N.F. Johnson, *Crowd-anticrowd theory of multi-agent market-games*, APFA2 Conference Belgium.
17. N.F. Johnson, M. Hart, P.M. Hui, D. Zheng, *Trader dynamics in a model market*, cond-mat/9910072.
18. Research in collaboration with Dr J. James, Bank One London.
19. J.P. Bouchaud, D. Sornette, J. Phys. I France **4**, 863 (1994).
20. J.P. Bouchaud, M. Potters, *Theory of Financial Risks* (Cambridge University Press, 2000).

Predictability of Large Future Changes in a Competitive Evolving Population

D. Lamper and S. D. Howison

Oxford Centre for Industrial and Applied Mathematics, Oxford University, Oxford, OX1 3LB, United Kingdom

N. F. Johnson

Physics Department, Oxford University, Oxford, OX1 3PU, United Kingdom

(Received 12 May 2001; published 14 December 2001)

The dynamical evolution of many economic, sociological, biological, and physical systems tends to be dominated by a relatively small number of unexpected, large changes ("extreme events"). We study the large, internal changes produced in a generic multiagent population competing for a limited resource, and find that the level of predictability *increases* prior to a large change. These large changes hence arise as a predictable consequence of information encoded in the system's global state.

DOI: 10.1103/PhysRevLett.88.017902   PACS numbers: 87.23.Ge, 02.50.Le, 05.45.Tp, 87.23.Kg

Populations comprising many "agents" (e.g., people, species, data packets, cells) who compete for a limited resource are believed to underlie the complex dynamics observed in areas as diverse as economics [1–4], sociology [5], internet traffic [6], ecology [7], and biology [8,9]. The reliable prediction of large future changes ("extreme events") in such complex systems would be of enormous practical importance, but is widely considered to be impossible [10].

In this paper, we examine the predictability of large future changes produced within an evolving population of agents who compete for a limited resource. We find that the level of predictability in the system *increases* prior to a large change, implying that such a large change arises as a predictable consequence of information encoded in the system's global state, as opposed to being triggered by some isolated random event.

We consider a generic multiagent system comprising a population of N_{tot} agents of which no more than $L < N_{tot}$ agents can win at each time step; an everyday example would be a popular bar with a limited seating capacity L [5]. For the purpose of this paper, we consider a specific case of such a limited-resource problem with N_{tot} odd and $L = (N_{tot} - 1)/2$ [11], hence there are more losers than winners, noting that similar dynamics can also occur for more general L [12]. Each agent is therefore seeking to be in the minority group: for example, a buyer in a financial market may obtain a better price if more people are selling than buying; a driver may have a quicker journey if she chooses the route with less traffic. At each time step, an agent decides whether to enter a game where the choices are option 0 (e.g., buy, choose route A) and option 1 (e.g., sell, choose route B). Each agent holds a finite number of strategies and only a subset $N = N_0 + N_1 \leq N_{tot}$ of the population, who are sufficiently confident of winning, actually play: N_0 agents choose 0 while N_1 choose 1. If $N_0 - N_1 > 0$, the winning decision (outcome) is "1" and vice versa. If $N_0 = N_1$ the tie is decided by a coin toss. Hence N and the "excess demand" $N_{0-1} = N_0 - N_1$ both fluctuate with time. In contrast to the basic minority game

(MG) [11], this variable-N model has the realistic feature of accounting for agents' confidence [13,14]. Furthermore the variable-N model can be used to generate statistical and dynamical features similar to those observed in financial markets (archetypal examples of complex systems) [2,13]. Therefore, demonstration of predictability of extreme events in the present multiagent model would open up the exciting possibility of predictability of extreme events in real-world systems. Such predictability goes beyond the standard economic paradigm of the efficient market hypothesis [10].

The only global information available to the agents is a common bit-string "memory" of the m most recent outcomes. The agents can thus be said to exhibit "bounded rationality" [5]. Consider $m = 2$; the $2^m = 4$ possible history bit strings are 00, 01, 10, and 11. A strategy consists of a response, i.e., 0 or 1, to each possible bit string; hence there are $2^{2^m} = 16$ possible strategies. At the beginning of the game, each agent randomly picks q strategies and, after each turn, assigns one (virtual) point to a strategy which would have predicted the correct outcome. Agents have a time horizon T, over which virtual points are collected, and a threshold probability level τ; strategies with a probability of winning greater than or equal to τ, i.e., having $\geq T\tau$ virtual points, are available to be used by the agent. We call these *active* strategies. Agents with no active strategies within their individual set of q strategies do not play at that time step. Agents with one or more active strategies play the one with the highest virtual point score; any ties between active strategies are resolved using a coin toss. The excess demand N_{0-1}, which can be identified as the output from the model system, can be expressed as

$$N_{0-1} = \sum_i n_i(1 - 2s_i), \qquad (1)$$

where s_i is the prediction of the ith strategy, e.g., 0 or 1, and n_i is the number of agents using this strategy; the sum is taken over the set of active strategies at that time step.

Because of the feedback in the game, any particular strategy's success is short lived. If all the agents begin to use similar strategies, and hence make the same decision, such a strategy ceases to be profitable. The game can be broadly classified into three regimes: (i) The number of strategies in play is much greater than the total available: groups of traders will play using the same strategy and therefore crowds should dominate the game [15]. (ii) The number of strategies in play is much less than the total available: grouping behavior is therefore minimal. (iii) The number of strategies in play is comparable to the total number available: this represents a transition regime and is of the most interest, since it produces seemingly random dynamics with occasional large movements. Remarkably, however, we find that *large* changes over several consecutive time steps can be predicted with surprising accuracy.

Suppose we are given a time series $H(t)$ with increments $\Delta H(t)$ generated by a physical, sociological, biological, or economic system (e.g., a financial market [13]), whose dynamics are well described by the multiagent game for a fixed *unknown* parameter set m, N, τ, T and an *unknown* specific realization of initial strategy choices. We call this our "black-box" game. Even with complete knowledge of the game's state, subsequent outcomes are not perfectly predictable since the coin tosses which resolve ties in decisions (i.e., $N_0 = N_1$) and active-strategy scores inject stochasticity into the game's time evolution. Previous authors have demonstrated the existence of a degree of stationary predictability in the basic MG, e.g., via the histogram of bit-string occurrences [16]; our results are, by contrast, dynamic. Our goal is to identify "third-party" games which can be matched with the black-box game [$\Delta H(t)$ being proportional to the excess demand N_{0-1}, or a known nonlinear function thereof] and then used to predict large future changes in $H(t)$. For the remainder of this article, we focus on the following game parameters for the black-box game: $N = 101$, $m = 3$, $q = 2$, $T = 100$, and $\tau = 0.53$, although our conclusions are more general [17]. Since $\tau > 0.5$, an agent will not participate unless she believes she has a better than average chance of winning. Note that it is computationally impractical to have large values of m in the third-party game, because there are 2^{2^m} strategies. However, we have found that the reduced strategy space, comprising a subset of 2^{m+1} strategies which are either anticorrelated or uncorrelated with each other [11], can be used to match a black-box game which was generated using the full strategy space [17].

We start by running $H(t)$ through a trial third-party game in order to generate an estimate of S_0 and S_1 at each time step, the number of active strategies predicting a 0 or 1, respectively. This is obtained from the strategy space, or the pool of all available strategies in the third-party game, and is independent of the distribution of agents. We wish to predict $\Delta H(t)$, i.e., N_{0-1}; we will do this by linking S and N through an appropriate probability distribution. Provided the strategy space in the black-box game is reasonably well covered by the agent's random choice of initial strategies, any bias towards a particular outcome in

the active strategy set will propagate itself as a bias in the value of N_{0-1} away from zero. Thus we expect N_{0-1} to be approximately proportional to $S_0 - S_1 = S_{0-1}$. This is equivalent to assuming an equal weighting n_i on each strategy in Eq. (1), indicating that the exact distribution of strategies among the individual agents is unimportant in this regime [18]. In addition, the number of agents taking part in the game at each time step will be related to the total number of active strategies $S_0 + S_1 = S_{0+1}$, hence the error (i.e., variance) in the prediction of N_{0-1} using S_{0-1} will depend on S_{0+1}. Based on extensive statistical analysis of known simulations for the multiagent game [17], we have confirmed that it is reasonable to model the relationship by

$$N_{0-1} = bS_{0-1} + \varepsilon[0, f(S_{0+1})],$$

where ε is a noise term with mean zero and variance a function of S_{0+1}, and b is a constant. In particular, we describe the forecast for N_{0-1} as a normal distribution of the form $N_{0-1} \sim N(bS_{0-1}, cS_{0+1})$, where c is a constant. (We seek the simplest stable distribution as a density forecast, while acknowledging that the true distribution of N_{0-1} is indeed fat tailed.)

The variance of our forecast density function can be minimized by choosing a third-party game that achieves the maximum correlation between N_{0-1} and our explanatory variable S_{0-1}, with the unexplained variance being characterized by a linear function of S_{0+1}. We focus on the parameter regime known to produce realistic statistics (e.g., fat-tailed distribution of returns in financial markets). Within this parameter space we run an ensemble of third-party games through the black-box series $H(t)$, calculating the values of S_{0-1} from the reconstructed strategy space. We then identify the configuration that achieves the highest correlation between S_{0-1} and N_{0-1} produced by the original black-box game. As shown in Fig. 1, the third-party game that achieves the highest correlation is the one whose parameters coincide with the black-box game. From a knowledge of just $H(t)$, and hence N_{0-1}, we have therefore used next-step prediction to recover all the parameters of relevance to produce a "model" game for prediction purposes. The games reported here were all homogeneous in T and τ, but we have also carried out studies in which the values of these parameters vary between agents [17]. Even if the black-box game is heterogeneous, prediction by a homogeneous third-party game still exhibits a significant degree of correlation, indicating the robustness of our procedure.

We now extend this forecast an arbitrary number j of time steps into the future, in order to address the predictability of large changes in $H(t)$ over several consecutive time steps. This is achieved by calculating the net value of S_{0-1} along all the 2^{j-1} possible future routes of the third-party game, weighted by appropriate probabilities. In order to assign these probabilities, it is necessary to calculate all possible S_{0-1} values in the next j time steps. This is possible since the only data required to update the

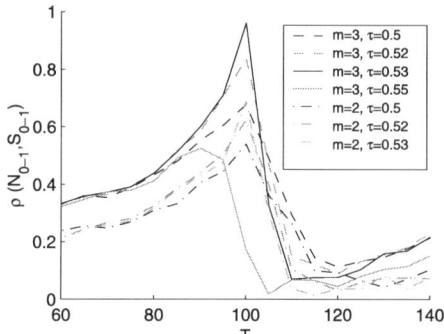

FIG. 1. Estimation of the parameter set for the black-box game. The correlation between N_{0-1} and S_{0-1} is calculated over 200 time steps for an ensemble of candidate third-party games. The third-party game that achieves the highest correlation is the one with the same parameters as the black-box game.

strategy space between time steps is knowledge of the winning decision, and hence the third-party game can be directed along a given path independent of the predictions of the individual agents in the black-box game. The change in N_{0-1} along a path indexed by k is given by a convolution of the predictions over the j individual steps and is distributed as

$$N(\mu_k, \sigma_k) \sim N\left(b \sum S_{0-1}, c \sum S_{0+1}\right),$$

where the summation is taken along the path represented by k. In general, the pdf for the change in N_{0-1} during the next j time steps is a mixture of normals:

$$P[\Delta N_{0-1}(i; i + j)] = \sum_{k=1}^{2^{j-1}} p_k N(\mu_k, \sigma_k), \qquad (2)$$

where p_k is the probability of path k being taken.

To test the validity of the density forecast, we perform a statistical evaluation using the realized variables. The one-step-ahead forecasts are normal distributions, and we define the test statistic Z_i as

$$Z_i = \frac{x_i - \mu_i^x}{\sigma_i^x}, \qquad (3)$$

where μ_i^x and σ_i^x are the mean and variance of the forecast distribution, and x_i is the realized value of N_{0-1} at time step i. The Z_i were found to be independent uniform $N(0, 1)$ variates for 1000 out-of-sample predictions, confirming that the predicted distributions are correct. To compare the forecasts to a naive "no-change" prediction, we calculate the Theil coefficient [19] which is the sum of squared prediction errors divided by the sum of squared errors resulting from the naive forecast. A coefficient of less than 1 implies a superior performance compared to the naive prediction; calculated values were typically in the region of 0.4. There is no accepted method in the literature

for evaluating multi-step-ahead forecasts [20]. However, the density function for an arbitrary time horizon is a mixture of normal distributions, see Eq. (2), each of which can be roughly characterized in terms of a single mean and variance:

$$E[X] = \sum_{k=1}^{2^{j-1}} p_i \mu_i \,,$$

$$\mathrm{Var}[X] = \sum_{k=1}^{2^{j-1}} p_i(\sigma_i^2 + \mu_i^2) - \left(\sum_{k=1}^{2^{j-1}} p_i \mu_i\right)^2 .$$

Hence the same test statistic as Eq. (3) can be calculated. Again, the predictions were found to be reliable.

Given that we can derive accurate distributions for the future changes in $H(t)$, these will be of most practical interest in situations where there is likely to be a substantial, well-defined movement. We characterize these moments by seeking distributions with a high value of $|\mu|$ and a low value of σ at a future time step, or over a specified time horizon. In Fig. 2 we plot $|\mu|$ vs σ for a number of separate forecasts, and take a fraction of points that are farthest from the average trend indicated by the regression line, i.e., we are interested in the outliers. The point with the highest residual is thus a candidate for the game to be in a highly predictable phase. We call these time periods *predictable corridors*, since comparatively tight confidence intervals can be drawn for the future evolution of the excess demand, a typical example of which is shown in Fig. 3. A standard autoregressive prediction AR(8), which is based on information from the previous eight time steps, does not pick up the large change. Furthermore, no significant

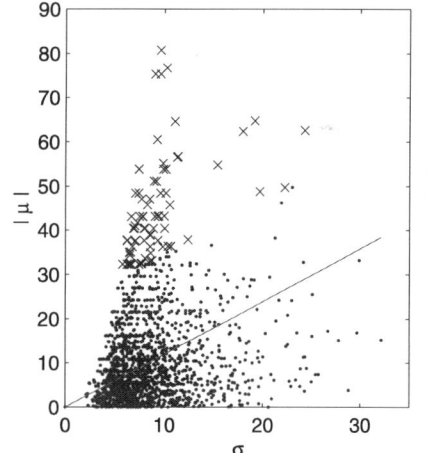

FIG. 2. A plot of $|\mu|$ vs σ for 500 separate four-step density forecasts. Items marked by "×" are forecasts with an unusually large value of $|\mu|/\sigma$. At these moments, the game is likely to be in a highly predictable phase.

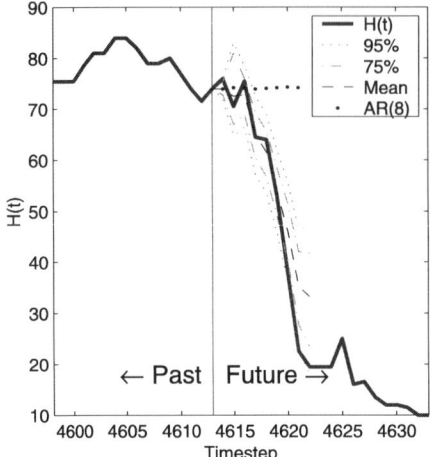

FIG. 3. Comparison between the forecast density function and the realized time series $H(t)$ for a typical large movement. The large, well-defined movement is correctly predicted. An AR(8)-based prediction has been included for comparison.

linear autocorrelation (at the 95% level) exists prior to the large movement studied. We subject these points to an identical test as described earlier to ensure that these potential outliers are well described by our probability distributions, and this is found to be true. We note that the coin-toss frequency does not change dramatically prior to the large changes, confirming our statement that the large changes are global and hence cannot be traced to a single nucleation event [17].

We performed extensive numerical simulations to check the validity of these predictive corridors [17]. Our procedure is to take a sample of 5000 time steps, then fit parameters using the first 3000 steps. We then look at the largest changes (extreme events) in our out-of-sample region. Extreme events are ranked by the largest movements in $H(t)$ over a given window size W. Hence we consider the top twenty extreme events and calculate the probability integral transform z_t of the realized variables with respect to the forecast densities. The z_t are found to be approximately uniform $U[0, 1]$ variates, confirming that the forecast distribution is essentially correct. About 50% of large movements occur in periods with tight predictable corridors, i.e., a large value of $|\mu|/\sigma$. Both the magnitude and sign of these extreme events are therefore predictable. The remainder correspond to periods with very wide corridors. Although the magnitude of the future movement is now uncertain, the present method predicts with high probability

the actual direction of change. Even this more limited information would be invaluable for assessing future risk in the physical, economic, sociological, or biological system of interest. Finally we note that some empirical support for our claim of enhanced predictability prior to extreme movements has very recently appeared for the case of financial markets [21].

We are very grateful to Michael Hart, Paul Jefferies, Pak Ming Hui, and Jeff Dewynne for their involvement in this project. D. L. thanks EPSRC for support.

[1] T. Lux and M. Marchesi, Nature (London) **397**, 498 (1999).
[2] See the Econophysics website, http://www.unifr.ch/econophysics
[3] R. Mantegna and H. Stanley, *Econophysics* (Cambridge University Press, Cambridge, UK, 2000).
[4] J. Bouchaud and M. Potters, *Theory of Financial Risks* (Cambridge University Press, Cambridge, UK, 2000).
[5] W. Arthur, Am. Econ. Rev. **84**, 406 (1994).
[6] B. Huberman, P. Pirolli, J. Pitkow, and R. Lukose, Science **280**, 95 (1998).
[7] J. L. Tella, M. A. R. de Cara, O. Pla, and F. Guinea, in *Sixth Granada Lectures in Computational Physics*, edited by P. L. Garrido and J. Marro, AIP Conf. Proc. 574 (AIP, New York, 2001).
[8] M. Nowak and R. May, Nature (London) **359**, 826 (1992).
[9] D. Sornette, Phys. World **12**, 57 (1999); see also A. Johansen and D. Sornette, cond-mat/0010050.
[10] See, for example, B. Malkiel, in *A Random Walk Down Wall Street* (Norton, New York, 1985).
[11] D. Challet and Y.-C. Zhang, Physica (Amsterdam) **246A**, 407 (1997); D. Challet and Y.-C. Zhang, Physica (Amsterdam) **256A**, 514 (1998). See Ref. [2] for a full bibliography of the minority game.
[12] N. F. Johnson, P. M. Hui, D. Zheng, and C. W. Tai, Physica (Amsterdam) **269A**, 493 (1999).
[13] P. Jefferies, N. F. Johnson, M. Hart, and P. M. Hui, Eur. Phys. J. B **20**, 493 (2001); see also I. Giardina, J. P. Bouchaud, and M. Mezard, Physica (Amsterdam) **299A**, 28 (2001).
[14] N. F. Johnson, M. Hart, P. M. Hui, and D. Zheng, Int. J. Theor. Appl. Fin. **3**, 443 (2000).
[15] N. F. Johnson, M. Hart, and P. M. Hui, Physica (Amsterdam) **269A**, 1 (1999).
[16] R. Savit, R. Manuca, and R. Riolo, Phys. Rev. Lett. **82**, 2203 (1999).
[17] Further details of the statistical tests and parameter sets are available from the authors. See http://www.maths.ox.ac.uk/~lamper
[18] An accurate estimate of n_i can be recovered using Kalman filters.
[19] H. Theil, *Applied Economic Forecasting* (North-Holland, Amsterdam, 1966).
[20] A. S. Tay and K. T. Wallis, J. Forecast. **19**, 235 (2000).
[21] R. Mansilla, cond-mat/0104472.

On a universal mechanism for long-range volatility correlations

Jean-Philippe Bouchaud[1,2], Irene Giardina[3] and Marc Mézard[4]

[1] Service de Physique de l'État Condensé, Centre d'Études de Saclay, Orme des Merisiers, 91191 Gif-sur-Yvette Cedex, France
[2] Science & Finance, 109–111 rue Victor-Hugo, 92532 France
[3] Service de Physique Théorique, Centre d'Études de Saclay, Orme des Merisiers, 91191 Gif-sur-Yvette Cedex, France
[4] Laboratoire de Physique Théorique et Modèles Statistiques, Université Paris Sud, Bat. 100, 91405 Orsay Cedex, France

Received 9 December 2000

Abstract

We propose a general interpretation for long-range correlation effects in the activity and volatility of financial markets. This interpretation is based on the fact that the choice between 'active' and 'inactive' strategies is subordinated to random-walk-like processes. We numerically demonstrate our scenario in the framework of simplified market models, such as the Minority Game model with an inactive strategy. We show that real market data can be surprisingly well accounted for by these simple models.

A well-documented 'stylized fact' of financial markets is volatility clustering [1–4]. Figure 1 compares the time series of the daily returns of the Dow Jones Index since 1900 and that of a Brownian random walk. Two features are immediately obvious to the eye: the volatility does indeed have strong intermittent fluctuations, and these fluctuations tend to persist in time. A more quantitative analysis shows that the daily volatility σ_t (defined, for example, as the average-squared high frequency returns) has a log-normal distribution [6], and that its temporal correlation function $\langle \sigma_t \sigma_{t+\tau} \rangle$ can be fitted by an inverse power of the lag τ, with a small exponent in the range $0.1 - 0.3$ [2, 5–7]. This suggests that there is no characteristic time scale for volatility fluctuations: outbursts of market activity can persist for short times (say a few days), but also for much longer times, months or even years. A very interesting observation is that these *long-range* volatility correlations are observed on many different financial markets, with qualitatively similar features: stocks, currencies, commodities or interest rates. This suggests that a common mechanism is at the origin of this universal phenomenon.

A first possibility is that the apparent lack of time scale associated with the power-law dependence of the correlation function is a consequence of the fact that human activity is naturally rhythmed by days, weeks, months, quarters and years. Now, the ratio between these successive time scales is roughly constant. The superposition of correlation functions with time constants uniformly distributed on a log scale may easily be confused with a single power law with a small exponent [8].

However, very important insights into market dynamics have recently been gained by the study of several agent-based models [9–17]. These models postulate some simple behaviour at the level of the agents and investigate the resulting price dynamics. Among others, the model by Lux and Marchesi [15] assumes that each agent can behave, as a function of time, either as a fundamentalist (i.e. determining his action by comparing the current market price to some fundamental 'true' price), or as a 'trend follower', influenced by observed past trends on the price itself. Agents switch between the two strategies as a function of their relative performance. Numerical simulations based on this model produce quite realistic price charts. In particular, long-range, power-law type volatility correlations are reported. Another family of models, the 'Minority Game' (MG) and its variants [10, 18, 19, 21, 22], has recently become the focus of intense theoretical scrutiny. The Minority Game describes

1469-7688/01/020212+05$30.00 © 2001 IOP Publishing Ltd PII: S1469-7688(01)21343-8

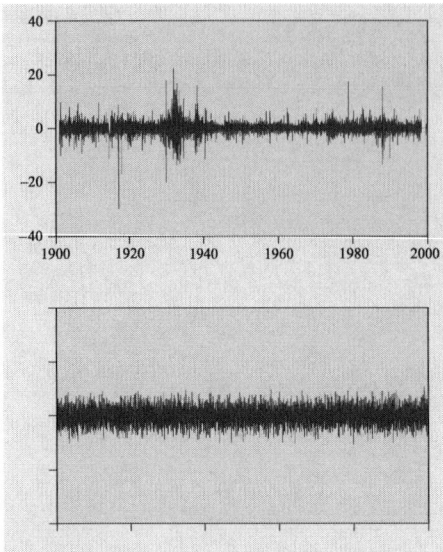

Figure 1. Top panel: daily returns of the Dow Jones Index since 1900. One very clearly sees the intermittent nature of volatility fluctuations. Note in particular the sharp feature in the 1930s. Lower panel: daily returns for a Brownian random walk, showing a featureless pattern.

the behaviour of competing agents that can choose between different individual strategies as a function of their past performance. In its original version, this model is remote from financial markets; in particular, there is no price dynamics. Several attempts have been made to generalize it and construct more realistic market models [18]. As first noticed in [19], if one allows the agents to be inactive, intermittent volatility fluctuations can be generated. We have ourselves studied a market model that allows traders to switch between a bond market and a stock market, and accounts properly for their wealth balance and for market clearing. The phenomenology of this model is very rich and a detailed account of our results will be published separately [23]. One of our main results is the existence of a 'turbulent' market phase where volatility fluctuations are intermittent and show a power-law-like correlation. A very important point is that all these models are different in their details but all show qualitatively similar behaviour, without the explicit introduction of any of the 'human' time scales mentioned above. In other words, these agent-based models assume a unique elementary time scale (say the 'day') and the long-range volatility correlations spontaneously emerge from the dynamics.

We wish to propose a simple and robust mechanism to account for the appearance of these long-range correlations in the above simplified models. We then argue that this mechanism also very naturally operates in real financial markets, and accounts well for the empirical findings. The

following discussion is intentionally qualitative; more detailed and technical results will be presented elsewhere [23].

The idea is the following: in the above models, scores are attributed by agents to their possible strategies, as a function of their past performance. In a region of the parameter space where these models lead to an efficient market, the autocorrelation of the price increments is close to zero, which means that to a first approximation, no strategy can, on average, be profitable. This implies that for *any* reasonable definition of the update of the scores, these scores will locally behave, as a function of time, as random walks. Furthermore, the scores associated with different strategies generically behave as *independent* random walks. Now, in all these models, the switch between two strategies occurs when their scores cross. Therefore, in the case where each agent has two strategies, say one 'active' (trading in the market) and one 'inactive' (holding bonds), the survival time of any one of these strategies will be given by the return time of a random walk (the difference between the scores of the two strategies) to zero. The interesting point is that these return times are well known to be power-law distributed (see below): this leads to the non-trivial behaviour of the volume autocorrelation function. In other words, the very fact that agents compare the performance of two strategies on a random signal leads to a multitime scale situation.

More formally, let us define the quantity $\theta_i(t)$ that is equal to 1 if agent i is active at time t, and 0 if inactive. The total activity is given by $a(t) = \sum_i \theta_i(t)$. The time autocorrelation of the activity is given by[5]:

$$C_a(t, t') = \langle a(t)a(t') \rangle = \sum_{i,j} \langle \theta_i(t)\theta_j(t') \rangle. \qquad (1)$$

We will actually use in the following the so-called activity variogram, directly related to the autocorrelation through:

$$V_a(t, t') = \left\langle \left[a(t) - a(t') \right]^2 \right\rangle = C_a(t, t) + C_a(t', t') - 2C_a(t, t'). \qquad (2)$$

One can consider two extreme cases which lead to the same result, up to a multiplicative constant: (a) agents follow completely different strategies and have independent activity patterns, i.e., $\langle \theta_i \theta_j \rangle \propto \delta_{i,j}$ or (b) agents follow very similar strategies, for example by comparing the perfomance of stocks to that of bonds, in which case $\theta_i = \theta_j$. In both cases, $C_a(t, t')$ is proportional to $\langle \theta_i(t)\theta_i(t') \rangle$. This quantity can be computed in terms of the distribution $P(s)$ of the survival time s of the strategies (in the following, we assume that both the inactive and active strategies have the same survival time distribution). Following [24], one first introduces the probability $p_n(t, t')$ that exactly n switches between the active and inactive strategies take place between times t' and t. The correlation function $C_a(t, t')$ is then given by:

$$C_a(t, t') = \sum_{n=0}^{\infty} \frac{[1 + (-1)^n]}{4} p_n(t, t'). \qquad (3)$$

Assuming that the survival times s are independent random quantities, one can establish simple recursion formulae for

---

[5] Up to an additive constant which disappears from the variogram.

$p_n(t, t')$ in Laplace space [24]. Indeed, the probability of observing n switches between t' and t is such that:

$$\sum_{i=1}^{n_0} s_i < t' < \sum_{i=1}^{n_0+1} s_i \quad \text{and} \quad \sum_{i=1}^{n_0+n} s_i < t < \sum_{i=1}^{n_0+n+1} s_i, \tag{4}$$

summed over all possible values of n_0.

Two cases must then be distinguished: (a) $P(s)$ has a finite first moment $\langle s \rangle$ (finite average lifetime of the strategies), then $C_a(t, t')$ is stationary, i.e., it only depends on the difference $\tau = t' - t$. Introducing the Laplace transforms $\mathcal{L}C_a(E)$ and $\mathcal{L}P(E)$ of $C_a(\tau)$ and $P(s)$, the general relation between the two quantities reads [24]:

$$E\mathcal{L}C_a(E) = \left(1 - \frac{2[1 - \mathcal{L}P(E)]}{\langle s \rangle E[1 + \mathcal{L}P(E)]}\right); \tag{5}$$

(b) if, on the other hand, $P(s)$ has an infinite first moment, then $C_a(t, t')$ depends both on t and t': this is known as the *aging* phenomenon [24, 25]. For an unconfined random walk, the return-time distribution decays as $s^{-3/2}$ for large s and therefore its first moment is infinite. However, in all the models mentioned above, there exist 'restoring' forces which effectively confine the scores to a finite interval [23]. This can be attributed, both in the case of the MG or of more realistic market models, to 'market impact', which means that good strategies tend to deteriorate because of their very use. There are many reasons to believe that such confining forces also operate in financial markets. For example, the finite memory time of market operators used to assess their strategies will result in such a confining force. The consequence of these effects is to truncate the $s^{-3/2}$ tail for values of s larger than a certain equilibrium time s_0. Therefore, the first moment of $P(s)$ actually exists, such that equation (5) is valid. Nevertheless, one can see from equation (5) that the characteristic $s^{-3/2}$ behaviour of $P(s)$ for short time scales leads to $E\mathcal{L}C_a(E) \sim 1 - B/\sqrt{E} + \ldots$, for $s_0^{-1} \ll E \ll 1$. This in turn leads to a singular behaviour for the variogram $V_a(\tau)$ at small τ, as $V_a(\tau) \propto \sqrt{\tau}$, before saturating to a finite value for $\tau \sim s_0$. Intuitively, this means that the probability of the activity having changed significantly between t and $t+\tau$ is proportional to $\int_0^\tau ds\, s\,P(s) \propto \sqrt{\tau}$ (for $\tau \ll s_0$), where $sP(s)$ is indeed the probability to be, at time t, playing a strategy with lifetime s.

Let us illustrate this general scenario with the example of the MG with an inactive strategy, first introduced in [19]. Each agent has a certain number of fixed strategies to choose from. A strategy is a mapping from a signal (for example the past history) into a decision, say $+1$ or -1. The aim of the game at each time step is to make the decision that is chosen by the minority of the agents at that time [10]. If a strategy is successful (or would have been if it had been played), its score increases, conversely, if the wrong decision is made (or again, would have been if it had been played), the score decreases. The chosen strategy is the one that has the highest score at a given instant of time. If all the strategies of an agent have negative scores, then the agent does not play. The relevant parameter α of this model is the ratio of the

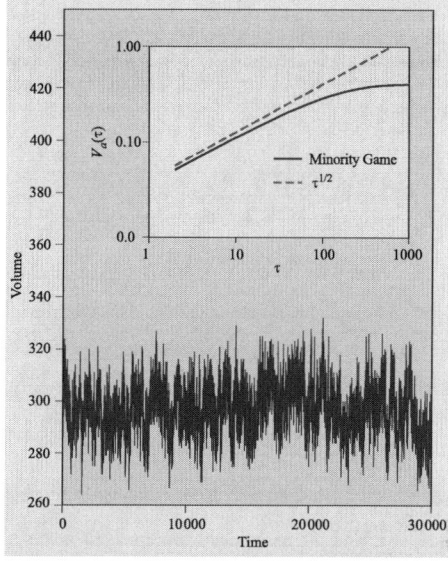

Figure 2. Volume of activity (number of active agents) as a function of time in the MG with two active strategies and one inactive strategy per agent, and for $\alpha = 0.51$ ($\alpha_c \simeq 1.$). The number of agents is 501. Inset: the corresponding activity variogram as a function of the lag τ, in a log–log plot to emphasize the $\sqrt{\tau}$ singularity at small τ.

number of possible histories to the number N of agents. The history is given by the M past steps of the game, therefore $\alpha = 2^M/N$. One finds [20, 23] that there is a critical value α_c above which all agents finally become inactive. Below this value, the activity is non-zero. A plot of the activity as a function of time in this model is given in figure 2, for a value of α smaller than α_c. In the inset, we have plotted the activity variogram $V_a(\tau)$, which reveals the characteristic $\sqrt{\tau}$ singularity discussed above, before saturating for large τ ($\sim s_0$). This $\sqrt{\tau}$ singularity is present in the whole active phase $\alpha < \alpha_c$, although s_0 is large compared to 1 only if α is not too small. Very similar variograms have also been found in the more realistic market model that we have investigated, showing the universality of this result [23]. Note that a similar mechanism might also be present in the Lux–Marchesi model, where it has been observed that the activity bursts are associated with a large number of agents switching from being 'fundamentalists' to being 'trend followers' [15].

It is interesting to compare the above results with real market data. Figure 3 shows the volume of activity on the S&P 500 futures contract in the years 1985–1998. This plot is, to the eye, very similar to that of figure 2, obtained with the MG, although very low frequency patterns, probably related to human time scales (holidays, etc) or the upsurge of activity at the end of the 1990s, are obviously missed by the MG. The similarity is quantitatively confirmed by the activity variogram, shown in the inset. On the same graph, we have reproduced

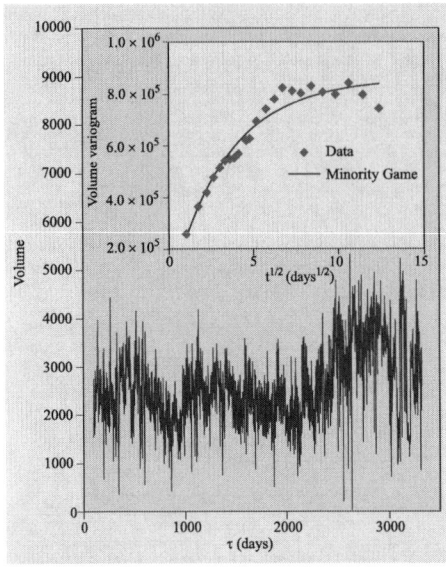

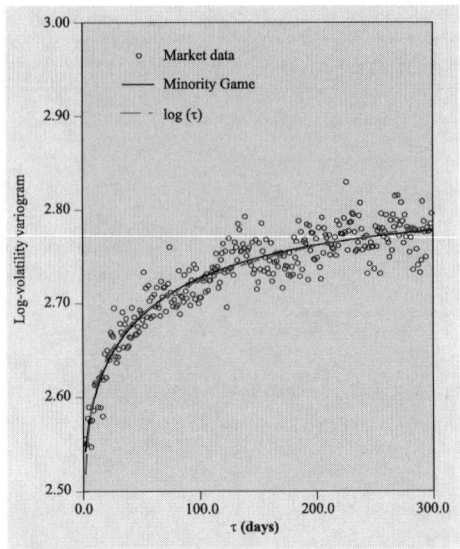

Figure 3. Total daily volume of activity (number of trades) on the S&P 500 futures contracts in the years 1985–1998: compare with figure 2. Inset: corresponding variogram (diamonds) as a function of the square root of the lag. Note the clear linear behaviour for small $\sqrt{\tau}$. The full curve is the MG result, with both axes rescaled and a constant added to account for the presence of 'white noise' trading.

Figure 4. Variogram of the log volatility, $\langle \log^2(\sigma_t/\sigma_{t+\tau}) \rangle$, as a function of τ, averaged over 17 different stock indices (American, European, Asian). The full curve is the MG result, with again both axes rescaled and a constant added to account for the presence of 'white noise' trading. The dashed curve is the prediction of the multifractal model of [7], and is nearly indistinguishable from the MG result.

the MG result. Both the time scale and the volume scale (arbitrary in the MG model) have been adjusted to get the best agreement. Furthermore, a constant has been added to V_a (corresponding to a $\delta_{\tau,0}$ contribution to C_a), to account for the fact that part of the trading activity is certainly white noise (e.g. motivated by news or by other non-strategic causes). As can be seen, the agreement is good. Most significant is the clear $\sqrt{\tau}$ behaviour at small τ ($\tau < 50$ days). We therefore suggest that the effect captured by the MG (figure 2) or more sophisticated variants [23], namely the subordination of the activity on random walk like signals, is also present in real markets. It seems to us that this makes perfect sense since market participants indeed compare the results of different strategies to decide whether they should remain active in a market or leave it. Note, furthermore, that although our scenario is based on the comparison between the scores of strategies, similar results would be obtained if the volume was subordinated to the difference between the price and certain 'psychological levels' (i.e. the value 1000 for the S&P, etc). It is very clear that such levels do indeed play a role in determining the activity on financial markets.

Since the volatility and the volume of activity are strongly correlated in financial markets [26, 27], our interpretation should carry over to volatility fluctuations as well. This is illustrated in figure 4, where the variogram of the log volatility for major stock indices is shown, together with

the very same MG result. Again, the agreement is very good. We have also shown for comparison the prediction of the multifractal model of [7], $V_a(\tau) = 2\lambda^2 \log(\tau/\tau_0)$. We note that the two models, although very different, lead to nearly indistinguishable numerical fits. It would be interesting to investigate other statistics that would distinguish clearly between the 'cascade' idea underlying the multifractal model of [7] and the mechanism proposed here. Note however that more subtle effects, such as the negative volatility/return correlation described in [28], should also be taken into account.

The analogy between volatility clustering in financial markets and intermittency effects in turbulent flows has recently been emphasized [7,29,30]. It is tempting to speculate that the mechanism discussed here might also be at work in turbulent flows, where outbursts of activity are due to localized structures [31]. If the motion of these localized structures locally resembles that of a random walk, similar conclusions can be expected.

In summary, we have proposed a very general interpretation for long-range correlation effects in the activity and volatility of financial markets. This interpretation is based on the fact that the choice between different strategies is subordinated to random-walk like processes. We have numerically demonstrated our scenario in the framework of simplified market models, and showed that, somewhat

215

surprisingly, real market data can actually be quite accurately accounted for by these simple models (see figures 3 and 4).

Acknowledgments

We wish to thank M Potters for several important discussion on this topic, and A Matacz and Ph Seager for providing the data for figures 3 and 4 and for interesting remarks. Useful interactions with G Canat, A Cavagna, D Farmer, E Moro, J P Garrahan, N Johnson, M Marsili, D Sherrington and H Zytnicki are acknowledged.

References

[1] Lo A 1991 *Econometrica* **59** 1279

[2] Ding Z, Granger C W J and Engle R F 1993 *J. Empirical Finance* **1** 83

[3] Mantegna R and Stanley H E 1999 *An Introduction to Econophysics* (Cambridge: Cambridge University Press)

[4] Bouchaud J-P and Potters M 1997 *Théorie des Risques Financiers* (Aléa-Saclay: Eyrolles)
(Engl. transl. Bouchaud J-P and Potters M 2000 *Theory of Financial Risks* (Cambridge: Cambridge University Press))

[5] Cont R, Potters M and Bouchaud J-P 1997 Scaling in stock market data: stable laws and beyond *Scale Invariance and Beyond* ed B Dubrulle, F Graner and D Sornette (Les Ulis: EDP Sciences)
Potters M, Cont R and Bouchaud J-P 1998 *Europhys. Lett.* **41** 239

[6] Liu Y, Cizeau P, Meyer M, Peng C-K and Stanley H E 1997 *Physica* A **245** 437
Cizeau P, Liu Y, Meyer M, Peng C-K and Stanley H E 1997 *Physica* A **245** 441

[7] Arnéodo A, Muzy J-F and Sornette D 1998 *Eur. Phys. J.* B **2** 277
Muzy J-F, Delour J and Bacry E 2000 *Preprint* cond-mat/0005400

[8] Bouchaud J-P 2000 Power laws in economics and finance: some ideas from physics *Quantitative Finance* **1** 105

[9] Bak P, Paczuski M and Shubik M 1997 *Physica* A **246** 430

[10] Challet D and Zhang Y C 1997 *Physica* A **246** 407

[11] Bouchaud J-P and Cont R 1998 *Eur. J. Phys.* B **6** 543
Cont R and Bouchaud J-P 2000 *Macroeconomics Dynamics* **4** 170

[12] Farmer J D 2000 *Int. J. Theor. Appl. Finance* **3** 425
(Farmer J D 1998 Market force, ecology and evolution *Preprint* adap-org/9812005)

[13] Sornette D, Stauffer D and Takayasu H 1999 Market fluctuations, multiplicative and percolation models, size effects and predictions *Preprint* cond-mat/9909439 and references therein

[14] Brock W and Hommes C 1997 *Econometrica* **65** 1059

[15] Lux T and Marchesi M 1999 *Nature* **397** 498
Lux T and Marchesi M 2000 *Int. J. Theor. Appl. Finance* **3** 675

[16] Iori G 1999 *Int. J. Mod. Phys.* C **10** 149
(Iori G 1999 A microsimulation of traders activity in the stock market: the role of heterogeneity, agents' interactions and trade frictions *Preprint* adap-org/9905005)

[17] For a review, see Farmer J D 1999 Physicists attempt to scale the ivory towers of finance *Comput. Sci. Engng* November 1999
(Reprinted in Farmer J D 2000 *Int. J. Theor. Appl. Finance* **3** 311

[18] Challet D, Marsili M and Zhang Y C 1999 Modeling market mechanism with Minority Game *Preprint* cond-mat/9909265
Challet D, Marsili M and Zecchina R 2000 *Int. J. Theor. Appl. Finance* **3** 451

[19] Jefferies P, Hart M, Hui P M and Johnson N F 2000 From market games to real world markets *Preprint* cond-mat/0008387
Jefferies P, Hart M, Hui P M and Johnson N F 2000 *Int. J. Theor. Appl. Finance* **3** 443

[20] Canat G, Zytnicki H and Mézard M 2000 *Ecole Polytechnique Internal Report (June 2000)*

[21] Cavagna A 1999 *Phys. Rev.* E **59** R3783
Cavagna A, Garrahan J P, Giardina I and Sherrington D 1999 *Phys. Rev. Lett.* **83** 4429

[22] Garrahan J P, Moro E and Sherrington D 2000 *Phys. Rev.* E **62** R9

[23] Giardina I, Bouchaud J-P and Mézard M 2001 in preparation

[24] Godrèche C and Luck J M 2000 Statistics of the occupation time of renewal processes *Preprint* cond-mat/0010428

[25] For a review, see Bouchaud J-P, Cugliandolo L, Kurchan J and Mézard M 1998 Out of equilibrium dynamics in spin-glasses and other glassy systems *Spin-Glasses and Random Fields* ed A P Young (Singapore: World Scientific) and references therein

[26] Bonnano G, Lillo F and Mantegna R 1999 Dynamics of the number of trades in financial securities *Preprint* cond-mat/9912006

[27] Plerou V, Gopikrishnan P, Amaral L A, Gabaix X and Stanley H E 1999 *Preprint* cond-mat/9912051

[28] Bouchaud J-P, Matacz A and Potters M 2001 *Preprint* cond-mat/0101120

[29] Ghashghaie S, Breymann W, Peinke J, Talkner P and Dodge Y 1996 *Nature* **381** 767

[30] Bouchaud J-P, Potters M and Meyer M 199 *Eur. Phys. J.* B **13** 595

[31] Frisch U 1997 *Turbulence: The Legacy of A Kolmogorov* (Cambridge: Cambridge University Press)

216

Criticality and market efficiency in a simple realistic model of the stock market

Damien Challet[1] and Matteo Marsili[2]

[1]Theoretical Physics, Oxford University, 1 Keble Road, Oxford OX1 3NP, United Kingdom
[2]Istituto Nazionale per la Fisica della Materia (INFM), Trieste-SISSA Unit, Via Beirut 2-4, Trieste 34014, Italy

(Received 4 December 2002; published 26 September 2003)

We discuss a simple model based on the minority game which reproduces the main *stylized facts* of anomalous fluctuations in finance. We present the analytic solution of the model in the thermodynamic limit. Stylized facts arise only close to a line of critical points with nontrivial properties, marking the transition to an unpredictable market. We show that the emergence of critical fluctuations close to the phase transition is governed by the interplay between the signal to noise ratio and the system size. These results provide a clear and consistent picture of financial markets, where stylized facts and verge of unpredictability are intimately related aspects of the same critical systems.

DOI: 10.1103/PhysRevE.68.036132   PACS number(s): 89.65.Gh, 02.50.Le, 05.20.Dd, 64.60.Ak

Understanding the origin of the anomalous collective fluctuations arising in stock markets poses novel and fascinating challenges in statistical physics. Stock market prices are characterized by anomalous collective fluctuations—known as *stylized facts* [1]—which are strongly reminiscent of critical phenomena: Prices do not follow a simple random walk process, but rather price increments are fat tailed distributed and their absolute value exhibits long range autocorrelations, called volatility clustering.

The connection with critical phenomena is natural, because financial markets are indeed complex systems of many interacting degrees of freedom—the traders. However, the nature of the two phases is still unclear. By means of agent based modeling, it has been realized [2–6] that stylized facts are due to the way in which the trading activity of agents interacting in a market "dresses" the fluctuations arising from economic activity—the so-called *fundamentals*. Reference [6] has shown that very simple models based on the minority game [7] can reproduce a quite realistic and rich behavior. Their simplicity makes an analytical approach to these models possible, using tools of statistical physics. Although minority game models do not capture the full complexity of financial markets [8–10], the emergence of anomalous fluctuations in such simple models, besides providing a picture for the behavior of real markets, also poses novel questions in statistical physics which deserve interest in their own.

In this paper, we first introduce the simplest possible grand canonical minority game (GCMG) which reproduces the main stylized facts, i.e., fat tails and volatility clustering. Then we present the analytic solution of this model in the relevant thermodynamic limit. It shows that the behavior of GCMG, in this limit, exhibits Gaussian fluctuations for all parameter values, but on a line of critical points which marks a phase transition at which the market becomes informationally efficient (i.e., unpredictable). For finite size systems, numerical simulations reveal that stylized facts emerge close to the transition line, but they abruptly disappear as the system size increases. Remarkably, the vanishing of stylized facts when the system's size increases also occurs in a variety of models of financial markets [11]; note that the models of Refs. [8,9] are not affected by finite size effects. We present

a theory of finite size effects which is fully confirmed by numerical simulations. This allows us to conclude that i) anomalous fluctuations are properties of the critical point in GCMG and ii) their occurrence is a consequence of markets being close to efficiency. Put differently, the standard model of mathematical finance where markets are efficient and price fluctuations are Gaussian [2] is never realized. It is exactly in the limit where markets become efficient that anomalous fluctuations arise.

The phase transition is quite unique as it mixes features which are typical of first order phase transitions—as discontinuities and phase coexistence—and of second order phase transitions—such as the divergence of correlation volumes and finite size effects.

In the market described by the minority game [7], agents $i=1,\ldots,N$ submit a bid $b_i(t)$ to the market in every period $t=1,2,\ldots$. Agents whose bid has the opposite sign of the total bid $A(t)=\Sigma_i b_i(t)$, win whereas the others lose. Agents bid according to a *trading strategy* which prescribes a bid $a_i^{\mu(t)}=\pm 1$ for each possible value of the public information variable $\mu(t)$, which is drawn uniformly from the integers $1,\ldots,P$ at each time. Each agent is assigned one trading strategy a_i^μ, randomly chosen from the set of 2^P possible strategies of this type. Agents are adaptive and may decide to refrain from playing if their strategy is not good enough [3,4]. More precisely, the bids of agents take the form $b_i(t)=\phi_i(t)a_i^{\mu(t)}$ where $\phi_i(t)=1$ or 0 according to whether agent i trades or not. In order to assess the performance of their strategy, agents assign scores $U_i(t)$ which they update by

$$U_i(t+1)=U_i(t)-a_i^{\mu(t)}A(t)-\epsilon_i, \qquad (1)$$

where $A(t)=\Sigma_i\phi_i(t)a_i^{\mu(t)}$. Agents trade ($\phi_i=1$) only if their score $U_i(t)$ is large enough. Here we suppose that [12]

$$\text{Prob}\{\phi_i(t)=1\}=\frac{1}{1+e^{\Gamma U_i(t)}}, \qquad (2)$$

where $\Gamma>0$ is a constant. The connection with markets goes along the lines of Refs. [4–6,10], which show that $A(t)$ is proportional to the difference of price logarithms; here, we take $\ln p(t+1)=\ln p(t)+A(t)$.

1063-651X/2003/68(3)/036132(4)/$20.00

In words, an agent reward his strategy if it prescribes bids a_i^μ which tend to coincide with those $b(t) = -\text{sign}\, A(t)$ of the minority of agents. If $-a_i^{\mu(t)} A(t)$ is larger than ϵ_i, the score U_i increases. The threshold ϵ_i in Eq. (1) models the incentives of agents for trading in the market. Investors who need to trade in the market for exchanging goods or assets will have $\epsilon_i < 0$. On the contrary, speculators who only trade for profiting of price fluctuations typically have $\epsilon_i > 0$. Of course there may be a whole range of types of traders, from prudent investors ($\epsilon_i > 0$) to risk-lover speculators ($\epsilon_i < 0$). Here we focus, for simplicity, on the case $\epsilon_i = \epsilon$ for $i \leqslant N_s$ and $\epsilon_i = -\infty$ for $N_s < i \leqslant N$. The $N_p = N - N_s$ agents who have $\epsilon_i = -\infty$, called *producers* after Refs. [13,14], trade no matter what, whereas the remaining N_s, the *speculators*, trade only if their strategy puts them on the minority side often enough.

If the conditional time average $\langle A|\mu \rangle$ of $A(t)$ given $\mu(t) = \mu$ is nonzero, then the knowledge of $\mu(t)$ allows a statistical prediction of the sign of $A(t)$. A measure of predictability is hence given by

$$H_0 = \overline{\langle A \rangle^2} = \frac{1}{P} \sum_{\mu=1}^{P} \langle A|\mu \rangle^2,$$

where we introduced the notation $\overline{(\cdots)}$ for averages over μ whereas $\langle \cdots \rangle$ denotes averages on the stationary state. When $H_0 = 0$ the market is unpredictable or *informationally efficient*. Volatility is instead defined as $\sigma^2 = \overline{\langle A^2 \rangle}$ and it measures market's fluctuations. A further quantity of interest is the number of active speculators, $N_{\text{act}}(t) = \Sigma_i \langle \phi_i(t) \rangle$ in the market.

Exact results can be obtained in the thermodynamic limit, which is defined as the limit $N_s, N_p, P \to \infty$, keeping constant the reduced number of speculators and producers $n_s = N_s/P$ and $n_p = N_p/P$. In this limit, both σ^2 and H_0 diverge with the system size, since $A(t) \sim \sqrt{N}$. Hence we shall consider the rescaled quantities H_0/P or σ^2/P. A detailed account of the calculation will be given elsewhere [15]. Here we just discuss the main step and the results. Following Ref. [16], we derive an Ito stochastic differential equations for the strategy scores $y_i(\tau) = U_i(t)$ in the rescaled continuous time $\tau = t/N$:

$$\frac{dy_i}{d\tau} = -\overline{a_i \langle A \rangle}_y - \epsilon + \eta_i. \tag{3}$$

Here η_i is a zero average Gaussian noise term with

$$\langle \eta_i(\tau) \eta_j(\tau') \rangle = \frac{1}{N} \overline{a_i a_j \langle A^2 \rangle}_y \delta(\tau - \tau'). \tag{4}$$

In Eqs. (3, 4) averages $\langle \cdots \rangle_y$ are taken on the distribution of $\phi_i(t)$ in Eq. (2), which depends on $y_i(\tau)$ in a nonlinear way: $\text{Prob}\{\phi_i(t) = 1\} = 1/[1 + e^{\Gamma y_i(\tau)}]$. Hence Eq. (3) is a quite complex system of nonlinear equations with a noise strength proportional to the time dependent volatility $\overline{\langle A^2 \rangle}_y$. This feedback will be responsible for the emergence of volatility buildups.

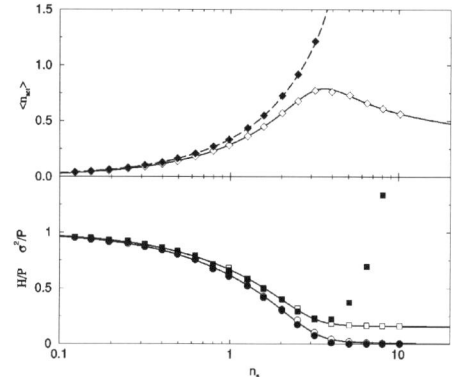

FIG. 1. Theory and numerical simulations: n_{act} (top) and σ^2/P and H/P (bottom) as a function of n_s for $\epsilon = 0.1$ (solid line) and $\epsilon = -0.01$ (dashed line). Numerical results for $\epsilon = 0.1$ (open symbols) and $\epsilon = -0.01$ (full symbols) are averages over 200 runs, with $N, P = 10\,000$ fixed and $\Gamma = \infty$.

Following Refs. [16,17] we find that the fraction $\langle \phi_i \rangle$ of times that agent i plays his active strategy in the stationary state is the solution of the minimization of the function

$$H_\epsilon = \frac{1}{P} \sum_{\mu=1}^{P} \left[\sum_{i=1}^{N} \langle \phi_i \rangle a_i^\mu + \sum_{i=N_s+1}^{N_s+N_p} a_i^\mu \right]^2 + 2\epsilon \sum_i \langle \phi_i \rangle, \tag{5}$$

with respect to $\langle \phi_i \rangle$. Note that for $\epsilon = 0$ this function reduces to the predictability H_0. For $\epsilon \neq 0$, the solution to this problem, i.e. the stationary state, is unique. An exact statistical mechanics description of the solution $\{\langle \phi_i \rangle\}$ can be carried out with the replica method, because the replica symmetric ansatz is exact. Furthermore, the solution to the Fokker-Planck equation corresponding to Eq. (3) can be well approximated by a factorized ansatz for $\epsilon > 0$. This means that the off-diagonal correlations vanish $[\langle (\phi_i - \langle \phi_i \rangle)(\phi_j - \langle \phi_j \rangle) \rangle = 0$, for $i \neq j]$ and, as a consequence, the volatility turns out to be given by $\sigma^2 = \overline{\langle A^2 \rangle} = H_0 + \Sigma_{i=1}^{N_s} \langle \phi_i \rangle (1 - \langle \phi_i \rangle)$. The solution $\{\langle \phi_i \rangle\}$ of the minimization of H_ϵ provides a complete description of the model in the limit $N \to \infty$ for $\epsilon > 0$. In particular the behavior of σ^2 is independent of Γ.

Figure 1 shows that all these conclusions are perfectly supported by numerical simulations: With a fixed number n_p of producers, as the number n_s of speculators increases, the market becomes more and more unpredictable, i.e., H_0 decreases. At the same time also the volatility σ^2 decreases. In a market with few speculators ($n_s < 1$ in Fig. 1), most of the fluctuations in $A(t)$ are due to the random choice of $\mu(t)$ (i.e., $\sigma^2 \approx H_0$) and the number n_{act} of active speculators grows approximately linearly with n_s.

When n_s increases further, the market reaches a point where it is barely predictable. Then, for $\epsilon > 0$ the number of

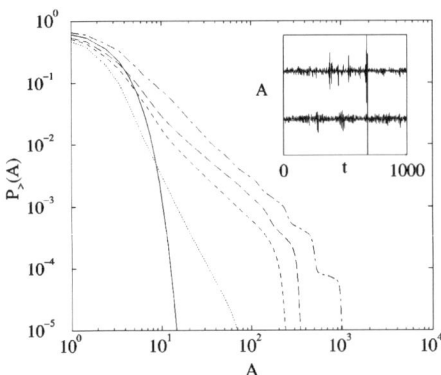

FIG. 2. Probability distribution of $A(t) > A$ for $n_s = 10$ (continuous line), 20, 50, 100, and 200 (dash-dotted line) ($PN_s = 16\,000$, $n_p = 1$, $\epsilon = 0.01$, $\Gamma = \infty$). Inset: time series of returns $A(t)$ showing volatility clustering for $n_s = 20$ (lower curve), but not for $n_s = 200$ (upper curve).

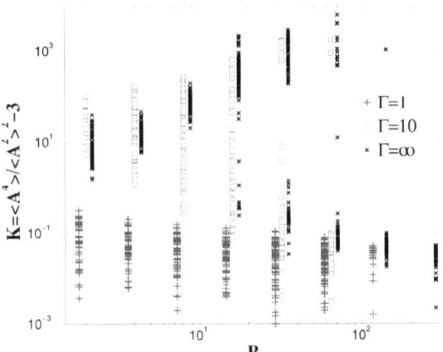

FIG. 3. (Color online) Excess kurtosis of $A(t)$ in simulations with $\epsilon = 0.01$, $n_s = 70$, $n_p = 1$, and several different system sizes P for $\Gamma = 1$, 10, and ∞.

active traders decreases and finally converges to a constant. This means that the market becomes highly selective: Only a negligible fraction of speculators trade ($\phi_i(t) = 1$) whereas the majority is inactive ($\phi_i(t) = 0$). The volatility σ^2 also remains constant in this limit.

For $\epsilon < 0$ we see a markedly different behavior: The number of active speculators continues growing with n_s even if the market is unpredictable $H_0 \approx 0$. The volatility σ^2/P has a minimum and then it increases with n_s in a way which depends on Γ. In other words, $\epsilon = 0$ for $n_s \geq n_s^\star(n_p)$ ($= 4.15 \ldots$, for $n_p = 1$) is the locus of a first order phase transition across which N_{act} and σ^2 exhibit a discontinuity. This same picture applies to a wider range of GCMG models such as that of Ref. [6].

Numerical simulations reproduce anomalous fluctuations similar to those of real financial markets close to the phase transition line. As shown in Fig. 2, the distribution of $A(t)$ is Gaussian for small enough n_s, and has fatter and fatter tails as n_s increases; the same behavior is seen for decreasing ϵ. In particular the distribution of $A(t)$ shows a power law behavior $P(|A| > x) \sim x^{-\beta}$ with an exponent which we estimated as $\beta \approx 2.8$ and 1.4 for $n_s = 20$ and 200 respectively and $\epsilon = 0.01$. Note that a realistic value $\beta \approx 3$ [19] is obtained for $n_s = 20$.

This is inconsistent, at first sight, with the theoretical results discussed previously for $N \to \infty$. Indeed, if the distribution of ϕ_i factorizes, $A(t)$ is the sum of N_s independent contributions and it satisfies the Central Limit Theorem. This implies that for $\epsilon \neq 0$ the variable $A(t)/\sqrt{N}$ converges in distribution to a Gaussian variable with zero average and variance σ^2/N in the limit $N \to \infty$ at fixed α. There are no anomalous fluctuations and no stylized facts. Figure 3 indeed shows that the anomalous fluctuations of Fig. 2 are finite size effects which disappear abruptly as the system size increases (or if Γ is small).

In order to understand these finite size effects, we note that volatility clustering arises because the noise strength in Eqs. (3,4) is proportional to the time dependent volatility $\langle A^2 \rangle_y$. The noise term is a source of correlated fluctuations because $a_i a_j \langle A^2 \rangle_y / N \sim 1/\sqrt{N}$ is small but nonzero, for $i \neq j$. It is reasonable to assume that the dynamics will sustain collective correlated fluctuations in the y_i only if the correlated noise is larger than the signal $-a_i \langle A \rangle_y - \epsilon$, which agents receive form the deterministic part of Eq. (3). Time dependent volatility fluctuations would be dissipated by the deterministic dynamics otherwise. A quantitative translation of this insight goes as follows: The noise correlation term is of order $\overline{a_i a_j \langle A^2 \rangle_y}/N \sim \sigma^2/P^{(3/2)}$, for $i \neq j$. This should be compared to the square of the deterministic term of Eq. (3) $[a_i \langle A \rangle_y + \epsilon]^2 \sim [\sqrt{H_0/P} + \epsilon]^2$. Rearranging terms, we find that volatility clustering sets in when

$$\frac{H_0}{\sigma^2} + 2\epsilon \sqrt{\frac{H_0}{P}} \frac{P}{\sigma^2} + \epsilon^2 \frac{P}{\sigma^2} \approx \frac{K}{\sqrt{P}}, \qquad (6)$$

where K is a constant. This prediction is remarkably well confirmed by Fig. 4: In the lower panel we plot the two sides of Eq. (6) as a function of n_s for different system sizes. The upper panel shows that the volatility σ^2/N starts deviating from the analytic result exactly at the crossing point $n_s^c(P)$ where Eq. (6) holds true. Furthermore the inset shows that the region $n_s > n_s^c(P)$ is described by a different type of scaling limit. Indeed the curves of Fig. 4 collapse one on top of the other when plotted against $n_s/n_s^c(P)$.

The nonlinearity of the response of agents is crucial for the onset of volatility time dependence. If Γ is small the response becomes smooth and anomalous fluctuations disappear (see Fig. 3). This picture is not affected by the introduction of a finite memory in the learning process of agents, for example in Ref. [18]. In particular the exponents of Fig. 2 do not depend on the memory.

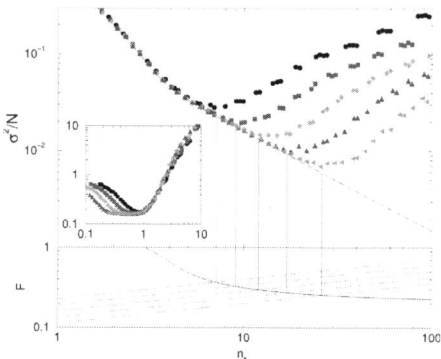

FIG. 4. (Color online) Onset of the anomalous dynamics for different system sizes. Top: σ^2/N for different series of simulations with $L \equiv PN_s$ constant: $PN_s = 1000$ (circles), 2000 (squares), 4000 (diamonds), 8000 (up triangles) and 16 000 (left triangles). In all simulations $n_p = 1$, $\epsilon = 0.1$, and $\Gamma = \infty$. Bottom: Left-hand side of Eq. (6) (full line) from the exact solution and $K/\sqrt{P} = K(n_s/L)^{1/4}$ (parallel dashed lines) as a function of n_s ($K \approx 1.1132$ in this plot). The intersection defines $n_s^c(P)$. Inset: Collapse plot of σ^2/N as a function of $n_s/n_s^c(P)$.

The fact that, in finite systems, stylized facts arise only close to the phase transition is reminiscent of finite size scaling in the theory of critical phenomena: In d-dimensional Ising model, for example, at temperature $T = T_c + \varepsilon$ critical fluctuations (e.g., in the magnetization) occur as long as the system size N is smaller than the correlation volume $\sim \varepsilon^{-d\nu}$. But for $N \gg \varepsilon^{-d\nu}$ the system shows the normal fluctuations of a paramagnet.

Equation (6) and $H_0/P \sim \epsilon^2$ imply that the same occurs in the GCMG with $d\nu = 4$. In other words, the critical window shrinks as $N^{-1/4}$ when $N \to \infty$. However, because of the long range nature of the interaction, anomalous fluctuations either concern the whole system or do not affect it at all, as clearly shown in Fig. 3. In the critical region the Gaussian phase coexists probabilistically with a phase characterized by anomalous fluctuations. This and the discontinuous nature of the transition at $\epsilon = 0$, are usually typical of first order phase transitions.

The picture of collective correlated fluctuations controlled by the signal to noise ratio appears to be universal for minority games. Finite size effects close to the phase transition of the standard minority game [7,15] are indeed explained by the same generic argument: When the signal to noise ratio H_0/σ^2 is of order $1/\sqrt{P}$ self-sustained collective fluctuations arise. In addition, finite size effects appear at a distance of order $P^{-1/4}$ from the critical point.

Volatility clustering also occur only close to the phase transition in the GCMG. The effect, in real markets is known to be due to wild fluctuations in the volume of trades [19]. Volume is the number of active traders $N_{act} + N_p$ in the GCMG. Wild volume fluctuations can only occur because of correlated collective fluctuations which arise close to criticality. Numerical simulations suggest that exponents vary continuously on the line of critical points. This raises the question of why real markets self-organize close to the critical surface with $\beta \approx 3$.

We conclude that the GCMG exhibits a critical behavior which is very similar to that observed in real markets. This, with the observation that real markets are indeed close to being informationally efficient, strongly suggests that real markets operate close to criticality. The phase transition is quite peculiar, with properties of both continuous and discontinuous transitions. The extension of renormalization group approaches to this system promises to be a quite interesting challenge.

This work was supported in part by the European Community's Human Potential Programme under Contract HPRN-CT-2002-00319, STIPCO, and in part by EPSRC under Oxford Condensed Matter Theory Grant No. GR/M04426.

[1] M. M. Dacorogna et al., An Introduction to High-Frequency Finance (Academic Press, London, 2001), Chap. V.
[2] See J.D. Farmer, Comput. Sci. Eng. 1, 26 (1999).
[3] F. Slanina and Y.-C. Zhang, Physica A 272, 257 (1999).
[4] P. Jefferies et al., Int. J. Theor. Appl. Finance 3(3), 443 (2000).
[5] D. Challet et al., Quant. Finance 1, 168 (2001).
[6] D. Challet, M. Marsili, and Y.-C. Zhang, Physica A 294, 514 (2001).
[7] D. Challet and Y.-C. Zhang, Physica A 246, 407 (1997).
[8] M. Marsili, Physica A 299, 93 (2001).
[9] I. Giardina and J.-Ph. Bouchaud, e-print cond-mat/0206222.
[10] J.V. Andersen and D. Sornette, Eur. Phys. J. B 31, 141 (2003).
[11] E. Egenter, T. Lux, and D. Stauffer, Physica A 268, 250 (1999).
[12] C. Camerer and T.-H. Ho, Econometrica 67, 827 (1999).
[13] D. Challet, M. Marsili, and Y.-C. Zhang, Physica A 276, 284 (2000).
[14] Y.-C. Zhang, Physica A 269, 30 (1999).
[15] D. Challet and M. Marsili (unpublished).
[16] M. Marsili and D. Challet, Phys. Rev. E 64, 056138 (2001).
[17] D. Challet, M. Marsili, and R. Zecchina, Phys. Rev. Lett. 84, 1824 (2000).
[18] M. Marsili et al., Phys. Rev. Lett. 87, 208701 (2001).
[19] V. Plerou et al., Phys. Rev. E 62, R3023 (2000).

PHYSICA Ⓐ

www.elsevier.com/locate/physa

Market mechanism and expectations in minority and majority games

Matteo Marsili*

*Istituto Nazionale per la Fisica della Materia (INFM), Via Beirut 2-4, Unità di Trieste-SISSA,
I-34014 Trieste, Italy*

Abstract

We present a derivation of the minority game from a market mechanism. This shows that the minority nature of the interaction crucially depends on the expectation model of agents. The same market mechanism with different expectations leads indeed to the majority game. We study in detail the minority game without information and clarify the role of initial conditions on the dynamics. The stronger and the more heterogeneous the prior beliefs which agents hold on the best choice, the more efficient is the final stationary state. We also review the effect of market impact. Finally we discuss mixed minority–majority games in order to address the issue of whether the dynamics of the market satisfies the expectations of agents. We find that in both a minority and a majority game expectations are self-fulfilled. ⓒ 2001 Elsevier Science B.V. All rights reserved.

1. Introduction

The minority game has been proposed [1,2] to model speculative behavior in financial markets. Agents sell and buy asset shares or currencies with the only goal of profiting from market's fluctuations. The minority game is a highly simplified picture of this context where agents can take, in each period, one of two actions. The agents who take the minority action win, whereas the majority loses. The connection with financial markets is established naively by observing that markets are instruments for reallocating goods. No arbitrage implies that no gain can be made, in principle, by pure trading. Hence the market should be a zero sum game. Transaction costs and other frictions make it an unfavorable game, on average, i.e., a minority game.[1] With this or similar motivations, a large body of numerical and analytical work [4] has been done in order

---

* Tel.: +39-040-2240461; fax: +39-040-3787528.

E-mail address: marsili@sissa.it (M. Marsili).

[1] Ref. [3] expands these types of arguments in much more details.

0378-4371/01/$ - see front matter ⓒ 2001 Elsevier Science B.V. All rights reserved.
PII: S 0378-4371(01)00285-0

---

to understand the collective behavior of such a complex system. This has finally led to a coherent picture [5–7,22] of how agents, processing public information, make a market informationally efficient, what is the role of market impact and how features such as excess volatility [8–10], fat tails and volatility clustering [3,11,12] arise.

But are financial markets really minority games? Naive common sense suggests that when everybody is going to buy the price will raise and hence it is convenient to buy. According to this argument, speculative markets should be rather similar to majority games. One may argue that only the minority of agents who buy first win whereas the other lose and eventually enter into endless arguments. Definitely something still needs to be clarified on the very basic relation between minority games and financial markets.

The problems with arguments in support of either the minority or the majority game essentially arise from the difficulties related with the definition of the payoff of a single transaction. Strictly speaking, buying or selling an asset does not change agent's wealth but just the composition of his portfolio. His wealth changes with the price of the assets he holds. Furthermore current prices cannot be used to compare the value of two portfolios with different composition: The actual sequence of trades necessary in order to liquidate them will not occur at present prices. The difference with realized prices is particularly relevant for high frequency speculative activity, which "lives" on the risky margin of price fluctuations. Therefore, the objective assessment of the validity of a trading strategy is a complex inter-temporal problem and cannot be based on a single transaction. The ultimate conclusion of these arguments is that financial markets cannot be described by simple markovian agent based models, but rather require rather sophisticated models of traders' behavior.

However, probably agents do not solve very complex problems in real-markets: For example, a trader may not want to compute the third decimal digit of his loss before deciding to dismiss a trading strategy! It may be reasonable to assume that traders first form an expectation on the behavior of the market and then optimize their behavior with respect to this expectation. Expectations are eventually revised and modified, on a longer time-scale, if they contrast with actual market behavior.

The first aim of this paper is to show that the minority game can be derived assuming that agents follow this behavior, from a market mechanism. From this viewpoint, expectations lie at the very basis of the definition of the minority game as a market model. Depending on the expectations of agents we can distinguish between *fundamentalists* or *contrarian* traders—who perceive the market as a minority game—and *trend followers*—who perceive it as a majority game.

We discuss the properties of the minority game—when there are only fundamentalists—in the simplest case, where no information is present. In particular we clarify the role of heterogeneity in the initial conditions, which represents the prior beliefs which agents hold on what strategy is the best. The larger the spread of initial conditions, the more the stationary state is efficient. Then we discuss the consequences of price-taking behavior: As soon as one allows agents to deviate from this behavior accounting even approximately for their market impact, the collective behavior of the system changes dramatically [10].

Finally we analyze the mixed case, where both fundamentalists and trend followers are present in the market. These two groups have opposite expectations on the price process. Which of these expectations is fulfilled by the actual price process? We find that the price process satisfies the expectations of whatever group is more numerous: In a market with a majority of fundamentalists the minority mechanism will prevail and the expectations of fundamentalists will be satisfied. On the contrary, if trend followers are the majority their expectations will be satisfied and price process will acquire a trend. In other words, we recover the well known fact that expectations of traders in a market can be self-fulfilling prophecies.

We conclude by discussing how these results generalize to the more complex case where public information is also present.

2. Minority and majority games as a market models

Let us imagine that time t is discrete, there are N agents and they submit all together their orders $a_i(t)$ to the market ($i = 1, \ldots, N$).

The single time step is split into three phases:

time $t - \varepsilon$. Agents take their choices on the basis of their accumulated experience up to time $t - 1$ and submit their orders $a_i(t)$.

time t. The market aggregates orders $a_i(t)$ from traders and forms a price $p(t)$.

time $t + \varepsilon$. Agents learn: they update their experience by evaluating the success of their actions. This will enter into the decision process at time $t + 1 - \varepsilon$.

Agents do not know the price at which the transaction will actually take place. Secondly, given that agents cannot define a real payoff for the present transaction as discussed above, they have to resort to "perceived" or "expected" payoffs in the learning phase.

We shall discuss later how agents take their decisions and how they update their behavior on the basis of perceived payoffs. For the moment being let us focus on the second-step and define the market interaction in detail. Let $a_i(t) > 0$ mean that agent i contributes $a_i(t)\$$ to the demand for the asset. Likewise $a_i(t) < 0$ means that i sells $-a_i(t)/p(t-1)$ units of asset, which is the current equivalent of $|a_i(t)|\$$. With $a_i(t) = \pm 1$ and $A(t) = \sum_i a_i(t)$, the demand is given by $D(t) = N + A(t)/2$, whereas the supply is $S(t) = N - A(t)/2\, p(t-1)$. Price is fixed by the market clearing condition, $p(t) = D(t)/S(t)$, i.e.,

$$p(t) = p(t - 1)\frac{N + A(t)}{N - A(t)} \, . \tag{1}$$

Consider an agent who buys 1\$ of asset at time t (i.e., $a_i(t) = 1$): He exchanges 1\$ with $1/p(t)$ units of asset. Was the choice $a_i(t) = 1$ the "best" one?

In order to answer this question, we may imagine that agent i considers selling $1/p(t)$ units of assets at time $t + 1$. This leads to a payoff

$$u_i(t) = \frac{p(t + 1)}{p(t)} - 1 \quad \text{if } a_i(t) = +1 \, . \tag{2}$$

95

However, the price $p(t + 1)$ will only be revealed after agents communicate their investments decisions $a_j(t + 1)$ for all j. If agents want to use Eq. (2) to revise their choice rule before deciding $a_i(t + 1)$, they have to replace $p(t + 1)$ in it by their expectation at time t, denoted by $E_t^{(i)}[p(t + 1)]$. Let us assume that:

$$E_t^{(i)}[p(t + 1)] = (1 - \psi_i)p(t) + \psi_i p(t - 1). \tag{3}$$

Then $E_t^{(i)}[u_i(t)|a_i(t) = +1] = -\psi_i[p(t) - p(t - 1)]/p(t)$ and, using Eq. (1) we find $E_t^{(i)}[u_i(t)|a_i(t) = +1] = -2\psi_i A(t)/[N + A(t)]$.

Likewise, if agent i sells $1/p(t - 1)$ units of assets at time t (i.e., $a_i(t) = -1$) and buys it back at the expected price $E_t^{(i)}[p(t + 1)]$, elementary algebra leads to $E_t^{(i)}[u_i(t)|a_i(t) = -1] = 2\psi_i A(t)/[N - A(t)]$. This means that:

$$u_i[a_i(t), A(t)] = E_t^{(i)}[u_i(t)] = -2\psi_i a_i(t) \frac{A(t)}{N + a_i(t)A(t)} . \tag{4}$$

Notice that agents who took the majority action $a_i(t) = \text{sign} A(t)$ "receive a payoff" $-2\psi_i |A(t)|/[N + |A(t)|]$ whereas agents in the minority get $2\psi_i |A(t)|/[N - |A(t)|]$. If $\psi_i > 0$ the minority is the winning side and indeed Eq. (4) reduces to the usual payoffs of the minority games.[2] Agents with $\psi_i > 0$ may be called *fundamentalists* as they believe that market prices fluctuate around a fixed value, so that future price is an average of past prices. They may also be called *contrarians* since they believe that the future price increment $\Delta p(t + 1) = p(t + 1) - p(t)$ is negatively correlated with the last one

$$E_t^{(i)}[\Delta p(t + 1)] = -\psi_i \Delta p(t) .$$

On the other hand, if $\psi_i < 0$ the game turns into a majority game. More precisely, agent i perceives the game as one in which he prefers to stay in the majority. These type of agents may be called trend followers since they believe that future price increments $\Delta p(t + 1)$ are positively correlated with past ones, as if the price were following a monotonic trend.

The expectations of agents play a key role in the definition of the model. We shall discuss below in some detail the collective behavior of the market, depending on the expectation models of agents, in the simplest possible setting.

In the real world, agents revise and calibrate their expectations according to the real price history. Given that they all consider the same price history, expectations should converge. Hence we expect that either all agents play a minority game or they all play a majority game. We shall see that in both cases expectations of agents are fulfilled. So, even if with totally different outcomes, both models may provide a description of market dynamics.

---

[2] It turns out that, in the minority game ($\psi_i > 0 \ \forall i$) $A(t) \sim \sqrt{N}$ is negligible compared to N in the denominator and it can be dropped. Then one recovers the linear payoffs used in Refs. [13,14,5,6].

3. Minority game

In the minority game the quantities of interest are the first two moments of $A(t)$:

$$\langle A \rangle = \lim_{t_0, T \to \infty} \frac{1}{T} \sum_{t=t_0+1}^{t_0+T} A(t),$$

$$\sigma^2 \equiv \langle A^2 \rangle = \lim_{t_0, T \to \infty} \frac{1}{T} \sum_{t=t_0+1}^{t_0+T} A^2(t).$$

If agents are rational at all, we expect that they will drive the system to a state where none of the two actions $a_i = \pm 1$ identifies systematically the minority side. Hence, we expect $\langle A \rangle = 0$. σ^2 gives instead a measure of the efficiency of the systems because it tells how many more losers than winners are there. For illustrative purposes, let us compare the state where $A(t) = 0$ $\forall t$ to the state where $A(t) = (-1)^t N$. Both have $\langle A \rangle = 0$ however in the former no agent loses ($\sigma^2 = 0$) whereas in the latter all agents lose ($\sigma^2 = N^2$).

Let us consider a simple version of the MG [10] where the collective behavior can be easily understood with quite simple mathematics.

Agents learn from past experience which action $a_i(t)$ is the best one. The learning dynamics is the one used in general in minority games and it is well rooted in the economic literature [15]. The past experience of agent i is stored in the "score" $\Delta_i(t)$: $\Delta_i(t) > 0$ means that the action $a_i = +1$ is (perceived as) more successful than $a_i = -1$ and *vice-versa*. Agents use the information accumulated in $\Delta_i(t)$ to take decisions:[3]

$$\text{Prob}\{a_i(t) = \pm 1\} \equiv \frac{e^{\Delta_i(t)}}{e^{\Delta_i(t)} + e^{-\Delta_i(t)}} \tag{5}$$

and they update $\Delta_i(t)$ by

$$\Delta_i(t+1) = \Delta_i(t) - \Gamma \frac{A(t)}{N}. \tag{6}$$

This learning dynamics is easily understood: if $A(t) < 0$ agents observe that the best action was $+1$ at time t. Hence they increase Δ_i and the probability of playing $a_i = +1$ (see Eq. (5)). The parameter Γ modulates the strength of the response in the behavior of agents to the "stimulus" $A(t)/N$. Let us finally assume that the initial conditions $\Delta_i(0)$ are drawn from a distribution $p_0(\Delta)$ with a standard deviation s. How does the collective behavior depends on the parameters Γ and s?

Notice that $y(t) = \Delta_i(t) - \Delta_i(0)$ does not depend on i, for all times. For $N \gg 1$, the law of large numbers allows us to approximate $A(t)/N$ by its average value.[4] In

---

[3] The exponential form, which results from a Logit discrete choice model, is taken here for simplicity. Any increasing continuous function $\chi_i(x)$, with $0 \leqslant \chi_i(x) \leqslant 1$ for all real x, $\chi(x) \to 0$ as $x \to -\infty$ and $\chi(x) \to 1$ as $x \to \infty$, leads to the same results [10].

[4] The average value of $A(t)/N$ is computed using Eq. (5), which gives $\langle a_i(t) \rangle = \tanh \Delta_i(t)$, and averaging over the distribution $p_0(\Delta)$ of initial conditions $\Delta_i(0)$.

Eq. (6), this yields a dynamical equation for $y(t)$:

$$y(t+1) \cong y(t) - \Gamma \langle \tan h[y(t) + \Delta(0)] \rangle_0 , \qquad (7)$$

where the average $\langle \cdots \rangle_0$ is on the distribution p_0 of initial conditions. This equation admits a fixed point solution $y(t) = y^*$ for all t, where y^* is the solution of

$$\langle \tan h[y^* + \Delta(0)] \rangle_0 = \langle A \rangle = 0 . \qquad (8)$$

If this solution is stable, the distribution of relative scores $\Delta_i(t)$ shift bodily from the initial conditions and settles around the origin, in order to satisfy $\langle A \rangle = 0$ (Eq. (8)). Given that $\langle a_i \rangle = \tan h[y^* + \Delta_i(0)]$, it is not difficult to find that

$$\sigma^2 = \sum_{i=1}^{N} (1 - \langle a_i \rangle^2) = N \{ 1 - \langle \tan h[y^* + \Delta(0)]^2 \rangle_0 \}$$

for this state. Notice that $\sigma^2 \propto N$ and it *decreases* with the spread of the distribution of initial conditions.

When is this a stationary state of the dynamics? To answer this question it suffices to study the linear stability of the dynamics. We set $y(t) = y^* + \delta y(t)$ and expand Eq. (7) to linear order. It is easy to find that the fixed point y^* is stable only for

$$\Gamma < \Gamma_c = \frac{2}{1 - \langle \tan h[y^* + \Delta(0)]^2 \rangle_0} = \frac{2N}{\sigma^2} . \qquad (9)$$

When $\Gamma > \Gamma_c$ we find periodic solutions $y(t) = y^* + z^*(-1)^t$ where y^* and z^* satisfy

$$\frac{\langle \tan h[y^* + z^* + \Delta(0)] \rangle_0 + \langle \tan h[y^* - z^* + \Delta(0)] \rangle_0}{2} = 0 , \qquad (10)$$

$$\frac{\langle \tan h[y^* + z^* + \Delta(0)] \rangle_0 - \langle \tan h[y^* - z^* + \Delta(0)] \rangle_0}{2} = \frac{2z}{\Gamma} . \qquad (11)$$

The parameter z^* plays the role of an order parameter of the transition at Γ_c ($z^* = 0$ for $\Gamma < \Gamma_c$). Again we have $\langle A \rangle = 0$, but now it is easy to check that

$$\sigma^2 \cong N^2 \frac{\langle \tan h[y^* + z^* + \Delta(0)] \rangle_0^2 + \langle \tan h[y^* - z^* + \Delta(0)] \rangle_0^2}{2} = \left(\frac{2Nz^*}{\Gamma} \right)^2$$

is proportional to N^2. Hence this is a much less efficient state. Fig. 1 shows the behavior of σ^2/N^2 as a function of Γ. The inset shows how Γ_c depends on the spread of initial conditions. We conclude that the more heterogeneous the initial condition is, the more efficient is the final state and the more the fixed point y^* is stable.

The transition from a state where $\sigma^2 \propto N$ to a state with $\sigma^2 \propto N^2$ is generic in the minority game, and it has been discussed by several authors [13,14,16,17].

3.1. Market impact

Agents in Eq. (6) behave as price takers: They totally neglect the fact that price changes—i.e., $A(t)$—also depend on their choice $a_i(t)$. This may seem reasonable given

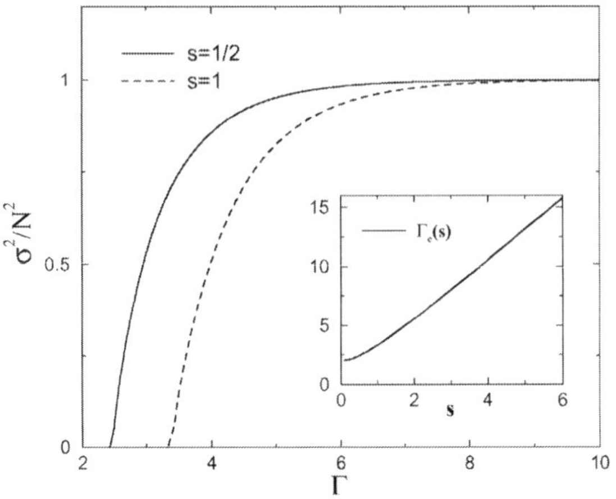

Fig. 1. Global efficiency σ^2/N^2 as a function of Γ for two different sets of initial conditions: $\Delta_i(0)$ is drawn from a Gaussian distribution with variance s^2. The full line corresponds to $s = 1/2$ whereas the dashed line is the result for $s = 1$. The inset reports the critical learning rate Γ_c as a function of the spread s of initial conditions.

that agents are very many and the impact of each of them is very small. As we shall see in a while (see also Refs. [5,6,10]), this argument is misleading because indeed price taking behavior has very strong consequences. Let us consider a slightly different learning dynamics:

$$\Delta_i(t+1) = \Delta_i(t) - \frac{\Gamma}{N}[A(t) - \eta a_i(t)] .\qquad(12)$$

The η term in Eq. (12) describes the fact that agent i accounts for his own contribution to $A(t)$. For $\eta = 1$ indeed, agent i considers only the behavior of other agents $A(t) - a_i(t)$ and does not react to his own action $a_i(t)$. In other words, η measures the extent to which agents account for their "market impact".

For $\eta = 0$ we recover the results discussed above. But the situation changes drastically as soon as agents start to account for their market impact, i.e., for $\eta > 0$. To see this, let us take the average of Eq. (12) in the long time limit and define $m_i = \langle a_i \rangle$. We note that

$$\langle \Delta_i(t+1) \rangle - \langle \Delta_i(t) \rangle = -\frac{\Gamma}{N}\left[\sum_{j \in N} m_j - \eta m_i\right] = -\frac{\Gamma}{N}\frac{\partial H_\eta}{\partial \eta} ,\qquad(13)$$

where

$$H_\eta = \frac{1}{2}\left(\sum_{i \in N} m_i\right)^2 - \frac{\eta}{2}\sum_{i \in N} m_i^2 .\qquad(14)$$

A close inspection[5] of these equations implies that m_i are given by the minima of H_η.

Note that H_1 is an Harmonic function of m_i's. Hence, it attains its minima (and maxima) on the boundary of the hypercube $[-1, 1]^N$. So for $\eta = 1$ all agents take always the same actions $a_i(t) = m_i = +1$ or -1 and the waste of resources is as small as possible: Indeed $\sigma^2 = 0$ or 1 if N is even or odd, which is a tremendous improvement with respect to the case $\eta = 0$ (where $\sigma^2 \sim N$ or N^2). These states are indeed Nash equilibria [10] of the associated N persons minority game. This argument extends to all $\eta > 0$: The stationary states of the learning process for any $\eta > 0$ are Nash equilibria.[6] Hence, as soon as agents start to account for their market impact ($\eta > 0$) the collective property of the system changes abruptly and inefficiencies σ^2 are drastically reduced.

Again the asymptotic state is not unique and it is selected by the initial conditions. However, now the set of equilibria is discrete and the system jumps discontinuously from an equilibrium to another, as the initial conditions $\Delta_i(0)$ vary. This contrasts with the $\eta = 0$ case, where the equilibrium shifts continuously as a function of the initial conditions [10].

4. Mixed minority–majority game

The derivation of inter-agent interaction depends on the expectations of agents on the nature of the market process. It is then crucial to ask whether expectations are consistent with market dynamics. We shall pose this question in a more general model where a fraction θ of agents is fundamentalist and behaves as in the minority game, whereas a fraction $1 - \theta$ of agents behaves as a trend follower. More precisely let $i = 1, \ldots, \theta N$ label fundamentalist, who have $\psi_i > 0$ and follow Eq. (6). Trend followers—who have $\psi_i < 0$—are labeled by $i = \theta N + 1, \ldots, N$ and we assume that they follow the usual choice rule Eq. (5) with

$$\Delta_i(t+1) = \Delta_i(t) + \Gamma \frac{A(t)}{N} . \tag{15}$$

By this dynamics, agents reward the action taken by the majority and increase the probability of choosing $a_i(t + 1) = \operatorname{sign} A(t)$.

Let us assume for simplicity $\Delta_i(0) = 0$ for all i. Then we shall have that $\Delta_i(t) = y(t)$ for $i \leqslant \theta N$ (fundamentalists) and $\Delta_i(t) = -y(t)$ for $i > \theta N$ (trend followers). The same

---

[5] The first-order conditions on H_η imply that if $-1 < m_i < 1$ then $\langle \Delta_i(t + 1) \rangle = \langle \Delta_i(t) \rangle$, i.e., the process $\Delta_i(t)$ is stationary. Else if $m_i = +1$ (or -1) one should have $\Delta_i(t) \to +\infty$ (or $-\infty$), which is precisely what constrained minimization and Eq. (13) say.

[6] The proof of this statement goes as follows: Suppose that m^* is an equilibrium with $-1 < m_k^* < 1$ for $k = 1, \ldots, n$ and $m_i^* = \pm 1$ for $i > n$. The conditions for a minimum requires that H_η is locally positive definite around m^*. At least n eigenvalues of the matrix $\partial^2 H_\eta / \partial m_i \partial m_j$ must be non-negative. But this matrix has only one positive eigenvalue $\lambda = N - \eta$ and $N - 1$ negative eigenvalues $\lambda = -\eta$. Hence n can at most be 1, which can occur for N odd.

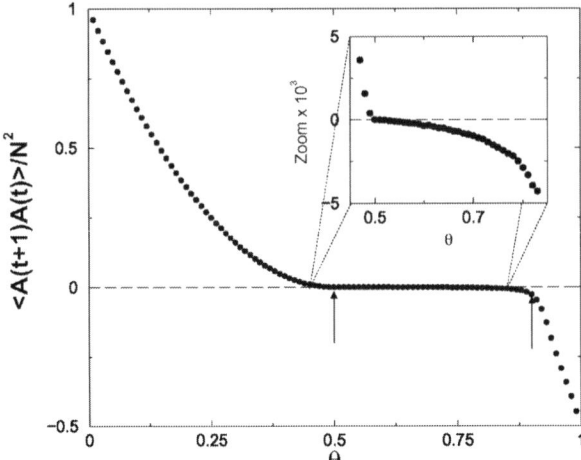

Fig. 2. Autocorrelation of successive returns as a function of the fraction θ of fundamentalists in the market. Autocorrelation is taken in the stationary state of a system of $N = 10^4$ agents with $\Gamma = 2.5$. Arrows mark the transitions between the three regimes described in the text, which occur at $\theta = 0.5$ and at $\theta = 0.9$. The inset shows a detail of the central part of the graph.

steps leading to Eq. (7) give this time

$$y(t+1) = y(t) + \Gamma(1 - 2\theta) \tan h \, y(t) . \tag{16}$$

Again there is fixed point solution $y^* = 0$. The linear stability analysis requires $-2 < \Gamma(1 - 2\theta) < 0$. We have then three regimes:

$\theta > 1/2$, $\Gamma < (2\theta - 1)^{-1}$. The fixed point y^* is stable and hence $\langle A \rangle = 0$ and $\sigma^2 \propto N$. We are in the regime of a minority game.

$\theta > 1/2$, $\Gamma > (2\theta - 1)^{-1}$. The fixed point y^* is unstable and a bifurcation to period two orbits occurs as in the previous section. We have $\langle A \rangle = 0$ and $\sigma^2 \propto N^2$ as for the minority game for $\Gamma > \Gamma_c$.

$\theta < 1/2$. The fixed point y^* is unstable but a novel dynamical solution $y(t) = y_0 + vt$ sets in, with $v = \pm \Gamma(1 - 2\theta)$. In this solution trend followers all behave coherently $a_i(t) = a_{tf}$ for $i > \theta N$, whereas all fundamentalists choose the opposite action $a_i = -a_{tf}$ for $i \leqslant \theta N$. As a result $\langle A \rangle = \pm (2\theta - 1)$ and $\sigma^2 \propto N^2$.

Summarizing we see that the character of dynamics which prevails is that of the minority game when fundamentalists are the majority ($\theta > 1/2$) and that of the majority game when trend followers are in majority ($\theta < 1/2$). Furthermore the expectations of the majority group are fulfilled. This is easy to understand when trend followers dominate: Indeed for $\theta > 1/2$ we find $\langle A \rangle \neq 0$ which means that indeed the price dynamics acquires a trend. Fig. 2 shows that the same happens also for $\theta = 1/2$: When fundamentalists are the majority the correlation coefficient $\langle [p(t+1) - p(t)][p(t) - p(t-1)] \rangle \propto$

$\langle A(t+1)A(t)\rangle$ is negative, indicating that large price fluctuations are likely to be corrected by future price fluctuations in the opposite direction.

In a more general model agents would likely revise their expectations and correct them if they are wrong, i.e., the parameters ψ_i, and hence θ, should be slowly functions of time. The only possible stationary states where expectations are self-fulfilling are those with $\theta = 1$—which corresponds to the minority game—and $\theta = 0$—the majority game. This picture would still be an highly idealized situation: On one hand market rallies such as those described by the majority game cannot last forever because of budgets constraints not taken into account here, and/or lack of liquidity: The behavior of the majority game is typical of a market bubble. On the other, even in a market of fundamentalists only, a price trend could appear by stochastic fluctuations. This may convince some agent to revise his expectations and change from fundamentalist to trend follower.

The interplay between these two groups of agents—fundamentalists and trend followers—has indeed been studied by many authors [18]. The switch between market phases dominated by fundamentalists ($\theta > 1/2$) and speculative bubbles caused by trend followers ($\theta < 1/2$) provides an explanation for the origin of non-trivial statistical properties of price processes in agent based models [19]. Even though alternative explanations based entirely on a minority game mechanism exist [3,12,11], mixed minority–majority games as the ones discussed here are definitely worth of more detailed investigations.

5. Conclusion and perspectives

The results discussed above for the minority game generalize to much more complex models with heterogeneous agents. Agents are heterogeneous because they react differently to the "state of the market", i.e., because they are endowed with different trading strategies. As long as agents are many, one again finds [7,10] a transition in Γ for $\eta = 0$, between a fixed point like stationary solution for $\Gamma < \Gamma_c$ and a turbulent state for $\Gamma > \Gamma_c$. Again as soon as η is "switched on" the market's efficiency σ^2 increases with a discontinuous jump at $\eta = 0^+$ as long as the number of agents N is large enough [5,6].

The case of the majority game and of mixed models has instead received much less attention. On one hand, results from numerical simulations have been reported in Ref. [20]. On the other, the analytic approach of Ref. [5] extends naturally to these models and leads to the analysis of well known models in the neural network community. Results on this line of research shall be presented elsewhere [21].

Acknowledgements

I gratefully acknowledge D. Challet, A. De Martino and Y.-C. Zhang for discussions.

References

[1] D. Challet, Y.-C. Zhang, Emergence of cooperation and organization in an evolutionary game, Physica A 246 (1997) 407.

[2] Y.-C. Zhang, Evolving models of financial markets, Europhys. News 29 (1998) 51.

[3] D. Challet, A. Chessa, M. Marsili, Y.-C. Zhang, From minority games to real markets, Quant. Fin. I (2001) 168.

[4] For a commented collection of papers and preprints on the minority game see the web site http://www.unifr.ch/econophysics/.

[5] D. Challet, M. Marsili, R. Zecchina, Statistical mechanics of systems with heterogeneous agents: minority games, Phys. Rev. Lett. 84 (2000) 1824.

[6] M. Marsili, D. Challet, R. Zecchina, Exact solution of a modified El Farol bar problem, Physica A 280 (2000) 522.

[7] M. Marsili, D. Challet, On the continuum time limit and stationary states of the minority game, 2001, e-print cond-mat/0103024.

[8] P. Jefferies et al., Int., J. Th. Appl. Fin. 3 (2000) 3.

[9] T.S. Lo et al., From market games to real-world markets, 2000, e-print cond-mat/0008387.

[10] M. Marsili, D. Challet, Trading behavior and excess volatility in toy models of financial markets, Adv. Compl. Systems 4 (2001) 5.

[11] J.-P. Bouchaud, I. Giardina, M. Mezard, On a universal mechanism for long ranged volatility correlations, 2000, e-print cond-mat/0012156.

[12] D. Challet, M. Marsili, Y.-C. Zhang, Stylized facts of financial markets and market crashes in minority games, 2001, e-print cond-mat/0101326.

[13] D. Challet, M. Marsili, Phase transition and symmetry breaking in the minority game, Phys. Rev. E 60 (1999) 6271.

[14] A. Cavagna et al., A thermal model for adaptive competition in a market, Phys. Rev. Lett. 83 (1999) 4429.

[15] C. Camerer, T.-H. Ho, Experience-weighted attraction learning in normal form games, Econometrica 67 (1999) 827.

[16] R. Savit, R. Manuca, R. Riolo, Adaptative competition, market efficiency and phase transition, Phys. Rev. Lett. 82 (1990) 2203.

[17] N.F. Johnson et al., Crowds effects and volatility in a competitive market, Physica A 269 (1999) 1.

[18] C. Chiarella, The dynamics of speculative behavior, Ann. Oper. Res. 37 (1992) 101.

[19] T. Lux, M. Marchesi, Scaling and criticality in a stochastic multi-agent model of a financial market, Nature 397 (1999) 498.

[20] M.A.R. de Cara, O. Pla, F. Guinea, Competition efficiency and collective behavior in the El Farol bar problem, Eur. Phys. J. B 10 (1999) 187–191.

[21] A. De Martino, M. Marsili, 2001, in preparation.

[22] J. Berg, M. Marsili, A. Rustichini, R. Zecchina, Statistical mechanics of asset markets with private information, Quant. Finance 1 (2) (2001) 203–216.

THE EUROPEAN
PHYSICAL JOURNAL B

The $-game

J. Vitting Andersen[1,2] and D. Sornette[2,3,a]

[1] UFR de Sciences Économiques, Gestion, Mathématiques et Informatique[b], and Université Paris X-Nanterre,
92001 Nanterre Cedex, France
[2] Laboratoire de Physique de la Matière Condensée[c] and Université de Nice-Sophia Antipolis, 06108 Nice Cedex 2, France
[3] Institute of Geophysics and Planetary Physics and Department of Earth and Space Science
University of California, Los Angeles, California 90095, USA

Received 5 June 2002 / Received in final form 21 November 2002
Published online 27 January 2003 – © EDP Sciences, Società Italiana di Fisica, Springer-Verlag 2003

Abstract. We propose a payoff function extending Minority Games (MG) that captures the competition
between agents to make money. In contrast with previous MG, the best strategies are not always targeting
the minority but are shifting opportunistically between the minority and the majority. The emergent
properties of the price dynamics and of the wealth of agents are strikingly different from those found in
MG. As the memory of agents is increased, we find a phase transition between a self-sustained speculative
phase in which a "stubborn majority" of agents effectively collaborate to arbitrage a market-maker for
their mutual benefit and a phase where the market-maker always arbitrages the agents. A subset of agents
exhibit a sustained non-equilibrium risk-return profile.

PACS. 89.65.Gh Economics, business, and financial markets – 89.75.Fb Structures and organization in
complex systems – 02.50.Le Decision theory and game theory

The Minority Game (MG)[1] is perhaps the simplest in the
class of multi-agent games of interacting inductive agents
with limited abilities competing for scarce resources. Many
published works on MG have motivated their study by
their relevance to financial markets, because investors exhibit a large heterogeneity of investment strategies, investment horizons, risk aversions and wealths, have limited resources and time to dedicate to novel strategies
and the minority mechanism is found in markets. Here,
our goal is to point out that the minority mechanism is
a relatively minor contribution to the self-organization of
financial markets. We develop a better description based
on a financially motivated payoff function. Following the
standard specification of MG, we assume that markets are
purely speculative, that is, agents profit only from changes
in the stock price. In addition, agents are chartists or technical analysts who only analyze past realization of prices,
with no anchor on fundamental economic analysis.

A MG is a repeated game where N players have to
choose one out of two alternatives at each time step based
on information represented as a binary time series $B(t)$.
Those who happen to be in the minority win. Each agent i
possesses a memory of the last m digits of $B(t)$. A strategy gives a prediction for the next outcome of $B(t)$ based
on the history of the last m digits of B. Since there are 2^m
possible histories, the total number of strategies is given

[a] e-mail: sornette@unice.fr
[b] CNRS UMR7536
[c] CNRS UMR6622

by $S = 2^{2^m}$. Each agent holds the same number s of
(but in general different) strategies among the S possible strategies. At each time t, every agent uses her most
successful strategy (in terms of payoff, see below) to decide whether to buy or sell an asset. The agent takes an
action $a_i(t) = \pm 1$ where 1 is interpreted as buying an asset
and -1 as selling an asset. The excess demand, $A(t)$, at
time t is therefore given as $A(t) = \sum_{i=1}^N a_i(t)$. The payoff
of agent i in the MG is given by:

$$g_i(t) = -a_i(t)A(t). \qquad (1)$$

As the name of the game indicates, if a strategy i is in the
minority $(a_i(t)A(t) < 0)$, it is rewarded. In other words,
agents in MG try to be anti-imitative. To ensure causality, the notation $-a_i(t)A(t)$ in (1) must be understood as
$-a_i(t-1/2)A(t)$ since the actions/strategies of the agents
take place *before* the price (and thus the payoff) can be determined. The richness and complexity of minority games
stem from the fact that agents have to be different; theories based on an effective representative agent are bound to
fail because she would represent the majority. MG are intrinsically frustrated and fluctuations and heterogeneities
are the key ingredients.

In order to model financial markets, several authors
have used the following or slight variants of the following
equation for the return $r(t)$ [2,3]

$$r(t) \equiv \ln(p(t)) - \ln(p(t-1)) = A(t)/\lambda, \qquad (2)$$

where $\lambda \propto N$ is the liquidity. The fact that the price goes
in the direction of the sign of the order imbalance $A(t)$

We wish to thank the authors and Springer-Verlag, for granting us permission to reprint this paper.

is well-documented [4–9]. By constructing and analyzing a large database of estimated market-wide order imbalances for a comprehensive sample of NYSE stocks during the period 1988–1998 inclusive, Chordia *et al.* [10] confirm that contemporaneous order imbalance $A(t)$ exerts an extremely significant impact on market returns in the expected direction; the positive coefficients of their regressions imply that excess buy (sell) orders drive up (down) prices, in qualitative agreement with (2).

Let us assume that an agent thinks at time $t - 1/2$ that the unknown future price $p(t)$ will be larger than the known previous quote $p(t-1)$ and larger than the next future quote $p(t+1)$, thus identifying $p(t)$ as a local maximum. Her best strategy is to put a sell order at time $t - 1/2$ in order for the sale to be realized at time t at the local price maximum, allowing her to profit from future drops at later times. She will then profit and cash in the money equal to the drop from the local maximum at time t to a smaller price realized at $t + 1$ or later. In this case, the optimal strategy is thus to be in the minority as seen from the relation between the direction of the price change given by the sign of $r(t)$ and the direction of the majority given by the sign of $A(t)$. Alternatively, if the agent thinks at time $t - 1/2$ that $p(t-1) < p(t) < p(t+1)$, her best strategy is to put a buy order at time $t - 1/2$, realized at the price $p(t)$ at time t. She will then profit by the amount $p(t+1) - p(t)$ if her expectation that $p(t) < p(t+1)$ is born out. In this case, it is profitable for an agent to be in the majority, because the price continues to go up, driven by the majority, as seen from (2). In order to know when the price reaches its next local extremum and optimize their gains, the agents need to predict the price movement over the next *two* time steps ahead (t and $t + 1$), and not only over the next time step as in the standard MG. This pinpoints the fundamental misconception of MG as models of financial markets. Indeed, by shifting from minority to majority strategies and vice-versa, an agent tries at each time step to gain $|p(t + 1) - p(t)|$ whatever the sign of $p(t + 1) - p(t)$: an ideal strategy is a "return rectifier." Because an agent's decision $a(t - 1/2)$ at time $t - 1/2$ is put into practice and invested in the stock market at time t, the decision will bring its fruit from the price variation from t to $t + 1$. From (2), this price variation is simply proportional to $A(t)$. Therefore, the agent has a positive payoff if $a(t - 1/2)$ and $A(t + 1/2)$ have the same sign. As a consequence, in the spirit of the MG (and using the MG notation without half-time scales), the correct payoff function is[1]

$$g_i^\$(t + 1) = a_i(t)A(t + 1). \tag{3}$$

The superscript $ is a reminder that the action taken by agent i at time t results at time $t + 1$ in a percentage gain/loss of $g_i^\$(t + 1)/\lambda$ (see (2)). We will refer to the game where the agents use (3) as the "$-game" since, by

using this payoff function, the agents strive to increase their wealth. This reasoning stresses that, in real markets, the driving force underlying the competition between investors is not a struggle to be in the minority at each time step, but rather a fierce competition to gain money.

In reference [12], Marsili presents an interesting derivation of the minority game based on a reasonable approximation of market mechanisms by emphasizing the role of agents' expectations. By playing with the nature of the agents' expectation, Marsili also shows that the majority rule can emerge naturally and he studies mixed minority-majority games to find that, in both a minority and a majority game, expectations are self-fulfilled. The difference with our present work is multifold. First, Marsili postulates beliefs that are of a very simple nature and imposes the fraction of trend-followers (majority players) and contrarians (minority players). This leads to different market regimes depending on this fraction. In contrast, our agents do not belong to fixed populations of either majority or minority players but any agent freely shifts from trend-follower to contrarian by using an adaptive behavior. Thus, Marsili's paper emphasizes expectations at the cost of freezing the division between the two categories of trend followers and contrarians. We do not use expectations but only the objective of maximizing a payoff in order to address the problem of adaptation leading to possible shifts between the two classes of strategies. We believe that our approach is more relevant to understanding concretely real markets. There are many evidences well-documented in the finance literature that investors may be mainly contrarian in certain phases of the market and become trend-followers in other phases (see for instance Ref. [13] in which Frankel and Froot found that, over the period 1981–1985, the market shifted away from the fundamentalists and towards the chartists to fuel the speculative bubble on the US dollar). Thus, rather than being either minority or majority players, our agents change adaptively from trend-followers to contrarians and *vice versa*. Our agents are thus both opportunistic majority and minority players, as they should to represent real investors.

In the simplest version of the model, each trade made by an agent is the exchange of one quanta of a riskless asset (cash) for one quanta of a risky one (asset) irrespective of the agent's wealth or the price of the asset. The wealth of the ith agent at time t is given as

$$W_i(t) = N_i(t)p(t) + C_i(t), \tag{4}$$

where $N_i(t)$ is the number of assets held by agent i and $C_i(t)$ the cash possessed by agent i at time t. In order to illustrate the differences between the payoff functions (1) and (3), we have plotted in Figure 1 an example of the payoff (upper plot) of the best as well as the worst performing MG agent using (1). Each agent is allowed to take either a long or a short position, and we furthermore assume that the agents stay in the market at all times. This means that if *e.g.* an agent has taken a long position (*i.e.* taken the action $a_i = 1$ to buy a asset) the agent will not open new positions (and therefore does not contribute to the excess demand and price change) but keep the long

---

[1] A similar rule for the update of scores was recently considered in another model [11] but with a different sign. After appearance of our present paper in cond-mat, we were notified by the authors of [11] that their sign difference was a misprint, so that ours and their rule are the same.

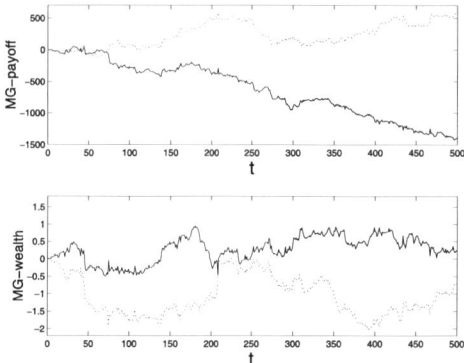

Fig. 1. Payoff function (1) (upper graph) and wealth (lower graph) for the MG-game showing the best (dotted line) and worst (solid line) performing agent for a game using $N = 501$ agents, memory of $m = 10$ and $s = 10$ strategies per agent. No transaction costs are applied.

to zero [10]. As shown in [15], this can be achieved by the following generalization of (2):

$$r(t) \equiv \ln(p(t)) - \ln(p(t-1)) = (A(t) - S_M(t))/\lambda, \quad (5)$$

with $S_M(t) = -\sum_{t=0}^{t-1} A(t)$. Expression (5) implies that, the larger is the long position the market-maker is holding, the more he will lower the price in order to attract buyers, and *vice versa* for a short position. Another way to ensure the same behavior is to introduce a spread or change the available liquidity [17].

We first study the price formation using (2) and resulting from a market competition between agents with payoff function (3) and compare it with the MG case (1) in the case with no constraint on the number of stocks held by each agent (*i.e.*, an agent can open a new position at each time step). Contrary to the MG case, we find that the price always diverges to infinity or goes zero within a few tens or hundreds of time steps. This behavior is observed for all values of N, m, s. Similar results are found if we replaced the price equation (2) with (5) which includes the market-maker strategy. The reason for this non-stationary behavior is that agents, using (3) as pay-off function, are able to collaborate to their mutual benefit. This happens whenever a majority among the agents can agree to "lock on" for an extended period of time to a common decision of either to keep on selling or buying. A constant sign of $A(t)$ is seen from either (2)-(4) or (3)-(5) to lead to a steady increase of the wealth of those agents sticking to the majority decision. A "stubborn majority" manages to collaborate by sticking to the same common decision – they all gain by doing so at the cost of the market-maker who is arbitraged. The mechanism underlying this cooperative behavior is the positive feedback resulting from a positive majority $A(t)$ which leads to an increase of the price (5) which in turn confirms the "stubborn majority" to stick to their decision and keep on buying, leading to a further confirmation of a positive $A(t)$. This situation is reminiscent of wild speculative phases in markets, such as occurred prior to the October 1929 crash in the US, before the 1994 emergent market crises in Asia, and more recently during the "new economy" boom on the Nasdaq stock exchange, in which margin requirements are decreased and/or investors are allowed to borrow more and more on their unrealized market gains. This situation is quite parallel to our model behavior in which agents can buy without restrain, pushing the prices up. Of course, some limiting process will eventually appear, often leading to the catastrophic stop of such euphoric phase.

We turn to the more realistic case where agents have bounded wealth, and study the limiting case where agents are allowed to keep only one long/short position at each time step. With this constraint, the previous positive feedback is no longer at work. Holding a position, an agent will contribute to future price changes only when she changes her mind. Thus, a "stubborn majority" can not longer directly influence future price changes through the majority term $A(t)$, but only now indirectly through the impact on the market maker strategy $S_M(t)$ in (5). Figure 2a show typical examples of price trajectories using (3)-(5) with

position until she gets a signal to sell $(a_i = -1)$ [14]. The lower plot of Figure 1 shows the wealth (4) corresponding to the agents of the upper plot. The consistently bad performance of the optimal MG-agent in terms of her wealth and reciprocally the relatively good performance for the worst MG-agent in terms of her wealth is a clear illustration of the fact that a minority strategy will perform poorly in a real market. This does not exclude however the potential usefulness of MG strategies in certain situations, in particular for identifying extrema, as discussed above and as illustrated recently in the prediction of extreme events [18]. In contrast, for the "$-game" (3) presented here, the performance of the payoff function (3) matches by definition the performance of the wealth of the agents. The superficial observance by some MG of the stylized facts of financial time series is not a proof of their relevance and, in our opinion, express only the often observed fact that many models, be they relevant or irrelevant, can reproduce superficially a set of characteristics (see for instance a related discussion on mechanisms of power laws and self-organized criticality in chapters 14 and 15 of [19]).

In order for trading to occur and to fully specify the price trajectory, a clearing mechanism has to be specified. Here, we use a market maker who furnishes assets in case of demand and buys assets in case of supply [15]. The price fixing equation (2) implicitly assumes the presence of a market-maker, since the excess demand of the agents $A(t)$ always finds a counterpart. For instance, if the cumulative action of the agents is to sell 10 stocks, $A(t) = -10$, the market-maker is automatically willing to buy 10 stocks at the price given by (2). As pointed out in reference [15], expression (2) leads to an unbound market-maker inventory $S_M(t)$. In order to lower his inventory costs and the risk of being arbitraged, a market-maker will try to keep his inventory secret and in average close

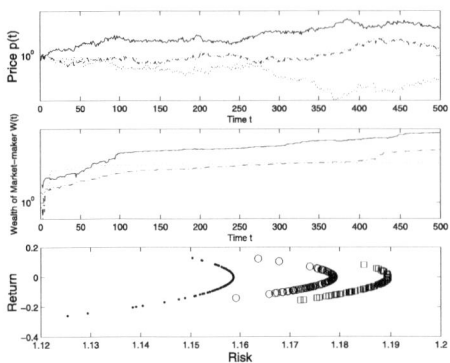

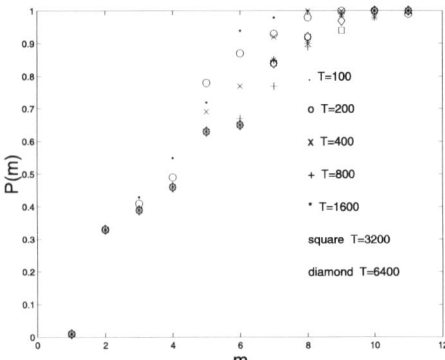

Fig. 2. Price, wealth of market-maker and risk-return plots for three different parameter choices using the payoff function (3) and the constraint that agents can only accumulate one position at a time. Solid line and black circle: $m = 10, s = 4$; dashed-dotted line and circle: $m = 10, s = 10$; dotted line and square: $m = 8, s = 10$.

Fig. 3. Probability $P(m)$ for the market-maker to arbitrage the group of agents using (3)-(5) as a function of the memory length m. $P(m)$ is determined from the market-maker wealth after T time steps and by averaging over 100 simulations with different initial configurations. The parameters used are $N = 101, s = 5$. Similar results are found using different N, s.

agents keeping a single position (short/long) at any times, for three different choices of parameter values (N, m, s). The time series are quite similar to typical financial price series and possess their basic stylized properties (short-range correlation of returns, distribution of returns with fat tails, long-range correlation of volatility [20]). The corresponding wealth of the market maker is shown in Figure 2b. It exhibits a systematic growth, interrupted rarely for some short periods of time with small losses. The stochastic nature of the price trajectories is translated into an almost deterministic wealth growth for the market-maker, who is an almost certain winner (as it should and is in real market situations to ensure his survival and profitability). The market maker is similar to a casino providing services or entertainments and which profits from a systematic bias here resulting from the lack of cooperativity of the agents.

For each agent i, we define a risk parameter

$$R_i(t) = \langle (dW_i(t) - \langle dW_i \rangle_t)^2 \rangle_t \qquad (6)$$

where $dW_i(t)$ is the change of wealth of agent i between t and $t - 1$. $R_i(t)$ is the volatility of the wealth of agent i. The average return per time step $\langle dW_i \rangle$ for each of the $N = 101$ different agents as a function of his volatility R_i is shown in Figure 2c (each point corresponds to one agent). Since agents choose either a short or a long position at each time step, a perfect performing agent is a return rectifier taking no risk. Similarly, the worst performing agent is consistently moving against the market, again with the risk defined from (6) equal to zero. This explains why the risk-return behavior seen in Figure 2c is an mirror image of the risk-return efficient frontier in Markovitz standard portfolio theory [16]. The figure shows that even though the market-maker arbitrages the agents as a group, some "clever" agents are still able to profit from their trade with

a risk-return profile which should be unstable in the sense of standard economic theory. It is however a robust and stable feature of our model. This property results fundamentally from the heterogeneity of the strategies and can not be captured by a representative agent theory.

To study further the competition between the agents as a group and the market-maker, we let the $-game evolve for T time steps and measure if the market-maker has arbitraged the agents, *i.e.*, if his wealth is positive at the end of the time period T. Figure 3 shows the probability $P(m)$ for the market-maker to arbitrage the agents *versus* the memory of the agents m. For $m = 1$, the agents always exploit the market-maker according to the positive feedback mechanism involving the "stubborn majority" described above. As m increases, $P(m)$ increases and, for the largest memory $m = 11$ of the agents, the market-maker arbitrages the group of agents with probability 1. This correspond to the examples illustrated in Figure 2. In between, there is a competition between cooperativity between the agents and the destructive interferences of their heterogeneous strategies. The finite-size study of $P(m)$ as a function of T suggests the existence of a sharp transition in the large T limit for $m \approx 9$. Below this memory length, the set of strategies available to agents allow them to sometimes cooperate successfully. As the complexity of the information increases, their strategies are unable to cope with the large set of incoming information and the chaotic desynchronized behavior that results favors the market maker. This could be termed the curse of intelligence.

We will report elsewhere on extensions of this model with traders who act at different time scales and with different weights and on the detection of large price movements in the spirit of [18].

D.S. gratefully acknowledges support from the James S. McDonnell Foundation 21st Century Scientist award/studying complex systems.

References

1. For an introduction to the Minority Game see *e.g.* the papers: D. Challet, Y.-C. Zhang, Physica A **246**, 407 (1997); *ibid.* **256**, 514 (1998); R. Savit, R. Manuca, R. Riolo, Phys. Rev. Lett. **82**, 2203 (1999); A. Cavagna, Phys. Rev. E **59**, R3783, (1999). See also the special webpage on the Minority Game by D. Challet at `www.unifr.ch/econophysics/minority/minority.html` For more specific applications of the Minority Game to financial markets see *e.g.* D. Challet *et al.*, Quant. Fin **1**, 168 (2001); N.F. Johnson *et al.*, Int. J. Theor. Appl. Fin. **3**, 443 (2001)

2. Bouchaud, J.-P., R. Cont, Eur. Phys. J. B **6**, 543 (1998)

3. J.D. Farmer, *Market force, ecology and evolution*, preprint at `adap-org/9812005` (1998)

4. R.W. Holthausen, R.W. Leftwich, D. Mayers, J. Fin. Econ. **19**, 237 (1987)

5. J.A. Lakonishok, R. Shleifer, Thaler, R.W. Vishny, J. Fin. Econ. **32**, 23 (1991)

6. L.K.C. Chan, J. Lakonishok, J. Fin. Econ. **33**, 173 (1995)

7. S. Maslov, M. Mills, Physica A **299**, 234 (2001)

8. D. Challet, R. Stinchcombe, Physica A **300**, 285 (2001)

9. V. Plerou, P. Gopikrishnan, X. Gabaix, H.E. Stanley, Phys. Rev. E **66**, 027104 (2002)

10. T. Chordia, R. Roll, A. Subrahmanyam, (2001) forthcoming in J. Fin. Econ., UCLA working paper

11. I. Giardina, J.-P. Bouchaud, M. Mézard, Physica A **299**, 28 (2001)

12. M. Marsili, Physica A **299**, 93 (2001)

13. J.A. Frankel, K.A. Froot, Greek Economic Rev. **10**, 49102 (1988); Am. Econom. Rev. **80**, 181185 (1990)

14. A similar conclusion as seen in Figure 1 is found in the absence of constraint on the number of stocks each agent is allowed to hold, that is, when agents are allowed to open a new position at each time step so as to leverage their strategy

15. P. Jefferies *et al.*, Eur. Phys. J. **20**, 493 (2001)

16. H. Markovitz, *Portfolio selection* (John Wiley and Sons, New York, 1959)

17. We do not expect any qualitative difference in the results represented in this paper depending on which of these different mechanisms is implemented, since a "stubborn majority" can manifest itself independent of which of these mechanisms is used

18. N.F. Johnson *et al.*, Physica A **299**, 222 (2001); D. Lamper, S.D. Howison, N.F. Johnson, Phys. Rev. Lett. **88**, 017902 (2002)

19. D. Sornette, *Critical Phenomena in Natural Sciences* (Springer, Heidelberg, 2000)

20. Notice that because each agent only keep one (long/short) position each time step, they switch between active/inactive states. A somewhat similar switching happens in the Grand Canonical version of the MG [1]. In [11] this switching has been mentioned as a necessary condition to obtain volatility clustering

145

PHYSICA Ⓐ

www.elsevier.com/locate/physa

Dynamical spin-glass-like behavior in an evolutionary game

František Slanina[a,*], Yi-Cheng Zhang[b]

[a]*Institute of Physics, Academy of Sciences of the Czech Republic, Na Slovance 2,
CZ-18221 Praha, Czech Republic*
[b]*Institut de Physique Théorique, Université de Fribourg, Pérolles, CH-1700 Fribourg, Switzerland*

Received 21 August 2000

Abstract

We study a new evolutionary game, where players are tempted to take part by the premium, but compete for being the first who take a specific move. Those, who manage to escape the bulk of players, are the winners. While for large premium the game is very similar to the Minority game studied earlier, significant new behavior, reminiscent of spin glasses is observed for premium below certain level. © 2001 Elsevier Science B.V. All rights reserved.

PACS: 05.65.+b; 02.50.Le; 87.23.Ge

Keywords: Stochastic processes; Economics

1. Introduction

The transfer of physical ideas and procedures to traditionally social disciplines and a parallel backflow of inspiration for statistical physics from these disciplines has been increasing in the last decade.

Among other applications, the field of econophysics [1,2] has attracted much attention. An important approach seems to be, modeling the collective effect found in the economic systems by assemblies of individually acting heterogeneous agents. One of the basic models is the Minority game [3,4], an evolutionary game which mimics the adaptive behavior of agents with bounded rationality, studied by Arthur in his El Farol bar problem [5].

In the Minority game, each player faces the choice between two possibilities, which can be buying or selling stock, entering or not a business, selecting first or second drive

* Corresponding author. Fax: +420-2-858-8605.
E-mail address: slanina@fzu.cz (F. Slanina).

and so on. The winning side is that of the minority of players. Each player possesses a set of $S \geqslant 2$ strategies. Each strategy collects its score, indicating the virtual gain of the player, if she had played that strategy all the time. In each round, the player choose among their strategies, the one with highest score. This sort of an on-line learning and adaptation leads to better-than-random performance of the system as a whole. It was found that the properties of the game depend on the memory length M and number of players N through the scaling variable $\alpha = 2^M/N$ [4,6,7]. The Minority game was thoroughly studied both numerically and analytically [8–19] along with the study of the original bar attendance problem [20,21] and various modifications of the Minority game [22–29]. An important role is attributed to the observation that the dynamics of the memorized pattern and the strategies' scores are decoupled in certain regimes [30–32] and that the thermal noise can be introduced in the players' decisions [33–35].

The most intriguing feature is the minimum of volatility, which occurs for the value $\alpha = \alpha_c \simeq 0.34$ [4,6,7,20]. A phase transition occurs here, the properties of which are well studied both numerically [36] and analytically [37–41].

The Minority game is essentially symmetric. The players can choose between two sides, none of which is a priori preferred. The situation is somewhat different in the bar attendance model [20,21], where the optimal attendance is set from outside. There are also variants of the game, in which the players can decide to participate or not, depending on their accumulated wealth [27,39]. The number of players who influence the outcome of the game can thus vary in time.

In this work we want to study a more abstract version of these models with variable number of players. We implement a scheme, in which the players struggle to be "ahead" of the other players, i.e., to come in before the others and not to stay if others have already left. This behavior is relevant in situations, where the early comers have advantage, irrespective of what is the direction of the movement. We can think, for example, of a bunch of apes exploring a virgin land. The first animal coming to the place finds enough food, but much less is left for the followers. In an infinite space, we could have stationary movement of the bunch in one direction. When the space available is limited, frustration comes into play. The bunch should oscillate between the borderlines and no one can steadily win. Our aim is to formalize and simulate this situation in a manner similar to the formalization of the inductive behavior in the Minority game.

2. Escape game

We introduce a new mechanism, which leads to frustration in the agent's actions. Similar to the Minority game, we have N agents. The agents can choose between two options: to participate (1) or not (0) in the business. If we denote $a_j \in \{0,1\}$ the action of jth player, the attendance is $A = \sum_j a_j$. We measure the success of the jth player by her wealth W_j. The players who decide to participate can be either rewarded or punished by the corresponding change in their wealth, while the wealth of non-participating agents remains unchanged.

There are two sources of the wealth change. First, there is a constant influx of wealth into the system, which we will call premium p. All the participating players receive the amount p/A. Second, we reward the players, who by some means induce the others to follow them in the next step. If a player decides to participate in step $t - 1$ and the attendance rises from $t - 1$ to t (i.e., $A(t) - A(t - 1) > 0$), we consider that the player is "ahead" of her companions and gets a point. If, on the other hand, the attendance decreases (i.e., $A(t) - A(t - 1) < 0$), the player is considered as "behind" and looses a point. If the attendance remains unchanged, no points are assigned. Thus, each player tries to "escape" the bulk of the other players. That is why we have nicknamed the present dynamical multi-agent system as "Escape game".

As in the Minority game, the record is maintained about the past M changes of the attendance, $\mu(t) = [c(t - 1), c(t - 2), \ldots, c(t - M)]$. We denote $c = 1$ as increase in A, and $c = -1$ as decrease in A. There are two possibilities to deal with the case when the attendance does not change. It is possible to attribute $c = 0$ to such a situation; then the state variable will have values from the set $c \in \{-1, 0, +1\}$. Alternatively, we can merge the cases of decrease and no change, so $c = -1$ also in the case when the attendance is constant. In this case we distinguish only two states, $c \in \{-1, +1\}$. We found, that both choices give qualitatively similar results, while the former one leads to slightly more demanding simulations. Therefore, throughout this article we will investigate the latter choice, with two states only.

The agents look at the record $\mu \in \{-1, +1\}^M$. They have a set of S strategies ($S = 2$ in our simulations). The sth strategy of the jth player prescribes, for the record μ the action $a_{j,s}^\mu \in \{0, 1\}$. For each strategy, the score is computed, which is the virtual gain of the player, if she played constantly that strategy. The update of the strategies' scores can be written as

$$U_{j,s}(t + 1) = U_{j,s}(t) + a_{j,s}^{\mu(t-1)} \left(\frac{p}{A(t - 1)} + G(A(t) - A(t - 1)) \right). \tag{1}$$

For the function G, weighting the attendance changes, we use the signum function, $G(x) = \text{sign}(x)$. Note that the delivery of the player's gain is delayed: the action taken at time $t - 1$ can be rewarded only at time t, so that it influences the scores at time $t + 1$. Again with close analogy to the Minority game, the actions the players take are prescribed by the strategies with highest score, $a_j = a_{j,s_M}$, where s_M denotes the most successful strategy at the moment, $U_{j,s_M} = \max_s U_{j,s}$.

To clearly see the points of difference from the Minority game, note first that in the Escape game the non-participation $a_j = 0$ cannot change the wealth of the player. Second, the strategie's update rule (1) contains derivative of the attendance, not the attendance itself.

3. Evolution of attendance and glassy behavior

Let us first observe qualitatively the time dependence of the attendance. We have found that for large enough premium, the Escape game behaves in a manner very

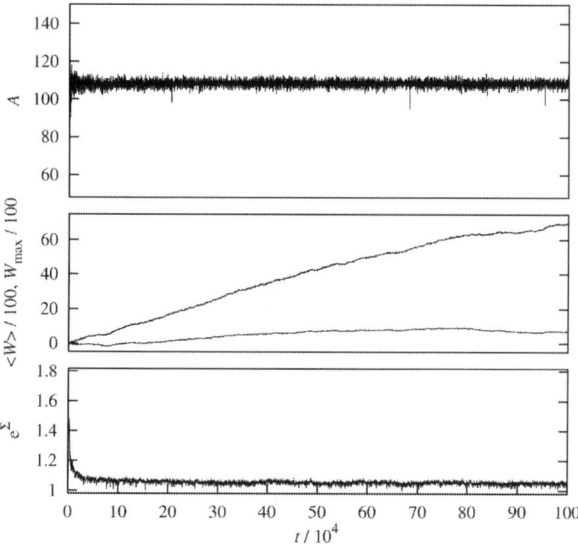

Fig. 1. Example for the time dependence of the attendance (top frame), the effective number of strategies (bottom frame), and average wealth (middle frame, lower curve) and maximum wealth among all players (middle frame, upper curve). The number of players is $N = 200$, memory $M = 5$ and premium $p = 1$.

similar to the Minority game. The fluctuations in attendance decrease from their initial value until they stabilize at a stationary value. The average attendance is shifted from its random value $N/2$ above, as a response to the incentive, posed by the premium, for the players to prefer presence over absence. We can see in Fig. 1 an example of such a behavior. The stationary state is reached in a short time (shorter than 10^5 steps for $N = 200$). The wealth of the most successful player grows constantly at a high rate and also the average wealth grows slightly. This means that due to the premium, the game is a positive-sum game on average.

We can also observe, e^Σ, the time dependence of the effective number of strategies per player. We define it through the average entropy of the usage of the strategies

$$\Sigma(t) = \frac{1}{N} \sum_{j,s} v_{j,s}(t) \log v_{j,s}(t), \tag{2}$$

where $v_{j,s}$ is the time-averaged frequency of the usage of sth strategy of jth player. We performed the time averaging over a relatively short window using the exponential weighting, $v_{j,s}(t) = (1 - \lambda)u_{j,s}(t) + \lambda v_{j,s}(t - 1)$, where the usage index $u_{j,s}(t) = 1$ if the player j used the strategy s at time t, and $u_{j,s}(t) = 0$ otherwise. We used $\lambda = 0.99$, which corresponds to effective time-window width of 100 steps.

We can see in Fig. 1 that the effective number of the strategies used stabilizes at a value above but close to 1, which also corresponds well to the behavior of the Minority game in the symmetry-broken phase.

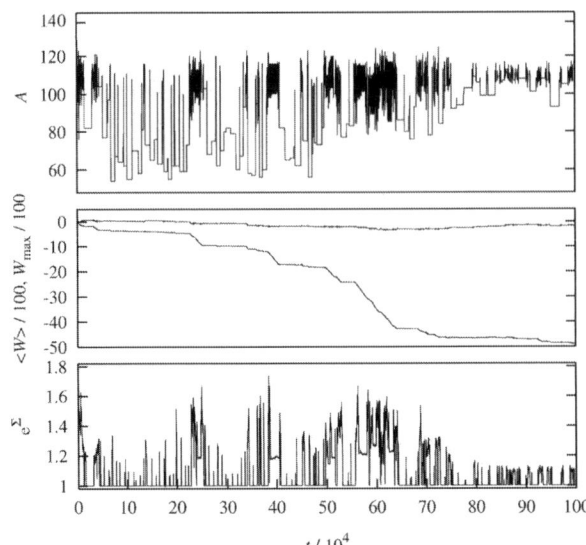

Fig. 2. The same as in Fig. 1, but for premium $p = 0.01$.

On the other hand, we can observe significant change of the behavior of the model, if the premium is decreased below certain level. An example can be seen in Fig. 2. First, the transient time before the system settles in a stationary state is significantly larger (we observed that it is nearly 10^6 steps). Then, we can see that periods with significant attendance fluctuations are alternating with periods with constant attendance, which can frequently last more than 10^4 steps. The fluctuating periods are characterized by decrease of the average wealth (the game is a negative-sum one) and effective number of strategies larger than 1. On the other hand, the periods of constant attendance exhibit nearly constant average wealth and effective number of strategies equal to 1. It means that within the constant periods the system is able to find a favourable configuration, in which the game is globally effective (avoids the losses due to fluctuations) and everybody is stuck at single strategy. Moreover, there are many such states: in different constant periods the attendance may differ considerably.

This behavior is further pronounced when we diminish the premium even more. We can see such a behavior in Fig. 3. We can observe long periods (sometimes longer than 10^5 steps) of constant attendance, separated by very short fluctuating periods. The effective number of strategies differs from 1 only during these short periods. Again, there are many configurations in which the attendance does not change for long time.

The situation is reminiscent of spin glasses. In the spin-glass behavior, there are many states, stable for long time, but mutually very different, in which the system can stay. If the barriers between these states are not infinite (which happens only in the

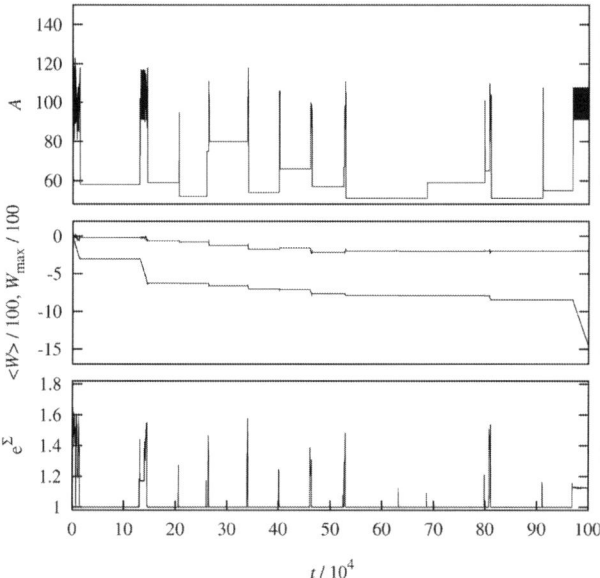

Fig. 3. The same as in Fig. 1, but for premium $p = 0.001$.

fully connected case in thermodynamic limit), the dynamics of such a system is very similar to our Escape game: long periods of stasis within one state, interrupted by short periods corresponding to the jumps from one state to another.

Therefore, we can describe the behavior with changing premium p as a kind of transition from "paramagnet" (high p) to "spin-glass" phase (low p). We have not studied in detail the phase diagram. However, we have observed that with fixed N the transition occurs at smaller p if the memory is longer.

4. Time-averaged attendance and its fluctuations

The response of the player's assembly to the premium was measured by the average attendance. Its dependence on the value of premium is shown in Fig. 4. As expected, it is an increasing function. We can see, that shorter memory leads to stronger response to the premium. The value of p at which the average attendance crosses its random value $N/2$ is smaller for shorter memory.

The dependence of the attendance fluctuations σ^2 on p is shown in Fig. 5. Again, the dependence on p is more pronounced for shorter memory. The minimum, which is located around $p = 3$ for $N = 200$ is probably connected with the transition from the "paramagnet" to "spin-glass" phase: for low p the fluctuations are mainly due to rare but large jumps of the attendance from one quasi-static value to another. Indeed,

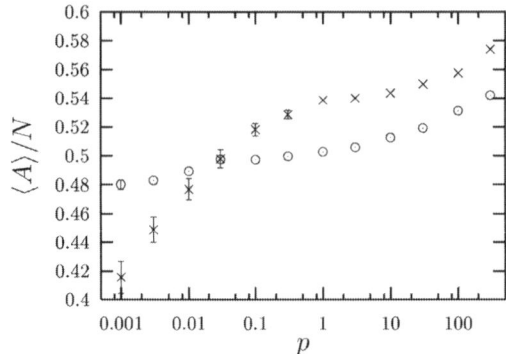

Fig. 4. Average attendance for $N=200$ and memory length $M=5$ ($\times$) and $M=7$ ($\bigcirc$). The data are averaged over 50 independent runs. Each run was 10^6 steps long and the average was taken over last 5×10^5 steps. Where not shown, the error bars are smaller than the symbol size.

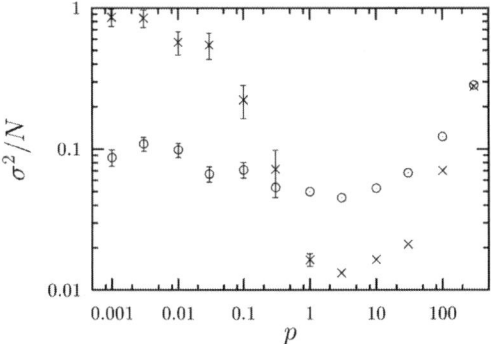

Fig. 5. Attendance fluctuations for $N = 200$ and memory length $M = 5$ ($\times$) and $M = 7$ ($\bigcirc$). The data are averaged over 50 independent runs. Each run was 10^6 steps long and the average was taken over last 5×10^5 steps. Where not shown, the error bars are smaller than the symbol size.

we observed qualitatively that the transition occurs slightly below the position of the minimum in σ^2.

The memory dependence of attendance fluctuations for several values of p is presented in Fig. 6. In the minimum of fluctuations, we recognize the same behavior as in the Minority game. Here, however, the position of the minimum depends strongly on the value of the premium. We can see that the long-memory phase does not depend much on the premium. On the other hand, the crowded phase is strongly influenced by the premium. For smaller p, the crowded phase occurs at longer memories.

In Fig. 7, the dependence of average attendance on M is shown. We can clearly observe that, as discussed already with Fig. 4, longer memory suppresses the response of the system to the premium. For shorter memories and sufficiently small p (for

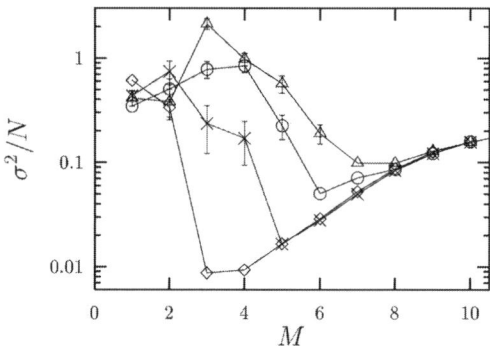

Fig. 6. Average attendance fluctuations for $N = 200$ and premium $p = 10$ ($\diamond$), 1 ($\times$), 0.1 ($\bigcirc$), and 0.01 ($\triangle$). The data are averaged over 50 independent runs. Each run was 10^6 steps long and the average was taken over last 5×10^5 steps. Where not shown, the error bars are smaller than the symbol size.

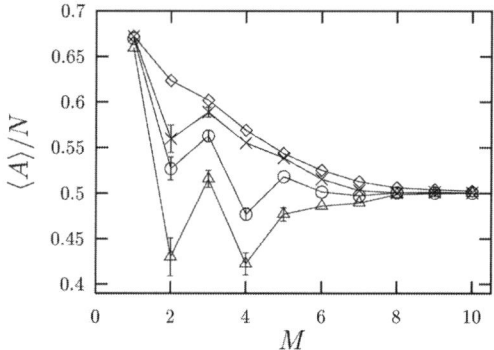

Fig. 7. Average attendance for $N = 200$ and premium $p = 10$ ($\diamond$), 1 ($\times$), 0.1 ($\bigcirc$), and 0.01 ($\triangle$). The data are averaged over 50 independent runs. Each run was 10^6 steps long and the average was taken over last 5×10^5 steps. Where not shown, the error bars are smaller than the symbol size.

$N = 200$ it means $M \leqslant 4$ and $p \leqslant 0.1$), we observe an interesting, yet not clearly understood behavior, characterized by non-monotonic dependence of the average attendance on M.

In the minority game, the relevant quantities are the functions of the scaling variable $2^N/N$. We tried the same scaling also in our Escape game. The results for $p = 0.1$ are in Fig. 8, while the case $p = 1$ is shown in Fig. 9. As we have already noted, larger p makes the game behave more similar to the usual Minority game. Here it is illustrated by the fact, that the data collapse is much better for $p = 1$ than for $p = 0.1$. We can also see again that in the large-memory phase the scaling works very well, while the crowded phase behaves differently.

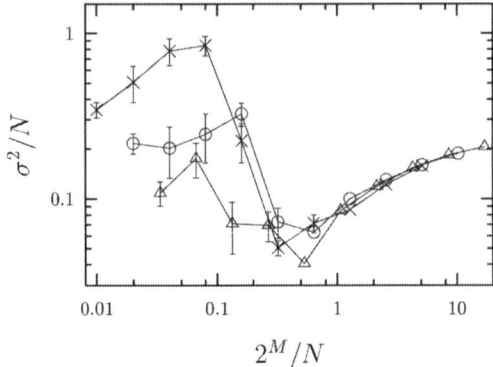

Fig. 8. Rescaled attendance fluctuations for premium $p = 0.1$ and number of players $N = 200$ ($\times$), 100 ($\bigcirc$), and 60 ($\triangle$). The data are averaged over 50 independent runs. Each run was 10^6 steps long and the average was taken over last 5×10^5 steps. Where not shown, the error bars are smaller than the symbol size.

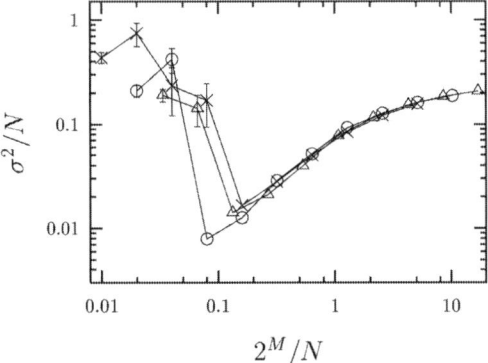

Fig. 9. The same as in Fig. 8, but for premium $p = 1$.

5. Conclusions

We have introduced an evolutionary game, which we call Escape game. The dynamical rules are similar in principle to the Minority game, but some substantial differences occur. We observed that in the large-memory phase the response to the premium is lower. At the same time, the behavior is closer to the Minority game, which is quantitatively seen in the fact that the relevant quantities depend on the scaling variable $2^M/N$ as in the Minority game. On the other hand, for fixed memory length the behavior is similar for large premium but differs from it for small premium.

The fact that the players are drawn into the play by the premium leads to enhanced attendance for high premium. On the other hand, for small premium the incentive is not strong enough and the system starts to exhibit a new dynamical phase, whose character is very close to a spin-glass.

This result can be qualitatively understood as follows. The presence of fluctuations makes the game a negative-sum one, if we neglected the premium. High premium overweighs the negative effect of fluctuations and the players choose the strategies, which give them highest possible attendance, irrespective of the fluctuations they cause. That is why for higher premium both the attendance and its fluctuations grow.

For small premium, the fluctuations are disastrous and the players tend to avoid them by not participating. The situations in which there are two groups, one of constantly participating players and second of constantly non-participating ones, are suitable for both groups. The first one receives steadily the small premium, the second one at least does not loose anything. After some time, however, the scores of the absent players change so that they would prefer being in over staying out. At that moment, the system is reshuffled and another configuration of participating and non-participating players is found. The mean period of such reshufflings must be longer for smaller premium, because in this case the scores change more slowly. We expect that the transition occurs at such a value of the premium, which would correspond to reshuffling period of order one. So, the "spin-glass" behavior is purely dynamical in origin.

To sum it up, we can draw a fuzzy line in the M versus p plane, which encloses the region of both p and M small. Outside this region the Escape game behaves merely as a slight modification of the usual Minority game, while inside we observe qualitatively new features, including the dynamical "spin-glass" behavior.

Acknowledgements

We would like to express our gratitude to P. De Los Rios and D. Challet for useful discussions and comments.

References

[1] R.N. Mantegna, H.E. Stanley, Introduction to Econophysics: Correlations and Complexity in Finance, Cambridge University Press, Cambridge, 1999.
[2] J.-P. Bouchaud, M. Potters, Theory of Financial Risks, Cambridge University Press, Cambridge, 2000.
[3] D. Challet, Y.-C. Zhang, Physica A 246 (1997) 407.
[4] D. Challet, Y.-C. Zhang, Physica A 256 (1998) 514.
[5] W.B. Arthur, Am. Econ. Rev. (Papers and Proceedings) 84 (1994) 406.
[6] R. Savit, R. Manuca, R. Riolo, adap-org/9712006.
[7] R. Savit, R. Manuca, R. Riolo, Phys. Rev. Lett. 82 (1999) 2203.
[8] N.F. Johnson, M. Hart, P.M. Hui, Physica A 269 (1998) 1.
[9] N.F. Johnson, D.J.T. Leonard, P.M. Hui, T.S. Lo, cond-mat/9905039.
[10] M. Hart, P. Jefferies, N.F. Johnson, P.M. Hui, cond-mat/0003486.
[11] M. Hart, P. Jefferies, N.F. Johnson, P.M. Hui, cond-mat/0005152.
[12] T.S. Lo, P.M. Hui, N.F. Johnson (2000), cond-mat/0003379.
[13] M.A.R. de Cara, O. Pla, F. Guinea, Eur. Phys. J. B 10 (1999) 187.
[14] M.A.R. de Cara, O. Pla, F. Guinea, Eur. Phys. J. B 13 (2000) 413.

[15] Y. Li, R. Riolo, R. Savit, Physica A 276 (2000) 234.
[16] Y. Li, R. Riolo, R. Savit, Physica A 276 (2000) 265.
[17] R. D'hulst, G.J. Rodgers, Physica A 270 (1999) 514.
[18] R. D'hulst, G.J. Rodgers, Physica A 278 (2000) 579.
[19] R. Mansilla, cond-mat/9906017.
[20] N.F. Johnson, S. Jarvis, R. Jonson, P. Cheung, Y.R. Kwong, P.M. Hui, Physica A 258 (1998) 230.
[21] N.F. Johnson, P.M. Hui, D. Zheng, C.W. Tai, Physica A 269 (1999) 493.
[22] N.F. Johnson, P.M. Hui, R. Jonson, T.S. Lo, Phys. Rev. Lett. 82 (1999) 3360.
[23] H. Ceva, Physica A 277 (2000) 496.
[24] T. Kalinowski, H.-J. Schulz, M. Briese, Physica A 277 (2000) 502.
[25] M. Paczuski, K.E. Bassler, Phys. Rev. Lett. 84 (2000) 3185.
[26] R. D'hulst, G.J. Rodgers, adap-org/9904003.
[27] F. Slanina, Y.-C. Zhang, Physica A 272 (1999) 257.
[28] F. Slanina, Physica A 272 (1999) 257.
[29] L. Ein-Dor, R. Metzler, I. Kanter, W. Kinzel, cond-mat/0005216.
[30] A. Cavagna, Phys. Rev. E 59 (1999) R3783.
[31] N.F. Johnson, P.M. Hui, D. Zheng, M. Hart, J. Phys. A 32 (1999) L427.
[32] D. Challet, M. Marsili, cond-mat/0004196.
[33] A. Cavagna, J.P. Garrahan, I. Giardina, D. Sherrington, Phys. Rev. Lett. 83 (1999) 4429.
[34] D. Challet, M. Marsili, R. Zecchina, cond-mat/0004308.
[35] J.P. Garrahan, E. Moro, D. Sherrington, Phys. Rev. E 62 (2000) R9.
[36] D. Challet, M. Marsili, Phys. Rev. E 60 (1999) R6271.
[37] D. Challet, M. Marsili, R. Zecchina, Phys. Rev. Lett. 84 (2000) 1824.
[38] M. Marsili, D. Challet, R. Zecchina, Physica A 280 (2000) 522.
[39] D. Challet, M. Marsili, Y.-C. Zhang, Physica A 276 (2000) 284.
[40] D. Challet, M. Marsili, R. Zecchina, Mathematical Models and Methods in Applied Sciences, World Scientific, Singapore, to appear.
[41] M. Marsili, D. Challet, cond-mat/0004376.

www.elsevier.com/locate/physa

A stochastic strategy for the minority game [☆]

G. Reents[*], R. Metzler, W. Kinzel

Institut für Theoretische Physik, Universität Würzburg, Am Hubland, Würzburg D-97074, Germany

Abstract

We present a new strategy for the Minority Game. Players who were successful in the previous timestep stay with their decision, while the losers change their decision with a probability p. Analytical results for different regimes of p and the number of players N are given and connections to existing models are discussed. It is shown that for $p \propto 1/N$ the average loss σ^2 is of the order of 1 and does not increase with N as for other known strategies. © 2001 Elsevier Science B.V. All rights reserved.

Keywords: Minority game; Markov process; Econophysics

1. Introduction

Game theory describes situations in which players must make decisions, i.e., choose between different alternatives, and receive payoffs according to their and other players' choices. The question how players decide on a strategy, i.e., how they find out what to do if the situation is too complicated for the player to grasp completely using deductive thinking, was addressed in Ref. [1]. There it was suggested that each player has a number of models that prescribe an action for a given state of the player's world, for example, for a given game history. The model that has proven most successful so far is actually used by the player.

This approach was applied in the Minority Game introduced and studied in Refs. [2–4] and other publications. The rules for this game and its variations are as

[☆] Expanded version of a talk presented at the NATO Advanced Research Workshop on Application of Physics in Economic Modelling, Prague, February 2001.
[*] Corresponding author.

follows:

- There is an odd number N of players.
- At each time step t each player i makes a decision $\sigma_i(t) \in \{+1, -1\}$, the majority is determined, $S(t) = \text{sign}\left(\sum_{i=1}^{N} \sigma_i(t)\right)$, and those players who are in the minority, $\sigma_i(t) = -S(t)$, win, the others lose.
- A measure of global loss is

$$\sigma^2 = \left\langle \left(\sum_{i=1}^{N} \sigma_i(t)\right)^2 \right\rangle_t . \tag{1}$$

Random guessing leads to $\sigma^2 = N$.

- The only information accessible to players is the history of the majority $(S(t-M), \ldots, S(t))$.
- Accordingly, no contracts between players are allowed.

In the original Minority Game, each player has a small number of randomly picked decision tables that prescribe an action for each possible history. Those tables receive points according to how well they have predicted the best action in the course of the game, and the best table is used to actually make the decision.

Other publications studied variants in which the agents used neural networks to make their decisions [7], or in which each agent has a probability that determines whether he chooses the action that was successful in the last step or its opposite [8,9].

In some cases, especially if one is only interested in long-time averaged quantities like σ^2/N, the history can be replaced by a random sequence without essentially affecting the results. For certain other quantities, however, and in most extensions of the Minority Game, random histories are not equivalent with real ones [5,6].

2. The Model

In this paper, we introduce a very simple prescription for the agents that is still a reasonable way of behaving in the absence of detailed information. It is in some ways related to Johnson's model [8,9], but different in decisive details. The model is as follows:

- If an agent i is successful in a given turn, he will make the same decision the next turn: $\sigma_i(t+1) = \sigma_i(t)$. After all, there is no reason to change anything.
- Otherwise, the agent will change his output with a probability p: $\text{prob}(\sigma_i(t+1) = -\sigma_i(t)) = p$. The agent is reluctant to give up his position, but eventually, something must change.

This is evidently a stochastic one-step process and can be handled well with the tools for Markov processes. We, therefore, introduce variables to describe an ensemble of games.

Instead of using the whole set $\{\sigma_i(t)\}_{i=1}^N$ of time dependent random variables we consider the stochastic process

$$K(t) = \frac{1}{2} \sum_i \sigma_i(t) . \tag{2}$$

The possible values k that $K(t)$ can take are half-integer and run from $-N/2$ to $N/2$ in steps of 1. Then, the probabilities

$$\pi_k(t) = \text{prob} \, (K(t) = k) \tag{3}$$

together with the transition probabilities

$$W_{k\ell} = \text{prob} \, (K(t+1) = k \, | \, K(t) = \ell) \tag{4}$$

are the basic quantities to describe the system. To shorten the notation, we consider the probabilities $\pi_k(t)$ as components of the state vector $\boldsymbol{\pi}(t) = (\pi_{-N/2}(t), \ldots, \pi_{N/2}(t))^{\mathrm{T}}$. The number of players in the majority at time t is $N/2 + |K(t)|$. Since the individual players perform independent Bernoulli trials, the transition probability $W_{k\ell} = W(\ell \to k)$ from a state with $K(t) = \ell$ to $K(t+1) = k$ is given by the binomial distribution

$$W_{k\ell} = \begin{cases} \binom{\frac{N}{2} + \ell}{\ell - k} p^{\ell-k}(1-p)^{N/2+k} & \text{for } \ell > 0, \\ \binom{\frac{N}{2} - \ell}{k - \ell} p^{k-\ell}(1-p)^{N/2-k} & \text{for } \ell < 0. \end{cases} \tag{5}$$

It is understood that

$$\binom{\frac{N}{2} + |\ell|}{m} = 0 \quad \text{for } m < 0 .$$

This stochastic process may be considered a random walk in one dimension, where steps of arbitrary size with probability (5) are allowed only in the direction of the origin.

Given the initial state $\boldsymbol{\pi}(0)$, the state $\boldsymbol{\pi}(t)$ is updated at each time step by multiplying it by the transition matrix $\mathbf{W}$:

$$\boldsymbol{\pi}(t+1) = \mathbf{W}\boldsymbol{\pi}(t) . \tag{6}$$

The mathematical theory dealing with this kind of problems is that of Markov chains with stationary transition probabilities [10]. Since $(\mathbf{W}^2)_{k\ell} > 0$, the chain is irreducible as well as ergodic [11], which implies that irrespective of the initial distribution the state $\boldsymbol{\pi}(t)$ converges for $t \to \infty$ to a unique stationary state $\boldsymbol{\pi}(\infty) \equiv \boldsymbol{\pi}^s$. In view of Eq. (6), $\boldsymbol{\pi}^s$ corresponds to an eigenvector of $\mathbf{W}$ with eigenvalue 1:

$$\mathbf{W}\boldsymbol{\pi}^s = \boldsymbol{\pi}^s \quad \text{and} \quad \sum_k \pi_k^s = 1 . \tag{7}$$

The properties of this eigenvector, which by the stated normalization condition becomes unique, are our main interest.

The problem can be simplified by exploiting the symmetry $W_{-k,-\ell} = W_{k\ell}$, which implies the symmetry $\pi^s_{-k} = \pi^s_k$ of the stationary state. Reformulating the eigenvalue problem for the independent components of $\boldsymbol{\pi}^s$, the eigenvector can be calculated numerically up to $N \approx 1200$ in a reasonable time with standard linear algebra packages.

3. Solution for small probabilities

A closer look reveals that as $N \to \infty$, there are two scaling regimes for σ^2, depending on how p depends on N. We will first consider $p = x/(N/2)$, where x is constant and much smaller than N. As N is increased, the number of players that switch sides every turn stays constant to first order: since the majority is approximately $N/2$, on the average, x agents will change their opinion.

In this case, the matrix elements $W_{k\ell}$ can be approximated by Poisson probabilities [10]:

$$W_{k\ell} \to W^P_{k\ell} = \begin{cases} e^{-x} \dfrac{x^{\ell-k}}{(\ell-k)!} & \text{for } \ell > 0 , \\[2mm] e^{-x} \dfrac{x^{k-\ell}}{(k-\ell)!} & \text{for } \ell < 0 , \end{cases} \tag{8}$$

where, again, $1/m!$ for negative m has to be interpreted as zero. In the limit $N \to \infty$ we are thus looking for an infinite component vector $\boldsymbol{\pi}^s$ satisfying the eigenvalue equation together with the proper normalization:

$$\mathbf{W}^P \boldsymbol{\pi}^s = \boldsymbol{\pi}^s \quad \text{and} \quad \sum_k \pi^s_k = 1 . \tag{9}$$

Making use of (8) and (9) we were able to derive equations for the moments of the stationary distribution:

$$\left\langle |k| - \frac{1}{2} \right\rangle = \frac{x}{2} ,$$

$$\left\langle \left(|k| - \frac{1}{2}\right)\left(|k| - \frac{3}{2}\right) \right\rangle = \frac{x^2}{3} ,$$

$$\left\langle \left(|k| - \frac{1}{2}\right)\left(|k| - \frac{3}{2}\right)\left(|k| - \frac{5}{2}\right) \right\rangle = \frac{x^3}{4}, \quad \text{etc} . \tag{10}$$

These in turn determine the characteristic function of π^s_k, and a Fourier transform finally leads to

$$\pi^s_k = \frac{1}{2\,(|k| - \frac{1}{2})!} \sum_{j=0}^{\infty} \frac{(-1)^j\, x^{j+|k|-1/2}}{j!\,(j + |k| + \frac{1}{2})} . \tag{11}$$

It has been proven that (11) indeed satisfies the eigenvalue equation (9) [12]. Note that π^s_k can be expressed by the incomplete gamma function:

$$\pi^s_k = \frac{\gamma(|k| + \frac{1}{2}, x)}{2x\,(|k| - \frac{1}{2})!} . \tag{12}$$

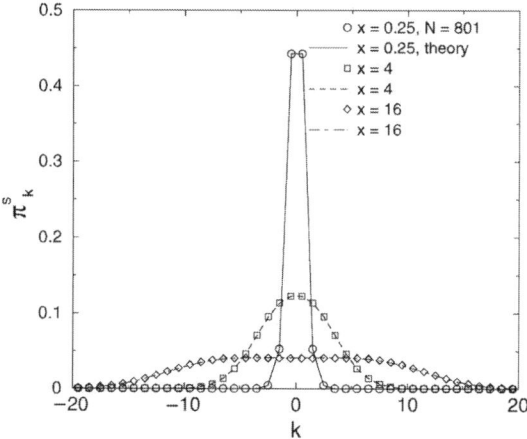

Fig. 1. Stationary solution π_k^s for $p = x/(N/2)$. The numerical solution for $N = 801$ (symbols) is in very good agreement with the analytical solution for $N \to \infty$.

A comparison with numerically determined eigenvectors of the matrix (5) for $N = 801$ gives excellent agreement, as seen in Fig. 1. The distribution is roughly flat for small $|k|$, has a turning point near $|k| = x$ and falls off exponentially with k for larger values of $|k|$. From (11), the variance $\sigma^2 = \langle (2k)^2 \rangle$ can be calculated:

$$\sigma^2 = 1 + 4x + \tfrac{4}{3}x^2 \ . \tag{13}$$

For small x, this approaches the optimal value $\sigma^2 = 1$ that occurs if the majority is always as narrow as possible, but even for larger x, σ^2 does not increase with N.

4. Solution for large probabilities

The other scaling regime assumes that p is of order one and $pN \gg 1$. To handle this regime, we will use a rescaled (continuous) coordinate $\kappa = k/N = \sum_i \sigma_i/(2N)$, the range of which is $-1/2 \leqslant \kappa \leqslant 1/2$. Multiplied by N, the stationary state π_k^s for large N turns into a probability density function $\pi^s(\kappa)$, and the matrix $W_{k\ell}$ becomes an integral kernel $W(\kappa, \lambda)$, hence (7) is transformed into an integral equation:

$$\pi^s(\kappa) = \int W(\kappa, \lambda)\, \pi^s(\lambda)\, \mathrm{d}\lambda \quad \text{and} \quad \int \pi^s(\kappa)\, \mathrm{d}\kappa = 1 \ . \tag{14}$$

Numerical calculations show that the eigenvector $\pi^s(\kappa)$ takes the shape of two Gaussian peaks centred at symmetrical distances $\pm \kappa_0$ from the origin (see Fig. 2). The physical interpretation is that the majority switches from one side to the other in every time step. Since approximately $(\kappa_0 + 1/2)pN$ agents switch sides every turn and the distance between the two peaks amounts to a number of $2\kappa_0 N$ agents, we get $\kappa_0 = p/(4 - 2p)$.

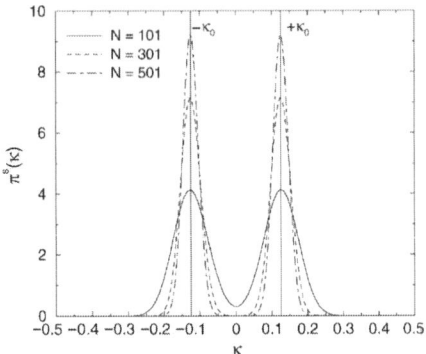

Fig. 2. Stationary solution $\pi^s(\kappa)$ for $p = 0.4$. With increasing N, the width of the peaks becomes narrower.

This reasoning can be made more precise, and also the width of the peaks for large but finite N can be calculated by the following argument: the well known normal approximation for the binomial coefficients in (5) leads to

$$W(\kappa, \lambda) = NW_{\kappa\ell} \approx \frac{1}{\sqrt{2\pi}\, s(\lambda)} \exp\left[-\frac{1}{2}\frac{(\kappa - f(\lambda))^2}{s^2(\lambda)}\right],$$

where

$$f(\lambda) = (1 - p)\lambda - \text{sign}(\lambda)\frac{p}{2}$$

and

$$s^2(\lambda) = \frac{p(1 - p)(\frac{1}{2} + |\lambda|)}{N}. \tag{15}$$

A double Gaussian of the form

$$\pi^s(\kappa) = \frac{1}{2}\frac{1}{\sqrt{2\pi}\, b}\left[\exp\left(\frac{(\kappa + \kappa_0)^2}{2b^2}\right) + \exp\left(\frac{(\kappa - \kappa_0)^2}{2b^2}\right)\right] \tag{16}$$

is transformed by the integral kernel (15) into a double peak of the same type if in the integral equation we approximate the variance $s^2(\lambda)$ of (15) by $s^2(\pm\kappa_0)$ and if the assumption $b^2 \ll \kappa_0^2$ is justified. It means that the peaks are well separated and that the integral can be extended from $-\infty$ to ∞. By requiring $\pi^s(\kappa)$ from (16) to satisfy the eigenvalue equation (14) we get

$$\kappa_0 = \frac{p}{2(2 - p)} \quad \text{and} \quad b^2 = \frac{1 - p}{(2 - p)^2 N}. \tag{17}$$

The result for κ_0 confirms the simple argument given above, whereas the term for b^2 is slightly surprising: it does not depend on p in the leading order, i.e., it is not simply the number of players who switch sides. Eq. (17) also allows to check whether the assumptions made for its derivation are true for a given p and N. For example, for $p = x/N$, $\kappa_0^2/b^2 \to 0$ for $N \to \infty$ according to (17), so one cannot expect the formation of

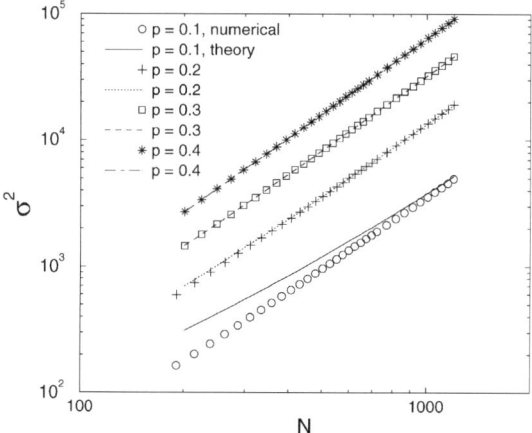

Fig. 3. σ^2 for several values of p and N, compared to predictions by Eq. (18).

double peaks in this limit. The crossover from single-peak to double-peak distribution occurs for $p \propto 1/\sqrt{N}$.

It is now easy to integrate over the probability distribution to get an expression for σ^2:

$$\sigma^2 = \frac{N}{(2-p)^2}(Np^2 + 4(1-p)). \tag{18}$$

This holds well if the condition $\kappa_0 \gg b$ is fulfilled, i.e., for sufficiently large p and N, as seen in Fig. 3. Numerical evidence shows that σ^2 scales like $\sigma^2 \propto N^2 p^2$ even when the condition $\kappa_0 \gg b$ is not fulfilled for $p \propto 1/\sqrt{N}$. In this case, we find $\sigma^2 \propto N$ as in the original game of Challet and Zhang and for random guessing. However, the behaviour of our system is different: the distribution of κ has a double-peak structure and the minority is still very likely to switch from one side to the other at consecutive timesteps.

5. Concluding remarks

It is possible (although not necessary) to include a longer history of minority decisions in our strategy. In that case every player would keep an individual decision table that tells him what is to be done if a given sequence of minority decisions occurs, similar to the tables that the players in the original Minority Game use. However, instead of changing to an entirely different table, each player changes individual entries in his table with probability p if he loses. It is easy to see—and a similar argument was given in Ref. [13] for the global decision table in Johnson's variant—that the entries for different histories are completely decoupled. Each entry or row in the table

259

corresponds to a one-step Markov process as described above, influenced only by the last time that the same history occurred.

In that sense, introducing a history changes the properties of the time series generated by the decisions, but not the average loss of the players in the stationary state. This has also been observed in other variants where the strategies are annealed rather than quenched [7,13]. Thus, it is possible for the system to generate a rather complex-looking time series, while still using the same simple rules.

The presented strategy shows similarities to the behaviour of the original minority game in the limit $\alpha \rightarrow 0$, i.e., a small ratio of possible histories compared to the number of players [14]. In the extreme case where each of the two decision tables that each player keeps consists of only one entry (i.e., only the last minority decision counts), the output of roughly 50% of the players is set to be either $+1$ or -1 independent of the history, whereas the other 50% can choose their output depending on their current score. Out of those players, those who chose the minority side will repeat their decision, whereas the update of the scores will cause some of the losers to switch sides. It has been observed that σ^2 shows a crossover from $\sigma^2 \propto N^2$ to $\sigma^2 \propto 1$ depending on the initial differences in players' scores [15,14]; these differences determine the typical number of players who switch sides when they lose. This situation is very much the same for players who use perceptrons with only one input unit [7], where a solution with $\sigma^2 = 1$ is reached if the learning rate η is smaller than the differences between the initial weights of the players. However, in the absence of frozen disorder, our stochastic strategy obviously does not lead to a separation of agents into frozen and oscillating players.

In summary, we have found an analytic solution of a stochastic strategy for the Minority Game. Although this strategy is very simple, it can yield an average loss of order one even in the limit of infinitely many agents for a suitably chosen p; for increasing p, a crossover to herd behaviour with $\sigma^2 \propto N^2$ is observed. Questions that will be discussed in future publications include the dynamics and relaxation time of the system, interactions with players using other strategies, and individual probabilities for each player.

Acknowledgements

R.M. and W.K. acknowledge financial support by the German-Israeli Foundation. We would like to thank Christian Horn, Andreas Engel, and Ido Kanter for their helpful discussions, and Jens Schipper for numerical simulations.

References

[1] W.B. Arthur, Am. Econ. Assoc. Papers Proc. 84 (1994) 406.
[2] D. Challet, Y.-C. Zhang, Physica A 246 (1997) 407.
[3] D. Challet, M. Marsili, Phys. Rev. E 60 (1999) R6271.

[4] M. Marsili, D. Challet, R. Zecchina, Physica A 280 (2000) 522.

[5] A. Cavagna, Phys. Rev. E 59 (1999) R3783.

[6] D. Challet, M. Marsili, Phys. Rev. E 62 (2000) 1862.

[7] R. Metzler, W. Kinzel, I. Kanter, Phys. Rev. E 62 (2000) 2555.

[8] N.F. Johnson, M. Hart, P.M. Hui, D. Zheng, cond-mat/9910072.

[9] T.S. Lo, P.M. Hui, N.F. Johnson, Phys. Rev. E 62 (2000) 4393.

[10] W. Feller, An Introduction to Probability Theory and its Applications, Vol. 1, Wiley, New York, 1970.

[11] F.R. Gantmacher, Application of the Theory of Matrices, Interscience, New York, 1959.

[12] Ch. Horn, Diploma Thesis, Universität Würzburg, 2001.

[13] E. Burgos, H. Ceva, cond-mat/0003179.

[14] J.A.F. Heimel, A.C.C. Coolen, cond-mat/0012045.

[15] J.P. Garrahan, E. Moro, D. Sherrington, Phys. Rev. E 62 (2000) R9.

Self-Segregation versus Clustering in the Evolutionary Minority Game

Shahar Hod[1] and Ehud Nakar[2]

[1]*Department of Condensed Matter Physics, Weizmann Institute, Rehovot 76100, Israel*
[2]*The Racah Institute of Physics, The Hebrew University, Jerusalem 91904, Israel*
(Received 26 December 2001; published 23 May 2002)

Complex adaptive systems have been the subject of much recent attention. It is by now well established that members ("agents") tend to self-segregate into opposing groups characterized by extreme behavior. However, the study of such adaptive systems has mostly been restricted to simple situations in which the prize-to-fine ratio R equals unity. In this Letter we explore the dynamics of evolving populations with various different values of the ratio R, and demonstrate that extreme behavior is in fact *not* a generic feature of adaptive systems. In particular, we show that "confusion" and "indecisiveness" take over in times of depression, in which case cautious agents perform better than extreme ones.

DOI: 10.1103/PhysRevLett.88.238702

PACS numbers: 02.50.Le, 87.23.Kg, 89.65.Ef

A problem of central importance in social, biological, and economic sciences is that of an evolving population in which individual agents adapt their behavior according to past experience, without direct interaction between different members. Of particular interest are situations in which members (usually referred to as "agents") compete for a limited resource, or to be in a minority (see, e.g., [1], and references therein.) In financial markets, for instance, more buyers than sellers implies higher prices, and it is therefore better for a trader to be in a minority group of sellers. Predators foraging for food will do better if they hunt in areas with fewer competitors. Rush-hour drivers, facing the choice between two alternative routes, wish to choose the route containing the minority of traffic [2].

Considerable progress in the theoretical understanding of such systems has been gained by studying the simple, yet realistic model of the minority game (MG) [3], and its evolutionary version (EMG) [1] (see also [4–13], and references therein). The EMG consists of an odd number of N agents repeatedly choosing whether to be in room "0" (e.g., choosing to sell an asset or taking route A) or in room "1" (e.g., choosing to buy an asset or taking route B). At the end of each turn, agents belonging to the smaller group (the minority) are the winners, each of them gains 1 point (the "prize"), while agents belonging to the majority room lose 1 point (the "fine"). The agents have a common "memory" look-up table, containing the outcomes of m recent occurrences (the particular value of m is of no importance [1]). Faced with a given bit string of recent m occurrences, each agent chooses the outcome in the memory with probability p, known as the agent's "gene" value (and the opposite alternative with probability $1 - p$). If an agent score falls below some value d, then its strategy (i.e., its gene value) is modified. In other words, each agent tries to learn from his past mistakes, and to adjust his strategy in order to survive.

A remarkable conclusion deduced from the EMG [1] is that a population of competing agents tends to self-segregate into opposing groups characterized by extreme behavior. It was realized that in order to flourish in such situations an agent should behave in an extreme way ($p = 0$ or $p = 1$) [1].

It should be emphasized, however, that previous analyses were restricted to the simple case in which the prize-to-fine ratio R was assumed to be equal unity. On the other hand, in many real life situations this ratio may take a variety of different values. In the extreme situation, the fine (e.g., a temporary worker getting fired of work after being late to the office due to a traffic jam, or a predator being starved to death while unsuccessfully trying to hunt in an area with many competitors) may be larger than the prize (a day's payment or a successful hunt which guarantees food for few days, respectively). Another example is that of a trader in a financial market which is under depression. In such circumstances, the trader usually loses more money in a bad deal than he gains in a successful one (due to overall reduction in market's value).

Moreover, we know from real life situations that extreme agents not always perform better than cautious ones. In particular, our daily experience indicates that in difficult situations (e.g., when the prize-to-fine ratio is low) human people tend to be confused and indecisive. In fact, in such circumstances they usually seek to do the *same* (rather than the opposite) as the majority.

Thus, of great interest for real social and biological systems are situations in which the prize-to-fine ratio is smaller (or larger) than unity. The aim of the present Letter is to explore the dynamics of evolving populations with various different external conditions (i.e., different values of the ratio R). Of main importance is the identification of the strategies that perform best in a particular situation.

Figure 1 displays the long-time frequency distribution $P(p)$ of the agents [the lifespan, $L(p)$, defined as the average length of time a strategy p survives between modifications, has a similar behavior]. We find three qualitatively different populations, depending on the precise value of the prize-to-fine ratio parameter R. For $R > R_c^{(1)}$ (this includes the case studied so far in the literature, $R = 1$. The value of $R_c^{(1)}$ depends on the number of agents and the parameter d) the distribution becomes peaked around $p = 0$

0031-9007/02/88(23)/238702(4)$20.00   © 2002 The American Physical Society   238702-1

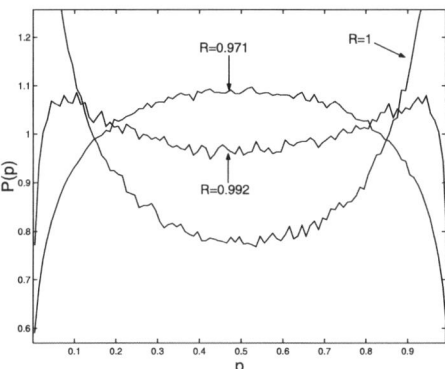

FIG. 1.   The strategy distribution $P(p)$ for different values of the prize-to-fine ratio: $R = 0.971$, $R = 0.992$, and $R = 1$. The results are for $N = 10\,001$ agents, $d = -4$. Each point represents an average value over 10 runs and 100 000 time steps per run.

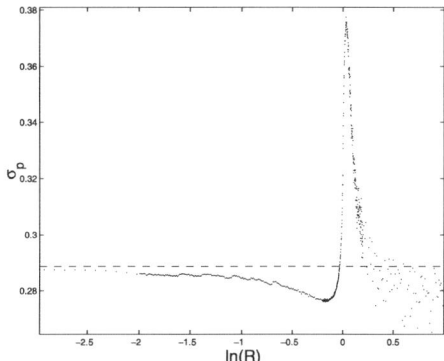

FIG. 2.   The root-mean-square separation (rms) of the strategies as a function of the prize-to-fine ratio R. The horizontal line represents the rms separation for a uniform $P(p)$ distribution. $N = 1001$, $d = -4$. Each point represents an average value over 10 runs and 10 000 time steps per run.

and $p = 1$; the population will self-segregate (this corresponds to always or never following what happened last time). To flourish in such a population, an agent should behave in an *extreme* way [1]. On the other hand, for $R < R_c^{(2)}$ (poor conditions, in which the fine is larger than the reward) the population tends to crowd around $p = \frac{1}{2}$. This corresponds to "confused" and "indecisive" agents. There is also an intermediate phase [for $R_c^{(2)} < R < R_c^{(1)}$], in which the population tends to form an M-shaped distribution, peaked around some finite p_0 and its counterpart $1 - p_0$ (with the absolute minimas of the distribution located at $p = 0$ and $p = 1$).

An important feature of the original EMG (for the $R = 1$ case [1]) is that the root-mean-square (rms) separation of the strategies is *higher* than the corresponding value for uniform $P(p)$. This indicates the desire of agents to do the *opposite* of the majority [1]. Figure 2 shows the rms separation of the population as a function of the prize-to-fine ratio R. Remarkably, we find that for small values of R the rms is in fact *smaller* than that obtained for a uniform $P(p)$ distribution. We therefore conclude that in times of difficulties agents desire to do the *same* (rather than the opposite) as the majority. This is exactly the type of behavior we anticipated in the introduction based on daily experience.

Qualitatively, we have found that the larger the number of agents N, the sharper the dependence of the system's behavior is on the prize-to-fine ratio R (that is, the peak in Fig. 2 is sharper for larger values of N). This may indicate a sharp phase transition (instead of a continuous change of the global behavior with R) in the limit of $N \to \infty$.

In the original EMG [1] it was found that the dynamics of the system leads to situations in which the size of the minority group is maximized, indicating that the efficiency of the system is maximized. The (scaled) efficiency of the

system is defined as the number of agents in the minority room, divided by the maximal possible size of the minority group, $(N - 1)/2$. Figure 3 displays the system's efficiency as a function of the ratio R. We also display the efficiency for agents guessing *randomly* between room 0 and room 1, and for a *uniform* distribution of agents. As previously found, there is a range of R (which includes the previously studied case $R = 1$ [1]) in which the efficiency of the system is *better* than the random case. However, for small values of the prize-to-fine ratio, the efficiency of the system is remarkably *lower* than that obtained for agents choosing via independent coin tosses. Thus, considering the efficiency of the system as a whole, the agents would

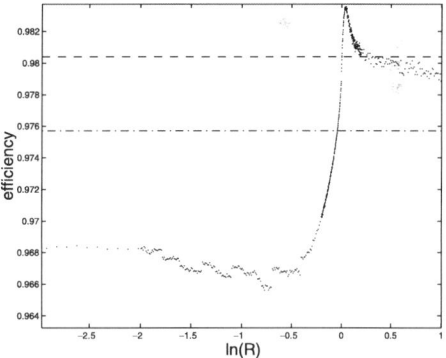

FIG. 3.   The (scaled) efficiency E of the system as a function of the prize-to-fine ratio R. Horizontal lines represents the efficiency for uniform $P(p)$ distribution (dashed) and a coin-tossing situation (dash-dotted). The parameters are the same as in Fig. 2.

be better off not adapting their strategies because they are doing *worse* than just guessing at random.

Note that an optimum utilization of the resources is obtained at some $R_{\max} > 1$ (with $R_{\max} - 1 \ll 1$). This implies that an evolving population requires a small positive feedback in order to exploit its resources in an optimal way. On the other hand, a wealthy society has an efficiency which is worse than that of a uniform $P(p)$ distribution (this occurs for prize-to-fine ratios which are too large). This reflects the fact that in a "spoiling" environment the agents have no real motivation to evolve (they have a long lifespan even without exploiting their resources in an optimal way).

In previous studies (of the $R = 1$ case) it has been established that the evolving population enters into a *stationary* phase, in which case the $P(p)$ distribution remains essentially constant in time [4,7]. In Fig. 4 we display the time dependence of the average gene value, $\langle p \rangle$, for different values of the prize-to-fine ratio R. The distribution $P(p)$ oscillates around $p = \frac{1}{2}$. The smaller the value of R the larger are the amplitude and the frequency of the oscillations. Thus, we conclude that a population which evolves in a tough environment never establishes a steady state distribution. Agents are constantly changing their strategies, trying to survive. By doing so they create global currents in the gene space.

We now provide some analytical analysis of the problem, a generalization of the one presented in [1] for arbitrary values of the prize-to-fine ratio R. The simplest example of our system contains $N = 3$ agents, and three discrete gene values $p = 0, \frac{1}{2}, 1$. We consider configurations for which the average gene value lies between $\frac{1}{3}$ and $\frac{2}{3}$, a reminiscent of the fact that $\langle p \rangle$ displays only mild oscillations around $p = \frac{1}{2}$. To obtain the average $P(p)$ distribution we weigh the various configurations according to the average points awarded per agent in each of

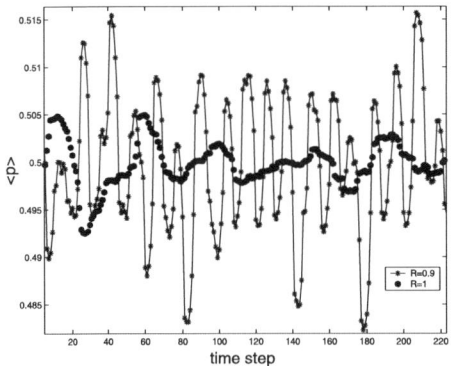

FIG. 4.   Time evolution of the average gene value $\langle p \rangle$, for different values of the prize-to-fine ratio: $R = 0.9$ and $R = 1$. The parameters are the same as in Fig. 1.

the configurations [14]. The analytical results are given in Table I [note that $P(0) = P(1)$]. We find that this simplified toy model provides a fairly good qualitative description of the complex system. In particular, it follows that the population self-segregates for prize-to-fine ratios larger than $R_c = \frac{5}{7}$, while for $R < R_c$ the agents tend to cluster around $p = \frac{1}{2}$. In addition, the efficiency of the system is maximal at *intermediate* values of the prize-to-fine ratio, while poor ($R < 2$) and wealthy ($R > 3$) populations display a lower efficiency.

One can improve the analysis of the evolutionary minority game with the aid of a semianalytical model [15]. The semianalytical model is based on the fact that the population never establishes a true stationary distribution (see Fig. 4). This fact has been ignored in previous studies of the evolutionary minority game. The probability of a particular agent to win is time dependent. In fact, the winning probability oscillates with time; the oscillation amplitude depends on both the value of the prize-to-fine ratio R, and on the agent's gene value p (the smaller the value of R, the larger is the oscillation amplitude; in addition, agents with $p = 0, 1$ have an oscillation amplitude larger than those with $p = 1/2$).

It turns out that the temporal oscillations of the winning probabilities explain the transition of the system's global behavior from self-segregation to clustering: For small values of R (when the prize is smaller than the fine) there is a negative global drift of the agents's score towards $-d$. Thus, agents with an equal number of winnings and losses will eventually perish [after approximately $2d/(1 - R)$ turns]. In order to survive in harsh conditions ($R < 1$) agents must win more times than they lose. Agents with $p = 0, 1$ have a winning probability which oscillates in time with a large amplitude, and therefore most of these agents win and lose the same number of times in each cycle of the oscillations. On the other hand, agents with $p = 1/2$ have a winning probability which is practically constant ($\approx 1/2$) in time. Thus, these are the only agents that can win more times than they lose. Therefore, for small values of the prize-to-fine ratio, agents tend to cluster around $p = 1/2$.

In summary, we have explored the evolution of complex adaptive systems with an arbitrary value of the prize-to-fine ratio R. The main results and their implications are as follows:

(i) It has been widely accepted that *self-segregation* is a generic characteristic of an evolving population of competing agents. This belief was based on studies of the

TABLE I.   Distribution of strategies and efficiency of a three agents system.

R	$P(0){:}P(\frac{1}{2})$	Efficiency
$R < 2$	$\frac{19R-53}{26R-58}$	$\frac{57R-150}{64R-164}$
$2 \leq R \leq 3$	2.5	1
$R > 3$	$\frac{23R-49}{23R-61}$	$\frac{85R-191}{92R-212}$

$R = 1$ case. Our analysis, however, turns over this point of view. In particular, in times of difficulties agents tend to *cluster* around $p = \frac{1}{2}$; cautious agents perform better (live longer) than extreme ones. Stated in a more pictorial way, confusion and indecisiveness take over at tough times.

(ii) In previous analyses it was found that agents desire to do the opposite of the majority [1]. We have shown that this property is in fact not a generic one. In particular, in a tough environment agents try to do the *same* as the majority [the rms separation of strategies is in fact *smaller* than that obtained for a uniform $P(p)$ distribution].

(iii) For small values of the prize-to-fine ratio (poor external conditions) the efficiency of the system is well below the efficiency achieved by random agents (ones who choose via independent coin tosses). It seems that "panic" and "confusion" (clustering around $p = \frac{1}{2}$) prevent the agents from achieving a reasonable utilization of resources. Similarly, a wealthy population, for which there is no real motivation for adaptation, displays a poor efficiency. On the other hand, an evolving population achieves an optimum utilization of its resources when it receives a (*small*) positive external reinforcement (that is, for $0 < R_{max} - 1 \ll 1$).

(iv) The gene distribution $P(p)$ displays temporal oscillations around $p = \frac{1}{2}$. The smaller the value of the prize-to-fine ratio, the farther the system is from a steady-state distribution. This in particular implies that the steady-state assumption used to analyze the EMG (in the $R = 1$ case) [7] is no longer valid for smaller values of R.

S. H. thanks Mordehai Milgrom for his kind assistance, and a support by the Dr. Robert G. Picard fund in physics. The research of S. H. was supported by Grant No. 159/99-3 from the Israel Science Foundation.

[1] N. F. Johnson, P. M. Hui, R. Jonson, and T. S. Lo, Phys. Rev. Lett. **82**, 3360 (1999).
[2] B. Huberman and R. Lukose, Science **277**, 535 (1997).
[3] D. Challet and C. Zhang, Physica (Amsterdam) **246A**, 407 (1997); **256A**, 514 (1998); **269A**, 30 (1999).
[4] R. D'Hulst and G. J. Rodgers, Physica (Amsterdam) **270A**, 514 (1999).
[5] H. Ceva, Physica (Amsterdam) **277A**, 496 (2000).
[6] E. Burgos and H. Ceva, Physica (Amsterdam) **284A**, 489 (2000).
[7] T. S. Lo, P. M. Hui, and N. F. Johnson, Phys. Rev. E **62**, 4393 (2000).
[8] P. M. Hui, T. S. Lo, and N. F. Johnson, e-print cond-mat/0003309.
[9] M. Hart, P. Jefferies, N. F. Johnson, and P. M. Hui, e-print cond-mat/0003486; e-print cond-mat/0004063.
[10] E. Burgos, H. Ceva, and R. P. J. Perazzo, e-print cond-mat/0007010.
[11] T. S. Lo, S. W. Lim, P. M. Hui, and N. F. Johnson, Physica (Amsterdam) **287A**, 313 (2000).
[12] Y. Li, A. VanDeemen, and R. Savit, e-print nlin.AO/0002004.
[13] R. Savit, R. Manuca, and R. Riolo, Phys. Rev. Lett. **82**, 2203 (1999).
[14] For $R < 2$ all configurations have a negative average yield. The relative weight of each configuration is inversely proportional to its yield. For $R \geq 2$ we weight those configurations that have a positive average gain, the weight being proportional to this yield. Consider, for instance, the configuration in which there is one agent in each of the gene values. In this case, each of the extreme agents wins with probability $\frac{1}{2}$, whereas the "confused" agent ($p = \frac{1}{2}$) cannot win. Thus, the average number of points gained per agent per time step is $(R - 2)/3$. The relative weight of this configuration is therefore proportional to $[(R - 2)/3]^{-1}$ in the $R < 2$ case, and to $(R - 2)/3$ for $R \geq 2$.
[15] S. Hod and E. Nakar (to be published).

LETTER TO THE EDITOR

Broken ergodicity and memory in the minority game

J A F Heimel[1] and A De Martino[2]

[1] Department of Mathematics, King's College London, Strand, London WC2R 2LS, UK
[2] International School for Advanced Studies (SISSA/ISAS) and INFM, via Beirut 2-4, 34014 Trieste, Italy

E-mail: heimel@mth.kcl.ac.uk, andemar@sissa.it

Received 9 August 2001
Published 28 September 2001
Online at stacks.iop.org/JPhysA/34/L539

Abstract
We study the dynamics of the 'batch' minority game with market-impact correction using generating functional techniques to carry out the quenched disorder average. We find that the assumption of weak long-term memory, which one usually makes in order to calculate ergodic stationary states, breaks down when the persistent autocorrelation becomes larger than $c_c \simeq 0.772$. We show that this condition, remarkably, coincides with the AT line found in an earlier static calculation. This result suggests a new scenario for ergodicity breaking in disordered systems.

PACS numbers: 02.50.Le, 75.10.Nr

The minority game (MG) models a market of speculators interacting through a simple supply-and-demand mechanism [1, 2]. One of the key behavioural assumptions of the original model is that agents act as so-called price-takers, meaning that at every stage of the game each of them only perceives the aggregate action of all agents, i.e. the total bid. Recently, in [3], a generalization has been introduced in which agents are able to estimate their own contribution to the total bid and use this additional information to adjust their learning dynamics and optimize their performance. The statics of this model has been tackled by spin-glass techniques in [3,4] along the lines of [5]. The system was found to approximately minimize a disordered Hamiltonian H whose minima could be calculated with the replica method. It was shown that replica-symmetry breaking (RSB) can occur, implying the existence of multiple stationary states.

In this Letter we adapt the dynamical method used in [6] to analyse the 'batch' version of this model. Assuming time-translation invariance, finite integrated response and weak long-term memory [7] we obtain exact results for the stationary state which are in excellent agreement with computer experiments and with earlier static approaches. Moreover, we derive a condition for the continuous onset of memory, where the assumption of weak long-term memory is found to fail while time-translation invariance still holds. This appears to be different from the usual

0305-4470/01/400539+07$30.00 © 2001 IOP Publishing Ltd Printed in the UK

---

aging scenario in non-ergodic disordered systems. Remarkably, the memory-onset condition coincides with the AT line found in statics.

We begin by recalling the definition of the model. We consider N agents labelled by roman indices. At each iteration round n all agents receive the same information pattern $\mu(n)$ drawn at random with uniform probability from $\{1, \ldots, \alpha N\}$. Each agent has at his disposal S different strategies (labelled by $g = 1, \ldots, S$) to convert the acquired information into a trading decision. Strategies are denoted by αN-dimensional vectors: $a_{ig} = \{a_{ig}^\mu\}_{\mu=1}^{\alpha N} \in \{-1, 1\}^{\alpha N}$, where a_{ig}^μ is the trading action (e.g. $+1$ for 'buy', -1 for 'sell') prescribed to agent i by his g-th strategy given receipt of information μ. By assumption, each component a_{ig}^μ is selected randomly and independently from $\{-1, 1\}$ with uniform probabilities before the start of the game, for all i, g and μ. This introduces quenched disorder into the model. Each strategy of every agent is given an initial valuation $p_{ig}(0)$, which is updated at the end of every round. At the start of round n, given $\mu(n)$, every agent selects the strategy with the highest valuation, $\widetilde{g}_i(n) = \arg\max p_{ig}(n)$, and subsequently makes a bid according to the trading decision set by the selected strategy: $b_i(n) = a_{i\widetilde{g}_i(n)}^{\mu(n)}$. The total bid at round n is defined as $A(n) = N^{-1/2} \sum_{i=1}^{N} b_i(n)$. Finally, for all i and g all payoffs are updated according to a reinforcement learning dynamics of the form

$$p_{ig}(n + 1) = p_{ig}(n) - a_{ig}^{\mu(n)}\left[A(n) - \frac{\eta}{\sqrt{N}}\left(a_{i\widetilde{g}_i(n)}^{\mu(n)} - a_{ig}^{\mu(n)}\right)\right] \tag{1}$$

and agents move to the next round. The first term in square brackets embodies the minority rule, in that the valuation of a strategy is increased every time it predicts the correct minority action, independently of it having been actually used. The term proportional to η adjusts the total bid for the possibility that agent i is not using strategy $\widetilde{g}_i(n)$. For $\eta = 0$ one returns to the original MG, while for $\eta = 1$ the total bid is completely adjusted.

We focus on the case $g = 1, 2$. Introducing the variables $y_i(n) = [p_{i1}(n) - p_{i2}(n)]/2$, as well as the αN-dimensional vectors $\omega_i = (a_{i1} + a_{i2})/2$, $\Omega = N^{-1/2} \sum_{i=1}^{N} \omega_i$ and $\xi_i = (a_{i1} - a_{i2})/2$, and defining $s_i(n) = \text{sgn}[y_i(n)]$ one has

$$y_i(n + 1) = y_i(n) - \xi_i^{\mu(n)}[\Omega^{\mu(n)} + \frac{1}{\sqrt{N}}\sum_{j=1}^{N} \xi_j^{\mu(n)} s_j(n) - \frac{\eta}{\sqrt{N}} s_i(n) \xi_i^{\mu(n)}]. \tag{2}$$

Following [6] we study in this paper a 'batch' version of the model, which is obtained by averaging (2) over information patterns:

$$y_i(t + 1) = y_i(t) - h_i - \sum_{j=1}^{N} J_{ij} s_j(t) + \eta \alpha s_i(t) + \theta_i(t) \tag{3}$$

where t is a re-scaled time, $h_i = (2/\sqrt{N}) \Omega \cdot \xi_i$ and $J_{ij} = (2/N) \xi_i \cdot \xi_j$. The external field $\theta_i(t)$ has been added for later use. In contrast to the more usual 'on-line' model (2), where the y_i's are updated after every iteration step, in the 'batch' case the updates are made on the basis of the average effect of all possible choices of μ. This modified dynamics yields results for the stationary state which are quantitatively very similar to those of the original model [8]. The theoretical advantage of the 'batch' formulation is that it circumvents the difficulty of constructing a proper continuous time limit. The numerical advantage is that one can simulate larger systems for a longer time. Following [6], one derives the effective non-linear single-agent equation

$$y(t + 1) = y(t) - \alpha \sum_{t' \leqslant t}(1 + G)_{tt'}^{-1} s(t') + \alpha \eta s(t) + \sqrt{\alpha} z(t) + \theta(t) \tag{4}$$

where $s(t) = \text{sgn}[y(t)]$ and $z(t)$ is a Gaussian noise with zero mean and temporal correlations given by

$$\langle z(t)z(t')\rangle \equiv H_{tt'} = \sum_{ss'}(1 + G)_{ts}^{-1}(E + C)_{ss'}(1 + G^T)_{s't'}^{-1} \tag{5}$$

The matrices C and G appearing here are the noise-averaged single-agent correlation and response functions for the process (4), with elements

$$C_{tt'} = \langle s(t)s(t') \rangle \qquad \text{and} \qquad G_{tt'} = \left\langle \frac{\partial s(t)}{\partial \theta(t')} \right\rangle \tag{6}$$

respectively, while I is the identity matrix and E denotes the matrix with all entries equal to one. The link between the Markovian multi-agent system (2) and the non-Markovian single-agent process (4) is established by the fact that, for $N \to \infty$, $C_{tt'}$ and $G_{tt'}$ become identical to the disorder- and agent-averaged correlation and response functions of (2):

$$C_{tt'} = \frac{1}{N} \sum_{i=1}^{N} [s_i(t)s_i(t')]_{\text{dis}} \qquad \text{and} \qquad G_{tt'} = \frac{1}{N} \sum_{i=1}^{N} \left[\frac{\partial s_i(t)}{\partial \theta_i(t')} \right]_{\text{dis}}. \tag{7}$$

Equations (4)–(6) describe the dynamics of the system exactly in the $N \to \infty$ limit. We now move to the stationary states of (4) upon making the following assumptions:

- Time-translation invariance (TTI) $\quad \lim_{t \to \infty} C_{t+\tau,t} = C(\tau) \quad \lim_{t \to \infty} G_{t+\tau,t} = G(\tau).$

- Finite integrated response (FIR) $\quad \lim_{t \to \infty} \sum_{t' \leqslant t} G_{tt'} = \chi < \infty.$

- Weak long-term memory (WLTM) $\quad \lim_{t \to \infty} G(t, t') = 0 \quad \forall t' \text{ finite}.$

For the re-scaled quantity $\tilde{y} = \lim_{t \to \infty} y(t)/t$ one finds

$$\tilde{y} = -\frac{\alpha s}{1+\chi} + \alpha \eta s + \sqrt{\alpha} z + \theta \tag{8}$$

where $s = \lim_{\tau \to \infty} \tau^{-1} \sum_{t < \tau} \text{sgn}[y(t)]$ and $z = \lim_{\tau \to \infty} \tau^{-1} \sum_{t < \tau} z(t)$, while θ is a static field. The variance of the zero-average Gaussian random variable z can be calculated from (5), yielding

$$\langle z^2 \rangle = \lim_{\tau, \tau' \to \infty} \sum_{t \leqslant \tau} \sum_{t' \leqslant \tau'} H_{tt'} = \frac{1+c}{(1+\chi)^2} \tag{9}$$

with the persistent correlation $c \equiv \langle s^2 \rangle = \lim_{\tau \to \infty} \tau^{-1} \sum_{t < \tau} C(t)$. The effective agent is 'frozen' if $\tilde{y} \neq 0$, so that $s = \text{sgn}(\tilde{y})$ and he is always employing the same strategy. Setting $\theta = 0$, this is easily seen to be the case if $|z| > \gamma$ with $\gamma = \sqrt{\alpha}[(1+\chi)^{-1} - \eta]$, provided $\gamma \geqslant 0$. He is instead fickle when $\tilde{y} = 0$ or $|z| < \gamma$, and in this case $s = z/\gamma$. A self-consistent equation for c can now be derived by separating the contribution of the frozen agents from that of the fickle ones. Upon defining $\lambda = \gamma/\sqrt{\langle z^2 \rangle}$ one finds

$$c = \langle \Theta(|z| - \gamma) \rangle + \left\langle \Theta(\gamma - |z|) \frac{z^2}{\gamma^2} \right\rangle = \phi + \frac{1}{\lambda^2} \left[\bar{\phi} - \lambda \sqrt{\frac{2}{\pi}} e^{-\lambda^2/2} \right] \tag{10}$$

where Θ is the step function, $\bar{\phi} = \text{erf}(\lambda/\sqrt{2})$ is the fraction of fickle agents, and $\phi = 1 - \bar{\phi}$ is the fraction of frozen agents. For $\chi = \left\langle \frac{\partial s}{\partial \theta} \right\rangle = \alpha^{-1/2} \left\langle \frac{\partial s}{\partial z} \right\rangle$ one obtains

$$\chi = \frac{1}{\sqrt{\alpha}} \langle \Theta(|z| - \gamma) 2\delta(\sqrt{\alpha}z) \rangle + \frac{1}{\gamma\sqrt{\alpha}} \langle \Theta(\gamma - |z|) \rangle = \frac{\bar{\phi}}{\gamma\sqrt{\alpha}}. \tag{11}$$

Equations (9)–(11) form a closed set from which one can solve for ϕ, c and χ for any α and η. Results for c are shown in figure 1.

For negative η, one observes an excellent agreement between theory and experiment for all values of α, implying that none of our assumptions is ever violated.

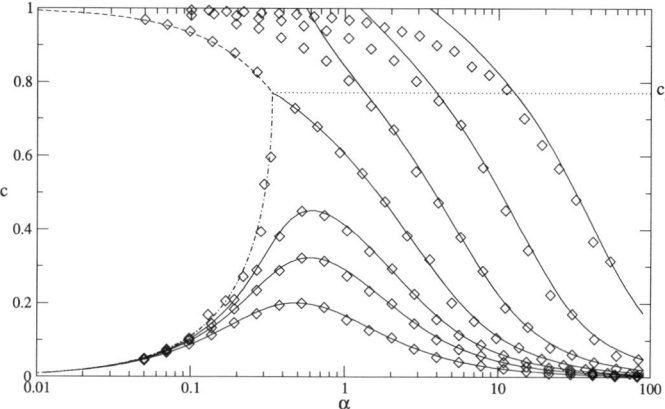

Figure 1. The persistent correlation c as a function of α for different values of η. Lines represent theoretical predictions. Solid lines: from bottom to top, $\eta = -1, -0.5, -0.25, 0, 0.25, 0.5, 0.7$. Dashed line: $y(0) \gg 0, \eta = 0$. Dot-dashed line: $\eta = 0^-$. Diamonds correspond to computer simulations with $\alpha N^2 = 10\,000$, run for 500 time steps and averaged over 50 disorder samples.

When $\eta = 0$, we recover the results of [3,6], which match the simulations perfectly for α larger than the critical value $\alpha_c \simeq 0.3374$. At this point the integrated response χ diverges (FIR is violated) and a transition to a highly non-ergodic regime takes place, where the stationary state depends on the initial conditions $y(0)$. Starting with $y(0) \simeq 0$ leads to a high volatility state, while starting with $|y(0)| \gg 1$ leads to relatively low volatility. The latter regime can be solved using the assumption that χ remains very large for all $\alpha < \alpha_c$. In fact, if $\chi \gg 1$ then $\gamma \simeq \sqrt{\alpha}/\chi$ so that $\overline{\phi} = \alpha$, which is equivalent to $\mathrm{erf}(\lambda/\sqrt{2}) = \alpha$. Solving this for λ and inserting the resulting value in (10), we obtain the top left branch of the $\eta = 0$ curve in figure 1, which is again in excellent agreement with numerical results.

For positive η, one sees that when $c > c_c \simeq 0.77$ our theoretical predictions deviate from the experimental observations, whereas the agreement is perfect for $c < c_c$. Finding no violation of FIR, we have to conclude that either TTI or WLTM is violated. However, we have found no evidence of aging. Therefore we expect the deviations to be related to the breakdown of WLTM only. To find the onset of memory, we split $G_{tt'}$ in its TTI part and its non-TTI part:

$$\lim_{t \to \infty} G_{tt'} = \widetilde{G}(t - t') + \widehat{G}(t, t'). \tag{12}$$

During the initial stages of the game, small perturbations can cause some agents, which would otherwise have remained fickle, to freeze and vice versa, thus creating a persistent part $\widehat{G}$ in the response function. As the agents freeze, their state (and consequently their contribution to G) becomes independent of t, so that we expect $\lim_{t \to \infty} \widehat{G}(t, t') = \widehat{G}(t')$. After an initial equilibration period, for all frozen agents the difference between the strategy valuations have become very large, so they are virtually insensitive to perturbations. Hence we must assume that $\lim_{t' \to \infty} \widehat{G}(t') = 0$. The fickle agents, however, remain sensitive to small perturbations. The effects will wear out over time (finite response) and are given by $\widetilde{G}$.

Assuming $\widehat{G}$ is small, we expand $(1 + G)^{-1}$ in powers of $\widehat{G}$ up to first order:

$$(1 + G)^{-1} = (1 + \widetilde{G})^{-1} - \sum_{n=0}^{\infty} \sum_{m=0}^{n-1} (-\widetilde{G})^m \widehat{G} (-\widetilde{G})^{n-m-1} + O(\widehat{G}^2). \tag{13}$$

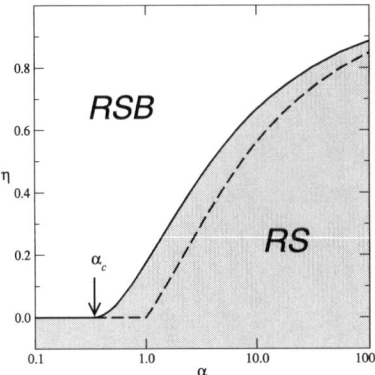

Figure 2. The solid line represents the MO(=AT) line. The dashed line corresponds to the AT line reported in [4].

Defining $\widetilde{\chi} = \sum_t \widetilde{G}(t)$ and $\widehat{\chi} = \sum_t \widehat{G}(t)$, one then finds asymptotically

$$\widetilde{y} = -\alpha \left(\frac{1}{1+\widetilde{\chi}} - \eta \right) s + \sqrt{\alpha} z.$$

$$+\alpha \sum_{n=0}^{\infty} \sum_{m=0}^{n-1} (-\widetilde{\chi})^m \sum_{t'} \widehat{G}(t') \sum_{t''} \left[(-\widehat{G})^{n-m-1} \right] (t', t'') s(t'') \tag{14}$$

Using the rectified linear function $f(x) = x$ for $|x| \leqslant 1$ and $\mathrm{sgn}(x)$ otherwise, we see that if $1/(1+\widetilde{\chi}) > \eta$ then

$$s = f\left(\frac{1}{\widetilde{\gamma}} \left[z + \sqrt{\alpha} \sum_{n=0}^{\infty} \sum_{m=0}^{n-1} (-\widetilde{\chi})^m \sum_{t'} \widehat{G}(t') \sum_{t''} \left[(-\widehat{G})^{n-m-1} \right] (t', t'') s(t'') \right] \right) \tag{15}$$

$$\widetilde{\gamma} = \sqrt{\alpha} \left(\frac{1}{1+\widetilde{\chi}} - \eta \right).$$

As before, we have $\widetilde{\chi} = \alpha^{-1/2} \left\langle \frac{\partial s}{\partial z} \right\rangle$, whereas

$$\widehat{G}(t) = \left\langle \frac{\partial s}{\partial \theta(t)} \right\rangle = \frac{\sqrt{\alpha}}{\widetilde{\gamma}} \sum_{n=0}^{\infty} \sum_{m=0}^{n-1} (-\widetilde{\chi})^m \sum_{t'} \widehat{G}(t') \sum_{t''} \left[(-\widehat{G})^{n-m-1} \right] (t', t'') \widetilde{G}(t'', t). \tag{16}$$

Up to first order in $\widehat{G}$ one finds $\widehat{\chi} = \widehat{\chi} \widetilde{\chi} \sqrt{\alpha} / [\widetilde{\gamma}(1+\widetilde{\chi})^2] + O(\widehat{G}^2)$. Although $\widehat{\chi} = 0$ is always a solution of this equation, a bifurcation occurs when $\widetilde{\chi} \sqrt{\alpha} / [\widetilde{\gamma}(1+\widetilde{\chi})^2] = 1$, which is equivalent to $\overline{\phi} = \alpha[1 - \eta(1 + \chi)]^2$, and can be written in terms of λ as

$$\lambda^2 [1 + c(\lambda)] = \overline{\phi}(\lambda). \tag{17}$$

We call this line in the (α, η) plane the memory-onset (MO) line, see figure 2. It coincides remarkably with the AT line (see appendix), and implies that the bifurcation occurs at $c_c \simeq 0.7722$ for $\eta > 0$. Above this value, WLTM can be broken, and indeed one sees from figure 1 that numerical results deviate from our theoretical predictions for $c > c_c$. To give further evidence of memory, we have analysed the time evolution of two identical copies a and b of the system, starting from slightly different initial conditions. We plotted in figure 3 the distance d of the stationary states, given by $(1/N) \sum_i (s_i^a - s_i^b)^2$, where s_i^m is the long-time average of $\mathrm{sgn}(y_i^m)$ ($m = a, b$), versus the persistent autocorrelation of copy a, c^a. As c^a approaches c_c, the two copies end up in different stationary states, proving that they remember

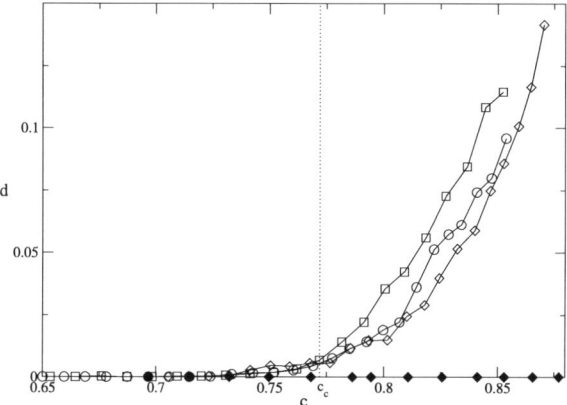

Figure 3. Distance between the stationary states of two identical copies of the system (see text) as a function of their persistent autocorrelation. Simulations are for various levels of η with $N = 450$, averaged over 100 samples. Open markers correspond to a perturbation at $t = 0$ ($\bigcirc$, $\square$, $\lozenge$ for $\alpha = 1, 2, 4$, respectively). Closed markers correspond to a perturbation at $t = 500$ ($\blacklozenge$ for $\alpha = 2$). All simulations are run up to 500 steps after the perturbation occurs. Time averages are over the last 300 steps.

initial conditions[3]. At the same time, if a perturbation is applied much later during the run the copies end up in the same stationary state, indicating that indeed $\widehat{G}(t') \to 0$ as $t' \to \infty$.

Summarizing, we have shown that in this model the usual connection between broken ergodicity and broken TTI (aging), as seen for instance in mean-field spin glasses [9], does not occur. In contrast, we derive from the dynamics a condition for breakdown of WLTM and continuous onset of memory within the TTI regime, which is found to be equivalent to the AT line found in the static approach. This remarkable deviation from the well-known RSB/aging picture is possibly due to the fact that the microscopic dynamics of our model does not satisfy detailed balance.

We gratefully acknowledge support from and useful discussions with A C C Coolen and M Marsili, and with S Franz. We also thank SISSA and King's College London for reciprocal hospitality. This work originated at the International Seminar on Statistical Mechanics of Information Processing in Cooperative Systems (Dresden, March 2001).

Appendix

While investigating the possible relation between our MO line and replica-symmetry breaking, it became apparent that in the very final step of the AT line calculation in [4] a small error has occurred. It was found that the replica-symmetric solution becomes unstable when

$$\lim_{\beta \to \infty} \left\langle \beta^2 \left(\langle s^2 \rangle - \langle s \rangle^2 \right)^2 \right\rangle_z = (1 + \chi)^2 \tag{18}$$

---

[3] The slight bump that occurs before c_c is likely due to the fact that in our simulation the perturbation can not be infinitesimal, but is at least $1/N$.

where $\langle f(s) \rangle = Z_\beta(z)^{-1} \int_{-1}^{1} f(s) e^{-\beta V_z(s)} ds$ and $Z_\beta(z) = \int_{-1}^{1} e^{-\beta V_z(s)} ds$, with $V_z(s) = \frac{1}{2}\gamma s^2 - zs$. The brackets $\langle \cdots \rangle_z$ denote a Gaussian average over z having zero mean and variance $\langle z^2 \rangle_z = (1+q)/(1+\chi)^2$, q being the overlap between two different replicas (off-diagonal overlap matrix element). We have absorbed a spurious factor $\sqrt{\alpha}$ in β. If we now define $F(z) = -\lim_{\beta \to \infty} \beta^{-1} \log Z_\beta(z)$, the AT line can be written as $\langle F''(z)^2 \rangle_z = (1+\chi)^2$. By Laplace's method we find $F(z) = V_z(s_0)$, s_0 being the minimum of V_z in $[-1, 1]$. For $|z/\gamma| < 1$, s_0 lies inside this interval and $V_z(s_0) = z^2/(2\gamma)$, while for $|z/\gamma| > 1$ s_0 is on the border and $V_z(s_0) = \gamma/2 - |z|$. This gives second derivatives that are $-\gamma^{-1}$ and 0, respectively. The AT line is therefore given by $\langle \gamma^{-2} \Theta(1 - |z/\gamma|) \rangle_z + \langle 0 \, \Theta(|z/\gamma| - 1) \rangle_z = (1+\chi)^2$. Recognizing the non-vanishing term on the lhs as the fraction $\bar{\phi}$ of fickle agents, we find

$$\alpha[1 - \eta(1+\chi)]^2 = \bar{\phi} \tag{19}$$

similar to the result of [4] where in place of $\bar{\phi}$ a 1 was reported. Written in terms of λ, the AT line is identical to the MO line (17). We learned that the AT line can also be derived from the dynamical stability of equation (2) [10].

References

[1] Challet D and Zhang Y-C 1997 *Physica A* **246** 407
[2] See the web page There is an extensive and commented overview of the existing literature at `www.unifr.ch/econophysics/minority`
[3] Marsili M, Challet D and Zecchina R 2000 *Physica A* **280** 522
[4] De Martino A and Marsili M 2001 *J. Phys. A: Math. Gen.* **34** 2525
[5] Challet D, Marsili M and Zecchina R 2000 *Phys. Rev. Lett.* **84** 1824
[6] Heimel J A F and Coolen A C C 2001 *Phys. Rev. E* **63** 56121
[7] Cugliandolo L F and Kurchan J 1995 *Phil. Mag. B* **71** 501
[8] Coolen A C C and Heimel J A F 2001 in preparation
[9] Bouchaud J-P, Cugliandolo L F, Kurchan J and Mézard M 1998 *Spin Glasses and Random Fields* ed A P Young (Singapore: World Scientific) pp 161–224
[10] Marsili M 2001 private communication

Self-Organized Networks of Competing Boolean Agents

Maya Paczuski,[1,2,3] Kevin E. Bassler,[3] and Álvaro Corral[1]

[1]*Niels Bohr Institute, Blegdamsvej 17, 2100 Copenhagen, Denmark*
[2]*NORDITA, Blegdamsvej 17, 2100 Copenhagen, Denmark*
[3]*Department of Physics, University of Houston, Houston, Texas 77204-5506*
(Received 6 May 1999; revised manuscript received 23 December 1999)

A model of Boolean agents competing in a market is presented where each agent bases his action on information obtained from a small group of other agents. The agents play a competitive game that rewards those in the minority. After a long time interval, the poorest player's strategy is changed randomly, and the process is repeated. Eventually the network evolves to a stationary but intermittent state where random mutation of the worst strategy can change the behavior of the entire network, often causing a switch in the dynamics between attractors of vastly different lengths.

PACS numbers: 02.50.Le, 05.65.+b, 87.23.Ge, 87.23.Kg

Dynamical systems with many elements under mutual regulation or influence are thought to underlie much of the phenomena associated with complexity. Such systems arise naturally in biology, as, for instance, genetic regulatory networks [1], or ecosystems, and in the social sciences, in particular the economy [2]. Economic agents make decisions to buy or sell, adjust prices, and so on based on individual strategies which take into account the heterogeneous external information each agent has available at the time, as well as internal preferences such as tolerance for risk. External information may include both globally available signals that represent aggregate behavior of many agents such as a market index, or specific (local) information on what some other identified players are doing. In this case each agent has a specified set of inputs, which are the actions of other agents, and a set of outputs, his own actions, that may be conveyed to some other agents. Thus, the economy can be represented as a dynamical network of interconnected agents sending signals to each other with possible, global feedback to the agents coming from aggregate measures of their behavior plus any exogenous forces.

Each agent's current strategy can be represented as a function which specifies a set of outputs for each possible input. In the simplest case the agents have only one binary choice such as either buying or selling a stock [3]. As indicated first by Arthur this simple case already presents a number of intriguing problems. In his "bar problem," each agent must decide whether to attend a bar or refrain based on the previous aggregate attendance history [4]. Challet and Zhang made a perspicuous adaptation, the so-called minority model, where agents in the minority are rewarded, and those in the majority punished [5]. Common to all these and related works [6] is that the network of interconnections between the agents is totally ignored. They are mean-field descriptions. Each agent responds only to an aggregate signal, e.g., which value (0 or 1) was in the majority for the last T_i time steps, rather than any detailed information he may have about other specified agents. It is not unexpected that an extended

system with globally shared information can organize. A basic question in studies of complexity is how large systems with only local information available to the agents may become complex through a self-organized dynamical process.

Here we explicitly consider the network of interconnections between agents, and for simplicity exclude all other effects. We represent agents in a market as a random network of interconnected Boolean elements under mutual influence, the so-called Kauffman network [1,7]. The market payoff takes the form of a competitive game. The performance of the individual agents is measured by counting the number of times each agent is in the majority. After a time scale, defining an epoch, the worst performer, who was in the majority most often, changes his strategy. The Boolean function of that agent is replaced with a new Boolean function chosen at random, and the process is repeated indefinitely. Note that it is not otherwise indicated to the agents what is rewarded, i.e., being in the minority. The agents are given only their individual scores and otherwise play blindly; they do not know directly that they are rewarded by the outcome of a minority game, unlike the original minority game model.

We observe that, irrespective of initial conditions, the network ultimately self-organizes into an intermittent steady state at a borderline between two dynamical phases. This border may correspond to an "edge of chaos" [1]. In some epochs the dynamics of the network takes place on a very long attractor, while, otherwise, the network is either completely frozen or the dynamics is localized on some attractor with a smaller period. More precisely, numerical simulation results indicate that the distribution of attractor lengths in the self-organized state is broad, with no apparent cutoff other than the one that must be numerically imposed, and consistent with power-law behavior for large enough attractor lengths. A single agent's change of strategy from one epoch to the next can cause the entire network to flip between attractors of vastly different lengths. Thus the network can act as a switch.

0031-9007/00/84(14)/3185(4)$15.00   © 2000 The American Physical Society   3185

Consider a network of N agents where each agent is assigned a Boolean variable $\sigma_i = 0$ or 1. Each agent receives input from K other distinct agents chosen at random in the system. The set of inputs for each agent i is quenched. The evolution of the system is specified by N Boolean functions of K variables, each of the form

$$\sigma_i(t+1) = f_i[\sigma_{i_1}(t), \sigma_{i_2}(t), \ldots \sigma_{i_K}(t)]. \quad (1)$$

There exist 2^{2^K} possible Boolean functions of K variables. Each function is a lookup table which specifies the binary output for a given set of binary inputs. In the simplest case defined by Kauffman, *where the networks do not organize,* each function f_i is chosen randomly among these 2^{2^K} possible functions with no bias; we refer to this case as the random Kauffman network (RKN).

We will now briefly review some facts about Kauffman networks. First, a phase transition occurs on increasing K. For $K < 2$ RKN starting from random initial conditions reach frozen configurations, while for $K > 2$ RKN reach attractors whose length typically grows exponentially with N and are called chaotic. RKN with $K = 2$ are critical and the distribution of attractor lengths that the system reaches, starting from random initial conditions, approaches a power law [8], for large enough system sizes, when averaged over many network realizations. This phase transition in the Kauffman networks can also be observed by biasing the random functions f_i so that the output variables switch more or less frequently if the input variables are changed. Boolean functions can be characterized by a "homogeneity parameter" P which represents the fraction of 1's or 0's in the output, whichever is the majority for that function. In general, on increasing P at fixed K, a phase transition is observed from chaotic to frozen behavior. For $K < 2$ the unbiased, random value happens to fall above the transition in the frozen phase, while for $K \geq 3$ the opposite occurs [1]. Kauffman networks are examples of strongly disordered systems and have attracted attention from physicists over the years (see, for example, Refs. [9–11]). Note that the phase transition previously observed in Kauffman networks arises by externally tuning parameters such as P or K.

We consider random Boolean networks of K inputs, and with lookup tables chosen independently from the 2^{2^K} possibilities with equal probability. With specified initial conditions, generally random, each agent is updated in parallel according to Eq. (1). The agents are competing against each other and at each time step those in the minority win. Thus there is a penalty for being in the herd. One may ascribe to agents a reluctance to change strategies. Only in the face of long-term failure will an agent overcome his barrier to change. In the limiting case of high barriers to change, the time scale for changing strategies will be set by the poorest performer in the network. The change of strategies is approximated as an extremal process [12] where the agent who was in the majority most often over a

long time scale, the epoch, is chosen for "Darwinian" selection. In our simulations, the network was updated until either the attractor of the dynamics was found, or the length of the attractor was found to be larger than some limiting value which was typically set at 10 000 time steps, solely for reasons of numerical convenience. The performance of the agents was then measured over either the attractor or the portion of the attractor up to the cutoff length.

The Boolean function of the worst player is replaced with a new Boolean function chosen completely at random with equal probability from the 2^{2^K} possible Boolean functions. If two or more agents are the worst performers, one of them is chosen at random and changed. The performance of all the agents is then measured in the new epoch, and this process is continued indefinitely. Note that the connection matrix of the network does not evolve; the set of agents who are inputs to each agent is fixed by the initial conditions.

Independent of initial conditions, a $K = 3$ network evolves to a statistically stationary but intermittent state, shown in Fig. 1. Initially the attractors that the system reaches are always very long, consistent with all previous work on Kauffman networks. But after many epochs of selecting the worst strategy, short attractors first appear and a new statistically stationary state emerges. In this figure we roughly characterize an attractor as "chaotic" or long if its length is greater than $l = 10 000$ time steps. On varying l a similar picture is obtained as long as l is sufficiently large to distinguish long period attractors from short period ones. In the stationary state, one observes that the network can switch behaviors on changing a single strategy. Intriguingly, Kauffman initially proposed random Boolean networks as simplified models of genetic regulation where it is known that switches exist and are an important aspect of genetic control [13].

To be more precise, the histogram of the distribution of the lengths of the attractor in the self-organized state was

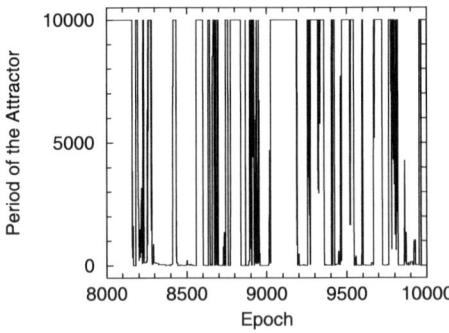

FIG. 1. Time series of the length of attractor in each epoch for $K = 3$, $N = 999$ in the stationary state.

3186

measured as shown in Fig. 2 for different system sizes with the same numerically imposed cutoff l. The apparent peak at small periods is due to the relative presence or absence of prime numbers, and numbers which can be factored many ways. The last point represents all attractors larger than our numerically imposed cutoff 10 000, which is why a bump appears. In between these two regions, the behavior suggests a power law, $P_{\text{atr}}(t) \sim 1/t$ asymptotically, as is the case at the phase transition in RKN [8]. If we increase or decrease our numerically imposed cutoff, then the bump at l correspondingly moves left or right and the intermediate region expands or contracts, both consistent with the power law. Also the power law behavior becomes more apparent for increasing system size suggesting that the self-organized state we observed is not merely an effect of finite system size, but becomes more distinct as the system size increases.

The process of evolution towards the steady state is monitored by measuring the average value of the homogeneity parameter P in the network from epoch to epoch. As shown in Fig. 3, for $K = 3$, the average value of P tends to increase from the random value set by the initial conditions during the transient. For finite N, there are fluctuations in P in the steady state, as well as finite size effects in the average value $\langle P \rangle$. For $N = (99, 315, 999, 3161)$ we measured an average value in the steady state $\langle P \rangle = (0.656(1), 0.664(1), 0.669(1), 0.671(1))$ and root-mean-square fluctuations $\Delta P_{\text{rms}} \simeq (0.015, 0.007, 0.004, 0.001)$. These numerical results suggest that in the thermodynamic limit $N \rightarrow \infty$, P is approaching a unique value $P_c \simeq 0.672$. This value is below the $P_c \simeq 0.792438$ [14,15] of random Kauffman $K = 3$ networks, but is many standard deviations away from the initial value.

The dynamical state that the system evolves toward is different from the phase transition of Kauffman networks

in other (less trivial) ways. In particular, the phase transition in RKN is a freezing transition where most elements do not change state. Only a few elements, strictly $[< \mathcal{O}(N)]$, are changing state [1,14] at the phase transition of RKN, whereas in our self-organized networks there can be short attractors associated with many elements $[\sim \mathcal{O}(N)]$ changing state. This can occur only if the Boolean tables in the network become correlated by the evolutionary process, which, by construction, is not allowed for RKN. Thus our initially chaotic networks are not freezing as in Kauffman networks at the phase transition, but are somehow phase locking many elements together.

The distribution of performances of agents in the network fluctuates a great deal from epoch to epoch. The performance is measured by counting the fraction of times each agent is in the majority. In the case where the network has period one, there are obviously two peaks, one corresponding to the group always in the minority and the other corresponding to the group always in the majority. In fact we find that even on the long attractors encountered in the steady state, typically a significant fraction of the agents are frozen. The number of these frozen agents fluctuates from epoch to epoch.

Figure 4 is a histogram of performances for agents in a self-organized network in a particular epoch which had a period greater than 10 000. Note that the relative performances vary considerably. The two peaks represent the frozen agents. As indicated in the figure, the frozen agents are typically divided between the two states unevenly. In any given instant, despite the uneven division between the frozen agents, the total number of agents in the two states (0,1) is almost evenly divided with fluctuations that are much smaller than in RKN. Active agents, who are changing their state in response to the inputs of others, comprise the remainder of the histogram outside of the two peaks. As shown in this figure, some agents who are inflexible and do not respond to their environment perform better than some agents who respond to their changing inputs and change states. This suggests that somehow the losers

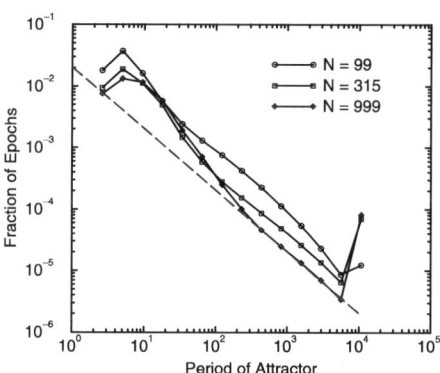

FIG. 2. Histogram of attractor lengths for $K = 3$ networks. The dashed line has a slope of 1.

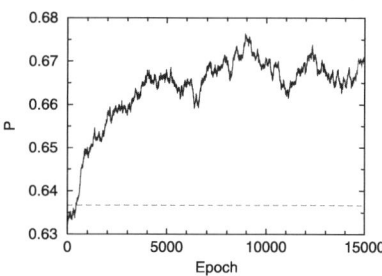

FIG. 3. Self-organization of the homogeneity parameter P for the same network as in Fig. 1. The dashed line corresponds to the unbiased random value.

3187

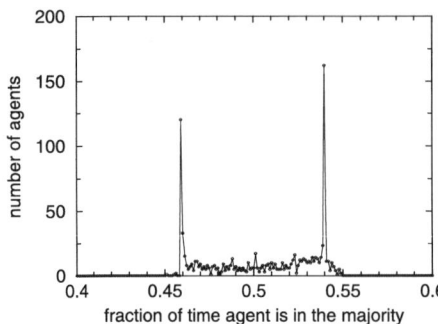

FIG. 4. Histogram of performances in a particular epoch, for $N = 999$ and $K = 3$ in the self-organized state. Those with high scores are poor performers.

are being exploited by some information traveling in the network that they respond to. Also, somewhat counterintuitively, a large group of agents who take the same action, corresponding to the left-hand peak, can compete very well in spite of the fact that the minority game tends to punish herd behavior.

Although we currently have no adequate theoretical description of our numerical observations, we can still discuss, to some extent, the generality and robustness of our results. First, if, instead of changing the entire Boolean table of the worst performer, just one element in it is changed, the self-organization process still takes place. If on the other hand, the Boolean function of the worst performer and those who receive input from it are changed, no self-organization takes place. Of course it does not make sense to change the Boolean functions of the agents who listen to the worst performer because in our context the barrier to change is an internal function of the performance for each individual. The precise behavior on varying K is not determined at present. For $K = 6$, we have simulated systems with $N = 99$ as long as 10^6 epochs, and never observed the system to reach any frozen state when starting from a random, unbiased state in the chaotic phase, so it is possible that the self-organization process as described here using completely random tables does not occur for high enough K.

However, other significant modifications were done where the self-organization process survives. For example, if, instead of changing the Boolean tables of the worst performer, we keep the Boolean tables fixed at their initial state, but change the inputs for the worst performer by rewiring the network, then the $K = 3$ networks still self-organize to a similar state at an "edge of chaos" with similar statistical properties for the periods of the attractors and performances of the agents. This occurs despite the fact that in this case the average homogeneity parameter P of the network cannot evolve.

Rather than define an arbitrary fitness, and select those agents with lowest fitness, an approach that was used by Bak and Sneppen [12], to describe coevolution, we eliminate the concept of fitness and define a performance based on a specific game. Clearly if the agents are rewarded for being in the majority, then the behavior of the system is completely trivial; the agents gain by cooperating instead of competing and the network is driven deep into the frozen phase. This naturally raises the question of which types of games lead to self-organized complex states. In our model, selection of agents in the majority for random change tends to increase the number in the minority. Even in the absence of interactions, eventually those in the minority would become the majority and lose. We suspect that, in general, the game must make agents compete for a reward that depends on the behavior of other agents in a manner that intrinsically frustrates any group of agents from permanently taking over and winning. This frustration may be an essential feature of the dynamics of many complex systems, and our model may be interpreted as, for instance, describing an ecosystem of interacting and competing species.

We thank P. Bak, S. Kauffman, and K. Sneppen for stimulating discussions. This work was funded in part by EU Grant No. FMRX-CT98-0183.

[1] S. A. Kauffman, *The Origins of Order* (Oxford University Press, New York, 1993).
[2] W. B. Arthur, Science **284**, 107 (1999).
[3] P. Bak, M. Paczuski, and M. Shubik, Physica (Amsterdam) **246A**, 430 (1997).
[4] W. B. Arthur, Am. Econ. Rev. **84**, 406 (1994).
[5] D. Challet and Y.-C. Zhang, Physica (Amsterdam) **246A**, 407 (1997); Y.-C. Zhang, Europhys. News **29**, 51 (1998).
[6] See, for example, R. Savit, R. Manuca, and R. Riolo, Phys. Rev. Lett. **82**, 2203 (1999).
[7] S. A. Kauffman, J. Theor. Biol. **22**, 437 (1969); S. A. Kauffman, Physica (Amsterdam) **10D**, 145 (1984).
[8] A. Bhattacharjya and S. Liang, Phys. Rev. Lett. **77**, 1644 (1996); U. Bastolla and G. Parisi, J. Theor. Biol. **187**, 117 (1997).
[9] B. Derrida and Y. Pomeau, Europhys. Lett. **1**, 45 (1986).
[10] U. Bastolla and G. Parisi, Physica (Amsterdam) **115D**, 203 (1998).
[11] S. Bornholdt and K. Sneppen, Phys. Rev. Lett. **81**, 236 (1998).
[12] P. Bak and K. Sneppen, Phys. Rev. Lett. **71**, 4083 (1993); M. Paczuski, S. Maslov, and P. Bak, Phys. Rev. E **53**, 414 (1996).
[13] M. Ptashne, *A Genetic Switch* (Cell Press, Cambridge, 1992).
[14] B. Derrida, in *Fundamental Problems in Statistical Mechanics VII*, edited by H. van Beijeren (North-Holland, Amsterdam, 1990).
[15] Note that the homogeneity parameter P is not equal to p in Ref. [14], but can be related to it.

3188

J. Phys. A: Math. Gen. **33** (2000) L141–L147. Printed in the UK   PII: S0305-4470(00)11132-1

LETTER TO THE EDITOR

Dynamics of interacting neural networks

W Kinzel†, R Metzler† and I Kanter‡

† Institut für Theoretische Physik, Universität Würzburg, Am Hubland, D-97074 Würzburg, Germany
‡ Minerva Center and Department of Physics, Bar Ilan University, 52900 Ramat Gan, Israel

Received 17 January 2000

Abstract. The dynamics of interacting perceptrons is solved analytically. For a directed flow of information the system runs into a state which has a higher symmetry than the topology of the model. A symmetry-breaking phase transition is found with increasing learning rate. In addition, it is shown that a system of interacting perceptrons which is trained on the history of its minority decisions develops a good strategy for the problem of adaptive competition known as the bar problem or minority game.

Simple models of neural networks describe a wide variety of phenomena in neurobiology and information theory. Neural networks are systems of elements interacting by adaptive couplings which are trained by a set of examples. After training they function as content addressable associative memory, as classifiers or as prediction algorithms. Using methods of statistical physics many of these phenomena have been elucidated analytically for infinitely large neural networks [1, 2].

Up to now, only isolated neural networks have been investigated theoretically. However, many phenomena in biology, social science and computer science may be modelled by a system of interacting adaptive algorithms. Nothing is known about general properties of such systems. In this letter we present the first analytic solution of a system of interacting perceptrons. For simplicity, we restrict ourselves to simple perceptrons with binary output.

The dynamics of a set of perceptrons learning from each other by a directed flow of information is solved analytically. Starting from a non-symmetric initial configuration, the system relaxes to a final state which has a higher symmetry than the ring-like flow of information. The system tries to stay as symmetric as possible. In some cases we find a phase transition: when the learning rate is increased the system suddenly breaks the symmetry and relaxes to a state with non-symmetric overlaps.

In addition, we show that a system of interacting neural networks can develop a good strategy for a model of adaptive competition in closed markets, the El-Farol bar problem [3]. In this problem N agents are competing for limited resources and the individual profit depends on the collective behaviour. Recently, a variation of this problem known as the minority game has been studied theoretically in a series of publications [4–8]. The minority game model has several peculiarities.

(a) The strategies of the agents are quenched random variables (decision tables), given in advance, and each agent can only choose between a few of these tables.

(b) Some of the agents are frozen as losers, at least in some regions of the parameter space. In a realistic situation permanent losers would change the strategy after some time.

(c) A good performance is only achieved if the number of time steps each agent is using for his/her decision is adjusted to the number of agents.

Our approach shows none of these drawbacks. Each agent uses one perceptron for his/her decision with couplings which are trained to the minority of all the outputs. Hence the strategies develop according to the dynamics of the system. We analytically calculate the statistical properties of such a system of interacting perceptrons. The system performs optimally in the limit of small learning rates and is insensitive to the size of the number of time steps taken for the decision. Each agent receives the same profit in the long run.

The perceptron is the simplest model of a neural network. It has one layer of synaptic weights $w = (w_1, \ldots, w_M)$ and one output bit σ which is given by

$$\sigma = \text{sign} \sum_{i=1}^{M} w_i x_i = \text{sign}(w \cdot x) \tag{1}$$

where x is the input vector of dimension M; for instance, it is given by a window of a bit sequence $S_t \in \{+1, -1\}, t = 1, 2, \ldots, M$, with $x_i = (S_{t-M+1}, \ldots, S_t)$, or it consists of random binary or Gaussian variables. A training example is a pair consisting of an input vector and an output bit (x, σ); a perceptron learns this example by adjusting its weights to it. Here we consider three well known learning rules [1]:

H: Hebbian learning:

$$w_{\text{new}} = w_{\text{old}} + \frac{\eta}{M} \sigma x. \tag{2}$$

P: Perceptron learning:

H is applied only if the example is misclassified, $w_{\text{old}} \cdot x\sigma < 0$.

PN: Learning with normalization:

After each step P the weights are normalized, $w_{\text{new}} \cdot w_{\text{new}} = 1$.

η is the size of the learning step. In the following we mainly consider the limit of infinitely large networks, $M \rightarrow \infty$, in which the learning step η becomes a learning rate for a continuous presentation of examples. In this case we can use the analytical methods for on-line training which are well developed [2, 9, 10]. In this letter we study a system of N perceptrons with weight vectors $w^1, w^2, \ldots, w^N$ which are trained by a common input vector x and their mutual output bits $\sigma^1, \ldots, \sigma^N$.

We consider a set of N interacting perceptrons with a directed cyclic flow of information. At each training step all of the networks receive the same randomly chosen input vector x. Now perceptron w^1 learns the output from w^2, perceptron w^2 learns from $w^3, \ldots$, perceptron w^N learns from perceptron w^1. Our analytical and numerical calculations give the following result: starting from random initial weight vectors with length $w_0 = |w_0|$ and using the perceptron learning rule P for each of the networks, the system runs into a state of complete symmetry with identical overlaps $w^i \cdot w^j$ for all pairs (i, j). The stationary state is given by the equation

$$\eta\theta\sqrt{1 + (N-1)\cos\theta} = \sqrt{2\pi} w_0(1 - \cos\theta) \tag{3}$$

where θ is the common mutual angle between all weight vectors. Figure 1 shows the result. For a small learning rate all perceptrons agree with each other, and their mutual angle θ is

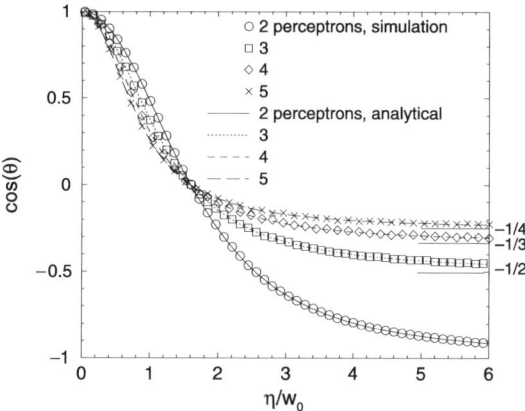

Figure 1. Fixed point of cyclic learning with algorithm P: simulations with $M = 100$ for two to five perceptrons and solutions of equation (3). θ is the common mutual angle between all weight vectors.

close to zero. With increasing learning rate the angle increases to its maximal possible value. The sum of the weight vectors $\sum_{i=1}^{N} w^i$ is constant under this learning rule, because for every perceptron that learns the pattern with a positive sign there is a subsequent neighbour that learns it with a negative sign. For $\eta \to \infty$ the norm of this sum is negligible compared to $|w^i|$, and the vectors form a hypertetrahedron which gives $\cos \theta = -1/(N-1)$. Note that the final stationary state has a higher symmetry than the ring flow of information. This symmetry seems to be robust to details of the model: in simulations where each perceptron had a different quenched learning rate, all the angles between the perceptrons again converged to the same value.

The effective repulsion between the weight vectors can be understood geometrically in the case of two perceptrons: the sum $w^1 + w^2$ is conserved; the fixed point results from an equilibrium between learning the component of x parallel to the w^1–w^2-plane (which decreases θ) and the component perpendicular to this plane (which increases θ).

The symmetric behaviour turns out to be different with learning rule PN, where all the weight vectors w^i remain on a sphere $|w^i| = 1$. For small learning rate the system runs into a symmetric state given by

$$\eta \theta = \sqrt{2\pi}(1 - \cos \theta) \tag{4}$$

(cf equation (3)). However, this equation can only be realized geometrically up to a critical value $\eta_c(N)$, where the hypertetrahedron configuration is reached and the sum of the w^i vanishes. In the case of two perceptrons, geometrical constraints do not play a role; however, there is a maximal $\eta_{c,2} \doteq 1.82$, above which no solution of equation (4) exists. For larger learning rates $\eta > \eta_c(N)$ our numerical simulations give the following results as shown in figure 2.

- For $N = 2$, there is a discontinuous transition to $\cos \theta = -1$ at the mentioned $\eta_{c,2}$.
- For $N = 3$ the state remains in the triangular configuration $\cos \theta = -\frac{1}{2}$.
- For $N \geqslant 3$ the symmetry is broken spontaneously. The angle θ_{ij} between perceptrons i and j now depends on their distance on the ring. However, the symmetry of the ring is still conserved. This means, for instance, that for $N = 7$, θ_{13} is the same as θ_{24} and θ_{35}, but

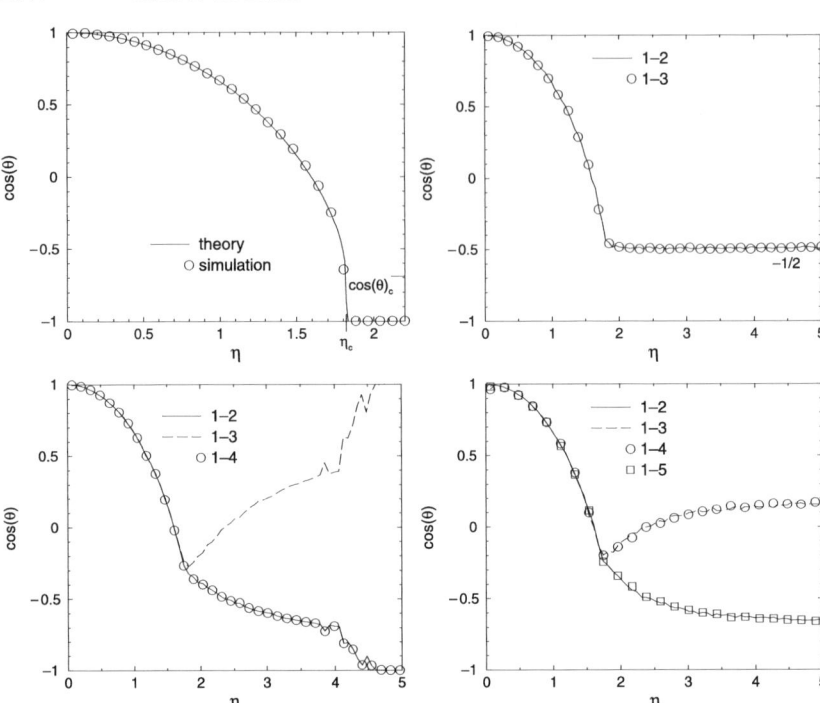

Figure 2. Fixed points of $\cos\theta$ in cyclic learning using the rule PN for two to five perceptrons, respectively, in simulations with $M = 100$. For $\eta < \eta_c$ all the weight vectors have a common mutual angle θ. For $\eta > \eta_c(N)$ and a ring with more than three perceptrons, the symmetry is broken and the angle θ_{ij} depends on the distance between perceptrons i and j on the ring.

there are three different values of mutual angles θ_{12}, θ_{13} and θ_{14}. In general, there are now $N/2$ different angles for even N and $(N - 1)/2$ angles for odd N. Since the perceptrons try to increase the angle to their nearest neighbour, the angle to more distant perceptrons has to increase to satisfy geometric constraints.

- For even values $N \geqslant 4$ we observe an additional discontinuous transition to pairing: two subsets are formed with antiparallel alignment between the subsets. This fixed point is probably unstable in the $M \to \infty$ limit and is only observed in simulations because the self-averaging property of the ordinary differential equations breaks down at that point.

Hence, with increasing learning rate the symmetry of the system of interacting perceptrons is broken, but the state still has the symmetry of the ring. Note that according to equation (2) the learning step scales to zero with system size M. The prefactor alone triggers the first phase transition.

Now we show that a system of interacting networks can show better-than-random performance in a problem of adaptive competition which was introduced recently by Arthur [3] and is being studied intensively [4–8]. It is a model of a closed market where N agents are competing for limited resources and where the individual profit depends on the action of the whole community.

The model consists of N agents who at each time step have to choose between actions $\sigma^i = +1$ or $\sigma^i = -1, i = 1, \ldots, N$. The profit of each agent depends on the minority decision; each agent gains $g^i = +1$ if he belongs to the minority, and he pays $+1$ if he belongs to the majority of the common decision. Hence, one has $g^i = -\sigma^i \, \mathrm{sign}(\sum_{j=1}^{N} \sigma^j)$. The global profit is given by

$$G = \sum_{i=1}^{N} g^i = - \left| \sum_{j=1}^{N} \sigma^j \right| < 0$$

i.e. the cashier always makes profit. Now each agent uses an algorithm which should maximize his profit. In this model agents know only the history of the minority sign $S_t = - \mathrm{sign}(\sum_{j=1}^{N} \sigma_t^j)$ for each previous time step t, and the agents are not allowed to exchange information.

If each agent makes a random decision σ_i, the mean square global loss is

$$\langle G^2 \rangle = N. \tag{5}$$

It is non-trivial to find an algorithm which performs better than (5). Previous investigations studied algorithms where each agent has two or more quenched random tables that prescribe a decision for each of the 2^M possible histories $x_t = (S_{t-M+1}, \ldots, S_t)$. Each table receives a score, and the one with the larger score is chosen.

Here we introduce an approach where each agent uses the same dynamic strategy. We use a perceptron with adaptive weights for each agent to make the decision. The weights define the strategy of the agent, and our strategies change with time as the weights are updated according to the minority decision one time step earlier. We follow the usual scenario for training a perceptron: start from a randomly chosen set of initial weights and train each network by the usual Hebbian learning rule. At each time its decision of each agent is made by $\sigma_i = \mathrm{sign}(w^i \cdot x)$ and each perceptron is trained by the minority decision S_t,

$$w_{t+1}^i = w_t^i - \frac{\eta}{M} x_t \, \mathrm{sign} \left(\sum_{j=1}^{N} \mathrm{sign}(x \cdot w^j) \right). \tag{6}$$

Hence, the bit sequence (S_t) is generated by the negative output of a committee machine. From equation (6) it follows that each weight vector is changed by the same increment, hence only the centre of mass of the weight vectors changes during the learning process.

Our numerical calculations show that starting from a random set of weight vectors and initial input the systems relaxes to a state with a good performance. The global gain is of the order of N and for small learning rates the system performs better than random guessing. We succeeded in solving the dynamics of the interacting networks analytically for the case where the input vector is replaced by a random one.

Approximating the input x by a random one, we derived the equation of motion of the norm of the centre of mass; the fixed point describes the global gain in the long run. To simplify the calculation, the initial norms $|w_0^i|$ are set to 1, the sum $\sum_i^N w_0^i$ is 0, and the scalar products are symmetric: $w_0^i \cdot w_0^j = -1/(N - 1)$ for $i \neq j$. We obtain for the attractor of the dynamics

$$\langle G^2 \rangle / N = 1 + (N - 1) \left(1 - \frac{2}{\pi} \arccos \frac{A - 1/(N - 1)}{A + 1} \right) \tag{7}$$

$$A = \frac{\pi \eta^2}{16} \left(1 + \sqrt{1 + \frac{16(\pi - 2)}{\pi N \eta^2}} \right). \tag{8}$$

For random patterns, A is the square norm of the centre of mass at the fixed point. Equation (7) agrees with simulations of both the real time series and random patterns, as shown in figure 3.

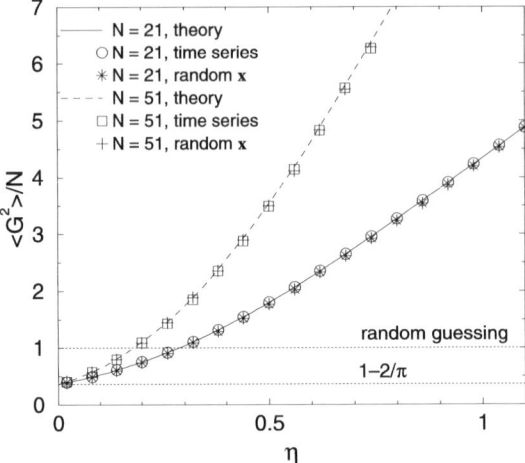

Figure 3. Average loss $\langle G^2 \rangle / N$ versus the learning rate in the bar problem, using the learning rule H. Simulations used $M = 100$.

Very similar results (up to factors of $1 + 1/\sqrt{N}$) are found analytically and in simulations by starting with uncorrelated random vectors. For a small learning rate $\eta \to 0$ we obtain the best global gain

$$\langle G^2 \rangle = \left(1 - \frac{2}{\pi} \right) N \simeq 0.363N. \qquad (9)$$

It is interesting that this result is also obtained for a scenario where we use a distribution of learning rates η instead of a fixed one. For every perceptron at every time step a different learning rate is chosen. Hence the centre of mass is not fixed during learning and the weight vectors increase their lengths similarly to a random walk. This process decreases the average learning rate compared to the length and leads to the performance given in equation (9).

Hence, the system of interacting networks performs better than the random decision. In fact, there are several advantages of the system of neural networks compared to the algorithm of scoring quenched random tables.

Firstly, the size M of the history does not have to be adjusted to the number of agents in order to perform better than random. Our analysis implicitly assumes that $N \leqslant M$ and both M and N are large, but simulations show good qualitative agreement even for $N = 21$, $M = 4$. For small M, $\langle G^2 \rangle / N$ even tends to be smaller than predicted for $M = \infty$. We suspect that a strong dependence on the ratio of players to possible strategies only occurs when players have to pick from a set of fixed strategies, and is absent when they fine tune one strategy. However, this point still needs further investigation.

Secondly, on average all of the agents perform identically—this is also a consequence of the absence of quenched disorder. There is no phase transition between a set of successful agents and losers, as found in [5] for the random tables. This is clear from the geometrical interpretation: the centre of mass does a random walk on a hypersphere around the origin. The radius depends on the learning rate; if the radius is smaller than $\sqrt{N}$ (obtained from when adding up N random vectors of norm 1), the 'strategies' are distributed better than random. As the centre of mass moves, each perceptron shifts from the current majority side to the minority

Letter to the Editor   L147

side and back.

Equation (9) represents the optimum obtainable for perceptrons as long as the symmetry among them is not broken. It would be interesting to study other network architectures to see whether the profit of a system of competing neural networks can still be improved.

This work benefited from a seminar at the Max-Planck Institut für Physik komplexer Systeme, Dresden and was supported by the German Israeli Foundation for Scientific Research and Development (GIF). The authors would like to thank Michael Biehl and Georg Reents for useful discussions, and Andreas Engel and Johannes Berg for their introduction to the minority game.

References

[1] Hertz J, Krogh A and Palmer R G 1991 *Introduction to the Theory of Neural Computation* (Reading, MA: Addison-Wesley)
[2] Opper M and Kinzel W 1995 *Models of Neural Networks* vol 3, ed E Domany, J L van Hemmen and K Schulten (Berlin: Springer) p 151
[3] Arthur B W 1994 *Am. Econ. Assoc. Papers Proc.* **84** 406
[4] Challet D and Zhang Y-C 1997 *Physica* A **246** 407
      Challet D and Zhang Y-C 1998 *Physica* A **256** 514–32
[5] Savit R, Manuca R and Riolo R 1999 *Phys. Rev. Lett.* **82** 2203
[6] Cavagna A 1999 *Phys. Rev.* E **59** R3783
[7] Marsili M, Challet D and Zecchina R 1999 *Preprint* cond-mat/9908480
[8] Challet D, Marsili M and Zhang Y-C 1999 *Preprint* cond-mat/9909265
[9] Biehl M and Schwarze H 1995 *J. Phys. A: Math. Gen.* **28** 643
[10] Saad D and Solla S 1995 *Phys. Rev. Lett.* **74** 4337

Intelligent systems in the context of surrounding environment

Joseph Wakeling and Per Bak

Department of Mathematics, Imperial College, 180 Queens Gate, London, SW7 2BZ, United Kingdom
(Received 5 April 2001; published 30 October 2001)

We investigate the behavioral patterns of a population of agents, each controlled by a simple biologically motivated neural network model, when they are set in competition against each other in the minority model of Challet and Zhang. We explore the effects of changing agent characteristics, demonstrating that crowding behavior takes place among agents of similar memory, and show how this allows unique "rogue" agents with higher memory values to take advantage of a majority population. We also show that agents' analytic capability is largely determined by the size of the intermediary layer of neurons. In the context of these results, we discuss the general nature of natural and artificial intelligence systems, and suggest intelligence only exists in the context of the surrounding environment (*embodiment*).

DOI: 10.1103/PhysRevE.64.051920   PACS number(s): 87.19.La, 07.05.Mh, 05.65.+b, 87.18.Sn

I. INTRODUCTION

Much research has been done into the computational possibilities of neural networks. Yet the engineering and industrial applications of these models have often eclipsed their use in trying to come to an understanding of naturally occurring neural systems.

Whereas in engineering we often use single neural networks to attack a single problem, in nature we see neural systems in competition. Humans, for example, invest in the stock market, attempt to beat their business rivals, or, in extreme examples, plan wars against each other. We are, as Darwin identified a century and a half ago, in competition for natural resources; our neural systems—i.e., our brains—are among the main tools we have to help us succeed in that competition.

In collaboration with Chialvo, one of the authors of this paper has developed a neural network model that provides a biologically plausible learning system [1], based essentially around "Darwinian selection" of successful behavioral patterns. This simple "minibrain"[1]—as we will refer to it from now on—has been shown to be an effective learning system, being able to solve such problems as the exclusive-OR (XOR) problem and the parity problem. Crucially, it has also been shown to be easily able to *unlearn* patterns of behavior once they become unproductive—an extremely important aspect of animal learning—while still being able to remember previously successful responses, in case they should prove useful in the future. These capabilities, combined with the simplicity of the model, provide a powerful case for biological feasibility.

In choosing a competitive framework for this neural network, we follow the example of Metzler, Kinzel, and Kanter [2], using the delightfully simple model of competition within a population provided by the minority model of Challet and Zhang [3] (itself based on the "El Farol" bar problem created by Arthur [4]). In this game, a population of agents has to decide, independently of each other, which of two groups they wish to join. Whoever is on the minority

---
[1]Source code for the programs used can be found at http://neuro.webdrake.net/.

side "wins" and is given a point. By combining these two models—replacing the fixed strategies of agents in Challet and Zhang's model with agents controlled by the minibrain neural system—we have a model of neural systems in competition in the real world.

This is not the first model of coevolution of strategies in a competitive game—a particularly interesting example is Lindgren and Nordahl's investigation of the prisoner's dilemma, where players on a cellular grid evolve and mutate strategies according to a genetic algorithm [5]. However, we believe that the biological inspiration for the minibrain model, and its demonstrated capacity for fast adaption, makes our model of special interest.

The structure of this paper is as follows. We begin with a discussion of what we mean when we talk about "intelligence," noting how historical influences have shaped our instinctive ideas on this subject in potentially misleading ways; in particular, we take issue with the suggestion that a creature's intelligence can be thought of as separate from its physical nature. We suggest that intelligence can only be measured in the context of the surrounding environment of the organism being studied: we must always consider the *embodiment* of any intelligent system.

This is followed by the account of the computer experiments we have conducted, in which we investigate the behavioral patterns produced in the minibrain/minority model combination, and the ways in which they are affected by changing agent characteristics. We show how significant crowding behavior occurs within groups of agents with the same memory value, and demonstrate how this can allow a minority of high-memory agents to take advantage of the majority population and "win" on a regular basis—and, by the same token, condemn a population of largely similar agents to continually losing. Indeed, perhaps the most startling implication of this model is that, in a competitive situation, having a "strategy" might well prove worse than simply making random decisions.

These results are in strong contrast with those of Metzler, Kinzel, and Kanter, whose paper inspired these experiments. In their simulations, a homogeneous population of perceptron agents relaxes to a stable state where all agents have an average 50% success rate, and overall population performance is better than random [2]. The perceptrons learn, in

1063-651X/2001/64(5)/051920(8)/$20.00

effect, to produce an efficient market system, and do not suffer from the crowding effect produced by minibrain agents. By the same token, however, it seems unlikely that a superior perceptron could win on a similar scale to a superior minibrain.

We conclude with further discussion on the nature of intelligence, suggesting a conceptual approach that we believe will enable easier investigation of both natural and artificially created intelligent systems. Having already suggested that we must consider "embodied" intelligences, we provide criteria for cataloguing that embodiment, consisting of hard-wired parts—the input and output systems of the organism, the feedback mechanism that judges the success or failure of behavioral patterns—alongside a dynamic decision-making system that maps input to output and updates its methodology according to the signals received from the feedback system.

II. WHAT IS "INTELLIGENCE"?

The *E. Coli* bacterium has a curious mode of behavior. If it senses glucose in its immediate surroundings, it will move in the direction of this sweet nourishment. If it does not, it will flip over and move a certain distance in a random direction, before taking stock again, and so on, and so on until it finds food.

Bacteria are generally not considered to be "intelligent." Yet this is a systematic response to environmental stimuli, not necessarily the *best* response but nevertheless a *working* response, a satisfactory response. The *E. Coli* bacterium is responding in an intelligent way to the problem of how to find food. How do we square this with our instinctive feeling that bacteria are *not* intelligent? Are our instincts mistaken? How, instinctively, do we define intelligence?

Historically, philosophers have often proposed the idea of a separation between "body" and "mind." The human mind, from this point of view, is something special, something distinct, something not bound up in the messy business of the real world. It is this, we are told, that separates us from the animals: we have this magical ability to *understand*, to *think*, to *comprehend*—the ability to view the world in a rational, abstract way and thus arrive at some fundamental *truth* about how the universe works.

The idea of separate compartments of reality for body and mind has lost its stranglehold over our way of thinking, but its influence lingers on in our concept of intelligence. Our minds, our consciousness, may be the result of physical processes, but we still cling to the idea that we have the ability to discover an abstract reality, and it's this idea that informs our notion of "intelligence." An intelligent being is one that can see beyond its own personal circumstances, one that is capable of looking at the world around it in an objective fashion. Given enough time, it can (theoretically) solve any problem you care to put before it. It is capable of rising above the environment in which it exists, and comprehending the nature of True Reality.

Naturally, this has informed our ideas about artificial intelligence. An artificially intelligent machine will be one that works in this same environmentally uninhibited manner. If

we tell it to drive a car, it will be able (given time to teach itself) to drive a car. If we tell it to cook a meal, it will be able to cook a meal. If we tell it to prove Fermat's last theorem ... All of these, of course, assume that we have given it some kind of hardware with which to gather input and make output to the relevant system, whether car, kitchen, or math textbook—assume, indeed, that we have these systems present at all—and it is this necessity that causes us to realize that in fact, *the mind and its surrounding environment (including the physical body of the individual) are inseparable*. Our brains are the product of evolution; they are not an abstract, infinite system for solving abstract, infinite problems, but rather a very particular system for solving the very particular problems involved in coping with the environmental pressures about us. In this respect, we are no different from the *E. Coli* bacterium we discussed earlier: the environments we inhabit are different, and consequently so are our behavioral patterns, but on a conceptual level there is nothing to choose between us.

Intelligence only exists in the context of its surrounding environment. So, if we are to attempt to create an artificial intelligence system, we must necessarily also define a world in which it will operate. And the question of *how* intelligent that system is can only be answered by examining how good it is at coping with the problems this world throws up, by its ability to utilize the data available to it to find working solutions to these problems.

III. "MINIBRAIN" AGENTS IN THE MINORITY MODEL

The "minibrain" neural system, developed by one of the authors in collaboration with Chialvo [1], is an extremal dynamics-based decision-making system that responds to input by choosing from a finite set of outputs, the choice being determined by Darwinian selection of good (i.e., successful) responses to previous inputs (negative feedback). We use the simple layered version of this model, consisting of a layer of input neurons, a single intermediary layer of neurons, and a layer of output neurons; each input neuron is connected to every intermediary neuron by a synapse, and similarly each intermediary neuron is connected to every output neuron. Every synapse is assigned a "strength," initially a random number between 0 and 1.

Competing against each other in the minority model, each agent receives data about the past, and gives as output which of the two groups—we label them 0 and 1—that it wishes to join. We follow the convention of Challet and Zhang's version of the game, that this knowledge is limited to knowing which side was the minority (i.e., winning) group at each turn in a finite number of past turns [3], so that agent input can be represented by a binary number of m bits, where m is the agent's memory. So, for example, if in the last three turns group 0 lost, then won, then won again, this would be represented by the binary number 110, where the left-most bit represents the most recent turn, and each bit is determined by the number of the *losing* (majority) group that turn (we choose these settings in order to match the way our computer code is set up).

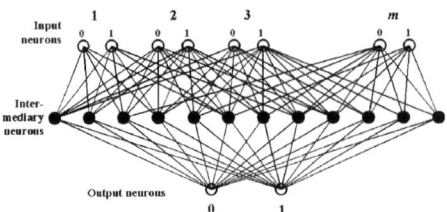

FIG. 1. Architecture of minibrain agents. Every input neuron is connected to every intermediary neuron, and every intermediary neuron is connected to every output neuron. For our setup, we have two outputs, and $2m$ inputs, where m is the agent's memory.

In order to preserve symmetry of choice between the two groups, an agent with a memory of m turns will have $2m$ input neurons, with the first of the ith pair of neurons firing if the bit representing the result i turns ago is 0, the second neuron of the ith pair firing if the result was 1. For example, if an agent with a memory of 3 (and hence with 6 input neurons) is given the past 110 as we discussed above, then the second, fourth, and fifth input neurons will fire. Figure 1 gives a picture of this architecture (to avoid over complicating the diagram, not all connections are shown).

To determine the intermediary neuron that fires, we take for each the sum of the strengths of the synapses connecting it to the firing input neurons. The intermediary neuron with the greatest such sum is the one that fires. Then, the output neuron that fires (0 or 1) is the one connected to the firing intermediary neuron by the strongest synapse.

Each turn, the synapses used are "tagged" with a chemical trace. If the output produced that turn is satisfactory (in this setup, if the agent joins the minority group), no further action is taken. If the output is not satisfactory, however, a global feedback signal (e.g., the release of some hormone) is sent to the system, and the tagged synapses are "punished" for their involvement in this bad decision by having their strengths reduced (in our model, by a random number between 0 and 1). As we noted in the Introduction, this Darwinian selection of successful behavioral patterns has already been shown to be an effective learning system when "going solo" [1]; how will it cope when placed in competition?

Figure 2 shows the success rates of agents of different memory values. A group of 251 agents has an even spread of memory values between 1 and 8; each agent has 48 intermediary neurons. The figure shows their success rates over a period of 2×10^4 turns.

To a certain extent, these results reflect those found by Challet and Zhang when they explore the behavior of a mixed population of fixed-strategy agents [3], inasmuch as performance improves with higher memory but tends to saturate eventually. Standard deviation within each memory group is much lower for minibrain agents, however, suggesting crowding behavior within memory groups, and we will later show that this does indeed occur.

Disappointingly, we see that not one agent achieves as much as a 50% success rate—they would all be better off

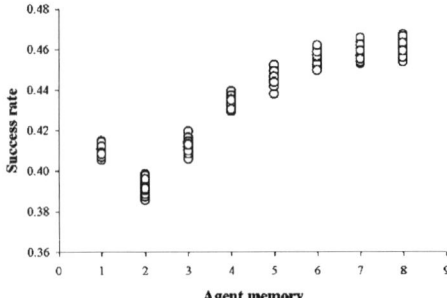

FIG. 2. Success rates of a mixed population of minibrain agents against their memory. Agents have 48 intermediary neurons.

tossing coins to make their decisions. The even spread of memory values throughout the population means that agents with higher-memory values cannot take full advantage of their extra knowledge: the crowding behavior between agents with the same memory cancels out most of the positive effects. It is no good having lots of data on which to base your decision if lots of other people have that same data—everyone will come to the same conclusion and, in the minority model, that means losing.

Necessarily, then, one of the conditions for an agent to succeed—i.e., to beat the coin-tossing strategy—is that there must be few other agents with the same amount of memory. This is demonstrated starkly in Fig. 3, displaying the results for a population of 251 agents of whom *one* has a memory of 3, the rest only 2.

The astonishing success of this "rogue" agent (it makes the right decision approximately 99.8% of the time) shows clearly just how important a factor this crowding behavior is in the success (or failure) of agents. The fact that this agent is the only one receiving the extra data means that he can use it

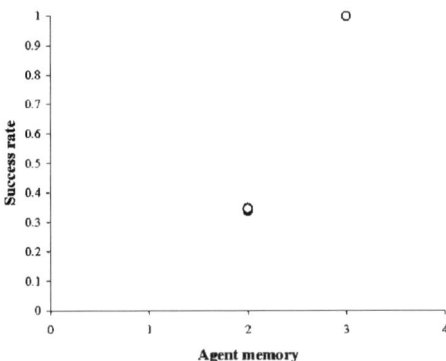

FIG. 3. Success rate of a single agent of memory 3, versus a 250-strong population of memory 2. Agents have 48 intermediary neurons.

051920-3

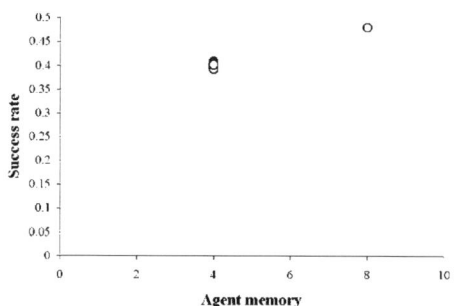

FIG. 4. Success rate of a single agent of memory 8, versus a 250-strong population of memory 4. Agents have 48 intermediary neurons.

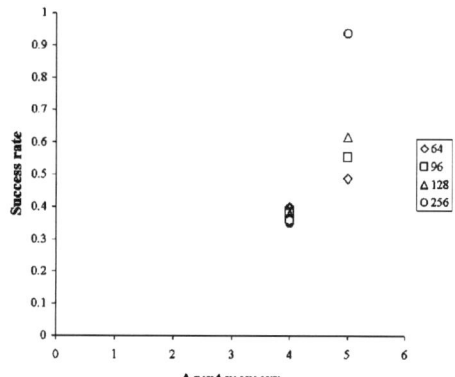

FIG. 5. Success rates of single agents of memory 5, versus a 250-strong population of memory 4, in simulations with 64, 96, 128, and 256 intermediary neurons per agent.

to his advantage. Contrast this with the other agents who, for all their careful thinking, fail miserably because *almost all of them think alike—entirely independently—almost all of the time.*

This example leads us to ask the more general question: given a population of agents who all have memory m, can we always find such a "rogue," an agent capable of understanding and thus beating the system? That it is not merely a matter of agent memory is amply demonstrated in Fig. 4, where we see a population of memory 4 pitted against a rogue with a memory of 8.

Despite its high memory value (twice that of the majority population) the rogue agent is unable to beat the coin-tossing strategy. Why is this? A higher memory value should, by our earlier results, always be an advantage. Certainly, since we have respected symmetry of choice between agent outputs, it should not be a *disadvantage*. What factor is it that prevents this agent from making full use of the memory available to it, memory that surely has within it useful data patterns that predict the behavior of the agents with memory 4, and thus should allow the rogue agent the success we expect it to achieve?

The answer becomes clear when we examine the nature of the input that each agent receives—a binary number of length m, where m is the value of the agent's memory. So, it follows that the total possible number of inputs will be 2^m. For an agent with memory 4, this means 16 possible inputs. For an agent with memory 8, the total number of possible inputs is 256. Compare this to the number of *intermediary* neurons possessed by each agent (48, in all the simulations we have run so far) and we realize that, while this is an adequate number for an agent receiving 16 different possible inputs, it is wholly inadequate for an agent having to deal with some 256 possible inputs. The number of intermediary neurons restricts the maximum performance of an agent by placing a limit on the amount of memory that can be effectively used.

Bearing this condition in mind, we run another set of games, again with a majority population of memory 4, but this time with a rogue of memory 5, and with the number of intermediary neurons given to each agent varying in each of

these games. Figure 5 shows the results of games where agents have intermediary layers of, respectively, 64, 96, 128, and 256 neurons.

The implications are clear—it is the number of intermediary neurons, as well as the amount of memory, that control whether or not a rogue agent can succeed, and, if it does, by how much. A higher memory value will always be an advantage, but the degree to which it is advantageous will be determined by the number of intermediary neurons possessed. Memory, obviously, determines how much information an agent can receive; the intermediary neurons are what provide agents' analytic capability.

Our computer simulations suggest that in situations such as the ones already discussed, with a majority population of memory m, it is the intermediary neurons, rather than the amount of memory possessed, that control the ability of a rogue agent to succeed. A memory of $m+1$ is all that is required, *provided* the rogue has enough intermediary neurons to be able to use it effectively.

We can muddy the waters, so to speak, by giving the majority population an evenly distributed *spread* of memory values (perhaps from 1 to m) rather than a single value. Where a single memory value is used, the crowding behavior observed within memory groups will easily allow rogue agents to predict the minority group. With a series of different, smaller groups in competition, it becomes significantly less easy to make accurate predictions, and rogue agent success rates fall significantly. Herding sheep is fairly easy; jumping into the middle of a brawl is dangerous for anyone, even a world champion martial artist.

All things considered, it seems as though this may be the key point in determining agent success. An agent can only be truly successful if it has plenty of "prey" whose weaknesses it can exploit. If the behavior of the prey is highly unpredictable, or the prey are capable of biting back, the agent's chances of success are vastly reduced.

IV. ANALYSIS OF CROWDING BEHAVIOR WITHIN MEMORY GROUPS

We have on several occasions referred to crowding behavior of minibrain agents within the same memory group. In this section, we give a brief mathematical analysis of what causes this to arise.

We begin with a simple case, assuming that all agents have the same memory value. Obviously, because of the nature of the game, a majority of these agents will behave in the same way each turn. What we show, however, is that this majority is significantly more than would be found if the agents were deciding randomly as to which group to join. Were agents to employ this strategy, the mean size of the (losing) majority group would be only a little over 50%.

We define by $0 \leq x_i(I) < 0.5$ the proportion of agents in the minority group given input I, where the subscript i is the number of times input I has occurred before. If an input has not been seen before by agents, it follows that they will decide randomly which group to join, and so we have $x_0(I) \approx 0.5$ for all possible inputs I.

If an input *has* been seen before, it follows that those agents in the minority group on that occasion—i.e., those who were successful—will make the same decision as last time. Those who were unsuccessful last time will make a random decision as to which group to join. We can expect, on average, half of them to change their minds, half to stay with their previous choice.

The effect of this, ironically, is that this last group—the unsuccessful agents who keep with their previous choice—will probably (in fact, almost certainly) form the minority group this time round. And so we can define a recurrence relation,

$$x_{i+1}(I) \approx \frac{1}{2}[1 - x_i(I)],$$

determining the expected proportion of agents joining the minority group for each occurrence of input I. This allows us to develop a more general equation,

$$x_{i+1}(I) \approx \varphi(i,I),$$

where

$$\varphi(i,I) = \frac{1}{3}\left(\frac{2^i + (-1)^{i-1}}{2^i}\right) + \frac{(-1)^i}{2^{i+1}}[1 - x_0(I)].$$

Observe that this holds for $i = 0$, as a little calculation reveals $x_1(I) \approx \frac{1}{2}(1 - x_0(I)) = \varphi(0,I)$. Now, assume the equation holds for $i = n-1$, with n any positive integer, so $x_n(I) \approx \varphi(n-1,I)$.

By the recurrence relation,

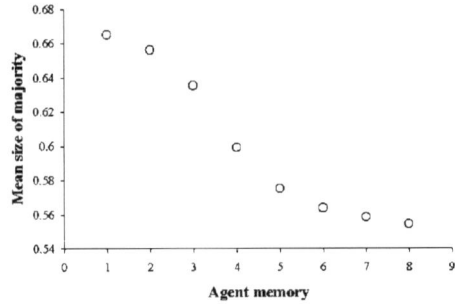

FIG. 6. Mean size of majority each turn in games with uniform agent memory, against different choices for this memory value. Agent population per game is 251, but majority size is given proportionally. Agents have 48 intermediary neurons.

$$x_{n+1}(I) \approx \frac{1}{2}[1 - x_n(I)]$$

$$= \frac{1}{2}[1 - \varphi(n-1,I)]$$

$$= \frac{1}{2}\left[1 - \left\{\frac{1}{3}\left(\frac{2^{n-1} + (-1)^{n-2}}{2^{n-1}}\right) + \frac{(-1)^{n-1}}{2^n}(1 - x_0(I))\right\}\right]$$

$$= \frac{1}{2}\left[\frac{1}{3}\left(\frac{3 \times 2^{n-1} - 2^{n-1} + (-1)^{n-1}}{2^{n-1}}\right) + \frac{(-1)^n}{2^n}(1 - x_0(I))\right]$$

$$= \frac{1}{2}\left[\frac{1}{3}\left(\frac{2^n + (-1)^{n-1}}{2^{n-1}}\right) + \frac{(-1)^n}{2^n}[1 - x_0(I)]\right]$$

$$= \frac{1}{3}\left(\frac{2^n + (-1)^{n-1}}{2^n}\right) + \frac{(-1)^n}{2^{n+1}}[1 - x_0(I)]$$

$$= \varphi(n,I).$$

Hence, $x_{n+1}(I) \approx \varphi(n,I)$, and so by the induction hypothesis $x_{i+1}(I) \approx \varphi(i,I)$ for all $i \geq 0$.

It follows, then, that as $i \to \infty$, so $x_i(I) \to \frac{1}{3}$, and so, with repeated exposure to the input I, we will find that on average $\frac{2}{3}$ of the agents will produce the same output. As a result, the average majority size per turn (regardless of input given) will also tend to $\frac{2}{3}$ as the agents become saturated by all the possible inputs.

This can be observed in Fig. 6, which shows the average proportion of agents joining the majority group each turn in eight different games involving single memory value populations, the first involving agents of memory 1, the second

051920-5

with agents of memory 2, and so on up to the final game, with agents of memory 8. Each game takes place over a time period of some 5×10^3 turns.

As memory increases, so the number of possible inputs also increases, meaning there is less repeated exposure to individual inputs, and hence less crowding for a given time period. Within a time scale of 5×10^3 turns, the behavior of agents with longer memories is random more often than not, and so the mean size of majority is similar to that of agents making random decisions. As the number of turns increases, so we can expect the mean size of the majority to tend to $\frac{2}{3}$ for all memory values, not just the lowest.

What implications does this have for games involving a mixed population of agents, such as that displayed in Fig. 2? Overall, the same principles will apply. Repeated exposure to the same input will produce the same crowding effect. But we note that the inputs given to this system—eight-digit binary numbers—are interpreted differently by different agents. For agents with lower memories, many of these "different" inputs are interpreted as being the same. For example, the inputs 11010010 and 11001011 are the same to an agent with a memory of 3 or less. So—as is demonstrated by Fig. 6—the crowding effect surfaces earlier in agents with lower memory values, and hence they are adversely affected to a greater degree.

The agents with higher memory values fail to beat the 50% success rate, however, because there are too many of them—any insights they might have into the crowding behavior of the lower memory groups is obscured by the actions of their fellow high-memory agents. Thus, the kind of behavior we see in Fig. 2: the lower-memory agents perform the worst, with the success rate increasing towards some "glass ceiling" as agent memory increases. It's only unique "rogue" agents, who don't have a large group of fellows, who can see the crowding effect and thus beat the system.

Even such rogue agents cannot succeed by any great margin in the case where they are pitted against a spread of memory values. The crowding behavior of the individual groups is obscured by the large number of them and predictions become difficult; the rogue has to work out, not just in which direction the crowding within each group will go, but how much crowding will be taking place in each group—a difficult task indeed.

If we increase the crowding, we also increase the rogue's chances of success. Figure 7 shows the results from two different games involving 251 agents. Five of them are "rogue" agents with memory values of, respectively, 4, 5, 6, 7, and 8. The rest have an even spread of memory values from 1 to 3. In order to allow the higher memory values to be useful, we give agents 256 intermediary neurons. The difference between the games is that in the first, when punishing unsuccessful synapses, we employ the principle that has been used throughout this paper—synapses are punished *once*. In the second game, the punishment does not stop until the agent has learned what would have been the correct output. The result is that, when an input has been seen before, we will have 100% agreement within memory groups.

We can see here how the increased crowding caused by "infinite" punishment allows the rogues to take advantage

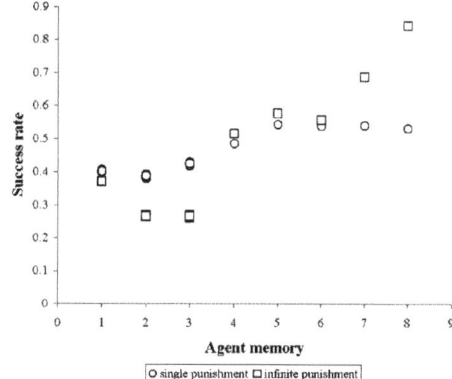

FIG. 7. Success rates of rogue agents of memory 5–8, versus a majority population with memory 1–3, in games involving single punishment and "infinite" punishment of unsuccessful synapses. Total agent population is 251. Agents have 256 intermediary neurons.

and be successful. A higher memory value is required for substantial success, but substantial success is possible—at the expense of the lower memory groups, whose success rates are substantially decreased by the extra crowding behavior they are forced to produce. The rogue agents in the game with single punishment, by contrast, are barely able to do better than a 50% success rate—though they can evidently glean *some* data from the crowding behavior displayed by the lower-memory groups, it is not sufficient for any great success and they are only barely able to beat the expected success rate, were they to make purely random decisions.

This is a striking result, to say the least. *The inevitable consequence of an analytic strategy is a predisposition to failure.* Challet and Zhang [3] and Arthur [4] have already shown that fixed strategies can prove to be a disadvantage compared to random decisions; this occurs when the number of available strategies is small compared to the number of agents. The crowding behavior that results from minibrain agents' imperfect analysis will inevitably reduce the number of strategies in use, thus dooming them to worse-than-random results.

We can see this at work in the real world, every day. Many strategies—whether for investments, business strategies, forming a relationship, or any of the myriad problems we have to solve—fail, because they are based on common knowledge, and as such, will be similar to most other people's strategies. We are often told, "Everybody knows that . . . ," but few people realize the negative side of following such advice: since *everybody* knows it, *everybody* will come to the same conclusions as you, and so your strategy will be unlikely to succeed. Perhaps the best recent example is the internet boom and bust: so many people thought the internet was the place to invest, the market overheated, and many companies went belly up.

As this paper was being prepared, a report was broadcast on UK television about an experiment in which a four-year-old child, picking a share portfolio, was able to outdo highly experienced City traders on the stock market. In such systems, with everyone's imperfect analysis competing against everyone else's, it seems highly likely that random decisions sometimes really are the best; the minibrain/minority model combination would appear to confirm this.

V. "INTELLIGENCE" RECONSIDERED

Another interesting conclusion to be drawn from the computer experiments here described is that, given some particular minibrain agent, there is no way of deciding if it will be successful or not unless we know about the other agents it will be competing with.

In a sense this is not surprising. We know, for example, that to be a high flier at an Ivy League university requires considerably more academic ability than most other educational institutions. The athlete coming last in the final of the Olympic 100 m can still run faster than almost anyone else in the world. We know that *in these contexts* the conditions to be the "best" are different, but there is surely still an overall comparison to be made between the whole of humanity. Or is there? Recall our suggestion in the introduction to this paper that the question of how intelligent a system is can only be answered by examining how good it is at coping with the problems its surrounding environment throws up. To return to minibrain agents: by the concepts we discussed earlier, it is agents' *intelligence*, and not just their success rate, that is dependent on their fellows', as well as their own, characteristics. Indeed, the two measures—success and intelligence—cannot be separated.

Contrast this with how we have identified a whole range of factors—memory, the number of intermediary neurons, the amount of punishment inflicted on unsuccessful synapses—that affect the manner in which an agent performs. There are objective comparisons that can be made between agents. While we might accept that any measure of "intelligence" we can conceive of will only hold in the context of the minority model, surely it is not fair to suggest that the only valid measure of intelligence is success rate in the context of the population of agents we place within that world?

Before we rush off to define our abstract "agent IQ," however, it is worth noting that all the measures of *human*, as well as minibrain, intelligence that we have put in place are in fact measures of success in particular contexts. When a teacher calls a pupil a "stupid boy," he is not commenting on the child's intelligence in some abstract sense, but rather the child's ability to succeed at the tasks he is set in the school environment. (Einstein was considered stupid in the context of a school environment where dyslexia and Asperger's syndrome were unknown.) When we say that human beings are more intelligent than other animals what we in fact mean is that human beings are more successful at manipulating their environment to their own benefit. High fliers at Ivy League universities are considered intelligent because of their academic success. Olympic athletes are considered

intelligent in the context of their sport because they are capable of winning consistently.

Even human IQ tests, long thought to provide an abstract and objective measure of intelligence, work in this fashion, being a measure of an individual's success in solving logical problems. More recently these tests have been shown to discriminate against certain individuals based on their cultural background—a further indication of their nonabstract, nonobjective nature—and in addition to this, psychologists are now proposing that there are other forms of intelligence, for example *emotional* intelligence or "EQ," which are just as important to individual success as intellectual ability.

Were abstract measures of intelligence possible, it would be reasonable to ask: "Who was more intelligent, Albert Einstein or Ernest Shackleton?" As it turns out, this question is impossible to answer. Shackleton probably lacked Einstein's capacity for scientific imagination, Einstein probably didn't know a great deal about arctic survival, but both were highly successful—and thus by implication intelligent—*in the context of their own chosen way of life*. The same is true of our hypothetical Ivy League student and Olympic runner. We suggest that no other possible measure of intelligence is truly satisfactory.

It is not an entirely easy concept to take on board. In particular, it conflicts with our instinctive sense of what it means to be "intelligent." Casually—and not so casually—we talk about people's intelligence in the context of their *understanding*, their *conceiving*, their *awareness*. In other words, we talk about it in the context of their *consciousness*. In their paper "Consciousness and Neuroscience" [6], Crick and Koch refer to the philosophical concept of a "zombie," a creature that looks and acts just like a human being but lacks conscious awareness. Using the concepts of intelligence we have been discussing, this creature is just as intelligent as a real human.

Yet, on closer examination, this is not such an unreasonable idea. Such a "zombie" is probably scientifically untenable, but it should be noted that our measures of "intelligence" do not measure consciousness, at least not explicitly. A digital computer can solve logical problems, for example, and it seems very unlikely that such computers are conscious. The "emotional intelligence" we referred to earlier almost certainly has some unconscious elements to it: our ability to respond to a situation in an appropriate emotional manner tends to be an instinctive, more than a conscious, response. Lizards, it is thought, lack a conscious sense of vision but they can still catch prey, find a mate, and so on, using their visual sense to do so. In fact, most of the organisms that exist on earth are probably not conscious. Consciousness, most likely, is a product of brain activity that is a useful survival aid, a useful aid for success. An *aid* for success, and thus for intelligence, rather than a requirement.

How, then, should we approach the question of what is an intelligent system? In their description of the construction of the minibrain neural system, Bak and Chialvo note: "Biology has to provide a set of more or less randomly connected neurons, and a mechanism by which an output is deemed unsatisfactory . . . . It is absurd to speak of meaningful brain processes if the purpose is not defined in advance. The brain

051920-7

JOSEPH WAKELING AND PER BAK   PHYSICAL REVIEW E **64** 051920

cannot learn to define what is good and what is bad. This must be given at the outset. From there on, the brain is on its own'' [1]. These concepts provide us with a way of thinking about intelligent systems in general, whether naturally occurring biological systems or man made artificial intelligence systems.

An intelligent system might be thought of as consisting of the following parts:

(i) *A hardwired set of inputs and outputs, which the system cannot change.* It can perhaps change which of them it takes notice of and which of them it uses, but its options are fixed and finite.

(ii) *A decision-making system.* Given an input, a systematic process is applied to decide what output to make. This can range from the purely deterministic (e.g., a truth table of required output for each given input) to the completely random. The *E. Coli* bacterium's behavior in response to the presence or otherwise of glucose—either moving in the direction of the food or, if none is to be found, in a random direction—is a perfect example.

(iii) *A hardwired system for determining whether a given output has been successful, and sending appropriate feedback to the system.* Again, the nature of this can vary. In our computer experiments, success is defined as being in the minority group. For the *E. Coli* bacterium, success is finding food. Possible types of feedback range from the positive reinforcement of successful behavior practiced by many neural network systems, to the negative feedback of the Minibrain model. The *E. Coli* bacterium provides perhaps the most extreme example: if it does not find food within a certain time period, it will die.

The last of these is perhaps the most difficult to come to terms with, simply because as human beings, we instinctively feel that it is a *conscious* choice on our part as to whether many of our actions have been successful or not. Nevertheless, the ultimate determination of success or failure must rest with hardwired processes over which the decision-making system has no control. If nothing else, we are all subject to the same consideration as *E. Coli*: if our actions do not provide our physical bodies with what they need to survive, they, and our brains and minds with them, will perish.

We should, perhaps, include an extra criterion that for a system to be *truly* intelligent, the feedback mechanism must in some way affect the operation of the decision-making system, whether it is punishing ``bad'' synapses in the minibrain neural network, changing the entries in a truth table, or

killing a bacterium. A system that keeps making the same decision regardless of how consistently successful that decision is, isn't being intelligent. With this in mind, we might consider systems such as *E. Coli* (i.e., systems that employ one single strategy, and when it becomes unsuccessful simply *stop*) to be *minimally intelligent* systems. They are nowhere near as smart as other systems, natural and artificial, but at least they know when to quit.

Intelligence, we suggest, is not an abstract concept. The question of what is intelligent behavior can only be answered in the context of a problem to be solved. So in the search for artificial intelligence, we must necessarily start with the world in which we want that intelligence to operate; we cannot begin by creating some ``consciousness in a box'' to which we then give a purpose, but must first establish what we want that intelligence to *do*, before building the systems—input/output, decision-making, feedback—that will best achieve that aim. Computer programmers already have an instinctive sense of this when they talk about, for example, the ``AI'' of a computer game. (Purpose: to beat the human player. No longer the deterministic strategies of Space Invaders—many modern computer games display a great subtlety and complexity of behavior.) This is not to denigrate attempts to build conscious machines. Such machines would almost certainly provide the most powerful forms of artificial intelligence. But we are still a long way from understanding what consciousness is, let alone being able to replicate it, and as we have noted here, consciousness is not necessarily needed for intelligent behavior.

The experiments discussed in this paper involve ``toy'' models. Comparing the minibrain neural system to the real human brain is like comparing a paper airplane to a jumbo jet [1]. But paper airplanes can still fly, and there are still lessons to be learned. These ``toy'' experiments provide us with a context to begin identifying what it means to be intelligent. We have been able to suggest criteria for identifying intelligent systems that avoid the controversial issues of consciousness and understanding, and a method of determining how intelligent such systems are that rests on one simple, useful, and practical question: how good is this system at doing what it is meant to do? In other words, we and others have begun to demystify the subject of intelligence and maneuver it into a position where we can begin to ask precise and well-defined questions. Paper airplanes can fly for miles if they're launched from the right places.

[1] D.R. Chialvo and P. Bak, Neuroscience **90**, 1137 (1999); P. Bak and D.R. Chialvo, Phys. Rev. E **63**, 031912 (2001).

[2] R. Metzler, W. Kinzel, and I. Kanter, Phys. Rev. E **62**, 2555 (2000).

[3] D. Challet and Y.-C. Zhang, Physica A **246**, 407 (1997).

[4] W.B. Arthur, Pap. Proc. Annu. Meet. Am. Econ. Assoc. **84**, 406 (1994).

[5] K. Lindgren and M.G. Nordahl, Physica D **75**, 292 (1994).

[6] F. Crick and C. Koch, Cereb. Cortex **8**, 97 (1998).

ELSEVIER

Available online at www.sciencedirect.com

SCIENCE @ DIRECT°

www.elsevier.com/locate/physa

The Interactive Minority Game: a Web-based investigation of human market interactions

Paolo Laureti, Peter Ruch, Joseph Wakeling*, Yi-Cheng Zhang

Département de Physique, Université de Fribourg, Pérolles, Fribourg, CH-1700 Switzerland

Abstract

The unprecedented access offered by the World Wide Web brings with it the potential to gather huge amounts of data on human activities. Here we exploit this by using a toy model of financial markets, the Minority Game (MG), to investigate human speculative trading behaviour and information capacity. Hundreds of individuals have played a total of tens of thousands of game turns against computer-controlled agents in the Web-based *Interactive Minority Game*. The analytical understanding of the MG permits fine-tuning of the market situations encountered, allowing for investigation of human behaviour in a variety of controlled environments. In particular, our results indicate a transition in players' decision-making, as the markets become more difficult, between deductive behaviour making use of short-term trends in the market, and highly repetitive behaviour that ignores entirely the market history, yet outperforms random decision-making.
© 2003 Elsevier B.V. All rights reserved.

PACS: 02.50.Le; 89.65.Gh; 89.70.+c

Keywords: Decision theory and game theory; Economics and financial markets; Information theory; Internet experiments

Experimental games and their theoretical offspring have been a fruitful research direction for various disciplines, particularly psychology [1–6] and economics [7–11], but elsewhere as well [12–14]. The advantage of this approach is that the simplified game environment allows for controlled investigation of human behaviour while still potentially maintaining the essential features of real-world situations. A notable example in recent years has been the so-called "market entry" games [9,11], where traders must decide whether or not to join a market based on knowledge of its capacity and of their

---

* Corresponding author.
 E-mail address: joseph.wakeling@unifr.ch (J. Wakeling).

0378-4371/$ - see front matter © 2003 Elsevier B.V. All rights reserved.
doi:10.1016/j.physa.2003.07.002

competitors' past actions. These games have generated much interest as examples of situations where the insight provided by classical economic theory is limited, and an experimental approach was thought essential [11,15,16].

By coincidence, a theoretical approach has been developed by the statistical physics community for an independently created game that has many similarities to the market entry class: the Minority Game (MG) [17]. Economic agents are endowed with simple strategies and learn inductively, as suggested by Arthur [18]. A rich market dynamics emerges, whose properties depend on only a few simple parameters [19–21]. These results have recently led some authors to return to more traditional experiments, playing the MG with small groups of humans [22,23].

Our approach here has instead been to make use of the understanding of the theoretical game, by having individual humans play against computer-controlled "MG agents". We can thus fine-tune the market situation the player encounters, and provide a variety of controlled environments in which to investigate human behaviour. Because we only ever engage individual players, we have been able to make use of the immense access provided by the World Wide Web,[1] presenting the game via an online interface. Since being launched a year ago [25], hundreds of players have played a total of tens of thousands of game turns in the *Interactive Minority Game*.

The player is presented with a "price" history of the past 50 time steps of a market (Fig. 1) in which he is one of N traders, the others being MG agents. At each time step t, each individual i must choose independently, based on the market history, between two actions, $a_i(t) = +1$ or -1 (say, "buy" or "sell").[2] They then receive points given by the formula,

$$g_i(t) = -a_i(t)A(t) , \qquad (1)$$

where $A(t) = \sum_{i=1}^{N} a_i(t)$ is the aggregate action of the population at time t. Thus, those whose choice is in the minority gain $|A(t)|$ points, and those in the majority lose this amount; a player's average gain per turn, $\langle g_i(t) \rangle$, can be taken as a measure of his success. (Note that the Minority Game is a non-zero sum game.) From the values $A(t)$ we can generate the price history[3] shown to the human player [26,27],

$$P(t+1) = P(t) + A(t) . \qquad (2)$$

Five different markets are available to choose from, whose names give a rough order of increasing difficulty. Broadly these can be divided into two groups, determined by a control parameter $\alpha = 2^M/N$, where M is the MG agents' game memory. (Table 1 gives the statistics for the different levels.) The first three markets are in a "symmetric" phase with large price fluctuations, informationally efficient if looked at with memory

---

[1] For instance, the SETI@home project (http://setiathome.ssl.berkeley.edu/) was able to gain the processing power of over a million computers by requesting net users to download a screensaver that also acted as a data analysis program [24].

[2] For ease of play, the human player is in fact asked to predict the direction of the next market price change (i.e., the next majority action); his own action (the opposite) is inferred from this. For more details on the MG, including details of computer-controlled agents' decision-making process, see Refs. [17,20,25].

[3] Technically $P(t)$ is the logarithm of the true market price, but presenting the market history in this form communicates far better what is actually occurring in the Minority Game being played.

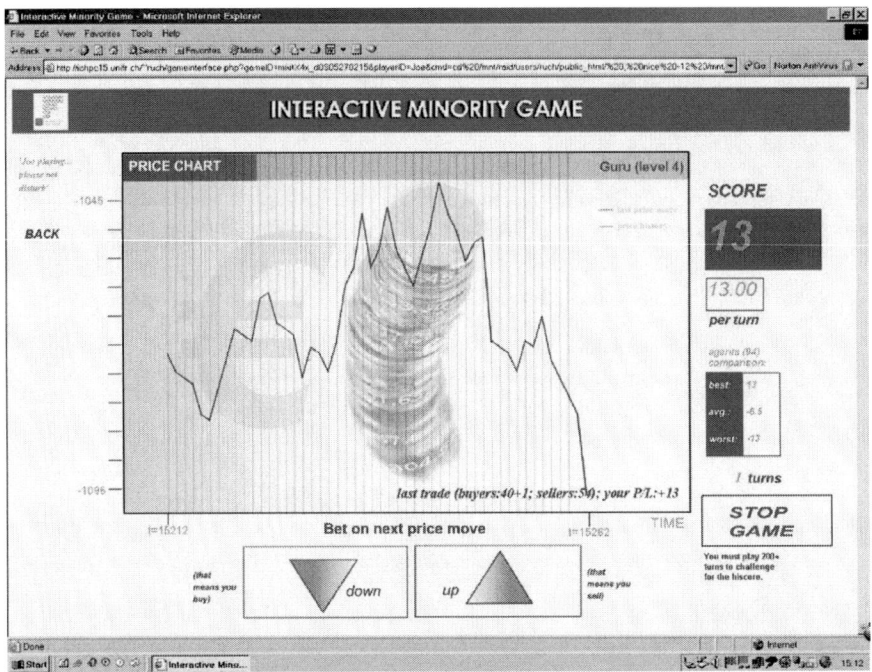

Fig. 1. The Interactive Minority Game online interface. The player is presented with a price history of the past 50 turns and must predict the direction of the next price movement.

Table 1

Statistics for the different markets of the Interactive Minority Game. Different market experiences are possible based on two parameters, MG agents' memory, M, and the number N of agents; the latter we have fixed (95 including the human) so that the market weight of the human is player is always the same. If the control parameter $\alpha = 2^M/N$ is below the critical value $\alpha_c \approx 0.3$, the market is in the "symmetric" phase; for $\alpha > \alpha_c$ the market phase is "asymmetric"

Level	Agents' memory, M	α	Market phase	Volatility[a] σ^2/N	No. of game turns played by humans[b]
Easy	2	0.04	Symmetric	7.58	15,400
Apprentice	3	0.08	Symmetric	3.71	11,000
Trader	4	0.17	Symmetric	1.46	9,400
Professional	6	0.67	Asymmetric	0.25	9,800
Guru	Mixed values	—	Asymmetric	0.24	16,000

[a]Data from simulations. $\sigma^2/N = 1$ means that fluctuations are the same as if agents were playing randomly.
[b]Data taken up until 05/2003. Note that this statistic only includes games of more than 100 turns in length.

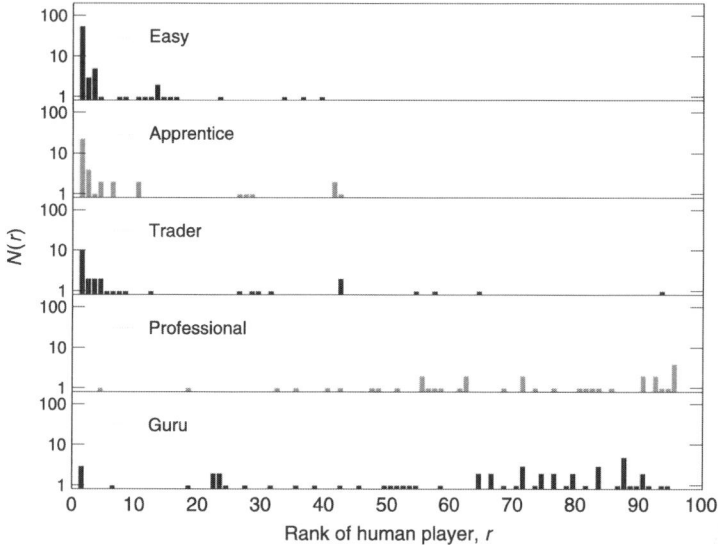

Fig. 2. Number $N(r)$ (log scale) of human players gaining rank r among computer-controlled agents. x and y scales are the same for all graphs.

M or less, yet inefficient if looked at with a longer memory value, with noticeable herding effects among MG agents [19]—*Easy*, *Apprentice* and *Trader*, with average fluctuations decreasing respectively. The other two levels, *Professional* and *Guru*, are in an "asymmetric" phase with fluctuations less than or equal to those which would result from players making random decisions—yet with small amounts of usable information still present in the price history if viewed with memory M.

Each market consists of $N = 95$ players, including the human. All were started with a 1000-turn introductory period with computer-controlled agents only; the subsequent interactive games are continuous, with each player picking up the price history where the last leaves it. Thus, a continuous price history (Eq. (2)) of each market can be generated.[4]

As a first step to analysing human performance, one can consider the human player's rank in the game compared to the computer-controlled agents (Fig. 2). A marked difference can be observed depending on the market phase. In the symmetric-phase markets humans almost always gain rank 1, clearly exploiting information the MG agents cannot see, while in the asymmetric markets humans do much worse, with most players being located in the lower half of the ranks (though their performance spans the complete range of possibilities)—a much fairer game.

---

[4] Games are only included in this history if they last more than 100 turns. The computer-controlled agents are also inherited from game to game, with evolutionary rules built in to allow them to adapt to each individual player and not become "frozen" into rigid responses.

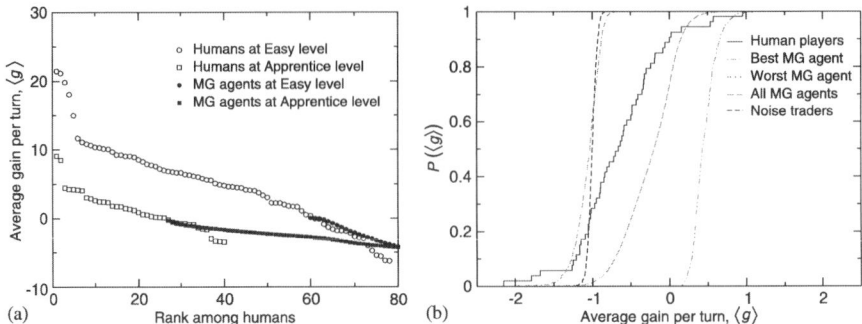

Fig. 3. (a) Score versus rank among other humans, at Easy (open circles) and Apprentice (open squares) levels, compared to scores of MG agents (filled symbols). In these easier markets, almost all human players are able to beat even the best MG agent. (b) Cumulative distribution of human scores at Guru level, compared to MG agents and noise trading. Simulation results averaged over 512 realisations; human results taken from all games of > 50 turns played up until 05/2003.

An alternative point of view is given by considering humans' average gain per turn in the game, as compared to average gain per turn for the regular MG agents and other types of computer-controlled player. One can use the distribution of scores as a function of rank among other humans, which we display for Easy and Apprentice levels (Fig. 3a), or (to better compare to computer-controlled players) the cumulative distribution of scores, which we display for Guru level (Fig. 3b). In the former case humans can easily exploit the herding effects in the market, doing much better than most MG agents and usually better than even the best MG agent. The latter, fairer market proves much more difficult: human performance covers a range from the very lowest to the very highest scores achieved by MG agents, but the MG agents generally do better (reflecting the results of Fig. 2). In all cases, however, humans do consistently better than random decision-making ("noise trading").

Insight into human decision-making processes can be gained by information-theoretic analysis. If we denote by $a_*(t)$ the human's action at time t, and $\mu_m(t)$ the market history of length m preceding this decision, then predictability of human action can be measured by the *information entropy* [28], $H(a_*|\mu_m)$, of the sequence $a_*(t)$ conditional on $\mu_m(t)$. More conveniently, we can use the *information gain ratio*[5] defined by

$$I_m := 1 - \frac{H(a_*|\mu_m)}{H(a_*)}, \tag{3}$$

which gives us extremal values $I_m = 1$ and 0, meaning, respectively, that human action is completely predictable or completely random with respect to market histories of length m.

---

[5] This measure of association between m-bit strings and subsequent actions is sometimes also referred to as the *uncertainty coefficient*. A similar analysis of actions in response to histories has independently been proposed in Ref. [22].

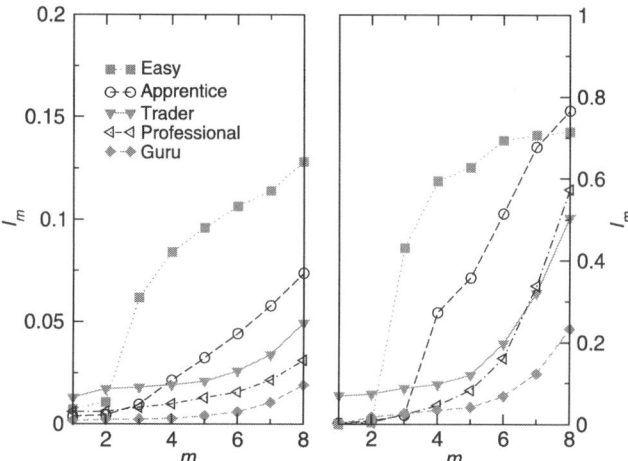

Fig. 4. Information gain ratio (Eq. (3)) in human decisions conditional on market histories of length m. *Left:* Average over entire continuous market history. *Right:* Handpicked individual players with high scores. (y-axes are on different scales to allow easier view of data.) The discontinuity in I_m at memory 3 and 4, respectively, in the Easy and Apprentice levels indicates that human actions become predictable with respect to histories of length $m = M + 1$. The jump is larger for the handpicked players, indicating greater exploitation of market trends.

Fig. 4 shows how I_m changes with m at different levels, both over the entire continuous market history (left) and for handpicked players with high scores (right) who had each played around 1000 turns. When computer-controlled agents have shorter memory values I_m (the Easy and Apprentice levels), all humans are able to spot these values and exploit resulting patterns, playing as if they were basing most of their decisions on market histories of length $M + 1$. This is particularly noticeable for the handpicked players, for whom the discontinuities in I_m are very large at Easy and Apprentice levels, and marked even at Trader—indicating considerable exploitation of patterns in the market.

In the more difficult levels, as agents' memory is increased, no clear discontinuities in I_m can be observed. Instead players tend to ignore the market history entirely and simply repeat their immediately preceding action with large probability (~ 0.8 at Professional and Guru). This repetitive behaviour is even stronger among the handpicked players. Further analysis shows that while human decisions in the easier markets are correlated with the long-term trend of the market, this correlation decreases as the markets become more difficult, being close to zero at Professional and Guru levels. Thus, at these levels players appear to be ignoring all aspects of the information presented by the market. This behaviour in the more difficult markets reflects the observations of other authors on humans playing the Minority Game in groups [22,23], but in our case the tendency to repetition is even stronger.

A final point of view is provided by examining the human's market impact, by considering how volatility and the average gain per turn of computer-controlled agents

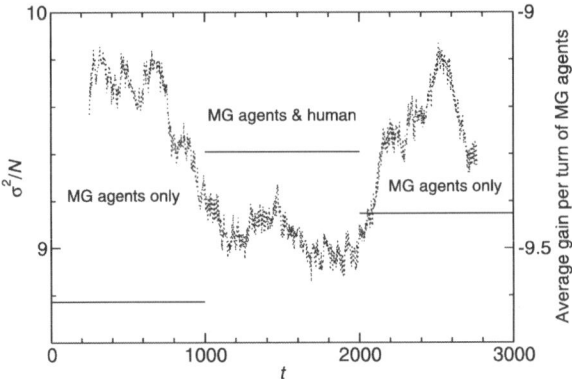

Fig. 5. Market volatility (Eq. (4)) at Easy level with and without a human player (Peter Ruch). The first 1000 turns of the game are with MG agents only, followed by 1000 turns with a human player, and finally, 1000 again with MG agents only. The dotted line (left axis) plots the mean value of normalized volatility averaged over the 500-turn window ($t - 250, t + 250$). The presence of the human player decreases σ^2/N. The solid histogram shows MG agents' average gain per turn over the different periods (right axis), with an observable benefit being derived from the human speculator's presence.

change as the human enters and leaves. The former can be measured by the normalized variance of the market fluctuations:

$$\frac{\sigma^2}{N} = \frac{\langle A^2(t) \rangle}{N} \ . \tag{4}$$

In the easier markets a good player can consistently decrease σ^2/N, most obviously at Easy level (Fig. 5, dotted line) but also observable at Apprentice. This has the unintended benefit of actually *increasing* the gain of the computer-controlled players (Fig. 5, solid line): thus, a symbiosis exists between the "selfish" human and the MG agents, who gain from a speculator decreasing volatility by exploiting market inefficiencies they cannot themselves observe. So to speak, the human is "doing good by doing well". By contrast at Trader, Professional and Guru levels the effect of the human player is too small to make any clear statement. Since volatility at Trader level is still greater-than-random, this suggests that there is a limit to untrained humans' ability to arbitrage: when volatility is below a certain level, there is not much they can do to decrease it further, despite inefficiencies still being present.

In summary, whereas most studies of market entry games have concentrated in the main on whether players can coordinate to an equilibrium [9,11,18], the different controlled environments provided by the analytically understood Minority Game allow for quantitative measurement of important factors in economic decision-making. The differences in performance between the levels are likely to be in part a result of the different memory values of computer-controlled agents, suggesting that humans may have a maximum length of market history over which they are able to consider patterns. However, emphasis must also be put on the smaller fluctuations in the more difficult markets, which mean that short-term patterns cannot survive for long under market impact.

The transition we observe, based on the market phase, between behaviour utilizing short-term patterns in the market and the long-term direction of price movement, and simple repetitive behaviour that ignores all aspects of the market history, provides a confirmation of Arthur's suggestion [18] that beyond a certain level of complexity human logical capacity can no longer cope. When observed elsewhere in human economic decision-making, repetitive behaviour has been criticized as "illogical" [22], as it potentially provides information that competitors could exploit. Yet, as we have seen here, this behaviour actually consistently outperforms random actions, which provide no such information. This might suggest that the transition is not between learning and ignorance, but between two different types of learning, the deductive and inductive.

Acknowledgements

Our sincere and warmest thanks to all those who played the Interactive Minority Game. We are grateful to Damien Challet, Maya Paczuski and Duncan J. Watts for comments and advice, and especially Fabio Mariotti and Fribourg University Chemistry Department for providing us with a web server and much computational assistance. This work was supported by the Swiss National Science Foundation.

The Interactive Minority Game is online at http://www.unifr.ch/econophysics/minority/game/

References

[1] A. Rapoport, A.M. Chammah, C.J. Orwant, Prisoner's Dilemma: A Study in Conflict and Cooperation, University of Michigan Press, Ann Arbor, 1965.

[2] M. Deutsch, Socially relevant science: reflections on some studies of interpersonal conflict, Am. Psychologist 24 (1969) 1076–1092.

[3] D. Kahneman, P. Slovic, A. Tversky, Judgment Under Uncertainty: Heuristics and Biases, Cambridge University Press, Cambridge, 1982.

[4] C. Wedekind, M. Milinski, Cooperation Through Image Scoring in Humans, Science 288 (2000) 850–852.

[5] E. Fehr, S. Gächter, Altruistic punishment in humans, Nature 415 (2002) 137–140.

[6] O. Huber, Risky decision making: Focus on risk defusing behavior, In: F. Columbus (Ed.), Advances in Psychology Research, Nova Sciences Publishers, New York, 2004.

[7] E.H. Chamberlin, An Experimental Imperfect Market, J. Polit. Econ. 56 (1948) 95–108.

[8] T.C. Schelling, Micromotives and Macrobehavior, W. W. Norton & Co., New York, 1978.

[9] J. Ochs, The coordination problem in decentralized markets: an experiment, Q. J. Econ. 105 (1990) 545–559;
    D.J. Meyer, J.B. Van Huyck, R.C. Battalio, T.R. Saving, History's role in coordinating decentralized allocation decisions, J. Polit. Econ. 100 (1992) 292–316.

[10] R.H. Day, V.L. Smith, Experiments in Decision, Organization and Exchange, North-Holland, Amsterdam, 1993.

[11] J.H. Kagel, A.E. Roth (Eds.), The Handbook of Experimental Economics, Princeton University Press, New Jersey, 1995.

[12] R. Axelrod, The Evolution of Cooperation, Basic Books, New York, 1984.

[13] M.A. Nowak, K.M. Page, K. Sigmund, Fairness Versus Reason in the Ultimatum Game, Science 289 (2000) 1773–1775.

[14] D.J. Watts, Small Worlds, Princeton University Press, New Jersey, 1999.

[15] T.C. Schelling, The Strategy of Conflict, Harvard University Press, Cambridge, MA, 1960.

[16] R.E. Lucas Jr., Adaptive behavior and economic theory, in: R.M. Hogarth, M.W. Reder (Eds.), Rational Choice: The Contrast between Economics and Psychology, University of Chicago Press, Chicago, 1986.

[17] D. Challet, Y.-C. Zhang, Emergence of cooperation and organization in an evolutionary game, Physica A 246 (1997) 407–418.

[18] W.B. Arthur, Inductive reasoning and bounded rationality, Am. Econ. Rev. 84 (1994) 406–411.

[19] R. Savit, R. Manuca, R. Riolo, Adaptive Competition, Market Efficiency, and Phase Transitions, Phys. Rev. Lett. 82 (1999) 2203–2206;
R. Manuca, Y. Li, R. Riolo, R. Savit, The structure of adaptive competition in minority games, Physica A 282 (2000) 559–608.

[20] D. Challet, M. Marsili, Y.-C. Zhang, Modeling market mechanism with minority game, Physica A 276 (2000) 284–315.

[21] M. Marsili, D. Challet, R. Zecchina, Exact solution of a modified El Farol's bar problem: Efficiency and the role of market impact, Physica A 280 (2000) 522–553.

[22] G. Bottazzi, G. Devetag, Coordination and Self-Organization in Minority Games: Experimental Evidence, LEM Working Paper 2002/09, http://sssup1.sssup.it/~LEM/WPLem/2002-09.html, 2002.

[23] T. Płatkowski, M. Ramsza, Playing minority game, Physica A 323 (2003) 726–734.

[24] T. Reichhardt, A million volunteers join the online search for extraterrestrial life, Nature 400 (1999) 804.

[25] P. Ruch, J. Wakeling, Y.-C. Zhang, The Interactive Minority Game: Instructions for Experts, arXiv.org, preprint cond-mat/0208310, 2002.

[26] J.D. Farmer, Market force, ecology, and evolution, Santa Fe Institute Working Paper 98-12-117, 1998; J.D. Farmer, Ind. Corp. Change 11 (2002) 895–953.

[27] N.F. Johnson, M. Hart, P.M. Hui, D. Zheng, Trader dynamics in a model market, Int. J. Theor. Appl. Finance 3 (2000) 443–450.

[28] D. MacKay, Information Theory, Inference and Learning Algorithms, Cambridge University Press, Cambridge, 2003.

Bibliography

Akerlof, G. A. (1970). The market for lemons: quality uncertainty and the market mechanism. *Quart. J. Econ.* **80**, pp. 488–500.

Andrecut, M. and Ali, M. K. (2001). Q learning in the minority game. *Phys. Rev. E* **64**, 067103.

Andersen, J. V. and Sornette, D. (2003). The $–game. *Eur. Phys. J. B* **31**, 141. cond-mat/0205423.

Arthur, B. W. (1990). Positive feedbacks in the economy. *Sci. Am.* **262**, 92–99.

Arthur, B. W. (1994). Inductive reasoning and bounded rationality: the El Farol problem. *Am. Econ. Rev.* **84**, 406–411.

Arthur, W. B. (1999). Complexity and the economy. *Science* **284**, 107–109.

Arthur, W. B., Holland, J. H., LeBaron, B., Palmer, R., and Tayler, P. (1997). Asset pricing under endogenous expectations in an artificial stock market. In Arthur, W. B., Durlauf, S., and Lane, D. (eds) *The Economy as an Evolving Complex System, II*, Vol. XXVII of *SFI Studies in the Sciences of Complexit*. Addison-Wesley. Redwood City.

Bacry, E., Delour, J., and Muzy, J. F. (2001). Modelling financial time series using multifractal random walks. *Physica A* **299**, 84–92.

Bak, P. and Chialvo, D. R. (2001). Adaptive learning by extremal dynamics and negative feedback. *Phys. Rev. E* **63**, 031912.

Berg, J. et al. (2001). Statistical mechanics of asset markets with private information. *Quant. Fin.* **1**(2). cond-mat/0101351.

Borgers, T. and Sarin, R. (1997). Learning through reinforcement and replicator dynamics. *J. Econ. Theory* **77**, 1–14.

Bottazzi, G., Devetag, G., and Dosi, G. (2002). Adaptive learning and emerging coordination in minority games. *Simul. Model. Pract. Theory* **10**.

Bottazzi, G., Devetag, G., and Dosi, G. (2003). In Adaptive Learning and Emergent Coordination in Minority Games. *Heterogeneous Agents, Interactions and Economic Performance*, Number 521 in Lecture Notes in Economics and Mathematical Systems. Springer Verlag. London.

Bouchaud, J.-P. (2001). Power laws in economics and finance: some ideas from physics. *Quant. Fin.* **1**, 105–112.

Bouchaud, J.-P. and Potters, M. (2000). *Theory of Financial Risks*. Cambridge University Press, Cambridge.

Bouchaud, J.-P., Giardina, I., and Mézard, M. (2001). On a universal mechanism for long ranged volatility correlations. *Quant. Fin.* **1**, 212. cond-mat/0012156.

Bouchaud, J.-P., Mézard, M., and Potters, M. (2002). Statistical properties of stock order books: empirical results and models. *Quant. Fin.* **2**, 251.

Burgos, E. and Ceva, H. (2000). Self organization in a minority game: the role of memory and a probabilistic approach. *Physica A* **284**, 489–495. cond-mat/0003179.

Caldarelli, G., Marsili, M., and Zhang, Y.-C. (1997). A prototype model of stock exchange. *Europhys. Lett.* **50**, 479–484.

Campbell, J. Y., Lo, A. W., MacKinlay, A. C., and Campbell, J. W. (1997). *The Econometrics of Financial Markets*. Princeton University Press. Princeton.

Caridi, I. and Ceva, H. (2003). Minority game: a mean-field-like approach. *Physica A* **317**, 247–258.

Casti, J. L. (1995/1996). Seeing the light at el farol. *Complexity* **1**, 7.

Cavagna, A. (1999). Irrelevance of memory in the minority game. *Phys. Rev. E* **59**, R3783–R3786. cond-mat/9812215.

Cavagna, A. et al. (1999). A thermal model for adaptive competition in a market. *Phys. Rev. Lett.* **83**, 4429–4432. cond-mat/9903415.

Cavagna, A., Garrahan, J. P., Giardina, I., and Sherrington, D. (2000). Reply to comment on 'thermal model for adaptive competition in a market'. *Phys. Rev. Lett.* **85**, 5009. cond-mat/9905134.

Challet, D. The minority game's web page www.unifr.ch/econophysics/minority.

Challet, D. (2000). Modelling Market Dynamics: Minority Games and Beyond. PhD Thesis, University of Fribourg.

Challet, D. (2003). *Efficiency and Back*. cond-mat/0210319 unpublished. London.

Challet, D. and Galla, T. (2003). Price return auto-correlation in mixed minority/majority games. Unpublished, cond-mat/0404264.

Challet, D. and Marsili, M. (1999). Symmetry breaking and phase transition in the minority game. *Phys Rev. E* **60**, R6271. cond-mat/9904392.

Challet, D. and Marsili, M. (2000). Relevance of memory in minority games. *Phys. Rev. E* **62**, 1862. cond-mat/0004196.

Challet, D. and Marsili, M. (2003*a*). Criticality and finite size effects in a simple realistic model of stock market. *Phys. Rev. E* **68**, 036132, cond-mat/0210549.

Challet, D. and Marsili, M. (2003*b*). Shedding light on el farol. *Physica A*. **332**, 469–482, cond-mat/0306445.

Challet, D. and Zhang, Y.-C. (1997). Emergence of cooperation and organization in an evolutionary game. *Physica A* **246**, 407. adap-org/9708006.

Challet, D. and Zhang, Y.-C. (1998). On the minority game: analytical and numerical studies. *Physica A* **256**, 514. cond-mat/9805084.

Challet, D., Chessa, A., Marsili, M., and Zhang, Y.-C. (2000*a*). From minority games to real markets. *Quant. Fin.* **1**, 168. cond-mat/0011042.

Challet, D., Marsili, M., and Zecchina, R. (2000*b*). Comment on 'thermal model for adaptive competition in a market'. *Phys. Rev. Lett.* **85**, 5008. cond-mat/9904392.

Challet, D., Marsili, M., and Zecchina, R. (2000*c*). Statistical mechanics of heterogeneous agents: minority games. *Phys. Rev. Lett.* **84**, 1824–1827. cond-mat/9904392.

Challet, D., Marsili, M., and Zhang, Y.-C. (2000*d*). Modeling market mechanisms with minority game. *Physica A* **276**, 284. cond-mat/9909265.

Challet, D., Marsili, M., and Zhang, Y.-C. (2001*a*). Minority games and stylized facts. *Physica A* **299**, 228. cond-mat/0103024.

Challet, D., Marsili, M., and Zhang, Y.-C. (2001*b*). Stylized facts of financial markets in minority games. *Physica A* **294**, 514. cond-mat/0101326.

Chialvo, D. R. and Bak, P. (1999). Learning from mistakes. *Neuroscience* **90**, 1137.

Cohen, J. E. (1998). Cooperation and self-interest: Pareto-inefficiency of nash equilibria in finite random games. *Proc. Natl Acad. Sci.* **95**, 9724–9731.

Cont, R. and Bouchaud, J.-P. (2000). Herd behaviour and aggregate fluctuation in financial markets. *Macroecon. Dyn.* **4**, 170.

Coolen, A. A. C. (2004). *The Mathematical Theory of Minority Games.* Oxford University Press, Oxford, in preparation.

Coolen, A. A. C. and Heimel, J. A. F. (2001). Dynamical solution of the on-line minority game. *J. Phys. A: Math. Gen.* **34**, 10783–10804.

Dacorogna, M. M., Genay, R., Müller, U. A., Olsen, R. B., and Pictet, O. V. (2001). *An Introduction to High-Frequency Finance.* Academic Press, London.

de Almeida, J. and Thouless, D. (1978). Stability of the Sherrington–Kirkpatrick solution of a spin glass model. *J. Phys. A: Math. Gen.* **11**, 983.

de Cara, M. A. R., Pla, O., and Guinea, F. (2000). Learning, competition and cooperation in simple games. *Eur. Phys. J. B* **13**, 413–416. cond-mat/9904187.

De Martino, A. D. and Marsili, M. (2001). Replica symmetry breaking in the minority game. *J. Phys. A: Math. Gen.* **34**, 2525–2537. cond-mat/0007397.

De Martino, A. D., Giardina, I., and Mosetti, G. (2003*a*). Statistical mechanics of the mixed majority-minority game with random external information. *J. Phys. A: Math. Gen.* **36**, 8935–8954.

De Martino, A. D., Marsili, M., and Mulet, R. (2003*b*). Adaptive drivers in a model of urban traffic. cond-mat/0308543.

D'hulst, R. and Rodgers, G. (1999). The hamming distance in the minority game. *Physica A* **270**, 514. cond-mat/9902001.

Drew Fudenberg, D. K. L. (1998). *The Theory of Learning in Games*. MIT Press.

Dyson, F. J. (1962). Statistical theory of energy levels of complex systems i. *J. Math. Phys.* **3**, 140–156.

Ein-Dor, L., Metzler, R., Kanter, I., and Kinzel, W. (2001). Multichoice minority game. *Phys. Rev. E* **63**, 066103. cond-mat/0005216.

Eissfeller, H. and Opper, M. (1992). New method for studying the dynamics of disordered spin systems without finite-size effects. *Phys. Rev. Lett.* **68**. 2094–2097.

Farmer, J. D. (1999a). Market force, ecology and evolution. Technical Report 98-12-117, Santa Fe Institute.

Farmer, J. D. (1999b). Physicists attempt to scale the ivory towers of finance. Computing in Science and Engineering, Nov–Dec, 26–39, adap-org 9912002.

Farmer, J. D. and Joshi, S. (1999). Santa Fe working Paper, 99-10-071. Santa Fe Institute.

Farmer, J. D. and Lillo, F. (2003). On the origin of power law tails in price fluctuations. cond-mat/0309416. Unpublished.

Farmer, J. D. and Lo, A. (1999). Frontiers of finance: evolution and efficient markets. *Proc. Natl Acad. Sci.* **96**, 9991–9992.

Follmer, H. (1974). Random economies with many interacting agent. *J. Math. Econ.* **1**, 51–62.

Fudenberg, D. and Tirole, J. (1991). *Game Theory*. MIT Press. Cambridge, MA.

Gabaix, X., Gopikrishnan, P., Plerou, V., and Stanley, H. (2003). A theory of power-law distributions in financial market fluctuations. *Nature* **423**, 267.

Galambos, J. (1987). *Asymptotic Theory of Extreme Order Statistics*, 2nd edn. Krieger, Malabar, Florida.

Garrahan, J. P., Moro, E., and Sherrington, D. (2000). Continuous time dynamics of the thermal minority game. *Phys. Rev. E* **62**, R9. cond-mat/0004277.

Giardina, I. and Bouchaud, J.-P. (2002). Crashes and intermittency in agent based market models.

Gopikrisnan, P., Plerou, V., Gabaix, X., and Stanley, H. (2000). Statistical properties of share volume traded in financial markets. *Phys. Rev. E* **62** R4493.

Gourley, S., Choe, S., Hui, P., and Johnson, N. (2003). Fairness and efficiency in competitive networked societies with limited global resources. Unpublished.

Hart, M., Jefferies, P., Hui, P., and Johnson, N. (2001). Crowd–anticrowd theory of multi-agent market games. *Eur. Phys. J. B* **20**, 547–550. cond-mat/0008385.

Hart, M. L., Jefferies, P., and Johnson, N. F. (2002a). Dynamics of the time horizon minority game. *Physica A* **311**, 275. cond-mat/0103259.

Hart, M. L., Lamper, D., and Johnson, N. F. (2002*b*). An investigation of crash avoidance in a complex system. *Physica A* **316**, 649–661.

Heimel, J. A. F. and Coolen, A. A. C. (2001). Generating functional analysis of the dynamics of the batch minority game with random external information. *Phys. Rev. E* **63**, 056121. cond-mat/0012045.

Heimel, J. A. F. and De Martino, A. D. (2001). Broken ergodicity and memory in the minority game. *J. Phys. A: Math. Gen.* **34**, L539–L545. cond-mat/0108066.

Heimel, J. A. F., Coolen, A. A. C., and Sherrington, D. (2001). Dynamics of the batch minority game with inhomogeneous decision noise. *Phys. Rev. E* **65**, 016126. cond-mat/0106635.

Hod, S. and Nakar, E. (2002). Self-segregation versus clustering in the evolutionary minority game. *Phys. Rev. Lett.* **88**, 238702.

Huang, K. (2001). *Introduction to Statistical Physics*. Taylor & Francis, London.

Hui, N. J. P., Zheng, D., and Hart, M. (1999). Enhanced winnings in a mixed-ability population playing a minority game. *J. Phys. A: Math. Gen.* **32**, L427.

Jefferies, P., M., Hart, Johnson, N. (2001). Deterministic dynamics in the minority game. *Phys. Rev. E* **65**, 016105. cond-mat/0102384.

Jefferies, P., Hart, M., Hui, P., and Johnson, N. (2001). From market games to real-world markets. *Eur. Phys. J. B* **20**, 493–502. cond-mat/0008387.

Jensen, H. J. (1998). *Self-organized Criticality: Emergent Complex Behavior in Physical and Biological Systems*, Number 10 in Cambridge lecture notes in physics. Cambridge University Press, Cambridge.

Johnson, N., Jarvis, S., Jonson, R., Cheung, P., Kwong, Y., and Hui, P. (1998). Volatility and agent adaptability in a self-organizing market. *Physica A* **256**, 230. cond-mat/9802177.

Johnson, N., Hart, M., and Hui, P. (1999*a*). Crowd effects and volatility in a competitive market. *Physica A* **269**, 1. cond-mat/9811227.

Johnson, N., Hui, P., Zheng, D., and Tai, C. (1999*b*). Minority game with arbitrary cutoffs. *Physica A* **269**, 493.

Johnson, N. et al. (1999*c*). Self-organized segregation within an evolving population. *Phys. Rev. Lett.* **82**(16), 3360–3363. cond-mat/9910072.

Johnson, N., Hart, M., Hui, P. M., and Zheng, D. (2000). Trader dynamics in a model market. *International Journal of Theoretical and Applied Finance*, **3**. cond-mat/9910072. pp. 443–450.

Kagel, J. H. and Roth, A. E. (1995). *The Handbook of Experimental Economics*. Princeton University Press. Princeton.

Kauffman, S. A. (1993). *The Origins of Order: Self-Organization and Selection in Evolution*. Oxford University Press. Oxford.

Kinzel, W., Metzler, R., and Kanter, I. (2000). Dynamics of interacting neural networks. *J. Phys. A: Math. Gen.* **33**, L141–147. cond-mat/9906058.

Krieger, A. J. (1992). *The Money Bazaar: Inside the Trillion-Dollar World of Currency Trading*. Random House. New York.

Lamper, D., Howison, S., and Johnson, N. (2002). Predictability of large future changes in a competitive evolving population. *Phys. Rev. Lett.* **88**, 017902–017905. cond-mat/0105258.

Laureti, P., Ruch, P., Wakeling, J., and Zhang, Y.-C. (2003). The interactive minority game: a web-based investigation of market human interaction. *Physica A*.

Levy, H., Levy, M., and Solomon, S. (2000). *Microscopic Simulation of Financial Markets: From Investor Behavior to Market Phenomena*. Academic Press, London.

Li, Y., Van Deemen A., and Savit, R. (2000*a*). The minority game with variable payoffs. *Physica A* **284**, 461–477. nlin.Ao/0002004.

Li, Y., Riolo, R., and Savit, R. (2000*b*). Evolution in minority games. (i). games with a fixed strategy space. *Physica A* **276**, 234–264. cond-mat/9903415.

Li, Y., Riolo, R., and Savit, R. (2000*c*). Evolution in minority games. (i). games with a fixed strategy space. *Physica A* **276**, (265–283). cond-mat/9906001.

Lo, T., Hui, P., and Johnson, N. (2000). Theory of evolutionary minority game. *Phys. Rev. E* **62**, 4393. cond-mat/0003379.

Lo, T. S., Hui, P. M., and Johnson, N. (2000). Theory of the evolutionary minority game. *Phys. Rev. E* **62**, 4393.

Luce, R. D. (1959). *Individual Choice Behavior: A Theoretical Analysis*. Wiley. New York.

Lux, T. and Marchesi, M. (1999). Scaling and criticality in a stochastic multi-agent model of a financial market. *Nature* **397**, 498–500.

Mansilla, R. (2000). From naive to sophisticated behavior in multiagents based financial markets models. *Physica A* **284**, 478–488. cond-mat/0002331.

Mantegna, R. and Stanley, H. G. (2000). *Introduction to Econophysics*. Cambridge University Press. Cambridge.

Manuca, R., Li, Y., Riolo, R., and Savit, R. (2000). The structure of adaptive competition in minority games. *Physica A* **282**, 559–608.

Marshall, A. (1932). *Elements of Economics*. Macmillan, London.

Marsili, M. (2001). Market mechanism and expectations in minority and majority games. *Physica A* **299**, 93–103.

Marsili, M. and Challet, D. (2001*a*). Continuum time limit and stationary states of the minority game. *Phys. Rev. E* **64**, 056138. cond-mat/0102257.

Marsili, M. and Challet, D. (2001*b*). Trading behavior and excess volatility in toy markets. *Adv. Complex Syst.* **3**(I), 3–17. cond-mat/0011042.

Marsili, M. and Ferreira, F. F. (2003). Is the market really a minority game? cond-mat/0311257 unpublished.

Marsili, M. and Piai, M. (2002). Colored minority games. *Physica A* **310**, 234–244. cond-mat/0202479.

Marsili, M., Challet, D., and Zecchina, R. (2000). Exact solution of a modified el farol's bar problem: Efficiency and the role of market impact. *Physica A* **280**, 522. cond-mat/9908480.

Marsili, M., Mulet, R., Ricci-Tersenghi, F., and Zecchina, R. (2001). Learning to coordinate in a complex and nonstationary world. *Phys. Rev. Lett.* **87**, 208701. cond-mat/0105345.

McFadden, D. (1981). Econometric models of probabilistic choice. In Manski, C. F. and McFadden, D. (Eds) *Structural Analysis of Discrete Data with Econometric Application*, pp. 171–260. MIT Press. Cambridge, MA.

Metzler, R. (2002). Antipersistent binary time series. *J. Phys. A: Math. Gen.* **35**, 721–730.

Metzler, R., Kinzel, W., and Kanter, I. (2000). Interacting neural networks. *Phys. Rev. E* **62**. cond-mat/0003051.

Mézard, M., Parisi, G., and Virasoro, M. A. (1987). *Spin Glass Theory and Beyond*. World Scientific. Singapore.

Neumann, J. V. and Morgenstern, O. (1944). *Theory of Games and Economic Behavior*. Princeton University Press, Princeton.

Niederhoffer, V. (1998). *The Education of a Speculator*. John Wiley & Sons Inc. New York.

Paczuski, M., Bassler, K. E., and Corral, A. (2000). Self-organized networks of competing boolean agents. *Phys. Rev. Lett.* **84**(14), 3185–3188. cond-mat/9905082.

Patkowski, T. and Ramsza, M. (2003). Playing minority game. *Physica A* **323**, 727–734.

Press, W. H., Flannery, B. P., Teukolsky, S. A., and Vetterling, W. T. (1993). *Numerical Recipes in C: The Art of Scientific Computing*. Cambridge University Press. www.nr.com. Cambridge.

Reents, G., Metzler, R., and Kinzel, W. (2001). A stochastic strategy for the minority game. *Physica A* **299**, 253–261. cond-mat/0007351.

Rustichini, A. (1999a). Optimal properties of stimulus response models. *Games Econ. Behav.*, **29**.

Rustichini, A. (1999b). Sophisticated players and sophisticated agents. *Tilburg University, Center for Economic Research Discussion Paper*, 110.

Samuelson, P. A. (1965). Proof that properly anticipated prices fluctuate randomly. *Ind. Manage. Rev.* **6**, 41.

Sato, A. and Takayasu, H. (1998). Dynamical models of stock market exchange: from microscopic determinism to macroscopic randomness. *Physica A* **250**, 231–252.

Savit, R., Manuca, R., and Riolo, R. (1999). Adaptive competition, market efficiency, and phase transitions. *Phys. Rev. Lett.* **82**, 2203–2206.

Savit, R., Koelle, K., Treynor, W., and Gonzalez, R. (2003). Man and superman: Human limitations, innovation and emergence in resource competition. Unpublished.

Sengupta, A. M. and Mitra, P. P. (1999). Distributions of singular values for some random matrices. *Phys. Rev. E* **60**, 3389. cond-mat/9709283.

Sherrington, D. and Galla, T. (2003). The minority game: effects of strategy correlations and timing of adaptation. *Physica A* **324**, 25–29.

Sherrington, D., Moro, E., and Garrahan, J. P. (2002). Statistical physics of induced correlation in a simple market. *Physica A* **311**, 527–535. cond-mat/0010455.

Simon, H. (1981). *The Sciences of the Artificial*. MIT Press. Cambridge, MA.

Slanina, F. and Zhang, Y.-C. (1999). Capital flow in a two-component dynamical system. *Physica A* **272**, 257–268. cond-mat/9906248.

Slanina, F. and Zhang, Y.-C. (2001). Dynamical spin-glass-like behavior in an evolutionary game. *Physica A* **289**, 290–300.

Sysi-Aho, M., Chakraborti, A., and Kaski, K. (2003). Adaptation using hybridized genetic crossover strategies. *Physica A* **322**, 701–709.

Vázquez, A. (2000). Self-organization in populations of competing agents. *Phys. Rev. E* **62**, R4497–R4500. cond-mat/0006179.

Veblen, T. (1898). Why is economics not an evolutionary science? *Quart. J. Econ.* **12**(4), 373–397.

Wakeling, J. and Bak, P. (2001). Intelligent systems in the context of surrounding environment. *Phys. Rev. E* **64**, 051920. nlin.AO/0201046.

Waldrop, M. M. (1994). *Complexity: The Emerging Science at the Edge of Order and Chaos*. Penguin Science. Harmondsworth.

Wigner, E. (1967). Random matrices in physics. *SIAM Rev.* **9**, 1–23.

Yeomans, J. (1992). *Statistical Mechanics of Phase Transitions*. Oxford University Press. Oxford.

Zhang, Y.-C. (1998). Modeling market mechanism with evolutionary games. *Europhys. News* **29**, 51.

Zhang, Y.-C. (1999). Towards a theory of marginally efficient markets. *Physica A* **269**, 30.

Index